Scriptural Authority in Early Judaism and Ancient Christianity

Deuterocanonical and Cognate Literature Studies

Edited by
Friedrich V. Reiterer, Beate Ego, Tobias Nicklas

Volume 16

De Gruyter

Scriptural Authority in Early Judaism and Ancient Christianity

Edited by
Isaac Kalimi, Tobias Nicklas, Géza G. Xeravits

in collaboration with
Heike Hötzinger

De Gruyter

ISBN 978-3-11-048795-4
e-ISBN 978-3-11-029553-5
ISSN 1865-1666

Library of Congress Cataloging-in-Publication Data
A CIP catalog record for this book has been applied for at the Library of Congress.

Bibliographic information published by the Deutsche Nationalbibliothek

The Deutsche Nationalbibliothek lists this publication in the Deutsche Nationalbibliografie; detailed bibliographic data are available in the Internet at http://dnb.dnb.de.

© 2013 Walter de Gruyter GmbH, Berlin/Boston

Printing: Hubert & Co. GmbH & Co. KG, Göttingen
∞ Printed on acid-free paper

Printed in Germany

www.degruyter.com

Vorwort / Preface

The Department of Bible at the Sapientia College of Theology (Budapest) organised an international conference entitled "The Concept of Authority in Early Judaism" (18–21 May, 2010). The core of the present volume consists of papers read at that conference. This material has been supplemented by additional papers in order to obtain a more comprehensive corpus.

The authors explore various aspects of scriptural authority from the late Old Testament literature to the emerging Christianity. Along with several recently published volumes, this collection shed light how ancient authors defined authority, how they used earlier texts and traditions when expressing their own thoughts. The readers of the volume obtain an introduction both into the plurality of authorities and the emergence of mainstream authoritative traditions around the turn of the era.

The editors express their gratitude to the editors of the series, especially Prof.s Dr. Friedrich Reiterer and Beate Ego for accepting this volume, to the staff of Walther de Gruyter publishing house and to the contributors for their kind cooperation and their patience. Thanks are due to the staff of the Department of Bible, Sapientia College of Theology for their invaluable help during the conference and to Dr. Heike Hötzinger and Michael Sommer, both assistants at the chair of New Testament Studies at the University of Regensburg for their help in the editorial process of this volume.

April 2013

Isaac Kalimi, Tobias Nicklas & Géza G. Xeravits

The Editors

Inhalt / Contents

VORWORT / PREFACE v

STEFAN SCHORCH
Which Kind of Authority? The Authority of the Torah
during the Hellenistic and the Roman Periods 1

JAMES L. CRENSHAW
Qohelet and Scriptural Authority 17

BENJAMIN G. WRIGHT
Pseudonymous Authorship and Structures of Authority
in the *Letter of Aristeas* 43

SEAN A. ADAMS
Reframing Scripture: A Fresh Look at Baruch's
So-Called "Citations" 63

KARIN SCHÖPFLIN
Scriptural Authority and the Ancestor as its Teacher and Example
in the Book of Tobit 85

BRADLEY C. GREGORY
Ben Sira as Negotiator of Authoritative Traditions 109

FRIEDRICH V. REITERER
Ein unkonventioneller Umgang mit der biblischen Autorität.
Siras Art in hellenistischer Umgebung aus seiner Bibel zu denken
und zu sprechen 129

ANDREW T. GLICKSMAN
"Set Your Desire on My Words": Authoritative Traditions in the
Wisdom of Solomon 167

JOHN C. ENDRES
Scriptural Authority in the Book of Jubilees 185

PAUL METZGER
Die geheime Offenbarung – Zur Autorität der Schrift im IV Esra 207

BALÁZS TAMÁSI
The Sources of Authority in Second Baruch 225

ROB KUGLER
Writing Scripturally in the Testament of Job.
Advancing Our Notions of Scripture and Authority in Judean
Literature of the Early Roman Era 251

LEVENTE B. MARTOS
Authority of a Forgiven King: David's Psalms in the Letter
to the Romans 261

PAUL FOSTER
Scriptural Authority in Q 279

HEIKE HÖTZINGER
Schriftgebrauch in der Stephanusepisode: Apg 6,1-8,3 305

TOBIAS NICKLAS
Frühchristliche Ansprüche auf die Schriften Israels 347

Index of References 369

Index of Subjects 377

Which Kind of Authority?
The Authority of the Torah during the Hellenistic and the Roman Periods

STEFAN SCHORCH

It is in very different ways that a text can own authority for a community. In the following, I would like to address the question, which kind of authority the Torah owned for Judaism during the Hellenistic and Roman periods. However, authority presupposes and is closely intertwined with actual presence, and in order to own authority for a community, a text must above all be present. Therefore, I would like to start with the question, how the Torah was present in Judaism at what is sometimes called Late Second Temple period, although this concept is maybe too focused on Jerusalem, as will be shown later.

1. The Torah in the Judean Desert

Regarding the circulation of the Torah in that period, we are of course best informed by the manuscripts which were found in the Judean Desert, especially those from Qumran. According to Emanuel Tov, 105 manuscripts of the different books of the Torah turned up in Qumran:[1]

    Gen 23
    Ex   21
    Lev 15
    Num 10
    Deut 35

In order to put these numbers in context, we may add that the Book of Psalms turned up in 36 copies, Isaiah in 21, Samuel in 4, as well as Enoch in 25 copies, and Jubilees in 21.

Thus, as evidenced by these numbers and as is well known, the book of Deuteronomy was especially popular among the five books of the Torah, although we should keep in mind that the interest in Deu-

---

1 See TOV, Textual criticism, 96-97.

teronomy still seems to have been equaled or even exceeded by some other literary compositions.

The Qumran manuscripts of the Torah date from the late 3rd through the 1st centuries BCE, and they exhibit some significant textual variations, which are commonly attributed to different textual types, determined on account of textual characteristics and text-historical dependencies, the latter especially prominent regarding the so-called proto-Masoretic and pre-Samaritan text type. Apart from these two a number of further textual types left there traces in the Qumran finds but cannot easily connected with certain streams of literary and textual tradition, as our knowledge is very fragmentary. However, the manuscripts from Qumran seem to create the picture of a Jewish sect in which different texts of the Torah were in parallel and contemporaneous use.

A very different picture emerges if we look at the manuscripts found at Masada, which date to the 1st and 2nd centuries CE., i.e. which are about 200 to 300 years younger. All the four Torah manuscripts from Masada, one containing the Book of Genesis, two Leviticus, and one Deuteronomy, belong to only one textual type, the proto-Masoretic, and the same is true for the other manuscripts attesting the books known from the later Biblical collection.[2]

Thus, although the small number of manuscripts calls for a cautious judgment, a certain change seems to have happened in the meantime, as in the Masada group only one textual type seems to have been in use, while other textual types are totally absent in this group. It seems that this evidence points towards the emergence of group specific texts, i.e. texts, which were specifically connected with a certain Jewish sect.

If we look back once again at the Qumran finds and their time, we will have to take into account yet further evidence regarding the presence of the Torah in ancient Judaism: The contemporary literary compositions demonstrate that the Torah was not only physically present in multiple copies, but that the text of the Torah was rather well known, as indicated by the fact that the textual sources from the late Second temple period refer to it in paraphrases, quotations, re-worked compositions and so on. References to the text of the Torah are of course well known already from earlier compositions, which became part of the later Biblical collections, as for instance and most prominently Chronicles. However, the references to the Torah, which appear in Chronicles as well as in other Biblical books, are rather freely phrased, they generally allude to the content rather than to the external form of the quoted

---

2 See TOV, Textual criticism, 29.

text, or, more accurate, to the deep structure³ of that text rather than to its surface,⁴ e.g.:

> 1 Chron 16:40
> "to offer burnt offerings to the Lord on the altar of burnt offering regularly, morning and evening, according to all that is written in the law of the Lord (לכל הכתוב בתורת יהוה) that he commanded Israel."

> 2 Chron 23:18
> "Jehoiada assigned the care of the house of the Lord to the levitical priests whom David had organized to be in charge of the house of the Lord, to offer burnt offerings to the Lord, as it is written in the law of Moses (ככתוב בתורת משה), with rejoicing and with singing, according to the order of David."

Most obviously, in these two examples as in the vast majority of explicitly marked inner-Biblical references to the Torah, the quotations are not word-by-word, but free. The only exception,⁵ where ככתוב indeed introduces a virtually literal quotation from the Torah in Chronicles, is 2 Chron 25:4:

> "But he did not put their children to death, according to what is written in the law, in the book of Moses (ככתוב בתורה בספר משה), where the LORD commanded, *The parents shall not be put to death for the children, or the children be put to death for the parents; but all shall be put to death for their own sins*."

Freely phrased references to the text of the Torah can be found in compositions from Qumran as well. However, besides this kind of references literal quotations from the Torah are much more frequent in the compositions from Qumran than in late Biblical literature, pointing to the emergence of a new pattern. Literal quotations from the Torah are especially prominent in the halakhic composition 4QMMT, where references of the Torah are several times introduced by the quotation formula כתוב "it is written", followed by the quotation itself appearing in direct speech. However, not always the passage referred to by כתוב seems to be a quotation in the strict sense, as the following example from 4QMMT may demonstrate:

---

3   For this terminology, see SCHORCH, "Libraries", 179-180.
4   More or less the same conclusions have been drawn e.g. by Lars Hänsel and Thomas Willi, although their terminology is different: „Desweiteren hat sich gezeigt, daß die Bezugnahme mit ככתוב keine festgefügte Zitateinleitungsformel im Sinne einer *Text*orientierung oder gar *Textstellen*orientierung darstellt, sondern meist einen Bezug im Sinne einer *Stoff*orientierung herstellt." (HÄNSEL, Studien zu Tora, 66); „Bei den genannten, immer wieder leicht abgewandelten Ausdrücken handelt es sich um *Schriftkonformitätsklauseln*, nicht um Zitationsformeln!" (WILLI, Leviten, 86; Italics by the authors). A full list of the cases, where Chronicles employs ככתוב and similar readings for references to the Torah includes the following: 1 Chron 16:40; 2 Chron 23:18; 25:4; 30:5. 18; 31:3; 34:21; 35:12. 26.
5   Compare DÖRRFUSS, Mose, 221: „Ein Bezug auf die – geschriebene – Tora oder gar das Buch des Mose findet sich jedoch nur in IIChr 25,4b, der innerhalb der Chronikbücher ganz singulär ist."

[וע]ל שא כתוב [איש כי ישחט במחנה או ישחט] מחוץ למחנה שור וכשב ועז

"[And re]garding what is written [If anyone of the house of Israel slaughters] an ox or a lamb or a goat in the camp, or outside the camp." (4QMMT - 4Q394 3–7 ii, 14–15)

Most obviously, 4QMMT here quotes Lev 17:3. However, a close comparison with the Biblical text shows that the quotation is not quite literal:

MT   איש איש מבית ישראל אשר ישחט שור או כשב או עז במחנה או אשר ישחט מחוץ למחנה

4QMMT   איש כי ישחט במחנה או ישחט מחוץ למחנה שור וכשב ועז

Thus, a certain tension appears: On the one hand side, the quoting text (i.e. 4QMMT) seems to suggest that the quotation is literal: "as is written". The quotation itself, on the other hand, doesn't seem to be literal, to the best of our knowledge, at least it is not attested in one of the preserved manuscripts of the Book of Leviticus in the same form in which it appears in 4QMMT. Additionally, and maybe more importantly, the deviation of the quotation from the wording known from the Leviticus manuscripts follows a clear interest, as has been demonstrated by Reinhard Kratz: The verse seems to have been reworked with the aim to focus the verse on the exact localization of the offering place.[6] Therefore, it is likely that the wording of the quotation was intentionally changed by the author of of 4QMMT, or maybe already by his *Vorlage*,[7] and that the literalness of the quotation is rather a fiction. This creates a difficulty, since 4QMMT attributes authority to the textual surface of the Torah, at the one hand, but seems to have changed this surface intentionally, on the other.[8] Thus, we can cautiously conclude at this point that 4QMMT attests a new tendency, namely to attribute authority to the wording of the Torah, although the textual surface is not yet a fixed entity, a fact which corresponds to the multitude of textual versions attested among the Qumran finds.

We should keep in mind, however, that Qumran could be a special case, and I therefore would like to proceed to the question whether the

---

6   See KRATZ, The place which He has chosen.
7   Compare MAIER, Die Qumran-Essener, 361.
8   Compare BROOKE, The explicit presentation of scripture, 85: "In particular the explicit citations of scripture, including those citations which are mild adjustments of scriptural word order or grammatical forms, show that the compilers of MMT had a lively attitude to scripture which was not bound by its precise letter but which was very careful to fit suitably, in its own phraseology, to the context of the debate."

evidence from Qumran is part of a general development, or a rather esoteric feature.

2. The Torah – esoteric or public among Jews of the Hellenistic and Roman periods?

The view that the Torah is a public text emerges for the first time in Deuteronomy: According to Deuteronomy, the Torah is presented by Mose to Israel (e.g. Deut 4:44), it is published on stone tabletts after the crossing of the Jordan river (Deut 27:2f), and the Book of the Torah is to be kept not in, but rather beside the ark of the covenant (Deut 31:26), i.e. not hidden, but with open access.

In which measure this claim for publicity was put into effect during the Hellenistic and Roman times is difficult to determine exactly. However, we seem to have a few leads:

(1) The public access to and maybe even the private property of manuscripts of the Torah, as well as the wide circulation of Torah manuscripts is presupposed by 1 Makk 1:54–57 for the first half of the 2nd century BCE:

> And on the fifteenth day of Chaseleu in the one hundred and forty-fifth year, he constructed an abomination of desolation on the altar, and in the cities around Iouda they built altars and burnt incense at the doors of the houses and in the city squares. And the books of the law which they found (καὶ τὰ βιβλία τοῦ νόμου ἃ εὗρον) they tore up and burned with fire. And wherever there was found in someone's possession a book of the covenant, or if someone was confirming to the law (καὶ ὅπου εὑρίσκετο παρά τινι βιβλίον διαθήκης καὶ εἴ τις συνευδόκει τῷ νόμῳ), the judgement of the king put them to death.[9]

This source implies that a multitude of Torah scrolls were publically available in different Jewish places, and some of these scrolls seem to have been in private hands.[10]

Starting from the 1st century CE onward the view that the Torah is a public document became a topos, well attested in Philo, Josephus and Rabbinic sources, as has been shown by Albert Baumgarten.[11]

(2) Further clear evidence that the Torah was accessible by a wide public is the multitude of textual versions of the Torah as attested by

---

9 Translation by George T. ZERVOS (NETS).
10 It is less important here, whether τὰ βιβλία τοῦ νόμου and βιβλίον διαθήκης refer to the Torah as a whole, or rather to certain parts of it, as for instance the Book of Deuteronomy. For a discussion of this problem see RAPPAPORT, The First Book of Maccabees, 120, and ABEL, Les Livres des Maccabées, 26.
11 See BAUMGARTEN, The Torah as a public document in Judaism.

the Qumran manuscripts. The fact of their textual diversity can only be explained when we acknowledge that a relatively high number of copies of the Torah circulated in different Jewish circles, which were not directly connected one with the other, and it may be not superfluous to note that this observations contradicts the theory that a library in the Temple of Jerusalem housed a standard text of the Torah. In fact, there is barely evidence for a library like this.[12]

We may therefore conclude, again with some caution, that the physical existence, circulation, reception and transmission of the Torah during the Hellenistic and Roman period took place in the environment of a wider Jewish public, and not only within the circles of a small Jewish elite. Therefore, there seems to be no reason to interpret the evidence from Qumran regarding the presence of the Torah as a group specific feature.

The same seems to be the case regarding the turn from a content-focused towards a form-focused or access to the text of the Torah, which is evidenced by some Qumran texts for the 2nd century BCE. Admiel Schremer and other scholars have pointed out the clear evidence that the same development is visible within the traditions which were incorporated in the early Rabbinic sources, although there it took place at a somewhat later time. In a clear and obvious opposition to the general trend in Rabbinic literature, halakhic arguments and decisions attributed to the authorities before the first century CE do generally not refer to scriptural quotations, and even the halakhic decisions attributed to Hillel the elder, who lived at the turn from the 1st century BCE to the 1st century BCE, and whom Rabbinic traditions regards as the founder of scriptural hermeneutics, in their vast majority do not appeal to scripture, which seems to be an indication that even within proto-Rabbinic movement this kind of authority feature was not common in the early 1st century CE., although it was wide spread already during the 2nd century CE.[13]

Therefore, the same developments with regard to the attitude towards the text of the Torah were at stake in the Qumran community as well as in the proto-Rabbinic and Rabbinic tradition of Judaism, although there is a significant difference regarding the time when these changes happened, since in the proto-Rabbinic movement this same development happened around 150 years later, and this difference in time needs to be explained in order to connect the two processes.

---

12 For a discussion of the theory that a library in the temple of Jerusalem was the driving force behind the canonization of the Biblical text see SCHORCH, Communio lectorum, 174-176; idem, The libraries, 173-174.

13 See SCHREMER, They did not read, 116.

Regarding this difference, I would like to suggest that a further factor should be taken into account, namely the emergence and creation of Jewish sub-groups with their own and distinct identities, which happened within Judaism during the Hellenistic and Roman periods. As a part of this process, group-specific forms of literature and textual compositions started to emerge, and as regarding the different versions of the Torah, at least some of these groups seem to have shaped their identity by choosing one specific textual form of the Torah as their group specific text. This development, which lead from a multitude of textual versions of the Torah, accessible to a wide Jewish public, as can be observed for the first half of the 2nd century BCE, towards group-specific textual versions of the Torah as part of the identity of these groups, can be described as a process of esoterization of the Torah, insofar at the end of this process only the members of a specific group had access to a specific version of the Torah. The first group-specific text of the Torah seems to have been created in the late 2nd century BCE as part of the creation of a distinct Samaritan identity.[14] More such group-specific texts may have been created, but did not materialize in the sources which survived, especially since our knowledge about the different Jewish groups of that period is of course very fragmentary.

Thus, to the best of my knowledge, only two groups can be clearly connected with specific textual versions of the Torah, which is the Samaritans and the proto-Rabbinic/Rabbinic movement. Therefore, I would like to turn now to these two groups and their respective texts, in order to outline this process of the creation of group-specific textual versions of the Torah, or, in other words, this process of esoterization of the Torah. My examples will be taken from the Book of Deuteronomy, since it seems to me that in this composition the process is the most obvious, as will be seen. Additionally, we should keep in mind that Deuteronomy was the most read book of the Torah, according to the evidence from Qumran[15] and appears therefore especially relevant.

3. The Samaritan and the Jewish Deuteronomy

As is well known, one of the central issues of Deuteronomy is the question of the chosen place. The formula "the place that the LORD your God will chose" (המקום אשר יבחר ההוה) appears in Deut 12:5 for the first time, and it is repeated within the book another 21 times. We are used to read this formula as reference to the temple in Jerusalem, and this

---

14 See SCHORCH, La formation de la communauté samaritaine, 10-14.
15 See above.

seems at least to be justified by many passages from the Book of Kings and Chronicles, e.g.:

> "Since the day that I brought my people out of the land of Egypt, I have not chosen a city from any of the tribes of Israel (לא בחרתי בעיר מכל שבטי ישראל) in which to build a house, so that my name might be there, and I chose no one as ruler over my people Israel; but I have chosen Jerusalem in order that my name may be there (ואבחר בירושלם להיות שמי שם), and I have chosen David to be over my people Israel." (1 Kings 8:16 LXX // 2 Chron 6:5–6)

Within the Book of Deuteronomy itself, however, we seem to encounter a different identification of the chosen place, namely that the chosen place refered to in Deut 12 is the altar which the Israelites are commanded to errect after entering the Holy Land, according to Deut 27:

Deut 11:31–12:18	**Deut 27:2–7**	
11:31	When you cross the Jordan (כי אתם עברים),	On the day that you cross over the Jordan (תעברו)	27:2
	to go in to occupy the land that the LORD your God is giving you …	into the land that the LORD your God is giving you …	
12:4-5	… you shall seek the place that the LORD your God chose out of all your tribes as his habitation to put his name there.	So when you have crossed over the Jordan, you shall set up these stones, about which I am commanding you today, on Mount Garizim, and you shall cover them with plaster. And you shall build an altar there to the Lord your God, an altar of stones …	27:4-6a
12:6	There you shall bring your burnt offerings (עלתיכם),	Then offer up burnt offerings on it (והעלית עולת) to the LORD your God,	27:6b
	and your sacrifices (וזבחיכם),	make sacrifices of well-being (וזבחת שלמים)	27:7
	your tithes and your donations, your votive gifts, your freewill offerings, and the firstlings of your herds and flocks.	–	
12:7	And you shall eat (ואכלתם) there in the presence of the LORD your God, you and your households together,	and eat them (ואכלת) there,	
	rejoicing (ושמחתם) …	rejoicing (ושמחת) before the LORD your God…	

The parallel structure of Deut 12 and Deut 27 seems to leave no doubt that for Deuteronomy itself, in the textual state which is preserved in both MT and the Samaritan Torah, the chosen place is explicitly mentioned in Deut 27:4. If we look at the different textual traditions regarding Deut 27:4, however, we encounter a further problem, namely that the Masoretic text and the Septuagint place this altar on Mount Ebal, the mount of curses (compare Deut 27:13), while the Samaritan Torah and the Old Greek translation[16] localize this altar on Mount Garizim, which is the mountain of blessing, according to Deut 27:12:

> "So when you have crossed over the Jordan, you shall set up these stones, about which I am commanding you today, on [MT/LXX:] *Mount Ebal* / [SP/Old Greek:] *Mount Garizim* and you shall cover them with plaster. And you shall build an altar there to the LORD your God, an altar of stones on which you have not used an iron tool." (Deut 27:4)

From a text-historical point of view this evidence clearly indicates that the oldest version of Deut 27:4 located the altar on Mount Garizim, since otherwise the reading "Garizim" would not be part of the Old Greek text, which is anything but suspect for pro-Garizim and anti-Jerusalem tendencies. On the other hand, the re-location of the altar from Mount Garizim to Mount Ebal turns out to be a text-historically secondary endeavor of followers of the Temple in Jerusalem, which tried to delegitimize the sanctuary on Mount Garizim, being claimed by the Samaritans as the only legitimate cultic place.

Yet a further textual correction of Deuteronomy seems to have entered the text in this context: The formula pointing to the chosen place, already quoted above and attested for the first time in Deut 12:5, is preserved in the Samaritan Torah and in the Old Greek version of the Pentateuch as: "the place that the LORD has chosen" (המקום אשר בחר יהוה), while the later, and again deliberately corrected reading of the Masoretic Text contains: "the place that the LORD will choose" (המקום אשר יבחר יהוה).[17]

The background of this change seems to be that the future verbal form can be understood as referring to a place beyond Deuteronomy, thus creating the identificatory link with Jerusalem as seen above. Therefore, both textual corrections, from Garizim to Ebal in Deut 27:4, and from "the LORD has chosen" to "the LORD will choose" in the deuteronomic centralization formula were carried out as part of a conflict about the localisation of the one and only legitimate sanctuary, be it

---

16 See SCHENKER, Le Seigneur choisira-t-il le lieu de son nom, and idem, Textgeschichtliches zum Samaritanischen Pentateuch.

17 The textual evidence was gathered and presented by Adrian Schenker in his two articles mentioned above, note 16.

Mount Garizim, as claimed by the Samaritans, or be it the Temple in Jerusalem, as presupposed by Jews.

The two textual corrections within the text of Deuteronomy can be dated with reasonable certainty: The Old Greek translation of Deuteronomy, dating to the 3rd century BCE exhibits the unchanged text of Deuteronomy, i.e. the reading Garizim in Deut 27:4 and the verbal form in the perfect "he has chosen" in the centralization formula. The reference to the centralization formula contained in 4QMMT (written around the middle of 2nd century BCE) preserves the reading in the perfect "he has chosen", while the Temple scroll (late 2nd century BCE) already contains the verb in the future:

4QMMT:

ירושלים היאה מחנה הקדש היא מקום שבחר בו מכל שבטי [ישראל ...] – "For Jerusalem is the holy camp. It is the place that He chose from all the tribes of [Israel ...]" (4Q394 f8 iv:9–11)

Temple scroll:

לפני תאוכלנו שנה כשנה במקום אשר אבחר – "You are to eat those before Me annually in the place that I shall choose." (11Q19 52:9)

ושמחתה לפני במקום אשר אבחר לשום שמי עליו – "and rejoice before Me in the place that I will choose to establish My name" (11Q19 52:16)

Thus, the textual change from "he has chosen" (בחר) to "he will chose" (יבחר) seems to have taken place around the middle of the 2nd century BCE.

However, the Book of Deuteronomy was of course already known in Judah long before this time, and thus long before this textual change, and there is no reason to believe that the centralization formula was taken by the Judeans as referring to any other place outside Jerusalem, even before the textual correction was carried out. Thus, how can be explained that the text was corrected only much later, around the middle of the 2nd century BCE? The answer to this question relies on the two observations already described above:

(1) On the one hand side, as was demonstrated, a new attitude towards the text of the Torah emerged during the 2nd century BCE. The central focus of this development was the creation of awareness of the textual surface, which increasingly attributed authority to the concrete wording of the text. Within the context of this new intellectual environment, it was the textual surface of the Book of Deuteronomy which became the basis for the mutually excluding holy geographies of Samaritans and Jews. The corrections carried out in the Jerusalem-text expressed the needs of the Jews who were followers of the Jerusalem temple.

(2) On the other hand side, and closely interrelated with the first development in the field of textual awareness, the 2nd century BCE saw the emergence of groups with distinct identities, which started to use their group specific textual versions as an esoteric medium of delimitation, as can be observed especially regarding the Samaritan community and their Torah. Most obviously, however, the creation and establishing of the Samaritan sect as an independent community cannot be separated from the challenges posed by the Hasmonean policy to sharpen the profile of Judean identity. The quarrels between pre-Samaritans and Jews culminated in 129/128 BCE, when the Hasmonean John Hyrkan destroyed the sanctuary on Mount Garizim, causing thereby the final break between the two communities and the break of a literal culture into two.[18]

4. The question of languages and the Greek tradition

If we look at this outline of the presence and the authority of the Torah within the Judaism of the Hellenistic and Roman periods, there emerges the picture of a development, which started in the 2nd century BCE and was effective at least until the 2nd century CE, a development which led from multitude of textual versions shared by all followers of the ancient Israelit-Judean traditions, towards a group specific and esoteric textual uniformity. In the course of this process, the attitude to the text of the Torah changed from a focus on the content towards a focus on the textual surface. In light of this latter point, we should try to clarify yet another question: How these changes affected the Hellenistic Jewish literary tradition, i.e. the Jewish literature in Greek, and especially the attitude towards the Septuagint? – In order to analyze this problem, it seems above all important to deal with the question of the different languages used by the Jews of this period and their respective role.

It has been demonstrated elsewhere[19] that within the Palestinian Jewish tradition, the 2nd century BCE saw the emergence of a new concept of Hebrew as the Holy language. Most prominently, this new concept is expressed in Jubilees 12:

> "Then the LORD God said to me: 'Open his mouth and his ears to hear and speak with his tongue in the revealed language.' For from the day of the collapse[20] it had disappeared from the mouth(s) of all mankind. I opened

---

18   See SCHORCH, La formation de la communauté samaritaine, 10.
19   See SCHORCH, The Pre-eminence of the Hebrew Language, 47-48.
20   I.e., of the tower of Babel, see VANDERKAM, The Book of Jubilees, 73.

his mouth, ears and lips, and began to speak Hebrew with him – in the language of the creation. He took his fathers' books (they were written in Hebrew), and copied them. From that time he began to study them, while I was telling him everything that he was unable (to understand)." (Jub 12:25-27)[21]

Hebrew appears here as that language, which was used by God in the creation of the world, which was the only language until the tower of Babylon was destroyed, and which was used for composing the holy scriptures. According to Jubilees 12 this forgotten language was taught to Abraham in a revelatory act, and it was used by him and his sead as a sign of their being God's elected ones. Being the original and godly language, Hebrew thus became the central element of an exclusive revelation and the holy language of Judaism. The first explicit reference to this new concept is found in a fragmentary text from Qumran (4Q464), dating to the 1st century BCE, where the term לשון הקודש "holy language" is used *expressis verbis*.[22]

The prologue of the Greek translator of Ben Sira shows that these concept of Hebrew as the holy language was augmented with a further concept by the end of the 2nd century BCE, namely that due to this special status of Hebrew texts cannot be translated adequately:

οὐ γὰρ ἰσοδυναμεῖ αὐτὰ ἐν ἑαυτοῖς Ἑβραϊστὶ λεγόμενα καὶ ὅταν μεταχθῇ εἰς ἑτέραν γλῶσσαν·– "For those things originally in Hebrew do not have the same force when rendered into another language."

Thus, according to the Greek translator of Ben Sira, there is no there is no ἰσοδυναμία "equal force" between the Hebrew and the Greek version of a text, and both do not have the same effect on the reader, since the Hebrew text is more meaningful and important from the outset.[23] Although the Hebrew text is not totally untranslatable, and even has to be translated for practical reasons, it is effected for bad by the translation in both its content and its meaning, and the reason is that the text doesn't use the holy language anymore. Thus, there cannot be real equivalence between the original Hebrew and the Greek translation.

We may therefore conclude that the translator of Ben Sira claims an exclusive authority for the Hebrew text. Without totally disapproving of translations, he declares them as being of secondary importance only, and thus applies the concept, that it is the surface of the text, which is granted authority, on the question for the status of translations. Obviously, this view must have posed a challenge to the translation of the Septuagint. However, among the Jews of Alexandria, this challenge seems not to have been realized, or it was unknown to them.

---

21 Translation by VANDERKAM, The Book of Jubilees, 73-74.
22 See ESHEL/STONE, The holy language, 170-174.
23 See SCHORCH, The Pre-eminence of the Hebrew Language, 49-51.

At least the Letter of Aristeas seems to show no traces of this challenge, as it bases the authority of the Septuagint on the acclamation of the Jewish community. It is only in Philo that the legend about the origin of the Septuagint[24] appears in a form which declares the external textual shape of the Greek text as holy, when the story says that 72 independently working translators produced exactly the same text, the consequence of which is that the text is inspired. To the best of my knowledge, this is the first attestation that the surface focused concept of text arrived in Alexandrias Hellenistic Jewish community and was applied to the Greek Torah.

Unlike Philo, Josephus repeats the legend about the origin of the Septuagint more or less in the same version as it is found in the Letter of Aristeas, which is maybe an indication that the concept of the Greek Torah as an inspired text was not adopted among the Greek speaking Jews of Palestine. This impression is even enforced when we look at the quotations from the Old Testament which the writings of the New Testament use, exhibiting features well known from the Biblical quotations in the Qumran texts:[25]

Thus, on the one hand side, the quotation formula which marks quotations from the Old Testament (e.g. καθὼς γέγραπται, λέγει) obviously displays awareness that the textual surface is acknowledged as authority. On the other hand, however, the quoted text *de facto* seems to have been rather flexible and could be changed by the author of the new composition in order to fit the aim of the quoting text. An illustrative example is found in Eph 4:7–8:

> "But each of us was given grace according to the measure of Christ's gift. Therefore it is said, *When he ascended on high he made captivity itself a captive; he gave gifts to his people.*"[26]

The text refers to the text of Psalm 68:19 (= Psalm 67 LXX). However, this verse originally uses the 2nd person:

> "You ascended on high; you led captivity captive; you received gifts by a person […]"

Most obviously, the author of Ephesians (or his *Vorlage*) re-phrased the original quote in the 3rd person, and created thus a scriptural prooftext which could be understood as a reference to Christ. This procedure of re-phrasing a given quotation seems even to have been augmented towards the creation of pseudo-quotations, i.e. verses which are intro-

---

24 For an overview about the history of the LXX-legend in Hellenistic antiquity see WASSERSTEIN/WASSERSTEIN, The Legend of the Septuagint, 19-50.
25 See above, p. 3.
26 Translation by Albert Pietersma as published in NETS.

duced and used as scriptural references, but do not appear to have their origin in the Old Testament writings. The books of the New Testament contain a number of such pseudo-quotations. One example is 1 Cor 2:9, where Paul says:

"[…] as it is written, "What no eye has seen, nor ear heard, nor the human heart conceived, what God has prepared for those who love him."

However, although Paul seems to claim so, this quotation appears in none of the writings available to us, and in light of the developments outlined before it seems much more likely to suggest that 1 Corinthians in that case used the quotation formula only for the sake of providing, or forging, higher authority to a certain view expressed in the pseudo-quotation.

To us, this attitude may seem problematic. Paul, however, and most obviously, just used a literary technique, which was in complete accordance with the contemporary ideas about scriptural authority in Palestinian Judaism.

Bibliography

ABEL, Félix-Marie, Les livres des Maccabées, Paris ²1949.

BAUMGARTEN, Albert I., The Torah as a public document in Judaism, in: Studies in Religion 14 (1985), 17-24.

BROOKE, George J., The Explicit Presentation of Scripture in 4QMMT, in: Bernstein, Moshe/García Martínez, Florentino/Kampen, John (eds.), Legal texts and legal issues: proceedings of the second Meeting of the International Organization for Qumran Studies, Cambridge, 1995: Published in honour of Joseph M. Baumgarten (STDJ 23), Leiden/New York/Köln 1997, 67-88.

DÖRRFUSS, Ernst Michael, Mose in den Chronikbüchern: Garant theokratischer Zukunftserwartung(BZAW 219), Berlin/New York 1994.

ESHEL, Esther/STONE, Michael, The Holy Language at the End of the Days in Light of a New Fragment Found at Qumran (in Hebrew) in: Tarbitz 62 (1992/93), 169-177.

HÄNSEL, Lars, Studien zu „Tora" in Esra-Nehemia und Chronik: Erwägungen zur Bezugnahme auf חוק, מזוה, דבר, משפט, תורה in Esra-Nehemia und Chronik im Horizont frühjüdischer Texte, Universität Leipzig, Theologische Fakultät, Dissertation, 1999.

KRATZ, Reinhard Gregor, "The place which He has chosen": The identification of the cult place of Deut. 12 and Lev. 17 in 4QMMTin: Meghillot V-VI (2007), 57-80.

MAIER, Johann, Die Qumran-Essener: Die Texte vom Toten Meer I-III, München 1995.

RAPPAPORT, Uriel, The First Book of Maccabees: Introduction, Hebrew translation, and commentary [hebr.], Jerusalem 2004.

SCHENKER, Adrian, Le Seigneur choisira-t-il le lieu de son nom ou l'a-t-il choisi?: l'apport de la Bible grecque ancienne à l'histoire du texte samaritain et massorétique, in, Voitila, Anssi (ed.), Scripture in transition: Essays on Septuagint, Hebrew Bible, and Dead Sea Scrolls in Honour of Raija Sollamo (JSJS 126), Leiden/Boston 2008, 339-351.

SCHENKER, Adrian, Textgeschichtliches zum Samaritanischen Pentateuch und Samareitikon, in: Mor, Menahem/Reiterer, Friedrich (eds.), Samaritans past and present: current studies (Studia Samaritana 5 / Studia Judaica 53), Berlin/New York 2010, 105-121.

SCHORCH, Stefan, La formation de la communauté samaritaine au 2e siècle avant J.-Chr. et la culture de lecture du Judaïsme, in: Himbaza, Innocent / Schenker, Adrian (eds.), Un carrefour dans l'historie de la Bible: Du texte à la théologie au IIe siècle avant J.-C.; [colloque international tenu à l'Université de Fribourg en Suisse les 4 et 5 novembre 2004] (OBO 233), Fribourg/Göttingen 2007, 5-20.

SCHORCH, Stefan, The libraries in 2 Macc 2:13-15, in: Xeravits, Géza G./Zsengellér, József (eds.), The books of the Maccabees: History, theology, ideology; papers of the Second International Conference on the Deuterocanonical Books, Pápa, Hungary, 9 - 11 June, 2005 (JSJ.S 118), Leiden 2007, 169-180.

SCHORCH, Stefan, Communio lectorum: Die Rolle des Lesens für die Textualisierung der israelitischen Religion, in: Schaper, Joachim (ed.), Die Textualisierung der Religion (FAT 62), Tübingen 2009, 167-184.

SCHORCH, Stefan, The Pre-eminence of the Hebrew Language and the Emerging Concept of the "Ideal Text" in Late Second Temple Judaism, in: Xeravits, Géza G./Zsengellér, József (eds.), The Book of Ben Sira. Papers of the Third International Conference on the Deuterocanonical Books, Pápa, Hungary, 2006 (JSJ.S 127), Leiden 2008, 43-54.

SCHREMER, Adiel, "[T]he[y] did not read in the sealed book": Qumran halakhic revolution and the emergence of Torah study in Second Temple Judaism, in: Goodblatt, David/Pinnick, Avital/Schwartz, Daniel R. (eds.), Historical perspectives: from the Hasmoneans to Bar Kokhba in light of the Dead Sea scrolls: proceedings of the Fourth International Symposium of the Orion Center for the Study of the Dead Sea Scrolls and Associated Literature, 27-31 January, 1999 (STDJ 37), Leiden/Boston/Köln 2001, 105-126.

TOV, Emanuel, Textual Criticism of the Hebrew Bible, Minneapolis ^{3}2011.

VANDERKAM, James C., The Book of Jubilees. Translated by James C. Vanderkam (CSCO; Scriptores Aethiopici 88), Louvain 1989.

WASSERSTEIN, Abraham/WASSERSTEIN, David J., The legend of the Septuagint: From classical antiquity to today, Cambridge 2006.

WILLI, Thomas, Leviten, Priester und Kult in vorhellenistischer Zeit: Die chronistische Optik in ihrem geschichtlichen Kontext, in: Ego, Beate/Lange, Armin/Pilhofer, Peter (eds.), Gemeinde ohne Tempel / Community without Temple (WUNT 118), Tübingen 1999, 75-98.

Qoheleth and Scriptural Authority
JAMES L. CRENSHAW

For many Christians, the age of scriptural authority is a relic of the past, like dinosaurs, duels, and d*esoto automobiles*. For others, every word of the Bible is divinely inspired, inerrant, and universally binding. Ironically, the opposing camps are united in selectively ignoring parts of sacred writ. No one, to my knowledge, obeys the specific command in Exod 22:29b, attributed to the deity, to sacrifice firstborn sons along with the first animals to leave the womb. Nor do devout Christians greet all the brothers with a holy kiss, even those who obey the ban on women speakers in congregational meetings. In short, the principle of "picking and choosing" the parts of scripture to obey is alive and well in both the progressive and conservative camps of Christendom.

For modern Jews, who are not burdened with the belief in an inerrant Bible, oral tradition formalized in Talmud and Mishnah stands alongside scripture and prevents a written text from becoming an idolatrous object. A theory of gradations in scriptural authority, with Torah carrying more weight than the *Prophets and Writings*, further weakens the possibility of making a fetish of the Bible. Nevertheless, Judaism, too, is marked by competing understandings of the degree to which contemporary conduct should be controlled by written texts.

The other Abrahamic tradition, Islam, also supplements the Bible with its own holy text. Here, too, this version of divine will, the Quran, carries greater authority for Muslims than the two testaments that precede it. That is also true of the Church of the Latter Day Saints, whose Book of Mormon is thought to embody divine truths that go beyond those within the Bible itself. Both religions, however, have produced groups with different degrees of adherence to the mandates of Mohammed and Joseph Smith.

A by-product of the selective process within Christianity is the creation of distinctions between priests and laity, with priests bearing the onus of more rigorous adherence to divine commands. In Judaism, a similar distinction occurs, although membership in the priesthood is by birth and not the result of a voluntary choice. Protestantism has resisted such distinctions on the basis of the principle of the priesthood of all believers, while elevating the ministry in ways approximating that of priests in Catholic and Episcopal circles. Authority has its own allure, especially when combined with the expected rewards of being holy.

I. Diminishing Scriptural Authority

Why has belief in scriptural authority become problematic? For one thing, globalization has exposed the localized nature of sacred texts. As a result, every claim of universality, whether found within a text or put forth by an interpreter of that particular religious tradition, becomes a case of special pleading. No text is self-validating, and claiming to be exclusively true does not make it so, however often the assertion is made.

Each "holy book" becomes the religious repository of a special group. Those who reside outside this community do not find its teachings authoritative, even if they grant the inspirational power of specific insights now and again. Christians may admire the *Bhagavad Gita* or the teachings of Confucius, but this appreciative response does not include obeisance. Similarly, the Buddhist who finds certain features of the Bible to be commendable is still free to reject all its mandates. In a word, only adherents of a special religious tradition are in any way obligated to regulate their lives according to its teachings.

This point can be broadened to include the non-religious. Vast numbers of people lack a sacred text at all. Regardless of the political or religious context in which they find themselves, atheists do not consider the Bible authoritative. To them, all talk about the authority of the Bible is meaningless. The same can be said of modern secularists, some of whom may prefer the agnostic label because of the atheist's necessity to make a leap of faith. Honesty compels agnostics to recognize that disproving a deity's existence is just as impossible as demonstrating that one exists.[1]

These three things, globalization, secularism, and diminishing scriptural authority, weigh heavily on Christians. Changes in the culture have rendered much of the Bible offensive to the intellect. All too frequently, the "narrated story" of God[2] depicts a warrior and like-

---

1 Arguments for the existence of God (e.g., the cosmological, ontological, teleological, proofs from design, morality, and consciousness) succeed if at all only in bringing comfort to theists.
2 Many readers of the Bible naively take the depiction of deity in its pages to be an accurate account of divine character and conduct. They would be better served to view the narrated story as a product of an active human imagination. The result

minded followers. The Bible treats slavery as an acceptable social practice, women as by nature subject to men, and anything other than heterosexuality as an offense to society and to the deity. In some places it sanctions genocide, adopts an ideology of a chosen people, and reports miracles that are scientifically implausible (e.g., the sun standing still or going backwards). It mandates customs with no rational basis such as restrictions in diet, mode of dress, the mixing of different kinds of cloth, and the like. In a word, some sections of the Bible belong in a museum that houses outmoded artifacts.

This same Bible depicts a loving God who is deeply involved in the lives of human beings, an involvement of pathos[3] and extreme suffering because of human sin. This God champions the cause of the defenceless – the widow, the orphan, the poor, the stranger; works with human agents to establish social justice; teaches the principle that we ought to love our neighbours as ourselves; gives meaning to history, instilling the imagination with a vision of peace on earth; transforms all of life into little moments of holiness; eliminates the sharp distinction between thought and deed; provides useful myths of origins and symbols that structure existence, and much more.

The Bible has been influential in shaping western culture, especially in providing hospitals to care for the sick and schools to train the mind. It has encouraged acts of charity toward the poor and philanthropy in general. Its teachings about a dependable universe have helped to provide a matrix for the rise of science, and its teleology has enriched literature from history to fiction. The Bible has shaped languages like English and German, and its rich spirituality has fed hungry souls for millennia.

In short, the embarrassing and the ennobling fill the pages of the Bible. The former arouses suspicion that the Bible is a huge lie;[4] the latter encourages those who hear a divine voice behind it. The modern controversy over the Bible began long ago. When two prophets, Jeremiah and Hananiah, proclaimed contradictory messages (surrender to the Babylonians; resist them) and each claimed to speak in YHWH's name, who was the true prophet? Not surprisingly, the resulting con-

---

would relieve them of trying to defend God's actions and force them to come to the defence of humans. Theodicy would give way to anthropodicy.
3   The name associated with the notion of divine pathos is Abraham Joshua Heschel, who turned the Aristotelian concept of the unmoved mover upside down. According to Heschel, YHWH was the most moved mover, and the prophets stood apart from others in society precisely because they participated in divine pathos. The similarity between Heschel's view of divine pathos and the Christian understanding of Jesus' death on the cross is obvious.
4   EHRMAN, Forged.

flict could not be resolved.⁵ Consequently, even today we are left with the naysayers and the defenders.

The extremes to which defenders of scriptural authority will go are richly illustrated in a recent publication of papers that were presented at a philosophical symposium held at Notre Dame University with the theme taken from Isa 55:8, "My ways are not your ways." The title of this volume, *DIVINE EVIL?*, is especially provocative.⁶ The interrogative reflects the controversy between progressive and conservative authors represented in its pages. Assertions of scriptural authority stand over against rejections, and proponents of these competing views refused to budge an inch. The main arguments of the defenders follow, with my response to each one.⁷

1. Whatever God does is right

By definition, God is good. It follows from this conviction that God can do no wrong. Human beings are mistaken when they attribute evil to the deity, for they do not understand the divine will sufficiently to make such a judgment. Although many acts of God may give the impression of being immoral and downright cruel, God must have a reason for behaving in this way. The giver of life can take it back, whether by a universal flood, by catastrophic forays against cities like Sodom and Gomorrah, by genocidal action against a single ethnic group like the Amalekites for being inhospitable, by punishing an infant for the sins of a father, the warrior king David, and so on. Such conduct by the deity need not be disturbing to believers,⁸ for they can count on the goodness of God to control divine action.

But a God whose power determines what is right is not worthy of worship. As early as Epicurus, the logical dilemma intrinsic to belief in

---

5   The struggle to distinguish authentic prophets from inauthentic ones led to the compilation of criteria by which to test those claiming to speak on YHWH's behalf. I have examined those tests of true prophecy and found them wanting. See my Prophetic Conflict, 2007.

6   Edited by Michael BERGMANN, Michael J. MURRAY, and Michael C. REA, Oxford 2011. The subtitle of this volume, *The Moral Character of the God of Abraham*, lacks a question mark.

7   The twelve arguments come from the defenders of the moral character of YHWH. In the elaboration, I have tried to strengthen some arguments by adding things the speakers could have said.

8   For a pastoral perspective on difficult biblical texts about YHWH, see SEIBERT, Disturbing Divine Behavior. Neither of Seibert's solutions solves the problem, for who is equipped to say when the depiction of YHWH strays from the actual character of deity, and how can a Christocentric reading of the Hebrew Bible do anything but distort its original intent?

divine goodness and power in the face of the reality of evil was recognized. Since evil is undeniable, one of the other two ideas has to be abandoned or at the very least modified. Either God is not fully good or not almighty. Often it is conceded that God freely chooses to limit divine power, but seldom is belief in divine goodness surrendered by believers. A rabbinic *midrash* makes the point emphatic by having angels advise the Creator that he cannot have both a world and justice.

To state the matter differently, surely God ought to exemplify an ethical standard equal to that of humans. Good people do not subject faithful friends to tests that involve murder, nor do they kill others and cause pain just to win a wager. Decent citizens do not engage in genocide, show irrational favouritism, and inflict suffering on those who do not reciprocate love. When God's actions in the Bible are examined against such an ethical standard, they often fail to measure up to it.

Furthermore, once a gift has been exchanged, it becomes the sole property of the recipient. We do not take back the book we have given to a friend any more than we ask for the return of a perennial we have bestowed on a fellow gardener. If life is a divine gift, it is no longer God's to take back.

2. The human concept of justice does not apply to God

Divine transcendence means that the deity remains outside every ethical argument about goodness. Only humans are subject to norms of behaviour that make society possible. God is not a member of society and does not have to abide by its rules. Abraham was completely mistaken when arguing that God act justly by sparing the condemned cities in which innocents resided. "Shall not the judge of all the earth do what is right?"[9] rests on the premise that mortals resemble God. The principle of similitude,[10] enunciated in the priestly account of creation and reinforced by the notion of *imitatio dei*, is rendered null and void by an absolute break between creator and creature.

Even the vilest act by human standards, the testing of an obedient servant by ordering him to sacrifice his beloved son[11] or killing another

---

9 This text provided the title for a Festschrift in my honor edited by David Penchansky and Paul Redditt (Winona Lake, Indiana: Eisenbrauns, 2000). Its contributors reveal the extent to which biblical texts trouble interpreters.

10 VAN DER TOORN, Sources in Heaven, 265-277, thinks the collapse of a worldview based on the principle that the gods resembled humans led to the idea of revelation and elitism. See also VAN DER TOORN, Why Wisdom Became a Secret. For a discussion of the concept of similitude in wisdom literature, see CRENSHAW, Sipping.

11 For analysis of Genesis 22, see CRENSHAW, Defending God, 57-65, 213-216. The story about Abraham sacrificing Isaac continues to fascinate interpreters; see the extensive

servant's sons and daughters to satisfy a bet with a celestial being[12] is acceptable because God is exempt from the standards of human decency. God has the right to find out whether Abraham loves him more than anything else and whether Job's goodness is calculated on being rewarded for service.

The numerous attempts to defend divine justice over the millennia are misguided and theodicy[13] is a fruitless enterprise, despite huge sections of the Bible that bear witness to the human struggle to understand the unthinkable in a universe governed by a good God.

But justice is justice, whether practiced by God or by humans. The peril of adducing two different standards of justice, one for God and another for human beings, was recognized by the author of Genesis 18 and by various other biblical thinkers.[14] That is why they struggled so valiantly to understand God's interaction with them. Like Jeremiah, they endeavoured to affirm divine justice as a mystery, but they were not willing to abandon the concept or to create a unique definition of justice for God alone. In short, they did not opt for a teleological suspension of the ethical in order to justify a horrific command like that issued to Abraham in Genesis 22.

3. God uses historical events to teach morality and to foster spiritual growth

For biblical authors, history was the arena of divine activity, just as it was for the intellectuals in surrounding cultures.[15] The rise and fall of city states occurs according to a divine plan, with sin determining the extent of decline. History was written and revised with this principle as

---

bibliography on page 214, note 9, to which may be added KALIMI, God, I Beg You; FELDMAN, Glory and Agony.

12 Equally intriguing is the story about Job and the dialogue that is associated with it. For my latest perspective on this book and its influence through the centuries to the present, see CRENSHAW, Reading Job.

13 Theodicy as a problem was not limited to the biblical world. For discussion of the broader context, see LAATO/DE MOOR (eds.), Theodicy in the World of the Bible. Biblical exclusivism, however, heightened the problem where YHWH was concerned. See CRENSHAW, Theodicy; and CRENSHAW, Theodicy in the Book of the Twelve. For a look at prophetic literature generally and the problem of theodicy see CRENSHAW, Theodicy and Prophetic Literature.

14 See CRENSHAW, Sojourner.

15 The earlier view that the biblical concept of YHWH's role in guiding history toward a favourable outcome for Israel was unique, placing Israel over against its environment, has given way to a new reading of the situation that emphasizes semblance. The ground-breaking monograph was ALBREKTSON, History and the Gods. Its impact is chronicled in GNUSE, Heilsgeschichte as a Model for Biblical Theology.

the guiding light. A failed kingdom was deemed guilty of serious transgression, and a prosperous one was believed to have been obedient to the deity. City states that worshiped gods other than YHWH did not deserve to survive because of the danger they posed to weaker Israelites. The threat of sin was serious, causing the downfall of both kingdoms, Ephraim and Judah.

This theory of history applied to all nations. God mandated the destruction of cities such as Jericho and larger ethnic groups like the Canaanites. In addition, God controlled the actions of the rulers of powerful kingdoms, even Assyria and Egypt. The world was a huge chess board, and God moved the pieces around to arrive at the ultimate goal, checkmate. The nature of the game requires that some pieces fall along the way, and the end justifies the means, even if there is no logical rationale for determining winners and losers.

But a pedagogy that involves mass destruction is abominable. Theological instruction that comes at the cost of dividing ethnic groups into hate mongers or that is achieved on false pretenses comes at too great a cost. Stories about the eradication of whole peoples damage those whose memory includes gruesome accounts, whether they are based on actual history or are no more than the fruit of an active imagination. Clearly, the ancient Near Eastern context makes it probable that at least some of the atrocities in the Bible were real. Fabrications certainly occurred, but so did battles that were fought in the name of YHWH. Survival depended on defending life and property, and the lure of power was often irresistible.

4. Some historical events in the Bible are merely symbolic

Ancient historiographers were more interested in propaganda than in reporting actual facts. They often wrote to promote the causes of their royal sponsors. Accordingly, they composed narratives that reflected favourably on the reigning monarch. In doing so, they employed rhetoric that appealed to the emotions. The victory over local powers was merely spiritual, and the transformation of a cultural battle into mortal conflict is motivated by a desire to stress the importance of total allegiance to YHWH.

Modern readers are wrong in thinking that God actually mandated the total destruction of cities or peoples, that celestial beings married women, that an Assyrian army consisting of 185,000 soldiers was slain by the divine breath, that the patriarchs engaged in morally questionable behaviour, and so on. Just as the Homeric stories of the gods were really about conflicts other than what seems on the surface to be the case, biblical accounts also point to something on a higher plane than the historical.

But an allegorical interpretation of scripture does not rule out the literal. Even the church fathers Origen and Tertullian, like their Alexandrian Jewish predecessor Philo who practiced a hermeneutic involving allegory, recognized that texts are first and foremost historical.[16] That is, literature derives from a specific context, and the primary task of an interpreter is to understand that setting and its implications for reading. The subjectivity of the allegorical method leaves its practitioners free to impose their own will on a text, for they do not acknowledge even the semblance of objective control. The text means what they want it to mean, and that leaves room for *eisegesis* of all sorts.

5. Both the canonical context and its larger ancient Near Eastern counterpart correct questionable features of the Bible

The composition of the Bible took place over centuries; during this time, many ideas changed for the better. In the process, some disturbing aspects of conduct were discarded. By this process, the Bible continually pointed to nobler instincts, at the same time interjecting a teleological hope that leads beyond the Hebrew Bible.

The distinctive nature of the Israelite people even bathed borrowed ideas in a radical negativity, changing them completely to fit into the world view of those who worshiped YHWH. Mythic themes dealing with the flood and proverbial teachings take on a unique character once they are combined with concepts peculiar to YHWH's followers.

But uplifting features of the Bible, no matter how sublime, do not atone for its many troubling aspects. As a matter of fact, sometimes the sublime and the obscene lie side by side. The best example of this phenomenon can be found in Job's Oath of Innocence in chapter 31 of the book bearing his name. Although it soars to the heavens in one moment, it descends to the lowest depths with its reprehensible view of women, acceptance of slavery, and condescending attitude toward the poor.[17]

Furthermore, the emphasis on progress through the centuries leads naturally to a view of Christianity as superior to Judaism from which it

---

16 Church fathers like Origen and Augustine depended on allegory to explain troublesome aspects of biblical literature, but they regarded the literal sense (historical) as primary and the figurative as secondary. The allegorical and topological meanings served more like window dressing.

17 CRENSHAW, A Good Man's Code of Ethics, and CRENSHAW, Reading Job; BALENTINE, Job, 471-510; GOOD, In Turns of Tempest, 309-318; NEWSOM, The Book of Job.

sprang and drives a wedge between sister faiths, making a mockery of the bond that the Apostle Paul considered the divine purpose behind the two. In addition, it overlooks the disturbing views that persist to the end of the Bible. Progress, that is, occurs but not in all things.

6. Metaphorical language and stylistic features in the Bible have been confused with literal discourse

An analogy with language involving modern athletes illustrates this point. Players frequently exaggerate the scope of their victory by saying something like "We slaughtered the opponents." Those who are familiar with the boasts of exuberant athletes easily recognize similar claims of victory in the field of battle. The story about Joshua conquering the people of Jericho and many other accounts of military exploits resulting in the death of whole populations are really boastful exaggeration. When stylistic phrases such as "Israel (or its agents) put everyone to the sword," appear several times, readers can conclude that the authors are using familiar stereotypical expressions to universalize a favourite view of the conquest. The language refers to cultural wars, not to success on the field of battle.

But even if the language of genocide were symbolic, which is doubtful, the effect of such metaphorical trumpeting of victory is harmful to the psyche. Children who are taught national history in which savagery is normal will be tempted to behave in a similar manner, especially if the historical record has nothing to indicate that the language is symbolic. The non-existence of Jericho in the thirteenth century does not erase the fact that canonical authors had no compunctions about attributing mass destruction to Joshua and his god. No linguistic slight of hand can divest *herem* of its sinister nature, and the eradication of a people's system of values is reprehensible aside from their disappearance at the hands of YHWH.

7. Stories of atrocities in battle are retrojections from a later time that illustrate a spiritual truth

The biblical record is governed by theological interests rather than historical fact. When much of the history was finally committed to writing, centuries had passed and the authors of stories dealing with national origins were far removed from the event themselves. By necessity, the history was fabricated out of the active imagination of writers. Only the experiences were highlighted that contributed to the religious insights the authors hoped to convey to a receptive audience. The conquest of

Canaan and the many atrocities associated with the early judges never took place. The spiritual conflict between the Israelites and neighbours did not leave a trail of mangled bodies.

The desire to put the best face on one's history is widespread, as citizens of the United States can easily appreciate. The popularity of a purist version of this nation's founding and even of the conflict between the North and the South shows how people tend to glorify their past. Ancient Israel was no different. Its historians wrote a story that justified the existence of a people fiercely eager to preserve its distinctiveness. Ideology prevailed, as usual, and the record of atrocities must be read through a lens that filters out the gory details.

But imposing one's own ideology on the recording of events from the past makes a mockery of history. The authors of the biblical stories present the narrative as factual. They may be writing imaginary stories but they do not offer a clue as to their rhetorical strategy. Throughout the entire process, they give the impression of transmitting facts. Worse still, they interject theories that have lasting repercussions, specifically the idea that Israel is a chosen nation and that the land has been set aside for them for posterity.

8. In reading the Bible, the rule of faith is primary

No one comes to a text without bringing a counter text to bear on it. The principle of interpretation and the linguistic system in which one has been educated determine the interpretation of a given text, as any history of hermeneutics amply documents. The approaches are endless (*midrash*, patristic and medieval exegesis, historical criticism, romantic criticism, feminist criticism, Afro-American readings, structuralism, post-modernism, cognitive criticism, queer criticism, and so on). Because complete objectivity is impossible and the mind is not blank, readers impose their own world on texts. Therefore the crucial task facing readers is to choose the most appropriate lens through which to view a written document. Readers have inherited a long tradition of interpretation; they can select a hermeneutic of suspicion or one of charity. Those who think the latter approach is the right one find guidance in the past. Fortunately, both Christians and Jews possess a rich interpretive tradition. For Christians, the rule of faith (doctrines codified in creeds over the centuries) illumines texts, and the Holy Spirit, protects against heresy. The rule of faith is both Christocentric and trinitarian.

But the rule of faith fails to do justice to a sacred text that belongs to two religions. The application of a Christian principle to the Hebrew

Bible yields a meaning that has nothing to do with its original sense and widens the gulf between Judaism and Christianity. Historical criticism is forced to take a back seat to patristic ways of interpreting scripture, and doctrinal issues shape the questions brought to the text and the answers derived from it. After all, one person's heretic is another person's saint.

9. Christology ought to shape all reading of the Bible

Just as Philip in Acts 8 explained the story of the suffering servant in Deutero-Isaiah as a proclamation about Jesus, readers look for typologies in the Hebrew Bible that are fully disclosed in the Galilean. Because Jesus is believed to be God's son and the Holy Spirit is God's presence after the son's departure to heaven, all talk about deity must take into account Jesus of Nazareth. The son was present at the moment of creation, as implied by the plural in God's initial words, "Let us make humankind in our own image" and he was present when God visited Abraham and Sarah to inform them that they would become the parents of a son in their old age. Similarly, the Holy Spirit guided the Israelites out of Egyptian bondage, communicated the divine will to prophets, and manifested itself to sages as personified wisdom.

But the earliest Christians did not agree about the trinity, a doctrine formally introduced into a creed of the church after much controversy. To use this late doctrine when interpreting the Hebrew Bible is to impose a theological dogma from very different times on literature that arose long before such a belief was introduced. The plural in Gen 1:26 derives from the celestial court; the visitors in Gen 18:2 are called men; and the spirit in the Hebrew Bible does not reflect trinitarian language.

10. God acts like a surgeon in removing a threat to the divine will

It is generally agreed that surgeons operate to remove cancerous growth or diseased organs. While the operation may cause pain, the ultimate goal is to heal patients. By analogy, the great Physician surgically removes sin from society in its various guises – idolatry, pride, rebellion, venality, and the like.

But surgeons remove diseased organs; they do not intentionally kill patients. Even if Exod 15:26 calls YHWH a healer, the analogy above is flawed, for it seeks to explain how God can take human lives, which is altogether different from healing the sick. In addition, this argument depends on the identification of whole peoples as cancerous primarily because they pay allegiance to gods other than YHWH. Groups do not fall into categories like sinful and innocent, for they consist of individuals, each with a distinctive character.

11. The existence of heaven makes everything relative

Originating in martyrdom and in an intense sense of divine presence,[18] belief in a future life with God in some heavenly abode acts as a powerful incentive to ethical conduct. It also has a negative side, legitimating poverty and social injustice by promising a better existence in the next life. Even an early departure can become less burdensome when it is explained as God's way of preventing later disobedience, or so it seemed to the unknown author of Wisdom of Solomon.

But no one really knows what happens after death; heaven therefore falls into the category of hope, one sustained by faith. The controversial idea was rejected by the authors of the books of Job, Ecclesiastes, and Sirach. And it is difficult to see how the prospect of heaven can make up for the injustices that occur on earth. Ethicists know that virtue is its own reward, and anyone who does good simply to attain heaven or to escape hell is not truly virtuous.

12. God can kill without inflicting pain

Because nothing is impossible to deity, God can make death completely devoid of suffering. Divine anesthesia removes one of the objections to the idea that the deity takes human lives either to promote the divine plan or as punishment for sin. Plague, sickness, warfare, natural disasters, or any other cause of death do not impugn the goodness of God.

But murder is murder whether administered with or without causing suffering. The notion of divine anesthesia merely dances around the real problem. It does not remove the fact that God is still responsible for killing human beings. No matter how peaceful the final moments of the dead, the agent of their demise is still culpable.

In summary, the Bible depicts a deity who often does disturbing things, and no amount of rationalizing erases the scandal created by such action. Modern attempts to defend God's justice are no improvements on the ancient ones that I have discussed at some length elsewhere. They are (1) the atheistic response; (2) alternative gods; (3) the demonic; (4) limited power and knowledge; (5) split personality; (6) divine discipline; (7) punishment for sin; (8) suffering as atonement; (9)

---

18 I advance this thesis in CRENSHAW, Love is Stronger than Death. See also D'SOUSA, Stronger than Death.

deferring justice until the next life; (10) mystery; and (11) questioning the problem.[19]

II. The Intrinsic Nature of Literature

Those of us who are surrounded by the written word can scarcely imagine the radical change brought about by the discovery of writing. One important transition was recognized in the remark by Thamous, the patron of literature, to the putative inventor, Thoth, that writing will lead to an eventual decline in the power of memory. With a few exceptions such as blind bards, religious preservers of sacred texts, and "idiot savants," Plato's description of the transition between an oral and a written culture is accurate.

Loss of memory is not the only result of this important shift in communication, as Plato perceived. So long as the messenger was present to deliver a word to an intended audience, anyone who had trouble grasping any part of the speech could ask for clarification. That access is missing when a text is substituted for a speaker. Written texts are mute, and the burden of interpretation shifts to readers.

While the burden of successful communication stays the same regardless of the mode of delivery, the clues change greatly. Gestures and tonal quality belong to oral delivery, and these aids to hearers range from the straight-forward to the subtle. Written texts have their own intrinsic clues to meaning, and these, too, vary with each composition.

The secret of good reading is to uncover the signifiers left by the author. Only after that task has been carried out in minute detail can readers go on to extrapolate meanings never considered by the author, insights that have arisen because of changed circumstances and that accommodate an old message to the very different world view of a reader.

I have described close reading as the demand imposed on readers by a text. In short, one examines each word in the same way he or she studies the body of a lover, slowly and admiringly, always searching for that which brings pleasure and creates awe. At the same time, flaws are not overlooked but are recognized as a necessary condition of being finite. Furthermore, lovers make the best critics, for they force us to acknowledge our own shortcomings.

Like lovers, every written text is unique. Each author has a distinctive style, vocabulary, and message. Only by discovering these three can readers hope to grasp what is actually said. That is why a knowl-

---

19   CRENSHAW, Defending God.

edge of the language in which a text appears is required for accurate reading. That is also why familiarity with the rhetorical patterns in the time of the author is essential. It also means that interpretation of the Bible is an esoteric discipline, however much one recoils from drawing this conclusion.[20]

When we turn from texts in general to the Bible, as I have just done, the issue of authority complicates things. In my own experience, I have observed that religious zealots have used the authority of the Bible to advance their conservative social agenda. In doing so, they have seldom shown love for Christian brothers and sisters who disagreed with them. As I survey the global scene, it seems undeniable that other sacred texts generate similar rancour among those who profess allegiance to them. As a rule, belief in the authority of sacred texts has tended to divide people rather than bringing them together.

The conclusion that I draw from this situation is that the idea of the authority of sacred texts is often a convenient tool for those who are interested in power above everything else. Unscrupulous manipulators of the weak have rightly seen that the text has no intrinsic authority, that in reality people exercise the only existing authority. The philosopher Ernest Sabatier understood this fact when observing that individuals who choose to ignore the mandate of scripture insert themselves into the position of authority. Everyone does just that. It follows logically that human beings are the final authority, and the Bible plays a subsidiary role.

Because the Bible was written in an age vastly different from the modern one, many of its ideas do not pass the test of reason. A pre-scientific world view, a pre-Copernican universe, and theo-centrism stand over against the secular society that has shaped our sensibilities. At what point does scriptural authority begin to erode? When the sun stands still, seas divide themselves for the benefit of a wandering band of former slaves, a corpse raises another to life, an army of 185,000 soldiers is stricken and Zion spared? Or does the erosion begin the moment foreign texts such as the *Instruction of Amenemopet* are incorporated into the Bible? Alternatively, does its sway over readers dwindle when a psalmist prays for the murder of the children of an enemy, when YHWH behaves worse than either you or I would ever do, when slavery, genocide, and anti-feminism surface; when God threatens de-

---

20 This statement is not to be construed as ruling out the study of scripture by nonspecialists. In my experience, they often bring new insights into the practical application of the Bible to life. Two distinct types of study are involved. One has as its goal the accurate interpretation of the author's words in their historical setting; the other aims at deriving spiritual sustenance from what has become normative for believers.

struction of the whole human race except for 144,000 men who have not lain with women, and when a basic story line contributes to anti-semitism?

This indication of only a few objectionable features in the Bible reveals why a shift from text to reader is mandatory, despite the dangers inherent to this move. Choosing a canon within the canon occurred in the earliest days of Christendom when Jesus was asked to name the greatest commandment of all. That process of selectivity continued with Marcion and to a lesser degree survives even today. For some Christians, the choice involves something as extensive as the Deutero-canonical literature in the Septuagint, while for others it comes down to individual observations about divorce, sex, military combat, and any number of commands and directives that no longer seem obligatory.

The facts demand a minimal view of scriptural authority. Because the Bible was written by humans rather than by God, it is flawed just like its authors. It is essentially their own perception of reality, one that is in many ways alien to contemporary readers. Nevertheless, it has nurtured Jews and Christians for a very long time, perhaps because of its humanity, not in spite of it. Skeptical philosophy on the edges of faith seems just about right,[21] and that is the position put forth by Qoheleth.

III. Qoheleth

What position is that? In the first place, Qoheleth speaks in his own voice, not that of God. In this regard, he stands alongside the other authors of the wisdom corpus, all of whom present their ideas as their very own.[22] Experience, not divine revelation, lies behind the observations by the various composers of the books of Proverbs, Job, Ecclesiastes, Sirach, and Wisdom of Solomon. In these books, revelation plays a minimal role, seldom occurring (e.g., in a report of a dream in Job 4:12-17, in the personification of wisdom, especially in Prov 8:22-31 and

---

21 The language is derived from the Nobel Prize winner Czeslaw Milosz, who writes "In any case, I discovered that what fits me is a skeptical philosophy. That doesn't ascribe to man any higher qualities, nor to the God man created" (MILOSZ, Second Space, 20).

22 CRENSHAW, Old Testament Wisdom; Collins, Jewish Wisdom; and PERDUE, Wisdom Literature; IBID., The Sword and the Stylus; and IBID. (ed.), Scribes, Sages, and Seers. Perdue ranges more widely than either Crenshaw or Collins in that he includes scribes and seers in his study of wisdom literature.

Sirach 24, and in speeches attributed to YHWH in Job 38:1-40:2; 40:6-41:26).[23]

Some other canonical books, especially Psalms and Song of Songs, also speak from a human perspective, in these instances either to bring human misery before the deity, along with praise,[24] or to celebrate the strong passions that accompany love between the sexes.[25] These works, however, are sufficiently different from the sapiential corpus to discourage scholars from including them in wisdom literature.

The uniqueness of the wisdom books has led to extreme views that label it an alien body and pagan,[26] on the one hand, and thoroughly YHWHistic, on the other hand.[27] A more moderate view in which difference is recognized but not judged to be deficient has held sway. The emphases in other canonical works are not a valid measure to apply to wisdom literature, for it has long been known that central features of Israel's past are missing from it until the early second century: the names of the patriarchs, Mosaic and Davidic traditions, the centrality of Jerusalem and its cult,[28] and narratives in the service of the Israelites. The early sages were interested in discovering how to cope with problems that arose in daily experience. Only with Ben Sira[29] and the un-

---

[23] In an article entitled "Is the 'Wisdom Tradition' a tradition?", Mark SNEED faults me for neglecting the place of revelation in biblical wisdom. Had he bothered to read the third edition of my *Old Testament Wisdom*, he would have seen the error in that assessment. Regrettably, his criticism of my views rests on the first edition from 1981 and on articles from 1969 and 1976.

[24] The three volume commentary by HAKHAM, The Bible Psalms with the Jerusalem Commentary, reveals the rich treasures within rabbinic interpretation, while ALTER, The Book of Psalms, brings his expertise in literary criticism to bear on the biblical text. GILLINGHAM, Psalms Through the Centuries, examines the reception-history of Psalms, and WIEDER, Words to God's Music, lends a poet's voice to transform ancient views into modern concerns.

[25] FOX, The Song of Songs, brings out the universal aspects of love songs; ASTELL, The Song of Songs in the Middle Ages, reveals their abiding presence, and BLOCH/BLOCH, The Song of Songs, provide a fresh translation and commentary for these expressions of desire.

[26] PREUSS, Einführung. His view is vigorously opposed by STEIERT, Die Weisheit Israels.

[27] VON RAD, Wisdom in Israel, best represents the continuity between sacred narrative and poetry in the rest of the canon and wisdom literature. Of the many advocates of this perspective, DELL, Get Wisdom, and DELL, The Book of Proverbs, gives the clearest presentation of the facts.

[28] PERDUE, Wisdom and Cult, is the most notable exception to the view that sages were not interested in the cult.

[29] Studies of Ben Sira have flourished lately; two collected works demonstrate the progress that has been made toward a fuller understanding of his teachings. They are PASSARO/BELLIA (eds.), The Wisdom of Ben Sira, and a collection of articles by REITERER, "Alle Weisheit stammt vom Herrn …".

known author of Wisdom of Solomon[30] did sages incorporate Israel's sacred traditions into their teachings, perhaps as a matter of national pride in the face of an aggrandizing hellenism.[31]

More than any other sage, Qoheleth calls attention to his own ego as the source of his teachings.[32] He goes out of his way to stress the investigative mode of discovery that lay behind everything he said. He says that he determined to explore wisdom and folly, even going so far as to examine madness too. This language is so pervasive in his observations that it has led Michael Fox to label Qoheleth the first empirical thinker in the Bible.[33]

Perhaps that judgment would be altered if the authors of Prov 7:6-27 and 24:30-34 had left more of their teachings to posterity.[34] In both instances, sages derive their insights from careful examination of behavior, which then leads to useful analogies. Experience taught them that sexual sleuths pose a threat to innocent youth and that laziness leads to want. In the absence of such additional data from these two authors, scholars are left to ponder Qoheleth's empiricism.

In doing so, they would do well to consider the numerous places in Qoheleth's teachings where an empirical approach would necessarily have left him speechless. It would never have taught him for example, that God made everything beautiful, or appropriate in its time, and put something in the human mind but made it inaccessible to the recipient of this peculiar gift (3:10-11). Nor would an exclusively empirical approach have enabled Qoheleth to conclude that God mysteriously bestows life breath on a fetus (11:5). The same judgment applies to the several observations about angering the deity, indeed to everything involving transcendence.[35] Divine activity, that is, lies outside the scope of empirical investigation. Anything that Qoheleth says about God is a conclusion based on unprovable assumptions. Even his many refer-

---

30 John Collins' valuable introduction to Jewish wisdom in the Hellenistic age has been supplemented by PERDUE, The Sword and the Stylus, 292-371, and PERDUE, Wisdom Literature, 267-324.
31 HENGEL, Judaism and Hellenism. ADAMS, Wisdom in Transition, shows how a changing world view affects a fundamental concept.
32 HÖFFKEN, Das Ego des Weisen.
33 FOX, Qohelet's Epistemology, and FOX, A Time to Tear Down.
34 CRENSHAW, Qoheleth's Understanding, shows how much Qoheleth depends on traditional teaching.
35 Qoheleth's view of God has been widely explored; see GORSSEN, Le cohérence; MÜLLER, Wie sprach Qohälät von Gott?; MICHEL, Gott bei Qohelet; DE JONG, God in the Book of Qohelet; SCHOORS, God in Qoheleth; and SMELIK, God in the Book of Qoheleth. For me, Qoheleth's use of Elohim rather than the Tetragrammaton, Shaddai, Eloah, or such nomenclature is telling.

ences to divine gifts show to what extent Qoheleth combines "cultural givens" with his empirical approach to knowledge.

In short, Qoheleth observes, examines, reflects on, ponders, and explores reality as it presents itself to him, but he brings a host of assumptions to bear on what he sees. These preconceived notions about the deity are the depository of human voices over the centuries, but they cannot be subjected to the test of logical verification. In his teachings, readers come face to face with a religious quest like their very own if they take religion seriously. The operative word is quest, not divine disclosure.

The second point to be made about scriptural authority and Qoheleth is that despite his emphasis on observation he is open to life's deep mysteries. Not only is the miracle of birth seen as the realm of divine activity,[36] but death is also plumbed for its relationship to the deity.[37] In a word, the life breath returns to its source. Life between these two episodic events is bathed in light that is sweet to look upon but laden with irksome toil (*'amal*). Nevertheless, adoration alone does not suffice, for in Qoheleth's mind God also demands awe and even fear.

Sometimes Qoheleth chooses language that reinforces a sense of mystery. That is particularly true of the unusual *bore'eyka* in 12:1, which has been taken to mean creator, grave, and well. Interpreters who think creator makes no sense in context understand the word to be a double reference symbolizing death and one's wife. The latter connection is based on the description in Prov 5:18 of a wife as the cistern from which a husband drinks.[38]

At other times, Qoheleth seems to bend over backwards to be ambiguous, as in 5:19 where the participle *ma'aneh* occurs with Elohim as subject.[39] Precisely what does God do with the joy of the mind? Answer? Afflict? Keep one busy? Because experience itself is capable of several interpretations, Qoheleth's language reflects actual reality. His choice of a verbal root with at least three different meanings seems to suggest indecisiveness inherent to reality.

His reading of daily events is profound, openly acknowledging the ambiguities of existence.[40] When the facts do not support a positive

---

36 CRENSHAW, From the Mundane to the Sublime, 61-72, 217-222.
37 BURKES, Death in Qoheleth.
38 SEOW, Ecclesiastes, 351-352, argues persuasively that Qoheleth may have meant all three of these (Creator, well (wife), and grave (death), which was indeed the interpretation put forth in the first century by Rabbi Akabya ben Mahallel.
39 LOHFINK, Qoheleth 5:17-19, views the entire context positively.
40 KRÜGER, Meaningful Ambiguities, and WILSON, Artful Ambiguity.

view of things, Qoheleth does not hide his face in the sand and pretend that things are rosy. The randomness of so much that we encounter forces him to question the reason for all human endeavour. With that simple step, the whole system of reward and retribution collapses, and with it the controlling principle that shapes the biblical record.

Third, Qoheleth's pedagogy is dialogic. He realizes that every important truth is complex, so much so that its opposite also holds some truth. Accordingly, he frequently contradicts himself, partly because his own thought has changed over the years and partly because he recognizes his own limitations as an observer of reality. Qoheleth would have agreed with the author of the Babylonian "Dialogue between a Master and a Slave," who saw positives and negatives for most choices available to humans, e.g. dining, marrying, hunting, going for a ride in the country, making war, agreeing to lend money or goods, giving one's possessions away, and committing suicide.[41]

That is why a rhetoric of erasure functions nicely for Qoheleth's thought.[42] One insight cancels another, erasing the original and substituting its opposite, at least for the moment. In his world, a "yes" is naturally followed by a "but."[43]

Fourth, under the sun, that is, on earth, all things are relative. Absolutes, if they exist at all, belong to another world. Wisdom is good, but only up to a point. The effort to arrive at knowledge brings considerable pain, and riches do not always follow success in acquiring wisdom. Poor but wise men actually exist, even if often ignored and unappreciated.[44] The profit motive is not reinforced by the actual results of any given effort, for chance inevitably enters the equation.

From these observations, it follows that Qoheleth acts as an iconoclast. He takes existing views and transforms them, in the process introducing chaos. The sequence is one of orientation, disorientation, and reorientation.[45] For those whose comfort zone requires the status quo, Qoheleth poses a huge risk. In his mind, nothing is sacrosanct, and everything is subject to questioning. Popular wisdom, the accumulation of the insights of astute observers from the past, does not escape Qoheleth's scrutiny, even when seemingly borne out in daily experience.

---

41 GREENSTEIN, Sages.
42 BERGER, Qohelet and the Exigencies of the Absurd, uses this felicitous language.
43 HERTZBERG, Der Prediger, makes frequent use of the idea conveyed by Zwar/aber, listing as many as twenty-four on page 30 of his commentary.
44 CRENSHAW, Poor but Wise (Qoh 9:13-16).
45 The commentary by Thomas KRÜGER, Qohelet, makes exemplary use of the concept of deconstruction in interpreting Qoheleth's thought.

That is how he can question the prevailing prejudice about women being morally corrupt (7:23-29).[46]

Fifth, more than any other biblical author, Qoheleth attends to time's passage. From birth to death we stand under this powerful force, but we can never bend time to make it serve us. Our moments are determined and we act like puppets in a powerful drama until death stills our voice and immobilizes us. Ironically, nature outlasts humans who have populated the earth.[47]

For Qoheleth, even in death we are not unique; animals join us in that experience. Our equality with beasts serves two purposes: to instill fear and to promote reflection. The result of his own thought processes is to underline human ignorance about our ultimate destiny, a shrugging of the shoulders and whispered question, *"mi yodea'* (Who knows?). In the face of rising speculation about a future life beyond death, Qoheleth soberly reminds us that nobody really knows what takes place after death, if anything other than decomposition.

Time does more than seal human destiny. It makes possible the multiple opportunities to love and hate, laugh and cry, speak and be silent, plant and uproot, sew and rip apart, and much more. And although we may not be able to read the time chart so as to profit from it in the way earlier sages thought they could, we are not paralyzed by ignorance. Instead, we risk loss and defeat, knowing that life always proceeds according to time's agenda.

Sixth, Qoheleth understood the essential nature of human existence, which he called *hebel*.[48] By this word he means something approximating mist, vapor, the transitory or ephemeral, foulness, futility and absurdity. Nothing fell outside this domain, in his view, unless it existed beyond the sun.[49] Under the sun, existence consisted of something akin

---

46 No satisfactory interpretation of 7:23-29 has appeared. The current trend is to see the misogynism as a traditional view that Qoheleth challenges. The literature is rapidly expanding (see note 57 on pages 16-17 in my article, Qoheleth's Quantitative Language).

47 SHARP, Ironic Representation, explores the possibilities inherent to an ironic reading of Qoheleth. Ironically, she does not see the extent to which her commitment to canonical criticism shapes her positive reading of Qoheleth.

48 The most thorough analysis of *hebel* in Ecclesiastes is that by MILLER, Symbol and Rhetoric in Ecclesiastes. DOR-SHAV, Ecclesiastes, Fleeting and Timeless, roots this concept firmly in cognition about death. Franz Rosenzweig has said that all thinking about God begins with the reality of death.

49 (1) "Under the sun, the tangled knots of human carnage expose envy, greed, and bloated ego, their frayed edges masking a pained journey from trust to abuse, promise to betrayal, passion to indifference.
(2) Above the sun, a master weaver twists diverse threads in many directions to reveal a pattern of hope and pardon for abused and abuser.

to a breath, vital yet elusive like the wind. Life evokes the images of human beings either feeding on or chasing after the wind.[50]

Precisely because he viewed everything in a negative light and came to hate life, Qoheleth sought to redeem things by seizing the moment insofar as possible.[51] Hence he advises the young to savour existence while possible. The bloom of youth fades quickly, and a dark future awaits, one made no less oppressive by exquisite metaphors describing the end. These images of a shattered lamp and a broken cord magnify the truth that everything is *hebel*.

Seventh, Qoheleth looked death in the face and did not flinch. Still, he was not able to persuade the messenger to play a game of chess to forestall the inevitable.[52] He would probably have agreed with an Egyptian sage who suggests that death's real name is "Come."[53] The appointment with death may not read Samarra, as in John O'Hara's first novel, *Appointment in Samarra*,[54] but it has been inscribed in stone. Time flows into a gaping abyss in which everyone sooner or later comes to rest.

This realization may explain why death hovers over everything Qoheleth says. That single reality lends urgency to what he sought to convey to the people (*ha'am*).[55] All instruction (1) originates in the human mind; (2) is open to transcendence but not privy to its secrets; (3) takes the form of a dialogue with opposing understandings; (4) scorns absolutes; (5) recognizes the dominance of time's passage; (6) identifies everything as *hebel*; and (7) stares death in the face even while submitting to its power.

To recapitulate, scriptural authority has diminished in modern society for understandable reasons. Even in biblical times a few authors do not make a pretense of deriving their insights from a divine source, and of these Qoheleth strikes nearly all readers as an intruder in a sa-

---

(3) Beneath the heavens, victims cry out for measured justice, an eye for an eye. "A moment's satisfaction for past wrongs, finally avenged."
(4) Beyond the sun, no one assesses guilt, or even merit! Forgiveness reigns in a kingdom that knows no end." CRENSHAW, Dust and Ashes, 18.

50 *Hebel* occurs thirty-nine times in Ecclesiastes, and the phrase *re'ut rûah* appears seven times. A variant, *ra'yon rûah* makes two appearances.
51 GIANTO, Human Destiny, puts a positive spin on the brevity of life. See also WHYBRAY, Qoheleth, Preacher of Joy, and FISCHER, Aufforderung.
52 This observation evokes the scene in a film by Ingmar BERGMAN, "Wild Strawberries."
53 Stela of Taimhotep. See LICHTHEIM, Ancient Egyptian Literature, 63.
54 O'hara got the title from Somerset Maugham's retelling of an old story in the Babylonian Talmud illustrating death's inevitability.
55 The peculiar use of *ha'am* instead of *lemudîm* to designate Qoheleth's audience may suggest a broadening of sapiential instruction to include everyone willing to listen.

cred canon. His teachings underscore the human element in scripture. For some readers, that is a problem, as it seems to have been for his first readers (12:9-14).[56] For others, it is a testament to the integrity of a courageous and original thinker. It may be that logical persuasion is the finest authority available to mortals. Authority based on anything else is surely *hebel*, transient, and at times even foul.[57]

Bibliography

ADAMS, Samuel L., Wisdom in Transition. Act and Consequence in Second Temple Instructions, Leiden/Boston 2008.

ALBREKTSON, Bertil, History and the Gods (Con BOT 1), Lund 1967.

ALTER, Robert, The Book of Psalms, New York/London 2007.

ASTELL, Ann W., The Song of Songs in the Middle Ages, Ithaca/London 1990.

BALENTINE, Samuel E., Job, Macon 2006.

BARR, James, "Scripture, Authority of," in: IDB, Supplementary Volume (1976), 794-797.

BERGER, Benjamin L., Qohelet and the Exigencies of the Absurd, in: Bib Inter 9 (2001), 141-179.

BERGMANN, Michael/MURRAY, Michael J./REA, Michael C. (eds.), Divine Evil? The Moral Character of the God of Abraham, Oxford/New York 2011.

BLOCH, Ariel/BLOCH, Chana, The Song of Songs, Berkeley 1995.

---

[56] ENNS, Ecclesiastes 1, focuses on *kol ha'adam* in 12:13 and the three other uses of this phrase in Ecclesiastes (3:13; 5:18 {English, 5:19}; and 7:2) to demonstrate continuity of thought between Qoheleth's words and those of a frame narrator. Enns thinks the epilogue "places Qoheleth's flesh-and-blood struggles into their larger and theologically ultimate context and perspective" (128). The difficulty with this interpretation is the existence of two epilogues, each with a distinctive viewpoint. The emphasis on fearing Elohim and keeping the commandments places Qoheleth at some distance, for this type of instruction is close to that of Ben Sira. On the relationship of Qoheleth and Ben Sira, see GILBERT, Qohelet et Ben Sira. Gilbert argues against positing an influence of Qoheleth on Ben Sira.

[57] Studies on scriptural authority reach diverse conclusions because of the assumptions lying behind them. See WORK, Authority of Scripture. Work writes that the collapse of belief in the unity of scripture and tradition in the Enlightenment produced "camps of historicists, spiritualists, experientialists, fundamentalists, pragmatists, liberationists, and outright sceptics" (353). He thinks the apostolic and patristic consensus is making a comeback. If so, it corresponds to the current movement toward the right in Christendom. Scriptural authority is treated extensively in ABD, vol. 5, 1017-1056. The entries cover Judaism, Eastern Orthodoxy, Roman Catholicism, the early Church, the medieval church, the Protestant Reformation, the wake of the Enlightenment, and the Post-Critical period. In the last of these entries, Walter Brueggemann emphasizes the authorizing feature of the bible, its summons to establish justice, and its classic nature that extends beyond faith communities and the academy into the public arena. He thinks these two categories overcome the tyranny of the church and the academy where authority is concerned, bringing newness of life. James BARR'S remarks in "Scripture, Authority of," are still some of the most astute in print.

BRUEGGEMANN, Walter, Scriptural Authority, in: ABD, vol. 5 (1992), 1017-1056.
BURKES, Shannon, Death in Qoheleth and Egyptian Biographies of the Late Period (SBL DS 170), Atlanta 1999.
COLLINS, John J., Jewish Wisdom in the Hellenistic Age, Louisville 1997.
CRENSHAW, James L., A Good Man's Code of Ethics (Job 31), in: ibid., Prophets, Sages, & Poets, St. Louis, Missouri 2006, 42-46.
CRENSHAW, James L., Defending God. Biblical Responses to the Problem of Evil, Oxford/New York 2005.
CRENSHAW, James L., Dust and Ashes. Poems, Eugene 2010
CRENSHAW, James L., From the Mundane to the Sublime: Reflection on Qoheleth 11:1-8, in: ibid., Prophets, Sages, & Poets, St. Louis, Missouri 2006, 61-72.
CRENSHAW, James L., Love is Stronger than Death: Intimations of Life beyond the Grave, in: Charlesworth, James H. (ed.), Resurrection: The Origin and Future of a Biblical Doctrine (Faith and Scholarship Colloquies Series), New York/London 2009, 53-78.
CRENSHAW, James L., Old Testament Wisdom: An Introduction, Louisville ³2010.
CRENSHAW, James L., Poor but Wise (Qoh 9:13-16) [forthcoming in a Festschrift for Carol Meyers].
CRENSHAW, James L., Prophetic Conflict. It's Effect upon Israelite Religion (BZAW 124), Berlin 1971.
CRENSHAW, James L., Qoheleth's Quantitative Language, in: Berlejung, Angelika/van Hecke, Pierre (eds.), The Language of Qohelet in Its Context, (OLA 164), Leuven 2007, 1-22.
CRENSHAW, James L., Qoheleth's Understanding of Intellectual Inquiry, in: Schoors, Antoon (ed.), Qohelet in the Context of Wisdom (BETL 136), Leuven 1998, 205-224.
CRENSHAW, James L., Reading Job. A Literary and Theological Commentary, Macon 2011.
CRENSHAW, James L., Sipping from the Cup of Wisdom, in: Moser, Paul K. (ed.), Jesus and Philosophy. New Essays, Cambridge 2009, 41-62.
CRENSHAW, James L., The Sojourner Has Come to Play the Judge: Theodicy on Trial, in: Linafelt, Tod/Beal, Timothy K. (eds.), God in the Fray: A Tribute to Walter Brueggemann, Minneapolis 1998, 83-92 (reprinted in: Crenshaw, James L., Prophets, Sages, & Poets, St. Louis, Missouri 2006, 195-200).
CRENSHAW, James L., Theodicy and Prophetic Literature, in: ibid., Prophets, Sages, & Poets, St. Louis, Missouri 2006, 183-194.
CRENSHAW, James L., Theodicy and Prophetic Literature, in: LAATO, Antti/DE MOOR, Johannes C. (eds.), Theodicy in the World of the Bible, Leiden/Boston 2003, 236-255.
CRENSHAW, James L., Theodicy in the Book of the Twelve, in: Redditt, Paul L./Schart, Aaron (eds.), Thematic Threads in the Book of the Twelve (BZAW 325), Berlin/New York 2003, 175-191 (reprinted in: Crenshaw, James L., Prophets, Sages, & Poets, St. Louis, Missouri 2006, 173-182).
CRENSHAW, James L., Theodicy, in: NIDB 5, 551-555.
D'SOUSA, Pius James DCD, Stronger than Death. Intimations of Afterlife in the Book of Psalms, Bangalore 2010.
DE JONG, Stefan, God in the Book of Qohelet. A Reappraisal of Qohelet's Place in Old Testament Theology, in: VT 47 (1997), 154-67.
DELL, Katherine, "Get Wisdom, Get Insight:" An Introduction to Israel's Wisdom Literature, Macon 2000.
DELL, Katherine, The Book of Proverbs in Social and Theological Context, Cambridge 2006.

EHRMAN, Bart, Forged: Writing in the Name of God: Why the Bible's Authors Are Not Who We Think They Are, San Francisco 2011.

ENNS, Peter, "Ecclesiastes 1, Book of", in: Longman, Tremper III/Enns, Peter (eds.), Dictionary of the Old Testament Wisdom, Poetry & Writings, Downer Grove 2008, 125-129.

FELDMAN, Yael S., Glory and Agony. Isaac's Sacrifice and National Narrative, Stanford 2010.

FISCHER, Stefan, Die Aufforderung zur Lebensfreude im Buch Kohelet und seine Rezeption der ägyptischen Harfnerleider (Wiener Alttestamentlichen Studien 2), Frankfurt 1999.

FOX, Michael V., The Song of Songs and the Ancient Egyptian Love Songs, Madison 1985.

FOX, Michael, A Time to Tear Down & a Time to Build Up. A Rereading of Ecclesiastes, Grand Rapids 1999.

FOX, Michael, Qohelet's Epistemology, in: HUCA 58 (1987), 137-55

GIANTO, Augustus, Human Destiny in Emar and Qohelet, in: Schoors, Antoon (ed.), Qohelet in the Context of Wisdom (BETL 136), Leuven 1998, 473-479.

GILBERT, Maurice, Qohelet et Ben Sira, in: Schoors, Antoon (ed.), Qohelet in the Context of Wisdom (BETL 136), Leuven 1998, 161-179.

GILLINGHAM, Susan, Psalms Through the Centuries, volume 1, Oxford 2008.

GNUSE, Robert, Heilsgeschichte as a Model for Biblical Theology (College Theological Society Studies in Religion 4), Lanham/New York/London 1989.

GOOD, Edwin M., In Turns of Tempest. A Reading of Job with a Translation, Stanford 1990.

GORSSEN, Leo, Le cohérence de la conception de Dieu dans l'Ecclésiaste, in: TThL 46 (1970), 282-324.

GREENSTEIN, Edward L., Sages with a Sense of Humor: The Babylonian Dialogue between the Master and His Servant and the Book of Qoheleth, in: Clifford, Richard J. (ed.), Wisdom Literature in Mesopotamia and Israel (Society of Biblical Literature Symposium Series 36), Leiden 2007, 55-65.

HAKHAM, Amos, The Bible Psalms with the Jerusalem Commentary, Jerusalem 2003.

HENGEL, Martin, Judaism and Hellenism, vols 1-2, Philadelphia 1974.

HERTZBERG, Hans Wilhelm, Der Prediger (KAT, n.s. xvii, 4), Gütersloh 1963.

HÖFFKEN, Peter, Das Ego des Weisen, in: TZ 4 (1984), 121-35.

JANZEN, J. Gerald, Job, Atlanta 1985.

KALIMI, Isaac, "God, I Beg You, Take Your Beloved Son and Slay Him." The Binding of Isaac in Rabbinic Literature and Thought", in: RRJ 13 (2010), 1-29.

KRÜGER, Thomas, Meaningful Ambiguities in the Book of Qoheleth, in: Berlejung, Angelika/van Hecke, Pierre (eds.), The Language of Qohelet in Its Context, (OLA 164), Leuven 2007, 63-74.

KRÜGER, Thomas, Qoheleth, Minneapolis 2004.

LAATO, Antti/DE MOOR, Johannes C. (eds.), Theodicy in the World of the Bible, Leiden/Boston 2003.

LICHTHEIM, Miriam, Ancient Egyptian Literature, vol. III, Berkeley 1980.

LOHFINK, Norbert, Qoheleth 5:17-19. Revelation by Joy, in: CBQ 52 (1990), 625-635.

MICHEL, Dietrich, Gott bei Qohelet: Anmerkungen zu Kohelets Reden von Gott, in: BK 45 (1990), 32-36.

MILLER, Douglas B., Symbol and Rhetoric in Ecclesiastes. The Place of Hebel in Qoheleth's Work, Atlanta 2002.

MILOSZ, Czeslaw, Second Space. New Poems, New York 2004.
MÜLLER, Hans-Peter, Wie sprach Qohälät von Gott?, in: VT 18 (1968), 507-21.
NEWSOM, Carol A., The Book of Job, in: NIB IV (1996), 548-557.
O'HARA, John, Appointment in Samarra, New York 1934.
PASSARO, Angelo/BELLIA, Giuseppe, The Wisdom of Ben Sira. Studies on Tradition, Redaction, and Theology (DCL 1), Berlin/New York 2008.
PENCHANSKY, David/REDDITT, Paul (eds.), Shall not the Judge of all the Earth do what is right? Studies on the Nature of God in Tribute to James L. Crenshaw, Winona Lake 2000.
PERDUE, Leo G. (ed.), Scribes, Sages, and Seers. The Sage in the Eastern Mediterranean World (FzRLANT 219), Göttingen 2008.
PERDUE, Leo G., The Sword and the Stylus. An Introduction to Wisdom in the Age of the Empires, Grand Rapids 2008.
PERDUE, Leo G., Wisdom and Cult (SBLDS 30), Missoula 1977.
PERDUE, Leo G., Wisdom Literature: A Theological History, Louisville/London 2007.
PREUSS, Horst-Dietrich, Einführung in die alttestamentliche Weisheitsliteratur (UT 383), Stuttgart 1987.
RAD, Gerhard von, Wisdom in Israel, Nashville 1972.
REITERER, Friedrich V., „Alle Weisheit stammt vom Herrn ..." Gesammelte Studien zu Ben Sira (BZAW 375), Berlin/New York 2007.
SCHOORS, Antoon, God in Qoheleth, in: Brandscheidt, Renate (ed.), Schöpfungsplan und Heilsgeschichte. FS Ernst Haag, Rome 2002, 251-270.
SEIBERT, Eric A., Disturbing Divine Behavior. Troubling Old Testament Images of God, Minneapolis 2009.
SEOW, Choon-Leong, Ecclesiastes, New York 1997.
SHARP, Carolyn J., Ironic Representation, Authorial Voice, and Meaning in Qohelet, in: Bib Inter 12 (2004), 37-68.
SMELIK, Klaas, God in the Book of Qoheleth, in: Berlejung, Angelika/van Hecke, Pierre (eds.), The Language of Qohelet in Its Context (OLA 164), Leuven 2007, 177-181.
SNEED, Mark, Is the 'Wisdom Tradition' a tradition?, in: CBQ 73 (2011), 50-71.
STEIERT, Franz-Josef, Die Weisheit Israels – ein Fremdkörper im Alten Testament? (FThSt 143), Freiburg 1990.
VAN DER TOORN, Karel, Sources in Heaven: Revelation as a Scholarly Construct in Second Temple Judaism, in: Hübner, Ulrich/Knauf, Ernst Axel (Hg.), Kein Land für sich allein: Studien zum Kulturkontakt in Kanaan, Israel/Palästina und Ebirnâri, FS Manfred Weippert zum 65 Geburtstag, Freiburg, Schweiz 2002, 265-277.
VAN DER TOORN, Karel, Why Wisdom Became a Secret: On Wisdom as a Written Genre, in: Clifford, Richard J. (ed.), Wisdom Literature in Mesopotamia and Israel, Atlanta 2007, 21-29.
WHYBRAY, R. Norman, Qoheleth, Preacher of Joy, in: JSOT 23 (1982), 87-98.
WIEDER, Laurance, Words to God's Music. A New Book of Psalms, Grand Rapids 2003.
WILSON, Lindsay, Artful Ambiguity in Ecclesiastes 1:1-11, in: Schoors, Antoon (ed.), Qohelet in the Context of Wisdom, Leuven 1998, 357-365.
WORK, Telford, Authority of Scripture, in: NIDB, volume 1 (2006), 352-353.

Pseudonymous Authorship and Structures of Authority in the *Letter of Aristeas*

BENJAMIN G. WRIGHT

The *Letter of Aristeas* belongs to a special group of Second Temple Jewish works that are pseudonymous but whose putative authors are non-Jewish and not some ancient Jewish hero, such as Moses or Enoch. In addition to *Aristeas*, Jews wrote in the guise of the Sibylline Oracles, of Orpheus and of various Greek poets.[1] The reasons that Jews might have resorted to pseudonymity of this sort certainly cannot be narrowed to only one or two, and the generally fragmentary remains of such writings complicate any attempt to identify those reasons.[2] Other than the Jewish Sibyllines, however, *Aristeas* is the most extensive surviving work that assumes the voice of a non-Jewish author. As is well known, the purported author goes by the name Aristeas, and he is presented as a court member and confidant of king Ptolemy II Philadelphus, who is credited with patronizing the translation of the Hebrew Pentateuch into Greek. He is the narrative voice of the work as well as its primary actor. Ps.-Aristeas frames his διήγησις or "narrative" as a communication between Aristeas and his brother Philocrates in which Aristeas will tell about "the meeting that we had with Eleazar, the high priest of the Jews" (§1).[3] This deputation, while the explicit motivation for Aristeas's narrative, forms the setting for a series of events that culminates in the production of the Septuagint.

---

1 On these, see CHARLESWORTH, Old Testament Pseudepigrapha, vol. 2. No one seriously questions *Aristeas*'s Jewish authorship, and I will not detail the reasons here; they can be found in almost any publication on the book. Some works that presumably have a Jewish author adopting a Greek pseudonym still engender scholarly disagreement. See, for example, Robert Doran's assessment of the fragments attributed to Hecataeus (CHARLESWORTH, Old Testament Pseudepigrapha, 2.905-19).
2 For instance, the fragments of the Greek poets probably originated as compositional reworkings of short passages. See Harold Attridge in CHARLESWORTH, Old Testament Pseudepigrapha, 2.823-30.
3 Translations of *Aristeas* are my own. They will be part of a commentary on the book to appear in the Commentaries on Early Jewish Literature (CEJL) series from Walter de Gruyter. I use the name Ps.-Aristeas as shorthand for the Jewish author of Aristeas. Since he pretends to be the character Aristeas, this designation is a convenient one for this anonymous Jew.

The question of why a Jewish writer would assume the character of a gentile courtier of Ptolemy II is to a certain extent tied up with the purpose of the work, and scholars have proposed a variety of motivations for the book. Perhaps the most basic question focuses on its audience. Was it written for Jews or Gentiles? Early scholarship on *Aristeas* assumed that it was intended as a propaganda piece directed at Gentiles that aimed to promote or defend Judaism. Ps-Aristeas's assumption of a gentile voice was seen as one means of accomplishing that goal. So, for example, Herbert Andrews, who translated *Aristeas* in R.H. Charles's *Apocrypha and Pseudepigrapha of the Old Testament*, claimed:

> The whole tone of the letter from beginning to end proves conclusively that its author was a Jew and that the Greek role was assumed to strengthen the force of the argument and to commend it to non-Jewish readers.[4]

Thus, for Andrews and for scholars who took the same position, the purpose of the letter was to present a comprehensive view of Judaism that Gentiles could understand and perhaps even admire. The story of the Septuagint comprised only a part of this larger aim.

In an influential article, Victor Tcherikover contended that these conclusions were wrong and that *Aristeas* was intended for a Jewish audience.[5] Without rehearsing all the details of the argument, Tcherikover held that *Aristeas* was intended to show Jews "that no abyss separates Judaism from Hellenism."[6] At the same time, the author was concerned not to allow Jews to lose their identity. As Tcherikover puts it, "He [i.e., the author of *Aristeas*] was not a preacher of assimilation."[7] For Aristeas's author, Jews held to a universalistic philosophy combined with a Jewish monotheism, a combination most evident in the remarks about Jewish beliefs found in Eleazar's defense of the Jewish Law in §§133-171. Naturally, the translation of the Pentateuch assumes a special importance in this construction, since the Hebrew Law, which contains these Jewish beliefs, is now put in "a universal language" and is granted the status of revelation equal to that of the original.[8] Suffice it to say here that most scholars subsequent to Tcherikover have accepted the main contours of his arguments, specifically that the main audience for *Aristeas* was Jewish. That Gentiles perhaps encountered the book or became acquainted with the story cannot be ruled out, of course, but the function of the pseudonymity employed in *Aristeas* must be assessed with a Jewish audience in view.

---

4   ANDREWS, Letter of Aristeas, 2.84.
5   TCHERIKOVER, Ideology.
6   TCHERIKOVER, Ideology, 69.
7   TCHERIKOVER, Ideology, 70.
8   TCHERIKOVER, Ideology, 73-74.

More recently, Sylvie Honigman has maintained that *Aristeas* should be read as constructing a "charter myth" for the translation of the Jewish Law.[9] Those sections that do not directly concern the Septuagint, often referred to as digressions, all function within this larger mythic framework. Honigman's arguments have two primary implications. First, contrary to many other assessments of *Aristeas*, its major concern actually is the Septuagint, and in putting forward this charter myth, Ps.-Aristeas places special emphasis on two aspects of the translation: its high literary quality and its sanctity. Second, the audience for such a work would have been Jews and not Gentiles. Honigman identifies in *Aristeas* what she calls an "Exodus paradigm," which employs themes from the biblical Exodus story, such as the liberation of Jewish slaves, to equate the status of the Law in Greek with that of the Hebrew given to Moses at Sinai. In effect, the translation of the Pentateuch is a second giving of the Law, but this time it comes to Greek-speaking Jews in the Alexandrian diaspora.[10]

In my own work on *Aristeas*, I have argued, much like Honigman, that the letter is intended as a myth of origins for the Septuagint.[11] The necessity for creating such a myth is the changing function of the Septuagint over time. Judging from the characteristics of the translations themselves together with the lack of coherence between the actual translations as we have them and what *Aristeas* would lead us to expect them to look like, it seems that at the stage of its *production*, the Septuagint was meant to be subservient to its Hebrew source, to function as a way of accessing the authoritative Jewish Law, which was in Hebrew. In its *reception history*, the Septuagint began to be used independently of the Hebrew on which it originally depended, and as a result, some justification for its independent use, as well as its developing status as sacred scripture, was needed. *Aristeas* provides just that set of justifications.[12] In the course of making this argument, Ps.-Aristeas tries to show that (1) the Septuagint is a highly prestigious example of Greek literature whose philosophical *bona fides* are tied to the superior phi-

---

9   HONIGMAN, Septuagint and Homeric Scholarship.
10 HONIGMAN, Septuagint and Homeric Scholarship, chap 2. She also identifies an "Alexandrian paradigm" that argues for the accuracy and trustworthiness of the translation, because it has been prepared according to the standards of Alexandrian grammatical scholarship. For another argument that *Aristeas* employs themes from the Exodus, see KOVELMAN, Between Alexandria and Jerusalem.
11 WRIGHT, Letter of Aristeas (reprinted in WRIGHT, Praise Israel, 275-295). I have made these arguments independently of Honigman's work. She and I agree on *Aristeas*'s mythic character. She would preserve some elements of the narrative as historical, however, whereas I would not.
12 For the details of the argument, see WRIGHT, Letter of Aristeas, 52-65.

losophical acumen of the translators, which is established through the series of symposia, and (2) its original intention was to serve as an independent sacred scripture for the Alexandrian Jewish community.

In order to make the case, Ps.-Aristeas employs several authority conferring strategies that work together to establish that the Septuagint was originally supposed to be an independent scriptural authority for Alexandrian Jews. These strategies all work together under the umbrella of pseudonymous authorship. In this sense, then, there is a discourse of authority in *Aristeas* that focuses on the translation of the Torah and on its subsequent status for Greek-speaking Jews. Thus, pseudonymity (where the presumptive author is a Gentile) in *Aristeas* might have overlaps in function with pseudepigraphy (where the presumptive author is from the Israelite past). Hindy Najman has argued that pseudepigraphy plays a central role in conferring authority on a text – both on its contents and on its claims.[13] Looking at what she has called "Mosaic Discourse," Najman argues that discourse tied to a founder provides a mechanism for authorizing interpretations of earlier tradition and for thinking about developing understandings of Mosaic Law. She writes:

> On this understanding of discourse tied to a founder, to rework an earlier text is to update, interpret and develop the content of the text in a way that one claims to be an authentic expression of the law already accepted as authoritatively Mosaic. Thus, when what *we* might call a "new" law – perhaps even what we might regard as a significant "amendment" of older law – is characterized as the Law of Moses, this is not to imply that it is to be found in the actual words of an historical individual called Moses. It is rather to say that the implementation of the law in question would enable Israel to return to the authentic teaching associated with the prophetic status of Moses.[14]

This sort of discourse tied to a founder appears most clearly in works such as *Jubilees* and the Temple Scroll. Yet, even a figure such as Philo can participate in Mosaic discourse, since by arguing that the Law of Moses is a copy of the Law of Nature as expressed in the life of the sage, Philo can see himself as an inspired interpreter whose interpretations are copies of the Mosaic original.[15]

While one can find participation in Mosaic discourse in specific passages in *Aristeas*, particularly in Eleazar's central and significant apology for the Law (see below), the use of a gentile pseudonym situates the work in a different place from works like *Jubilees*, the Temple

---

13 See primarily, NAJMAN, Seconduing Sinai.
14 NAJMAN, Seconding Sinai, 13.
15 NAJMAN, Seconding Sinai, chap 3.

Scroll, or even Philo, whose more systematic philosophical contemplations (and more voluminous literary output) give greater insight into his position. And indeed, we certainly do not find in Ps.-Aristeas's use of the pseudonym a discourse tied to a founder. Even granting this point, *Aristeas* is still about interpretation and authorizing or legitimating interpretations, and Najman's insights about pseudepigraphy point to pseudonymity playing an important role in that legitimation effort. From a broader perspective, in *Aristeas* the translation of the Pentateuch into Greek is a two-fold act, on the one hand, rendering the Hebrew text into Greek, but on the other hand, revealing the meaning of the text in the act of translating. The characterizations offered by different figures in *Aristeas*'s narrative point to a way of understanding the Pentateuch as central to Alexandrian Jewish identity and as a way of placing Judaism within the acceptable orbit of Hellenistic Alexandrian society. Scholars have treated several of these authority conferring strategies as separate issues, and to a degree rightfully so, but I think that they all work in concert, and thus, it is worth a brief overview before moving to the overarching issue of pseudonymity.

The initial motivation for the translation of the Law, inclusion in Ptolemy II's library, indicates the significance of the Mosaic legislation for Greeks as well as Jews. In Aristeas's hearing, the king asks how the gathering of books is proceeding. Demetrius, the librarian, notes that he expects soon to acquire the total of 500,000 volumes, and he adds that he has found out that the "laws of the Jews are worthy of transcription (μεταγραφῆς) and of inclusion in your library" (§10). When the king asks why they have not been included, Demetrius notes that they require translation (ἑρμενεία). The king, then, proposes to write to the Jewish high priest so that a translation can be accomplished. In this section, we observe an ambiguity that runs through *Aristeas* – the relationship between transcription and translation.[16] In this case, however, the meaning is clear. The law deserves to be copied for the library, but it needs to be translated first. Although Demetrius mentions "Egyptian" and "Syrian" languages, nothing indicates that the library project routinely resorts to translating books in other tongues. It would seem that the Jewish Law is the only one accorded enough significance to be treated this way. Thus, the cultural significance of the Mosaic Law to Hellenistic Alexandria is placed before the reader at the very beginning of the enterprise, since it will be part of a culturally central institution, the Alexandrian library. Moreover, it will function as an independent Greek

---

16 On this language in *Aristeas*, see WRIGHT, Transcribing, Translating.

text, since it will be located in the library, presumably available to Greek readers.

After the episode of the liberation of the Jewish slaves (§§12-27), the thread that directly concerns the Septuagint picks up again, now in the form of a memorandum from Demetrius to Ptolemy (§§28-32), proposing a plan to have the Jewish books translated. Demetrius explains that not only are the books of the Jewish Law in Hebrew, these manuscripts "have been written rather carelessly and not as is proper, just as it has been reported by the experts" (§30).[17] He goes on to say that these books, once they have been made accurate, ought to be in the library, "because this legislation is both very philosophical and uncorrupted, inasmuch as it is divine" (§31). The king will want to have the books of the law because of this two-fold character, but unfortunately the most reliable texts are not immediately available.[18] Later, when the translators arrive from Jerusalem, they bring with them manuscripts "on which the legislation had been written in golden writing in Jewish characters" (§176). Upon seeing them unrolled, the king actually bows before them and does obeisance, calling them "oracles" of the Jewish God (§177). Thus, in this manner is the Hebrew text vouchsafed as the best one possible. This scene forms the basis for several legitimating mechanisms by which the author of *Aristeas* emphasizes a genetic relationship between original and translation in which the character of the Hebrew is transferred to the Greek, thereby assuring that it can replace the Hebrew on which it was based. To take just one passage here, after the translated is completed, Demetrius informs the king of all that has taken place. The king subsequently "bowed and ordered that great care be taken of the books and that they be preserved reverently" (§317). This behavior mirrors the king's earlier response to the Hebrew books and indicates that he holds the same attitude toward the translation that he did toward the originals.

The exchange of letters between Ptolemy II and the high priest Eleazar highlights several themes of the book that had surfaced previously: the king's piety; his munificence in his treatment of the Jews; and

---

17 The interpretation of the word σεσήμανται has long been a bone of scholarly contention. Most scholars now disagree with Paul Kahle and those who follow him, who claimed that the term referred to Greek translations, and see it as indicating less-than-satisfactory Hebrew texts. See ZUNTZ, Aristeas Studies 2; GOODING, Aristeas and Septuagint Origins; HONIGMAN, Septuagint and Homeric Scholarship, 48-49; and WRIGHT, Transcribing, Translating, 147, 154.

18 HONIGMAN, Septuagint and Homeric Scholarship, 44, argues that anyone familiar with the language of Homeric scholarship in Alexandria would recognize this problem. For the translation to be of the highest character and value, the Hebrew text on which it is based must be the most reliable.

his desire to have the law translated for the library. We also get introduced to the translators, whose character has much to do with establishing the authority of the Septuagint. Ptolemy requests men "who have lived exemplary lives, who have experience in the law and are able to translate, six from each tribe, so that from the majority there may be found agreement..." (§39).[19] Eleazar sends these men, whom the king receives and fêtes with a series of symposia. We later learn another, quite significant, characteristic of these prospective translators – they "had not only acquired experience in the literature of the Jews, but also not incidentally they had given heed to preparation in Greek literature" (§121). These are men who are at home in both worlds, the world of Jewish and of Greek texts, reflecting the two primary adjectives that Demetrius applied to the Hebrew law, philosophical and divine. Furthermore, Honigman points out that the language of the letter shows that these men employed the methods of the Alexandrian grammarians to produce a text in Greek that would assure its literary merit.[20]

The translators' double expertise is reinforced in several ways. They are explicitly said to be "zealous for the middle way" (§122), a reference to Aristotelian thought, in their conversations about the Jewish law. Thus, they embody both perspectives, Jewish and Greek. During the seven symposia, which together make up the single longest section of the letter, the king questions each translator individually about some aspect of kingship. The translators' replies are in each case applauded, and most importantly, in §§200-201, 235, and 296 their philosophical prowess is explicitly said to equal or even to excel that of the king's own philosophers. Moreover the translators are called learned or cultured (πεπαιδευμένοις, §321) and virtuous (ἀρετή, §§200, 235, 293-296). Finally, religious and moral rectitude also characterize the translators. When they finally get down to working, our author informs us that they "washed their hands in the sea, and they offered prayer to God" (§305). When Aristeas asks the reasons for these actions, the translators

---

19 The twelve tribes and the number 72 are significant. The letter's author seems to be representing Jerusalem as an ideal Greek *polis* for which the appearance of the twelve tribes is significant. The number 72 might also allude to the 70 elders who go up on the mountain with Moses in Exodus 24. That the later tradition rounds the number to 70 (hence the name Septuagint) is recognition of this significance. See HONIGMAN, Septuagint and Homeric Scholarship, 56-58. Harry Orlinsky argues that the twelve tribes are invoked precisely to recall Exodus 24 and the elders who ascended the mountain with Moses. This allusion certifies that all of Israel certified the enterprise of translation (see §§ 41-51) and that the translation was indeed revealed scripture. See ORLINSKY, Septuagint as Holy Writ, 98.
20 HONIGMAN, Septuagint and Homeric Scholarship, 42-49.

reply that by doing this they make clear that they have done no wrong. Not coincidentally, immediately following this claim to righteousness, the author offers the only indication that God has somehow been involved in the translation enterprise – "And thus it happened that the work of transcription was completed in seventy-two days, appearing as if this circumstance happened by some plan" (§307).

If we consider the translators' qualities in the context of the language of translation employed in the letter, in which the verbs ἑρμηνεύω and διερμηνεύω in particular walk a critical line between meaning "translation" or "interpretation," then we are presented with men who are more than functionaries who will render one language into another. They are divinely led authors, who bequeath to the translation their piety and learning. They *have insight* into the law, and their product embodies both the words *and* meaning of the original. Thus, the Septuagint, as the result of the work of righteous philosophers using the principles of the grammarians, is a highly prestigious literary document, philosophical and flawless in the same way as the original. These are cultured men who produce a text of high literary, philosophical and divine character for a cultured elite.[21]

Before the translators leave for Egypt, however, Aristeas inquires of Eleazar about certain Jewish practices (§§128-170). This question leads to a rather extended soliloquy that our author puts into the mouth of the high priest. A great deal has been written about Eleazar's so-called apology for the law, much of the focus centering on what looks to be an uncharacteristic detour on the part of Ps.-Aristeas into arguments about Jewish particularity and separateness. Scholars have taken both sides in this debate, some arguing that this speech promotes the superiority of Judaism over Hellenistic culture and religion and some arguing that the section is not out of character with the universalistic impulse of the rest of the letter and that the criticisms leveled in this section would not offend elite Hellenes, since these are rather stock critiques.[22] The other major characteristic of this speech is Eleazar's allegorical interpretation of Jewish kosher law, which bears on the particularistic/universalistic problem of the text and plays an important role in the authority structures of *Aristeas*. Indeed, Eleazar's speech is positioned strategically almost in the middle of the work, between the claim that the translators

---

21 For more detailed arguments on these issues, see WRIGHT, Transcribing, Translating.
22 So, for example, on the superiority side, see GRUEN, Heritage and Hellenism, 215-218; IDEM, Jewish Perspectives; BARCLAY, Jews in the Mediterranean Diaspora, 145; and BIRNBAUM, Allegorical Interpretations, 311-314. On the other side, see COLLINS, Between Athens and Jerusalem, 191-1–95; HADAS, Aristeas to Philocrates, 62-64; and HONIGMAN, Septuagint and Homeric Scholarship, 21-23.

are experts in both Jewish law and Greek literature and the symposia at which these men display their intellectual skills. His speech appears to be the transition from the Law in Hebrew to the Law in Greek, and its position is likely meant to suggest that the translators share Eleazar's views on the Law.

The premise for the entire section is Aristeas's question about the meaning of kosher law since, "most people have some curiosity about those matters in their [i.e., the Jews] legislation concerning food and drink and the beasts considered unclean" (§128). Before answering that question, Eleazar gives a discourse on the problem of human associations and conduct, claiming that "people who associate with evildoers become perverted, and they are miserable in the whole of life" (§130). He then addresses a foundational issue for Judaism: God's unique nature. Eleazar contrasts the Jewish belief that there is only one God, who knows the deeds of all, with a critique of gentile idol worship, offering a euhemeristic explanation of idol worship and condemning the Egyptian practice of theriolatry. This section concludes with the justly famous passage that Moses the lawgiver "fenced us around with unbroken palisades and with iron walls so that we might not intermingle at all with any other nations, being pure in both body and soul, having been set free from vain opinions ..." (§139). Thus, the law keeps Jews from worshiping anything other than God.

An important aspect of this section is that Eleazar has not delineated any of the laws as yet. He makes the point, both with associations and with idols, that Jewish separateness is about the desire to avoid moral taint. I do not view these sections as a blanket condemnation of all things non-Jewish, but rather they set up the discussion of the kosher law, which was supposed to be the topic of Eleazar's answer in the first place, as playing a central role in maintaining moral righteousness. Just as importantly, it also serves to reveal why Moses legislated in the way that he did, a purpose that becomes clearer with the explanation of kosher law.

Then, Eleazar comes right to the point about food laws: "Do not come to the contemptible conclusion that Moses legislated these matters on account of a curiosity with mice and weasels or similar creatures" (§144). He proceeds to argue in detail that observing foods laws really is about being reminded that the Jews need to practice justice and not to oppress others, that they must "separate each of our actions that they might turn out well" (§150) and that they must remember the "ruling and preserving nature of God" (§157). In the same way, Jews use tefillin and mezuzot in order to be reminded that all actions must be accomplished with justice (§§158-161).

In this entire section, Eleazar's speech shows the true character of the Law, which is revealed in the allegorical interpretations that he gives to the food laws. They are not about eating *per se* but about moral formation. Yet, Ps.-Aristeas takes this approach even another step; Eleazar's understanding of the law is not presented as his (or the translators') interpretation of the law, but rather he presents these interpretations as Moses' own intention for the laws. Where later in Alexandria, Philo can and will distinguish between Mosaic Law and his own interpretation of it, in Eleazar's speech no such distinction is made. Thus, here in *Aristeas*, we find a nice example of Najman's Mosaic discourse, which fits all the criteria that she establishes: (1) Eleazar's explanation of the law reworks and expands older traditions "through interpretation." (2) Although the text does not "ascribe to itself the status of Torah," the fact that Eleazar does not separate the allegorical interpretation from the original meaning or intention of the law in a *de facto* manner claims Torah status for it. (3) Even though Sinai is not mentioned in *Aristeas*, the Jewish community's acceptance of the Septuagint parallels the biblical scenes of binding to the law (§§308–311, see below) and the possible connections of the 72 translators with the 70 elders who go up to the mountain with Moses in Exodus 24. Although not explicit, the Sinai event seems to lurk behind the scenes in several places.[23] (4) Eleazar's interpretations of the law are clearly presented as being "associated with, or produced by, the founding figure. ... The new text can then be seen as an extension of earlier ancestral discourse."[24]

By presenting these interpretations as *the* law of Moses in the place that he does, Ps.-Aristeas makes the transition from the position already established that the original Jewish law is philosophical and divine to the claim that through the philosophical and pious translators, whom Eleazar himself selected for this momentous task, the Greek translation will indeed have the same character. The translation constitutes a second Sinai, or in Najman's language, we have "an authentic expression of the law already accepted as authoritatively Mosaic."[25] The same ideas that Moses enshrined in the original legislation would inhabit the Septuagint. In the narrative world of the *Letter of Aristeas*, no longer would someone like Aristeas need to ask Eleazar about these matters, they could be discovered by reading the text in its Greek form, which is endowed with all the characteristics of the original.

---

23 ORLINSKY, Septuagint as Holy Writ, 98.
24 On these criteria, see NAJMAN, Seconding Sinai, 16-19.
25 NAJMAN, Seconding Sinai, 13.

In one of the final scenes in *Aristeas*, after the completion of the translation, the Jewish community assembles together to hear the translation read aloud. The leaders of the community then proclaim that the translation "has been made well, piously, and accurately in every respect" (§310) and that no changes should be made to it. The approbation that the Jews give to the translation affirms its scriptural status. Harry Orlinsky showed that all of the elements of this scene are found in biblical scenes where a document is accepted as "official and binding, in other words, as divinely inspired scripture" (cf. Exod 24.3-7; 2 Kings 22-23; Jer 36.1-10).[26] In addition, the proclamation in §310 that nothing should be changed in the translation parallels the injunction in Deut 4.1-2 that the law that Moses is giving must be preserved without any changes whatsoever.[27] In *Aristeas*, then, the Jewish community acts *en masse* to accept the Septuagint as its sacred scripture without reservation, since it has all the same attributes as the Hebrew original from which it has derived.

Thus, there are two considerations that need to be kept in mind at this juncture. First, Ps.-Aristeas takes pains to establish that the Septuagint at the point of its origin was intended to be a prestigious literary work of Greek philosophy and that, because it was endued with all the characteristics of the Hebrew original and it expressed Moses' legislative intent, it would take the place of the Hebrew as the scriptural corpus of the Jews of Alexandria. This contention forms the nucleus of the myth of origins that we find in *Aristeas*. Second, all of the various strategies outlined above, which work to confer authority on the Septuagint, contribute to this larger effort of constructing this myth.

In light of these considerations, we have to confront the question of why use a gentile pseudonym to narrate this series of events. Does this technique accomplish something that an explicitly Jewish voice would or could not? Scholars have not generally addressed this question head-on with any significant detail or nuance. Other than scholars who thought that *Aristeas* was addressed to Greeks,[28] Tcherikover theorized that since Ps.-Aristeas was trying to portray the Septuagint as having been a gentile idea, "it was therefore necessary to disguise the author as a Greek and to present him as the hero of the story. Forgeries of this kind are nothing but a literary convention."[29] John Barclay understands Ps.-Aristeas's use of a fictional pseudonym as intending to create a

---

26 ORLINSKY, Septuagint as Holy Writ, 94.
27 ORLINSKY, Septuagint as Holy Writ, 95.
28 See, for example, ANDREWS, SCHÜRER, III.1, 679 and MEECHAM, Oldest Version of the Bible, 113-114.
29 TCHERIKOVER, Jewish Apologetic Literature, 175.

window "into the intimate discussions of the court and the private impressions of a courtier as he observes Jewish representatives and Jewish customs. The stance of the narrator...thus lends authority to the massively favorable impression of Jews which the work provides."[30] Both of these assessments do not really tell us much, however. Tcherikover might well be correct that we have here a literary convention, but literary conventions usually serve some purpose and are not mindlessly employed. Barclay, at least, sees the matter as one of authority, but his conclusion that this device shows us how Jews wanted Gentiles to see them in some ways begs the question of the purpose and audience of the book and how pseudonymity works as an authority conferring mechanism.

Sara Raup Johnson takes a slightly different tack. As she understands the fictional and Gentile Aristeas, his sentiments are often not distinguishable at all from those of a Hellenized Jew, and in them we see the commitments of *Aristeas*'s Jewish author. As it functions in the narrative, the character of Aristeas shows that other than certain religious laws, such as kosher, which enlightened Gentiles like Ptolemy and Aristeas respect anyway, Jews and Greeks do not have to be divided in philosophy or religion. "The fictional Aristeas personifies the harmonious relationship possible between the two cultures."[31] Regarding the purpose of *Aristeas*, Johnson affirms that Ps.-Aristeas writes to establish the Septuagint as an accurate and perfect translation made by perfectly qualified translators. In her view, however, the payoff is that the Septuagint confirms the authenticity of Alexandrian Jewish religiosity, that "an Alexandrian Jew who kept the Law according to the Septuagint was every bit as pious as a Jew who attended the Temple at Jerusalem."[32] I see no evidence in *Aristeas*, however, that conflicts, either potential or real, between Jerusalem and Alexandria are at stake for the author, although as I have argued above, I do think that the Septuagint is central to the work.

The one scholar who has dealt with the pseudonymous narrator in *Aristeas* in some detail is Honigman. Her position has two components: (1) the use of first-person narrative (what she calls "ego-narrative") and

---

30 BARCLAY, Jews in the Mediterranean Diaspora, 139.
31 JOHNSON, Historical Fictions, 36.
32 JOHNSON, Historical Fictions, 38. She also maintains that the immediate Jewish audience of *Aristeas* would have been very well aware that this was a fictitious account. As she says, "His [i.e., the author's] loyalty, however, is not to the truth of history, but to truth of another sort." I am not convinced that this fiction would be quite so apparent and well known, even if the author's allegiance was to a truth other than historical. For a longer review of Johnson's book, see my article, History, Fiction and the Construction of Ancient Jewish Identities.

(2) the use of a gentile pseudonym.³³ Ego-narrative was primarily employed by historians and is identified first with Herodotus. In *Aristeas* it serves the same function as it does for the historians; "[i]t strengthens the claim to truth-telling in the narrative."³⁴ She further notes that this type of narrative expanded into a variety of genres in the Hellenistic period and was used to convey a sense of veracity to the text. Whereas with earlier authors, such as Herodotus or Polybius, the ego-narrative was employed in factual accounts, later authors used the technique for fictional ones. Thus, the use of ego-narrative in the Hellenistic period actually blurred the boundary between factual and fictional, and ancient historians and novelists might be equally liable to employ it. In this respect, Honigman compares *Aristeas* to writers such as Euhemerus and composers of social utopias and religious pamphlets.³⁵ She also points out that for *Aristeas*, because certain fantastical elements such as paradoxography in the description of Jerusalem and its environs are missing in the work, "the interwoven dimension of charter myth prompted the author to refrain from inserting purely entertaining features in his narrative, in order to establish his work as an account of undisputable veracity."³⁶

Yet, unlike Herodotus and Polybius, who wrote in their own names, our author effaces his Jewish identity in favor of pseudonymity, a device found only in fictional works in the Hellenistic period. Honigman offers several reasons for this choice. First, this fictive identity lends a coherence to the narrative that makes it seem more likely — so, verisimilitude is at least part of the goal. Second, the primary frame of the story, the translation's origins in royal patronage, would almost require a court official as the narrator. Thus, the author constructs a consistent and logical narrative world. Third, a Jewish narrator would create insurmountable obstacles for our author. So, Honigman asks, within *Aristeas*'s narrative world, how would a Jew narrate Eleazar's apology, especially if Ps.-Aristeas were to keep the question-and-answer format in this section, a format that she claims is quite common in Hellenistic literature? As she puts it, "It would have been very clumsy to have a Jewish ambassador ask the High Priest Eleazar to enlighten him about the peculiarities relating to the Law of the Jews ... In short, inasmuch as B.Ar.'s author was interested in securing for his account the benefits of ego-narrative, the best, if not the sole possible option was to choose not only a Greek, but very precisely a court offi-

---

33   HONIGMAN, Septuagint and Homeric Scholarship, 67-71.
34   HONIGMAN, Septuagint and Homeric Scholarship, 67.
35   HONIGMAN, Septuagint and Homeric Scholarship, 68.
36   HONIGMAN, Septuagint and Homeric Scholarship, 69.

cial to impersonate the narrator." In her estimation, "A charter myth was not parochial, but universal—and 'universal,' in the Greek cultural context, meant Greek. Only this Greek voice could give the text a universal dimension."[37]

Honigman's position essentially starts from Tcherikover's and then moves somewhat beyond it. Having the story told from a first-person perspective is indeed a literary convention. Honigman maintains that once the author chose that approach, which would provide for the reader a historiographical veneer, a Greek narrator was the only way to go. As I see it, Honigman may be correct as far as she goes, but in the end, her arguments boil down to a similar approach that other scholars have suggested, that the Greek "Aristeas" serves to bring a sense of convincing verisimilitude to the narrative. I think, though, that we need to look a bit more deeply at how this Greek narrator functions as the overarching voice under which all of these other authority conferring strategies are introduced. If, in an analogous way to Najman's discourse tied to a founder, there is a discourse in *Aristeas* that confirms the authority and centrality of the Septuagint as the sacred scriptures for Alexandrian Jews, the fictitious Aristeas must play an important role in it, since at least within the narrative world of the text, he reports and articulates all the other ways that authority is conferred on the Septuagint.

The Gentile Aristeas is truly omnipresent in this work, and there is almost never a moment where he does not let the reader know that he observed the goings on first-hand. So, for example, Aristeas hatches the idea to free the Jewish slaves, and he pitches it to the king personally. In §91, Aristeas can tell about the water reservoirs in Judea, since he was taken to see them. Aristeas asks Eleazar about the significance of the Jewish food laws. And on and on. And to reinforce the veracity of his first-hand testimony, he cites "official" documents that support his account.[38] So, he can quote a *prostagma* of the king to show that the slaves were actually freed and that the king was magnanimous in doing so, or he can claim to have consulted the official records of the symposia as a check on and confirmation of his own first-hand testimony (§§298-300). In short, we are never allowed to lose sight of the fact that this court insider, someone whom the king "held in honor" (§40, 43), is the teller of the story.

---

37 For all these reasons, see HONIGMAN, Septuagint and Homeric Scholarship, 70-71.
38 Much has been written on the authenticity of these documents, but whether they are authentic or not does not bear on my arguments here. See HONIGMAN, Septuagint and Homeric Scholarship, 71-74.

If we combine this omnipresent narrator and primary actor with the work's purpose to serve as a charter myth or myth of origins for the Septuagint, then I think that we can see some specific reasons for a gentile pseudonym—and the centrality of the Septuagint is key here. The *Letter of Aristeas* is indeed, as other scholars have argued, about Jewish identity in a larger Hellenistic world, but that identity revolves around the Septuagint, the foundational text of Jewish identity. Certainly there is a tension in *Aristeas* between Jewish particularism or separateness and a universal appeal, but the Septuagint is at the center of it, as is Eleazar's re-presentation of Jewish law as well.

As I noted above, I think that *Aristeas* is primarily concerned with the changing function of the Septuagint and establishing as sacred scripture for the Jewish community in Alexandria a text that had *become* independent by the author's time.[39] The ways that Ps.-Aristeas argues for its authority and status all point in that direction. If *Aristeas* is any indicator, the Alexandrian community of Ps.-Aristeas was not looking in the direction of Jerusalem and the Temple for its primary Jewish identity and orientation. It now possessed in Greek the legislation that Moses had given, and its laws formed the foundation of its communal life. Ps.-Aristeas makes this clear in the letter.

Eleazar's speech about the law, then, takes on added importance, since it should be understood as a paradigmatic statement about the identity of Jews like Ps.-Aristeas. And while we might focus especially on the allegorical meaning of these laws as they are articulated here, it does seem that Eleazar's discourse presumes actual Jewish observance of the Jewish food laws. Paragraphs 145 and 150 indicate that there is a close relationship between Jews actually eating (or not eating) certain foods and recalling their significance as signs that they need to act with justice. Eleazar's interpretations do not only offer an allegorical meaning; they also justify a set of religious/ethnic practices.

The letter also reveals a strong sense that Jews share values with the larger Hellenistic world. The Jews and Ptolemy get along just well; the king makes sure that the translators are treated according to Jewish customs; Eleazar writes to the king as if he were his equal.[40] This harmony is nowhere better stated than in the famous §16 where Aristeas tells the king about the Jews, "These people revere God, the overseer and creator of all things, whom all also, even we, worship, O King, using different names, Zeus and Dis." As many have pointed out, this statement presumes that it is the *Jewish* God who is in control and who

---

39 See WRIGHT, Letter of Aristeas.
40 The form of the letter that Eleazar sends to Ptolemy uses a greeting form that indicates equal status.

goes by these names in Hellenistic worship. But, even so, this claim is rightly viewed as trying to establish that Jews and Greeks hold important values in common.

Our gentile narrator is situated in the midst of this tension, observing, inquiring, and explaining – and all to an intended audience of Jews. A gentile narrator and primary actor can affirm that in the eyes of Greeks Jewish particularism, when expressed in the language of the Eleazar's exposition, is not a barrier to close and beneficial relations between Jews and the larger Hellenistic world. Judging from the literary forms and allusions that he makes in *Aristeas*, it would appear that Ps.-Aristeas has clearly had the benefit of a Hellenistic education, and he would appear to be someone who has an interest in advocating Jewish participation in the larger cultural world of Alexandria. "Aristeas" confirms that Hellenistic Alexandria has already recognized the importance of the Jewish law – it was considered worthy of inclusion in the king's library along with all of the other prestigious books of Greek culture.

Thus, I think that having a gentile narrator performs two related tasks in *Aristeas*, both of which would be important to a Jewish audience. First, it reasserts the central and scriptural status of the Septuagint for the Jewish community. If the function of the Septuagint had changed over time from being dependent on the Hebrew and serving as a gateway to the Hebrew, which was still considered the scriptural authority, to becoming an independent replacement and self-standing scriptural corpus, then a Gentile who narrates the process can provide testimony that the Septuagint was produced under the most ideal circumstances, with a royal patron who was able to acquire the most reliable Hebrew manuscripts and the best possible translators to do the job. That is, he confirms its merits as a *Greek* text. Moreover, the Gentile attests that at the moment of the translation's production, the Jewish community recognized that the Septuagint had everything that the original Hebrew did and accepted it as its sacred scripture – that it was central to Jewish identity from the moment of its creation. This line of thinking actually coheres broadly with Honigman's views about the function of the gentile narrator.

Second, a gentile narrator can assure Jewish readers that non-Jewish Hellenistic Alexandria recognizes the centrality of Moses as legislator and the Septuagint for Jewish identity and that the law's requirements pose no obstacles to Jewish participation in the larger culture. As high a figure as the king recognized the Jewish law's philosophical and divine character, and the Septuagint combines the best of Moses and Greek thought. Gentiles already recognize all of this. It may be true that Jews only eat certain foods or pray in strange ways, but Gentiles understand that Moses instituted these customs for an end that Gentiles shared – the inculcation of the highest moral standards. Barclay has understood the basic thrust of what I am trying to get at here. As he says, *Aristeas* is "a document which demonstrates the extent of his [i.e., the author's] acculturation and the limits of his assimilation … His pride in the law (i.e., the LXX) is evident throughout, and he has taken care to interpret its more puzzling regulations as both rational and moral."[41] Yet, Barclay does not connect this insight to the use of the pseudonymous Aristeas as the narrator, but *it is precisely that gentile voice that gives these ideas their punch or force.*

In the one instance where Barclay does refer to the narrator, he contends that because Eleazar's speech is addressed to a Gentile in the narrative, that this indicates an implied gentile reader.[42] I disagree that the implied reader of this section or any other is Gentile simply because we have a gentile figure doing the storytelling. By using "Aristeas" to tell the story, the author is not hoping to inform Gentiles about Jews; he is trying to tell Jews that Gentiles who inhabit the upper echelons of Alexandrian society "get" Judaism. They understand and accept that the Jewish law in the form of the Septuagint is the foundational Jewish "legislation," and it is a central facet of Jewish identity. Thus, Jews should feel no anxiety about participating in the larger culture *as Jews*, but even more, they can take pride in the Septuagint and any ethnic customs based on it, since the highest officials in the land had recognized its prestige and value from the very beginning.

The decision to employ a gentile narrator, then, goes beyond broad scholarly explanations that Jews could engage in the broader Hellenistic culture or that the letter intended to promote Jewish customs to a gentile audience. Our author, a Jewish intellectual in Alexandria in the middle of the second century BCE, was making very specific claims about the Septuagint in this work. It possessed all the qualities of the Hebrew text on which it was based, and, because learned and cultured Jewish translators who came from Jerusalem executed it based on the best Hebrew manuscripts, it could serve as the sacred scripture of the Jews in Alexandria. The Sinai event had been played out in Greek for Jews in Alexandria, and this time the Gentiles facilitated it.[43] He also gave gentile approval and acceptance of the centrality of the Law in Greek for the Jews. Following their ethnic customs would presumably not prevent Jews from being part of Alexandrian society, since after all,

---

41   BARCLAY, Mediterranean Diaspora, 149.
42   BARCLAY, Mediterranean Diaspora, 148.
43   HONIGMAN'S "Exodus Paradigm" in Septuagint and Homeric Scholarship, 53-63.

the Gentiles understood that these customs helped Jews to embody ideals of monotheism, piety, and high moral standards that enlightened Gentiles shared. According to Ps.-Aristeas, this vision of Jewish identity, with a most philosophical and divine text at its center, held out the best possibility that he could imagine for *Jewish* engagement with the Hellenistic world.

Bibliography

ANDREWS, H., The Letter of Aristeas, in: Charles, Robert H. (ed.), Apocrypha and Pseudepigrapha of the Old Testament, Oxford 1913, vol. 2.

BARCLAY, John M. G., Jews in the Mediterranean Diaspora: From Alexander to Trajan (323 BCE–113 CE), Berkeley, CA 1996.

BIRNBAUM, Ellen, Allegorical Interpretations and Jewish Identity among Alexandrian Jewish Writers, in: Aune, David E. et al. (eds.), Neotestamentica et Philonica: Studies in Honor of Peder Borgen (NTSup 106), Leiden 2003, 307-329.

CHARLESWORTH, James H., Old Testament Pseudepigrapha. 2 vols., Garden City, NY 1985.

COLLINS, John J., Between Athens and Jerusalem: Jewish Identity in the Hellenistic Diaspora, Grand Rapids, MI ²2000.

GOODING, David W., Aristeas and Septuagint Origins: A Review of Recent Studies, in: VT 13 (1963), 357-379.

GRUEN, Erich S., Heritage and Hellenism, Berkeley, CA 1998.

GRUEN, ERICH S., Jewish Perspectives on Greek Culture and Ethnicity, in: Collins, John J./Sterling, Gregory E. (eds.), Hellenism in the Land of Israel (Christianity and Judaism in Antiquity Series 13), Notre Dame 2001, 61-93.

HADAS, Moses, Aristeas to Philocrates (Letter of Aristeas), New York 1951.

HONIGMAN, Sylvie, The Septuagint and Homeric Scholarship in Alexandria, London 2003.

JOHNSON, Sara Raup, Historical Fictions and Hellenistic Jewish Identity: Third Maccabees in its Cultural Context, Berkeley, CA 2004.

KOVELMAN, Arkadij B., Between Alexandria and Jerusalem: The Dynamic of Jewish and Hellenistic Culture (Brill Reference Library of Judaism 21), Leiden 2005.

MEECHAM, Henry G., The Oldest Version of the Bible: 'Aristeas' on its Traditional Origin. A Study in Early Apologetic, London 1932.

NAJMAN, Hindy, Seconding Sinai: The Development of Mosaic Discourse in Second Temple Judaism (JSJSup 77), Leiden 2003.

NEWSOM, Carol A., The Self as Symbolic Space: Constructing Identity and Community at Qumran, Leiden 2004.

ORLINSKY, Harry, The Septuagint as Holy Writ and the Philosophy of the Translators, in: HUCA 46 (1975), 89-114.

SCHÜRER, Emil, The History of the Jewish People in the Age of Jesus Christ (G. VERMES, F. MILLAR, and M. GOODMAN, eds.), Edinburgh 1986, III.1:677-687.

TCHERIKOVER, Victor, Jewish Apologetic Literature Reconsidered, in: Eos 48 (1956), 169-193.

TCHERIKOVER, Victor, The Ideology of the Letter of Aristeas, in: HTR 51 (1958), 59-85.

WEITZMAN, Steven, Surviving Sacrilege: Cultural Persistence in Jewish Antiquity, Cambridge 2005.

WRIGHT, Benjamin G., History, Fiction and the Construction of Ancient Jewish Identities, in: Prooftexts 26 (2006), 449-467.

WRIGHT, Benjamin G., The Letter of Aristeas and the Reception History of the Septuagint, in: BIOSCS 39 (2006), 47-67.

WRIGHT, Benjamin G., Praise Israel for Wisdom and Instruction: Essays on Ben Sira and Wisdom, the Letter of Aristeas and the Septuagint (JSJSup 131), Leiden 2008.

WRIGHT, Benjamin G., Transcribing, Translating, and Interpreting in the *Letter of Aristeas*: On the Nature of the Septuagint, in: Voitila, Anssi/Jokiranta, Jutta (eds.), Scripture in Transition: Essays on Septuagint, Hebrew Bible and Dead Sea Scrolls in Honour of Raija Sollamo (JSJSup 126), Leiden 2008, 147-161.

ZUNTZ, Günther, Aristeas Studies 2: Aristeas and the Translation of the Torah, in: JSS 4 (1959), 109-126.

Reframing Scripture: A Fresh Look at Baruch's So-Called "Citations"

SEAN A. ADAMS

Introduction

Many papers could and have been written on Baruch's use of Israel's Scripture. Not only do the Jewish Scriptures strongly influence Baruch in literary and linguistic selections, but some scholars have argued that Baruch is just a "pastiche" of Scriptural references in which the author "string[s] together passages borrowed or adapted from canonical sources".[1] Although I disagree with some of the pejorative terms used to describe Baruch in the past, it is clear with any reading of Baruch that this work is heavily influenced and draws repeatedly on Jewish Scripture.

The impetus for this article arose when I was investigating intertextuality in Bar 1:15-3:8 at which time I became disturbed by the lack of terminological precision and nuance scholars used when discussing the way Baruch uses scripture.[2] This, I believe, has led to a confusion of meaning and an overstating of positions. Tackling the entire issue of intertextuality in Bar 1:15-3:8 would far outstrip the word limitations of this article. Accordingly, I will focus on the so-called "quotations" in Baruch's penitential prayer section. After providing a brief introduction to some important preliminary issues, including a small section to discuss terminology, the bulk of the paper will look at Baruch's four so-called "quotations". Here I will argue that Baruch makes use of the deuteronomic tradition to frame the penitential prayer, but through a Jeremianic frame. In this I will primarily respond to Watson's recent

---

1   BURKE, Poetry of Baruch, 21.
2   There are a number of compositional theories of Baruch, though I am inclined to follow the view of STECK (Das apokryphe Baruchbuch, 265), who has argued that the different parts of Baruch form an intentional unity. We also do not know who wrote/compiled Baruch, although we are quite sure that it was not Baruch ben Nariah, but for convenience this paper will use Baruch when referring to the author(s) of the Book of Baruch. For a more thorough discussion of group authorship, see STECK, Das apokryphe Baruchbuch, 306-307.

proposal. Finally, we will look at the rhetorical significance of using quotation formulas and how they function in Baruch.

Text of Baruch

There are no extant texts of Baruch in Hebrew. This, however, has not stopped scholars from positing a Hebrew original, at least for certain sections.[3] The first and most notable retroversion was attempted by J.J. Kneucker, whose textual work and study of Baruch translations have laid the foundation for Baruchan study.[4] More recently, E. Tov has provided a retroversion of Baruch 1:1-3:8, holding the view that the remainder of Baruch lacks sufficient evidence for either a Hebrew original or sufficient data to create a Hebrew text with confidence.[5] Despite this caution by Tov, D.G. Burke has provided a reconstruction of the "original" Hebrew text of 3:9-5:9.[6]

Although these attempts at reconstructing the Hebrew behind the Greek Septuagint version are interesting, the enterprise of retroverting a text has recently been called into question.[7] In his article, "(How) Can We Tell if a Greek Apocryphon or Pseudepigraphon has been Translated from Hebrew or Aramaic?," Jim Davila thoroughly problematises the enterprise of retroversion by highlighting the retroverter's ignorance of key textual issues, such as: difficulties in determining Greek from Semitic grammar; possible language and dialect of origin, and the inadequacy of the bipolar scale of "literal" vs. "free" translation technique. Furthermore, Davila questions whether or not we can even securely establish Semitic interference.

Our ability to do such retroversion is further hampered in light of James Barr's insightful questioning of what the term "literal" means in respect to translations.[8] Nevertheless, that a number of scholars see Hebrew structure and influence behind the Greek provides insight in to understanding the Greek language of Baruch. This, however, is likely due to the Hebrew influence on the LXX which influenced the author(s) of Baruch. This perspective suffices sufficiently as an explanation for the Greek style of Baruch and undermines the need to postulate and reconstruct a Hebrew *Vorlage*.

---

3   TORREY, The Apocryphal Literature, 62.
4   KNEUCKER, Das Buch Baruch.
5   TOV, The Book of Baruch.
6   BURKE, The Poetry of Baruch.
7   DAVILA, (How) Can We Tell, 3-61.
8   BARR, The Typology of Literalism.

In light of this understanding and Davila's critique, I will be making use solely of the existing Greek text of Baruch and will not consult or interact with various retroversions. Furthermore, as we will be discussing below, the relationship and parallels between Baruch and the Jewish Scriptures in Greek suggests that the author of Baruch was drawing on Greek texts for his composition. Consequently, unless otherwise specified, all references are to the Greek, rather than the Hebrew, text.

Definitions of "Citation"

One of the first challenges of interpreting Baruch, particularly in this study, is adequately defining the terms and concepts of citation, allusion, etc.[9] Although scholarship is moving towards a greater definitional consensus, it is apparent that further work is still needed. Clearly, comprehensive definitions to each of these categories would require extended treatments well beyond the limits of this present study. Issues relating to definitions are complex, touching on numerous and often nuanced subtleties. The goal pursued in this article is much more modest, seeking to look more comprehensively at Baruch's so-called "citations". This investigation will commence with a brief discussion of this term before turning our attention to specific textual examples.

The primary definition needed for this study is that of citation. One of the challenges in dealing with Baruch and other "apocryphal" and "pseudepigraphal" literature is that there are few explicit quotations.[10] Echoes abound, but citations are is short supply. Christopher Stanley has attempted to delineate the existance of a citation in terms of either a "reader-centered" or an "author-centered" approach.[11] In the former, a passage can only be labelled a citation when it provides the reader with at least some indication that a quotation is present. In the latter approach, any verse that exhibits substantial verbal agreement with a known passage of Scripture, whether marked or not, can be classified as a "citation". What the reader-centered approach gains in conservatism, it

---

9 Some scholars, such as Hammill, have attempted to evaluate citation techniques in Apocryphal and Pseudepigraphal works. Hammill does rightly discern between quotations in which interpretation is involved and quotations which are "only convenient literary phrases which the author has taken over, or had become idioms or clichés in common use among the people" (p. 16 n.1). However, in his attempt to distinguish "acceptable" and "unacceptable" interpretation (pp. 52-131), Hammill imposes modern criteria on ancient practices. HAMMILL, Biblical Interpretation. For a further discussion of Hammill's work, see SCHULTZ, The Search for Quotation, 146-149.
10 STANLEY, Paul and the Language of Scripture, 308-309.
11 STANLEY, Paul and the Language of Scripture, 34.

loses in number of examples. Conversely, the author-centered approach is much more encompassing and allows for a more diverse handling of the texts, but runs the risk of including heterogeneous examples.

In light of this challenge, Dieter-Alex Koch has proposed a methodologically concise way of identifying citations from a reader's perspective.[12] Here Koch describes seven conditions under which a statement (in his case Pauline) might legitimately be identified as a quotation: (1) when accompanied by a clear formula; (2) when the same words appear in another context where they are marked clearly as a citation; (3) when followed by an interpretive gloss; (4) when the words in question stand out syntactically from their (Pauline) context; (5) when the passage differs stylistically from the verses that surround it; (6) when introduced by a light particle of emphasis; and (7) when the verse reproduces a tradition that the author clearly assumes will be familiar to his readers.[13]

Koch's conditions help provide a more robust methodology for identifying and labelling quotations within a particular author. There are, however, some limitations. For example, condition seven is much more subjective than condition one, which provides a clear criterion for evaluation. Moreover, certain conditions (e.g., two, four, and seven) rely on sufficient knowledge of the author in question. This is problematic for authors that have a limited corpus from which to draw, such as Baruch. As a result, this article will only use the first of Koch's conditions: "accompanied by a clear formula".[14] This is not to suggest that other means of determining citations cannot or should not be applied to Baruch. Rather, this article will solely focus on Baruch's explicit citations in which a named source (Moses or "Prophets") is given.

Unfortunately, this type of definitional rigour has been absent from many studies of Baruch. For example, Emanuel Tov in his work comparing Baruch to LXX Jeremiah regularly uses the terms "citation" and "quotation" to indicate a wide range of textual relationships. In many of these cases Tov merely wishes to identify textual inspiration and errs in labelling a one-word overlap as a quotation.[15]

---

12   KOCH, Die Schrift als Zeuge des Evangeliums, 11-15.
13   KOCH, Die Schrift als Zeuge des Evangeliums, 13-15. Challenging many of the above criteria, Stanley only adheres to categories 1, 3, and 4 of Koch. STANLEY, Paul and the Language of Scripture, 36-37. A similar approach was previously advanced by FOX, The Identification of Quotations in Biblical Literature, 416-431.
14   This is also the methodology adopted by STANLEY, Paul and the Language of Scripture.
15   For a list of examples, see TOV, The Septuagint Translation of Jeremiah and Baruch, 122-124.

One of the additional challenges of investigating Baruch's use of scripture is securely determining and identifying passages in which Baruch appropriates a LXX text. Not only is identifying which text Baruch cited a potential problem, but identifying the textual tradition(s) available to him is nearly impossible.[16] As a result, the commentator of Baruch is left making suggestions of source verses, which might have influenced the author of Baruch: "The greater part of Bar(uch) is a mosaic of biblical passages; it quotes or elaborates upon many biblical phrases, sentences and sections ..."[17] Though this article will not avoid the discussion of intertextual references in the "citations" – they will be an important focus – our investigation will not end there. Rather it will look to determine how Scripture is holistically used in Baruch through the use of citation formulae.

"Citations" in Baruch

Turning to the penitential text of Baruch (1:15-3:8), it appears that there are four passages that meet Koch's first criterion: Bar 2:2, 20, 24, and 28. Although we will only be discussing the four instances in which it appears that Baruch claims to be explicitly citing Jewish Scripture, it will be apparent that these passages are not exact citations so coveted and required by modern scholarship. Rather, it will be shown that they are mostly composite in character, drawing from a variety of sources. These sources, however, are not randomly selected. On the contrary, they are compiled and filtered in a way that channels the reader's interpretation through a Jeremianic frame.

---

16 STANLEY, Paul and the Language of Scripture, 293. Stanley's summarises further issues: "Several explanations can be posited for this comparative neglect: the complex and uncertain text-history of the biblical materials themselves; the difficulty in fixing an individual author's biblical *Vorlage*; the loss of original language versions of many of the works in question; a notable lack of comparative studies on other documents; and especially the higher visibility and relative accessibility of an author's exegetical techniques as compared to the way he handled the wording of Scripture. Comparing hermeneutical models is certainly a more promising enterprise than entering into a labyrinthine discussion of the relationship between a series of quotations and their presumed biblical *Vorlage*. In the long run, however, there is no escaping the close analysis that is required to render an adequate portrait of an author's approach to the biblical text."
17 TOV, The Septuagint Translation of Jeremiah and Baruch, 125-126.

Baruch 2:2-3

The first example of a "citation" in Baruch occurs at 2:2, which contains the phrase "according to that which is written in the Law of Moses" (κατὰ τὰ γεγραμμένα ἐν τῷ νόμῳ Μωυσῆ), which appears to introduce a specific quotation: "that we should eat, a person the flesh of his son and a person the flesh of his daughter" (τοῦ φαγεῖν ἡμᾶς ἄνθρωπον σάρκας υἱοῦ αὐτοῦ καὶ ἄνθρωπον σάρκας θυγατρὸς αὐτοῦ, Bar 2:3).

Upon inspection of the books of Moses it becomes apparent that this promise of cannibalizing of children is present, not only in the book of Deuteronomy and its lists of curses (Deut 28:53), "Then you shall eat the offspring of your own body, the flesh of your sons and of your daughters whom the LORD your God has given you, during the siege and the distress by which your enemy shall oppress you" καὶ φάγῃ τὰ ἔκγονα τῆς κοιλίας σου κρέα υἱῶν σου καὶ θυγατέρων σου ὅσα ἔδωκέν σοι κύριος ὁ θεός σου ἐν τῇ στενοχωρίᾳ σου καὶ ἐν τῇ θλίψει σου ᾗ θλίψει σε ὁ ἐχθρός σου), but also in Lev 26:29 "You will eat the flesh of your sons and the flesh of your daughters" (καὶ φάγεσθε τὰς σάρκας τῶν υἱῶν ὑμῶν καὶ τὰς σάρκας τῶν θυγατέρων ὑμῶν φάγεσθε).[18]

Outside of the Pentateuch, there are a couple references to eating ones own flesh. Isaiah 9:20 states that the Lord will be against Israel and that each person will eat the flesh of his own arms, both right and left, but will still be hungry. However, the best parallel outside the Mosaic Law for Bar 2:3 would clearly be Jer 19:9. In the passage leading up to this verse, Israel has once again failed to heed the word of the Lord. As a result, the Lord promises that he will punish Jerusalem by the sword. The climax of this curse is Jer 19:9, "And they will eat the flesh of their sons, and the flesh of their daughters; and they will eat every one the flesh of his neighbour in the blockade, and in the siege which their enemies will besiege them" (καὶ ἔδονται τὰς σάρκας τῶν υἱῶν αὐτῶν καὶ τὰς σάρκας τῶν θυγατέρων αὐτῶν καὶ ἕκαστος τὰς σάρκας τοῦ πλησίον αὐτοῦ ἔδονται ἐν τῇ περιοχῇ καὶ ἐν τῇ πολιορκίᾳ ᾗ πολιορκήσουσιν αὐτοὺς οἱ ἐχθροὶ αὐτῶν) (cf. Lam 2:20; 4:10; Ezek 5:10; 2 Kgs 6:28-29).

Although there is a change of person from second person to first person in Baruch, as well as a difference in number and construction, it is apparent that Lev 26:29 is the best fit for the reference in Bar 2:3, particularly in light of Baruch's explicit reference of the Law of Moses. The observant reader, however, would not only note this key Mosaic passage, but also pick up the allusive reference to Jeremiah. Similar to the

---

18 Unfortunately this reference to the Law of Moses and the possible allusion to Deuteronomy is not discussed in length by MARTTILA, Deuteronomistic Ideology and Phraseology in the Book of Baruch, 327.

Leviticus parallel, Jer 9:19 also changes the person reference (third to first person) and uses the plural as opposed to the singular when referencing sons and daughters.

On the other hand, the Jeremiah passage, unlike Leviticus, shares the same referent as Baruch, Jerusalem (Bar 2:2; Jer 19:3), and explicitly situates this punishing event in the Jewish capital: "It was not done under all of heaven as he did in Jerusalem" (οὐκ ἐποιήθη ὑποκάτω παντὸς τοῦ οὐρανοῦ καθὰ ἐποίησεν ἐν Ιερουσαλημ, Bar 2:2). The role of Jerusalem is prominent in Baruch, particularly in the final section of Baruch where Jerusalem has an extended speaking role (4:8-5:9). Similarly, the opening of Baruch (1:1-14) sets Jerusalem as the geographic destination of the work. Although not in the quotation itself, Baruch's framing of the quotation with a reference to Jerusalem in 2:2 helps the reader interpret the quotation and draw the parallels from Jeremiah 19. This explicit geographical referent is too important to overlook and provides the framework for understanding Baruch's "citation".

Rodney A. Werline has put forward an alternate view to interpret this passage, claiming that Baruch's penitential prayer section is thoroughly dependent on Daniel 9. According to Werline, at the time at which the author wrote Baruch (following the Jewish victories over the Seleucid armies)[19] the temple was no longer profaned as it was in Daniel. "To compensate for this, he incorporates an account of cannibalism during Antiochus V's siege."[20] This citation of Moses, according to Werline, is then inserted by Baruch into Daniel's invoking of the Mosaic Law in Dan 9:11. The major difference is that the author of Baruch changed Daniel's "we sinned against him" into an account of cannibalism.

The relationship between Daniel and Baruch in the penitential prayer section is complex. Many authors have attempted to discern exactly what is going on between these two works, and their arguments are not able to be discussed in full here.[21] Although I am not entirely convinced of Werline's reading of Baruch in light of the events and reign of Antiochus V, I appreciate Werline's discussion of penitential parallels between Baruch and Daniel and his attempt to incorporate the importance of Jeremiah for Baruch. In particular, Werline identifies

---

19   Werline follows Goldstein for his dating of Baruch. WERLINE, Penitential Prayer, 87; GOLDSTEIN, The Apocryphal Book of I Baruch, 179-199. For other dating views, see BURKE, Poetry of Baruch, 26-28.
20   WERLINE, Penitential Prayer, 96.
21   For further consideration, see WAMBACQ, Les prières de Baruch, 463-475; MOORE, Toward the Dating of the Book of Baruch, 312-320; TOV, The Relation between the Greek Versions, 27-34.

Baruch's continued use of Jeremiah and Deuteronomy and how both are important for understanding Baruch's message.²² This is especially the case as Baruch intentionally inserted a "citation" from the Law of Moses which has a strong parallel in Jeremiah.

As a result, though it is clear that Baruch is invoking the Mosaic tradition and his prophetic curse, it is not possible to disassociate the Baruch passage from its Jeremianic parallel. Nor is this what the author intended. Here in Bar 2:3 we have the fulfillment of the prophetic announcement by both Moses and Jeremiah. The specific geographic referent, Jerusalem, supplied by Jeremiah and understandably absent in Leviticus and Deuteronomy, guides the observant reader to interpret this Mosaic reference through the lens of Jeremiah. As we will soon see, Baruch's method of reframing the Mosaic tradition through Jeremiah is a recurring pattern.

Baruch 2:20-23

Continuing through the penitential prayer section, there are three other passages in Baruch (2:20, 24 28) whose citation technique adheres to Koch's category. Additionally, Baruch also provides a referent along with a corresponding citation phrase, in the case of Bar 2:20 it is λέγων "saying". What follows in each passage is a conglomeration of verses from different sources that have been arranged into a single quotation. In each case the language of the original verses has been so thoroughly adapted by the author to fit his literary agenda that, despite his identification of an author, determining the identity and location of the verses behind the quote is challenging.

It is interesting to note that at least one ancient reader possibly did not see this as a quotation. In the critical edition of the *Septuaginta* by Rahlfs/Hanhart Bar 2:20 reads καθάπερ ἐλάλησας ἐν χειρὶ τῶν παίδων σου τῶν προφητῶν λέγων. However, in both codex Vaticanus and the Syro-Hexapla the "saying" (λέγων) is absent. Although this omission in Vaticanus could be explained by *homoioteleuton*, the scribe skipping over λέγων because it shares the same ending as προφητῶν, it is possible that the scribe recognised that this was not an actual quotation from one of the prophets and dropped the signalling λέγων.²³

---

22 For example, Werline has a much more explicit and coherent integration of Deuteronomy, Jeremiah, Daniel, and Baruch than MOORE, Daniel, Esther, and Jeremiah; and KNEUCHER, Das Buch Baruch.

23 The scribe of Vaticanus was quite conscientious and careful with his copying. Furthermore, the corrector was quite thorough in catching the few mistakes. As a result, the λέγων might have been previously omitted and the scribe of Vaticanus faith-

Baruch 2:20, references un-named prophets, "just as you said through the hand of your servants the prophets, saying ..." (καθάπερ ἐλάλησας ἐν χειρὶ τῶν παίδων σου τῶν προφητῶν λέγων)

> For you have brought your anger and your wrath against us, as you had spoken by the hand of your servants the prophets, saying: "Thus did the Lord say: 'Incline your shoulder, and work for the king of Babylon, and sit upon the land which I gave to your fathers. And if you do not obey the voice of the Lord to work for the king of Babylon, I will make to fail from the towns of Judah and from outside Jerusalem a voice of merriment and a voice of delight, a voice of bridegroom and a voice of bride, and all the land will become untrodden by inhabitants'" (Bar 2:20-23).

Although there is an explicit reference to the prophets, which prophet(s) Baruch is intending is obscure. However, upon closer inspection Baruch seems to be only paraphrasing one prophet, Jeremiah.[24] For example, Zink claims that Baruch combines Jer 27[34]:11-14 and 7:34 to form this passage.[25] Moore follows by affirming the references of Jer 27[34]:11-12 and 7:34, but also adds Jer 16:9; 33:10-11.[26] Stanley endorses the identification of Jer 27:11-14, but challenges the reference of 7:34, seeing instead Jer 33:10-11 and 34:22b.[27] Recently, Večho has attempted to advance our understanding and agrees that this "quotation" is drawn from Jeremiah. However, she identifies a much larger number of parallel texts claiming that Baruch has drawn from every part of Jeremiah.[28] This strong emphasis on Jeremiah reinforces the Jeremianic perspective developed in this section and strengthens the ties between Jeremiah and Baruch.[29]

---

fully copied his exemplar. Either way, the fact that a good manuscript omits λέγων here is interesting and may suggest more than an accidental slip of the eye.

24 The references to the King of Babylon in Ezekiel are warnings to Israel and lack specific parallels.
25 ZINK, The Use of the Old Testament in the Apocrypha, 109-113. WHITEHOUSE (Baruch, 586) also notes the influence of Jer 27:11-12, but also adds Jer 29:5f, 7:34, 16:9, and 33:10-11.
26 MOORE, Daniel, Esther, and Jeremiah, 288.
27 STANLEY, Paul and the Language of Scripture, 310.
28 VEČHO, There is Hope for the Scattered People, 90. Večho's identification of (MT) Jeremiah passages in Bar 2:21-23: v. 21a // Jer 27:4,7f.,10f.,12f.; v. 21b // Jer 35:15; 25:5; v. 22 // Jer 26:4; 3:25; 7:24-28; 9:11-12; 11:4-5; 26:12-13; 32:23; 38:20; 42:13,21-22; 44:23; v. 23 //Jer 7:34; 16:9(-13); 25:10-11; 25:38; 26:9; 34:22; 33:10-11.
29 There is substantial scholarly discussion regarding the relationship between Baruch and Jeremiah (LXX). One of the more influential perspectives is that of E. TOV (The Book of Baruch; The Septuagint Translation of Jeremiah and Baruch) in which he argues that there was a similar translator/redactor used for Jer 29-52 (Jer B') and Baruch 1:1-3:9. Although this perspective is still accepted by a number of scholars, there is a growing awareness of the problems undermining Tov's perspective. I think that there is a much more dynamic use of Jeremiah by the author(s) of Baruch that cannot be limited to a similar redactor.

One issue with only being able to identify Jeremianic parallels in this Baruch "quotation" is the reference to multiple prophets (2:20). Although this is not the first time Baruch has referred to prophets in the plural (1:21), it is the first time that a saying has been attributed to them. A parallel example, however, also occurs in 2:24 (to be discussed below). Nevertheless, to anticipate that discussion, Bar 2:24 also primarily references Jeremiah despite the plural form of prophets. Nowhere in Baruch is a specific prophet referenced by name despite the abundance of intertextual parallels. The only author referenced by name is Moses (1:20; 2:2, 28). The paired references to Moses and the prophets in the penitential prayer section fit well with Baruch's holistic vision of the history of Israel and her ongoing relationship with God.[30] Not only does the author of Baruch remind the reader of God's promises with Abraham, Isaac, and Jacob (2:34), but he recalls God's repeated messages given through the prophets as a warning and promise of discipline.

Within Jewish Scripture it was not only Jeremiah who warned the people of Israel about God's impending judgement and exile, although he is arguably the most memorable voice. Rather, the prophets are seen as a chorus of voices warning the people of waywardness and trying to re-establish right actions and beliefs. As a result, it is possible that Baruch was attempting to bring the combined weight of the prophets to support his specific statements drawn from Jeremiah. In this way, Baruch's Jeremianic development of the "prophets" shapes the way that the reader views the prophets's message.

Baruch is not the only writer to make use of the "prophets" to support a claim despite not citing multiple prophets. For example, Ezra 9:11-12 speaks of a command from the prophets, but it is not to be found in the prophetic corpus. J.M. Myers in his commentaries claims that these verses are "a general summation of the message of the prophets"[31] and that "verses 11 and 12 represent a patchwork of Mosaic and prophetic ideas brought together by the writer."[32] H.G.M. Williamson also notes that "the citation does not come from a single passage, but is rather a mosaic of many passages and scriptural allusions." This, he claims, "is understandable in a liturgical context, but also is of significance as a pointer to the emergence of a view which came to regard Scripture as a uniform authority."[33]

Similarly, although writing somewhat later, Matthew 2:23 makes a parallel claim, "So was fulfilled what was said through the prophets:

---

30 KABASELE MUKENGE, Les Citations Internes en Ba. 1,15-3,8, 215.
31 MYERS, I and II Esdras, 93.
32 MYERS, Ezra, Nehemiah, 79.
33 WILLIAMSON, Ezra, Nehemiah. 137.

'He will be called a Nazarene'." Here, however, commentators have only found one possible referent, Isaiah, though there have been a number of theories proposed to answer this issue. R.T. France argues that Matthew is not providing a quotation from a specific passage, but is invoking the general theme of prophecy.[34] Others, such as U. Luz, suggest that Matthew used "prophets" because could not remember the exact location to cite the correct prophet by name.[35] Although this latter view is possible for Matthew, it unlikely that Baruch, whose work is so thoroughly influenced by Jeremiah, would have forgotten where these verses came from. W.D. Davies and D.C. Allison have posited that Matthew used "prophets" to signal that he was not going to cite scripture verbatim and that the reader should expect something else.[36]

A number of the theories given by commentators of Ezra and Matthew parallel what is happening in Baruch. Not only is there a patchwork of verses recalled in Baruch, but it appears that the author is intentionally developing a wide interpretive lens by which he wants the reader to approach Bar 2:20-23. This passage and the invoking of the "prophets", if seen in tandem with the other "citations", works well for Baruch's overall view of the unity of Scripture. Baruch not only wants Jeremiah, but the entire corpus of the prophets to bear witness to what has happened to the people of Israel. This perspective will be further developed below.

Baruch 2:24

The short citation at Bar 2:24, though missing λέγων or ὅτι to indicate a direct quotation, still fulfils Koch's criterion of citation as it explicitly references the words that the Lord spoke through his the prophets, "And we did not listen to your voice to work for the king of Babylon, and you have established your words, which you spoke by the hand of your servants the prophets". The words purported to be from the prophets include a promise that "the bones of our kings and the bones of our father would be carried out from their places". The omission of a direct speech marker, though not obscuring the invocation of the prophets, minimises the strength of the quotation and opens a greater possibility that the words following are not a direct quotation.

As with Bar 2:20-23 above, Baruch does not specify which prophet(s) he is referring to, but once again the closest text comes from

---

34 FRANCE, Matthew, 91.
35 LUZ, Matthew 1-7, 123.
36 DAVIES/ALLISON, Matthew 1-7, 174-175.

Jeremiah. Here the best parallel is Jer 8:1 which says "At that time, says the Lord, they shall bring the bones of the kings of Judah and the bones of its rulers and the bones of the priests and the bones of the prophets and the bones of the inhabitants of Jerusalem out of their tombs ..."

The similarities between these two texts were seen by some of the ancients as is indicated by Codex Alexandrinus (along with the Arabic text tradition), which makes an addition to Bar 2:24 to include more of Jer 8:1, specifically, καὶ τὰ ὀστᾶ τῶν ἀρχόντων ἡμῶν. Similarly, most modern scholars would agree that Jer 8:1 is the best fit for this verse. For example, Kabasele Mukenge identifies this as an "indirect citation" of Jer 8:1.[37] Although Kabasele Mukenge does an admirable job of discussing the differences between these two passage and the possible redactions that Bar 2:24 might have undergone, he does not adequately discuss the function of this verse, particularly Baruch's use of the plural prophets to reference only Jeremiah.[38] As mentioned above, it is clear from even a cursory study of Baruch that Jeremiah exerts much influence on the narrative. As a result, claiming that the author of Baruch did not know where this passage came from because he was drawing from memory is unconvincing. Rather, it is more likely that the author of Baruch knew that this was a reference to Jeremiah, but wanted to invoke the whole of the prophetic corpus.

Baruch 2:28-35

The final citation of this section, Bar 2:28-35, identifies Moses by name and provides a specific narrative context (καθὰ ἐλάλησας ἐν χειρὶ παιδός σου Μωυσῆ ἐν ἡμέρᾳ ἐντειλαμένου σου αὐτῷ γράψαι τὸν νόμον σου ἐναντίον υἱῶν Ισραηλ λέγων).

> As you spoke by the hand of your servant Moses in the day when you commanded him to write your law before the sons of Israel, saying: "If you do not obey my voice, surely this great, voluminous buzzing will turn into a small one among the nations, there where I will scatter them. For I knew that they would not obey me, because the people are stiff-necked. And they will return to their heart in the land of their exile, and they will know that I am the Lord their God. And I will give them a heart and hearing ears, and they will praise me in the land of their exile, and they will remember my name, and they will turn away from their hard back and from their wicked deeds, because they will remember the way of their fathers who sinned before the Lord. And I will return them to the land, which I swore to their fathers, to Abraham and to Isaac and to Jacob, and they will rule over it, and I will multiply them, and they will not diminish. I will establish with them

---

37 KABASELE MUKENGE, Les Citations Internes en *Ba.* 1,15-3,8, 216.
38 KABASELE MUKENGE, Les Citations Internes en *Ba.* 1,15-3,8, 219-223.

an everlasting covenant, that I be God to them and they be a people to me, and I will not disturb them again, my people Israel, from the land that I have given them" (Bar 2:28-35).

Here we find another supposed quotation that fits Koch's criteria. However, unlike the previous examples, this passage does not have a direct correspondent in the Torah.³⁹ Furthermore, unlike Bar 2:21-23 which reworks only Jeremiah, this "quotation" draws from a number of biblical books. Zink identifies the influences of Lev 26:12; 1 Kgs 8:47; Jer 16:15b; Gen 50:24b; and Jer 31:31, 33.⁴⁰ Stanley has made some further suggestions for this composite, indicating parallels between this passage and Jer 32:37-41, 29:6, and Deut 30:20.⁴¹ Whitehouse identifies Deut 27:62; 1 Kgs 8:47; Deut 6:10, Jer 19:6b; 31:31; 32:40,⁴² whereas Večho once again see numerous parallels primarily drawn from Deuteronomy and Jeremiah.⁴³

Francis Watson, however, is much more specific, suggesting that Bar 2:27-35 is a "free paraphrase of Deuteronomy 30.1-10," most likely based on Baruch's specific temporal reference, namely that "Baruch has in mind the depiction of a future beyond the curse in Deuteronomy 30.1-10."⁴⁴ Watson, furthermore, argues that Baruch is best understood as an elaboration of the deuteronomic schema,⁴⁵ identifying a number of instances where Baruch appears to be drawing on Deuteronomy and noting that these passages are pivotal for understanding Baruch's view of Israel. For example, in the beginning of this section (1:15-3:8), following an acknowledgement of guilt, Watson claims that Baruch frames the history of Israel as a history of disobedience:

> From the day when the Lord brought our fathers out of the land of Egypt even until this day, we were being disobedient to the Lord our God, and we were acting carelessly so as not to listen to his voice. And there have

---

39　KABASELE MUKENGE (Les Citations Internes en Ba. 1,15-3,8, 215-216) wants to differentiate between the different quotations by the use of "writing" or "saying" vocabulary. I am not convinced that this strong division can be made to indicate the author's direct use of citation or paraphrase.
40　ZINK, The Use of the Old Testament in the Apocrypha, 109-113.
41　STANLEY, Paul and the Language of Scripture, 310.
42　WHITEHOUSE, Baruch, 586.
43　VEČHO, There is Hope for the Scattered People, 92 n.45. The text is a mosaic of quotations from: v. 29 // Deut 28:15; Jer 26:4; Deut 4:27; 28:62; Jer 42:2; v. 30 // Deut 31:27-29; Jer 7:26-27; 17:23; 30:10; 46:27; v. 31 // Deut 4:39; Jer 24:7; Deut 29:3; Jer 24:7; 32:39; v. 33 // Deut 31:27; 2 Kings 17:14; Jer 17:26; 4:4; 21:12; 23:2,22; 25:5; 26:3, 13; 44:22; Deut 28:20; 1 Kings 8:47; Zech 1:4; Ps 79:8; v. 34 // Deut 30:1-10; Lev 26:42-45; Jer 32:37; 24:6; 30:3; 11:5; Deut 1:8; 6:10; Jer 32:23; Deut 30:5,16; Jer 3:16; 23:3; Zech 10:8; Jer 24:6; 42:10; v. 35 // Jer 50:5; 32:40,38; 31:31-34.
44　WATSON, Paul and the Hermeneutics of Faith, 461.
45　WATSON, Paul and the Hermeneutics of Faith, 455.

clung to us the bad things and the curse (τὰ κακὰ καὶ ἡ ἀρά) that the Lord instructed to his servant Moses in the day he brought out our ancestors from the land of Egypt, to give to us a land flowing with milk and honey, as this day … (Bar 1:19-21).

From the explicit reference to Moses and the curse given after the exodus, it is clear that Baruch is referencing Deuteronomy. Watson, however, states the "curse" here is the curse of Deuteronomy 27:26: "Cursed be every person who does not remain in all the words of this law and do them."[46] Although Watson is correct in connecting the Baruch passage to the wider set of deuteronomic curses, it is not apparent why Watson specifically associates Bar 1:19-21 only with Deut 27:26. True, curse language is found here; however, lexical similarities are lacking as there are two different terms used for curse, ἐπικατάρατος (Deut) and ἀρά (Bar).[47] Rather than advancing a specific passage, I would suggest that there are a number of parallels to Baruch from Deuteronomy 27 and 30, but also from other books in the Pentateuch, such as Lev 26.[48]

Watson is no doubt correct when he highlights deuteronomic influence; however, I would wish to emphasise the framework by which Baruch structures this "quotation". In Deuteronomy the scattering of the people of Israel is a threat given by God as a promised response to future disobedience. The geographic location of this scattering in Deuteronomy, though, is vague, lacking specific details. In Baruch, however, this citation of Moses is explicitly placed in the Babylonian exile. Although acknowledging the fore-promises of God through Moses, Baruch in this section is viewing those future promises as presently realised through the Babylonian exile. This is reinforced by the allusions to Jeremiah identified above, in which this geographic deictic marker anchors the Baruch narrative in the Babylonian exile and provides the literary context by which to interpret the later narrative.

Another shortcoming of Watson's otherwise insightful evaluation of Baruch is the lack of in-depth discussion of other, non-deuteronomic scriptural allusions. Although Watson is well aware of the parallels between Dan 9 and Bar 1:15-2:19 it is interesting that he downplays

---

46 WATSON, Paul and the Hermeneutics of Faith, 459.
47 There are many other vocabulary similarities in this passage between Baruch and Jeremiah against Deuteronomy. For example, ἀποικισμός (Bar 2:32) is a term for exile only found in Jeremiah and Baruch cf. Jer 50:11. Similarly, the root βομβ- is seen only in Bar 2:29 (βόμβησις); Jer 31:36; 38:36 and 1 Chron 16:32 (βομβέω). TOV, The Relation between the Greek Versions, 118. Though these are minor in importance, they do suggest a stronger literary relationship with Jeremiah than Deuteronomy.
48 VEČHO, There is Hope for the Scattered People, 85. Večho identifies parallels with Lev 26:14-39 and Deut 28:15-29:1.

Daniel's importance despite the fact that some of the literary and lexical similarities are stronger than the Deuteronomic ones. For example, there is a number of shared motifs between Daniel and Baruch, specifically: divine righteousness and human sinfulness (Bar 1:15-16; Dan 9:7-8); confession of sin (Bar 1: 17-18, 21; Dan 9:5-6); curses given by Moses (Bar 1:20; Dan 9:11, 13); destruction of the temple (Bar 2:2-3; Dan 9:12-13); remembering of the Exodus (Bar 2:11; Dan 9:15); appeal for a secession of divine anger (Bar 2:13; Dan 9:16); plea to be heard for God's sake (Bar 2:14; Dan 9:17); and prayer not based on one's own righteousness (Bar 2:19; Dan 9:18).[49] In Watson's defense, he is looking at the book of Baruch as a whole, not just the penitential prayer section and from this macro perspective Deuteronomy plays a more substantial role than Daniel.

More problematic, however, is Watson's lack of discussion of Jeremianic parallels. As shown above in the citations in the penitential prayer section, Baruch draws deeply from Jeremiah for its worldview.[50] Furthermore, Baruch portrays a particular relationship between Jeremiah and Deuteronomy; Deuteronomy or other books from the Pentateuch may be the specified referent, but it is to be understood through the lens of Jeremiah. In light of the strong relationship between Baruch and Jeremiah, it is surprising that mention of this affiliation is absent in Watson's study.

For example, though Watson discusses Baruch's three references to Moses (1:20; 2:2, 28), he overlooks the four references to the "prophets" (1:16, 21; 2:20, 24). It is this pairing of references that form the heart of the penitential prayer.[51] This is further confirmed by allusionary references to Jeremiah throughout the penitential prayer section. The very form of the passage, that of penitential prayer, reinforces the prophetic framework as this form of repentance is found almost exclusively in the prophetic literature.[52] These petitions, though grounded in a Deuteronomic worldview, are notably absent in practice outside of the pro-

---

49 Here the verbal similarities with Baruch are stronger with the Thedotian version of Daniel rather than the OG.
50 Baruch is also highly influenced by the text of Jeremiah. In the first half of Baruch alone, Tov has identified thirty-two "important agreements between Bar and Jer-R". Although I disagree with the strength and wording of some of Tov's claims, the number of similarities between Baruch and LXX-Jeremiah is impressive and demands consideration. TOV, Septuagint Translation, 122-124.
51 KABASELE MUKENGE, Les Citations Internes en *Ba.* 1,15-3,8, 215-216; FLOYD, Penitential Prayer in the Second Temple Period, 73.
52 For example, Bar 2:6-10 bears similarities to the closing of other penitential prayers (e.g., Ezra 9:15; Neh 9:33; Dan 9:14; cf. also Ex 9:27; 2 Kgs 10:9; Ezek 18:9). VEČHO, There is Hope for the Scattered People, 87.

phetic material and so any exegesis of this section must take into account that body of literature.

Although identifying allusions and parallel texts is important, it is insufficient – especially for Baruch – to merely state them without extrapolating on their significance. Unfortunately, a number of Baruchan scholars conclude their discussion at this point. If these are intentional allusions, one must ask about the intentionality of such connections. This is particularly relevant for Baruch which, as was seen above, draws on a number of scriptural texts. We turn now to understanding the function of Baruch's citations.

The Function of Baruch's "Citations"

It has been well documented that Baruch makes extensive use of Scripture, especially the books of Deuteronomy, Job, Isaiah, Jeremiah, Daniel, and Psalms of Solomon. However, this appropriation of Jewish Scripture has often been seen as a dependence on previous narratives and lacking any form of creativity.[53] Furthermore, some have taken this as a claim that Baruch offers little unique theological or exegetical contribution.

Turning to the "quotations" in Baruch, we discover that the "quotations" rarely match a specific biblical text or a singular author, which can often offend the sensibilities of modern readers and scholars. However, rigid lexical precision was not slavishly adhered to by the ancients. In Timothy Lim's investigation of the use of Scripture in Paul and the Qumran community he shows that "in both ideological orientation and exegetical tradition, the persherists did not consider the words of their biblical texts to be fixed and immutable."[54] Rather, Lim contends that these authors not only saw themselves as commentators of Scripture, but also might have seen themselves as biblical writers.[55]

A. Kabasele Mukenge claims that one reason for the differences in cited texts by the author of Baruch is a result of quotation from memory and not consulting the respective books.[56] Although this is likely the case for the author(s) of Baruch, this perspective does not do justice to all that we find in the text. It is insufficient to write off the differences as "authorial mistakes" and not to consider the holistic effect of the

---

53 So, MOORE, Daniel, Esther, and Jeremiah.
54 LIM, Holy Scripture, 120.
55 LIM, Holy Scripture, 120.
56 KABASELE MUKENGE, Les Citations Internes en *Ba.* 1,15-3,8, 213. Kabasele Mukenge explains the differences by also suggesting that the texts available to the writers of Baruch were different from the '*textus receptus*'.

"misquotation". This is especially so when approaching Baruch as it has a high number of allusions which assist in both shaping the text and assisting the reader in their interpretation.

As discussed above, there is a number of differences between the "quotations" in Baruch and their proposed source texts. Although I would agree with Kabasele Mukenge that it is unlikely that the author of Baruch had a roll of Jeremiah (or any other book) open before him, we must also appreciate, not only the changes from the source text, but also how they function in the book of Baruch.

First, the selection of specific texts is a creative act in itself. For example, Baruch could have selected any number of texts from Jeremiah, the Pentateuch, or the rest of Jewish Scripture, but rather he chose those that maintained a strong Jeremianic and deuteronomic perspective. This is seen in Bar 2:2 in which the "citation" from the Law of Moses has a near parallel in Jeremiah. Moreover, this Jeremiah parallel, though not explicitly referenced by the author, helps shape the interpretation of this passage by supporting the geographical location specified in Baruch and by providing a unified view of these verses's prophetic fulfillment.

Second, the supposed "changes" or "mistakes" in Baruch's citations need to be understood not solely in terms of carelessness or a free translation, but also as Baruch's tailoring his source text to his current context. The combination of exposition and composition is what we see in these Baruch "quotations". Here the author of Baruch composes a composite quotation from a number of biblical *excerpta* (cf. Luke 4:16-19)[57] in order to draw on a wide range of biblical texts and frame the deuteronomic promises through realized Jeremianic events.[58]

This is not a re-written version of Scripture, as rewriting Scripture implies a closer relationship to a text than reframing. Rather, this is an example of "reframing" Scripture by resituating it within a new setting. By placing allusions and explicit references in a new or different context the author has the ability to subtly reshape the original material and message. For Baruch, this is not a rejection of the original context, as often the author is drawing on the background context in his or her message. Rather, the reframing of Scripture allows the author to recast

---

57 "Here again the technique of conflating and adapting a series of verses to suit a later author's interpretive agenda finds a ready witness." STANLEY, Paul and the Language of Scripture, 310. Stanley further claims that "omissions of irrelevant material, condensing summaries, and additions designed to link the various selections into a coherent whole are the most visible forms of adaptation."

58 The citations are not the only deuteronomic influence seen in Baruch. Another example can be seen in the near parallel of Bar 1:19 and Deut 9:7. MARTTILA, Deuteronomistic Ideology and Phraseology in the Book of Baruch, 324-325.

the original message in a new and empowering way, one that is relevant for his current readers. In the case of Baruch, that way was to situate a deuteronomic worldview within a Jeremianic frame.[59] This allows the author of Baruch to appropriate the message of Deuteronomy, but to cast it in a manner that acknowledges its exilic setting. Furthermore, it allows Baruch to take hold of deuteronomic promises and claim them for his audience.

Helpful in this discussion, moreover, is the recognition of the type of text that these quotations occur in, namely, the penitential prayer section.[60] In this liturgical setting we have a group of people being led in a prayer as an act of repentance. The general thrust and function of the passage is to facilitate repentance by the Israelite people. In this case, there is a need to acknowledge that they have sinned by breaking the commandments given to them by Moses and the prophets, i.e., the whole of Jewish Scripture.[61] It would be insufficient to claim that they only disobeyed the words of Moses and Jeremiah, although this would be accurate. Rather, when it came to general repentance the author of Baruch, though drawing heavily from Jeremiah, did not wish to focus on Jeremiah alone, but indicate that the Jewish people had transgressed all the words of the prophets. The desire to indicate that the Jewish people had disobeyed all of the prophets, not just Jeremiah is the reason for the use of the plural prophets, rather than the use of the singular or specifying Jeremiah specifically.[62] This, I argue, is more convincing than the theory that the author of Baruch did not remember the book where these passages were taken.

---

59 STECK, Das apokryphe Baruchbuch, 110.
60 Although it is too much to discussion here, there is a strong scholarly discussion on the nature of penitential prayer in the Jewish Scriptures and the relationship between these passages. Of particular importance are the prayers of Deut 4:28-30 and 1 Kings 8:46-53, and their influence on the penitential prayers in Ezra 9; Neh 1; 9; Dan 9; and Bar 1:15-3:9. VEČHO, There is Hope for the Scattered People, 80. See also the three volumes of essays edited by BODA/FALK/WERLINE, Seeking the Favor of God.
61 WILLIAMSON, Ezra, Nehemiah, 137.
62 Although I have not substantially discussed the literary relationship between Baruch and Daniel in this paper, the role of Daniel in the penitential prayer section is quite important. Though I have limited this article to explicit citations that meet Hock's first criterion, I do not wish to underplay the importance of Daniel. Like Jeremiah, Daniel is not referenced by name; however, his influence is seen throughout. As a result, I would argue that Baruch's use of "prophets", though not functioning on the rhetorical level of the quotations discussed above, readily includes Daniel as an important member of the prophetic chorus who had warned Israel in the past. It should be noted, however, that reference to the person of Daniel in Baruch is understandably missing as its narrative is set in approximately 581 BCE and Daniel has not been born yet.

Conclusion

Much more work is needed in order to fully understand Baruch's use of Scripture. However, one way forward is consistent use terms. When dealing with texts that have a strong and complex relationship with Jewish Scriptures, such as Baruch, I believe we need much more precision in our use of terms. While finding synonyms is a standard procedure for making ones writing more interesting, we run the risk of diluting words that have particular meaning. For example, Watson, in discussing Baruch's relationship to Scripture, uses the terms "elaborates," "re-writes and expands," "amplifies," and "free paraphrase" all of which can be problematic in that he does not provide any boundaries to the relationship between the texts. Similarly, Lim rightly affirms that much more work needed before the relationship between a biblical text and its paraphrase is clarified.[63] Rather, these terms should only be used once they have been properly defined and delineated.

Turning to the text of Baruch, in light of the number of references and allusions to Jeremiah in this section it is imperative for interpreters to take into account possible Jeremianic associations in their interpretation. This is especially important when we attempt to interpret and evaluate the so-called "citations" in Baruch that refer to passages from the books of Moses. In these instances it is insufficient to only evaluate the Pentateuchal references. Rather, we see that these references to the Mosaic corpus are framed by and read through a Jeremianic lens. This understanding obligates future Baruch scholars to take seriously the creative and innovative constructions of Baruch and to understand the constructed relationships between Jeremiah and the Pentateuch, particularly Deuteronomy.

Finally, recognising the function of a text is important for interpreting how a text uses Scripture. In this article we have limited ourselves to Bar 1:15-3:8, or Baruch's penitential prayer section. It is this liturgical setting, I have argued, that makes the most interpretive sense for understanding Baruch's citations of Moses and the "prophets". In this case, there was a need to acknowledge that the people had sinned by breaking the commandments given to them by both Moses and the prophets, or the whole of Jewish Scripture. The desire to indicate that the Jewish people had disobeyed all of the prophets, not just Jeremiah is the reason for the use of the plural prophets, rather than the use of the singular or specifying Jeremiah specifically. This, I argued, is the most convincing theory for Baruch's use of the plural prophets.

---

63 LIM, Holy Scripture, 36.

Overall, this essay claims that, in its final form, Baruch displays an innovative and original reframing of Scripture to meet theological needs of the community. Accordingly, Baruch makes use of Scripture to frame the exile from Jerusalem to the Diaspora. But even more than this, Baruch uses Scripture to provide a theological understanding of the people's place within God's cosmos which allows them to come before God in an act of penitential prayer.

Bibliography

BARR, James, The Typology of Literalism in Ancient Biblical Translations (MSU 15), Göttingen 1979.

BODA, Mark J./FALK, Daniel K./WERLINE, Rodney Alan (eds.), Seeking the Favor of God: Vol. 1, The Origins of Penitential Prayer in Second Temple Judaism (SBLEJL 21), Atlanta 2006.

BODA, Mark J./FALK, Daniel K./WERLINE, Rodney Alan (eds.), Seeking the Favor of God: Vol. 2, The Development of Penitential Prayer in Second Temple Judaism (SBLEJL 22), Atlanta 2007.

BODA, Mark J./FALK, Daniel K./WERLINE, Rodney Alan (eds.), Seeking the Favor of God: Vol. 3, The Impact of Penitential Prayer Beyond the Second Temple Judaism (SBLEJL 23), Atlanta 2008.

BURKE, David G., The Poetry of Baruch: A Reconstruction and Analysis of the Original Hebrew Text of Baruch 3:9-5:9 (SBLSCS 10), Atlanta 1982.

DAVIES, William D./ALLISON, Dale C., A Critical and Exegetical Commentary on the Gospel According to Saint Matthew, Vol. I (ICC), London 1998.

DAVILA, James R., (How) Can We Tell if a Greek Apocryphon or Pseudepigraphon has been Translated from Hebrew or Aramaic?, in: JPS 15 (2005), 3-61.

FLOYD, Michael H., Penitential Prayer in the Second Temple Period from the Perspective of Baruch, in: Boda, Mark J./Falk, Daniel K./Werline, Rodney Alan (eds.), Seeking the Favor of God: Volume 2: The Development of Penitential Prayer in Second Temple Judaism (SBLEJL 22), Atlanta 2007, 51-81.

FOX, Michael V., The Identification of Quotations in Biblical Literature, in: ZAW 92 (1980), 416-431.

FRANCE, Richard T., The Gospel of Matthew (NICNT), Grand Rapids 2007.

GOLDSTEIN, Jonathan A., The Apocryphal Book of 1 Baruch, in: Proceedings of the American Academy for Jewish Research 46-47 (1979-80), 179-199.

HAMMILL, L.R., Biblical Interpretation in the Apocrypha and Pseudepigrapha, PhD dissertation, University of Chicago, 1950.

KABASELE MUKENGE, André, Les Citations Internes en Ba. 1,15-3,8: Un procédé rédactionnel et actualisant, in: Le Muséon 108 (1995), 211-37.

KNEUCKER, Johann J., Das Buch Baruch: Geschichte und Kritik, Übersetzung und Erklärung auf Grund des wiederhergestellten Hebräischen Urtextes, Leipzig 1879.

KOCH, Dietrich-Alex, Die Schrift als Zeuge des Evangeliums: Untersuchungen zur Verwendung und zum Verständnis der Schrift bei Paulus (BHT 69), Tübingen 1986.

LIM, Timothy H., Holy Scripture in the Qumran Commentaries and Pauline Letters, Oxford 1997.

LUZ, Ulrich, Matthew 1-7: A Commentary (Hermeneia), Minneapolis 2007.

MARTTILA, Marko, Deuteronomistic Ideology and Phraseology in the Book of Baruch, in: von Weissenberg, Hanne/Pakkala, Juha/Marttila, Marko (eds.), Changes in Scripture: Rewriting and Interpreting Authoritative Tradition in the Second Temple Period (BZAW 419), Berlin 2011, 321-346.

MOORE, Carey A., Towards the Dating of the Book of Baruch, in: CBQ 36 (1974), 312-320.

MOORE, Carey A., Daniel, Esther, and Jeremiah: The Additions: A New Translation with Introduction and Commentary (AB 44), London 1977.

MYERS, J.M., I and II Esdras: A New Translation with Introduction and Commentary (AB 42), New Haven 1995.

MYERS, J.M., Ezra, Nehemiah: A New Translation with Introduction and Commentary (AB 14), New Haven 1995.

SCHULTZ, Richard L., The Search for Quotation: Verbal Parallels in the Prophets (JSOTS 180), Sheffield 1999.

STANLEY, Christopher D., Paul and the Language of Scripture: Citation Technique in the Pauline Epistles and Contemporary Literature (SNTSMS 74), Cambridge 1992.

STECK, Odil Hannes, Das apokryphe Baruchbuch: Studien zu Rezeption und Konzentration "kanonischer" Überlieferung (FRLANT 160), Göttingen 1993.

TORREY, Charles C., The Apocryphal Literature: A Brief Introduction, New Haven 1945.

TOV, Emanuel, The Book of Baruch (Text and Translations 8; Pseudepigrapha Series 6), Missoula 1975.

TOV, Emanuel, The Septuagint Translation of Jeremiah and Baruch: A Discussion of an Early Revision of the LXX of Jeremiah 29-52 and Baruch 1:1-3:8 (Harvard Semitic Monographs 8), Missoula 1976.

TOV, Emanuel, The Relation between the Greek Versions of Baruch and Daniel, in: Stone, M.E. (ed.), Armenian and Biblical Studies, Jerusalem 1976, 27-34.

VEČHO, T.S., There is Hope for the Scattered People (Bar 1:15aβ-3:8), in: BV 67 (2007), 73-97.

WAMBACQ, Benjamin N., "Les Prières de Baruch (1,15-2,19) et de Daniel (9,5-19), in: Biblica 40 (1959), 463-475.

WATSON, Francis, Paul and the Hermeneutics of Faith, London 2004.

WERLINE, Rodney Alan, Penitential Prayer in Second Temple Judaism: The Development of a Religious Institution (SBLEJL 13) Atlanta 1998.

WHITEHOUSE, O.C., The Book of Baruch, in: Charles, R.H. (ed.), The Apocrypha and Pseudepigrapha of the Old Testament in English, Vol. 1. Oxford 1913, 569-595.

WILLIAMSON, Hugh G.M., Ezra, Nehemiah (WBC 16), Waco, TX 1985.

ZIEGLER, Josef, Jeremias, Baruch, Threni, Epistula Jeremiae. Septuaginta Volume XV., Göttingen ³2006 [1957].

ZINK, James K., The Use of the Old Testament in the Apocrypha, Ph.D. dissertation, Duke University, 1963.

Scriptural Authority and the Ancestor as its Teacher and Example in the Book of Tobit

KARIN SCHÖPFLIN

1. Introduction

By the time the book of Tobit was being composed[1] there existed obviously quite a number of writings considered to be authoritative by Jewish communities, though they were not yet part of an official canon of holy scriptures. Over and again critics have noticed that the book of Tobit abounds in intertextual references,[2] that is, it alludes to, imitates[3] or even quotes writings which must have been well-known to the author and his audience.[4] By employing references to established pieces of literature held quasi-canonical an author may claim the same or at least a similar authoritative status for his own writing as well.

This paper will endeavour to identify, interpret and critically evaluate at least some examples out of the network of allusions and

---

1   For a dating of Tob there is a range between the 4th century and 175 BCE; most scholars now assume that it was written in the late 3rd or early 2nd century BCE; cf. EGO, Buch, 899-900; FITZMYER, Tobit, 52.
2   Cf. e.g. ENGEL, Auf den Wegen, 85; NICKELSBURG, Search; EGO, Buch, 887-889. There are a number of exegetical contributions dealing with the influence of certain biblical books on Tob. The most important references identified are with Gen (e.g. RUPPERT, Buch; NOWELL, Book), Deut (e.g. DI LELLA, Background; SOLL, Misfortune), and Job (e.g. PORTIER-YOUNG, Eyes). KIEL, Tobit, holds that Tobit emulates the figure of Moses in Num and Deut.
3   Imitation may include use of vocabulary and style, but also literary form, patterns and motifs.
4   An important question is: which of the canonical-to-be and deuterocanonical and cognate books did exist at that time and were accessible to him and his readers? And in what state were they with regard to their respective genesis? Was their development still in process, maybe? So there is a certain factor of uncertainty because there may and will be a difference between the amount of writings regarded authoritative by modern exegetes and by the writer of Tobit and his contemporaries. For this problem cf. NICKELSBURG, Search.

analogies to writings obviously considered authoritative at the time when Tobit was composed.[5]

2. Quotation

Quotation is the most obvious type of intertextual reference. Three times writings nowadays canonical are quoted, twice these writings are explicitly mentioned by name. Tob 2:6 quotes Amos 8:10, and Tob 14:4 explicitly refers to Nahum's message of doom for Nineveh in S/G^{II}, whereas BA/G^I [6] attributes this prophecy to Jonah. First of all, it is interesting that these explicit references are taken from the writing prophets, namely the Book of the Twelve.

As has been remarked,[7] Tob 2:6 is not an exact quotation of Amos 8:10, though: God's first person perspective emphasizing his activity ("I will turn your feasts into mourning, and all your songs into lamentation.", NRSV) is turned into a passive ("Your festivals shall be turned into mourning, and all your songs into lamentation.", NRSV), thus shifting the attention to Amos, the prophet who uttered this (cf. the introductory phrases: καὶ ἐμνήσθην τῆς προφητείας Αμως καθὼς εἶπεν" and I remembered the prophecy of Amos as he said", TobG^I; καὶ ἐμνήσθην τοῦ ῥήματος τοῦ προφήτου, ὅσα ἐλάλησεν Αμως ἐπὶ Βαιθηλ λέγων "and I remembered the prophet's saying what Amos spoke against Bethel saying", TobG^{II}). The author quotes the prophet as an authority, that is, the mediator of God's word, not God himself as the book of Amos did. In addition, it is true what Friedrich Reiterer stated, namely that the change in the wording of Am 8:10 implies a generalization of the original divine threatening so that it becomes applicable as a statement to any current situation.[8] The context of the quotation is Tobit's autobiographical narrative. Tobit was about to celebrate *shavuot* when

---

5 This article will consider the two Greek versions BA/ G^I and S/ G^{II}, each in its own right. The relation of the two is not yet explained satisfactorily, cf. HANHART, Text, 37, who says that the comparison of the two Greek texts does not result in proving the priority of either of the two. So, the question which is to be preferred as the version that comes closest to an original one is still open to discussion. HANHART, Text, 37, thinks it more plausible, though, that G^I consciously abridged G^{II} so that the latter would represent a more original version. In this respect M. HALLERMAYER, Text, lately preferred G^I to G^{II}, however. For the complexity of the problem cf. EGO, Mehrfachüberlieferung, and especially NICKLAS/WAGNER, Thesen.
6 From now on TobG^I viz. TobG^{II}.
7 Cf. EGO, Buch, 931; REITERER, Prophet, 157.
8 REITERER, Prophet, 157.

his son informed him about a murdered, maybe executed,[9] Israelite who remained unburied so that Tobit left his house to hide the corpse in order to bury it at night (2:1-4). That a fellow countryman had been murdered and the body treated disrespectfully extremely grieves Tobit; therefore, he is eating his food in sorrow (2:5). He employs the quotation to comment on his distress (2:6). The prophecy taken from Amos is literally applied to Tobit's situation.[10] The word originally addressed to the people of Israel as a collective is now applied to Tobit as an individual, and other individuals may also regard this quotation as reflecting their respective situation. Maybe Amos 8:10 is also intended to function as a comfort for Tobit in distress. He accepts his affliction more willingly being aware that his experience is in accordance with God's saying and plan.[11]

Critical readers identified Amos 8:10 as a relatively late addition to that book.[12] An exact dating is hard to give, but nevertheless: is the fact that the author of Tobit explicitly mentions his source an indication that the book of Amos in its final form was not yet well-known at that time? The author of Tobit obviously regards Amos as an authoritative book, i.e. as quasi-canonical. But maybe he could not be sure that his audience would recognize that verse as being taken from Amos. Would Tob 2:6 then testify to the gradual development of the future canon in that the writing prophets were not yet as established as authoritative books as was the Torah?

In Tob 14:4 on his deathbed Tobit recommends that his son move from Nineveh to Media because of a prophecy of doom for Nineveh. According to TobG^{II} this prophecy is found in Nahum (ἃ ἐλάλησεν Ναουμ, "what Nahum spoke").[13] TobG^{I}, however, refers to Jonah (ὅσα ἐλάλησεν Ιωνας, "what Jonah spoke") and quotes the wording of the only prophecy in the book of Jonah, namely the verb καταστραφήσεται ("to be overthrown, ruined", Jonah 3:4), the most characteristic element in Jonah's six-word prophecy in LXX [four in Hebrew]. In fact, both minor prophets may be claimed as authorities for predicting the fall of Nineveh. Very probably Nahum is Jonah's senior, that is, the prophecies of doom addressed to Nineveh in Nah 2-3 preceded the composi-

---

9 As the corpse was left in the market place, MOORE, Tobit, 128, thinks so. At least the dead Jew was exposed to humiliation and shame through this.
10 Would it be saying too much when we find also Tobit's nearest future foreshadowed in the quotation, since Tobit will turn blind that very night? – At any rate, quoting Amos, who prophesied in the Northern Kingdom, fits in with the perspective of Tobit, the Naphtalite (cf. DESELAERS, Buch, 460).
11 In this sense he is an analogy of Job as depicted in Job 1-2, maybe.
12 Cf. e.g. JEREMIAS, Amos, 114, 119.
13 This would call Nah 3:7 or 2:8-10; 3:18-19 to mind, cf. MOORE, Tobit, 290.

tion of the story of Jonah – the latter is dated in the 4th or 3rd century rather unanimously now. Regarding the two Greek versions of Tobit this would mean that TobG^I refers to a more modern writing and TobG^{II} to a more established one.

What is the effect in the immediate context of either quoting Nahum or Jonah? With regard to the destruction of Nineveh Nahum would clearly be the better choice, because in Jonah readers will learn that Nineveh is not destroyed yet because of the Ninevites' conversion. But TobG^I might hold that Nineveh would still be demolished even if Jonah himself did not witness it,[14] thus actually implying that the fulfilment of Jonah's prophecy is imminent now – cf. Tobit's later remark in 14:8.9, when the reference to Jonah is resumed after the general outlook on Israel's future as the prophets predict it (Tob 14:8.9): καὶ νῦν τέκνον ἄπελθε ἀπὸ Νινευη ὅτι πάντως ἔσται ἃ ἐλάλησεν ὁ προφήτης Ιωνας ("and now, child, go away from Nineveh because it will happen for sure what the prophet Jonah spoke", G^I). Instead, TobG^{II}'s choice of Nah fits in with an eagerness to emphasize that God's word as uttered by the prophets principally never fails,[15] but every word will come true at the appointed time (14:4): ὅσα ἐλάλησαν οἱ προφῆται τοῦ Ισραηλ οὓς ἀπέστειλεν ὁ θεὸς πάντα ἀπαντήσει καὶ οὐ μηθὲν ἐλαττονωθῇ ἐκ πάντων τῶν ῥημάτων καὶ πάντα συμβήσεται τοῖς καιροῖς αὐτῶν ("everything the prophets of Israel, whom God sent, spoke will happen; none of all their sayings will fall short, and everything will happen at their appointed times"). For the readers of Nahum, Jonah and Tobit, Nineveh may be understood as representing any powerful regime oppressing the Jewish people; and the destruction of the oppressor will still occur for sure in the future.

In this context Tobit also gives a kind of summary of the writing prophets' message: the Israelites will be scattered and taken as captives from the land; the land of Israel, including Samaria and Jerusalem, will be desolate and the temple will be burned (14:4). But afterwards God will bring the people back into the land of Israel, and after their return from exile they will rebuild the temple (14:5). There even follows an outlook on the conversion of the nations who will worship the eternal God (14:6). For each of these items biblical scholars could point to sev-

---

14 "Schon vor der Entdeckung des Codex Sinaiticus hatten Grotius und Ilgen darauf aufmerksam gemacht, daß eine Prophetie von der Zerstörung Ninives, die, wie es hier vorausgesetzt wird, in Erfüllung gegangen ist, nicht Jona, sondern Nahum oder Zephania zuzuschreiben wäre. Ilgen gab die Möglichkeit, dass der in G^I überlieferte Text dennoch ursprünglich sei, mit der Erklärung zu, ‚dass Tobi also meinte, dass doch noch eintreffen würde, was einst Jonah gedroht hätte, obgleich damals die Drohung nicht wäre erfüllt worden'" (HANHART, Text, 34).

15 Cf. Isa 54:10; 55:11.

eral passages in OT prophecy.[16] The author of Tobit obviously had in mind a wide range of the canonical-to-be books of the (writing) prophets.[17]

In both the versions' final verse (14:15) the reader learns that Tobias is informed about Nineveh's fall before he dies. Because of Nineveh's end and because of the fulfilment of God's words Tobias is very happy. So the author of Tobit is careful to have the prophecy come true in the lifetime of the son to whom the father addressed it formerly. The fact that Tobit understood the prophetical writings correctly and was right to believe them makes him an authority in his own kind and an example of how to deal with these writings. The pattern that prophetic prediction is doubtless fulfilled corresponds to one of the concepts of prophecy in Deuteronomy and Deuteronomists' theology (cf. Deut 18:21-22).

Tobit is an example of a man trusting the prophets, who are intermediaries, as he – naturally – takes their message to be God's own words. And that is why he is absolutely sure that these prophecies will be fulfilled. This carries further associations: Tobit – and his son as well – listen to the prophets' words. This is in accordance with a second concept of prophecy in Deut and Deuteronomist theology (e.g. 2Kgs 17:13-14; punishment came upon Israel as they did not listen to the prophets' warnings) and it makes them devout persons.

As Reiterer put it: Tob 2:6 and 14:4 indicate that the author of Tobit (and his audience) appreciated the Book of the Twelve as authoritative.[18] Prophets predict future events, their words are trustworthy and reliable. If you listen to them and apply their message to your own situation you will take benefit from it. In fact, Tobit even functions as a prophet himself on his deathbed when he predicts the future to Tobias. Tobit thus shares prophetic identity[19] – in a former context he said to his son: υἱοὶ προφητῶν ἐσμεν ("we are prophets' offspring" or "we belong to the prophets", 4:12). The word "prophet" is, however, not the modern technical term, but embraces the general notion of a person elected by God and worthy of being spoken to by him, either directly –

---

16 Cf. MOORE, Tobit, 292: Zeph 2:13; Micah 5:5; Isa 10:5,12; 14:25.
17 In addition, the narrative of the former prophets describes Israel's history up to the destruction of Jerusalem, and Ezra and Neh cover the period of restoration. These history books, however, do not include any eschatological perspective, hoping for a conversion of the people.
18 But still: Tob explicitly mentions Amos and Jonah viz. Nahum because these writings were not yet as well-known and as accepted as authoritative as the Torah or, say, Isaiah.
19 REITERER, Prophet, 159-161.

Tobit mentions Noah, Abraham, Isaac, and Jacob[20] immediately afterwards (4:12) – or as a person familiar with and respecting prophetic revelations.

In contrast to these quotations from the writing prophets Tob 8:6 does not mention the origin of the quotation from Gen 2:18 in the course of Tobias' prayer during the first night after the wedding ceremony. The quotation – οὐ καλὸν εἶναι τὸν ἄνθρωπον μόνον ποιήσωμεν αὐτῷ βοηθὸν ὅμοιον αὐτῷ ("it is not good that the man should be alone, we will make a helper for him, similar to him") – is introduced by a short summary of the narrative of the creation of Adam[21] (σὺ ἐποίησας τὸν Αδαμ, "you made Adam/ man") and by giving the reason for the creation of Eve (καὶ ἐποίησας αὐτῷ βοηθὸν στήριγμα Ευαν τὴν γυναῖκα αὐτοῦ, "and you made a helper for him, a support, Eve, his wife") and stating the effect that from their union there originated all mankind (καὶ ἐξ ἀμφοτέρων ἐγενήθη τὸ σπέρμα τῶν ἀνθρώπων, "and from both of them the human race has originated")[22] – the latter also alluding to Gen 3:20b. As Tob 8:6 is part of a prayer the reference to the creation of Adam and Eve is grammatically put as an address to God so that there is the ring of a confessionary statement acknowledging that God is the creator of all mankind. The quotation is marked off as God's word: "you said that" (καὶ σὺ εἶπας ὅτι). Obviously it was not necessary to say that God's utterance was quoted from the Torah – because the text was widely known already.[23]

3. Mentioning Authority

3.1. Mentioning Scripture as Authority

Apart from quoting an authority there is the option just to mention an authoritative writing without giving any precise information. In Tobit we find two ways of hinting at Moses and his writing, namely by referring either to the law of Moses (for the most part in TobG[I]) or to his book (in TobG[II] exclusively):

---

20 In Ps 105:15 God calls the three patriarchs "my prophets".
21 "Adam" is understood as a name in Tob, cf. SCHÜNGEL-STRAUMANN, Tobit, 135-136.
22 In TobG[I] the introduction slightly varies (σὺ ἐποίησας Αδαμ καὶ ἔδωκας αὐτῷ βοηθὸν Ευαν στήριγμα τὴν γυναῖκα αὐτοῦ ἐκ τούτων ἐγενήθη τὸ ἀνθρώπων σπέρμα), the quotation is of course identical.
23 Was it quoted in the course of the wedding ceremony as it is wont today? – Note that Sir 36:24 also alludes to Gen 2:18.

Tob 6:13: G^I κατὰ τὸν νόμον Μωυσῆ ("according to the law of Moses")
G^II κατὰ τὴν κρίσιν τῆς βίβλου Μωυσέως ("according to the judgment of the book of Moses")

Tob 7:12: G^II κατὰ τὴν κρίσιν τῆς βίβλου Μωυσέως καὶ ἐκ τοῦ οὐρανοῦ κέκριταί σοι[24]

Tob 7:13: G^I κατὰ τὸν νόμον Μωυσέως
G^II κατὰ τὸν νόμον καὶ κατὰ τὴν κρίσιν τὴν γεγραμμένην ἐν τῇ βίβλῳ Μωυσέως

Tob 7:14: G^II κατὰ τὴν κρίσιν τοῦ Μωυσέως

As Fitzmyer remarks,[25] similar phrases indicating references to authoritative writings are found in 2Chr 23:18 (καθὼς γέγραπται ἐν νόμῳ Μωυσῆ, "as it is written in the law of Moses"), 25:4 (κατὰ τὴν διαθήκην τοῦ νόμου κυρίου καθὼς γέγραπται ὡς ἐνετείλατο κύριος λέγων, "according to the covenant of God's law as it is written as the Lord commanded it, saying"), and 30:16 (κατὰ τὴν ἐντολὴν Μωυσῆ ἀνθρώπου τοῦ θεοῦ, "according to the commandment of Moses, man of God"). Hieke[26] directs attention to Ezra 6:18 (κατὰ τὴν γραφὴν βιβλίου Μωυσῆ, "according to the writing of the book of Moses") and 2Chr 35:12 (ὡς γέγραπται ἐν βιβλίῳ Μωυσῆ, "as it is written in the book of Moses"). Obviously, in these late biblical books[27] there is no single standard phrase for referring to the authoritative tradition laid down by Moses – as opposed to Tobit there is a still greater variety of vocabulary and phrases in 2Chr. In the instances mentioned, 2Chr has different topics in mind that occur in Moses' law viz. his book: the tasks of priests and Levites, especially offerings (2Chr 23:18; point of reference would be Lev, especially chapters 1-7), the prescription in Deut 25:4 (2Chr 25:4), celebrating Passover (2Chr 30:16, cf. Exod 12:1-20), offerings once more (2Chr 35:12) and Num 36 (Ezr 6:18).[28] It is clear that both Moses' law and his book appear in the singular form only – in 2Chr and Ezr as well as in Tobit. With regard to Moses' book this is remarkable, as the references comprise at least Exod, Lev, Num, and Deut, so very probably the Torah/ Pentateuch as a whole. In addition, it is striking that the phrases quoted above include references to Moses' κρίσις, "judgment" or "decision"; this evokes the impression that Moses himself is the decisive authority one relies

---

24 TobG^I just says κατὰ τὴν κρίσιν.
25 FITZMYER, Tobit, 51.
26 HIEKE, Endogamy, 109.
27 Cf. also the example from Sir: ταῦτα πάντα βίβλος διαθήκης θεοῦ ὑψίστου νόμον ὃν ἐνετείλατο ἡμῖν Μωυσῆς κληρονομίαν συναγωγαῖς Ιακωβ (Sir 24:23).
28 Note that one finds similar phrases also in the Torah: cf. Jos 23:6 ποιεῖν πάντα τὰ γεγραμμένα ἐν τῷ βιβλίῳ τοῦ νόμου Μωυσῆ;

on. That Moses' law, judgment, or book is of divine origin seems to go without saying, then. The phrasing in G^{II} presses the point that Moses' guidelines exist in written form, a detail G^I will very probably also take for granted, as it says in Tob 1:6: καθὼς γέγραπται παντὶ τῷ Ισραηλ ἐν προστάγματι αἰωνίῳ, "as it is written for all Israel in an everlasting ordinance" (G^{II} is nearly identical: καθὼς γέγραπται ἐν παντὶ Ισραηλ ἐν προστάγματι αἰωνίῳ, "as it is written in all Israel in an everlasting ordinance") which appears to be thinking of Deut 16:16, since Tobit is talking about his regular pilgrimages to Jerusalem.

To which passages in the Torah do Tob 6 and 7 refer? The context of all of these references to Moses is concerned with marriage, especially with choosing the right mate. In Tob 6 the angel prepares young Tobias for marrying Sara. Raphael informs Tobias that Sara is Raguel's only child, and he praises her beauty and disposition. It is most important, however, that Raguel is a close relative of Tobit so that Tobias is destined to become Sara's husband and to inherit Raguel's property through her (6:12). Raguel is obliged, even compelled by Mosaic Law to give Sara to Tobias (6:13). Critics take Raphael's statements as referring to legal directions in Num 27:1-17 and Num 36 (dealing with inheritance of brotherless daughters)[29] and maybe also in Deut 25:5-10 (levirate law and the redemption of property).[30] As Collins[31] has shown neither Num nor Deut include any suggestion that it would be equivalent to a crime worthy of capital punishment if Raguel did not give his daughter to Tobias. Neither does Collins find any regulation like this elsewhere in the Torah. That is why he thinks "that the 'book of Moses' in Tobit does not point to a specific biblical law, but rather to ancestral traditions, which derive authority from Moses even when they go beyond what is written in the Torah."[32]

This explanation may be true, of course. Nevertheless, there are several legal regulations connecting a certain crime – though not a father's unwillingness to marry off his daughter to a close kinsman – with capital punishment, most prominent in the Book of the Covenant (cf. e.g. Exod 21:12-17; 22:14-15). Instances of severe compensations of offence might easily come to the mind of readers familiar with the To-

---

29 Cf. SCHÜNGEL-STRAUMANN, Tobit, 120.
30 Cf. COLLINS, Judaism, 31. "To be sure, the Law / Book of Moses is of concern to the narrator, even in places where the phrase itself is absent (e. g. 3:15,17, which allude to Levirate marriage)", MOORE, Tobit, 204.
31 COLLINS, Judaism, 31-32.
32 COLLINS, Judaism, 32. GAMBERONI argued that the author followed ideals he found inherent in the Pentateuch (Gesetz, 228). It is impossible to unmistakably identify the Pentateuch as it is known to us in Tobit. He reckons that the author of Tobit regarded texts as authoritative that were not canonized later on (Gesetz, 239-240).

rah.³³ So the angel's divine voice would not only remind Tobias (and the readers) of the directions given in Num, but he would also evoke the impression that severe consequences, too, were announced in Mosaic Law. Through this the author has the angel assure Tobias that he is the one and only husband designated for Sara. At the same time he highlights the prominence of endogamy which is a most important motif in the book's narrative.³⁴

The passage in Tob 7 presents the negotiations with Raguel concerning the marriage. Raguel acknowledges the fact that Tobias is the only one entitled to marry Sara (7:10). His words in the course of the following wedding ceremony sound like a formula spoken by a father on the occasion when he is giving away the bride (7:12). This action is authorized by "the law" (TobG^I) viz. "the book (TobG^II) of Moses".³⁵ As a last step both versions stress the legal character of the wedding by mentioning that Raguel wrote a marriage contract (7:13) – as TobG^II has it, according to Moses' Law again. Writing a contract underlines the binding and lasting quality of an undertaking³⁶ as, in this case, marriage. It is true that none of the canonical biblical books attests to the custom of writing a marriage certificate, so that again at least this detail is taken to originate in Jewish tradition.³⁷ But still, there is a second aspect to the marriage, because in giving off his daughter to Tobias, the kinsman, Raguel is acting in agreement with the example of the patriarchs,³⁸ their endogamous practice is described in the narratives on Isaac and Jacob getting kinswomen for their wives, as their respective father arranged (Gen 24) or ordered it (Gen 28:1-2). These narratives were obviously interpreted as equivalent to legislation so that Raguel

---

33 GAMBERONI, Gesetz, 229, assumes that death had become sort of standard penalty associated with Law.
34 For a detailed discussion of marriage in Tobit cf. NICKLAS, Marriage, and of endogamy cf. HIEKE, Endogamy.
35 G^II is eager to emphasize this by presenting the reference to Moses twice: first as Raguel pronounces his intention, then when he puts it into practice afterwards. Therefore, Moses is mentioned three times within the context of the wedding in this version.
36 Note that there are analogous expressions in the Torah, e.g. Exod 24:4, 7, or Deut 31:9, and in Josh 24:26.
37 Cf. EGO, Buch, 971. MOORE, Tobit, 230-232, quotes Jewish marriage contracts from findings from Elephantine (5th century BCE). Cf. FITZMYER, Tobit, 235-236. COLLINS, Judaism, 32, says that the Bible does not specify the wedding ceremony. He finds "a widespread tendency in Second Temple Judaism to construe 'the law of Moses' as something more inclusive than the written text of the Torah, and roughly equivalent to 'normative Jewish tradition' as a given author understood it." (Judaism, 34).
38 Thus endogamy is not so much motivated by the prohibitions in Deut or Ezra, but by the example of Abraham; cf. COLLINS, Judaism, 30.

might say that he acts according to Moses, i.e. Genesis, in this sense as well.[39]

Besides the legal significance of a written document its authoritative meaning is emphasized. Both aspects are intertwined with one another considering Moses. Near the end of Tobit this becomes clear in another way, too: Raphael tells father and son to write down everything that has happened to them (12:20, TobG^{II} γράψατε πάντα ταῦτα τὰ συμβάντα ὑμῖν, "write down all these [events] that happened to you"); in TobG^{I} Raphael even explicitly mentions a book (γράψατε πάντα τὰ συντελεσθέντα εἰς βιβλίον, "write down everything that happened in a book").[40] The angel's order may be taken as a divine one, at this stage of the narrative not only by the readers, but also by Tobit and Tobias. The selfsame book of Tobit is the result of Raphael's command so that there is the claim that Tobit is an authoritative writing prompted by divine order.

3.2. Mentioning the Ancestor as Authority

Moses, his law or his book, is not the only authority the characters in Tobit rely on. This is most obviously seen in Tob 6. When Raphael has told Tobias that he is the one and only man destined to marry Sara, Tobias reacts hesitantly. He is frightened because of the danger to be killed by the demon like the seven bridegrooms before, and if he died there would be no son left to bury his parents: καὶ νῦν ἐγὼ φοβοῦμαι μὴ ἀποθάνω καὶ κατάξω τὴν ζωὴν τοῦ πατρός μου καὶ τῆς μητρός μου μετ' ὀδύνης ἐπ' ἐμοὶ εἰς τὸν τάφον αὐτῶν καὶ υἱὸς ἕτερος οὐχ ὑπάρχει αὐτοῖς ὃς θάψει αὐτούς ("and now I am afraid that I might die and will lead my father's and my mother's life down to their grave because of their grief for me; and there will not be left another son to them who will bury them", 6:15 TobG^{I}, only slight variations in TobG^{II}). So, regarding Tobit's instructions that the son should bury his parents (Tob 4:4-5), Tobias has learnt his lesson. But Raphael now reminds him of Tobit's order to marry a kinswoman (cf. Tob 4:12). Whereas TobG^{I} has the angel refer to Tobit's words by a verbal expression (μέμνησαι τῶν λόγων ὧν ἐνετείλατό σοι ὁ πατήρ σου ὑπὲρ τοῦ λαβεῖν σε γυναῖκα ἐκ τοῦ γένους σου, "remember the words your father commanded you that you take a wife from his family", 6:16), TobG^{II} uses the respective noun, ἐντολή, in addi-

---

39 The book of Tobit is not interested in explaining why Raguel – now acknowledging endogamy in principle – gave Sara off to seven men before.

40 Cf. the heading Tob 1:1 introducing the story explicitly as a "book". SOLL, Misfortune, 219, takes the title to be modelled on prophetic or wisdom literature. The author attempts "to model his narrative on the sacred literature of his people" (220).

tion, forming a *figura etymologica* (μέμνησαι τὰς ἐντολὰς τοῦ πατρός σου ὅτι ἐνετείλατό σοι λαβεῖν γυναῖκα ἐκ τοῦ οἴκου τοῦ πατρός σου, "remember your father's commands/orders that he commanded you to take a wife from your father's house"). This instruction from Tobit's wisdom speech gains the advantage over the order of burying in this context where the focus is on the issue of marriage. And it is the angel, who explains this to scared young Tobias.

The semantic field of the verb, "to command, order" (ἐντέλλεσθαι), and the noun in its plural form, "commands, orders" (ἐντολαί) is worth noticing, also because a difference in usage within the two Greek versions is found elsewhere in the book: In Tob 1:8 Tobit talks about his practice of delivering tithe and mentions his grandmother Debora, who brought him up and who taught him this cultic practice:

TobG^I καθὼς ἐνετείλατο Δεββωρα ἡ μήτηρ τοῦ πατρός μου ("as Debora, my father's mother had commanded it").

TobG^II κατὰ τὸ πρόσταγμα τὸ προστεταγμένον περὶ αὐτῶν ἐν τῷ νόμῳ Μωσῆ καὶ κατὰ τὰς ἐντολὰς ἃς ἐνετείλατο Δεββωρα ἡ μήτηρ Ανανιηλ τοῦ πατρὸς ἡμῶν ("according to the ordinance set down about them in the law of Moses and according to the orders that Debora commanded, the mother of Hananiel, our father").

Whereas TobG^I employs a verbal expression, TobG^II uses the noun-verb-combination (*figura etymologica*) again, and puts a reference to the Law of Moses in front, thereby combining the authority of the ancestress with that of the Torah. Syntactically TobG^II creates an analogy between Moses and Debora by referring to their utterances by the preposition κατά, "according to", which is a typical way of pointing to authoritative words or texts besides καθώς, which TobG^I uses here.

Tobit calls his own instructions to Tobias "commands" when he finishes his speech addressed to his son: TobG^I καὶ νῦν παιδίον μνημόνευε τῶν ἐντολῶν μου ("and now, child, remember my commands"; TobG^II καὶ νῦν παιδίον μνημόνευε τὰς ἐντολὰς ταύτας, "and now, child, remember these commands"). The minor variation of possessive pronoun (μου, TobG^I) versus demonstrative pronoun (ταύτας, TobG^II) makes the difference that the demonstrative possibly gives a more impersonal, and therefore authoritative, ring to the "commands". In both versions Tobit uses the noun; in reacting to his father's speech Tobias chooses the verb: πάτερ ποιήσω πάντα ὅσα ἐντέταλσαί μοι ("father, I shall do everything you told me", TobG^I), πάντα ὅσα ἐντέταλσαί μοι ποιήσω πάτερ ("everything you told me, I shall do, father", TobG^II), thereby focusing on the father's activity of teaching him.

In addition, TobG^II explicitly characterizes Tobit's words on his deathbed as orders given to his offspring: in Tob 14:3 the narrator introduces Tobit's words: καὶ ὅτε ἀπέθνῃσκεν ἐκάλεσεν Τωβιαν τὸν υἱὸν αὐτοῦ καὶ ἐνετείλατο αὐτῷ λέγων ("and as he was about to die, he called his son Tobias and commanded/ told him"). And after his prophecy on Israel's future Tobit introduces his instructions by saying καὶ νῦν παιδία ἐγὼ ὑμῖν ἐντέλλομαι ("and now, children, I command/ tell you" TobG^II 14:8.9).

The plural form of the term ἐντολή also occurs three times in Tobit referring to divine orders: In the context of his prayer (3:1-6) Tobit says that his ancestors did not listen to God's commandments/ orders: παρήκουσαν γὰρ τῶν ἐντολῶν σου ("since they did not listen to your commandments", G^I, G^II: παρήκουσα "I did not listen") (3:4) and did not put God's orders into practice: οὐκ ἐποιήσαμεν τὰς ἐντολάς σου (3:5), thereby provoking divine fury and judgment. In the beginning of his speech to Tobias Tobit warns his son not to transgress God's commandments (4:5 μὴ θελήσῃς ἁμαρτάνειν καὶ παραβῆναι τὰς ἐντολὰς αὐτοῦ). It is a noteworthy observation that in a few instances canonical biblical writings share the usage of ἐντολαί as we find it in Tob, in that it refers both to the divine and to human – namely Mosaic and Davidic – authority.[41]

So, the words ἐντέλλεσθαι and ἐντολαί establish ancestral authority besides the authority of God and generally accepted human authorities, especially Moses and the Torah. TobG^II prefers the noun and the *figura etymologica* to the verbal expression, thereby creating a feeling of something to be generally applied, something more than an act of speaking bound to a single occasion.

---

41 Cf. the phrase κατὰ τὰς ἐντολάς: Deut 26:13 says in the context of the regulations concerning liturgical practice when delivering the first fruit and the tithe including a declaration κατὰ πάσας τὰς ἐντολάς ἃς ἐνετείλω μοι οὐ παρῆλθον τὴν ἐντολήν σου καὶ οὐκ ἐπελαθόμην. On his deathbed David addresses Salomon telling him φυλάσσειν τὰς ἐντολὰς αὐτοῦ καὶ τὰ δικαιώματα καὶ τὰ κρίματα τὰ γεγραμμένα ἐν νόμῳ Μωυσέως ἵνα συνίῃς ἃ ποιήσεις κατὰ πάντα ὅσα ἂν ἐντείλωμαί σοι (1Kgs 2:3). Similarly, God addresses Solomon: ποιεῖν κατὰ πάντα ἃ ἐνετειλάμην αὐτῷ καὶ τὰ προστάγματά μου καὶ τὰς ἐντολάς μου φυλάξῃς (1Kgs 9:4). David admonishes the people: φυλάξασθε καὶ ζητήσατε πάσας τὰς ἐντολὰς κυρίου τοῦ θεοῦ ἡμῶν (1Chr 28:8). Solomon sacrifices κατὰ τὰς ἐντολὰς Μωυσῆ (2Chr 8:13), and the singers in the temple are acting κατὰ τὰς ἐντολὰς Δαυιδ (2Chr 35:15).

4. The Ancestor as an Authoritative Example: Tobit's Autobiographical Narrative (Tob 1:3-2:14)

In the beginning of the book of Tobit the author has Tobit, the senior protagonist, give an account of his life from an autobiographical perspective (1:3-2:14). Tobit's autobiography offers a mixture of matters as he talks about the circumstances of his life and his experience on the one hand, and about his own conduct on the other hand so that events and ethics are interwoven. For the present purpose the focus is on Tobit's behaviour since Tobit's description of it includes manifold allusions to biblical writings held authoritative, that is quasi-canonical, at the time the author of Tobit composed the book.

The impression that Tobit is continually describing his own behaviour in relation to authoritative rules is effected by the use of catchwords and vocabulary characteristic of well-known traditions or even passages from scriptures, especially the Torah. It may suffice to give a few prominent examples out of the numerous instances for this technique,[42] which Steven Weitzman called the "allusive strategy"[43] of Tobit.

After an introductory summary (1:3) the first autobiographical section (1:4-8) is dedicated to cultic practice.[44] As a young man, when he still lived in Israel, Tobit experienced the apostasy of his own tribe Naphtali which meant to abandon the prescription found in Deut 12 to worship God in the Jerusalem temple, the place God had chosen out of all Israelite tribes (Tob 1:4; cf. Deut 12:5).[45] For the tribes' idolatry TobG^I employs the keyword "calf" (δάμαλις) identified with "Baal", whereas TobG^{II} explicitly refers to King Jeroboam who erected the statue of a bull in Dan, which makes the allusion to 1Kgs 12:28 even more obvious.[46] Both versions make the reader think of the concept of Jeroboam's sin (1Kgs 12:30); according to Deuteronomist writers[47] it was repeated

---

42   For the huge amount of references and allusions in Tob 1:3-22 cf. the commentaries by MOORE; EGO, Buch; FITZMYER, Tobit.
43   WEITZMAN, Allusion, 50.
44   As Tob 1:4-8 focusses on Tobit's piety towards Jerusalem, some critics suspect that the lines may be "secondary additions"; cf. COLLINS, Judaism, 25.
     For Tobit's offerings and donations delivered in Jerusalem, the first fruit and first born of the cattle and the tithe, many passages of reference are found in Exod, Lev, Num, and Deut. Cf. the commentaries for this. It is important to remember the example of Abraham giving the tithe to Melchisedek (Gen 14:20).
45   Deut 12:11 God will choose the place as a dwelling for his name.
46   Possibly, the version TobG^{II} is even more sophisticated, as the bovine is not called δάμαλις as in TobG^I and 1Kgs 12:28, but μόσχον as in the episode of the Golden Calf in Exod 32:4.
47   Cf. e.g. 1Kgs 15:26,30,34; 16:19,26,31; 2Kgs 17:22.

by all of his successors to the Israelite throne, a religious offence of fatal consequence as it resulted in destruction and exile. Thus the term "calf" or "(young) bull" combined with either "Baal" or "Jeroboam" produces a chain of associations connected with Deuteronomist theology.

Tobit remarks that, still in Israel, he married a kinswoman, γυναῖκα ἐκ τοῦ σπέρματος τῆς πατριᾶς ἡμῶν, "a woman from the offspring of our ancestral lineage" (1:9).[48] As he says this in a brief statement as in passing it seems as if it is quite natural to him and not to be disputed. This reveals a contrast both to prohibitive legal regulations like Exod 34:15 or Deut 7:3 which intend to prevent Israelites from mingling with non-Israelite people in order to preserve Jewish religious identity, and to the narratives about the patriarchs in Genesis where it is emphasized that Isaac and Jacob marry their cousins (Gen 24:3-4,7,37-38; 28:1-2; 29:10).[49] Even in these narratives we find a prohibition not to marry a foreigner preceding the command to wed a kinswoman. We will find the ideal of endogamy again later in Tobit's speech to his son (4:12), though.

When he had come to Niniveh as a captive, Tobit, in contrast to his fellow exiles (1:10), strictly observes the rules of ritual purity by avoiding to consume any gentile food (1:11), that is, he is acting according to regulations as found in Lev 11, or Deut 14:3-20; the book of Daniel says the same about its protagonist (Dan 1:8-16), so does the book of Judith (12:2,20). In Tobit's statement that he was mindful of God with all his soul (ἐμεμνήμην τοῦ θεοῦ ἐν ὅλῃ τῇ ψυχῇ μου, 1:12) the phrase "with all my soul" (ἐν ὅλῃ τῇ ψυχῇ μου) immediately calls to one's mind the imperative in Deut 6:5: "you shall love the LORD your god with all your heart and with all your soul and with all your might" (NRSV)[50] whereas the combination with the verb μιμνήσκομαι ("remember, to be mindful of") is characteristic of Tobit.[51]

Tob 1:17 defines what is to be understood by the acts of charity he performed for his brothers, i.e. fellow Jewish people (ἐλεημοσύνας πολλὰς ἐποίησα τοῖς ἀδελφοῖς μου 1:16, cf. 1:3),[52] namely giving alms and burying the dead (1:17). What is mentioned as Tobit's general practice here, will function as effecting a turning point on a special occasion in Tobit's biography as we learn in the following chapter (Tob 2). As opposed to the allusions in the previous verses for the most part harking back to the

---

[48] The wording is similar to Jdt 8:2: ὁ ἀνὴρ αὐτῆς Μανασσης τῆς φυλῆς αὐτῆς καὶ τῆς πατριᾶς αὐτῆς.
[49] For the motif cf. also Judg 14:3.
[50] Variants of the expression are found throughout Deut, e.g. 26:16, or 30:2,10.
[51] Cf. Tob 2:2; 4:5; 14:2,9 (G^II)
[52] „[C]harity is an in-group activity", FASSBECK, Tobit's Religious Universe, 179.

Torah (and Deuteronomistic history), there are hardly any directions to be found in the Torah explicitly regulating almsgiving or burial.[53]

Though Deut 15:7-11 demands that an Israelite helps a member of the community who is in need, the passage within the Torah does not precisely define how to help; but implicitly it comes closest to the idea of almsgiving.[54] The combination of feeding and clothing the poor as an act of charity is found in Ezek 18:7b,16b and Job 31:16-20.[55] And Sira appeals to give alms several times.[56] However, this conduct appears to be a *topos* of ethical behaviour considering that similar phrases are found in Egyptian literature, for instance.[57]

As to burying the dead one can see that remaining unburied is regarded as a shame and as indicating divine judgment in the Torah and prophetic writings so that from these passages one might deduce a responsibility or even an obligation to bury one's dead fellow countrymen.

The burial motif is based on the common Ancient Near Eastern idea that it was an extreme disgrace to remain unburied,[58] i.e. exposed to the weather and to wild animals and birds, but also to the view of passers-by. This is reflected in OT series of curses – most prominent in Deut 28:26 – and in prophetic words threatening punishment. For instance, Ahijah announces to Jeroboam that dogs will feed on the dead body of any member of his family dying in the city, and that birds will eat the bodies of those who die in the open country (1Kgs 14:11),[59] or Jeremiah predicts that Jehoiakim will be buried like a donkey, that is not buried at all (Jer 34:20). Jeremiah also announces that the people will be put to

---

53 Cf. COLLINS, Judaism, 27.
54 But cf. Lev 9:9-10 commanding to leave some of the harvest to the *personae miserae*.
55 In Deut 10:18 Moses declares that God himself is the one "who executes justice for the orphan and the widow, and who loves the strangers, providing them with food and clothing." (NRSV).
56 E.g. 4:1-3; 7:32. In Sira 7:32-33 almsgiving and the statement that charity embraces both the living and the dead occur side by side.
57 Confronting his divine judge the dead person says that he used to give bread to the hungry, water to the thirsty, and clothes to the naked. Cf. HORNUNG, Totenbuch, 240 (Spruch 125, 126-128); cf. also the texts from Egypt and Mesopotamia quoted by ENGEL, Auf den Wegen, 95-96.
58 A reflection of this is found in Isa 14:19, but also in Qoh 6:3.
59 Cf. the same curse on Baasha, 1Kgs 16:4; Elijah threatening Ahab, 1Kgs 21:24 (cf. 21:19); a young prophet sent by Elisha tells Jehu that the house of Ahab shall perish like the houses of Jeroboam and Baasha, and that the dogs shall eat Jezebel's dead body for she will remain unburied, 2Kgs 9:9-10 – this comes true in 2Kgs 9:25. For this *topos* of the denied burial cf. Zenger, Israel, 133.

death and that their corpses will be exposed to wild animals (7:33).[60] So remaining unburied is an effect of divine judgment. In Tobit it affects Israelites in exile, so that the people suffer exactly the punishment announced in Deut 28:25-26 ("The Lord will cause you to be defeated before your enemies [...]. You shall become an object of horror to all the kingdoms of the earth. Your corpses shall be food for every bird of the air and animal of the earth, and there shall be no one to frighten them away." NRSV). These texts of reference are dealing with judgment and envision untimely death and the negative potential of the way one could deal with dead bodies, namely leaving them to themselves, that is unburied. It is more of a collective perspective, and the atmosphere is one of menace and despair. It is noteworthy that some narratives (Josh 8:29 and 1Sam 31:11-13; 2Sam 21; note also Ezek 39:11-16) say that the corpse of a defeated ruler, though first exhibited in a humiliating way, is then buried at last. And Deut 21:22-23 demands that the corpse of a criminal executed by hanging on a tree has to be buried the same day in order to prevent the defilement of the land.

In addition, the Torah offers the model of the patriarchs: When Sarah has died Abraham purchases a field containing a cave in Machpelah and establishes a hereditary family tomb there (Gen 23). He is the first person in the book of Genesis to practice a funeral. Abraham's and Isaac's burials by their son(s) will also come to one's mind (Gen 25:9; 35:29[61]) as well as Jacob's (Gen 47:29-30; 49:29-32) and Joseph's (50:25) orders that their corpse should be taken to Canaan and be buried there. Joseph obeys his father's command immediately (Gen 50:2-13), his own dead body is taken to Canaan by Moses (Exod 13:19) and buried by Joshua (Josh 24:32).[62] Through the act of burying the bereaved pay respect and piety to their elders; the patriarchs as well as Moses die old and full of days because they are blessed men.

Throughout the autobiography Tobit's conduct is highlighted by allusions to the Torah and prophetical writings, as well. Even if it is not always possible to name an exact source, one feels reminded of the Torah and further writings. The references to the Torah include both Mosaic legislation and an interpretation of the patriarchs as models of action. On the whole, the achievement of this allusion strategy is the

---

60 Cf. Jer 16:4,6; 19:7; in addition there are similar predictions not mentioning wild animals; cf. Isa 34:3; Jer 9:21; 14:16; 36:30.
61 Gen 35:19 mentions Rachel's burial.
62 One might even remember that Moses was buried by God himself (Deut 34:6). Outside Genesis it is quite common to refer to the fact that a leader, judge, or king of Israel is buried and to mention the place where the tomb is to be found; cf. e.g. Josh 24:30; Judg 2:9; 8:32; 10:2,5; 12:7, 10, 12, 15; 1Sam 25:1; 31:15; 1Kgs 2:10.

readers' impression that Tobit always acted as a pious man, always paying attention to and obeying divine orders as they had been uttered and written by human intermediary authorities, or by imitating the example of the patriarchs. The autobiography in Tob 1 basically characterizes Tobit as a thoroughly ideal Jew.[63]

For Tobit's life the motif of burying the dead becomes crucial: the habitual practice of burying his countrymen endangered Tobit's life when a Ninevite informed the king about this (Tob 1:19), and it caused the loss of all his possessions (1:20). In chapter 2 we learn about another specific instance when Tobit buried a fellow countryman murdered and left unburied in the market-place, that is, exposed to disgrace (2:3, 7). Tobit's neighbours comment on this as an unwise action: to them it appears that Tobit has not learnt any lesson from his former experience (2:8). The narrative then evokes the impression that Tobit went also blind as a result of charitably burying the Jewish man (2:9).[64] This caused him not to enter his house[65] and therefore to be affected by the sparrows' excrements in the courtyard. So the reader gets the impression that there is a sequence of pious activities that results in Tobit's personal catastrophe: In the beginning he intends to celebrate *shavuot* piously respecting the order given in Deut 16:14 to include the *personae miserae* in joyfully performing the feast. Therefore, Tobit sends Tobias to invite any poor from among the exiles – thereby feeding the hungry; so there is a charitable aspect to *shavuot*. As Tobias finds a dead body instead, Tobit buries the man, and then, probably observing regulations of (cultic?) cleanliness, gets injured. In spite of Tobit's charitable acting on behalf of his countrymen, he personally experiences sorrowful events, and his autobiographical narrative culminates in his own misfortune, his blindness, want, and helplessness.

In the end, the readers learn through Raphael's words that besides his prayer it was exactly Tobit's perseverance in burying his fellow countrymen (ὅτε ἔθαπτες τοὺς νεκροὺς ὡσαύτως, 12:12) which – in addition to Tobit's prayer – prompted the angel's mission (12:13).[66] Tobit's charitable custom of burying his countrymen even at the risk of his own life is the decisive criterion for divine recompense, then.[67] There-

---

[63] In this respect he is similar to Job, who is comparatively briefly portrayed by a third person narrator, though, by way of a number of adjectives and a description of his blessed situation and religious prudence (Job 1:1-3,5).

[64] Cf. FITZMYER, Tobit, 130.

[65] Critics discuss whether Tobit did not enter his house for hygienic reasons or because of ritual impurity in the sense of Num 19.

[66] According to TobG^II 12:13 a second reason for the mission was to test Tobit (πειράσαι σε).

[67] Cf. BOLYKI, Burial, 94.

fore out of the number of exemplary actions performed by Tobit throughout his biography, the motif of burying the dead becomes a central ethical tenet within the book. This would be one of the reasons why Tobit's speech to Tobias begins with this subject.

5. The Ancestor as an Authoritative Teacher: Tobit's Wisdom Speech Addressed to His Son (Tob 4)

Tobit is, in fact, granted two occasions of holding a farewell discourse (Tob 4:3-19; 14:3-11).[68] In the second one, speaking on his deathbed as a very old man, he functions as a prophet[69] as we have seen already. In chapter 4 Tobit reckons that God might hear his prayer and let him die soon; that is why he addresses his son Tobias before he sends him on the journey to Media. The words of a dying person (cf. the book of Deuteronomy stylized as Moses' last words to the people), especially an ancestor (cf. Jacob in Gen 48 and 49) are characterized by a particular authority.

In Tob 4:3-19 the father functions as the wisdom teacher of his son,[70] offering a catalogue of good counsel[71] for blameless conduct expected from persons fearing the LORD.[72] The autobiographical narrative comprised Tobit's exemplary behaviour in the fields of (cultic) worshipping of God, endogamy, observance of dietary regulations, and charity

---

[68] In this sense, he is as privileged as Moses who also gives two testaments (Deut 31-32; 33), cf. MOORE, Tobit, 293.

[69] Tob 14:3-11 includes a few orders, though: a general call to practice righteousness/charity, and the order to bury Tobit (14:8-10).

[70] As for the genre of testament literature developed in Second Temple Judaism, cf. RABENAU, Studien, 28 note 8. It is extant in TestXII and TestIob and modelled according to a pattern the central part of which consists of an autobiographical retrospective (cf. Tob 1-2), admonishing advice / wisdom (cf. Tob 4), and a preview of future events / prophecy (cf. Tob 14).

[71] It is, in fact, a collection of proverbs and aphorisms" (FITZMYER, Tobit, 166), consisting of commands and prohibitions combined with causal clauses (14:3b-14, 19), and short exhortations (14:14-18). RABENAU, Studien, 28-65, studies the passages diachronically and finds that the short sentences are redactional additions. As NIEBUHR, Gesetz, 205-206, has it, though, the author of Tob used a traditional sequence of exhortations which can be seen by those sayings (e.g. demanding sobriety, 4:15) that are not connected with elements of the narrative. This paraenetic tradition influenced the narrative, on the one hand, but the narrative also had an effect on the formulation of the wisdom speech, on the other hand.

[72] Similar catalogues are found in Ezek 18:5-9 and Job 31; for a comparison of Job 31 and Tob 4 cf. OEMING, Ethik. They have differing functions as they are included in different genres. Critics also compare Isa 58:6-8; Job 22:6-9; Sira 3-4; 7:32-35 (ENGEL, Auf den Wegen, 96). With Sira, there are numerous points of contact, though. For catalogues of ethics cf. NIEBUHR, Gesetz.

(almsgiving and burying). From these Tobit resumes endogamy (4:12-13) and charity (4:6-11,16-17) in his instructions to Tobias.[73] As Fitzmyer says

> "[t]he counsels that Tobit gives are relatively few, but they are meant as examples of the advice given to educate Tobiah in the way that he should live as a young Jew. [...] Tobiah is urged to honor his mother (vv.3-5), pursue righteousness (4:5-6), practise almsgiving (vv. 6-11), avoid fornication and marry a woman within his ancestral lineage (vv. 12-13a), and avoid pride, shiftlessness, and drunkenness (vv. 13b, 15b). He is advised to pay the wages of laborers promptly (v.14), care for the poor and homeless (v. 16), seek proper advice (v. 18a), exercise piety and reverence for God (v. 19), and adhere to the Golden Rule (v. 15a). In short, Tobiah is to care for others, be faithful to the law, and trust in God."[74]

Again, also Tobit's exhortation abounds in manifold allusions to biblical (Deut, Prov[75]) and early Jewish literature, especially in parallels found in Sira.[76] These analogies in Sira are most important in the field of almsgiving[77] which is heavily emphasized in Tobit's teaching.[78] As the focus in Tobit's biography is on burying viz. in the narrative on Tobias on endogamy, these two elements in the sapiential speech may serve as examples. With burying, the attention now shifts from Tobit's practice to inter anonymous fellow countrymen (Tob 1-2) to the inner circle of the family: Tobit asks young Tobias to bury him (4:3)[79] and his mother as well (4:4), and to put them in a tomb side by side (4:4; cf. 14:10).

The command to honour the mother recalls the commandment in the Decalogue (Ex 20:12; Deut 5:16) in the first place, but it also echoes curses in Prov,[80] and finds analogies in Sira 3:1-16 and 7:27-28. Especially the phrase ordering to entomb the parents side by side (4:4) would remind readers of Abraham and Sarah (Gen 25:10). Respecting and honouring one's parents is expressed by an appropriate burial in the book of Tobit where the burial motif is prominent,[81] a fact that is

---

73 As for the father teaching his children God's commandments, cf. Deut 6:6-7.
74 FITZMYER, Tobit, 166.
75 Tob 4:10 even quotes Prov 10:2b = 11:4b; cf. Tob 12:9; 14:10 (ENGEL, Auf den Wegen, 95).
76 Cf. MOORE, Tobit; EGO, Buch; FITZMYER, Tobit.
77 Cf. Sira 28:8-13; 4:3-5; 7:10b; 35:9-10; 40:17, 24 (FITZMYER, Tobit, 169).
78 Note what most critics explain, namely that Hebrew צְדָקָה "righteousness" was "translated at times in the LXX as ἐλεημοσύνη, almsgiving" (COLLINS, Judaism, 30; cf. GAMBERONI, Gesetz, 238; MOORE, Tobit, 176-177; EGO, Buch, 917-918; FITZMYER, Tobit, 169). This accounts for the prominence of the motif in Tob.
79 Tobit repeats this order on his deathbed according to TobG¹.
80 19:26; 20:20; 28:24; 30:17.
81 Cf. BOLYKI, Burial, 91-95.

also due to the example given by the patriarchs who clearly function as authoritative models in the book.

When Tobit commands Tobias to practice endogamy (4:12-13) the same combination of allusions to legal instructions (forbidding to marry a foreign woman) and to narratives about the patriarchs[82] is found. So, the author of Tobit employs the same "allusion strategy" in Tobit's wisdom speech as in the protagonist's autobiographical narrative.

Tobit's counselling is confirmed by Raphael's wisdom focussing on social ideals (12:7-9), as he emphasizes the decisive importance of Tobit's practicing burial, afterwards (12:12-14). This divine voice thus explicitly approves of Tobit's teaching and acting. In the end the reader learns that the request Tobit uttered in 4:3-4 is done – though not as soon as Tobit thought at the time, as he outlives his expectations and dies a very old man many years later. That he dies extremely old (alike to the patriarchs, again) indicates that he is a blessed person because of his conduct for which he is recompensed. At the same time, Tobias has learnt his lesson from his father's instructions, first burying his father (καὶ ἔθαψεν αὐτὸν ἐνδόξως; 14:11[TobG^I][83]), afterwards also his mother by the side of her husband (14:12), and later on his wife's parents as well (14:13). This makes Tobias an example of filial obedience and respect.

6. Conclusion

On the whole, scriptural authority plays a very important part in the book of Tobit in several respects.

Scriptures regarded as authoritative are explicitly quoted, both the Torah and the prophets, the latter are even named. Moses and the prophetic writings represent scriptural authority, then.[84]

Authoritative words are attributed to Moses – his law viz. his book –, especially in the context of Tobias' endogamous marriage, one of the book's central topics.

---

82 Noah is added to these in 4:12 because of a tradition reflected in Jub 4:33 (cf. FITZMYER, Tobit, 173).

83 14:11 does not say explicitly that it is Tobias who buries Tobit; neither does 14:11 according to G^{II} employing the passive form: καὶ ἐτάφη ἐνδόξως.

84 DESELAERS, Buch, diachronically analyzed G^I, which he takes to be the "original" (19). He holds that the book consists of a basic narrative and three redactional layers. He regards those passages focussing on Jerusalem (1:4-8; 5:14b; 13:10b-18; 14:4-8) and law (1:4-8; 1:10-12; 2:1*; 4:12; 6:13) as well as those elements dealing with prophetic tradition (2:6*; 14:4,5b,8; 4:12b) as additions he ascribes to the third and last redactional layer (51-53) which was very conscious of tradition (488) and originated about 185 BCE (500).

The semantic field "command", "order" (ἐντέλλεσθαι, ἐντολαί) establishes ancestral authority besides already generally accepted (written) authorities, Moses in particular. TobG^II is more tradition oriented than TobG^I, mentioning Moses more often and evoking the impression of a more established status of the authority who uttered the command through the use of the noun ἐντολαί.

The righteous ancestor is characterized as an authority – both through his acting and his teaching – by an almost overall allusion strategy[85] employed by the author: throughout the book he constantly refers to writings regarded as authoritative or quasi-canonical in Judaism at the time; the allusions comprise legal instruction from the Torah, ethic counselling from wisdom literature and narrative texts describing the lives of the patriarchs, Moses, and Job; and they help to characterize Tobit as an ideal member of the Jewish community. The ancestor is representative of tradition and at the same time a living example of the reliability of these authoritative traditions which are granting prosperity as divine recompense and, most important, Jewish identity. In obeying and imitating his father's example Tobias becomes a model of perfect conduct himself. Finally, Tobit as a book written on Raphael's demand claims to be authoritative scripture in itself. It invites the audience to imitate the examples of Tobit (and Tobias).

Notably, God is kept in the background, he remains transcendent; only rarely is God mentioned as the origin of authoritative regulations.[86] It is through (authoritative) media and mediators that God's authoritative will is communicated: the law / book of Moses, the writings of the prophets – and the ancestor who teaches these and acts according to scriptural authority. So, obviously it would go without saying that God is the source of law as it is promulgated by Moses, and of prophecy as uttered by the prophets – and both phenomena as represented and illustrated in the lives of the patriarchs whom God had elected as the forefathers of his people. Scriptural authority and its ancestral application are confirmed and encouraged by God's own representative, Raphael, the angel, when he reveals his identity in the course of the happy ending. By highlighting the ancestor as a representative

---

85 ENGEL, Auf den Wegen, refers to Dancy's commentary (1972) who characterized the relation of the author of Tobit to scripture: "like all pious Jews of the last centuries B.C., he was living in a community where the events and sayings recorded in the scriptures were in a sense more *real* than what he saw and heard about him every day. It was not that he quoted from the Bible; rather he thought and felt naturally in biblical terms." (6, quoted by ENGEL, Auf den Wegen, 93, note 29).

86 Cf. Tob 3:4,5; 4:5 as exceptions to this rule; cf. also Tob 8:6 where Gen 2:18 is quoted as God's utterance.

and interpreter of authority the book of Tobit establishes an element of tradition combined with scriptural authority.

Bibliography

RAHLFS, Alfred/HANHART, Robert (ed.), Septuaginta. Editio altera, Stuttgart 2006.

BOLYKI, János, Burial as an Ethical Task in the Book of Tobit, in the Bible and the Greek Tragedies, in: Xeravits, Géza G./Zsengellér, József (ed.), The Book of Tobit. Text, Tradition, Theology. Papers of the First International Conference on the Deuterocanonical Books, Pápa, Hungary, 20-21 May 2004 (JSJS 98), Leiden/Boston 2005, 89-101.

COLLINS, John J., The Judaism of the Book of Tobit, in: Xeravits, Géza G./Zsengellér, József (ed.), The Book of Tobit. Text, Tradition, Theology. Papers of the First International Conference on the Deuterocanonical Books, Pápa, Hungary, 20-21 May 2004 (JSJS 98), Leiden/Boston 2005, 23-40.

DESELAERS, Paul, Das Buch Tobit. Studien zu seiner Entstehung, Komposition und Theologie (OBO 43), Fribourg/Göttingen 1982.

DI LELLA, Alexander A., The Deuteronomic Background of the Farewell Discourse in Tob 14:3-11, in: CBQ 41 (1979), 380-389.

EGO, Beate, Buch Tobit, (JSHRZ II 6), Gütersloh 1999, 873-1007.

EGO, Beate, Die Mehrfachüberlieferung des griechischen Tobitbuches, in: Kraus, Wolfgang/Munnich, Oliver (ed.), La Septante en Allemagne et en France / Septuaginta Deutsch und Bible d'Alexandrie (OBO 238), Fribourg/Göttingen 2009, 100-117.

ENGEL, H., Auf zuverlässigen Wegen und in Gerechtigkeit. Religiöses Ethos in der Diaspora nach dem Buch Tobit, in: Braulik, Georg et al. (ed.), Biblische Theologie und gesellschaftlicher Wandel (FS Norbert Lohfink), Freiburg/Basel/Wien 1993, 83-100.

FASSBECK, Gabriele, Tobit's Religious Universe Between Kinship Loyalty and the Law of Moses, in: JSJ 36 (2005), 173-196.

FITZMYER, Joseph A., Tobit (CEJL), Berlin/New York 2003.

GAMBERONI, Johann, Das „Gesetz des Mose" im Buch Tobias, in: Braulik, Georg (ed.), Studien zum Pentateuch (FS Walter Kornfeld), Wien/Freiburg/Basel 1977, 227-242.

HALLERMAYER, Michaela, Text und Überlieferung des Buches Tobit (DCLS 3), Berlin/New York 2008.

HANHART, Robert, Text und Textgeschichte des Buches Tobit (MSU 17), Göttingen 1984.

HIEKE, Thomas, Endogamy in the Book of Tobit, Genesis, and Ezra-Nehemiah, in: Xeravits, Géza G./Zsengellér, József (ed.), The Book of Tobit. Text, Tradition, Theology. Papers of the First International Conference on the Deuterocanonical Books, Pápa, Hungary, 20-21 May 2004 (JSJS 98), Leiden/Boston 2005, 103-120.

HORNUNG, Erik (ed.), Das Totenbuch der Ägypter, Zürich/München 1980.

JEREMIAS, Jörg, Der Prophet Amos (ATD 24,2), Göttingen 1995.

KIEL, Micah D., Tobit and Moses Redux, in: JSP 17 (2008), 83-98.

MOORE, Carey A., Tobit (AncB 40A), New York 1996.

NICKELSBURG, Georg W., The Search for Tobit's Mixed Ancestry. A Historical and Hermeneutical Odyssey, in: RdQ 17 (1996), 339-349.

NICKLAS, Tobias, Marriage in the Book of Tobit. A Synoptic Approach, in: Xeravits, Géza G./Zsengellér, József (ed.), The Book of Tobit. Text, Tradition, Theology. Papers of the First International Conference on the Deuterocanonical Books, Pápa, Hungary, 20-21 May 2004 (JSJS 98), Leiden/Boston 2005, 139-154.

NICKLAS, Tobias/WAGNER, Christian, Thesen zur textlichen Vielfalt im Tobitbuch, in: JSJ 34 (2003), 141-159.

NIEBUHR, Karl-Wilhelm, Gesetz und Paränese. Katechismusartige Weisungsreihen in der frühjüdischen Literatur (WUNT II 28), Tübingen 1987, 201-206.

NOWELL, Irene, The Book of Tobit: An Ancestral Story, in: Corley, Jeremy/Skemp, Vincent (ed.), Intertextual Studies in Ben Sira and Tobit. Essays in Honor of A. A. Di Lella (CBQ.MS 38), Washington 2005, 3-13.

OEMING, Manfred, Ethik in der Spätzeit des Alten Testaments am Beispiel von Hiob 31 und Tobit 4, in: Mommer, Peter/Thiel, Winfried (ed.), Altes Testament. Forschung und Wirkung (FS Henning Graf Reventlow), Frankfurt a. M. 1994, 159-173.

PORTIER-YOUNG, A., „Eyes to the Blind": A Dialogue Between Tobit and Job, in: Corley, Jeremy/Skemp, Vincent (ed.), Intertextual Studies in Ben Sira and Tobit. Essays in Honor of A. A. Di Lella (CBQ.MS 38) Washington 2005, 14-27.

RABENAU, Merten, Studien zum Buch Tobit (BZAW 220), Berlin/New York 1994.

REITERER, Friedrich V., Prophet und Prophetie in Tobit und Ben Sira. Berührungspunkte und Differenzen, in: Xeravits, Géza G./Zsengellér, József (ed.), The Book of Tobit. Text, Tradition, Theology. Papers of the First International Conference on the Deuterocanonical Books, Pápa, Hungary, 20-21 May 2004 (JSJS 98), Leiden/Boston 2005, 155-175.

RUPPERT, Lothar, Das Buch Tobias – ein Modellfall nachgestaltender Erzählung, in: Schreiner, Josef (ed.), Wort, Lied und Gottesspruch. Beiträge zur Septuaginta (FS Joseph Ziegler), Würzburg 1972, 109-119.

SCHÜNGEL-STRAUMANN, Helen, Tobit (HThKAT), Freiburg i. Br. 2000.

SOLL, Will, Misfortune and Exile in Tobit: The Juncture of a Fairy Tale Source and Deuteronomic Theology, in: CBQ 51 (1989), 209-231.

WEITZMAN, Steven, Allusion, Artifice, and Exile in the Hymn of Tobit, in: JBL 115 (1996), 49-61.

ZENGER, Erich, Das alttestamentliche Israel und seine Toten, in: Richter, Klemens (ed.), Der Umgang mit den Toten. Tod und Bestattung in der christlichen Gemeinde (QD 123), Freiburg 1990, 132-152.

Ben Sira as Negotiator of Authoritative Traditions
BRADLEY C. GREGORY

1. Introduction

In the book which bears his name Ben Sira, a sage living in Jerusalem in the late third and early second centuries BCE, saturates his teaching with topics and language drawn from Israel's literary heritage. While the sacred texts of Israel are by no means the only sources for Ben Sira's teaching, they do constitute an essential aspect for the authoritativeness of his teaching insofar as the scribe was the guardian and interpreter of that tradition.[1] Leaving aside the heavily debated issue of canon at the time of Ben Sira, it is at least safe to say that the Torah and the sapiential tradition, as found principally in the book of Proverbs, were authoritative for Ben Sira.

Yet, as many scholars have pointed out, the teaching of these texts is not simply reproduced in a prosaic way by Ben Sira; rather he understands himself as an inspired interpreter of these traditions. He and other select scribes were *Schriftgelehrten*, whose deep study of the tradition was enabled by God to bring forth true and authoritative understandings. This is clear from his autobiographical statements in which he characterizes his instruction as like "prophecy" (24:33) and as the result of divine blessing and inspiration (33:16-18; 39:6-7). Because the Scriptures are "subtle" and "obscure", containing "hidden meanings", the sage's reception of these divinely provided abilities enables him to develop privileged understandings.[2] In his study of biblical interpretation in Sirach, Benjamin Wright examines Sir 16:6-10; 17:1-12; and 19:13-17 as case studies. He concludes that "Ben Sira does not simply reproduce his sources. He manipulates, transforms, and otherwise shapes

---

1 HORSLEY, Politics of Cultural Production, 127.
2 See BEENTJES, Prophets and Prophecy in the Book of Ben Sira; PERDUE, Ben Sira and the Prophets; STADELMANN, Ben Sira als Schriftgelehrter; WRIGHT, The Role of the Sage (my thanks to the author for making this essay available to me).

them to fit his own agenda, even if at times what he produces looks to us to contravene what he found there."³

In this paper I wish to contribute to our understanding of this interface between authoritative texts and traditions and the self-described authoritative, inspired nature of Ben Sira's interpretation by focusing on a particular issue. How does Ben Sira handle topics about which his authoritative traditions are in conflict? This is a relatively rare phenomenon in Sirach, the exploration of which is methodologically complicated by a couple of factors. Sometimes Ben Sira simply conflates what modern scholars would consider a conflict, but on the assumptions of Ben Sira would not have been viewed as a conflict at all. For example, he simply identifies Sinai and Horeb in Sir 48:7, though modern scholars would see these two names for the same mountain as significant in that they are characteristic of different Pentateuchal sources (P and D, respectively). A second issue can be seen in Ben Sira's "Praise of the Ancestors." In Ben Sira's portrait of David he simply conflates the pictures of David in Samuel and Chronicles; yet, when Samuel-Kings and Chronicles conflict, as in the reason for the division of the monarchy or regarding which kings were good (cf. 49:4), he consistently opts for the version in Samuel-Kings.⁴ It becomes methodologically problematic to begin guessing why he does so. Is it because Samuel-Kings is more authoritative than Chronicles?⁵ Is Chronicles even considered authoritative by Ben Sira? And if so, how can we even be sure Ben Sira is aware that Chronicles and Samuel are in conflict? Perhaps, his preference for Samuel is not hermeneutical at all, but merely one of familiarity. In addition, his proclivity for Samuel-Kings over Chronicles may simply suit his rhetorical and theological goals better, without reflecting anything about their relative authoritative status. For someone who is a *Schriftgelehrter* all of these options are possible for any one example.

Therefore, in order to reduce the methodological problems involved, I would like to focus on two cases in which Ben Sira's negotiation of an issue involves interacting with texts whose status as known and authoritative for him is certain. In addition, I think that for these two cases it is highly likely that Ben Sira is aware of different options

---

3 WRIGHT, Biblical Interpretation in the Book of Ben Sira, 382 (my thanks to the author for making this essay available to me).
4 I am convinced that Ben Sira knew Chronicles, at least in regard to David. For a fuller discussion see my article, The Warrior-Poet of Israel.
5 The degree to which Ben Sira uses Samuel-Kings and the fact that he uses what Beentjes has identified as "inverted quotations" (e.g. 1 Sam 12:3 in Sir 46:19) suggests to me that it was, in some sense, considered authoritative by Ben Sira. See BEENTJES, Canon and Scripture in the Book of Ben Sira, 175-177.

because of their importance for him and the fact that other extant texts at the time were advocating different approaches to these issues. Since these other authors would have appealed to the traditions which supported their view, it stands to reason that in advocating his position Ben Sira would have been aware of these alternate traditions. By focusing on how Ben Sira navigates the traditions that are authoritative and in conflict, I believe we will be able to get a new angle on how Ben Sira understands his own role as an inspired *Schriftgelehrter* of these authoritative traditions.

2. Surety (Sir 8:13; 29:14-20)

The first issue is that of going surety for a neighbor.[6] The practice of going surety for another's loan is mentioned several times in Proverbs. Representative examples can be seen in Prov 11:15 and 17:18:

11,15 To guarantee loans for a stranger brings trouble
but there is safety in refusing to do so

17,18 It is senseless to give a pledge
to become surety for a neighbor

The book of Proverbs reflects a consistently negative view of the practice, believing that it is senseless, bringing only trouble. In Prov 6:1-5 the sage admonishes the student to try everything possible to extricate himself from such a situation if he has been foolish enough to go surety. Interestingly, the Torah gives no legislation about the practice of a third-party surety, though Judah does offer to go surety for Benjamin in Gen 43:9. Likewise, the practice is not a focus of attention in the prophets, but it is noteworthy that in Isa 38:14 Hezekiah asks God to go surety for him: "O Lord, I am oppressed; be my security!" (NRSV, אדני עשקה לי ערבני). Thus, one might infer from the actions of Judah and the statement of Hezekiah that surety is not altogether bad, but in terms of direct teaching on the matter the sapiential tradition views the practice of going surety to be foolish and dangerous, while the Torah is practically silent. In light of this, Ben Sira's treatment of the subject is remarkable.

In Ben Sira's first mention of the topic, in 8:13, he merely warns against the dangers of going surety for someone who is more powerful than the student:

---

6 This section is adapted from my discussion in Like an Everlasting Signet Ring, 128-170.

8:13 Do not go surety for someone greater than you
   but if you do go surety, consider it something you have to repay

The larger context of chapter 8 shows a cautious concern for the vulnerability of the sage and his students and Ben Sira's advice on surety fits within this concern. While the first stich warns of the danger involved in going surety, the second stich seems to provide a disjunctive concession (ואם). Since the student would have little leverage to make a more powerful person repay the loan Ben Sira advises his students to consider going surety for such a person as a loan that they will have to pay in the end. Given that the second stich is probably concessive, this passage hints that Ben Sira is mildly permissive of the practice, even if he is pessimistically cautious about its prudence. Thus, his stance is, for the most part, in basic continuity with the warnings against going surety in Proverbs (Prov 6:1-5; 11:15; 17:18; 22:26-27). This situation changes, however, in Ben Sira's much longer instruction on surety in chapter 29.

In Sirach 29 Ben Sira addresses various topics related to the use of finances. After discussing loans (vv. 1-7) and almsgiving (vv. 8-13) he turns to a discussion of going surety:

14 A good person will go surety for (his) neighbor
    but the one who has lost any sense of shame will abandon him.

15 Do not forget the goodness of your guarantor
    for he has given his life on your behalf.

16 A sinner ruins the goods of the guarantor

17 and the one inclined towards ungratefulness abandons his rescuer.

18 Surety has ruined many prosperous people
    and tossed them about like waves of the sea.
    It has exiled powerful people
    and they wondered around foreign nations.

19 The sinner falls in going surety
    and his pursuit of profit causes him to fall into lawsuits.

20 Go surety for (your) neighbor as you are able
    but be careful that you do not fall yourself.[7]

---

[7] Unfortunately, the Hebrew for this passage is not extant. My translation is mostly based on the Greek, though I have slightly emended the text in two places. In v. 18a I have followed most commentators in emending the participle κατευθύνοντας, assuming the Greek has misread מְאֻשָּׁרִים as מְאֻשָּׁרִים. Likewise, at the beginning of v. 20 I follow most commentators in opting for the Syriac's "go surety" instead of the Greek's more general ἀντιλαβοῦ ("help"). See my Like an Everlasting Signet Ring, 151-152.

Ben Sira begins the pericope by stating the principle that going surety for one's neighbor is a characteristic of the good person. Because of this, the borrower who leaves his surety to pick up the tab for his debt is described as someone who has lost all sense of shame (ὁ ἀπολωλεκὼς αἰσχύνην).⁸ Over against the shameless one, the student should remember the goodness of his guarantor and be faithful to repay the loan.

The reason, according to Ben Sira, is that "he has given his life on your behalf." Di Lella comments that this reason is "an exaggeration to dramatize the point," though if so, it is not by much.⁹ The precarious position of the guarantor can be seen in v. 18 where a guarantor runs the risk of complete financial ruin and of becoming a wanderer in foreign lands. His instability and loss of control are vividly pictured as being "tossed about like waves of the sea." The reference in the following pericope to the insults of the creditor (v. 28) suggests that the miserable life of the one who must serve in the house of a foreigner, a fate worse than poverty (vv. 22-24), is to be identified as that of those who have come to ruin through surety.¹⁰ Elsewhere Ben Sira tells his students that it is "better to die than to beg" and that being dependent on a stranger is "not to be considered a life" (40:28-29). From this vantage point, the comment in v. 15b that the guarantor risks his life should not be downplayed as less serious than it is.

Verses 16-17 give ample testimony that there were plenty of people who were so callous and ungrateful that they thought nothing of ruining those who had been nice enough to aid them in their time of need. The scope of this tendency is accented in v. 18 when Ben Sira refers to "many prosperous and powerful people". Not even the wealthy and powerful are able to extricate themselves once they are at the mercy of an unscrupulous borrower. According to Ben Sira, there are "many" examples of people who were rich and powerful but were plunged into financial disaster by going surety.

---

8 The Greek for v.14b is ambiguous. It could refer either to a potential guarantor or to a potential borrower. If the former, the sense is that someone who abandons someone in need by refusing to go surety is shameless. This would then contrast with the previous stich. If the latter, the sense is that abandoning one's guarantor is especially shameless because it was out of the goodness of his heart that he helped the debtor. The latter scenario is suggested by the fact that the idea is recapitulated in v. 17 but there the subject and object are identified. So also, GILBERT, Prêt, aumône et caution, 184. Cf. SKEHAN/DI LELLA, The Wisdom of Ben Sira, 371.
9 SKEHAN/DI LELLA, The Wisdom of Ben Sira, 371. Note the similar "life and death" stakes involved in Prov 6:1-5.
10 See GILBERT, Prêt, aumône et caution, 184; SAUER, Jesus Sirach, 211; SKEHAN/DI LELLA, The Wisdom of Ben Sira, 376; contra PETERS, Das Buch Jesus Sirach, 240-242; EBERHARTER, Das Buch Jesus Sirach, 105-106.

In light of the financial danger involved, the silence of the Torah on the matter, and the advice of Proverbs to avoid going surety, one might expect the sage to take a negative view of the practice. This is, in fact, the position of 4QInstruction, where going surety is also described as putting the *mevin*'s life at stake and as something to be avoided at all costs (4QInstruction^b 2 ii 4-6; 2 iii 3-8; 4QInstruction^c 2 i 21-24). The *Damascus Document* takes this line of thinking even further. There, going surety is associated with lending on interest and therefore is prohibited legally (4QD^b 4 8-11). In other words, it is not just a bad idea; it is raised to the level of a sin.[11]

However, Ben Sira moves in exactly the opposite direction. He concludes his pericope with an imperative to stand surety for one's neighbor. This positive command provides a counterpart to the indicative regarding the goodness of the practice in v. 14 and frames the discussion with an *inclusio*, in which the practice of going surety is urged as an ethical obligation. Granted, it is also tempered with a caution. One should go surety only according to one's means in order to prevent financial ruin. Yet, in light of the dangerous social situation portrayed in the pericope it is surprising that he advocates the practice at all. Given the silence in the legislative portions of the Torah and the uniformly negative assessment in Proverbs, how should Ben Sira's position be explained?[12]

Rybolt, Segal, Smend, and Snaith explain the difference between Proverbs and Sirach in terms of a change in the socio-economic climate whereby loans on surety had become an economic necessity by the time of Ben Sira.[13] While this might explain why Ben Sira concedes the practice, as in 8:13, this observation is not sufficient to explain why he believes it is characteristic of a *good* person (29:14) and urges his students to go surety, albeit cautiously (29:20). One factor that may have contributed to this change of perspective seen in Sirach is that, while the Torah legislation is silent regarding surety, Judah does go surety for Benjamin in the narrative portion of the Torah. Even more suggestively, since Hezekiah requests that God go surety for him in Isa 38:14 one

---

11   See MURPHY, Wealth in the Dead Sea Scrolls, 45-47.
12   Sandoval believes that the difference between Proverbs and Sirach is primarily derived from the fact that they have different social relationships in mind, i.e. Prov 6 concerns going surety for a stranger while Sir 29 concerns going surety for a neighbor (The Discourse of Wealth and Poverty in the Book of Proverbs, 111). For why I do not think the difference can be sufficiently explained in this way see my Like an Everlasting Signet Ring, 159-160.
13   RYBOLT, Sirach, 63; SEGAL, ספר בן־סירא השלם, 179; SMEND, Die Weisheit des Jesus Sirach, 259; SNAITH, Ecclesiasticus, 146. Snaith adds that a contributing factor was "Ben Sira's own deep sense of piety."

could conclude that surety done for the right reasons could be permissible, or even virtuous.

More importantly, it seems that Ben Sira had come to regard surety as a type of generosity.[14] The structure of chapter 29 in which the topics of loans and surety frame a discussion of almsgiving suggests that when Ben Sira works out his view of surety here it is within a theological context of generosity. This is why Ben Sira begins the passage with an appeal to acting out of a sense of mercy (29:1). A consideration of the chapter as a whole suggests that Ben Sira understands surety along similar lines as two-party loans. When one accepts risk in these financial transactions, one does so either because there is something to be gained (e.g. collecting interest) or because one is motivated by compassionate piety. Thus, to engage in either practice without the goal of profiting from the needy person is by definition an act of mercy which is fundamental to the social vision of the Torah, even if surety is not explicitly addressed within it.[15] The drive towards using one's wealth to help those in need, itself a significant component of the biblical tradition, was strong enough that once surety was understood as a kind of merciful loan it became an ethical obligation to help one's neighbor through surety despite the lack of precedent in the tradition and the practical risks involved.[16]

An assessment of Ben Sira's teaching on surety raises some important points about how he interacts with authoritative traditions. With regard to this issue Ben Sira moves in the opposite direction of his sapiential predecessors and other wisdom texts of his day, such as 4QInstruction. Given his familiarity with Proverbs and the rival positions current at the time, Ben Sira cannot have been unaware of the statements on surety in Proverbs. But, unlike other sapiential thinkers, Ben Sira is a strong advocate of surety. This is because, as we have seen, surety is being viewed by Ben Sira through the lens of the Torah's teaching on financial generosity. Ben Sira does *not* make the mistake of thinking surety is advocated in the Torah; this is clear from the fact that in Sirach 29 he appeals to the commandments when he advocates loans and almsgiving, but not for his teaching on surety. Rather, the structure of Sirach 29 suggests that Ben Sira frames almsgiving with the related topics of loans and surety and thus his instruction regarding surety is

---

14 So DUESBERG/FRANSEN, who remark that "Ben Sira riporta la cauzione a una forma di elemosina" (Ecclesiastico, 223).
15 The aspect of supporting social cohesion as fundamental to 29:1-20 is accented by SAUER, Jesus Sirach, 210-211.
16 For a fuller discussion of 29:14-20 and the larger context of 29:1-20, see my Like an Everlasting Signet Ring, 128-170.

embedded within a larger discourse of a mercy-ethic which he has derived from the Torah. One helps a neighbor, whether through loans, surety, or almsgiving, either out of a sense of self-interest or out of a pious compassion. Once viewed from this angle, the teaching of Proverbs is subordinated, not just to an explicit statement in the Torah, but to *Ben Sira's understanding of the Torah* and its ethical implications.

3. Ben Sira and the Priesthood

A second issue which illuminates how Ben Sira negotiates authoritative traditions concerns the nature and scope of the priesthood.[17] At the outset it is important to observe that, contrary to the claims of some scholars, the work of Perdue, Stadelmann, Olyan, Hayward, and Wright has conclusively shown that Ben Sira is fundamentally supportive of the Jerusalem priesthood.[18] This positive support is clear from several angles. First, and strikingly, he explicitly states that it is a religious obligation to support the priests in 7:29-31.

> 29 With all your heart fear God
> and revere his priests.
>
> 30 With all your strength love your Maker
> and his ministers do not neglect.
>
> 31 Glorify God and honor the priest
> and give them their portion as you have been commanded.
> The suet, the guilt-offering, and the contribution of (your) hand
> righteous sacrifices and the holy contribution.[19]

In this passage, Ben Sira equates honoring God with honoring his servants, the priests, and he points out that the support of the latter is an issue of obedience to the Torah (v. 31b). Second, Ben Sira's famous praise of Wisdom in Sir 24 identifies the Jerusalem temple as the residence of Wisdom.[20] In addition, Wisdom herself operates as a priest in her ministry before God. Thirdly, Wright has shown that Ben Sira de-

---

17 This section is adapted from my discussion in Like an Everlasting Signet Ring, 222-253.
18 PERDUE, Wisdom and Cult, 188-211; STADELMANN, Ben Sira als Schriftgelehrter; OLYAN, Ben Sira's Relationship to the Priesthood, 261-86; HAYWARD, Sacrifice and World Order, 22-34; WRIGHT, Fear the Lord and Honor the Priest, 189-222.
19 The text-criticism of 7:31 is highly problematic, but does not affect the argument I wish to make here. For a discussion of the text-criticism of this passage see my Like an Everlasting Signet Ring, 304-307.
20 József ZSENGELLÉR makes an important point that while Ben Sira's theology of the priesthood and his theology of the temple are related, they are also conceptually distinct (Does Wisdom Come from the Temple, 136).

fends the priesthood by supporting a lunar calendar (43:6-8), opposing epistemologies that introduce new revelation that is perceived as extraneous to the received traditions (3:21-24; 34:1-8), and "domesticates" the figure of Enoch. These positions appear to counter the critiques of the Jerusalem priesthood put forth by the marginalized authors of the *Astronomical Book*, the *Book of the Watchers*, and *Aramaic Levi*.[21] Fourth, the "Praise of the Ancestors" glorifies the Aaronic priesthood and culminates in the praise of the high priest Simon II.[22]

Given this positive disposition towards the priesthood, Ben Sira must negotiate his authoritative traditions in multiple ways. First, Ben Sira must negotiate between conflicting theological traditions regarding who is a legitimate priest. The Hebrew Bible embodies competing perspectives on the legitimate parameters of the priesthood, depending on where one places the line of demarcation along the lineage of Levi – Aaron – Phinehas – Zadok. In the Deuteronomic tradition all Levites are eligible to be priests (Deut 18:1-14; Jer 33:18), but in P the sphere of legitimacy is narrowed to just Aaron and his descendants. Finally, in Ezekiel 40-48 it is the Zadokites alone who are eligible to be priests (cf. Ezek 40:46). The socio-political antagonism in this struggle for the rights of the priesthood is detectable in the texts themselves. The redactor of Ezek 40-48 attributes the exclusion of the Levites to idolatry and unfaithfulness (Ezek 48:11) and a second P redactor of Num 16 has inserted a polemic against the Korahites into a narrative originally about Dathan and Abiram.[23]

This debate over the parameters of the priesthood continued until the turn of the Common Era and Saul Olyan has argued persuasively that Ben Sira's view of the priesthood aligns with that of P. He states, "Ben Sira alludes to P passage after P passage in order to tell his tale, ignoring for all intents and purposes other Pentateuchal narrative."[24] In 45:15 and 25 it is the whole family of Aaron who receives the priesthood, while in 45:23-24 Phinehas's actions secure the right to the high priesthood for him and his descendants.[25] In Sirach 50 Simon is not identified as a Zadokite, and in 50:13 he makes a point of saying that "all the sons of Aaron" brought offerings. Therefore, Ben Sira appears

---

21 WRIGHT, Fear the Lord and Honor the Priest, 202-222.
22 For a fuller explanation of these four elements see my Like an Everlasting Signet Ring, 225-230.
23 See ALBERTZ, A History of Israelite Religion, 480-493; BLENKINSOPP, Sage, Priest, Prophet, 83-98.
24 OLYAN, Ben Sira's Relationship to the Priesthood, 270.
25 In Num 25:6-13 the covenant is for "perpetual priesthood." Regarding Ben Sira's modification see POMYKALA, The Covenant with Phinehas in Ben Sira, 17-36.

to have approved of all Aaronids as priests and ascribed the rights of the high priesthood to the descendants of Phinehas, without explicitly limiting it further to the sons of Zadok.[26] While Simon was a Zadokite, Ben Sira does not mention it.[27] However, even if Olyan is correct that Ben Sira believed all those of the line of Phinehas were eligible for the high priesthood, this still affirms the legitimacy of the high priests of the Zadokite line, such as Simon.[28]

Therefore, with regard to the legitimate priests, Ben Sira apparently rejects the most restrictive view of Ezek 40-48, even though he praises Ezekiel as a true prophet in Sir 49:8.[29] Instead he opts for a view of the priesthood found in the Torah. Yet, with respect to the conflicting traditions within the Torah itself, Ben Sira opts for the view of P rather than the view of D. Aside from the issue of whether Ben Sira was or was not a priest, he evidently moved in priestly circles.[30] On the basis of the above data Olyan poses the question, "Does this not imply that in the second century BCE, a 'pure' P tradition is being taught in the Aaronid schools which presumably existed to train young priests?" Likewise, in his study of the "Praise of the Ancestors" Burton Mack argues that

---

26 OLYAN, Ben Sira's Relationship to the Priesthood, 275-276.
27 Whoever inserted the poem after 51:12 explicitly narrows the parameters of the priesthood to the Zadokites (in line with Ezek 40-48) by stating, "Give thanks to him who has chosen the sons of Zadok as priests." DI LELLA, The Hebrew Text of Sirach, 101-105, believes this poem was added within a couple of decades after Ben Sira's death, but OLYAN, Ben Sira's Relationship to the Priesthood, 275 n.41, argues that this is debatable.
28 Boccacini critiques Olyan by arguing that Ben Sira takes a Zadokite view of the high priesthood, noting that the biblical genealogies do not mention any other descendants of Phinehas besides Zadok. It is possible, though, to see Ben Sira's view as pan-Aaronid regarding priests, while also limiting the high priesthood to the line of Phinehas and/or Zadok. Cf. BOCCACCINI, Where Does Ben Sira Belong, 30-31. For a defense of Olyan see WRIGHT, Ben Sira and the *Book of the Watchers* on the Legitimate Priesthood, 245-246.
29 While Ben Sira mentions Ezekiel in his "Praise of the Ancestors" (Sir 49:8), he only makes reference to the chariot vision. However, his statement regarding Wisdom in Sir 24:25-28 appears to depend on the vision in Ezek 47. Since the Zadokite-only view of the priesthood was probably a stable part of the text of Ezekiel by the time of the Chronicler, there is no reason to doubt that the copy of Ezekiel available to Ben Sira contained this view as well.
30 Stadelmann and Olyan both believe he was a priest. Others, however, have found the evidence that Ben Sira was a priest inconclusive. See the critique of Stadelmann in BEENTJES, Recent Publications, 191-194. Among those who remain agnostic are WISCHMEYER, Die Kultur des Buches Jesus Sirach, 62-63, and WRIGHT, Fear the Lord and Honor the Priest, 196. It is worth pointing out that a supportive attitude of the priesthood and even their ideology does not in itself require that Ben Sira was a priest. Ben Sira's position as a member of the retainer class can equally account for these affinities.

"Ben Sira's hymn reflects a view of the Pentateuch very much like that of the priestly redactor."[31]

Of course, Ben Sira does not think in the modern literary-critical categories of D and P, but in terms of one authoritative Torah and so while Ben Sira agrees with P over against D on the issue of *who* can be a priest, this issue becomes more complicated when set within the larger issue of supporting these priests. That Ben Sira advocated supporting the priesthood is clear enough from passages like Sir 7:29-31, but this position was complicated considerably by the socio-political climate of Seleucid Judea. In Ben Sira's time Judea was headed by a temple aristocracy that placed the priesthood in a position of considerable social, economic, and political power. The exploitation of the poor was, unfortunately, a common element in this socio-economic climate and Sir 13:2-23 makes it clear that Ben Sira was not blind to the social sins of the aristocracy.[32]

Over against this, he is a strong advocate of treating the poor well and does not mince words in condemning those who participate in social injustice (Sir 4:1-10; 7:32-36; 29:8-13; 34:21-35:26). This emphasis on justice for the poor in these passages is also grounded in the prescriptions of the Torah. While there is an element of concern for the poor throughout the Torah, including in P and H,[33] Ben Sira's concern for the poor seems most heavily indebted to Deuteronomy, especially chapter 15. Thus, when Ben Sira advocates generosity to those in need in Sir 29 he supports his teaching through multiple appeals to the commandments in Deut 15. This comports with Di Lella's observation that in regard to Ben Sira's thought "his pervading theological outlook is Deuteronomic."[34]

Though support of the priesthood and concern for the poor may seem to stand in tension within Seleucid Judea, Ben Sira apparently thought a choice between the two to be a false dichotomy. The fact that the Torah both legitimates the priesthood and also calls for justice to the poor requires both, despite any perceived complications in the implementation of such a vision. For Ben Sira these two allegiances run

---

31 MACK, Wisdom and the Hebrew Epic, 117.
32 On this passage see my Like an Everlasting Signet Ring, 61-72.
33 Less expensive sacrifices are permitted for the poor in the case of the purification offering in Lev 5:1-13, for the purification after childbirth in Lev 12:1-8, and for the purification from disease in Lev 14:21-32. Reduced rates are also permitted in the case of votive offerings in Lev 27:1-18. In the Holiness Code there is a more pronounced emphasis on the protection of the poor. Leviticus 19 demands paying a laborer on time and the Sabbatical year and the year of Jubilee in Lev 25 provide for the release of the indigent from debt-slavery.
34 SKEHAN/DI LELLA, The Wisdom of Ben Sira, 75.

much deeper than surface commitments; they are understood to be crucial components of the Torah. Hayward has perceptively pointed out that the only two places in Sirach where the phrase "for the sake of the commandment" (χάριν ἐντολῆς) occurs are in the instructions regarding almsgiving (29:9; cf. 29:11) and in the instruction not to neglect the sacrificial cult (35:7; cf. 7:31).³⁵

This observation about Ben Sira's phrasing reflects his larger belief that support of the cult (drawn mostly from P) and concern for the poor (drawn mostly from D) are parallel ideals of a Wisdom-Torah ethic. It cannot be a coincidence that the two places where Ben Sira casts almsgiving in sacrificial language (3:30-31; 35:1-5) are juxtaposed with the passages that are most adamant about the need for social justice (4:1-10; 34:21-27; 35:14-26). Likewise, the two passages that are the most insistent on the virtue of supporting the Jerusalem cult (7:29-31; 35:6-13) are juxtaposed with passages about the need to care for the poor (7:32-36; 35:14-26).³⁶ This pattern of juxtaposing the two is understandable since the Torah shows the same tendency. For example, in Deut 14:22-27 the Israelites are instructed regarding the bringing of their tithes to the sanctuary and in Deut 15:1-18, a passage already seen to be highly important for Ben Sira, there is a concern for social justice regarding the poor. In the few verses that bridge these two sections there is an intertwining of priests and the socially vulnerable as the recipients of the tithes:³⁷

> Every third year you shall bring out the full tithe of your produce for that year, and store it within your towns; the Levites, because they have no allotment or inheritance with you, as well as the resident aliens, the orphans, and the widows in your towns, may come

---

35 HAYWARD, Sacrifice and World Order, 29. Of course, there are other places in Sirach where appeal to the commandments is made in different language, but almost all of these are generic admonitions to keep the commandments. In context, a few of them are linked to particular issues (e.g. 28:6-7; 29:1-7).

36 It should be remembered that charity and social justice are not the same. Pleins argues that the latter seeks structural, institutional change to bring about an end to poverty while the former, at least in the book of Proverbs, is not so much out of concern for injustice, but in order to receive a reward from God. Pleins has been criticized by Kimilike, who observes that a compartmentalization of charity and social justice does not hold if the former is considered ineffective without the latter. Then charity and social justice are two components of one strategy to address poverty. Perhaps even more than Proverbs, this is the direction both Job and Sirach are moving (cf. Sir 34:21-35:26). See the discussions in KIMILIKE, Poverty in the Book of Proverbs, 64-66; MALCHOW, Social Justice in the Wisdom Literature, 120-124; PLEINS, Poverty in the Social World of the Wise, 61-78.

37 Pointed out by DI LELLA, The Wisdom of Ben Sira, 207, in connection with 7:29-36.

and eat their fill so that the LORD your God may bless you in all the work that you undertake. (Deut 14:28-29)

The fact that Ben Sira's strongest statements concerning either justice for the poor or the sacrificial cult always evoke teaching about the other demonstrates that, for him, they are inseparable dimensions of obedience to the Torah.

But the inseparable nature of these two aspects of Torah goes even deeper for Ben Sira. For him, both of these have their ultimate theological antecedent in the nature of Wisdom. Wisdom dwells in the Jerusalem temple and, like Simon the high priest, acts as a priest, sending forth her incense (Sir 24:15). Likewise, the layperson attains wisdom through the study of Torah (39:1-11) and his praise is also like incense (39:14), as is the legacy of the righteous (49:1). Thus, for Ben Sira the pursuit of Wisdom must necessarily lead to a convergence, not an opposition, of supporting the cult and concern for the poor.

Hayward is certainly correct when he concludes that, "As far as Ben Sira is concerned, there can be no question of a dichotomy between ritual and moral commandments. Both kinds of commandment derive from Wisdom-Torah, and the wise man, the righteous, pious and learned man, is the one who, in tune with the divine order of the universe, observes all the commandments – ritual and ethical."[38] In other words, even if members of the priestly aristocracy of Seleucid Judea oppress the poor, the sage's allegiance to the Torah as a whole does not allow him to choose to support *either* the priesthood *or* the poor. He must seek out a way to try to accomplish both because both the priests and the poor function as "theological conduits" to God. One cannot honor God through one and despise him through the other. The way of Wisdom requires the sage to hold the two together and, as such, Ben Sira's ethic might be characterized as an *imitatio sapientiae*.

In sum, concerning the question of who can be a priest, Ben Sira answers 'Aaronids' in agreement with P and against Deuteronomy (as well as others, e.g. Ezek 40-48). This is significant since Deuteronomy is very influential on Ben Sira and the view of Deuteronomy, where all Levites are eligible to be priests, may be advocated by works roughly

---

38 HAYWARD, Sacrifice and World Order, 30-31. Earlier Perdue, Wisdom and Cult, 199, came to the same conclusion: "The most striking element is Sirach's equating righteous behavior with cultic devotion, since both achieve the same end: forgiveness and acceptance by the deity (33:1-3 [= 35:1-5]). This should not be interpreted to mean that Sirach exalts righteous actions over cultic participation, but rather that he places them both on an equal plane in his depiction of sapiential piety. The true wise man, therefore, is righteous and cultically observant, and to distinguish between the two is a dichotomy completely foreign to Sirach's understanding".

contemporary with Ben Sira, such as *Jubilees*, *Testament of Levi*, and possibly *1 Enoch* and *Testament of Moses*.[39] Yet, a wider consideration of the nature of the priesthood shows that Ben Sira often contextualizes his positive view of the priesthood with a social understanding drawn directly from Deuteronomy. Here we can see an analogy with his treatment of surety. Despite the difficult socio-economic situation of his day, he advocates support of the priesthood and the needy in light of his understanding of the whole Torah. He apparently felt free to leave aside one aspect of Deuteronomy's teaching, i.e. that concerning the Levitical priests, while integrating it within a broader social ethic derived primarily from Deuteronomy. In his teaching on the priesthood, therefore, Ben Sira reveals a complex mediation between his conflicting traditions and his own social context. Regarding who can be a priest, Ben Sira simply opts for one strand of the Torah over another, but in terms of practical support of these same priests he seeks to hold together both ritual and ethical prescriptions of the Torah despite the practical difficulty in doing so. At no point does he subordinate the Torah's social demands to its cultic demands, or vice versa.

Here one can begin to see the complex interconnection between the authority of Israel's sacred literary tradition and the authority of Ben Sira as a sage. On one hand, Ben Sira's authority and that of the positions he advocates are derived from the authority of the texts to which he appeals. Through appeals to the commandments both support of the priesthood and concern for the poor are grounded in the authority of the Torah's demands. This gives Ben Sira an angle from which to criticize his socio-political superiors among the temple aristocracy.[40] On the other hand, Ben Sira does not simply reproduce the texts in which he grounds his views, but appropriates and transforms them within his framework of a wisdom piety. Thus, paradoxically, his authority is derived from the literary heritage of Israel and yet this authority also invests him with the freedom to adapt and transform the teaching

---

[39] FABRY, Jesus Sirach und das Priestertum, 280; OLYAN, Ben Sira's Relationship to the Priesthood, 278-280.

[40] Cf. "They view their own authority as grounded in 'the wisdom of all the ancients' and their faithful 'study of the law of the Most High' (38:34-39:1). They thus derive their authority, independent of the priestly aristocracy, from God and the revered cultural tradition. This suggests also that they had their own sense of how the temple-state should operate; that is, it should operate according to the sacred cultural tradition of which they were the professional guardians and interpreters. Despite their dependence on and vulnerability to their patrons among the ruling aristocracy, therefore, scribes such as Ben Sira could both criticize the aristocracy and take measures to mitigate its oppression of the poor (4:8-10; 13:3-4, 18-19; 29:8-9; 34:21-27)." HORSLEY, Politics of Cultural Production, 127.

within this literary heritage in new ways. In other words, the authority of the sacred texts and the authority of the sage stand in a dialogic and reciprocal relationship.

4. Ben Sira as Authoritative Interpreter of Authoritative Traditions

With these two case studies in mind, let us now return to the question of how Ben Sira as an inspired *Schriftgelehrter*, functions as an authoritative interpreter of authoritative texts. First, it is imperative to note that we should be careful not to extrapolate from just two case studies to broader statements regarding the authority of these texts. I think it would be a mistake to take the case of surety and conclude that, simply on the basis of this one example, that the Torah is more authoritative than the book of Proverbs. Rather, as we saw, it is not so much the explicit teaching of the Torah as Ben Sira's understanding of the Torah ethic that is determinative. A similar dynamic can be seen in the discussion of the priesthood. There is no formula for how Ben Sira negotiates his various authoritative traditions. This reason, already highlighted at the beginning, is that a considerable component of this negotiation resides, not so much in the authority of the texts relative to one another, but in the authority of Ben Sira as a learned sage who is able to "penetrate the subtleties of parables; to seek out the hidden meanings of proverbs" (39:2-3), trusting that "the Lord will direct his counsel and knowledge as he meditates on his mysteries and shows the wisdom of what he has learned" (39:7-8).

This interaction between authoritative texts and the authority of the sage, I believe, does *not* constitute a tension in Ben Sira's thought. Contrary to the way we, as post-Enlightenment Westerners, understand the authority of sacred texts as creating a certain distance between text and interpreter, one of the remarkable aspects of Second Temple Judaism is that it was apparently precisely the authoritative nature of the texts that drives interpreters to appropriate them, transform them, and even alter their content.[41]

Building on the work of Carr, Najman, and Newsom, Benjamin Wright has shown how the notion of appropriated discourse is a helpful way to think about how Ben Sira both uses texts to authorize his

---

[41] See TEETER, Exegesis in the Transmission of Biblical Law. This is by no means unique to the wisdom tradition. The notion of authoritative tradition as living and developing, captured in the German word *Vergegenwärtigung*, was shared by many in Second Temple Judaism. For this see the discussion in DUNN, The Living Word, 53-68.

own discourse while also transforming these authoritative texts for his own ends.[42] I would like to elaborate a little on the dynamic elucidated by Wright, by highlighting what James Kugel calls "the anthological temper" of wisdom literature. Kugel notes that the wisdom literature shows an awareness that wisdom is by nature anthological and therefore it is something that is acquired, studied, and then passed to the next generation. There was a keen awareness that even the most insightful sage could not master everything and therefore growth in wisdom is a collective, transgenerational affair. One generation extends the horizon by discovering more wisdom and passes it to the next generation, which, after mastering what has already been discovered and charted, can proceed to expand the horizon even more.[43] Extending this understanding of wisdom into the *textual sphere* results in the conclusion that the task of comprehending texts and their significance is never completed, but is a transgenerational, anthological endeavor. What has been missed by Kugel and by many others is that this perspective is an integral part of Ben Sira's statements on his own divine inspiration:[44]

24:33 I will again pour out teaching like prophecy
and leave it to all future generations.

33:16 Now I was like the last to keep vigil
I was like a gleaner following the grape-pickers.

33:17 by the blessing of the Lord I arrived first
and like a grape-picker I filled my wine press.

33:18 Consider that I have not labored for myself alone
but for all who seek instruction.

---

42 WRIGHT, The Use and Interpretation of Biblical Tradition in Ben Sira's Praise of the Ancestors. The works discussed by Wright are CARR, Writing on the Tablet of the Heart; NAJMAN, Seconding Sinai; and NEWSOM, The Self as Symbolic Space.
43 KUGEL, Wisdom and the Anthological Temper, 18.
44 In the final sentence of his essay, Ben Sira on the Sage as Exemplar, Benjamin WRIGHT hints in this direction: "sapiential exemplarity (if we can call it that) locates inspiration, understood both as revealed by God and in a prophetesque manner and as developed from the interpretations of the inherited tradition, in the corporate work of the sages as a class of people who produced, transmitted and preserved the Israelite wisdom/literary tradition." (182)

Ben Sira's mode of prophetic-like activity[45] is oriented around the transmission of his learning to future generations and he envisions himself as picking the grapes of others, but blending them in his own winepress. This is an extraordinarily apt metaphor for how Ben Sira understands the dialogic relationship between his authoritative source material and his own product. This is why, I believe, Ben Sira describes the sage in Sirach 39 as one who studies the Law of the Most High, is concerned with prophecies, and preserves and probes the sayings of the famous. The fact that this is all characterized by a divinely enabled ability to penetrate the subtle and seek out the mysterious and obscure highlights the fact that Ben Sira understands his relationship to the authoritative texts of Israel as a *hermeneutically anthological* endeavor.

In the concrete cases of surety and the priesthood we can see the dialogical and anthological dynamics at work. Ben Sira is indebted to the earlier authoritative works, both for their teaching and for their authorization of him as a sage, but he also goes beyond them and feels free to transform their teaching in light of a new synthesis of understanding, either regarding financial generosity or regarding one's social relationship with the aristocracy and the poor. In both cases, his divine inspiration enables him to take the wisdom charted in the Torah and Proverbs and then expand its horizons for his students who should in turn do the same for future generations. Sometimes, as we have seen here, this even involves setting aside the teaching of an earlier authoritative text in light of new insights. In describing how Ben Sira as an authoritative *Schriftgelehrter* stands in relation to his authoritative texts we might return to the wine imagery Ben Sira used above. In savoring Ben Sira's discourse, the student can at once taste the grapes that Ben Sira has gathered from others, but he has blended and fermented them into a concoction all his own.

---

45 PERDUE, Ben Sira and the Prophets, 153, argues that Ben Sira understood himself "to stand in succession to the long line of prophets when the prophets for at least two centuries had been discredited and when the priests no longer had the ability to obtain divine revelation through the casting of lots". I differ slightly from Perdue in that I think it is significant that 24:33 characterizes Ben Sira's teaching as being poured out *like* prophecy. The inspiration underlying his teaching and his abilities to interpret earlier writings is analogous and approximates the divine inspiration the prophets had, but I do not think Ben Sira quite understood himself to stand in succession to the prophets.

Bibliography

ALBERTZ, Rainer, A History of Israelite Religion in the Old Testament Period, Volume II. From the Exile to the Maccabees (OTL), Louisville 1994.

BEENTJES, Pancratius C., Canon and Scripture in the Book of Ben Sira, in: id., "Happy the One who Meditates on Wisdom" (Sir. 14,20): Collected Essays on the Book of Ben Sira (CBET 43), Leuven 2006, 169-186.

BEENTJES, Pancratius C., Prophets and Prophecy in the Book of Ben Sira, in: id., "Happy the One who Meditates on Wisdom" (Sir. 14,20): Collected Essays on the Book of Ben Sira (CBET 43), Leuven 2006, 207-229.

BEENTJES, Pancratius C., Recent Publications on the Wisdom of Jesus Ben Sira (Ecclesiasticus), in: Bijdr 43 (1982), 191-194.

BLENKINSOPP, Joseph, Sage, Priest, Prophet: Religious and Intellectual Leadership in Ancient Israel (Library of Ancient Israel), Louisville 1995.

BOCCACCINI, Gabriele, Where Does Ben Sira Belong? The Canon, Literary Genre, Intellectual Movement, and Social Group of a Zadokite Document, in: Xeravits, Géza G./Zsengellér, József (eds.), Studies in the Book of Ben Sira. Papers of the Third International Conference on the Deuterocanonical Books, Shime'on Centre, Pápa, Hungary, 18-20 May 2006 (SJSJ 127), Leiden 2008, 21-41.

CARR, David, Writing on the Tablet of the Heart. Origins of Scripture and Literature, New York 2005.

DI LELLA, Alexander A., The Hebrew Text of Sirach. A Text-Critical and Historical Study (Studies in Classical Literature 1), Hague 1966.

DUESBERG, Hilaire/FRANSEN, Irénée, Ecclesiastico (La Sacra Bible), Rome 1966.

DUNN, James D. G., The Living Word, Minneapolis ²2009.

EBERHARTER, Andreas, Das Buch Jesus Sirach oder Ecclesiasticus übersetzt und erklärt (Die Heilige Schrift des Alten Testamentes übersetzt und erklärt in Verbindung mit Fachgelehrten, VI/5), Bonn 1925.

FABRY, Heinz-Josef, Jesus Sirach und das Priestertum, in: Fischer, Irmtraud/Rapp, Ursula/Schiller, Johannes (eds.), Auf den Spuren der schriftgelehrten Weisen. Festschrift für Johannes Marböck (BZAW 331), Berlin 2003, 265-282.

GILBERT, Maurice, Prêt, aumône et caution, in: Egger-Wenzel, Renate/Krammer, Ingrid (eds.), Der Einzelne und seine Gemeinschaft bei Ben Sira (BZAW 270), Berlin 1998, 179-189.

GREGORY, Bradley C., Like an Everlasting Signet Ring. Generosity in the Book of Sirach (DCLS 2), Berlin 2010.

GREGORY, Bradley C., The Warrior-Poet of Israel. The Significance of David's Battles in Chronicles and Ben Sira, in: Corley, Jeremy/van Grol, Harm (eds.), Rewriting Biblical History. Essays on Chronicles and Ben Sira, Berlin 2012, 79-96.

HAYWARD, C. T. Robert, Sacrifice and World Order. Some Observations on Ben Sira's Attitude to the Temple Service, in: Sykes, Stephen W. (ed.), Sacrifice and Redemption. Durham Essays in Theology, Cambridge 1991, 22-34.

HORSLEY, Richard, The Politics of Cultural Production in Second Temple Judea. Historical Context and Political-Religious Relations of the Scribes Who Produced 1 Enoch, Sirach, and Daniel, in: Wright, Benjamin G./Wills, Lawrence M. (eds.), Conflicted Boundaries in Wisdom and Apocalypticism (SBLSS 35), Atlanta 2005, 123-145.

KIMILIKE, Lechion Peter, Poverty in the Book of Proverbs. An African Transformational Hermeneutic of Proverbs on Poverty (BTA 7), New York 2008.

KUGEL, James, Wisdom and the Anthological Temper, in: Prooftexts 17 (1997), 9-32.

MACK, Burton L., Wisdom and the Hebrew Epic. Ben Sira's Hymn in Praise of the Fathers (Chicago Studies in the History of Judaism), Chicago 1985.

MALCHOW, Bruce V., Social Justice in the Wisdom Literature, in: BTB 12 (1982), 120-124.

MURPHY, Catherine M., Wealth in the Dead Sea Scrolls and in the Qumran Community (STDJ 40), Leiden 2002.

NAJMAN, Hindy, Seconding Sinai. The Development of Mosaic Discourse in Second Temple Judaism (SJSJ 77), Leiden 2003.

NEWSOM, Carol, The Self as Symbolic Space. Constructing Identity and Community at Qumran (STDJ 52), Leiden 2004.

OLYAN, Saul M., Ben Sira's Relationship to the Priesthood, in: HTR 80 (1987), 261-286.

PERDUE, Leo G., Ben Sira and Prophets, in: Corley, Jeremy/Skemp, Vincent (eds.), Intertextual Studies in Ben Sira and Tobit. Essays in Honor of Alexander A. Di Lella, O.F.M. (CBQMS 38), Washington 2005, 132-154.

PERDUE, Leo G., Wisdom and Cult. A Critical Analysis of the Views of Cult in the Wisdom Literatures of Israel and the Ancient Near East (SBLDS 30), Missoula 1977.

PETERS, Norbert, Das Buch Jesus Sirach oder Ecclesiasticus übersetzt und erklärt (EHAT 25), Münster 1913.

PLEINS, J. David, Poverty in the Social World of the Wise, in: JSOT 37 (1987), 61-78.

POMYKALA, Kenneth E., The Covenant with Phinehas in Ben Sira (Sirach 45:23-26; 50:22-24), in: Pomykala, Kenneth E. (ed.), Israel in the Wilderness. Interpretations of the Biblical Narratives in Jewish and Christian Traditions (TBN 10), Leiden 2008, 17-36.

RYBOLT, John E., Sirach (CBC 21), Collegeville 1986.

SANDOVAL, Timothy J., The Discourse of Wealth and Poverty in the Book of Proverbs (BINS 77) Leiden 2007.

SAUER, Georg, Jesus Sirach/Ben Sira. Übersetzt und erklärt (ATD 1), Göttingen 2000.

SEGAL, Mosheh Z., ספר בן־סירא השלם, Jerusalem ⁴1997.

SKEHAN, Patrick W./DI LELLA, Alexander A., The Wisdom of Ben Sira. A New Translation with Notes, Introduction and Commentary (AB 39), New York 1987.

SMEND, Rudolph, Die Weisheit des Jesus Sirach erklärt, Berlin 1906.

SNAITH, John, Ecclesiasticus or the Wisdom of Jesus Son of Sirach, Cambridge 1974.

STADELMANN, Helge, Ben Sira als Schriftgelehrter. Eine Untersuchung zum Berufsbild des vor-makkabäischen Sōfēr unter Berücksichtigung seines Verhältnisses zu Preister-, Propheten-, und Weisheitslehrertum (WUNT 2/6), Tübingen 1980.

TEETER, David Andrew, Exegesis in the Transmission of Biblical Law in the Second Temple Period. Preliminary Studies, Ph.D. dissertation, University of Notre Dame, 2008.

WISCHMEYER, Oda, Die Kultur des Buches Jesus Sirach (BZNW 77), Berlin 1995.

WRIGHT, Benajamin G., Ben Sira and the Book of the Watchers on the Legitimate Priesthood, in: Corley, Jeremy/Skemp, Vincent (eds.), Intertextual Studies in Ben Sira and Tobit. Essays in Honor of Alexander A. Di Lella, O.F.M. (CBQMS 38), Washington 2005, 241-254.

WRIGHT, Benjamin G., Ben Sira on the Sage as Exemplar, in: id., Praise Israel for Wisdom and Instruction. Essays on Ben Sira and Wisdom, the Letter of Aristeas and the Septuagint (SJSJ 131), Leiden 2008, 165-182.

WRIGHT, Benjamin G., Biblical Interpretation in the Book of Ben Sira, in: Henze, Matthias (ed.), Companion to Biblical Interpretation in Early Judaism, Grand Rapids 2012, 363-388.

WRIGHT, Benjamin G., 'Fear the Lord and Honor the Priest'. Ben Sira as Defender of the Jerusalem Priesthood, in: Beentjes, Pancratius C. (ed.), The Book of Ben Sira in Modern Research. Proceedings of the First International Ben Sira Conference 28-31 July 1996, Soesterberg, Netherlands (BZAW 255), Berlin 1997, 189-222.

WRIGHT, Benjamin G., The Role of the Sage. Ben Sira at the Boundary, Unpublished Paper delivered at the Society of Biblical Literature Annual Meeting, Boston, Massachusetts (Wisdom and Apocalypticism Group), 2008.

WRIGHT, Benjamin G., The Use and Interpretation of Biblical Tradition in Ben Sira's Praise of the Ancestors, in: Xeravits, Géza G./Zsengellér, József (eds.), Studies in the Book of Ben Sira: Papers of the Third International Conference on the Deuterocanonical Books, Shime'on Centre, Pápa, Hungary, 18-20 May 2006 (SJSJ 127), Leiden 2008, 183-207.

ZSENGELLÉR, József, Does Wisdom Come from the Temple? Ben Sira's Attitude to the Temple of Jerusalem, in: Xeravits, Géza G./Zsengellér, József (eds.), Studies in the Book of Ben Sira: Papers of the Third International Conference on the Deuterocanonical Books, Shime'on Centre, Pápa, Hungary, 18-20 May 2006 (SJSJ 127), Leiden 2008, 135-149.

Ein unkonventioneller Umgang mit der biblischen Autorität

Siras Art in hellenistischer Umgebung aus seiner Bibel zu denken und zu sprechen

FRIEDRICH V. REITERER

Dieser Beitrag steht im Kontext von „Scriptural Authority in Early Judaism and Ancient Christianity". Aus dem Gesamtthema ergeben sich einerseits Grundfragen allgemeiner Art und weiters spezifische Fragestellungen des Buches Ben Sira. Daher wird die Untersuchung in zwei Schritten vorgenommen: 1. In einem ersten Schritt werden Beobachtungen gesammelt, auf Grund derer man die Autorität bzw. die Verbindlichkeit der „Schrift" darstellen kann, wobei *Schrift* auch ein zu untersuchender Bereich ist. 2. Im zweiten Schritt wird Sira behandelt.

1. Verschriftetes und dessen Verbindlichkeit

Die Worte „scriptural authority" setzen voraus, dass schriftliches Material vorgegeben ist, das einen verpflichtenden Anspruch erhebt – oder dem ein verpflichtender Charakter zugesprochen wird. Wenn das zutrifft, kann man von „Schriftautorität" sprechen. Nun fragt man sich, ob die „Autorität von Offenbartem und schriftlich Zugänglichem" auf eine neuzeitlich-hermeneutische Fragestellung zurückgeht oder der Anspruch auf Verbindlichkeit schon in der Bibel als integrierender Bestandteil zu belegen ist. Hingewiesen sei darauf, dass sich die vorliegende Untersuchung nicht nach literarischen Strängen ausrichtet, sondern nach thematisch Vorfindlichem und inhaltlich Nahestehendem folgt. Als Einstieg bietet sich der Bericht über die Auffindung des „Buches" im Tempel zur Zeit des Königs Joschija als Modell an. Die Szene wird als Zufallsereignis beschrieben. Daher werden 2 Kön 22,3-20 und dessen Parallele in 2 Chr 34,8-28 auf unsere Thematik hin untersucht werden.

1.1 Schreiber und Verschriftetes

Nach der Mitteilung, dass Joschija als Achtjähriger seine 31 Jahre dauernde Regentschaft angetreten hatte und er sich kompromisslos an den guten, von David vorgezeichneten Weg hielt, folgt unvermittelt der uns interessierende Teil. Es heißt, dass der König im 18. Jahr seiner Regierung „Schafan, den Sohn Azaljas, des Sohnes Meschullams [fehlt in 2 Chr 34,8], den *Schreiber* (הַסֹּפֵר)" (2 Kön 22,3) zum Priester Hilkija schickte, um Geld für Reparaturarbeiten am Tempel überbringen zu lassen. Inzwischen haben Bauarbeiter zufällig eine Rolle gefunden, die der Hohepriester dem Schreiber Schafan gibt. Dieser liest sie und berichtet davon in großer Erregung dem König.

Ein wichtiger Akteur ist *Schafan*, der *Schreiber*. In diesem Abschnitt liest man sowohl von שָׁפָן הַסֹּפֵר[1] als auch nur von שָׁפָן, wobei bei zweimaligem Vorkommen im näheren Kontext durchwegs שָׁפָן הַסֹּפֵר an erster Stelle steht.[2] In Jer 36,10 wird der leitende Beamte Gemarja, dem keine seinem Ahnen vergleichbare Berufsbenennung beigefügt wird, durch seinen Vorfahren „Schafan den Schreiber" (גְּמַרְיָהוּ בֶן־שָׁפָן הַסֹּפֵר) näher hin qualifiziert, ein weiterer Beleg dafür, dass mit Schafan das Stichwort „Schreiber" markant und zugleich unverzichtbar verbunden ist. – Nun steht nichts davon da, dass Schafan etwas geschrieben habe, sodass sich die Frage erhebt, warum סֹפֵר so nachdrücklich herausgestellt wird. Wie Jer 26,24; 29,3; 36,11f; 39,14; 40,5.9.11; 41,2; 43,6 und Ez 8,11 zeigen, ist Schafan eine politisch sehr einflussreiche Persönlichkeit gewesen und das hängt mit seiner Rolle als סֹפֵר zusammen, doch wird damit nicht geklärt, was ein סֹפֵר, wenn kein Hinweis auf Schreibtätigkeit gegeben ist, kann. Darauf geben aber die untersuchten Schlüsseltexte selbst Antwort.

(1) Der Hohepriester Hilkija übergab Schafan das im Haus des Herrn gefundene Buch des Gesetzes (סֵפֶר הַתּוֹרָה; 2 Kön 22,8 // 2 Chr 34,15). Nun steht das Stichwort סֵפֶר – von der gleichen Wurzel wie סֹפֵר –, welches innerhalb des untersuchten Abschnittes noch in 2 Kön 22,10 // 2 Chr 34,18; 2 Chr 34,21 und dann noch mehrfach in der CsV als דִּבְרֵי הַסֵּפֶר (2 Kön 22,13 [zweimal] // 2 Chr 34,21; 2 Kön 22,16) steht.

---

1   Vgl. 2 Kön 22,8 // 2 Chr 34,15; 2 Kön 22,9; 2 Kön 22,10 // 2 Chr 34,18; 2 Kön 22,12 // 2 Chr 34,20.
2   Vgl. 2 Kön 22,8 // 2 Chr 34,15; 2 Kön 22,10 // 2 Chr 34,18; 2 Kön 22,12 // 2 Chr 34,20; weiters steht שָׁפָן in 2 Chr 34,16 ohne den in der Parallelstelle 2 Kön 22,9 verwendeten סֹפֵר wie auch in 2 Kön 22,14, wozu es in 2 Chr keine direkte Parallele gibt.

(2) Dass es sich tatsächlich um Geschriebenes handelt, wird auch ausdrücklich notiert: כָּל־הַכָּתוּב (2 Kön 22,13 // 2 Chr 34,21); vgl. 2 Chr 34,24): כָּל־הָאָלוֹת הַכְּתוּבוֹת עַל־הַסֵּפֶר.[3]

(3) Während nicht gesagt wird, auf welche Weise der Hohepriester Hilkija feststellte, um welches Werk es sich bei dem gefundenen gehandelt hat, wird von Schafan berichtet, er habe das Buch gelesen (וַיִּקְרָאֵהוּ; 2 Kön 22,8).

(4) Ob der König Joschija lesen konnte, wird nicht klar, denn in 2 Kön 22,16 meint Hulda zwar, dass der König das Buch gelesen habe (קָרָא מֶלֶךְ יְהוּדָה), doch heißt es in der chronistischen Parallele – und die Formulierung macht durchaus den Eindruck einer „Korrektur" –, dass man ihm das Buch vorgelesen hat (קָרְאוּ לִפְנֵי מֶלֶךְ יְהוּדָה; 2 Chr 34,24). Dies entspricht auch dem Duktus der anderen Belege: Schafan, der Schreiber, las vor dem König das Buch (וַיִּקְרָאֵהוּ שָׁפָן לִפְנֵי הַמֶּלֶךְ [2 Kön 22,10] bzw. וַיִּקְרָא־בוֹ שָׁפָן לִפְנֵי הַמֶּלֶךְ [2 Chr 34,15]) und der König hörte (כִּשְׁמֹעַ הַמֶּלֶךְ; 2 Kön 22,11 // 2 Chr 34,19) das Gelesene bzw. reagierte auf das Gehörte.

(5) In diesem Buch stehen Worte, welche es zu erfüllen gilt (לַעֲשׂוֹת; 2 Kön 22,13 // 2 Chr 34,21).

Bei דְּבָרִים handelt es sich sowohl einerseits um schon früher *verschriftete* wie andererseits um die von Hulda *mündlich formulierten Worte* (2 Kön 22,16-20 // 2 Chr 34,24-28). In ihrer Argumentation bezieht sich Hulda auf die Worte des Buches (קָרָא מֶלֶךְ יְהוּדָה אֵת כָּל־דִּבְרֵי הַסֵּפֶר אֲשֶׁר; 2 Kön 22,16 // 2 Chr אֵת כָּל־הָאָלוֹת הַכְּתוּבוֹת עַל־הַסֵּפֶר אֲשֶׁר קָרְאוּ לִפְנֵי מֶלֶךְ יְהוּדָה; 34,24).

1.2 Niederschrift – Konservierung der תּוֹרַת יְהוָה

Bevor wir wieder auf 2 Kön 22,3-20 // 2 Chr 34,8-28 eingehen, werden Stellungnahmen gesammelt, die uns die Bedeutsamkeit und Auswirkung von niedergeschriebener Gottesweisung von anderen Seiten her beleuchten. In 1 Sam 10,25 liest man, schon Samuel habe zuerst das Regelwerk des Königtums (מִשְׁפַּט הַמְּלֻכָה) vorgetragen und dann schrieb

---

3 Das Partizipium passiv כָּתוּב ist häufig in Verbindung mit סֵפֶר belegt (vgl. Dtn 28,58.61; 29,19f.26; 30,10; Jos 8,31.34; 10,13; 23,6; 2 Sam1,18; 1 Kön 11,41; 14,19.29; 15,7.23.31; 16,5.14.20.27; 21,8f.11; 22,39.46; 2 Kön 1,18; 8,23; 10,1.6.34; 12,20; 13,8.12; 14,6.15.18.28; 15,6.11.15.21.26.31.36; 16,19; 20,20; 21,17.25; 23,3.21.24.28; 24,5; 1 Chr 9,1; 2 Chr 25,4.26; 27,7; 28,26; 34,21.24.31; 35,12.27; 36,8; Neh 12,23; Ps 40,8; Jer 25,13 und Dan 12,1); des Weiteren stehen verschiedene Formen bzw. Derivate von כתב und ספר noch im engeren Kontext in Ex 17,14; 32,32; Num 5,23; Dtn 17,18; 24,1.3; 31,24; Jos 1,8; 18,9; 24,26; 1 Sam 10,25; 2 Sam 11,14f; 2 Kön 22,13; 1 Chr 24,6; 2 Chr 16,11; 20,34; 24,27; 32,17.32; Neh 7,5; 13,1; Est 1,22; 2,23; 3,12; 8,5.9f; 9,20.32; 10,2; Ijob 19,23; 31,35; Ps 69,29; 87,6; 139,16; Jes 30,8; Jer 30,2; 32,10.12.44; 36,2.4.18.32; 45,1; 51,60 und Mal 3,16.

er (וַיִּכְתֹּב) dieses in *dem* „Buch" (בַּסֵּפֶר) – der Artikel scheint sich auf ein *besonderes* Werk zu beziehen – nieder. Dieses Niedergeschriebene hinterlegte er anschließend *vor Gott* (לִפְנֵי יְהוָה). Der Ort, an dem man die schriftliche Urkunde deponierte, bürgt für Verlässlichkeit, ist doch JHWH *selbst* der Garant dafür, und weist auf den außergewöhnlichen und zugleich verpflichtenden Charakter des Deponierten hin.

Die gewichtige Rolle *des Ortes der Hinterlegung* wird auch andernorts hervorgehoben und bezeugt die unbedingte Autorität des Niedergeschriebenen: „Nehmt diese Urkunde der Weisung (סֵפֶר הַתּוֹרָה הַזֶּה) entgegen, und legt sie neben die Lade des Bundes des Herrn, eures Gottes (מִצַּד אֲרוֹן בְּרִית־יְהוָה אֱלֹהֵיכֶם)! Dort wird sie als Zeuge gegen dich dienen (וְהָיָה־שָׁם בְּךָ לְעֵד)"; (Dtn 31,26).

Bei Missachtung der Tora JHWHs droht allerlei Übel, wie z.B. bei Jesaja steht: „Darum: Wie des Feuers Zunge die Stoppeln frisst und wie das Heu in der Flamme zusammensinkt, so soll ihre Wurzel verfaulen und ihre Blüte wie Staub aufgewirbelt werden. Denn sie haben die Weisung des Herrn der Heere von sich gewiesen (כִּי מָאֲסוּ אֵת תּוֹרַת יְהוָה צְבָאוֹת) und über das Wort des Heiligen Israels gelästert"; (Jes 5,24).

Eine vergleichbar ernste Situation hält Joschija auf Grund der Worte des im Tempel gefundenen Buches für gekommen, zerreißt zum Zeichen der Unterordnung unter Gottes Offenbarung seine Kleider und sieht den Zorn Gottes hereinbrechen, „weil unsere Väter auf die Worte dieses Buches [2 Chr 34,21: auf das Wort des Herrn] nicht gehört und weil sie nicht getan haben (לֹא־שָׁמְעוּ ... לַעֲשׂוֹת), was in ihm niedergeschrieben ist (כְּכָל־הַכָּתוּב)" (2 Kön 22,13 // 2 Chr 34,21 [אֶת־דִּבְרֵי יְהוָה לַעֲשׂוֹת] [כְּכָל־הַכָּתוּב עַל־הַסֵּפֶר הַזֶּה]).

Bevor wir uns weiter mit der Ausführung und der Erfüllung des in dem/den Wort(en) Angeordneten beschäftigen, wenden wir uns einer vorher zu klärenden Materie zu: Ist in dem Verschriften überhaupt *all* das zu finden, was man einzuhalten hat? Denn was passiert dann, wenn man das in der Schriftrolle Geschriebene durchführt, aber es anderswo auch verpflichtende Regelungen gibt, die aber nicht eingehalten werden, weil sie nicht in der Rolle stehen? Kann – nach schriftlichem Zeugnis – dieser Fall eintreffen?

1.3 Vollständigkeit der Verschriftung

Ohne hier alle möglichen Belegstellen zu behandeln, stellt sich also die Frage, ob es Hinweise darauf gibt, wonach sich die Autoren der Problematik bewusst waren, dass man auf Vollständigkeit Bedacht nehmen sollte bzw. wieweit sich die Autoren bemühten, die wichtigen Daten umfassend zu verschriften. – Die großen Schreiber – so die theologische

Überzeugung – haben *alle* Worte der göttlichen Offenbarung in dem entsprechenden Buch niedergeschrieben, wie es anhand von Mose in Dtn 31,24 dargestellt wird: „Es geschah, als Mose fertig [damit] war (כְּכַלּוֹת מֹשֶׁה), die Worte dieser Weisung (אֶת־דִּבְרֵי הַתּוֹרָה־הַזֹּאת) auf einer Buchrolle (עַל־סֵפֶר) niederzuschreiben (לִכְתֹּב), – vollständig bis zu [deren letzten Wort] (עַד תֻּמָּם), befahl er …". Das Thema der Vollständigkeit ist zentral und es zeigt sich, dass auf die Vollständigkeit der – zuerst mündlichen – Weitergabe der Worte JHWHs auch andernorts und in verschiedenen Zusammenhängen Gewicht gelegt wird.

Das kann singuläre Agenden betreffen. So teilt *Mose* bei seiner Rückkehr nach Ägypten dem Aaron, der ihm in die Wüste entgegen ging, alle Worte bzw. Taten JHWHs mit (כָּל־דִּבְרֵי יְהוָה) welche er selbst mitgeteilt bekommen hatte (Ex 4,28). Als das Volk einen König verlangte, klärte *Samuel* dieses auf über alle von Gott in dieser Causa geäußerten Worte (כָּל־דִּבְרֵי יְהוָה; 1 Sam 8,10). Ähnlich steht in Ez 11,25, dem Schlussvers der Vision (Ez 11,14-25), dass Gott nach der Exilierung sein Volk wieder in das Land zurückbringen werde und dass *Ezechiel* den Verschleppten alle Worte (כָּל־דִּבְרֵי יְהוָה) mitteilte, welche JHWH ihn sehen ließ. – Nach der Ermordung Gedaljas kam das Volk verängstigt zu Jeremia, um durch ihn von Gott jenen Weg, den das Volk in Zukunft einschlagen sollte, zu erfahren (Jer 42,1-6). Nach dem erfolgten Gotteswort (Jer 42,7-22) wird nochmals summiert, dass Jeremia „dem ganzen Volk alle Worte JHWHs, ihres Gottes, mit denen ihn JHWH zu ihnen gesandt hatte, mitteilte," und zudem, wohl um die Vollständigkeit zu bekräftigen, wird abschließend – nachhängend und auffällig – nochmals betont „alle diese Worte" (כָּל־הַדְּבָרִים הָאֵלֶּה; Jer 43,1).

Die eben dargestellten Belege stammen aus verschiedenen literarischen Bereichen, doch wird aus allen – besonders aus dem letzten – deutlich, dass die Autoren großen Nachdruck auf die Vollständigkeit der Vermittlung der göttlichen Offenbarung legen. Der Aspekt der Vollständigkeit wird deshalb hervorgehoben, weil es um die דִּבְרֵי יְהוָה, also *JHWHs mündliche,* in unterschiedlichem Zusammenhang mitgeteilte *Offenbarung* geht.

Neben eben behandelten Einzelereignissen gibt es solche, welche sich auf *die gesamte Offenbarung* und auf das ganze Volk beziehen. Sobald das Volk den Jordan überquert hatte, hatte es große Steine aufzustellen und darauf „alle Worte dieser Weisung" (כָּל־דִּבְרֵי הַתּוֹרָה הַזֹּאת) zu schreiben (Dtn 27,3). „JHWH wird die Schläge, die er dir und deinen Nachkommen versetzt, über alles Gewohnte hinaus steigern zu gewaltigen und hartnäckigen Schlägen, zu schlimmen und hartnäckigen Krankheiten", steht bei Nichterfüllung als Drohung in Dtn 28,59. Diese Auswirkungen werden durch das Fehlverhalten verursacht, welches darin besteht, dass das Volk nicht darauf achtet (אִם־לֹא תִשְׁמֹר), alle Worte der Weisung (אֶת־כָּל־דִּבְרֵי הַתּוֹרָה) – eine andere Umschreibung der gesamten Offenbarung – durchzuführen (לַעֲשׂוֹת; Dtn 28,58). In Ex 24,3 steht, dass Mose dem Volk alle Worte JHWHs auflistete (וַיְסַפֵּר לָעָם אֵת כָּל־דִּבְרֵי יְהוָה) und dann alle diese JHWH-Worte (אֵת כָּל־דִּבְרֵי יְהוָה; Ex 24,4) nieder schrieb. Das Volk bekräftigte in diesem Zusammenhang, „alle Worte (כָּל־הַדְּבָרִים), welche JHWH der Herr gesagt hat (אֲשֶׁר־דִּבֶּר יְהוָה), werden wir tun (נַעֲשֶׂה)" (Ex 24,3). Die häufigen Wiederholungen wirken nahezu überbordend, lassen aber die Stichworte und zugleich Programme „כֹּל – דְּבָרִים – יהוה", also *Gesamtheit / alle – Worte / Offenbarung – JHWH* plakativ in den Mittelpunkt treten. Wie schon in Dtn 28,58 liegt ein weiterer Akzent auf der Zusage, der Offenbarung zu *entsprechen* bzw. die Offenbarung *durchzuführen*: עשה. Die *Erfüllung* bzw. *Durchführung* stellt demnach eine zentrale Forderung dar.

1.4 Die konkrete Durchführung der Worte JHWHs

Mose teilte dem Volk, „alle diese Worte (כָּל־הַדְּבָרִים הָאֵלֶּה), die JHWH aufgetragen hatte" (Ex 19,7), mit. Daraufhin erklärte sich das Volk ausdrücklich einverstanden und stimmte zu: „Alles (כֹּל), was JHWH gesagt hat, werden wir *tun*" (נַעֲשֶׂה; Ex 19,7). – Die *Durchführung* wird also zum großen Thema. Dies gilt einerseits – wie in der vorher zitierten Stelle – für eben erst „frisch" verkündete Worte, wie auch für die Reaktion auf die Verlesung schon verschrifteten Materials. Mose nimmt die Bundesurkunde (סֵפֶר הַבְּרִית; Ex 24,7), liest sie vor und das hörende Volk antwortet: „Alles (כֹּל), was der Herr gesagt hat, werden wir tun und wir werden gehorsam sein" (נַעֲשֶׂה וְנִשְׁמָע; Ex 24,7). – Das Tun ist demnach keine äußerliche Erfüllung, sondern ein Zeichen des Gehorsams gegenüber dem JHWH-Wort (vgl. Neh 9,29) und weist auf dessen *verbindlichen* und *bindenden* Charakter hin.

1.5 Die konkrete Durchführung der Worte der Tora

Bisher haben wir uns mit den *Worten JHWHs* beschäftigt. Häufiger als auf Worte JHWHs trifft man auf alle Worte der Tora (כָּל־דִּבְרֵי הַתּוֹרָה), wobei auffällt, dass der erste Beleg erst in Dtn 17,19 steht. Man erfährt, dass die Worte der Tora – mitunter unter dem Hinweis auf ein Buch – *geschrieben* (כתב; Dtn 27,3.8; 31,24; vgl. Jos 24,26), *vorgelesen* (קרא; Jos 8,34; vgl. Neh 8,18) oder zur *Geltung gebracht* (קום; Dtn 27,26; 2 Kön 23,24) werden und man sie *hören* (שמע; 2 Kön 23,24; 2 Ch 34,19; Neh 8,9) und *kennen lernen* (שׂכל hi.; Neh 8,13) kann. Daneben wird – vor allem im Deuteronomium – betont, dass man die Worte der Tora auch *zu beachten* (שמר; Dtn 17,19 und שִׂים לֵבָב; Dtn 32,46) und *durchzuführen*[4] (עשׂה) hat: לַעֲשׂוֹת אֶת־כָּל־דִּבְרֵי הַתּוֹרָה הַזֹּאת (Dtn 29,28; vgl. 27,26; 28,58; 31,12). Unter diesem Gesichtspunkt stehen demnach die Worte JHWHs und die Worte der Tora auf der gleichen Ebene.

1.6 Versagen in der Praxis

Im folgenden Abschnitt sehen wir, dass sich in der Praxis nach und nach negative Erscheinungen ergeben haben. Wir greifen auf die oben genannten Ausgangstexte zurück, da König Joschija nach der „Lektüre" zerknirscht bekennt, dass der Istzustand gemessen an dem schriftlich Geforderten falsch ist, woraufhin nur Schrecklichstes zu erwarten sei. Während man oft von der „guten alten Zeit" spricht,[5] sieht man im folgenden Beispiel, dass gerade die Vorfahren keineswegs so gelebt haben, wie es Gott gewollt hat. – Die Überlieferung und die in ihr greifbaren Textveränderungen zeigen, dass es zu Abnützungserscheinungen gekommen war, sodass Präzisierungen und Klarstellung vorgenommen und neue Aufgaben hinzugefügt werden mussten.

Oben wurde schon hervorgehoben, dass Sanktionen zu erwarten sind, wenn man nicht das, was Gott aufträgt, tut (vgl. Jer 42,5). Zudem können die negativen Auswirkungen des Fehlverhaltens über Generationen hinweg nachwirken; vgl. 2 Chr 34,21. Wenn die eigenen Vorfahren (אֲבוֹתֵינוּ) die im einschlägigen Buch (עַל־הַסֵּפֶר הַזֶּה) schon schriftlich (כָּתוּב) niedergelegten Worte (דִּבְרֵי הַסֵּפֶר) nicht eingehalten hatten und sich aber auch nicht vom falschen Weg abbringen ließen, dann muss damit gerechnet werden, dass Sanktionen – diese werden mit dem Stichwort „Zorn" formuliert – folgen werden. Wenn aber eine grundle-

---

4   Vgl. auch die Hinweise auf die konkrete Umsetzung in Jos 1,7f; 22,5; 23,6; 1 Kön 2,3; 2 Kön 17,34.37; 21,8; 2 Chr 14,3; 33,8; Ezra 7,10; Neh 9,34; 10,30.

5   Das „goldene Zeitalter" stand schon in der Antike am Anfang und dann gab es eine beständige Abwärtsentwicklung; vgl. die Ausführungen in Wikipaedia unter dem Stichwort: „Goldenes Zeitalter (altgriechisch χρύσεον γένος *chrýseon génos* ‚Goldenes Geschlecht', lateinisch *aurea aetas* oder *aurea saecula* ‚Goldenes Zeitalter') ist ein Begriff aus der antiken Mythologie. Er bezeichnet eine als Idealzustand betrachtete friedliche Urphase der Menschheitsgeschichte vor der Entstehung der Zivilisation. Dem griechischen, von den Römern übernommenen Mythos zufolge waren die sozialen Verhältnisse damals optimal und die Menschen hervorragend in ihre natürliche Umwelt eingebettet. Kriege, Verbrechen und Laster waren unbekannt, die bescheidenen Lebensbedürfnisse wurden von der Natur gedeckt. Im Verlauf der folgenden Zeitalter trat jedoch ein moralischer Verfall ein, Macht- und Besitzgier kamen auf und die Lebensbedingungen verschlechterten sich drastisch. In der Gegenwart (der Lebenszeit des Mythenerzählers) hat diese Entwicklung einen Tiefstand erreicht. Manche römischen Autoren verkündeten aber den Anbruch einer neuen Epoche des Friedens und der Eintracht als Erneuerung des Goldenen Zeitalters."

gende Korrektur vorgenommen wird, d.h. eine grundlegende Änderung zum Guten eintritt, dann tut sich ein Ausweg auf. Voraussetzung für eine gute Entwicklung ist ein echter und zugleich richtiger Neubeginn, wie folgendes Beispiel zeigt: „Der König trat an seinen Platz, er schloss vor JHWH einen Bund (הַבְּרִית לִפְנֵי יְהוָה): Er wolle dem Herrn folgen, auf seine Gebote, Satzungen und Gesetze (מִצְוֹתָיו וְעֵדְוֹתָיו וְחֻקָּיו) von ganzem Herzen und ganzer Seele achten und die Vorschriften des Bundes (דִּבְרֵי הַבְּרִית) durchführen (לַעֲשׂוֹת), die in diesem Buch niedergeschrieben sind (הַכְּתוּבִים עַל־הַסֵּפֶר הַזֶּה)" (2 Chr 34,31).[6]

Eine gerade für unsere Untersuchung bedeutsame Abweichung in 2 Chr ist hervorzuheben. In 2 Kön 23,3 steht לְהָקִים [אֶת־דִּבְרֵי הַבְּרִית הַזֹּאת] הַכְּתֻבִים עַל־הַסֵּפֶר הַזֶּה gegenüber 2 Chr 34,31 לַעֲשׂוֹת [אֶת־דִּבְרֵי הַבְּרִית] הַכְּתוּבִים עַל־הַסֵּפֶר הַזֶּה; (2 Chr 34,31). Während in 2 Kön 23,3 herausgestellt wird, dass der Bund formal installiert wird, legt der spätere Text von 2 Chr 34,31 gerade auf die Konkretion Gewicht. Die Differenz ist wohl das Ergebnis der zwischenzeitlichen Erfahrung mit dem Scheitern: Die besten Regeln und Vorsätze nützen nichts, wenn sie zwar theoretisch gelten, aber nicht praktiziert werden. Derartige Beobachtungen weisen darauf hin, dass die Praxis immer mehr und mehr in Schräglage geraten ist, woraus erklärlich wird, warum im Laufe der Zeit immer größeres Gewicht auf die *Durchführung*, auf die *Praxis* gelegt wird.

1.7 Erweiterungs- und Reduktionsverbot

Nun mag man die Frage stellen, ob der verbindliche Charakter am konkreten Buchstabenbestand haftet oder ob es um einen verpflichtenden Charakter des Intendierten geht, sodass der Wortbestand selbst weniger ausschlaggebend ist. Sira schrieb sein Werk um die Wende vom dritten zum zweiten vorchristlichen Jahrhundert und hatte sich vorher, so schreibt der Enkel, beste Kenntnis des TaNaK (0,8-10) angeeignet. Bei diesem Bibelstudium hat er ja auch über jene Texte nachgedacht, welche oben behandelt worden sind. Was hat also Sira im Rahmen der Autorität und der Verbindlichkeit des Geoffenbarten beeindruckt und wie hat er diese Fundstellen interpretiert?

Zum einen kann man auf die bisherigen Ausführungen zurückverweisen, doch dann stellt sich die Frage, warum er bei den Themen,

---

6 In 2 Kön 23,3 stand ja schon der Paralleltext und dieser ist weitgehend identisch und die nachfolgen angegebenen Differenzen sind nicht schwerwiegend. Die Belege aus 2 Kön 23,3 stehen an erster und jene aus 2 Chr 34,31 an zweiter Stelle: מִזְוֹתָיו / אַחֲרֵי / אַחַר; / הַבְּרִית הַזֹּאת / נַפְשׁוֹ / נֶפֶשׁ ;לְבָבוֹ / לֵב ;וְחֻקֹּתָיו / וְחֻקָּיו ;וְאֶת־חֻקָּיו תָיו / וְעֵדְוֹתָיו ;אֶת־עֵדְוֹתָיו ;אֶת־מִצְוֹתָיו / הַבְּרִית.

die auch im TaNaK vorkommen, seine „Bibel" nie ausführlicher zitiert hat. Das wäre ja nicht ungewöhnlich gewesen, wie folgende Belege zeigen. Im gegen Jeremia aufbrandenden Aufruhr mahnen „einige von den Ältesten des Landes (זִקְנֵי הָאָרֶץ)" (Jer 26,17) zur Besinnung und verweisen auf den seinerzeitigen Umgang mit Micha von Moreschet, der mit Jeremia vergleichbar gegen Jerusalem gewettert und den Untergang angesagt hatte. Belegt wird dieser Mahnruf mit einem Zitat, das wörtlich von Mi 3,12 übernommen wurde.[7] Tobit erinnert sich an Amos und zitiert ihn, weicht jedoch leicht von Am 8,10[8] ab (Tob 2,6); in Tob 14,4 wird entweder auf die Untergangsankündigung für Ninive durch Jona (G I) oder Nahum (G II) verwiesen, ohne dass ein wörtliches Zitat angeführt wird. In der Praxis hat man also einen mit einer biblischen Persönlichkeit untermauerten *inhaltlichen Hinweis*, ein bei der Übernahme *leicht verändertes Zitat* und ein *wort-wörtliches Zitat* vor sich. Sind diese Angaben unterschiedlich verbindlich? – Wo findet man eine klärende Entscheidung?

Zur Beantwortung der aufgeworfenen Frage wenden wir uns an folgende Belege:

Dtn 4,2:

לֹא תֹסִפוּ עַל־הַדָּבָר אֲשֶׁר אָנֹכִי מְצַוֶּה אֶתְכֶם
וְלֹא תִגְרְעוּ מִמֶּנּוּ לִשְׁמֹר אֶת־מִצְוֹת יְהוָה אֱלֹהֵיכֶם אֲשֶׁר אָנֹכִי מְצַוֶּה אֶתְכֶם

Dtn 13,1:[9]

אֵת כָּל־הַדָּבָר אֲשֶׁר אָנֹכִי מְצַוֶּה אֶתְכֶם אֹתוֹ תִשְׁמְרוּ לַעֲשׂוֹת לֹא־תֹסֵף עָלָיו וְלֹא תִגְרַע מִמֶּנּוּ

Klar ist, dass nichts hinzugefügt und nichts weggenommen werden darf (לֹא תֹסִפוּ und לֹא־תֹסֵף bzw. וְלֹא תִגְרְעוּ und תִגְרַע מִמֶּנּוּ וְלֹא). Aber wovon darf nichts weggenommen werden? Es ist das *Wort*, das Mose aufgetragen hat (כָּל־הַדָּבָר אֲשֶׁר אָנֹכִי מְצַוֶּה und הַדָּבָר אֲשֶׁר אָנֹכִי מְצַוֶּה). Die Verwendung des Artikels und der kollektive Singular הַדָּבָר betonen einerseits die Bedeutsamkeit und andererseits die Breite des Gemeinten. Das *Wort* ist wohl gleich zu setzen mit Offenbarung. An dieser Stelle wird *nicht ausdrücklich* darauf hingewiesen, dass diese Worte auch verschriftet worden sind, was man häufig unwillkürlich in den Text legt. Vielmehr konzentriert sich der Autor auf das Ziel des Auftrages: Die Worte sind samt und sonders, ganz und gar *zu beachten* (לִשְׁמֹר) bzw. zu beachten, um sie *durchzuführen* (תִשְׁמְרוּ לַעֲשׂוֹת). Auf diesen le-

---

[7] Die identischen Worte sind צִיּוֹן שָׂדֶה תֵחָרֵשׁ וִירוּשָׁלַיִם עִיִּים תִּהְיֶה וְהַר הַבַּיִת לְבָמוֹת יָעַר („Zion wird umgepflügt zu Ackerland, Jerusalem wird zum Trümmerhaufen, der Tempelberg zur waldigen Höhe.").
[8] Vgl. ausführlich REITERER, Tobit 1.2.
[9] Vgl. die Aktualisierung der Gegenüberstellung in Offb 22,18-19.

benspraktischen Aspekt legt auch Ps 78 Wert, wenn er schreibt, dass die Vorfahren zentrale Inhalte als *erzähltes* Gut weitersagen[10] (Ps 78,3-6), und Gewicht darauf gelegt wird, dass die Ereignisse mit Gott regelmäßig und immer wieder *weitererzählt* werden. Die immer wieder neu erzählte Geschichte hat ein pädagogisches und ethisches Ziel: Die kommende Generation soll „nicht werden wie ihre Väter, jenes Geschlecht voll Trotz und Empörung, das wankelmütige Geschlecht, dessen Geist nicht treu zu Gott hielt" (Ps 78,9), sondern aus den historischen Fakten belehrt sich nach Gott ausrichten.

Wenn die Gottes- bzw. Toraworte so bedeutsam sind, dann ist die Frage aufzuwerfen, wie denn die Kenntnis erhalten bleibt. Es ist unausweichlich, dass sich eine Tradition der Weitergabe entwickelt, um das Vergessen zu verhindern. Wie wird die Kenntnis in den aufeinander folgenden, d.h. immer späteren Generationen, erhalten?

1.8 Weitergabe und Aneignung der Gottes- bzw. Tora-Worte

Wo bekommen das Volk und vor allem diejenigen, die das Volk belehren, ihre Informationen her, sodass es gewährleistet ist, dass das Richtige auch weiter gesagt wird?

Mose, so wird der Eindruck vermittelt, tut sich ja leicht, weil er direkt von Gott die Regeln und Offenbarungen empfängt. Als sein Schwiegervater beobachtet, dass sich Mose in den Leitungs- und Entscheidungsfunktionen aufreibt und sich zu überarbeiten droht, wendet er sich mit einem Ratschlag seinem Schwiegersohn zu: „Nun höre (שְׁמַע), ich gebe dir einen Rat (אִיעָצְךָ), und Gott wird mit dir sein. Vertritt du das Volk vor Gott! Du wirst ihre Reden (אֶת־הַדְּבָרִים) vor Gott bringen, du wirst ihnen die Gesetze (אֶת־הַחֻקִּים) und Weisungen (וְאֶת־הַתּוֹרֹת) einschärfen (וְהִזְהַרְתָּה), du wirst ihnen den Lebensweg (אֶת־הַדֶּרֶךְ) zur Kenntnis bringen (וְהוֹדַעְתָּ), auf dem sie sich bewegen (יֵלְכוּ בָהּ), und die Handlung (וְאֶת־הַמַּעֲשֶׂה), die sie ausführen sollen (יַעֲשׂוּן);" (Ex 18,19f). Entsprechend diesem Rat wird das Volk durch die *konkrete Belehrung* in die Lage versetzt, selbst die Grundlagen zu kennen, nach denen es zu leben hat. Die Offenbarung ist keine Geheimbotschaft, es gibt keine Arkandisziplin. Ein zusätzlicher Lehrer neben Mose wird vorerst nicht erwähnt. Aber was ist bzw. was wird sein, wenn das Volk vergesslich ist oder wenn einfach die Zeit fort schreitet und die erste bzw. die ersten Generationen, die noch Augenzeugen gewesen sind, verstorben sind? Dann kann man auf das im „Gesetz des Mose" Niedergeschrie-

---

10 Vgl. unter anderem Ex 13,8: „Du wirst deinem Sohn [gewiss] sagen / וְהִגַּדְתָּ לְבִנְךָ בַּיּוֹם הַהוּא" und Ex 13,14; Dtn 6,20-21; Jos 4,6-7 und 4,21-22. Vgl. REITERER, Elders.

bene verweisen (vgl. die Belege für כתב und ספר) unter der Voraussetzung, dass alle lesen können und sich auch regelmäßig damit beschäftigen. Da das offensichtlich in der Praxis nicht der Fall gewesen ist (vgl. den kommenden Abschnitt), liest man die erinnernden Mahnungen, das Geoffenbarte im Gedächtnis zu behalten.

Aber die Frage ist noch offen, wie die Lehrer der Offenbarung in der späteren Zeit Kenntnis von den überlieferten Grundlagen erhielten und was sie mit dem, was sie eruiert hatten, tun. Dafür bietet Esra 7,10 eine instruktive Information: „Esra war von ganzem Herzen (לְבָבוֹ) darauf aus (הֵכִין), das Gesetz des Herrn (אֶת־תּוֹרַת יְהוָה) zu erforschen (לִדְרוֹשׁ) und danach zu handeln (וְלַעֲשֹׂת) und es als Satzung (חֹק) und Recht (וּמִשְׁפָּט) in Israel zu lehren (לְלַמֵּד)." Vier Ebenen werden hier aufgezählt, welche zur Tradierung der JHWH-Offenbarung nötig sind. Esra ist ein lebendes Beispiel dafür:

(1) כון לבב: *das Herz festigen*, die ganze Persönlichkeit mit allen Anlagen und Fertigkeiten ist gefordert,

(2) דרש: *forschen, erforschen*, in Wortlaut und Intention eindringen und durchdringen,

(3) עשה: *durchführen, machen*, vermutlich als lebendiges „Anschauungsmaterial" danach leben,

(4) למד: *unterrichten* und die anderen *lehren*, sodass auch die Textkenntnis vermittelt wird.

Nun ist darauf hinzuweisen, dass sich Esra als ein direkter Nachfahre Aarons versteht (Esra 7,1f), in dessen Geschlechterliste eine so bekannte Gestalt wie Pinhas geführt wird. Daher spielt der soziale Stand als *Priester* eine besondere Rolle. Von dieser Stelle ausgehend wird man daher die genannten vier „Säulen" des Umganges notieren, jedoch *nicht* den Schluss ziehen, das sei ein Programm für jeden Israeliten. Das persönliche Engagement, die Erforschung und die Lehrtätigkeit sind Spezifika der Priester, die Einhaltung und die Umsetzung, das wurde schon in den früheren Schritten herausgestellt, wird jedoch von jedem JHWH-Gläubigen erwartet und auch eingefordert.

1.9 *Volksbildung*: Vortrag – Erklärung – Sanktionsdrohung

Bisher wurden einige Belege (Ex 24,3-4; 1 Sam 10,25) angeführt, denen zufolge Worte der Offenbarung öffentlich vorgetragen und dann verschriftet worden sind. – Jetzt geht es um die weitere Fragestellung: Wie erfuhr das Volk, wenn es nicht direkt Zeuge ist bzw. wenn die Offenbarung schon vor Generationen ergangen war, von dem zuvor Niedergeschriebenen? Einst lehrte Mose die Israeliten (וַיִּכְתֹּב מֹשֶׁה ... וַיְלַמְּדָהּ אֶת־בְּנֵי יִשְׂרָאֵל; Dtn 31,22). Was oben für die Verschriftung festgehalten wurde, gilt jetzt auch für den mündlichen Vortrag, dass auf die Vollständigkeit des Gesagten Wert zu legen ist (vgl. וַיְדַבֵּר ... עַד תֻּמָּם; Dtn 31,30).

Lange „nach Mose" richtete das Volk die Bitte an den Schreiber Esra, das Gesetzbuch zu holen[11] (וַיֹּאמְרוּ לְעֶזְרָא הַסֹּפֵר לְהָבִיא אֶת־סֵפֶר תּוֹרַת מֹשֶׁה; Neh 8,1). Dieses Buch wird dann in Abschnitten laut vorgelesen und mit verständlichen Erläuterungen versehen (וְשׂוֹם שֶׂכֶל; Neh 8,8). Im Unterschied zur pluralisch formulierten hebräischen Version konzentriert sich die LXX nur auf Esra als Lehrer (ἐδίδασκεν Εσδρας). Zu notieren ist vor allem, dass über den hebräischen Text hinausgehend angefügt wird, dass sich auch Esra selbst um das Verständnis Gottes bemüht hatte (καὶ διέστελλεν ἐν ἐπιστήμῃ κυρίου). So wird hervorgehoben, dass Esra, der das Volk (λαός) unterrichtet, selbst auf eine vertiefte Kenntnis und Einsicht verweisen kann. Zwar begegnet man in Neh 8 ungewöhnlich häufig dem Substantiv כֹּל (8,1ff.5f.9.11f), doch bezieht es sich nie auf das Gesetz. Daher kann man an dieser Stelle auch nicht ausdrücklich nachweisen, dass in betonter Form das *ganze* Gesetz mitgeteilt wurde. Die Gesetzesunterweisung erfolgt aber für das *ganze Volk*. Da viele Akteure bei der Erklärung mitwirkten und die Aktion den ganzen Tag in Anspruch nahm (vgl. Neh 8,4.7), kann man annehmen, dass eine umfangreiche Textmenge bearbeitet wurde.

Wohl weniger aus religiösem Förderungsinteresse, als aus politischem Kalkül wird König Artaxerxes aufgetragen haben, dass Esra jenen, die das Gesetz nicht kennen, ebendieses zu lehren hat (וְדִי לָא יָדַע תְּהוֹדְעוּן; Esra 7,25). Man weiß, dass es eine lange Tradition gibt, nach der in Israels Umwelt wichtige Verträge im Tempel so angebracht worden sind, dass man sie immer „vor Augen" hatte. Auszuschließen ist nicht, dass das Buch auch im Tempelbereich aufbewahrt wurde, bevor der Priester Esra das geschriebene Gesetz wegen der großen Menge von Leuten im Freien vortrug. Wenn man eine Analogie zu den offiziell politisch verbindlichen Texten herstellen darf, dann kann man von jenen lernen, dass diese, die sich nicht an die Verordnungen halten, harte Sanktionen[12] erwarten. Gleich sind auch die Drohungen durch Artaxerxes: „Doch über jeden, der das Gesetz deines Gottes (דָּתָא דִי־אֱלָהָךְ) und das Gesetz des Königs (וְדָתָא דִי מַלְכָּא) nicht befolgt, halte man streng Gericht und verurteile ihn je nachdem zum Tod (הֵן לְמוֹת), zum Ausschluss (aus der Gemeinde) (הֵן לִשְׁרֹשִׁי)[13], zu einer Geldstrafe oder zu Gefängnis (הֵן־לַעֲנָשׁ נִכְסִין וְלֶאֱסוּרִין)!" (Esra 7,26). Die Durchsetzung dieser

---

11 Zur Aufbewahrung der Gesetzesniederschrift vgl. 1.2.
12 Vgl. oben 1.6.
13 So Qre', geschrieben steht jedoch הֵן לִשְׁרֹשִׁי; שְׁרֹשׁ im Sinne von „Entwurzelung, Expatriierung" (GESENIUS, HAHW, ¹⁷1962, 929; DONNER, HAHW, 2010, 1543).

drakonischen Strafen fordert der persisch-weltliche König hinsichtlich der Befolgung der Gesetze in der Offenbarung!

1.10 Die Lebenszusage

Der verpflichtende Aspekt der Gottesgebote wird vor allem häufig in der theologischen Argumentation betont, strebt jedoch praktische Ziele an und ist vor allem nicht Selbstzweck. Die Stellung Israels zu den Gottesgeboten kann zu zwei konträren Konsequenzen führen, einer negativen und einer positiven:

Zum einen wird ähnlich wie in den Vertragstexten der Umwelt bei Nichtbeachtung Strafe angedroht. Auffällig ist dabei, dass festgehalten wird, dass Israel seit eh und je und auch noch kontemporär zum biblischen Autor die Gebote JHWHs ignoriert,[14] sodass Gott gar nichts Anderes übrig blieb, als gegen sein Volk vorzugehen (vgl. 2 Kön 17,34-41).[15] Vor allem die Verschleppung ins Exil und die Fremdherrscher im zugesagten Land sind das Ergebnis der fehlenden Bereitschaft, das zu tun, was Gott will (Neh 9,29-37; Jer 32,23).

Zum anderen heißt es, dass Israel auf die Gebotserfüllung hin bei seinen Tätigkeiten Erfolge haben werde (vgl. z.B. „damit du bei allem, was du tust [אֵת כָּל־אֲשֶׁר תַּעֲשֶׂה], und in allem, was du unternimmst, Erfolg haben wirst [תַּשְׂכִּיל];" [1 Kön 2,3])[16]

Beide Wege haben warnend oder unterstützend ein Ziel vor Augen, das geradezu klassisch mit folgendem Zitat zusammengefasst werden

---

14 „Bis zum heutigen Tag (עַד הַיּוֹם הַזֶּה) handeln sie nach ihren früheren Bräuchen. Sie fürchten den Herrn nicht und halten sich nicht an die Satzungen und Bräuche, an das Gesetz und die Gebote (וְאֵינָם עֹשִׂים כְּחֻקֹּתָם וּכְמִשְׁפָּטָם וְכַתּוֹרָה וְכַמִּצְוָה), auf die der Herr die Nachkommen Jakobs, dem er den Namen Israel gegeben hatte, verpflichtet hat (צִוָּה יְהוָה)" (2 Kön 17,34). „Unsere Könige (מְלָכֵינוּ), Vorsteher (שָׂרֵינוּ) und Priester (כֹּהֲנֵינוּ) und unsere Väter (וַאֲבֹתֵינוּ) befolgten dein Gesetz nicht (לֹא עָשׂוּ תּוֹרָתֶךָ); sie missachteten deine Gebote und die Warnungen, die du an sie gerichtet hast. Sie lebten in ihrem eigenen Königreich, in der Fülle des Reichtums, den du ihnen gewährt hast, in dem weiten, fruchtbaren Land, das du vor sie hingebreitet hast; sie aber haben dir trotzdem nicht gedient und sich nicht von ihrem bösen Treiben abgewandt. Darum sind wir heute Knechte (הִנֵּה אֲנַחְנוּ הַיּוֹם עֲבָדִים). Du hast unseren Vätern dieses Land gegeben, damit sie seine Früchte und seinen Reichtum genießen; wir aber leben darin als Knechte (הִנֵּה אֲנַחְנוּ עֲבָדִים עָלֶיהָ)" (Neh 9,34-36).
15 Vgl. „…. Ahab ging Elija entgegen. Sobald er ihn sah, rief er aus: Bist du es, Verderber Israels? Elija entgegnete: Nicht ich habe Israel ins Verderben gestürzt, sondern du und das Haus deines Vaters, weil ihr die Gebote des Herrn (מִצְוֹת יְהוָה) übertreten habt und den Baalen nachgelaufen seid" (1 Kön 18,16-18).
16 Vgl. „Über dieses Gesetzbuch sollst du immer reden und Tag und Nacht darüber nachsinnen, damit du darauf achtest, so zu handeln (לְמַעַן תִּשְׁמֹר לַעֲשׂוֹת), wie darin geschrieben steht. Dann wirst du auf deinem Weg Glück und Erfolg haben"; (כִּי־אָז תַּצְלִיחַ אֶת־דְּרָכֶךָ וְאָז תַּשְׂכִּיל; Jos 1,8).

kann: „Der Mensch wird [gewiss] durch sie[17] leben (אָדָם] וְחָיָה בָהֶם]; Neh 9,29)". Es geht also um Leben, Lebenserhaltung und Intensivierung des Lebens. Auf dieser Basis wird später Sira die Wortverbindung תורת חיים prägen.[18] Der Weisheitslehrer fasst mit dieser Phrase zusammen, worauf weisheitliches Leben ausgerichtet ist, wobei er neue, *universale* Gesichtspunkte herausstellt: Gottes Offenbarung führt für alle, also nicht nur für die Israeliten, zum Leben. Dieses wird deshalb möglich, weil Sira in seiner Rede von der Offenbarung die Tora sowie die Einzelvorschriften mit einbezieht und *zudem darüber hinaus geht*, sodass auch übrige Schriften wie die weisheitliche Lehre, aber auch einfache Beobachtungen, z.B. in der Schöpfung relevant werden, denn auch dort begegnet man dem Gotteswillen bzw. der Planung Gottes.[19]

1.11 Zwischensumme

– Basis für die Überlegungen, wie sich inneralttestamentlich die Autorität der Bibel darstellt, bildet jene Buchsammlung, welche man mehr oder weniger unscharf als *Altes Testament / Alter Bund* bezeichnet; vgl. 2 Kor 3,14: κάλυμμα ἐπὶ τῇ ἀναγνώσει τῆς παλαιᾶς διαθήκης; Vulgata: velamen in lectione veteris testamenti.

– Vielfach ist belegbar, dass es sich um Mitteilungen JHWHs und nicht um Menschenwort handelt. Unterschiedlich sind die Bereiche und Bezeichnungen: es kann sich um das *Wort JHWHs* und um die *Tora JHWHs* handeln.

– Die oben untersuchten Belege stammen aus allen verschiedenen Bereichen des TaNaK. Es ist jedoch auch hervorzuheben, dass in vorsirazidischer Zeit noch keine blockweise Zusammenstellung in verschiedene Buchgruppen, wie z.B. *Propheten*, belegt werden kann.

– Neben der Schriftlichkeit wird darauf Wert gelegt, dass alles, was JHWH mitgeteilt hat, auch tatsächlich weitergegeben und dann auch aufgeschrieben worden ist.

– Nicht nur die Vollständigkeit, sondern auch die Korrektheit der Erhaltung wird betont. Dies äußert sich darin, dass es keine nachträgliche Veränderung geben darf.

– Der Wert der Niederschrift wird auch dadurch hervorgehoben, dass sie in der Nähe Gottes hinterlegt wird.

– Das von Gott Geoffenbarte darf nicht in Vergessenheit geraten. Daher gibt es unterschiedliche Anhaltspunkte und Anregungen, dass

---

17 „Sie" bezieht sich allgemein auf das Gesetz, wie auch auf die Einzelvorschriften.
18 Vgl. den Beitrag REITERER, Akzente; MARBÖCK, hat diese Erkenntnis übernommen „als Eigenprägung Siras ..." (Jesus, 216); vgl. WITTE, ,Kanon', 245-246.
19 Vgl. REITERER, Alles, 121-133.

die „lehrmäßige" Weitergabe regelmäßig zu erfolgen hat. Ebenso wird das „Wie" der Verkündigung und Lehre thematisiert.

– Im Konvolut der verschrifteten Offenbarung finden sich Belege, die festhalten, dass das Ergehen des Volkes von der Erfüllung der schriftlich vorliegenden Worte abhängt. Diese Thematik wird breit ausgefaltet. Es geht wesentlich darum, wie das Leben infolge des von Gott Geoffenbarten geführt wird. Die Lebenspraxis ist entscheidend, ja das Leben an sich und die Lebenserhaltung werden zum Offenbarungsziel.

– Die Erhaltung des Wissens und des Gewichtes des früher Geoffenbarten wird ausdrücklich eingeschärft.

– Wenn sich Autoren auf konkrete ältere Passagen beziehen, kann das auf verschiedene Art geschehen:
- Es kann ein direktes Zitat angeführt werden.[20]
- Es kann eine teilweise wörtliche, teilweise veränderte Zitation erfolgen.
- Es kann ohne ausdrückliches Zitat inhaltlich auf eine nachweislich früher belegbare Aussage verwiesen werden.

Daraus ergibt sich, dass sich die Schriftautorität innerhalb des Sira vorliegenden Buchbestandes relativ gut beschreiben lässt. Auffällig ist, dass die Praxis, d.h. die Umsetzung des Verschrifteten, eine hervorgehobene Rolle spielt. Die Konkretisierung der Offenbarung ist gefordert.

2. Ben Siras Umgang mit seiner biblischen Tradition

Um Sira richtig zu verstehen, ist die Vorfrage zu beantworten, welche Rolle für Sira die „Bibel" spielt. – Von zwei Seiten kann man dafür Informationen erwarten: einerseits von Sira selbst und andererseits vom Enkel, der sich ausdrücklich mit dieser Thematik beschäftigt.

2.1 Ben Sira

Da es keinen Abschnitt im sirazidischen Werk gibt, in welchem er Bibelautorität ausdrücklich thematisiert, muss man die Anspielungen analysieren und diese sind informativ. Als Ausgangspunkt greifen wir 38,34-39,1 heraus,[21] wofür es keinen hebräischen, wohl aber einen grie-

---

20 Wenn jemand die Schriften des TaNaK in späterer Zeit als Autorität ansieht, zitiert er wörtlich, wie z.B. καθὼς γέγραπται ἐν τῷ Ἠσαΐᾳ τῷ προφήτῃ· [ἰδοὺ ἀποστέλλω τὸν ἄγγελόν μου πρὸ προσώπου σου, ὃς κατασκευάσει τὴν ὁδόν σου] (Mk 1,2).

21 WITTE, ‚Kanon', 238, sieht „einen im Rahmen der biblischen Literatur einmaligen Lobpreis des weisen Schreibers" und verweist in der Fußnote darauf, dass sich „umfangreiche Parallelen ... im ägyptischen Bereich (finden), vgl. z.B. die aus der Zeit

chischen und einen syrischen Text gibt. Zur folgenden deutschen Übersetzung ist eine Notiz anzubringen: Da die Partizipien von 38,34c.d erst im Verb von 39,1a.b aufgelöst werden, und gerade die verbale Glättung, wenn man die Partizipien in einen vollen Satz auflöst, infolge der Übersetzung eine Akzentverlagerung bei 38,34c.d zur Folge hat, wird die für unsere Fragestellung gewichtige Stelle unter Beibehaltung der im Griechischen[22] vorliegenden Eigenheiten verdeutscht:

38,34c „Nur der sein Leben (τὴν ψυχὴν αὐτοῦ) Hingebende
     d und im Rahmen des Gesetzes des Höchsten (ἐν νόμῳ ὑψίστου) Denkende (διανοουμένου)
39,1 a wird die Weisheit (σοφίαν) aller Alten durchforschen (ἐκζητήσει)
    b und sich innerhalb der Prophetien (ἐν προφητείαις) beschäftigen.
39,2 a Die Erörterungen (διήγησιν) der berühmten Männer wird er einhalten (συντηρήσει)
    b und in die Strophen (ἐν στροφαῖς) der Sinnsprüche (παραβολῶν) wird er eindringen,
39,3 a das Hintergründige (ἀπόκρυφα) der Sprichworte (παροιμιῶν) wird er durchforschen (ἐκζητήσει)
    b und in den dunklen Reden (ἐν αἰνίγμασιν) der Sprichworte (παροιμιῶν) wird er sich bewegen."

Wer sich also ganz und gar engagiert (τὴν ψυχὴν αὐτοῦ; *sein Leben*) einsetzt und wer sich bei seinem Nachsinnen im Rahmen des Gesetzes des Höchsten bewegt, der *wird*[23] die Prophetien und die unterschiedlichen Ebenen der mit Hintersinn ausgestatteten Sprüche er- bzw. durchforschen. Die Unterscheidung von der *Weisheit* in Sinnsprüchen einerseits und den *Prophetien* andererseits weist auf zu unterscheidende Schriftsätze. Das ergibt: Hier setzt der Schreiber voraus, dass er zwei verschiedene Typen von Literatur vor sich hat.

In 39,8 steht dann καὶ ἐν νόμῳ διαθήκης κυρίου καυχήσεται, also „und im Gesetz des Bundes des Herrn wird er sich rühmen": Die Formulierung „im Gesetz des Bundes des Herrn" weist darauf hin, dass er mit einem νόμος διαθήκης κυρίου rechnet, also mit einem *Gesetz des Gottesbundes*. Diese seltene Phraseologie berührt sich mit 2 Chr 25,4, ein Vers aus einem Corpus später Schriften, dessen Nähe zu Sira auch an ande-

---

    der 12. Dynastie stammende, aber bis in ptolemäische Zeit tradierte Lehre des Cheti, die möglicherweise auch Ben Sira bekannt war".
22 Πλὴν τοῦ ἐπιδιδόντος τὴν ψυχὴν αὐτοῦ καὶ διανοουμένου ἐν νόμῳ ὑψίστου (38,34c.d) σοφίαν πάντων ἀρχαίων ἐκζητήσει καὶ ἐν προφητείαις ἀσχοληθήσεται (39,1a.b) διήγησιν ἀνδρῶν ὀνομαστῶν συντηρήσει καὶ ἐν στροφαῖς παραβολῶν συνεισελεύσεται (39,2a.b) ἀπόκρυφα παροιμιῶν ἐκζητήσει καὶ ἐν αἰνίγμασιν παραβολῶν ἀναστραφήσεται (39,3a.b).
23 Die Futurformen weisen auf hebräische Präfixkonjugationsformen hin, womit Vorgänge und nicht Zeitstufen wie die in der griechischen Sprache vorzuliegen scheinen.

rer Stelle gegeben ist:[24] κατὰ τὴν διαθήκην τοῦ νόμου κυρίου (vgl. die hebräische Version: כְּכָתוּב בַּתּוֹרָה בְּסֵפֶר מֹשֶׁה). Wenngleich die LXX-Version und die Masoretenversion markant voneinander abweichen, nehmen beide inhaltlich Bezug auf Dtn 24,16 (vgl. 2 Kön 14,6), d.h. auf ein Werk im Pentateuch.

Eben wurde beschrieben, was ein Schriftgelehrter zu erforschen hat, um Schriftgelehrter (סופר bzw. γραμματεύς; Sir 38,24)[25] zu sein: Es sind dies als Stichworte die *Weisheit* in den Sinnsprüchen, die *Prophetien* und der *nomos*/die *Tora*. – Damit sind wir aber noch nicht am Ende, denn erst die Weisheit des Schriftgelehrten (חכמת סופר / σοφία γραμματέως / ܚܟܡܬܐ ܕܣܦܪܐ; 38,24a) vermehrt die Weisheit (חכמה תרבה; 38,24a; Syr versteht diesen Satz reflexiv: ܬܣܓܐ ܠܗ ܚܟܡܬܐ). Also ist danach zu fragen, wie sich die Weisheit des Schriftgelehrten darstellt.

Der Übersetzer ins Griechische bezeugt die Ausdrucks- und Vorstellungswelt der hellenistischen Bildung und Kultur: Wenn es jemand nicht nötig hat, auf der Basis bezahlter[26] Tätigkeit sein Leben zu fristen, weist das auf dessen herausgehobene gesellschaftliche Stellung. Und im Regelfall gilt nur der als wirklich gebildet und weise, der – ausgenommen die Mitwirkungen in der Gesellschaft und der eventuelle militärische Einsatz – sich in Muße mit den „geistigen" Dimensionen des Lebens, ohne Erwerbstätigkeit, hingeben kann.[27] Das setzt voraus, dass der Betreffende entsprechend begütert ist: Weisheit entwickelt sich im Zustand der Muße, und das gilt auch für die Weisheit des Schriftgelehrten: σοφία γραμματέως ἐν εὐκαιρίᾳ σχολῆς;" (38,24a).

Festzuhalten ist zudem, dass Sira der erste Autor ist, der eine Dreiteilung dessen, was wir mit der *Bibel* zusammenfassen, insinuiert. Das bedeutet natürlich keinen Hinweis auf einen fixierten Kanon, doch wird man danach fragen, ob und welche Art von Autorität diesen Schriften zugeschrieben werden, womit wir wieder mitten in unserer Kernfrage sind.

---

24 REITERER, Aarons's, 31 „in late writings of the Old Testament (2 Chr 26,18)"; in diesem Artikel finden sich immer wieder einschlägige Hinweise.
25 Vgl. dazu MARBÖCK, Weise, 29-32.
26 Wer sich die Lehre bezahlen lassen muss, wird als Banause bezeichnet; vgl. CHRISTES, Bildung, 71-129. Sira „gehört zur reichen, städtischen Oberschicht, hat keine finanziellen Sorgen und ist, wie man im deutschen Mittelalter sagte, ein ehrbarer Müßiggänger. Er hat Zeit, sich mit anderen Dingen als denen zu beschäftigen, die dem Broterwerb dienen. Er ist ein Intellektueller und hat Mittel zum Reisen und Studieren. …". So beschreibt LANG, Propheten, 102, treffend. Leider ist dem Autor nicht bewusst, dass er sich hier auf klassischen Spuren im hellenistischen Ambiente befindet, sodass gar manche Frage über die Gebildeten von dort her bearbeitet werden müsste.
27 Vgl. dazu ausführlich CHRISTES, Bildung, 176-182.

2.2 Der Enkel des Ben Sira

2.2.1 Die Probleme mit einer Übersetzung

Der Enkel Ben Siras, auf den die griechische Version zurückgeht, setzt offensichtlich voraus, dass der Großvater hebräisch *geschrieben* hat, da er um Nachsicht bittet, wenn es ihm nicht gelungen seine sollte, in seinen griechischen Worten die Intention der hebräischen Vorlage korrekt wiedergegeben zu haben:[28]

> „0,15 Lasst euch also ermahnen, 0,16 mit Wohlwollen und Aufmerksamkeit 0,17 die Lektüre zu betreiben 0,18 und Nachsicht zu haben, 0,19 in diesen [wo] wir scheinen 0,20 versagt zu haben, obwohl wir uns gemäß der Übersetzungskunst um bestimmte Redewendungen[29] emsig bemüht haben. 0,21 Denn nicht ist gleich imstande (ἀδυναμεῖν)[30] 0,22 das in hebräischer Eigenart (ἐν ἑαυτοῖς Ἑβραϊστί) Gesagte (λεγόμενα) und wann immer es in eine andere Sprache übertragen wird. 0,23 Nicht allein nur das, 0,24 sondern selbst auch das Gesetz und die Prophezeiungen 0,25 und die sonstigen Bücher 0,26 haben einen nicht geringen Unterschied in Bezug auf das in ihnen Gesagte."

---

28 Basis der hier verwendeten Übersetzung ist LXXD.

29 In 0,20 „obwohl wir uns gemäß der Übersetzungskunst um (bestimmte) Redewendungen für einige (Leser) emsig bemüht haben" mag man der LXXD aus folgenden Gründen nur teilweise folgen. Denn τισὶν τῶν λέξεων hat man wohl *auf einander* und nicht das vor τῶν λέξεων (ein genetivus partitivus, den man inhaltlich als *Redewendungen* verstehen kann) stehende τισίν auf ein ganz anderes, gar nicht genanntes Subjekt zu beziehen. Dieses wurde zudem in der Übersetzung in Klammern ergänzend hinzugefügt – wohl ein Hinweis auf die Unsicherheit der vorliegenden Übersetzungsarbeit? – Erst die bei der Übersetzung vorgenommenen Umstellungen im Deutschen ermöglichen die vorgenommenen Bezüge.

30 Auch bei 0,21-22 sind Abweichungen von der in LXXD vorgelegten Übersetzung unausweichlich. οὐ γὰρ ἰσοδυναμεῖ (0,21) liest man als „Denn dasselbe ist in sich nicht gleichbedeutend". Das Verb ἰσοδυναμέω gehört nicht in das Arsenal von Fachausdrücken der Übersetzungstechnik im hier vorgenommenen Sinne: „in sich ... gleichbedeutend". LIDDELL/SCOTT, s.v. [837] gibt als Bedeutung von ἰσοδυναμέω an: „have equal power ... to be equivalent to". *In sich gleichbedeutend sein* weist auf anderes als „aequivalent sein". – Der nähere Kontext gibt die Deutung vor, folgt doch auf ἀδυναμεῖν (0,20) ἰσοδυναμεῖν (0,21). Erst zu begründen wäre es, sollte man dem Grundverb δυναμεῖν unterschiedliche Bedeutungen zumessen müssen. Da in 0,20 die Bedeutung „imstande sein, die Kraft zu etwas haben" (deutend in 0,20: „emsig bemüht haben") in negierter Form gegeben ist, ist hier der Gleichklang gemeint. Das Verb ἰσοδυναμέω ist zusammengesetzt aus ἴσος und δυναμέω (siehe δύναμαι): also „zum Gleichen imstande sein, das Gleiche vermögen". Auch das wird negiert (οὐ; 0,21). Es ist nicht nur nicht gleichbedeutend, sondern es ist überhaupt nicht möglich, das im Hebräischen Gesagte in eine andere Sprache – gemeint ist offensichtlich Griechisch – sinngleich zu übersetzen. Der Autor dieser Worte setzt demnach voraus, dass er nicht nur beiläufig Hebräisch und Griechisch kann, sondern dass er die sprachlichen Möglichkeiten beherrscht.

Es ist davon auszugehen, dass Ben Sira *hebräisch* geschrieben hat. Diese Feststellung wird auch durch die Textfunde in Qumran aus vorchristlicher Zeit bestätigt, wogegen (bisher) keine griechischen Belege von Ben Sira aus jener Zeit zu finden sind. Man kann nicht nachweisen, dass der heutige hebräische Bibeltext des TaNaK identisch ist mit jenem, den Ben Sira für seine Studien zur Verfügung hatte. Ebenso wenig kann man zeigen, welcher hebräische Text des TaNaK jener Übersetzung vorgelegen ist, die der Enkel voraussetzt. Wahrscheinlich ist es aber, dass die in der hebräischen Bibel vorliegenden „Bücher" in einem Naheverhältnis zu jenen Texten stehen, die auch Sira las.

Wenn auch die kontextgemäße Übersetzung von ἀδυναμεῖν in 0,21 kompliziert ist, so ist doch inhaltlich verständlich gesagt, dass das, was hebräisch vorliegt, in diesen Dimensionen, welche die hebräische Sprache besitzt, *nicht in das Griechische übertragen werden kann*. Darin mag auch einer der Gründe liegen, dass der Enkel nicht selten eine Nach- bzw. Neudichtung des großväterlichen Textes vornimmt. Man mag einmal darüber nachdenken, was dieser freie Umgang mit der Vorlage für die Autorität eines übersetzten Textes bedeutet. Wie sollte man also „Autorität des zu übersetzenden und des übersetzten" Textes verstehen? Hatte in den Augen des Enkels die mit viel Mühe vorgenommene Übersetzung das gleiche Gewicht wie der hebräische Ausgangstext? – Ja, man fragt sich, warum hat denn der Enkel überhaupt eine griechische Version vorgelegt?

2.2.2 Übersetzung als Bildungstransporteur

Wenn auch der Anlass für die Nennung anderer literarischer Bereiche durch den Enkel darin liegt, dass in der Übersetzung des TaNaK gleiche Probleme wie bei der Übersetzung des großväterlichen Werkes auftreten, bietet der Enkel – beiläufig – eine für uns interessante *Einteilung* der um 132 v. Chr. schon ins Griechische übersetzten und wichtigen Schriften. Danach gibt es drei Bereiche, die er als schon übersetzt voraussetzt, nämlich:

1) „das Gesetz" (0,24: ὁ νόμος; vgl. 0,1.8),
2) „die Prophetien" (αἱ προφητεῖαι [0,24] und ἐν προφητείαις [39,1a.b]; vgl. προφῆται; 0,1.9),
3) „den Rest der Schriften" (καὶ τὰ λοιπὰ τῶν βιβλίων [0,25; vgl. 0,2.10]).

Leider findet sich keine genauere Umschreibung,[31] wie umfangreich damals diese Schriften waren bzw. welche einzelne Schriften zu welchem Block zu rechnen sind.[32] Für unsere Fragestellung sind die Erwähnungen, dass das traditionelle Buchmaterial in drei Teile sortiert werden kann, an sich Randbereiche. Doch helfen uns in diesem Kontext eher beiläufig gemachte Notizen weiter: Sowohl die *sorgfältige Übersetzung* (0,22: ὅταν μεταχθῇ εἰς ἑτέραν γλῶσσαν) wie vor allem auch die *Empfehlung zum* (intensiven) *Lesen* (0,17: τὴν ἀνάγνωσιν ποιεῖσθαι) weisen auf eine *Literatur*, die auf *besondere Weise zu behandeln ist*.

Uns wird mitgeteilt, wozu in den Augen des Enkels, der ja ein interpretierender und informierender Zeuge seiner Zeit ist, die ihm vorliegende Übersetzung des TaNaK dient: Es geht um den prinzipiellen Nachweis von *Bildung* und *Weisheit* (0,3: παιδεία καὶ σοφία). Nach eigener Angabe kam der Enkel nach Ägypten und lebte – ohne es ausdrücklich zu sagen – vermutlich in Alexandria. Auch eine andere Stadt würde nichts an den für uns wichtigen Zusammenhängen ändern, da auch die anderen genauso vom hellenistischen Denksystem geprägt waren. Dass auch der Enkel der Oberschicht angehört, lässt sich aus

---

31 Es ist nach WITTE, ‚Kanon', 242, „deutlich, dass Ben Sira mit Ausnahme der Bücher Ruth, Hoheslied, Esther, Daniel und Esra offenbar mit allen in der späteren Hebräischen Bibel versammelten Schriften mehr oder weniger stark arbeitet, auf diese anspielt und sie mitunter zitiert ..." Weiters lässt sich die Tatsache, „dass sich keine Bezüge zu den in den späteren Kanon der Septuaginta aufgenommenen Büchern Tobit, Judit und Baruch finden, ... einfach mit der wohl in der Zeit Ben Siras (Tob, Bar) oder kurz danach (Jdt) zu verortenden jüngeren Entstehung dieser Schriften ... (erklären); dies gilt erst recht für die aus dem ausgehenden 1. Jahrhundert v.Chr. oder frühen 1. Jahrhundert n. Chr. stammenden Sapientia Salomonis;" (WITTE, ‚Kanon', 242-243).

32 In dem um etwa vor 100 n.Chr. entstandenen Werk schreibt Josephus Flavius, Contra Apionem I.8, dass man im Gegensatz zu den griechischen Myriaden von Büchern, welche sich zudem widersprechen, im Judentum nur 22 Büchern zu Recht vertraut (δύο δὲ μόνα πρὸς τοῖς εἴκοσι βιβλία τοῦ παντὸς ἔχοντα χρόνου τὴν ἀναγραφήν, τὰ δικαίως πεπιστευμένα). Fünf dieser Bücher stammen von Mose (καὶ τούτων πέντε μέν ἐστι Μωυσέως), 13 werden nach Mose den Propheten zugerechnet (οἱ μετὰ Μωυσῆν προφῆται τὰ κατ' αὐτοὺς πραχθέντα συνέγραψαν ἐν τρισὶ καὶ δέκα βιβλίοις) und die restlichen vier beinhalten Gotteslob und Lebenslehren für Menschen (δὲ λοιπαὶ τέσσαρες ὕμνους εἰς τὸν θεὸν καὶ τοῖς ἀνθρώποις ὑποθήκας τοῦ βίου περιέχουσιν). Nach LOBOW, Flavius, 33. Anm. 89, wurde Esra von Josephus als Prophet angesehen. Auch weitere Schriften werden erwähnt, die nicht die gleiche Dignität und Akzeptanz haben, womit nach LOBOW, Flavius, 33. Anm. 90, die Deuterokanonen gemeint sind: ἀπὸ δὲ Ἀρταξέρξου μέχρι τοῦ καθ' ἡμᾶς χρόνου γέγραπται μὲν ἕκαστα, πίστεως δ' οὐχ ὁμοίας ἠξίωται τοῖς πρὸ αὐτῶν διὰ τὸ μὴ γενέσθαι τὴν τῶν προφητῶν ἀκριβῆ διαδοχήν. Grundsätzlich gilt, dass es niemand wagt, „etwas hinzuzufügen, weg zu nehmen oder zu verändern (οὔτε προσθεῖναί τις οὐδὲν οὔτε ἀφελεῖν αὐτῶν οὔτε με-ταθεῖναι τετόλμηκεν). Diese Werke sind verbindlich und im Extremfall sterben Gläubige auch gerne für diese Gottesgabe (καὶ ὑπὲρ αὐτῶν, εἰ δέοι, θνήσκειν ἡδέως)".

seiner elitären Sprache, seiner Perfektion im Griechischen und aus seiner Leichtigkeit, schwierige Passagen durch Umschreibungen und z.T. Neudichtungen zu überwinden, entnehmen. Zudem ist auch davon auszugehen, dass nicht jedermann (von der Straße [wie man sagen könnte]) von damals die von seltenen Worten gespickte Version verstanden hat. Das zeigt, dass sich der Enkel an die Schicht der Gebildeten von damals wandte, gerade jene Schicht, die ihre Identität in der hellenistischen Gräzität und den damit verbundenen Werten sieht. Dort nun ist die „Erziehung", „Kultur" – oder wie immer man versucht παιδεία wieder zu geben – Zentrum und Ziel des Lebens der Gebildeten, sie ist Kern der Identität. Das Parallelwort zu παιδεία ist *Weisheit*. *Weisheit* ist häufig in den griechischen Tugendkatalogen zu finden, ist aber nicht so zentral wie δικαιοσύνη.[33] Ein Grieche hätte wohl δικαιοσύνη gewählt. Bei der Verwendung von σοφία nimmt der Enkel ein in der alttestamentlichen Tradition bedeutsames Wort – zugleich Programm – auf. Im Speziellen ist *Weisheit* im Werk des Großvaters ein, vielleicht das bedeutsamste Schlüsselwort, welches eine gute Brücke zum Hellenentum schlagen lässt. Das bedeutet aber, dass schon die Übersetzung des TaNaK in erster Linie nicht für den liturgischen Gebrauch und vermutlich auch nicht für breite Kreise erstellt wurde, sondern als Rüstzeug für die elitäre Begegnung mit der Kultur und Bildung der nicht-israelitischen Zeitgenossen anzusehen ist.

2.2.3 Die Bedeutung der Bildung

Das Werk Ben Siras zeigt, dass er sich mit verschiedenen Kulturen der Umgebung beschäftigt hat. Die Hinweise u.a. auf seine Reiseerfahrung, die Bedeutung der Freunde im Sinne einer politischen, der griechischen Welt vergleichbaren Solidargemeinschaft Gleichgesinnter,[34] die Gastmähler usw. lassen weitere Schlüsse zu. Unterschiedlich sind die Beurteilungen des Verhältnisses zwischen Sira und der hellenistischen Umgebung. Er sei beim Bemühen um Abhebung vom Gegenüber unbeabsichtigt mitgeprägt worden, doch halte er sich nationalistisch orientiert vom griechischen Einfluss zurück. Demgegenüber werden die positiven Berührungspunkte herausgehoben. „Persönlich möchte ich

---

33 Vgl. z.B. Platon, Symp. 196 c.d: δικαιοσύνη, σωφροσύνη, ἀνδρεία, σοφία; Weish 8,7: καὶ εἰ δικαιοσύνην ἀγαπᾷ τις οἱ πόνοι ταύτης εἰσὶν ἀρεταί σωφροσύνην γὰρ καὶ φρόνησιν ἐκδιδάσκει δικαιοσύνην καὶ ἀνδρείαν ὧν χρησιμώτερον οὐδέν ἐστιν ἐν βίῳ ἀνθρώποις.

34 „Ein ... zentrales Strukturelement hellenistischer Monarchien sowohl auf innen- als auch auf außenpolitischem Gebiet bildeten die philoi des Königs" schreibt MITTAG, Antiochos, 59. Er verweist auf WEBER, der sich u.a. mit der Funktion als königliche Berater beschäftigte (Interaktion, 44-46).

die doch nicht geringen Berührungspunkte nicht nur als Unterstützung apologetischer Interessen der Selbstvergewisserung Israels in der Welt des Hellenismus sehen, sondern auch als Ausdruck einer gewissen Offenheit des Weisen gegenüber der griechischen Kultur. Er betrachtet den Hellenismus nicht als Schreckensgespenst, vollzog aber die Unterscheidung ständig durch den Bezug auf den Maßstab der biblischen Überlieferung."³⁵ – Nach diesen Worten ist für Sira Norm und Maß die „biblische Überlieferung", aber in welchem Sinne ist das zu verstehen?

Bevor wir uns dieser Fragestellung zuwenden, sei nochmals ein Blick in die hellenistische Welt gemacht. „The Homeric poems began to be recited at the prestigious Panaathenaic festival, which was among the central events of the public life of the city and of the whole of Greece. They also formed the basis of elementary education, to be memorized at schools all over the Greek world and, since the fourth century BCE, stood in the focus of attention both in the grammatical schools, which formed the first level of the higher education, and the rhetorical schools, its second and highest level. ... This unique position of Homer in Greek education finds further corroboration in the amount of Homeric quotations found in ancient authors."³⁶ Die zentrale Stellung ließ sogar die Formulierung vornehmen, dass Homers Werk als „Bibel der Griechen" angesehen worden ist.³⁷ – Es ist hier nicht der Ort, die Rolle Homers intensiv zu behandeln, doch zeigen sich manche sehr gewichtige Implikationen. Denn es fragt sich, warum denn ein Adeligen-Heldenepos (!), in dem die soziale Stellung zugleich auch das Selbstverständnis prägt, zur zentralen Bildungsgrundlage für eine demokratische Stadtorganisation werden kann?

Dies liegt in den allgemein anerkannten und angestrebten Werten, wie man sie in den Tugendkatalogen aufgelistet und selbst im biblischen Corpus nach griechischer Manier in Weish 8,7³⁸ zitiert findet, wobei nachdrücklich hervorzuheben ist, dass in dieser Liste σοφία nicht

---

35 MARBÖCK, Gerechtigkeit, 184-185.
36 FINKELBERG, Canonicity, 146.
37 „Homer die Bibel der Griechen zu nennen ist kaum eine Übertreibung. Seine Epen wurden zum pädagogischen Standardwerk, zum Knigge korrekten Benehmens während der ganzen griechischen Geschichte;" (POLIAKOFF, Kampfsport, 155-156). Weiteres zur Verwendung Homers in der Ausbildung während der hellenistisch-römischen Ära vgl. MORGAN, Education, 69.105; CRIBIORE, Gymnastics, 140-142.194-197. Zu ergänzen ist, dass man in der Grundschule das Schreiben mit einem an Homer erinnernden Merksatz einübte: „Die Kenntnis des Homer ist Bildung"; vgl. ZIEBARTH, Schule, passim.
38 Vgl. Weish 8,7: „Wenn jemand Gerechtigkeit liebt (δικαιοσύνην ἀγαπᾷ), in ihren Mühen findet er die Tugenden (ἀρεταί). Denn sie lehrt Maß (σωφροσύνην) und Klugheit (φρόνησιν), Gerechtigkeit (δικαιοσύνην) und Tapferkeit (ἀνδρείαν), die im Leben der Menschen nützlicher sind als alles andere".

vorkommt! Alles überstrahlt aber die „Ehre" als höchster Wert und höchstes Ziel. Diese kann man dann erlangen, wenn man der Beste ist. Während vom Ausgang her gesehen der Krieg um Troja, und dort vor allem Achill das anschaulichste und wirkungsvollste Beispiel darstellt, wird dieser Drang, ja Trieb, – selbst unter Einsatz des Lebens[39] – der Erste und Beste zu sein, auf alle gesellschaftlichen Ebenen ausgedehnt, wie z.B. mit den Wettkämpfen der Rhapsoden[40] zu belegen ist. An verschiedene politische Systeme anpassungsfähige Werte prägen und bestimmen daher die Vorstellung und man lässt sich freiwillig und gerne in ein straffes, hoch geachtetes Wertesystem einzwängen: „the basic values of the society were given, predetermined, and so were a man's place in the society and the privileges and duties that followed from his status."[41] Diese Orientierung an den eben genannten Werten wird nicht nur zur einenden, sondern zur das Leben bestimmenden Triebfeder der griechischen Gesellschaft. In der hellenistischen Zeit, als die Überschaubarkeit und die Geborgenheit in der Polis und die dadurch mögliche Abgrenzung von anderen *Poleis* nicht mehr gegeben war, sondern durch die Machtöffnung in die gleichsam unbegrenzte Umwelt von damals (Vorderasien, Ägypten, Asien) neue und geradezu berauschende Dimensionen aufgerissen werden, wurden der Durchsetzungswille und das für diesen nötige Instrumentarium zur alles bestimmenden Mitte und zur bindenden Klammer. Auf der politischen und militärischen Ebene mag man zustimmen, dass "together with risking one's life in war, these expectations also embraced assistance to and the protection of those to whom the person was tied by the mutual obligations of military alliance, guest-friendship, or vassal relations"[42]. Diese unumgehbare, aber auch oft beängstigend bedrängende Bindung führt zur Entwicklung neuer Verbindlichkeit, der Ausbildung und Bildung, und jetzt sind wir wieder bei παιδεία angekommen. Die Bildung ist nicht nur Mittel und Zweck, sondern vor allem Identitätszentrale und die Basis des Kontaktes in geographischen Dimensionen zuvor ungeahnten Ausmaßes. – Diesen Nucleus der Vorstellung und des Selbstwertes interpretiert Sira, so verstand es der Enkel, von seiner eigenen biblischen Tradition her, – und der Enkel kann mit folgenden Worten seine Einleitung beginnen: „Vieles und Großes (πολλῶν καὶ

---

39 Vgl. das Zitat aus Platons Symposion unten in der Zusammenfassung.
40 Vgl. z.B. den Dialog des Ion mit Sokrates. Von Sokrates gefragt, wo Ion herkomme, brüstet er sich mit dem ersten Platz (τὰ πρῶτα τῶν ἄθλων ἠνεγκάμεθα; man beachte den pluralis majestaticus) beim Rhapsodenwettkampf zur Interpretation der homerischen Epen bei einem Asklepiosfest zu Epidauros; (Plat. Ion 530a-b).
41 FINLEY, World, 115.
42 FINKELBERG, Canonicity, 144.

μεγάλων) ist uns durch das Gesetz, die Propheten und die anderen Schriften, die ihnen folgen, geschenkt worden. Dafür ist Israel zu loben wegen seiner Bildung und Weisheit" (παιδείας καὶ σοφίας; 0,1-3).

2.2.4 Der gelehrte Großvater als Bildungsvermittler

Auf diesem Hintergrund ist es – hellenistisch gedacht – nicht nur konsequent, sondern unausweichlich, dass die Bildungsinhalte nicht (nur) zur privaten Vertiefung und zum individuellen Nutzen dienen, sondern als gesellschaftliches Angebot und Anliegen anzusehen sind. Schon der Großvater hatte registriert, dass jene, die die gesellschaftserhaltenden Berufe wie Schmied, Landwirte usw. innehaben, undiskutiert *notwendig* sind. Doch genügen sie kontemporär nicht in einer pluralen, sehr schnell weiter pluriform werdenden Welt.

Der Enkel kennt die hellenistischen Prinzipien, die ihn zur „Volksbildung" drängen. Aber ihm war sein Großvater schon zuvor gekommen und stellt in dessen Sinne gleich am Anfang als These auf, dass die, die das Privileg besitzen, sich in Wort und Schrift äußern und mitteilen zu können, auch den Auftrag haben, die anderen an ihrem Vorteil teilhaben zu lassen. Die Verbreitung der Kenntnis ist kein Zugeständnis, kein Wunsch, sondern Notwendigkeit: „Nötig ist, dass nicht nur die Lesefähigen Verständige (= Gebildete) werden, sondern dass sie auch gute Dienste leisten müssen (χρησίμους εἶναι) den zusätzlichen (τοῖς ἐκτός = außerhalb des Bildungsprivilegs) Bildungswilligen (τοὺς φιλομαθοῦντας), und zwar in Wort und Tat;"[43] (0,4-6). Es ist Aufgabe des Weisheitslehrers und es gehört zu seiner Verantwortung, für breite Volksbildung zu sorgen, indem er seinen Wissensschatz auch für die aufbereitet, die selbst nicht des Lesens fähig sind.

Aber niemand kann etwas geben, was er selbst nicht hat. Das bedeutet, dass jener, der Bildung vermitteln will, sich selbst zuvor einschlägige Bildung angeeignet haben muss.[44] Tatsächlich steht dort: „So befasste sich mein Großvater Jesus sorgfältig (ἐπὶ πλεῖον ἑαυτὸν δούς) mit (εἰς) dem Gesetz, mit den Propheten und mit den anderen von den Vätern überkommenen Schriften".[45] – Man weiß nicht so recht, wie man ἐπὶ πλεῖον ἑαυτὸν δούς εἰς ... korrekt wiedergeben sollte: Klar scheint, dass der Enkel festhalten will, dass sich der Großvater weit über das zu erwartende Maß hinaus (ἐπὶ πλεῖον) mit der ihm vorliegenden schriftlichen Tradition auseinandergesetzt hatte, wobei er intensive

---

43 Καὶ ὡς οὐ μόνον αὐτοὺς τοὺς ἀναγινώσκοντας δέον ἐστὶν ἐπιστήμονας γίνεσθαι ἀλλὰ καὶ τοῖς ἐκτὸς δύνασθαι τοὺς φιλομαθοῦντας χρησίμους εἶναι καὶ λέγοντας καὶ γράφοντας.
44 So richtig LANG, Propheten, 103: „Sein Bildungsgut ist die Bibel."
45 Man achte wiederum auf die drei Bereiche.

und häufige Lektüre (ἀνάγνωσις) pflegte. Die Intensität ergibt sich aus der eigenartigen Formulierung, dass er sich selbst *gibt in ...*, gleichsam „hin-" oder „hineingibt" (ἑαυτὸν δούς), also ganz und gar im Gelesenen versunken erscheint, sich diesem Gelesenen auslieferte. Das Partizipium als Form (δούς) beschreibt im Hebräischen sicher, im Griechischen möglicherweise die Dimension langer Dauer. Man hört geradezu das für die griechische Bildung so entscheidende Wort σχολή durchklingen, das der Übersetzer in vergleichbarem Kontext (38,24) verwendet.

Was der Großvater sich angeeignet hat, geht weit über die übliche Wissensaneignung innerhalb einer Familie hinaus, in der ja auch der Großvater aufgewachsen war. Dies trifft auch dann zu, wenn man so, wie in Ps 78,5-6 gefordert worden war, gehandelt haben sollte: „Er gebot unseren Vätern, ihre Kinder das alles zu lehren, damit das kommende Geschlecht davon erfahre, die Kinder späterer Zeiten; sie sollten aufstehen und es weitergeben an ihre Kinder". – Das intensive Studium weist darauf hin, dass er sich auf eine bisher nicht übliche Art dem Textstudium widmete. Da Sira keine praktische Erfahrung mit priesterlichen Vorgängen hat,[46] wird man hier keinen Vergleich mit einer Priesterschulung versuchen, doch zeigt das Ergebnis, dass es auch nicht um berufsmäßiges Traditionswissen geht, wie das z.B. bei den Priestern der Fall ist.

Obwohl wir den Umfang der Ben Sira angediehenen Grundschulung nicht kennen, war die Kenntnis der Tradition vorher offensichtlich nicht hinreichend, um sich mit dem hellenistischen Bildungsstand messen zu können. Daher lesen wir, dass „er sich eine ἱκανὴν ἕξιν von ihnen (den drei Buchkomplexen) verschaffte" (περιποιησάμενος; vgl. wieder das Partizipium); (0,11). Während man ἱκανός als „einschlägig", zugleich „umfassend" und „sachgemäß" verstehen kann, ist das Substantiv ἕξις schwerer zu deuten. In diesem Falle trifft es besonders zu, dass eine Übersetzung schon eine Deutung ist, weshalb die Vorschläge auch ziemlich unterschiedlich sind, wobei sich das Verständnis – vergröbernd gesprochen – auf „Wissen/Kenntnis"[47], „Urteilsfähigkeit" und „Fertigkeit" konzentriert. Von der Ausgangsbedeutung für ἕξις[48], nämlich *transitivem* ἔχω, her geht es nicht nur um Wissen/Kenntnis, was zwar eingeschlossen ist, aber nicht die Pointe trifft. Auch die Urteilsfä-

---

46 Vgl. den Nachweis bei REITERER, Aaron's , 46.52.
47 Herder: "eine gründliche Kenntnis davon"; HAMP, Echter Bibel (1951): "eine entsprechende Kenntnis"; The New Jerusalem Bible: "become very learned"; New Revised Standard Version: "considerable proficiency" [beträchtliche Kenntnisse]; SAUER, ATD (2000): „um die Kenntnis ... bemüht hatte"; MARBÖCK, Jesus, 37: "eine hinreichende Vertrautheit"
48 Als Bedeutung listet GEMOLL, Schul- und Handwörterbuch, 289, auf: „Halten, Besitz, ... Haltung, Beschaffenheit, ... Fähigkeit, ... Eigenschaft".

higkeit⁴⁹ mag inkludiert sein, doch greift diese Bedeutung im Hinblick auf das Werk zu wenig weit. Die Fertigkeit⁵⁰ ist zu unspezifisch. Was soll er sich für eine Fertigkeit mit Hilfe des intensiven Bibelstudiums angeeignet haben?

Der restliche Gebrauch in der LXX konzentriert sich weitgehend auf eine Bedeutungsschiene, nämlich ἕξις als dinglich „äußere Gegebenheit, Erscheinung, Zustand"⁵¹. Bei Sira kann es sich jedoch nur um eine geistige Dimension handeln, und da kann man die Theodotion-Version von Dan 7,15 als Vergleichstext heranziehen: „Mein Geist erschauerte in *meinem Zustand*, ich, Daniel, und die Schauungen meines Kopfes wühlten mich auf" (LXX^D; ἔφριξεν τὸ πνεῦμά μου ἐν τῇ ἕξει μου ἐγὼ Δανιηλ καὶ αἱ ὁράσεις τῆς κεφαλῆς μου ἐτάρασσόν με). – Sira hat sich ein Objekt erworben, und das *prägt* sein *Bewusstsein* und ist die Grundlage für sein ganzes Werk: Er hat sich die dreiteilige Bibel angeeignet, sie ist sein Besitz, er beherrscht sie: Dies ist sowohl im innerlichen (vgl. ἑαυτὸν δούς) wie im äußerlichen (ἀνάγνωσιν) Sinne gemeint. Sira besitzt die Bibel im Inneren, sie prägt ihn, sie hat ihrerseits ihn in Besitz, die Bibel ist Siras Identität, wofür auch das Wort Autorität sehr unscharf erscheint. Die dreiteilige Bibel prägt Sira, sodass sein Denken und seine Argumentationsform von ihr bestimmt wird, und zwar im umfassenden Sinne; vgl. περί + ποιησάμενος; 0,11. Siras umfassender, verinnerlichter Bibelbesitz realisiert die Intention, weshalb er auch keine Zitate einzubauen braucht und sich frei weiß von missverständlichen Worthülsen, was ihn zu vielen Neuformulieren und der Entwicklung neuer Aspekte treibt.

Nach diesem intensiven Aneignungsprozess „ging [der Großvater] daran, auch selbst etwas aufzuschreiben von dem, was zur Bildung und Weisheit (εἰς παιδείαν καὶ σοφίαν) gehört;" (0,12). Der Besitz im Inneren – der den Formulierungen nach mehr als nur gelernter Stoff ist – drängt transitiv danach, sich mitzuteilen. Jetzt macht der Großvater das, was er selbst mitgemacht hat: Er hat sich in „Gesetz, Propheten und Schriften" hineinbegeben, sie haben sein Bewusstsein ergriffen. *Analog* fühlt er sich jetzt dazu angetrieben (προήχθη; vgl. das Passivum), zeitangepasst die ihn prägende Weltsicht als Offenbarungsergriffener wieder für andere zu deuten und in der Interpretation der Zeitereignisse Anleitungen für konkrete Lebensentscheidungen zu formulieren. Er

---

49 King James Version Apocrypha: "good judgment"; Brenton LXX with Apocrypha: "good judgment"
50 French Bible Jerusalem: "une grande maîtrise"; French Bible en francais courant: "un véritable expert en ce domaine"; Becker, LXXD (2009): „eine angemessene Fertigkeit".
51 Vgl. Ri 14,9; 1 Sam 16,7; Sir 30,14; Hab 3,16; Dan 1,15; 7,28.

ist nicht mehr Vermittler der Offenbarungsworte, sondern *Deuter seiner Zeit* infolge der Offenbarungsworte.[52]

Dass wir den zeitgeschichtlichen Hintergrund als eine beständig präsente Folie zu berücksichtigen haben, zeigt die Weiterführung, da sich der Großvater gedrängt fühlte, auch „etwas von dem zur [eigentlichen] Bildung und Weisheit Gehörenden" (τι τῶν εἰς παιδείαν καὶ σοφίαν ἀνηκόντων; 0,12) zu schreiben. Offenbarung an sich und die in ihr selbst formulierte autoritative Gültigkeit (vgl. oben 1.), so scheint es, ist nicht mehr das Argument, das zu überzeugen imstande ist. Zu Siras Zeit, vor allem dort, wo der Enkel übersetzt, war Bildung – wie oben auch behandelt – Kernelement der Identität der hellenistischen Welt: Sie war mehr als nur Wissensvermittlung, Aneignung von damals unerlässlichen Fähigkeiten oder Persönlichkeitsbildung, sie war offensichtlich auch die religiöse Existenzversicherung (vgl. die Zerstörung des Heiligen durch Holofernes in Jdt 3,8). Ist das richtig, argumentierte Sira vom religiösen Terrain aus, und es ergibt sich geradezu von selbst, dass Sira kyrio-zentristisch argumentiert und die Achtung vor dem Herrn permanent präsent weiß.[53] Jedenfalls sieht auch der Enkel des Großvaters Botschaft erst dann richtig verstanden, wenn jemand seine Worte in „einer Lebensführung innerhalb der Offenbarungsregeln" (τῆς ἐν-νόμου βιώσεως) realisiert, das heißt in konkrete Taten umsetzt. So kommt Siras Enkel auf subtilem Umweg auf ein vergleichbares Ziel, welches in der Tradition zentral gewesen war.

2.3 Beispiele

Wenn wir uns einzelnen Beispielen zuwenden, geht es als erstes um die Frage, ob und wie sich im Werke Ben Siras das bisher Beobachtete widerspiegelt. Die Antwort ist aus dem Werk zu erheben. Wer das Buch liest, stellt die Dominanz von folgenden Bereichen fest: „Weisheit"[54] und „Achtung vor dem Herrn", dem folgen andere wichtige Themen, wobei es ein Kriterium für die Bedeutsamkeit ist, ob Sira der jeweiligen Materie eine eigene „Abhandlung" (exegetisch neuzeitlich ausgedrückt: „literarische Einheit") widmet. Unter diesem Gesichtspunkt sind dann weiters die Freundschaftsperikopen und jene zum Bereich der Gastmähler wie auch zur Schöpfung zu nennen.

---

52 LANG ist auf der rechten Spur, wenn er Sira als „Laien" (Propheten, 102) und „Privatgelehrten" einstuft (Propheten, 102), jedoch wird man Zweifel anmelden, wenn er Sira dann weiters als „Erbauungsautor" (105) qualifiziert.
53 Vgl. auch unten die Zusammenfassung.
54 Vgl. die über 100 Stellen umfassende Belegstellensammlung für hebräisch, syrisch und griechisch Verse bei REITERER, Verhältnis, 228-231.

Man kann also von Basisthemen sprechen, doch ist vorweg ein durchwegs präsenter, nicht in einer Einheit thematisierter Kernpunkt, der Nukleus Ben Siras, herauszustellen, nämlich die zentrale Rolle und Position des *Herrn* (seltener Gottes) und seine alle anderen Materien überstrahlende Bedeutung. Dies ist auch statistisch belegbar, kommt doch κύριος mehr als 180[55] Mal vor, dazu kommen noch 15[56] Stellen mit θεός. Zu erwarten ist, dass man in diesen Kontexten auf geprägte Theologumena trifft, sodass die sirazidische Version Übereinstimmungen und abweichende Besonderheiten herausarbeiten lässt.

2.3.1 Die Rede vom Kyrios

Die Rede vom Kyrios ist nicht so zu verstehen, dass Sira erwartet, dass seine Hörer ihre Lebensführung nach dem Kyrios ausrichten, während andere Völker andere Götter[57] haben. Die Rede vom Kyrios ist auch nicht als Bekenntnis zu verstehen: „Höre (שְׁמַע / ἄκουε), Israel! Jahwe, unser Gott, Jahwe ist einer (יְהוָה אֱלֹהֵינוּ יְהוָה אֶחָד / κύριος ὁ θεὸς ἡμῶν κύριος εἷς ἐστιν);" (Dtn 6,4). Es geht vielmehr um eine nicht weiter zu diskutierende Feststellung, die auf einer umfassenden Kundigkeit basiert, womit man sich an die griechische Version von Jes 45,6 erinnert sieht: „damit sie erfahren/erkennen (יֵדְעוּ) vom Aufgang der Sonne bis zu ihrem Untergang, dass nichts außer mir ist. Ich bin JHWH (אֲנִי יְהוָה), und sonst niemand". In der LXX steht nun ἵνα γνῶσιν οἱ ἀπὸ ἀνατολῶν ἡλίου καὶ οἱ ἀπὸ δυσμῶν ὅτι οὐκ ἔστιν πλὴν ἐμοῦ ἐγὼ κύριος ὁ θεὸς καὶ οὐκ ἔστιν ἔτι, sodass יְהוָה als κύριος ὁ θεός präzisiert wird. Mit der gleichen religiösen Feststellung endet auch das Gebet um Rettung in Sir 36,1-22: γνώσονται ... ὅτι σὺ εἶ κύριος ὁ θεὸς τῶν αἰώνων; (36,22d), wofür in H^B der nicht ganz erhaltene Text steht: „[...] ...[58] וידעו כי אתה אל". Syr folgt dem hebräischen Text zugleich wie überall die Gottesbezeichnung vereinheitlichend, wobei die Einzigkeit betont wird, sodass anzunehmen ist, dass Syr ein teilweise von H und G abweichender Text vorgelegen ist: ... ܕܐܢܬ ܗܘ ܐܠܗܐ ܕܠܥܠܡܝܢ.

---

55 Vgl. Sir 1,1.9.11ff.16.18.20.26ff.30; 2,1.7ff.14ff; 3,2.6.16.18.20; 4,13f.28; 5,3f.7; 6,16f.37; 7,4f.29.31; 9,16; 10,4f.7.12ff.19f.22.24; 11,4.12.14.17.21f.26; 14,11; 15,1.9ff.13.18; 16,2.17.26.29; 17,1.17.20.25.28f; 18,2.6.11.13.23.26; 19,20; 21,6.11; 23,1.4.19.27; 24,12; 25,1.6.10f; 26,3.14.16.28; 27,3.24; 28,1.3.23; 30,19; 32,14.16.24; 33,1.8.11.17; 34,13ff; 35,3f.7.10.12.19; 36,4.11.16f; 37,21; 38,1.4.9.12.14; 39,5f.8.14.16.33.35; 40,26f; 41,4; 42,15ff; 43,5.9.29f.33; 44,2.16; 45,16.19.21.23; 46,3.5f.9ff.13f.16f.19; 47,5f.11.18.22; 48,3. 20.22; 49,3.12; 50,13.17.19f.29; 51,1.8.10.12.22.

56 Vgl. Sir 4,28; 7,9; 23,4; 24,23; 36,1.4.17; 41,8.20; 45,1; 47,13.18; 50,17.22; 51,1.

57 Vgl. „... denn alle Völker gehen ihren Weg, jedes ruft den Namen seines Gottes an (בְּשֵׁם אֱלֹהָיו / –); wir aber gehen unseren Weg im Namen Jahwes, unseres Gottes, (בְּשֵׁם־יְהוָה אֱלֹהֵינוּ / ἐν ὀνόματι κυρίου θεοῦ ἡμῶν) für immer und ewig" (Mi 4,5).

58 Vgl. die Variantlesart in HBm: ויראו.

Um nun zu überprüfen, wie eng sich Sira an einer bedeutsamen Stelle an seine Tradition gebunden hat, wird zuerst die hebräische und dann die griechische Phraseologie untersucht, welche der sich der Übersetzungsprobleme bewusste Enkel gekannt haben kann.

„[וידעו] ... כי אתה אל [...]"

Im Kontext von grundsätzlich theologischen Positionierungen sind diese Worte im Sinne der Einzigkeit gemeint – so ja schon in 36,5: כי אין אלהים זולתך / ὅτι οὐκ ἔστιν θεὸς πλὴν σου κύριε –, wie sich aus der Gegenposition zur theo-politischen Eigendefinition der Feindesmacht in 36,12 (אין זולתי / οὐκ ἔστιν πλὴν ἡμῶν) ergibt. Überprüft soll nun werden, wie die Ausdrucksweise bei gleichen Inhalten vorgenommen wird. So kann man auch aufzeigen, ob es einen geprägten Sprachgebrauch gibt und wie dieser aussieht.

Ein Beleg findet sich für אַתָּה יְהוָה, wobei ausdrücklich auch der Bezug zur Alleinigkeit JHWHs hergestellt wird in Jes 37,20 (כִּי־אַתָּה יְהוָה לְבַדֶּךָ). Mehrfach folgt nach יְהוָה auch אֱלֹהִים, so in 1 Kön 18,37 (כִּי־אַתָּה יְהוָה הָאֱלֹהִים) und Neh 9,7 (אַתָּה־הוּא יְהוָה הָאֱלֹהִים); vgl. 1 Chr 17,26 (וְעַתָּה יְהוָה אַתָּה־הוּא הָאֱלֹהִים). In 2 Kön 19,19 folgt noch der Hinweis auf die Einzigkeit (כִּי אַתָּה יְהוָה אֱלֹהִים לְבַדֶּךָ). אַתָּה אֱלֹהִים wird durchwegs mit Gottes elitärer Position verknüpft: 2 Kön 19,15 (... אַתָּה־הוּא הָאֱלֹהִים לְבַדְּךָ); Ps 86,10 (אַתָּה אֱלֹהִים לְבַדֶּךָ); Jes 37,16 ... (אַתָּה־הוּא הָאֱלֹהִים לְבַדְּךָ). Gottesnamen sind demnach in dieser Phrase: יְהוָה und/oder אֱלֹהִים.

Dort wo אל als Vorlage dient, steht ὁ θεός: ἐγώ εἰμι ὁ θεός (אֲנִי־אֵל) [καὶ οὐκ ἔστιν ἄλλος] (Jes 45,22); ὅτι ἐγώ εἰμι ὁ θεός (אָנֹכִי אֵל) [καὶ οὐκ ἔστιν ἔτι πλὴν ἐμοῦ] und διότι θεὸς ἐγώ εἰμι (כִּי אֵל אָנֹכִי) (Hos 11,9).

Im TaNaK findet sich mit „du / אַתָּה" und der Gottesbezeichnung אל keine Parallele. Als Ergebnis zeigt sich, dass Sira sehr selbständig formuliert. Es ist zwar durchaus möglich, Sir 36,22 mehr oder weniger ausschließlich aus dem Kontext zu deuten. Hilfreich sind die angeführten Vergleichstexte allemal, wenngleich eine direkte literarische Abhängigkeit nicht gegeben ist, ja das Gegenteil ist der Fall, da Sira die in vergleichbaren geprägten Phrasen sonst nicht belegbare Vokabel אל wählt.

(γνώσονται) ... κύριος ὁ θεός

Obgleich in der H-Vorlage nur *eine* Gottesbezeichnung steht (אל) und H auch durch Syr gestützt wird (ܐܠܗܐ), stehen in G: (γνώσονται ...) σὺ εἶ κύριος ὁ θεὸς τῶν αἰώνων in 36,22.

> Κύριος ὁ θεός ist in der LXX eine gebräuchliche Phrase und geht auf כִּי־אַתָּה יְהוָה [הָ]אֱלֹהִים zurück: 1 Kön 18,37: ὅτι σὺ εἶ κύριος ὁ θεός (כִּי־אַתָּה יְהוָה [הָ]אֱלֹהִים); Neh 9,7: σὺ εἶ κύριος ὁ θεός (אַתָּה־הוּא יְהוָה הָאֱלֹהִים); vgl. 1 Chr 17,26: νῦν κύριε σὺ εἶ αὐτὸς ὁ θεός. Es ist zu notieren, dass in Jes 37,20 auch JHWH als ὁ θεός wiedergegeben wird (ὅτι σὺ εἶ ὁ θεὸς μόνος / כִּי־אַתָּה יְהוָה

לְבַדֶּךָ). אֱלֹהִים erscheint mehrmals als ὁ θεός (2 Kön 19,15.19; Jes 37,16; Ps 86,10). Wenn man auch das Verb berücksichtigt, steht der Sirastelle der nur griechisch belegte Vers Dan 3,45^(LXX +Th) am nächsten: γνώτωσαν ὅτι σὺ εἶ μόνος κύριος ὁ θεός.

Die griechische Version folgt der dem in der LXX üblichen Übersetzungsusus, bietet aber für eine Gottesbezeichnung zwei und bringt eine kyriologische Ergänzung an.

2.3.2 Die Rede von der „Gottesfurcht"

Schon die große Anzahl von Belegen für „Achtung vor Gott", auf die man bei Sira „über 60 Mal"[59] trifft, zeigt, dass φόβος κυρίου[60] bzw. φοβούμενος / φοβούμενοι [τὸν] κύριον[61] zentrale Themen sind. In einem derart wichtigen Bereich muss man ja gut greifen können, wie Sira zu seiner Tradition steht. Im Kontext von ירא finden sich bei Sira unterschiedliche Gottesbezeichnungen, wie אל (6,16^A); אלהים (10,20^A.B.24^A) und ייי (15,1^A.B; 16,4^A.B; 26,3^C; 32,16^B; 33,1^B.F).

Ein Blick in den TaNaK zeigt Folgendes: Als hebräische Vorlage für φόβος κυρίου dienen יִרְאַת יְהוָה[62], יִרְאַת הָאֱלֹהִים[63]; dazu kommt יִרְאַת אֱלֹהִים[64], פַּחַד und חִתַּת אֱלֹהִים[65] אֱלֹהִים[66]. In Jes 2,10.19.21 geht φόβος κυρίου jeweils auf פַּחַד יְהוָה[67] zurück und meint den von Gott ausgehenden Schrecken. Auch in 2 Chr 19,7 schwingt bei פַּחַד־יְהוָה ein drohender Unterton mit, soll doch erreicht werden, dass die frisch eingesetzten Richter wegen der Angst vor Gottes Sanktion (וְעַתָּה יְהִי פַחַד־יְהוָה עֲלֵיכֶם) ihr Amt gut ausfüllen und nicht missbrauchen. Auch φόβος θεοῦ (vgl. Sir 7,31: φοβοῦ τὸν κύριον) hat in Spr 1,7; 2,5; 15,33; Jes 11,3 יִרְאַת יְהוָה als Ausgang. – Die in dieser Phrase verwendeten Gottesnamen sind יְהוָה und/oder אֱלֹהִים.

Anders als im TaNaK findet sich bei Sira der Gottesname אל im Kontext der „Gottesfurcht". Diesen Wortgebrauch kann er nicht der Tradition entnommen haben. Dort war der Wortgebrauch geprägt und anders vorgegeben.

---

59 REITERER, Jesus Sirach, 24.
60 Vgl. Sir 1,11f.18.27f.30; 9,16; 10,22; 16,2; 19,20; 21,11; 23,27; 25,6.11; 27,3; 40,26 (2 Mal).27; 45,23.
61 Vgl. Sir 1,13f.16.20; 2,7ff.15ff; 6,16f; 7,31; 10,19f.24; 15,1; 21,6; 25,10; 26,3; 32,14.16; 33,1; 34,13ff.
62 Vgl. 2 Chr 19,9; Ps 19,10; 34,12; Ps 111,10; Spr 1,29; 2,5; 8,13; 9,10; 10,27; 10,29; 14,26; 15,16; 15,27; 19,23; 22,4; 23,17; 31,30.
63 So in 2 Chr 26,5; vgl. τῷ κυρίῳ ἐν φόβῳ in Ps 2,11 für אֶת־יְהוָה בְּיִרְאָה.
64 So in Neh 5,9.15.
65 So in Ps 36,2.
66 So in Gen 35,5.
67 In einer abweichenden Übertragung von פַּחַד אֵלִי steht in Ijob 31,23 φόβος γὰρ κυρίου [= פַּחַד אֵל]. Wenn es sich um die Wiedergabe des Masoretentextes handelt, dann ist der Übersetzer einer Verlesung erlegen.

Aber auch in anderer Hinsicht erweist sich Sira als „emanzipiert". Das Verb פחד impliziert auch bei Sira Angst und Schrecken. Gott soll den Gottesschrecken über die Gegner ausgießen (36,1) und Sira verbindet dieses Wort ausdrücklich mit dem Tod; vgl. 9,13; 41,12. Daher ist es auffällig, wenn man in 7,29a liest:

בכל לבך פחד אל
ܚܕܠܡܐ ܠܡܪܝܐ ܘܒܠ ܡܢ ܐܠܗܐ
ἐν ὅλῃ ψυχῇ σου εὐλαβοῦ τὸν κύριον

Alle protokanonischen Vorkommen von בְּכָל־לֵב (16mal) bzw. בְּכָל־לֵבָב (29 mal), häufig in direkter Parallele zu וּבְכָל־נֶפֶשׁ[68], stehen in positiven und direkt oder indirekt auf JHWH bezogenen Kontexten. Die Wortverbindung ist fest in der Tradition verwurzelt. Das Verb in 7,29a ist פחד, weshalb überprüft werden soll, ob es sich auch dabei um eine traditionelle Formulierung handelt. Wenn mit בְּכָל־לֵב bzw. בְּכָל־לֵבָב ein Verhalten zu Gott oder zu einem ihm zustehenden Bereich, wie z.B. die Gebote, qualifiziert wird, werden folgende Verben verwendet: אהב[69]; בטח[70]; דרש[71]; אַחֲרֵי הלך ב[73]; הלך לִפְנֵי[74]; חלה פָּנִים[75]; ידה[76]; ידע[77]; נטע[78]; נצר[79]; עבד[80]; עלז[81]; קרא[82]; שבע[83]; שוב אֵל[84]; שוב עַד[85]; שמע[86]; שמע[87] und שמר[88]. Daher ist zu summieren, dass „an keinem der protokanonischen Belege ... der Gedanke vorkommt, Gott sei aus ganzen Herzen zu *fürchten*, wie Sira formuliert."[89]

---

68 Vgl. Dtn 4,29; 6,5; 10,12; 11,13; 13,4; 26,16; 30,2.6.10; Jos 22,5; 23,14; 1 Sam 12,20; 1 Kön 2,4; 18,48; 2 Kön 23,25; 2 Chr 15,12; 34,31.
69 Vgl. 6,5; 13,4; 30,6.
70 Vgl. Spr 3,5.
71 Vgl. Dtn 4,29; 2 Chr 15,12; 22,9; Jer 29,13; Ps 119,10.
72 Vgl. 1 Kön 14,8.
73 Vgl. 2 Kön 10,31.
74 Vgl. 1 Kön 2,4; 8,23; 2 Chr 6,14.
75 Vgl. Ps 119,58.
76 Vgl. Ps 9,2; 86,12; 111,1; 138,1.
77 Vgl. Jos 23,14; 2 Chr 32,31.
78 Vgl. Jer 32,41.
79 Vgl. Ps 119,2.69.
80 Vgl. Dtn 10,12; 11,13; 1 Sam 12,20.24; Jos 22,5.
81 Vgl. Zef 3,14.
82 Vgl. Dtn 26,16; 2Chr 31,21.
83 Vgl. Ps 119,145.
84 Vgl. 2Chr 15,15.
85 Vgl. Dtn 30,10; 1 Sam 7,3; 1 Kön 8,48; 2 Kön 23,25; 2 Chr 6,38; Jer 3,10; 24,7.
86 Vgl. Joel 2,12.
87 Vgl. Dtn 30,2.
88 Vgl. 2 Kön 23,3; 2 Chr 34,31; Ps 119,34.
89 REITERER, Gott, 140-141; in der Kommentierung bringt MARBÖCK, Jesus, 132, zu dieser eigenwillige Phraseologie keine Notiz an.

Aus der Parallele zu den Verben אהב (7,30a) und כבד (7,31a) ergibt sich, dass bei פחד keineswegs der Akzent auf der sonst üblichen Bedeutung „sich ängstigen, vor jemand beben" liegt. – Traditionell sind יְהוָֹה יְרָא / יְראוּ אֶת (Spr 3,7; 24,21 / Jos 24,14; 1 Sam 12,24; Ps 34,10) bzw. אֶת־הָאֱלֹהִים (Koh 5,6), doch Sira verwendet diese Phrase trotz des im sirazidischen Werk häufigen Gebrauchs von ירא nicht.

Wie aber mag der Autor auf die Idee gekommen sein, so ungewöhnlich zu sprechen? Als erstes wirken seine Worte infolge seiner Formulierung verfremdend und damit erreicht er gesteigerte Aufmerksamkeit, die er zur Einschärfung seiner Schwerpunktsetzungen nutzt. Zudem ist bei ihm *Achtung vor dem Herrn* anders besetzt denn als konkret einforderbare Aktion. *Achtung vor dem Herrn* beschreibt eine permanent anwesende Grundhaltung und kann gleich gesetzt werden mit dem vertieften Glauben als Zustand und als Haltung und ist daher Folie aller Worte Siras. Sie ist das israelitische Pendant zur hellenistischen Persönlichkeitsprägung in der παιδεία. Sira setzt damit einen anderen Akzent als jenen, der in der traditionell geprägten Phrase anvisiert ist. Erläuternd helfen die parallelen Verben אהב und כבד das Gemeinte zu beschreiben. Traditionell kommen weder das Paar אהב und כבד noch vergleichbare Aussagen im näheren Zusammenhang der oben zitierten ירא את־יהוה-Sätze vor. – Hinsichtlich unserer Fragestellung ergibt sich, dass Sira sich nicht an den tradierten Sprachgebrauch hält.

3. Zusammenfassung

Im ersten Teil (Teil 1.) wurde die Ernsthaftigkeit, mit der man die Worte und die Weisung JHWHs (vgl. 1.4 und 1.5) aufzunehmen (1.1), vollständig (vgl. 1.3) aufzuzeichnen (vgl. 1.2), aufzubewahren (vgl. 1.2), ohne Veränderung lehrend (vgl. 1.9) weiterzugeben (vgl. 1.7 und 1.8) und vor allem in die Tat umzusetzen hat (vgl. 1.9 und 1.10), dargestellt. Es handelt sich um die verbindliche und verpflichtende Offenbarung, deren Missachtung zu Sanktionen bzw. deren fehlende Aktualisierung zu negativen Reaktionen Gottes führen. Es gibt einen unmissverständlich formulierten Katalog von Rahmenbedingungen, mit Hilfe derer sich die autoritative Funktion der Offenbarung beschreiben lässt.

Sira hat sich nach seinem eigenen Ausweis und der Beschreibung des Enkels intensiv mit der – ihm vorliegenden – geoffenbarten Literatur auseinandergesetzt (Teil 2.): Unter diesen Voraussetzungen ist es gar nicht anders möglich, als dass Sira alle die genannten Verbindlichkeiten gelesen, studiert und sich einver*leibt* hat. Er hat die Regeln über die Autorität nicht nur durchgesehen und zur Kenntnis genommen, sondern jene Texte in seinen vollständigen Besitz gebracht. – Zugleich lebt Sira in einer Zeit, in der identitätstiftende Literatur in der damaligen „Weltkultur" zentral war: Bildung und Kultur eignet man sich im hellenistischen Bereich durch das Studium von überkommener Literatur (z.B. Homer, Hesiod) an. Wie zu seiner Zeit üblich, dient die Ausbildung nicht nur der Aneignung eines Arbeits- und Handlungsinstrumentariums, sondern zur Persönlichkeitsbildung, sodass die Ausbildung der Prägung der eigenen Identität dient.

Auf dem Wege dieser intensiven Beschäftigung erkennt er, dass Gott so zu handeln imstande ist, wie er will, und dem Weisen auch Worte schenken kann, um in verschiedensten Bereichen des Lebens die konkreten Herausforderungen im individuellen wie im gesellschaftlichen Leben zu bewältigen. Sira ist sich dessen bewusst, dass es nicht menschliche Leistung ist, wenn man das Leben auf der Basis der Gottesachtung zu gestalten imstande ist. Vor allem aber gilt, dass es die Gaben Gottes sind, welche die Bildung eines Schriftgelehrten erst ermöglichen – welch ein Gegensatz zum erlernbaren Wissen der profan argumentierenden Umwelt! „Wenn der Herr (κύριος), der Höchste, es will, wird er [= der Schriftgelehrte] mit dem Geist der Einsicht (πνεύματι συνέσεως) vollgefüllt (ἐμπλησθήσεται). Er fließt über (ἀνομβρήσει) von eigenen weisen Reden (ῥήματα σοφίας αὐτοῦ), und im Gebet preist er (ἐξομολογήσεται) den Herrn;" (39,6). – Sira beherrscht die Tora, die Propheten und die übrigen Schriften. Hätte er einen Satz sagen können, wie „errichte einen Zaun um die Tora"? – Nie, denn es geht nicht um das äußere Wahrnehmen der überkommenen Sprüche. Deren Tradierungsregeln stehen innerhalb der schriftlich vorliegenden Zeugnisse und bedürfen keiner zusätzlichen Verstärkung. Bei Sira geht es um die Einstellungsprägung, und dort kann man keinen Zaun errichten.

Die Folge seiner innig-engen Verbindung mit dem Herrn ist die, dass er das System des Glaubens drastisch verinnerlicht und sich offensichtlich nicht an den Wortlaut der überkommenen schriftlichen Offenbarung gebunden sieht. Zugleich hat er diese so verinnerlicht, dass sie gleichsam sein Vokabular geworden ist. – So kommt es, dass er herkömmlich fest geprägte Gedankenverbindungen auf originell unerwartete Weise in anderen Kontexten zur Sprache bringt: Oben (1.7) wurde nachgezeichnet, dass es nachdrücklich untersagt wird, etwas hinzuzufügen oder etwas wegzunehmen. Diese Opposition greift Sira im Kontext der Schöpfung auf und sagt: „Wer kann seine [= des Herrn] gewaltige Größe (κράτος μεγαλωσύνης αὐτοῦ) vermessen (ἐξαριθμήσεται) und seine Liebestaten (τὰ ἐλέη αὐτοῦ) aufzählen? Weder kann man [etwas] wegnehmen (ἐλαττῶσαι) noch hinzusetzen (προσθεῖναι), nicht aufzuspüren (ἐξιχνιάσαι) sind die erstaunlichen Taten (θαυμάσια) des Herrn;" (Sir 18,5-6; vgl. 42,21).

Wie stark sich Sira auch mit den hellenistisch bedeutsamen *Werten* auseinanderzusetzen hat, zeigt sich auch an seiner zentralen Denkkategorie φόβος κυρίου, und natürlich muss sich der oben beschriebene Denkansatz im Zentrum bewähren und wird tatsächlich bei der ersten Erwähnung des Schlüsselwortes thematisiert: „Die Achtung vor dem Herrn ist Ruhm und Ehre (δόξα καὶ καύχημα), Hoheit ist sie und eine prächtige Krone (στέφανος ἀγαλλιάματος);" (1,11). Ehre ist alles, könnte man sagen. Nachhaltigere Auswirkungen hat zwar im TaNaK das Vermeiden von Schande. Das Risiko, dieser zu verfallen, gilt als Drohung. Und wenngleich die Ehre an sich allenthalben recht positiv gesehen wird, mutet die Anhäufung einschlägiger Ausdrücke in 1,11 doch eigenartig an. Auffällig ist die Ansammlung von Ehrenausdrücken aber nicht, wenn man auf hellenistischem Hintergrund zu Ehre und Kranz Folgendes bedenkt:

Die außergewöhnlich weise Diotima („ὦ σοφωτάτη Διοτίμα"; Sym. 208b) fasst das Ziel des menschlichen Strebens mit einem Wort zusammen: φιλοτιμία, d.h. es geht um „Liebe zur Ehre" oder „Streben nach Ehre". Diotima hält fest, dass die Menschen einen „gewaltigen Trieb haben, berühmt zu werden und sich einen unsterblichen Namen auf ewige Zeiten zu erwerben und sich in jedes noch so gefährliche Abenteuer zu werfen (ἔρωτι τοῦ ὀνομαστοὶ γενέσθαι καὶ κλέος ἐς τὸν ἀεὶ χρόνον ἀθάνατον καταθέσθαι· καὶ ὑπὲρ τούτου κινδύνους τε κινδυνεύειν ἕτοιμοί εἰσι πάντας" (Sym. 208c), um zu guter Letzt unvergänglichen Ruhm und dauerndes Andenken zu erlangen (ἀθάνατον κλέος καὶ μνήμην; Sym. 209d)"[90]. – Auch gegen die Freude am halsbrecherischen Wagemut und Kampfeswillen wendet sich der Enkel, wohl im Sinne seines Großvaters: „καρδία σκληρὰ κακωθήσεται ἐπ' ἐσχάτων καὶ ὁ ἀγαπῶν κίνδυνον ἐν αὐτῷ ἀπολεῖται" (Sir 3,26).

Bei Philostrat[91] liest man, dass der Pankratiast Arrichion, „der siegend den Tod fand, den Kranz erhält und der olympische Richter ihn damit bekränzte. ... Denn obwohl es sicher etwas Großes ist, dass er bereits zweimal in Olympia gewonnen hat, so ist doch dies jetzt größer, dass er den Sieg mit dem Leben erkaufte ..." Die Gier nach dem Kranz wirkt wie eine Droge und Philon[92] schreibt dazu: „Ich weiß, dass Ringer und Pankratiasten oft aus Ehrgeiz und Siegesstreben (ὑπὸ φιλοτιμίας καὶ τῆς εἰς τὸ νικᾶν σπουδῆς), obwohl ihr Körper schon aufgibt und sie allein durch die Kraft der Seele weiteratmen und -kämpfen, die sie sich

---

90 REITERER, Politik, 131.
91 PHILOSTRATUS, Imagines 2.6.
92 PHILON, Prob. Quod omnis probus liber sit 1:110,113.

daran gewöhnt haben, die Furcht zu überwinden (τῶν φοβερῶν ἐγκαρτεροῦσιν), bis zum Eintritt des Todes durchhalten (ἄχρι τῆς τοῦ βίου τελευτῆς). ... Den Wettkämpfern gilt der Tod für einen Ölbaum- oder Selleriekranz als ehrenvoll (ἀλλὰ γὰρ οὖν κοτίνων μὲν χάριν καὶ σελίνων εὐκλεὴς ἀγωνισταῖς ἡ τελευτή)".

Der Gewinn eines Kranzes war im hellenistischen Bereich der Inbegriff des Erstrebenswerten und die Wettkämpfe, bei denen das Erringen eines solchen möglich war, können „die heiligen Kranzspiele"[93] genannt werden. – Den Kranz erlangt man bei Sira nicht im Wettkampf, sondern durch die Achtung vor dem Herrn. Um deren Wert und Anziehungskraft herauszuheben, bedient sich Sira der gesellschaftlichen Signalwörter seiner Zeit.

Etwas später umschreibt er die Erlangung der Gottesfurcht als die Erringung eines Kranzes der Weisheit. Damit verbunden ist Friede und Heilung: στέφανος σοφίας φόβος κυρίου ἀναθάλλων εἰρήνην καὶ ὑγίειαν ἰάσεως; (1,18). Wie kommt man denn auf die Idee, hier Gesundheit und Heilung zu erwähnen? Sira will seine Lehre als Alternative jenen Zeiterscheinungen gegenüberstellen, in denen Kranz, Friede, Heilung und Gesundheit gefährdet waren. Damit sind wir mitten in der Thematik der vielen Wettkämpfe in der hellenistischen Welt. Man halte sich vor Augen, dass z.B. Theogenes von der Insel Thasos wegen der vielen Siege, vor allem aber nach Olympiasiegen im Boxen (480 v.Chr.) und im Pankration (476 v.Chr.) nach seinem Tod als Gottheit verehrt wurde und man ihm opferte. Wie Pausanias[94] und Lucian[95] bezeugen, schreiben ihm „sowohl Griechen aus anderen Städten als auch Nichtgriechen ... magische Kräfte für das Heilen von Krankheiten zu."[96] Die Erwähnung des Kranzes und der Heilung besitzen auf diesem Hintergrund religiösen Charakter. Wenngleich Plutarch über ihn später schreiben wird: „Ich kann seine übergroße Ehrliebe und Streitlust nicht preisen"[97], zeigen diese Zeugnisse, dass Sira ein konkretes, sehr aktuelles Zeitthema aufgreift. Denn „in einem ... Epigramm hören wir von einem Boxer, dessen Verletzungen so entstellend sind, dass er sich im Spiegel nicht wieder erkennt. Ein anderer verliert sein Erbteil, weil niemand bestätigen will, dass dieser Mann ohne Gesichtszüge der Sohn des Verstorbenen ist."[98] Dann sieht man, wo der Anlass für die Zerstö-

---

93 POLIAKOFF, Kampfsport, 32.
94 PAUSANIAS, Graeciae description 6.11.9.
95 LUCIAN, Deorum Concilium 12.
96 POLIAKOFF, Kampfsport, 168.
97 PLUTARCH, Praecepta gerendae rei publice 15; vgl. DERS., Moralia 811d-e.
98 POLIAKOFF, Kampfsport, 119-120, wobei in der Antike Boxen als jene Sportart gilt, in der die meisten Verletzungen zugefügt werden.

rung der Gesundheit liegt. Daher ist es verständlich, wenn Sira später notiert: „Besser ist es, in die Hände des Herrn zu fallen als in die Hände der Menschen;" (Sir 2,18).

Man könnte die Auswirkungen der sirazidischen Studien und seiner Durchdringung des TaNaK noch um vieles erweitern, wie z.B. durch den Hinweis, dass die Elternehre und die Wohltaten an den alten Eltern in neue Dimensionen hineingestellt werden, wie das folgende Zitat zeigt: „Denn die Wohltat am Vater (ἐλεημοσύνη γὰρ πατρός) wird nicht vergessen, sie wird als Sühne für deine Sünden (ἀντὶ ἁμαρτιῶν) eingetragen. Zur Zeit der Bedrängnis wird sie dir vergolten werden; wie Wärme den Reif werden aufgelöst deine Sünden (ἀναλυθήσονταί σου αἱ ἁμαρτίαι);" (3,14-15).[99] Hier brechen sich neue religiös-theologische Sichtweisen Bahn, die sich in Bereiche der – im Regelfall – kultisch praktizierten Sündenvergebung einmischen. Wenn jetzt das Stichwort Kult gefallen ist, ist also gleich zu erwähnen, dass Sira auch die Opferthematik, aber auch Gebote aus dem TaNaK aufgreift und sie mit unerwarteten, neuen Aspekten verbindet: „Den Nächsten mordet (φονεύων τὸν πλησίον), der ihm den Lebensunterhalt (ἐμβίωσιν) nimmt, Blut vergießt (ἐκχέων αἷμα), wer dem Lohnarbeiter den Lohn (μισθὸν μισθίου) vorenthält" (34,26-27). „Wer das Gesetz (νόμον) einhält (ὁ συντηρῶν), vermehrt die Opfer (προσφοράς), ein Heilsopfer bringt dar (θυσιάζων σωτηρίου), der die Vorschriften hält (ὁ προσέχων ἐντολαῖς). Der Liebe erweist (χάριν), bringt [damit] Speiseopfer dar, der eine Wohltat macht (ὁ ποιῶν ἐλεημοσύνην), spendet (θυσιάζων) [damit] ein Dankopfer (αἰνέσεως);" (35,1-2). – Die Verinnerlichung der Offenbarung befreit Sira vom Zwang wörtlicher Zitate und lässt ihn mit geprägten Phraseologien unkonventionell umgehen. In einem weiteren Schritt stellt er viele der überkommenen religiösen Übungen und Gebräuche, aber auch gewöhnliche Alltagsthemen, wie Kindererziehung und Geldgeschäfte, im Lichte der Vertiefung neu dar.

Bibliographie

BOHLEN, Reinhold, Die Ehrung der Eltern bei Ben Sira. Studien zur Motivation und Interpretation eines familienethischen Grundwertes in frühhellenistischer Zeit (TThSt 51), Trier 1991.

CRIBIORE, Raffaella, Gymnastics of the Mind. Greek Education in Hellenistic and Roman Egypt, Princeton 2001.

CHRISTES, J., Bildung und Gesellschaft. Die Einschätzung der Bildung und ihrer Vermittler in der griechisch-römischen Antike (EF 37), Darmstadt 1975.

---

99 Vgl. dazu BOHLEN, Ehrung, 168-180.

DONNER, Herbert/RÜTERSWÖRDEN, Udo, Wilhelm Gesenius, Hebräisches und Aramäisches Handwörterbuch über das Alte Testament ש-ת , begonnen D.R. Meyer, Heidelberg ¹⁸2010.

FINLEY, Moses I., The World of Odysseus, Harmmondsworth ²1978.

FINKELBERG, Margalit, The Canonicity of Homer, in: Becker, Eve-Marie/Scholz, Stefan (Hg.), Kanon in Konstruktion und Dekonstruktion. Konanonisierungsprozesse religiöser Texte von der Antike bis zur Gegenwart. Ein Handbuch, Berlin/New York 2012, 137-151.

GESENIUS, Wilhelm, Hebräisches und aramäisches Handwörterbuch über das Alte Testament, Leipzig ¹⁷1915.

GLICKSMAN, Andrew T., Wisdom of Solomon 10. A Jewish Hellenistic Reinterpretation of Early Israelite History through Sapiential Lenses (DCLS 9), Berlin/New York 2011.

LABOW, Dagmar, Flavius Josephus, Contra Apionem, Buch I. Einleitung, Text, Textkritischer Apparat, Übersetzung und Kommentar (BWANT 167), Stuttgart 2005.

LANG, Bernhard, Vom Propheten zum Schriftgelehrten. Charismatische Autorität in verschiedenen Kulturkreisen, in: Stietencron, Heinrich von (Hg.), Theologen und Theologien in verschiedenen Kulturkreisen, Düsseldorf 1986, 89-114.

LIDDELL, Henry G./SCOTT, Robert/JONES, Henry St., A Greek-English Lexicon, Oxford 2001.

MARBÖCK, Johannes, Gerechtigkeit Gottes und Leben nach dem Sirachbuch. Ein Antwortversuch in seinem Kontext, in: Ders., Weisheit und Frömmigkeit. Studien zur alttestamentlichen Literatur der Spätzeit (ÖBS 29), Frankfurt 2006, 173-197 (= in: Jeremias, Jörg (Hg.), Gerechtigkeit und Leben im hellenistischen Zeitalter. Symposion anlässlich des 75. Geburtstages von Otto Kaiser [BZAW 296], Berlin/New York 2001, 305-319].

MARBÖCK, Johannes, Jesus Sirach 1-23. Übersetzt und ausgelegt (HThK.AT), Freiburg/Basel/Wien: Herder 2010.

MARBÖCK, Johannes, Sir 38,24-39,11: Der schriftgelehrte Weise. Ein Beitrag zu Gestalt und Werk Ben Siras, in: Ders., Gottes Weisheit unter uns. Zur Theologie des Buches Sirach, hg. Fischer, I. (HBS 6), Freiburg u.a. 1995, 25-51.

MITTAG, Peter Franz, Antiochos IV. Epiphanes. Eine politische Biographie (KLIO Beihefte 11), Berlin 2006.

MORGAN, Teresa, Literate Education in the Hellenistic and Roman Worlds, Cambridge 1998.

POLIAKOFF, Michael B., Kampfsport in der Antike. Das Spiel um Leben und Tod, Düsseldorf/Zürich 2004.

REITERER, Friedrich V., Aaron's Polyvalent Role according to Ben Sira, in: Corley, Jeremy/van Grol, Harm (eds.), Rewriting Biblical History. Essays on Chronicles and Ben Sira, FS Pancratius C. Beentjes (DCLS 7), Berlin/New York 2011, 27-56.

REITERER, Friedrich V., „Alles hat nämlich der Herr gemacht". Das Telos der Schöpfung bei Ben Sira, in: Nicklas, Tobias/Zamfir, Korinna (ed.) in coop. Braun, Heike, Theologies of Creation in Early Judaism and Ancient Christianity, FS Hans Klein, Berlin/New York 2010, 95-136.

REITERER, Friedrich V., Gott und Opfer, in: Ders., "Die Vollendung der Gottesfurcht ist Weisheit" (Sir 21,11). Studien zum Buch Ben Sira (Jesus Sirach) (SBAB 50), Stuttgart 2011, 133-175.

REITERER, Friedrich V., Religious identity and its development. What may Children learn from their Elders?, in: Passaro, Angelo, Family and Kinship in the Deuterocanonical and Cognate Literature (DCLY), Berlin/New York 2012, (in print).

REITERER, Friedrich V., Jesus Sirach / Jesus Sirachbuch / Ben Sira / Ecclesiasticus, in: Ders., "Die Vollendung der Gottesfurcht ist Weisheit" (Sir 21,11). Studien zum Buch Ben Sira (Jesus Sirach) (SBAB 50), Stuttgart 2011, 11-41; (Lit.).

REITERER, Friedrich V., Politik, Bildung und Religion. Der alttestamentliche Glaube im hellenistischen Ambiente. Teil 1, in: BN NF 149 (2011) 113-137.

REITERER, Friedrich V., Das Verhältnis von חכמה zur תורה im Buch Ben Sira. Kriterien zur gegenseitigen Bestimmung, in: Ders., „Die Vollendung der Gottesfurcht ist Weisheit" (Sir 21,11). Studien zum Buch Ben Sira (Jesus Sirach) (SBAB 50), Stuttgart 2011, 225-263.

WEBER, G., Interaktion, Repräsentation und Herrschaft. Der Königshof im Hellenismus, in: Winterling, A. (Hg.), Zwischen „Haus" und „Staat", Antike Höfe im Vergleich (HZ Beiheft 23), München 1997, 27-71.

WITTE, Markus, Der ‚Kanon' heiliger Schriften des antiken Judentums im Spiegel des Buches Ben Sira/Jesus Sirach, in: Becker, Eve-Marie/Scholz, Stefan (Hg.), Kanon in Konstruktion und Dekonstruktion. Konanonisierungsprozesse religiöser Texte von der Antike bis zur Gegenwart. Ein Handbuch, Berlin/New York 2012, 229-255.

ZIEBARTH, Erich (Hg.), Aus der antiken Schule. Sammlung griechischer Texte auf Papyrus, Holztafeln, Ostraka (Kleine Texte für Vorlesungen und Übungen 65), Bonn ²1913.

"Set Your Desire on My Words": Authoritative Traditions in the Wisdom of Solomon

ANDREW T. GLICKSMAN

Recent studies of the various textual traditions at Qumran have shed light on questions about scriptural authority in late Second Temple Judaism.[1] For several decades now, scholars have demonstrated that the pluriformity and multiplicity of certain traditions in the Dead Sea Scrolls point to a fluidity of scriptural authority, with no closed canon and "extrabiblical" traditions apparently holding the same level of authority as "biblical" ones.[2] While the scrolls provide a picture of scriptural authority for a particular group of Jews in Palestine, was this view of authoritative text and tradition shared by Jews in the rest of that region and beyond? What was the situation like in the communities of the Jewish Diaspora around the same time? What constituted "Scripture" and how was it interpreted in Alexandria, the major seat of Jewish learning in the Diaspora?[3] The Wisdom of Solomon provides some answers to this last question. The fundamental issue that I shall address is how the author of the Wisdom of Solomon (henceforth, Pseudo-Solomon) not only upholds many well-known traditions of the biblical text as authoritative but also includes extrabiblical traditions and implicitly urges his audience to revere his own work as authoritative text

---

[1] For example, see the multiple articles in ULRICH, Dead Sea Scrolls, especially IDEM, Bible, 17-33; IDEM, Canonical Process, 51-78; IDEM, Pluriformity, 79-98. For some of the most recent studies on this issue, see the various contributions in POPOVIĆ, Authoritative Scriptures.

[2] See GARCÍA MARTÍNEZ, Rethinking, 20-21; ULRICH, Bible, 17. Though I am fully aware of the anachronistic nature of the terms "biblical" and "extrabiblical" when speaking about authoritative texts before the late first century A.D., I use these terms in my investigation as a matter of convenience to designate those ancient Jewish writings and traditions that were once held as authoritative by some Jews and later accepted or rejected as either canonical or non-canonical by the Jewish community in Palestine. My use of the term extrabiblical applies to any tradition or interpretation, written or oral, not explicitly found in what eventually became the biblical text. For comments concerning the anachronistic nature of these terms, see REEVES, Scriptural Authority, 63; POPOVIĆ, Introducing, 1.

[3] By the term "Scripture," I mean any written work that a community deems authoritative and not only those biblical texts that were later canonized by the Jewish community. See REEVES, Scriptural Authority, 75.

and, therefore, as Scripture. That Pseudo-Solomon views extrabiblical traditions as authoritative alongside the traditions of the biblical text and stresses the authority of his own work attests to the complexity and fluidity of what constituted Scripture in his day, much like the situation at Qumran.

1. Pseudo-Solomon's Interpretive Milieu

As a hellenistic Jew living in Egypt in the early Roman era, Pseudo-Solomon revered the ancient Jewish ancestral traditions, which he knew primarily in their Greek form enshrined in the Septuagint. Though the Septuagint was not yet complete, Pseudo-Solomon had access to and used Greek versions of the Pentateuch, the Psalter, and major prophetic (especially Isaiah) and sapiential texts (especially Proverbs, Job, and Sirach).[4] Most relevant for him and his fellow Alexandrian Jews were the traditions of the Pentateuch, the bulk of which recount the trials of their ancestors who under Moses' leadership and God's direction escaped from Egyptian enslavement. While the Jewish community of Alexandria was very successful and prolific, anti-Jewish hellenistic groups often criticized its seemingly unphilosophical beliefs and exclusive customs, especially as expressed in the Pentateuch. Many Alexandrian Jewish interpreters before Pseudo-Solomon, such as Artapanus, Demetrius the Chronographer, and Ezekiel the Tragedian, had focused on defending, reinterpreting, and reapplying the Pentateuchal traditions in their works. They wrote these works not only because the Pentateuchal stories of the exodus and Sinai, so central for Jewish identity, were under attack but also because the Jews of Egypt could most readily relate to and draw encouragement from the trials endured by their ancestors who once lived in the same land.[5] Even in Pseudo-Solomon's own day, Philo attempted to synthesize Moses' teachings with the best that the Greek philosophical schools had to offer. As an inheritor of this Alexandrian interpretive tradition, Pseudo-Solomon joins their ranks by composing a lengthy *logos protreptikos* in which he encourages faithful Jews to hold fast to the ancient traditions of their ancestors. At the time, the Jewish community in Alexandria was subject to increasingly violent bouts of persecution at the hands of both Greek

---

4 See SKEHAN, Borrowings, 149-162; IDEM, Isaiah, 163-171; IDEM, Literary Relationship, 172-236. I shall treat this issue more extensively at a later point in my investigation.

5 For texts by these Jewish Alexandrian authors, see CHARLESWORTH, Pseudepigrapha, 2:803-819, 843-854, 889-903.

nationalists and Jewish apostates.⁶ As a result, many Jews were in danger of abandoning their faith to more fully embrace hellenistic thought and custom in order to gain social status and avoid further persecution. To combat this danger, Pseudo-Solomon argues that pagan, hellenistic philosophy and culture cannot lead one to true wisdom and glory, but rather these rewards come from pursuing the ancient Jewish traditions granted by God. The way that Pseudo-Solomon attempts to persuade his audience reveals something about his understanding of authoritative texts and traditions.

2. Authority in the Wisdom of Solomon

My point of departure for understanding authoritative texts and traditions in the Wisdom of Solomon is to determine Pseudo-Solomon's general perception of authority as manifested by his own words. Since our author was Jewish, it comes as no surprise that he presents God as the source of all authority. God is supreme ruler over the world (Wis 9:3; 12:15) and grants earthly authority (Wis 6:3). He mediates authority through divine wisdom, which Pseudo-Solomon often presents as a feminine figure, in keeping with previous Jewish wisdom tradition (see Proverbs 8; Sirach 24). *Sophia* or Lady Wisdom, as she is often called, is a personified divine attribute. At times, Pseudo-Solomon equates her with God's word (λόγος, Wis 9:1-2) by which he creates the world and associates her with divine law (νόμος, Wis 6:18) by which God communicates to his people the way to live righteously.⁷ The manifestation of God's wisdom as divine word and law within the past Israelite and present Jewish communities is at the heart of Pseudo-Solomon's understanding of authority.

Though many passages in the Wisdom of Solomon shed light on Pseudo-Solomon's understanding of authority, Wis 2:12-15, 6:9-11, and 18:9.22 best illustrate the authoritative nature of divine word and law and their role within the Jewish community. The last of these passages lays the foundation for understanding the other two. In chapter 18, Pseudo-Solomon retells two events from Israelite history in order to show that God saves and rewards the righteous and punishes the

---

6 For a full description of the situation of the Alexandrian Jewish community in the early Roman era, see TCHERIKOVER, Hellenistic Civilization, 308-332; SMALLWOOD, Jews Under Roman Rule, 220-255; MODRZEJEWSKI, Jews of Egypt, 161-183. One major point of contention in Pseudo-Solomon's day was the relegation of the Alexandrian Jewish population to the status of a lower-class, subjected people (λαός), thereby eliminating their exemption from paying the "poll tax" (capitatio or λαογραφία).

7 Wisdom's association with divine word and law is also present in Sir 24:3.23.

wicked. First, he describes God's salvation of his ancestors from the last two plagues in Egypt, that is, the plague of darkness and the death of the firstborn son. To avoid the last plague the Israelites carried out God's instructions for the first Passover, which Pseudo-Solomon recounts as follows:

κρυφῇ γὰρ ἐθυσίαζον ὅσιοι παῖδες ἀγαθῶν,
  καὶ τὸν τῆς θειότητος νόμον ἐν ὁμονοίᾳ διέθεντο,
τῶν αὐτῶν ὁμοίως καὶ ἀγαθῶν
  καὶ κινδύνων μεταλήμψεσθαι τοὺς ἁγίους,
    πατέρων ἤδη προαναμέλποντες αἴνους.

For the holy children of the good secretly offered sacrifice,
  and with one accord agreed to the divine law,
so that the holy ones would share alike the same things,
  both good things and dangers;
    already they were singing the praises of the ancestors.

The reference to the law here in Wis 18:9 is most likely God's Passover instructions in Exodus 12 and not the entire Mosaic law. However, an allusion to the Torah in general cannot be completely excluded, especially since the Israelite observance of the divine law here may foreshadow their unanimous acceptance of the law later at Sinai (Exod 24:3.7). Whatever the precise meaning of the phrase τὸν τῆς θειότητος νόμον in this passage, the law is authoritative because it has divine origins and, as authoritative, this same law unifies the community. Thus, authoritative traditions have a communal dimension. They form the life of a community by helping the community make sense of its surroundings. As Paul Achtemeier asserts, sacred traditions retain their authority within a community insofar as they possess the "ability to *author* reality."[8] In this particular case, Pseudo-Solomon looks back to a defining moment in the history of his community. In his interpretation of the original event, the Israelite ancestors believed that God was directing them in their common plight, which informed the early community's experience and solidified their identity as a group. By evoking and reflecting upon this tradition, Pseudo-Solomon allows it to author reality for his own generation in the same way. The Jews of the author's day, who endured hardship in Egypt because they were following God's commands, were unified in their struggles and perpetuated the heritage initiated by their ancestors long ago. The last line of this passage also reveals Pseudo-Solomon's understanding of authority, yet the referent of πατέρων αἴνους is ambiguous and hotly debated. Are these praises *about* the ancestors or, rather, sung *by* the ancestors?[9] The latter

---

8   ACHTEMEIER, Inspiration, 151.
9   See LARCHER, Livre de la Sagesse, 3:1006-1008; WINSTON, Wisdom, 316.

seems most likely, which means that Pseudo-Solomon retrojects the later Passover tradition of singing hymns (see 2Chron 30:21), a practice neither commanded nor mentioned in Exodus 12, to the time of the first Passover. The tradition of singing hymns at Passover in Pseudo-Solomon's day is an authoritative practice because of the perception that the enslaved ancestors of the Jews originally did so. Thus, practices or stories that are believed to originate from a community's distant past, and most especially from its inception, are considered to be authoritative.[10]

The second story that Pseudo-Solomon retells in chapter 18 is Aaron's saving of the Israelites from a plague in the wilderness by offering incense to God (Num 17:6-15). When he interprets this tradition, in v. 22 Pseudo-Solomon states:

ἐνίκησεν δὲ τὸν χόλον οὐκ ἰσχύι τοῦ σώματος,
οὐχ ὅπλων ἐνεργείᾳ,
ἀλλὰ λόγῳ τὸν κολάζοντα ὑπέταξεν,
ὅρκους πατέρων καὶ διαθήκας ὑπομνήσας.

He conquered the wrath not by strength of body,
not by force of arms,
But by word he subdued the avenger,
recalling the oaths of the ancestors and covenants (v. 22).

Aaron's words of supplication, represented by the incense rising up to God, are the means by which he averts further disaster. Even though the passage from Numbers does not reveal the content of Aaron's supplication, Pseudo-Solomon claims that Aaron reminded God of the covenants that he had made with their forebears (probably the patriarchs, especially, Abraham in Genesis 12; 15 ;17). Aaron's "word" is efficacious, and it is ultimately the divine word since he appeals to the oaths and covenants of old, which God originally spoke. He recalls the promises of God, the ancient and authoritative traditions of Israel's divine election, which are life-giving for the Israelite community in trouble. In addition, both this story from Numbers 17 and the previous example from Exodus 12 demonstrate the authoritativeness of traditions in the Pentateuch. And yet, Pseudo-Solomon embellishes the ancient traditions by adding more details, which suggests fluidity in authoritative traditions.

For Pseudo-Solomon, authority lies not only in ancient traditions that have divine origin but also in individuals, or whole communities, that live and pass on these traditions. Wis 18:9, which I mentioned earlier, hints at this point, but Wis 2:12-15 makes it even clearer. In this

---

10 See similar comments made by POPOVIĆ, Introducing, 2; VAN DER KOOIJ, Authoritative Scriptures, 55.

latter passage, a righteous individual by his words and deeds authoritatively admonishes and condemns the behavior of unrighteous individuals. Concerning the righteous individual, the wicked complain:

καὶ ὀνειδίζει ἡμῖν ἁμαρτήματα νόμου,
    καὶ ἐπιφημίζει ἡμῖν ἁμαρτήματα παιδείας ἡμῶν·[...]
ἐγένετο ἡμῖν εἰς ἔλεγχον ἐννοιῶν ἡμῶν·
    βαρύς ἐστιν ἡμῖν καὶ βλεπόμενος,
ὅτι ἀνόμοιος τοῖς ἄλλοις ὁ βίος αὐτοῦ,
    καὶ ἐξηλλαγμέναι αἱ τρίβοι αὐτοῦ·

And he reproaches us for sins against the law,
    and accuses us for sins against our training.[...]
He became to us a reproof of our thoughts;
    the sight of him is difficult for us,
because his life is unlike that of others,
    and his ways are unusual.

By his words, the righteous individual admonishes the wicked for transgressing the law. At the very least, νόμος here refers to the Torah if not *Halakah* in general. That the wicked speak of "our training" in conjunction with "the law" indicates that they, too, are Jews who have been instructed but have turned away from their upbringing. Both the words and deeds of the righteous one correct and annoy the apostates to the point that they plot evil against him. This passage demonstrates that the righteous one speaks and acts with authority because his ways are in line with the authoritative law, traditional Jewish instruction that ultimately comes from God and is imbued with his wisdom. Though the wicked do not consider the righteous one to have authority, they are mistaken in their judgment and will be condemned because they disregarded his righteous example (Wis 3:10). Thus, one who lives in accordance with authoritative traditions is considered to possess some level of authority. This understanding of authority bolsters the way that Pseudo-Solomon presents himself as an authoritative figure who proclaims an authoritative message.

In Wisdom 6-9, the author presents himself as wise King Solomon and claims that Wisdom herself taught him (7:22), implying that she is the source of his righteous behavior (9:9-11). With so great an instructress, and by identifying himself as the characteristically wise monarch, in Wis 6:9-11 Pseudo-Solomon has the authority to proclaim:

πρὸς ὑμᾶς οὖν, ὦ τύραννοι, οἱ λόγοι μου,
    ἵνα μάθητε σοφίαν καὶ μὴ παραπέσητε.
οἱ γὰρ φυλάξαντες ὁσίως τὰ ὅσια ὁσιωθήσονται,
    καὶ οἱ διδαχθέντες αὐτὰ εὑρήσουσιν ἀπολογίαν.
ἐπιθυμήσατε οὖν τῶν λόγων μου,
    ποθήσατε καὶ παιδευθήσεσθε.

> Therefore, O monarchs, my words are meant for you,
>> so that you might learn wisdom and not fall away.
> For those who observe holy things in a holy manner will be made holy,
>> And those who have been taught them will find a defense.
> Therefore set your desire on my words;
>> Long for them, and you will be instructed.

While Pseudo-Solomon appears to be addressing royal figures in these verses (and throughout the first part of the book, see 1:1), it seems more likely that his message is to those who generally pursue righteousness; in this case, his audience of faithful Jews.[11] In particular, the use of the terms παραπίπτω, " fall away," and ἀπολογία, "a defense," may hint at a Jewish audience that needs the wisdom that the author offers in order to avoid apostasy and defend its beliefs. Above all, Pseudo-Solomon asserts here that his own words are filled with "wisdom" and, by implication, with "holy things." What Pseudo-Solomon speaks is from God through Wisdom and, therefore, authoritative. As we will see, Pseudo-Solomon's authority extends beyond a mere reiteration of the ancient Israelite biblical traditions. Rather, he further exhibits his own authority and that of his work by including his own creative reinterpretation and reapplication of past events in new circumstances. In this way, he gives new life and relevance to the ancient traditions through extrabiblical material.

3. Pseudo-Solomon's Use of Biblical and Extrabiblical Traditions

Biblical and extrabiblical traditions pervade the Wisdom of Solomon. If we were to identify the origin of some of these traditions, then we would have a better understanding of which texts Pseudo-Solomon and his community perceived to be authoritative. This, of course, assumes that at least some of the traditions derive from specific texts rather than from oral tradition alone.[12] However, clearly identifying a tradition's source is not always possible, especially when dealing with extrabiblical traditions. Even identifying biblical traditions in other ancient Jewish works can be difficult because there are different ways

---

11 See SKEHAN, Borrowings, 385-386.
12 Presumably, the texts to which Pseudo-Solomon alludes are considered to be authoritative not only by himself but also by much of the Alexandrian Jewish community that he is addressing. If not, then why would he endanger the persuasiveness of his work by referencing texts that his community did not accept?

to reference a text, namely, through (1) direct quotation, (2) implicit citation, and (3) general allusion. Of these three types, direct quotation is the easiest to identify, though in some cases the direction of dependence is not so apparent. The task is made easier when the author uses an introductory formula such as "as it is written" or "as the prophet says." Implicit citation is less clear than direct quotation. This type of reference involves common imagery and significant terminology (preferably unique words or phrases) from the parent text. The last type, general allusion, can only be determined by extensive points of thematic contact which show that the imagery could only derive from a particular parent text. There must be enough thematic correspondences between the base text and the dependent text to make a clear judgment in favor of general allusion. This last case is often the most difficult to positively identify. With these three categories in mind, it is possible to analyze more effectively Pseudo-Solomon's references to specific biblical traditions.

Scholars have long recognized that Pseudo-Solomon makes extensive use of the stories found in the Pentateuch. Every major section of the Wisdom of Solomon exhibits dependence on this first part of Jewish scripture.[13] Most notable is the second half of the book (namely, chapters 10-19) which reinterprets key biblical figures and events from Adam to Moses in 10:1-11:1 and the Israelite exodus from Egypt and wilderness wanderings in 11:2-19:22. In referring to these Pentateuchal texts, Pseudo-Solomon never explicitly quotes extensive passages, rather some of his references are implicit citations while the majority can be categorized as general allusions.[14] In addition to this strong dependence on Pentateuchal texts, the vocabulary and imagery that

---

13 I espouse a bipartite structure for the Wisdom of Solomon (Part I = 1:1-11:1 and Part II = 11:2-19:22), with two major sections in the first part of the book (Part I,A = 1:1-6:21 and I,B = 6:22-11:1). The influence of Pentateuchal texts on Part I,B (especially in Wis 10:1-11:1) and Part II is most apparent. However, even Part I,A alludes to stories in Genesis. For example, note the discussion of the origin of sin and death in Wis 1:13-15 and 2:23-24 as dependent on Genesis 1-3 and the reference to Enoch in Wis 4:7-11 on Gen 5:24.

14 Scholars have noted the absence of extensive direct quotation of biblical passages in the Wisdom of Solomon, in general. See GILBERT, Sagesse, 93; MANFREDI, Trial, 162. However, some notable examples of implicit citation of Pentateuchal passages in the Wisdom of Solomon include: Abraham is ἄμεμπτος, "blameless," in Wis 10:4 and Gen 17:1; Lot's wife is a στήλη ἁλός, "pillar of salt," in Wis 10:7 and Gen 19:26; God performs σημεῖα, "signs," and τέρατα, "wonders," when saving the Israelites from Egypt in Wis 10:16 (in reverse order) and Exod 7:3; 11:9.10; the Israelites ἐσκύλευσαν, "plundered," their Egyptian oppressors in Wis 10:20 and Exod 12:36. For a more extensive list of implicit citations of Pentateuchal texts in Wisdom 10, see my discussion in GLICKSMAN, Wisdom, 152-153.

Pseudo-Solomon employs throughout his work further indicate his familiarity with and reverence for other biblical texts.

In the 1930s and 40s, Patrick W. Skehan conducted extensive investigations into Pseudo-Solomon's knowledge and use of biblical texts outside the Pentateuch.[15] He found that in addition to its clear concern with Pentateuchal themes, the Wisdom of Solomon also employs imagery and terminology from the Prophets and Writings. Though Pseudo-Solomon refers to many biblical books by means of implicit citation, most notable is his ubiquitous use of language and themes from Isaiah, the Psalter, and the wisdom corpus.[16] It makes sense that Pseudo-Solomon would borrow especially from the Psalms and wisdom literature because much of his composition is a sapiential reinterpretation of key biblical events and also a work of poetry that is modeled on the *parallelismus membrorum* exhibited in the Hebrew poetry of the Psalter.[17] From the wisdom literature, he extensively uses the language from Proverbs and Job. One could also mention possible allusions to Sirach, though in many cases the correspondences could be based primarily on Proverbs. Yet, as a wisdom writer, Pseudo-Solomon undoubtedly had extensive knowledge of Sirach, which was translated into Greek by Ben Sira's grandson at Alexandria near the end of the second century B.C.[18]

---

15 See n. 4 above.
16 Significant correspondences between the thought and language of Isaiah and the Wisdom of Solomon include: the suffering righteous individuals in Wis 2:10-5:23 (minus 3:15-4:13) and Isa 52:13-53:12; and the condemnation of idolatry in Wis 13:1-15:17 and Isaiah 44-45. See SUGGS, Wisdom, 26-33; NICKELSBURG, Resurrection, 63; SKEHAN, Isaiah, 163-171. For some clear examples of allusion to the Psalms, see the parallel between the reference to τρίβοι εὐθεῖαι, "straight paths," in Wis 10:10 and Ps 26:11 (Septuagint); correspondence between the address to kings in Wis 1:1; 6:9.11.21 and Ps 2:10.12 (Septuagint) and also between "knowing/not knowing the way of the Lord" in Wis 5:7 and Ps 24:4; 26:11; 94:10 (all from the Septuagint). For many other examples, see SKEHAN, Borrowings, 149-162.
17 When Pseudo-Solomon describes the Red Sea event from Exodus, some of his language and imagery derives from retellings of the same event in the Psalter (Septuagint version). For example, see the use of σκέπη, "shelter," to describe the pillar of cloud in Wis 10:17 and Ps 104:39; the use of ὕδωρ πολύ, "much water," in Wis 10:18 (singular) and Ps 76:20 (plural); and the use of ἄβυσσος, "abyss," in Wis 10:19 and Ps 105:9 (see also Isa 51:10; 63:12-13).
18 See the Prologue to Sirach. In his investigation of Pseudo-Solomon's use of wisdom texts, Skehan did not include the correspondences between Sirach and the Wisdom of Solomon. This is most likely because the correspondences are too numerous. He states: "Though the strong resemblances in thought and languages between Ben Sira and Wis were investigated in the preparation of my dissertation, it has been decided to omit discussion of them in the course of the present study. Were they added, the material presented would thereby be rendered too considerable and too unwieldy for convenient examination." SKEHAN, Literary Relationship, 173.

Finally, in terms of Pseudo-Solomon's use of biblical texts, Skehan asserts that the sage not only uses the Septuagint but also demonstrates that in some cases he must have consulted a proto-Massoretic text.[19] This finding suggests that Pseudo-Solomon considered both the Greek and Hebrew texts as authoritative. His access to and use of both versions indicates a general pluriformity and fluidity of textual traditions in Alexandria, which is similar to the situation at Qumran.

In addition to the prevalent biblical themes and terms in his work, Pseudo-Solomon masterfully integrates many expressions and themes not found in the biblical text. Though some of the added imagery and vocabulary have parallels in extrabiblical texts extant in his day (such as 1 Enoch, *Jubilees*, and the *Testament of the Levi*), there is no conclusive evidence that Pseudo-Solomon had direct familiarity with these texts, let alone considered them to be authoritative.[20] In the Wisdom of Solomon, there is no direct quotation or implicit citation of known extrabiblical texts, and neither can a strong case be made for general allusion. Nonetheless, Pseudo-Solomon does incorporate extrabiblical traditions in his interpretation of biblical texts even if their origin remains uncertain: it is unclear whether he borrows these insights into the text from specific written sources, uses well-known interpretive traditions circulating orally in Alexandria at the time, or presents his own creative reflections on the text (mediated, of course, by the light of God's eternal Wisdom – the author's instructress in all things). While it is impossible to determine which extrabiblical interpretive traditions originate with Pseudo-Solomon and which (or if) he borrows from other sources, it is likely that at least some of what he writes is *sui generis*. Like many skilled ancient biblical interpreters, Pseudo-Solomon weaves his own modes of expression and insights into his commentary on Scripture

---

19 In several instances, Skehan shows that the Wisdom of Solomon reflects readings in the Massoretic text (rather than the Septuagint) of Proverbs and Job. See SKEHAN, Literary Relationship, 175, 179-180, 192-194.

20 Parallels between the Wisdom of Solomon and these extrabiblical texts do not necessitate direct dependence of one upon the other. Rather, it is possible that they share a common oral or (currently undiscovered) written source. For examples of similarities between the Wisdom of Solomon and 1 Enoch, compare God's reward of the "elect" in Wis 3:9 with 1 Enoch 5:7-8; and the power of God's heavenly word to slay sinners in Wis 18:15-16 and 1 Enoch 62:2. For parallels between the Wisdom of Solomon and *Jubilees*, compare the way that Jacob's enemies "lie in wait" in Wis 10:12 and *Jub.* 34:1-9; and the interpretation in Wis 10:17 and *Jub.* 48:18 that the Israelite plundering of the Egyptians was payment for their slavery. For a list of similarities between the *Testament of Levi* and the Wisdom of Solomon, see WINSTON, Wisdom, 217. The most notable parallels include: the armor of God in Wis 5:17-19 and the garments of the priesthood in TestLevi 8:2; and the "light of the law" in Wis 18:4 and TestLevi 14:4.

without explicitly distinguishing between authoritative biblical text and extrabiblical interpretation. This lack of clear distinction in his work may indicate that Pseudo-Solomon does not perceive a difference between these categories – they are both ways that God communicates wisdom to his people.[21] In the late Second Temple period, there was not always a careful concern to keep the sacred text distinct from its interpretation. The mixing of biblical traditions with original, extrabiblical interpretation suggests that Pseudo-Solomon presents his own work as authoritative for his Alexandrian community.

4. The Wisdom of Solomon as Authoritative Scripture

As in any interpretive text, in the Wisdom of Solomon there is a dynamic interdependence between the authority of the interpreter of tradition and the authority of the very tradition that he is interpreting. While the interpreter presents himself as one worthy to expound the meaning of the tradition in an authoritative manner, the tradition retains its authority and relevance specifically because the interpreter decides to comment on it and apply its contents to circumstances that he and his community are experiencing.[22] This authoritative interplay between interpreter and tradition is well attested throughout the Wisdom of Solomon in three ways: (1) through the author's self-identification as wise king Solomon, (2) in the way that the author ingeniously combines originally unrelated texts and traditions in a new way; (3) and through the author's application of the traditions from Genesis and Exodus to make these texts relevant for a new generation of Jews enduring hardship in Egypt.

4.1 Solomonic Self-Identification

The most apparent interplay between authoritative author and authoritative tradition is the pseudepigraphic nature of Pseudo-Solomon's work. The author never reveals his true identity; however, in several

---

21 Some of the texts discovered at Qumran exhibit a similar phenomenon. For example, see the *Genesis Apocryphon* (1QapGen) and *Jubilees* (1Q17-18; 4Q216-224). In other texts from Qumran, such as the peshers, the sacred biblical text and commentary upon it are distinguished from one another. For example, see the *Habakkuk Pesher* (1QpHab), the *Hosea Pesher* (4Q167), the *Nahum Pesher* (4Q169), the *Zephaniah Pesher* (1Q15M 4Q170), and the *Psalms Pesher* (1Q16; 4Q171). However, even in the case of the peshers, the commentary interspersed among direct biblical quotations is presented as authoritative interpretation and application of the biblical text.
22 See similar comments by GARCÍA MARTÍNEZ, Rethinking, 28-29. See also BROOKE, Apocalyptic Community, 47, IDEM, Between Authority, 96.

passages, he implies that he is none other than the great King Solomon (see Wis 7:5; 8:14-15; 9:7), thereby appealing to a famed wise figure in Israel's past. With this Solomonic self-identification, two issues come to mind: (1) Why does the author find it necessary to associate himself with Solomon instead of revealing his true identity as sage? (for example, as Ben Sira unambiguously does in Sir 50:27); (2) And how would his audience have interpreted this claim of Solomonic authorship?

In response to the first question, it seems likely that the author of the Book of Wisdom was appealing to the authority of Solomon as a figure of Israelite antiquity to claim authoritative status for his own work. Solomon was well-known for his great wisdom (see 1Kgs 3:1-28; 5:9-14) and was traditionally linked to most wisdom books (see Prov 1:1; 10:1; 25:1; Eccl 1:1.12). To press this matter further: does the identification with Solomon hint at some self-perceived authoritative inadequacy on the author's part? In writing such an extensive exposition of Genesis and Exodus, the author of Wisdom undoubtedly perceived himself fit for such a task. However, perhaps he was not well-known or well-liked in the community and did not think his own interpretation would be accepted by the wider Jewish community and thus resorted to linking it with the great, sagacious king. Or perhaps he was well-known by both the Greek nationalists and apostate Jews in Alexandria and was hiding his identity to avoid persecution. While Pseudo-Solomon's true authoritative status as a sage is unknowable, his work most likely gained authority due to its connection with King Solomon.

Yet, would Pseudo-Solomon's audience really have thought that his overtly-hellenistic composition was an ancient work composed by Solomon himself? It is difficult to answer this question with certainty. On the one hand, some Alexandrian Jews may have literally believed that the text originated from the tenth-century king of Israel. For this literal-minded group, Solomon's awareness of Hellenistic thought and culture before the Greeks even existed might not have been perceived as problematic. In fact, such anachronistic knowledge may have served to reinforce the miraculous and unparalleled nature of Solomon's wisdom (see 1Kgs 3:10-12) in addition to underscoring the omniscience and omnipotence of the Jewish deity as the source and granter of this knowledge. Or, perhaps it was believed that the Greeks gained their knowledge from Solomon himself. This reading would be akin to Philo's claim that Moses influenced the Greek philosophers Heraclitus and Zeno.[23] On the other hand, there were most likely members of the community who did not literally believe that Pseudo-Solomon's work

---

23 See Philo, *Quis Rerum Divinarum Heres*, 214; *Quod Omnis Probus Liber*, 57.

was written by Solomon himself but nonetheless considered it to be an authoritative work. They may have perceived that the author was simply appealing to the authority and tradition of Solomon's wisdom in his work to show that his composition was in the same mode of thought as the sage-king. In other words, the pseudepigraphic Wisdom of Solomon was a participation in and extension of Solomon's original wisdom, which ultimately reflects God's Wisdom.

4.2 New and Creative Use of Scripture Combined with Original Interpretations

In addition to attributing his work to Solomon, the author of the Book of Wisdom also claims authority for his work by the new and creative ways that he weaves together biblical traditions and extrabiblical interpretations. His creativity and authority as interpreter is seen in the way that he embellishes and enhances the original biblical storyline (namely, Genesis and Exodus) with vocabulary and imagery from other biblical texts (Isaiah, Psalms, and wisdom literature) and with details not found in the Bible (either from other oral or written sources that were current at his time or from his own original mode of thought and expression).

When Pseudo-Solomon uses passages from other parts of the biblical text to reinterpret a biblical story from the Pentateuch, what emerges is a newly-combined tradition which is an authoritative way of understanding the original story. An example of this hermeneutical phenomenon is found in Wis 10:10cd, which speaks about Lady Wisdom's care for the patriarch Jacob:

ἔδειξεν αὐτῷ βασιλείαν θεοῦ,
    καὶ ἔδωκεν αὐτῷ γνῶσιν ἁγίων.

She showed him the kingdom of God
    and gave him knowledge of holy things.

In this passage, Pseudo-Solomon supplements the story of Jacob's vision of the ascending and descending angels in Gen 28:10-22 by the phrase γνῶσιν ἁγίων, "holy things," from the Septuagint of Prov 30:3, which states:

θεὸς δεδίδαχέν με σοφίαν,
    καὶ γνῶσιν ἁγίων ἔγνωκα.

God has taught me wisdom,
    and I have knowledge of holy things [or 'the holy one(s)'].

No matter how one translates the polyvalent term ἁγίων (perhaps meaning "holy matters," "Holy One" with God as the referent, or "holy ones" with angels as the referent), it ultimately introduces a new concept into the biblical story that did not exist before. Pseudo-Solomon suggests that through Jacob's vision the patriarch gained a special knowledge about the divine from Lady Wisdom.[24] This hermeneutical method shows that Pseudo-Solomon perceives continuity in Scripture; it is all God's revelation, and there is fluidity in the way that one passage can help interpret another. Furthermore, by using one tradition to interpret another, Pseudo-Solomon implicitly presents himself as having the authority to interpret traditions in this new and creative way.

Pseudo-Solomon also assumes authority for his own work when he places extrabiblical interpretations next to biblical traditions without distinguishing between the two. For example, in his recounting of the Red Sea event in Wis 10:18-21, Pseudo-Solomon claims that both mute individuals and infants were miraculously able to praise God after he saved the Israelites from Pharaoh's army (see v. 21):

ὅτι ἡ σοφία ἤνοιξεν στόμα κωφῶν,
    καὶ γλώσσας νηπίων ἔθηκεν τρανάς.

For Wisdom opened the mouth of the mute,
    and she made the tongues of infants speak clearly.

No such tradition is found anywhere in the biblical text. In fact, it is difficult to find such a tradition in Jewish literature before the first century A.D.[25] While it is impossible to know whether this tradition circulated in Pseudo-Solomon's day or was his own creative embellishment, the point is that he incorporates this detail as if it were an essential element in this central event of Israelite history. In the same way that Pseudo-Solomon presents continuity in Scripture by juxtaposing biblical traditions, he shows that the extrabiblical interpretations that he has written in his work have authoritative status and should be regarded as Scripture by his audience.

4.3 Application of Traditions for the Alexandrian Jewish Community

The last way that Pseudo-Solomon presents his work as having authority is through his application of the text to the situation of the Alexandrian Jewish community in his day. Part of the interplay between authoritative interpreter and tradition is that the interpreter helps to maintain the relevance and authoritativeness of traditions by reapply-

---

24 For further discussion of Wis 10:10cd, see BURROWS, Wisdom, 406-407; LARCHER, Livre de la Sagesse, 2:360, 629. See also my own extensive treatment in GLICKSMAN, Wisdom, 124-126.

25 Jewish traditions concerning infants praising God at the Red Sea are found in *Exod. Rab.* 23.8 and *Tg. Ps.-J.* Exod 15:2. In Wis 10:21, Pseudo-Solomon may be referencing and reapplying Ps 8:3 (Septuagint); however, such an allusion is uncertain.

ing them to new situations. As I mentioned earlier, Pseudo-Solomon composed his work in order to implore his fellow Jews to remain steadfast in the faith and to continue their pursuit of Jewish wisdom. In order to strengthen his case, Pseudo-Solomon evokes and reinterprets specific figures and events in the biblical tradition that would have resonated with his community, namely, (1) persecuted figures, mainly those abused by their own kinsmen and (2) Israelites who endured hardship at the hands of foreigners, especially Egyptians.

In the first case, Pseudo-Solomon's evocation of Deutero-Isaiah's "Suffering Servant Song" (Isa 52:13-53:12) in Wis 2:10-5:23 is apropos for encouraging the persecuted faithful Alexandrian Jews. Concurrent with the general theme of the "innocent sufferer" in the opening chapters of the book is the sub-theme of persecution at the hands of one's own brothers. As I mentioned previously, the phrases "sins against the law" and "sins against *our* training" in Wis 2:12 seem to indicate that the righteous sufferer (the faithful Alexandrian Jew) is persecuted by his own brothers, who have deviated from proper Jewish belief and practice, rather than by foreign oppressors. This theme of brotherly contention continues in the rest of the book. For example, in Wisdom 10 when Pseudo-Solomon presents a summary of figures from Adam to Moses, he specifically mentions two cases of brotherly anger: Cain's anger towards Abel, which leads him to kill his brother (10:3), and Esau's anger towards Jacob (10:10). The latter case is especially important because the Jews of Alexandria would have identified with their great forefather Jacob, who eventually lived and died in Egypt. The detail that Wisdom saved Jacob from his brother's wrath may have given the faithful Alexandrian Jews hope that she would save them as well from the wrath of their apostate brothers.

In another poignant application of the biblical text for his current situation, Pseudo-Solomon emphasizes figures who are oppressed by foreigners, especially by Egyptians. Examples include: Lot (Wis 10:6) who is treated with gross inhospitality in a foreign land (yet even his oppressors are not as wicked as the Egyptians who oppressed the Israelites and Alexandrian Jews, see Wis 19:17); Joseph (Wis 10:13-14) who was sold into slavery in Egypt, wrongly accused and imprisoned by Egyptians, but eventually rose to prominence – gaining power and glory; and, of course, the Israelites under Moses' leadership (Wis 10:15-11:1, which becomes the main theme in the rest of the book), who were enslaved in Egypt but escaped with much wealth in a miraculous way. The last two examples in particular must have been encouraging for the persecuted Jews of Pseudo-Solomon's day. Like their ancestors, they, too, were enduring injustice and hardship in Egypt, yet they hoped that their own situation could be reversed if, like their forebears, they pursued and trusted in the saving power of God's Wisdom. God saved his people from hardship in Egypt in the past, he could and would do the same for them in Pseudo-Solomon's time. Such reinterpretation and reapplication of biblical figures and events made them relevant for Pseudo-Solomon's community, thereby lending authority both to the biblical traditions and to his own work.

5. Conclusion

In the present study, I have demonstrated four major points concerning Pseudo-Solomon's perception of authoritative Jewish tradition. First, for Pseudo-Solomon and his community, in order for an oral or written tradition to be authoritative it must have divine origins. God communicates his authoritative message through his Wisdom, which is closely associated with his "word" and "law." When a righteous individual upholds God's word and law, he or she is seen as having authority by manifesting God's ways in the world. Second, Pseudo-Solomon esteems biblical texts in all three major sections of the later "canonical" *Tanak* as authoritative. He especially focuses on themes from Genesis and Exodus and favors language from Isaiah, the Psalms, and the wisdom literature. Third, he demonstrates familiarity with and acceptance of many extrabiblical interpretations of Jewish tradition. And fourth, Pseudo-Solomon presents his own composition as authoritative Scripture for his Jewish Alexandrian audience by attributing it to Solomon, presenting new ways of reading biblical traditions, and reapplying authoritative traditions for his own time. The manner in which Pseudo-Solomon integrates biblical and extrabiblical interpretations reveals a very fluid understanding of authoritative tradition in Alexandria in the early Roman era, as was the case at Qumran in the same period. Furthermore, there is no evidence in Pseudo-Solomon's work that textual traditions are more authoritative than oral traditions. The author juxtaposes biblical traditions and extrabiblical interpretations without clear delineation, which may suggest authoritative parity between these two categories. But even this assertion cannot be known with certainty since Pseudo-Solomon never explicitly makes such a claim. As has been the result of the recent studies of scriptural authority at Qumran, it is my hope that the findings of the present study further serve to remind modern Jewish and Christian biblicists to take great care not to impose upon late Second Temple thought and literature our own traditions of a fixed canon and textual priority.[26]

Bibliography

ACHTEMEIER, Paul J., Inspiration and Authority. Nature and Function of Christian Scripture, Peabody, Mass. 1999.
BROOKE, George J., Between Authority and Canon. The Significance of Reworking the Bible for Understanding the Canonical Process, in: Chazon, Esther G. et al. (ed.), Reworking the Bible. Apocryphal and Related Texts at Qumran, Leiden 2005, 85-104.
BROOKE, George J., The 'Apocalyptic' Community, the Matrix of the Teacher and Rewriting Scripture, in: Popović, Mladen (ed.), Authoritative Scriptures in Ancient Judaism (SuppJSJ 141), Leiden 2010, 37-54.
BURROWS, Eric. Wisdom X 10, in: Bib 20 (1939), 405-407.
CHARLESWORTH, James H. (ed.), The Old Testament Pseudepigrapha. 2 volumes (ABRL), New York 1983-1985.
GARCÍA MARTÍNEZ, Florentino, Rethinking the Bible – Sixty Years of Dead Sea Scrolls Research and Beyond, in: Popović, Mladen (ed.), Authoritative Scriptures in Ancient Judaism (SuppJSJ 141), Leiden 2010, 19-36.
GILBERT, Maurice, Sagesse de Salomon, in: Cazelles, Henri (ed.), DBSup 11, Paris 1991, 58-119.
GLICKSMAN, Andrew T., Wisdom of Solomon 10: A Jewish Hellenistic Reinterpretation of Early Israelite History through Sapiential Lenses (DCLS 9), Berlin/Boston 2011.
LARCHER, C., Le livre de la Sagesse ou la Sagesse de Salomon. 3 volumes, Paris 1983-1985.
MANFREDI, Silvana, The Trial of the Righteous in Wis 5:1-14 (1-7) and in the Prophetic Traditions, in: Passaro, Angelo/Bellia, Giuseppe (eds.), The Book of Wisdom in Modern Research: Studies on Tradition, Redaction, and Theology (DCLY 2005), Berlin 2005, 159-178.
MODRZEJEWSKI, Joseph M., The Jews of Egypt. From Rameses II to Emperor Hadrian, Philadelphia 1995 (transl. of id., Les Juifs d'Egypte. De Ramsès II à Hadrien, Paris 1992).
NICKELSBURG, George W. E., Resurrection, Immortality, and Eternal Life in Intertestamental Judaism, Cambridge, Mass. 1972.
POPOVIĆ, Mladen (ed.), Authoritative Scriptures in Ancient Judaism (SuppJSJ 141), Leiden 2010.
POPOVIĆ, Mladen, Introducing Authoritative Scriptures in Ancient Judaism, in: id. (ed.), Authoritative Scriptures in Ancient Judaism (SuppJSJ 141), Leiden 2010, 1-17.
REEVES, John C., Scriptural Authority in Early Judaism, in: Bowley, James E. (ed.), Living Traditions of the Bible: Scripture in Jewish, Christian, and Muslim Practice, St. Louis, Mo. 1999, 63-84.
SKEHAN, Patrick W., Borrowings from the Psalms in the Book of Wisdom, in: id., Studies in Israelite Poetry and Wisdom (CBQMS 1), Washington, D.C. 1971, 149-161 (repr. CBQ 10 [1948] 384-397).

---

26 I wish to thank Dr. Mark Goodwin, Dr. John Norris, Dr. Brian Schmisek, and Dr. Jerome Walsh for reading an earlier draft of this article and offering insightful comments and suggestions for its improvement.

SKEHAN, Patrick W., Isaiah and the Teaching of the Book of Wisdom, in: id., Studies in Israelite Poetry and Wisdom (CBQMS 1), Washington, D.C. 1971, 163-171 (repr. CBQ 2 [1940] 289-299).

SKEHAN, Patrick W., The Literary Relationship of the Book of Wisdom to Earlier Wisdom Writings, in: id., Studies in Israelite Poetry and Wisdom (CBQMS 1), Washington, D.C. 1971, 172-236.

SMALLWOOD, E. Mary, The Jews Under Roman Rule: From Pompey to Diocletian (SJLA 20), Leiden 1981.

SUGGS, M. Jack, Wisdom of Solomon 2 [10]–5: A Homily Based on the Fourth Servant Song, in: JBL 76 (1957), 26-33.

TCHERIKOVER, Victor, Hellenistic Civilization and the Jews, Peabody, Mass. 1999 (repr. Philadelphia 1959).

ULRICH, Eugene, The Dead Sea Scrolls and the Origins of the Bible (SDSSRL), Grand Rapids, Mich. 1999.

ULRICH, Eugene, The Bible in the Making. The Scriptures at Qumran, in: id., The Dead Sea Scrolls and the Origins of the Bible (SDSSRL), Grand Rapids, Mich. 1999, 17-33.

ULRICH, Eugene, The Canonical Process, Textual Criticism, and Latter Stages in the Composition of the Bible, in: id., The Dead Sea Scrolls and the Origins of the Bible (SDSSRL), Grand Rapids, Mich. 1999, 51-78.

ULRICH, Eugene, Pluriformity in the Biblical Text, Text Groups, and Questions of Canon, in: id., The Dead Sea Scrolls and the Origins of the Bible (SDSSRL), Grand Rapids, Mich. 1999, 79-98.

VAN DER KOOIJ, Arie, Authoritative Scriptures and Scribal Culture, in: Popović, Mladen (ed.), Authoritative Scriptures in Ancient Judaism (SuppJSJ 141), Leiden 2010, 55-72.

WINSTON, David, Wisdom of Solomon (AB 43), Garden City, N.Y. 1979.

Scriptural Authority in the Book of Jubilees
JOHN C. ENDRES

Assessing the authority of Scripture in the Book of Jubilees may begin with the observation that most of the text of Jubilees presents readers with a new version of first part of the Scriptures, i.e. Genesis and Exodus. Those with a good knowledge of the Torah, i.e. the Pentateuch, can follow in Jubilees 2-50 the basic story line of Genesis 1 to Exodus 24, which Jubilees renders in a unique rewriting. For this reason Jubilees is regularly considered a prime example of Jewish rewriting of the Scriptures in the Second Temple era. Studies of various sections of Jubilees in relation to the biblical text demonstrate these close connections between Jubilees and the Scriptures, reinforcing the notion that Scripture has great significance for this author. Vermes' study of Abraham traditions paid special attention to Jubilees in his description of the ways that authors were rewriting the Bible; thus began the usage of the term Rewritten Bible.[1] Modeled after Vermes' work, Endres studied biblical interpretation through rewriting in Jubilees 19-45 (treating the Jacob-family traditions, with significant emphasis on Rebekah).[2] Van Ruiten studied many individual texts in Jubilees with regard to the techniques of rewriting parts of the Bible, but his monograph focuses on the rewriting of Genesis 1-11 in Jubilees.[3] In each of these cases the study shows how Jubilees follows the narrative flow of the scriptural witness. In a different kind of study, Kugel draws attention to the interpretive role of Second Temple texts as they deal with biblical traditions; his work proceeds by a study of topics and themes, and observes how various writers dealt with them.[4] One outcome of these studies is to envision the Bible as holding authoritative status for Jubilees, a work which often follows biblical texts closely. This assessment may be main-

---

1 The study of rewriting biblical traditions began with VERMES, Scripture and Tradition in Judaism; in Section II: The Rewritten Bible (67-126) he initiated the study of "rewritten Bible" claiming *Jubilees* as a prime example.
2 ENDRES, Biblical Interpretation in Jubilees, argues that the author of Jubilees rewrote these traditions in order to convey a message about tradition, law, covenant, Levitical priorities, to the Palestinian Jewish community.
3 VAN RUITEN, Primaeval History Interpreted, studies Genesis 1-11 meticulously.
4 KUGEL, Traditions of the Bible. Jubilees stands as one of the most significant interpreters for Kugel.

tained whether or not one is satisfied with the term Rewritten Bible;[5] it concerns the authority of the Scriptures for the writer's project.

From a different angle, Jubilees' self-presentation and view of revelation depends on its imaginative setting at Mt. Sinai. According to this view, the entire text derives from experiences of Moses at this sacred site: at first God directly engages Moses in a dialogue (God speaks to Moses, 1:1-18, 22-26, and Moses responds, 1:19-21). This scene then is transformed into another, where the angel of the presence dictated to Moses, at Sinai, from the heavenly tablets (Jubilees Prologue; 1:4). Because readers also would know the traditions about Moses on Mount Sinai from Exod 24:12-18 and 34:1, 28, the text dictated to Moses by the angel of the presence constitutes a distinct though related revelation. One might consider the text in Scripture as the "first law," so Jubilees fills out its picture with further information from the heavenly tablets. The scriptural text tradition still provides the pattern and direction of the presentation in Jubilees, so we will use the term rewritten Scripture.

The most notable example of this distinction occurs when the Angel of the Presence explains the festival of Weeks to Moses in the midst of his narration of post-diluvian events in Jubilees 6, a chapter which includes several fundamentals of Jewish life whose origins Jubilees situated in the era of Noah. We may imagine this angel dictating to Moses a report of the covenant with Noah (Jub 6:1-16), which Moses is then commanded to make with the Israelites (6:11). As in Genesis 9, God made a covenant with Noah, but in a clear departure from the scriptural version he then told them to observe the festival of Weeks annually in the third month, in order to renew the covenant God made with Noah (Jub 6:17-22). Apparently God is speaking to Moses: "I have written (this) in the book of the first law in which I wrote for you that you should celebrate it at each of its times one day in a year" (Jub 6:22).

The reference to "the book of the first law" is usually understood as a direct reference to the Torah, i.e. the Pentateuch. Readers of Jubilees are expected not only to recognize the authority of this "first law", given at Sinai, but also that Jubilees stands under the same authoritative figure, Moses, as the scriptural text. The angel of the presence thus explains to Moses that this festival actually has a history prior to Noah, even though it was not narrated in this part of the scriptures.[6] What we

---

5 BERNSTEIN, Rewritten Bible, argued against using the term Rewritten Bible for Second Temple literature, since this literary activity pre-dated authoritative collections that could be termed the Bible. The most recent review of this issue appears in CRAWFORD, Rewriting Scriptures in Second Temple Times, 60-83 (on Jubilees).

6 In the "book of the first law", however, when the feast of Weeks is mentioned it is considered as an aspect of the Mosaic covenant, appearing in texts which legislate Is-

learn about the festival of Weeks in Jubilees, therefore, comes from the heavenly tablets and constitutes important additional knowledge and implications of the basic texts in the "first law".

In Jubilees' framework, therefore, Moses receives the Torah and the commandment at Sinai, and then God orders the angel of the presence to dictate to Moses the contents of the heavenly tablets. Presumably Jubilees 2–50 comprise what was dictated, a new version of the revelation, interpreting the first law from the heavenly tablets for this community. What import does this notion of the book of the first law have? It suggests an indissoluble connection between the Scriptures (Genesis and Exodus, at the least) and this text being written down by Moses as the angel of the presence reads it from the heavenly tablets.

How does this 'authorizing' strategy impact views of the Scriptures? Does it lessen or magnify the authority of the scriptural base? One could claim that re-writing which presents a new text lessens the authority of the base text: Wacholder argued that the re-writing in Jubilees was intended to rival Genesis-Exodus, that the book "repeatedly claims to be a super-biblical work, superior to Genesis and Exodus."[7] Perhaps, reasoned some critics, the writer of Jubilees intended to correct inadequacies of the Scriptures with this re-writing? If so, Scripture's authority would thereby be diminished. But does the writer of Jubilees intend to replace the sacred writings, Genesis and Exodus? That tactic seems doubtful, since Jubilees mentions the first law twice (Jub 6:22; 2:24), as if the reader might wish or need to consult the Scriptures for further information.[8] Later when retelling the Dinah story the writer seems to remind his audience of the fuller version of the narrative, which they should know from Genesis 34.[9] The writer of Jubilees

---

rael's pilgrimage festivals (Exod 23:16; 34:22; Lev 23:15-21) as part of covenant responsibility.

7   WACHOLDER, Jubilees as the Super-Canon, 195-211, esp. 196, 209. Expanding his thesis, he proposed that Jubilees and the Temple Scroll together form a 'super canon' intended to be a more important text than Genesis-Exodus. Also cf. WACHOLDER, The Relationship between 11Q Torah (the Temple Scroll) and the Book of Jubilees, 205-216.

8   The "first law" in 2:24 relates sabbath observance to the structure of the creation account in Gen 1:1–2:4b. In several other places when it mentions "the law" it seems to refer to the Torah/ Pentateuch: (1:12b) "They will persecute those too who study the law diligently"; (23:19) "One group will struggle with another – the young with the old, the old with the young; the poor with the rich, the lowly with the great; and the needy with the ruler – regarding the law and the covenant. For they have forgotten commandment, covenant, festival, month, sabbath, jubilee, and every verdict"; (23:26) "In those days the children will begin to study the laws, to seek out the commands, and to return to the right way."

9   Jubilees' rewriting of the Dinah story (Jubilees 30// Genesis 34) will be treated in more detail in the second part of this study.

reminds the audience of "the law" for different reasons: sometimes to offer clearer narrative context for a practice or law, at other times to bring out the full implications of that sacred text, including references to contemporary issues, religious practices and movements which form part of the full perspective of the readers of the time of the writer of Jubilees.[10]

So the question shifts: does the writer of Jubilees intend to present an interpretive guide to the Scriptures known in his day? In this essay I will argue that position, that the Book of Jubilees includes within itself markers of an interpretive perspective: returning to investigate the Scriptures for their proper appropriation in the teaching and life of the Jewish community. Thus Jubilees may enhance the authority of Scripture by demonstrating how its inspired retelling of the first law can address people of a different era (such as the writer's). Taking the figure of Moses as indicator of authority for the Scriptures, I will examine him and his authority where the writer seems to make claims about the meaning of Scripture, either its deeper meaning or the actions demanded by them.

Introductory Matters

Before proceeding, however, we set forth our assumptions about the Book of Jubilees. This book was written within the Palestinian Jewish community, probably in the middle of the second century B.C.E.[11] That it was written in Hebrew seems now to be certain, since approximately fifteen Hebrew manuscripts of this work were discovered at Qumran.[12] Subsequently the book was translated into Greek, and from the Greek into Latin, on the one hand, and then into various other languages, including Syriac and classical Ethiopic (Ge'ez).[13] The entire text is ex-

---

10 NAJMAN, Seconding Sinai, 44-45. NAJMAN, Interpretation, 379-410.
11 VANDERKAM, Jubilees 2001, 17-21 weighs different factors and suggests the "period between 160-150 BCE" (21). KNIBB, Jubilees and Qumran Origins, 252-254, locates Jubilees "in the prehistory of the Qumran sect" (253) and between 175 BCE and 167 BCE. SEGAL, Jubilees, surveys a number of positions and mentions VanderKam's as the most widely accepted (35-41); at the conclusion of his study which argues for a redactional level, he claims, with Kister, that Jubilees "was redacted within the same stream of Judaism within which one can locate the Qumran sect, and in a similar ideological climate", 322.
12 VANDERKAM, Textual and Historical Studies in the Book of Jubilees, argues this position, particularly by comparing Qumran fragments of Jubilees with the Ethiopic version, where both are extant. VANDERKAM, The Manuscript Tradition of Jubilees, 4-8, contains a recent, succinct overview of the manuscripts, their sources, and significance.
13 VANDERKAM, Jubilees Translated, vi-xxxiv.

tant only in Ethiopic, of which there are a good number of manuscripts available, and the number continues to grow.¹⁴ That so many manuscripts of Jubilees have been preserved in Ethiopia, especially in monastic collections, supports the claim that this book enjoys considerable authoritative status in the Ethiopian Orthodox church, where both Jubilees and the Book of Enoch are regularly printed with the other books of their Bible. The large number of Ethiopic texts of the book attests to its authoritative status in an ancient Christian church, and the large number of manuscripts of Jubilees found among the Dead Sea Scrolls attests to its special status and authority in that community and its community.

The notion of rewriting Scripture can easily be discerned through study of 1-2 Chronicles vis-a-vis Samuel and Kings. But the literary activity in Deuteronomy also provides helpful point of comparison. In an earlier era, Deuteronomy had appealed to the people to listen to God's word in the Exodus traditions, to hear anew its message about focused worship and all of the teaching and customs and laws of the Exodus generation. It evoked for them a new consciousness of the ancient narrative of their life as a covenant people. Similarly, Jubilees harkens back to traditions found in Genesis and Exodus, texts which had already attained a certain sacral status by mid-second century B.C.E.¹⁵ In Jubilees, however, Moses presents a narrative by writing down what the angel dictated to him, and this re-told story gives a "sense of their existence" by way of narratives that are redacted by both omissions and expansions;¹⁶ in addition, important laws are also embedded in the stories, yielding some new "structures of their existence." I would describe the entire work as a rewriting of the Scriptures, with many intriguing points not envisioned in the scriptural texts on which they seem to be based.

To probe the question of scriptural authority in Jubilees it helps to study the role of Moses, since he has long been considered as the recipient of revelation at Sinai that comprises Torah or Pentateuch (the

---

14 I am grateful to Ted Erho for information on newly-emerging manuscripts (letter of 30 November 2010). Among a number of manuscripts containing Jubilees, he suggested special attention to EMML 9001 (Gešan Maryam (Amba Gešan), Ambassal, Wallo; and EMIP 654 (Mekane Yesus Seminary 54; obtained through kindness of Prof. Steve Delamarter at George Fox College).

15 VANDERKAM, Moses Trumping Moses, 27.

16 SEGAL, The Book of Jubilees, presents a literary-critical theory for the composition of Jubilees in which the rewritten narratives were incorporated into the text of Jubilees, and since they were not written by this author, they do not reflect the author's ideology, perspective and theology in the same way it may be found in the legal passages, which he does attribute to this author.

"first law" in Jub 6:22). We suggest then that Jubilees provides the type of revelatory portrait of Moses which is lacking in Genesis when it launches directly into the creation text without any indications of the divine origin of the text. Since the scheme in Jubilees reminds the readers of the revelatory framework in Genesis-Exodus, we might imagine a complementary revelatory relationship between Jubilees and the Torah: Jubilees certainly depends on Genesis for authority, but the revelatory picture in Jubilees also helped to establish a basis for the authority of the Torah.

Preliminaries

The geographical location is significant, since the religious and imaginative world of Jubilees takes its cue from Moses' revelatory experiences at Mt Sinai, even for events in Genesis and Exodus which temporally preceded Sinai. This opening memory, God commanding Moses to ascend Mt. Sinai and to wait there until he (God) would give him tablets of stone with which to teach the people (Jub 1:1), teaches Jubilees' audience how earlier stories were recounted. Modeled on scenes in Exodus 24 and 31 (and Deuteronomy 9), we learn that Moses remained there forty days and forty nights (Exod 31:18 and Deut 9:11). The text includes traditional details of Moses journey to this mountain, where "the glory of the Lord took up residence on Mt. Sinai, and a cloud covered it for six days" (1:2). Beginning at Sinai reinforces the notion of Mosaic authorship for the Torah and also enhances the authoritative status of Jubilees.

More specifically, Jubilees carefully modeled the scene on Moses' first forty-day stay on Mt. Sinai, found in Exod 24:12-18. That Jubilees results from this first meeting may be intended to remind the hearers that this text continued intact, even though the first law and commandments engraved on the two stone tablets were lost when Moses cast them down and destroyed them. Thus "the revelation of *Jubilees* [remains] as the only product of Moses' first forty-day stay on Sinai."[17] In this case the book's claim to authority draws less from the biblical text than it does from Moses, the reputed 'author' of the Scriptures.

The book also opens with a chronological notice. This revelation occurred on the 16th day of the third month (III/16) of the first year of the Exodus of the Israelites from Egypt, and the date is significant because it follows by one day the celebration of the covenant at the feast of

---

17 VANDERKAM, Moses Trumping Moses, 31-32, noted this detail and brought out its subtle implications.

Weeks,[18] which Israel was commanded to celebrate on III/15.[19] Since God summoned Moses to Mt Sinai the very day after their celebration of covenant, the context suggests that this people should be well prepared and receptive to further revelatory messages from God. This revelation thus caps their experience of the special relationship with God concluded in the covenant.

The content and character of Jubilees are described in the Prologue, which characterizes its contents, implying that its words constitute an accurate record of everything that was revealed to Moses at Sinai when he was summoned there to "receive the stone tablets" (Prologue, 1). Moses apparently received much more than what was known from the Book of Exodus.

> [Prologue] These are the words regarding the divisions of the times of the *law* and of the *testimony*, of the events of the years, of the weeks of their jubilees throughout all the years of eternity as he related (them) to Moses on Mt. Sinai when he went up to receive the stone tablets – the law and the commandments – on the Lord's orders as he had told him that he should come up to the summit of the mountain.[20]

Jubilees thus contains "The divisions of the times ... of the events of the years, of the weeks of their jubilees", i.e. everything that happened, even before creation and continuing on not only until Sinai, but until the new creation, eternity. All these times and events fall under the umbrella of the chronological scheme of the book (years and jubilees and years of jubilees). These "words" recount both the Torah, "the law and the commandments", and the Testimony, a further category of revelation from God.

The words of Torah that Moses heard from the angel of the presence included the 'basic story' from Genesis 1 to Exodus 12, and the laws included therein. The Testimony, on the other hand, may refer to a more expansive reality, i.e. the "entity extant before Creation: the Torah and the *te'udah* engraved on the heavenly tablets before Creation."[21] This Testimony includes many things that would surprise one simply expecting a rewriting of Genesis: regulations for the sabbath (Jub 2:33),

---

18   The Hebrew word Shavuot could – by a slight change in pointing – be pronounced Shevuot, oaths, a basic element of covenant renewal ceremonies which many Jews, especially those at Qumran, connected with the feast annually celebrated in the third month.
19   Other events dated to III/15 in Jubilees include: Abraham celebrated first fruits of the harvest (15:1; 44:4); Isaac was born (16:13); Abraham died (22:1); Judah was born (28:15); Jacob and Laban bound themselves by vows (29:7); CHARLES, Jubilees, 1902, 2 f.n. ad loc.
20   All citations of Jubilees are taken from: VANDERKAM, Jubilees Translated.
21   WERMAN, *Jubilees* in the Hellenistic Context, 154.

and the law of purification for a parturient (Jub 3:14). The prohibition of consuming blood (animals, birds, and living thing) is written in a Testimony (Jub 6:12). Also the practice of intermarriage with Gentiles is prohibited by Jubilees' reading of the story of Dinah, Levi, Simeon and the Shechemites in Jubilees 30 (a Testimony, Jub 30:17). Thus the Testimony includes both legal and narrative contents.

To move a step further, the Testimony seems also to refer to heavenly teachings which are inscribed on the heavenly tablets. This term suggests a corpus with a much more comprehensive body of teaching and knowledge than the "law (*Torah*) and the commandments" found on the stone tablets which Moses received on Mt Sinai. Jubilees, then, is comprised of this heavenly revelation which interprets the scriptures (Genesis and Exodus 1-24). Without a knowledge of the Scriptures a reader would have no context in which to make sense of Jubilees. In this sense Jubilees receives its authority from the Scriptures, which it brings to a new life in its community.

Several other points about the character of the revelation received at Sinai need attention. From the stance of time, what is the temporal extent of this revelation of Torah and Testimony? The Testimony reaches back in time, perhaps even prior to creation. Later we hear that it extends from the time of creation to the building of God's temple in Zion/Jerusalem, to the new creation. Consider the italicized text in Jubilees 1.

> 1:29 The angel of the presence, who was going along in front of the Israelite camp, took the tablets (which told) of the divisions of the years from the time the law and the testimony were created – for the weeks of their jubilees, year by year in their full number, and their jubilees *from [the time of the creation until] the time of the new creation when the heavens, the earth, and all their creatures will be renewed like the powers of the sky and like all the creatures of the earth, until the time when the temple of the Lord will be created in Jerusalem on Mt. Zion.*

One might thus expect that Jubilees would narrate the "history" far into the future, to the time of the new creation; but that does not happen, and the story ends with the events paralleling Exodus 14.[22] Still, one might wonder why the angel of the presence did not continue dictating the history story, but perhaps this much suffices? Clearly we are to imagine that more than Genesis and Exodus 1-24 comprise the Testimony engraved on the heavenly tablets. The chronological framework of 49-year jubilees offers evidence that part of a jubilee of time yet remains (50:4; "it is still 40 years off (for learning the Lord's commandments) until the time when he leads (them) across to the land of

---

22 LOADER, Enoch, Levi, and Jubilees, 120.

Canaan ... 50:5 The jubilees will pass by until Israel is pure of every sexual evil ...") Jubilees thus looks towards the future.

Another surprising detail emerges in the geographical indicator in Jub 1:29b: the new creation occurs "when the temple of the Lord will be created in Jerusalem on Mt. Zion." As recipient of the words from the heavenly tablets, Moses gives authorization not only to Sinai traditions, but he also guarantees the words, the history till the construction of a Jerusalem temple. What appears elsewhere as part of the 'realm' of David (and Solomon) has become part of the Testimony given to Moses. Israelites of a much later time, even from Jubilees' time, must then consider the laws newly focused in this book to apply to their present situation, even though the voice speaks from a place (Sinai) and a time "long long ago".

Moses as Mediator: Authorizing this Book

Explicit attributions to Moses

With the history of Israel's life and obligations as the framework of this text, we now return to Moses, the person whose name connects Jubilees with the concept of Scripture through his role in formation of the Torah.[23] The writer explicitly invokes Moses as an authority in five locations, but there other events where Moses seems to play a significant role, even though his identity in the text is only implicit.[24] Later we will recognize how much more of the text works from these explicit orders to Moses and constitute an implicit authorizing presence elsewhere.

(1) In the opening scene on Mt. Sinai, Moses' name appears several times (Prologue; 1:1, 2, 3, 4, 19, 22, 27; 2:1) in the narrative that was clearly developed from the Torah in Exodus (Exod 24:12-13, 15-16; 31:27; 34:27; Lev 26:40). In these sections God directly addresses Moses in 1:1; 1:4b-18; 1:22-26. But Jub 1:27-29 brings in another character: the

---

23 VANDERKAM, Jubilees 2001, 24-25, notes that after the Prologue and 1:1-2:1, "there are 22 direct or indirect reminders that the angel is dictating to Moses and giving him orders: 2:26, 29 (sabbath); 6:13, 19, 20, 22, 32, 35, 38 (against eating blood, regarding the festival of weeks, the first law and the calendar); 15:28, 33 (circumcision); 23:32 (the future); 28:7 (against giving a younger daughter in marriage first); 30:11, 17, 21 (against intermarriage with foreigners); 33:13, 18, 19 (on Reuben's sin with Bilhah); 41:26 (against impurity); and 49:15, 22 (Passover)." All these cases concern matters of grave concern.

24 NAJMAN, Seconding Sinai, 60: "the contents of *Jubilees* are dictated by an angel to Moses, who transcribes what is revealed and who remains the initial addressee." On p. 66 f.n. 60 she lists a number of references to Moses in the book, mixing both the explicit and implicit references to Moses in the text.

Lord commands the Angel of the Presence to "dictate to Moses" all that has happened from the beginning of creation until the building of the temple (1:27-29).

> 1:27 Then he said to an angel of the presence: "*Dictate*[25] to Moses (starting) from the beginning of the creation until the time when my temple is built among: them throughout the ages of eternity.

The angel of the presence immediately obeys God's command, ordering Moses to write it all, beginning with the creation and the sabbath.

> 2:1 On the Lord's orders the angel of the presence said to Moses: "Write all the words about the creation – how in six days the Lord God completed all his works, everything that he had created, and kept sabbath on the seventh day. He sanctified it for all ages and set it as a sign for all his works.

Following VanderKam's translation and thus his interpretation of the scene, Moses' access to divine revelation has changed: in v. 26 he heard directly from God what to write down, but now there will be important material to write down that the angel of the presence will read, from the Law and the Testimony. Whether directly from God or mediated by the great angel, the source of the revelation to Moses comes from the heavenly realm. Segal comments that by dating this narrative on III/16, the day after the revelation of Torah and the covenant ceremony – understood as occurring on III/15 in Exod 19:1–24:11 the author wanted to signal that Jubilees was a "separate revelation" from the Pentateuch, even though "the author relied upon the Pentateuch, specifically the description of Moses' ascent in Exod 24:12-18, for a biblical source for this revelation."[26] Jubilees thus portrays its revelatory scheme from a well-known Scriptural narrative, which affords it some authority, but the author also distinguishes its message from that in Scripture: the revelation dictated by the angel of the presence is authorized, because of this author's understanding of the Sinai episode in Scripture, which he is rewriting for his community.[27]

(2) Directly after the death and burial of Abraham (23:1-8), there appears an eschatological text that has often been described as the *Jubilees* Apocalypse (23:9-31).[28] Fascinating in its own right, the text has been examined for the ways in which it has rewritten and redacted

---

25 VANDERKAM, Jubilees Translated, 6 gives cogent reasons for translating the verb as a causative "dictate" rather than "write" in this verse. Cf. also VANDERKAM, The Putative Author, 209-217.

26 SEGAL, Between Bible and Rewritten Bible, 21-22.

27 SEGAL, Between Bible and Rewritten Bible, 22, claims that the mediation of the angel has "the effect of distancing YHWH from direct contact with worldly matters."

28 For brief remarks on this text, cf. ENDRES, Eschatological Impulses in Jubilees, 332-336.

scriptural traditions, with references to Jer 6:23a (Jub 23:23b), Deut 28:49-50 (Jub 23:23) and Ps 79:2 (Jub 23:23),[29] and especially to Psalm 90.[30] Reading this text in the thought world of the deuteronomic covenant pattern would point to "four 'moments' of sin (vv. 16-21), punishment (vv. 22-25), a turning point (v. 26), and saving action of God (vv. 27-31)."[31] At its conclusion the writer makes clear that the angel of the presence has dictated to Moses all these things that he is to write (23:32).

> 23:32 Now you, Moses, write down these words because this is how it is written and entered in the testimony of the heavenly tablets for the history of eternity.

The apocalypse included in Jubilees also derives from the Testimony of the heavenly tablets.

The deuteronomic view of covenant life, however, plays an implicit role in this eschatological vision. The patterning of sin, punishment, turning point and saving action of God reminds those tutored in the Scriptures not only of Deuteronomy, but also of many recitals of Israel's past history found in the Books of Joshua, Judges, Samuel and Kings. Slightly novel in this text is the use of this patterning by the angel of the presence to help the community to imagine a future, and one which will include eschatological blessings of healing, happiness, punishment of enemies, just judgment from God and divine kindness (Jub 23:30-31). A vision of the future thus forms part of the testimony from the heavenly tablets which the angel dictates to Moses, providing a scriptural perspective for hope for those engaging fully in the covenant.

As an aside, we also note that the angel of the presence dictates to Moses in Jub 1:27 "from the beginning of the creation until the time when my temple is built among them throughout the ages of eternity." This description concludes another eschatological text (Jub 1:4b-29), with explicit indications of the heavenly tablets, the law and the testimony (Jub 1:29). As we noted earlier, those commands to Moses (Jub 1:26) and to the angel of the presence (Jub 1:27) set the revelatory schema of the entire book, and thus invoke the scriptural authority of

---

29 ENDRES, Biblical Interpretation, 52-62.
30 KUGEL, Jubilees Apocalypse, 323-324 introduces the notion that Jubilees' author enlisted the "revelation which Moses was ... urged to write down and restate in his own words ... our canonical Psalm 90." Kugel sees a time of suffering which is eventually concluded by a "golden age" (337). Since Ps 90 begins with "A Prayer of Moses, the man of God" the writer's interpretation in Jubilees demonstrates further the impact of the vision of the Scriptures revealed to Moses.
31 ENDRES, Eschatological Impulses, 334.

the deuteronomic covenantal patterning for the promise of a future of peace, healing, blessing.

(3) At Shechem Levi and Simeon were enraged after their sister Dinah had been defiled by Shechem, son of Hamor; they responded to his request to marry her by slaughtering all the men of the city (30:1-4). This event, rewritten in a very terse fashion, serves as a platform to discuss another issue:[32] to prohibit any Israelite man from giving his daughter in marriage "to Molech" (i.e. to a gentile). The legal stipulations, however, are addressed to Moses by the angel of the presence.

> 30:11 Now you, Moses, order the Israelites and testify to them that they are not to give any of their daughters to foreigners and that they are not to marry any foreign women because it is despicable before the Lord.
>
> 30:12 For this reason I have written for you in the words of the law everything that the Shechemites did to Dinah and how Jacob's sons said: 'We will not give our daughter to a man who has a foreskin because for us that would be a disgraceful thing'.
>
> 30:13 It is a disgraceful thing for the Israelites who give or take (in marriage) one of the foreign women because it is too impure and despicable for Israel.[33]

This addition to the story incorporates halakic traditions concerning intermarriage, found elsewhere in the Torah;[34] they address different issues than the rape of a young girl.[35] But the significance of the account for our purposes, however, is the claim that he had written about this event "in the words of the law," i.e. in the Pentateuchal text (Genesis 34). So "the law" contains a full account (even though it describes a different situation), but now the angel of the presence orders him to warn the Israelites about miscegenation in the Book of Jubilees. The figure of Moses has been enlisted for Jubilees' elucidation of the situation in two ways. The appropriate legislation about marriage to foreigners derives from law mediated through Moses (v. 12), but the text also implies the role of Moses in the writing of Jubilees. This narrative offers an excellent example of the rewriting of scriptural narrative in order to highlight laws from the heavenly tablets, which interpret the "first" law in an authentic way. Scripture has authorized the demands of the law, not only in the schema of the rewriting but also in the revelatory 'picture' of Moses. To deepen the message the angel of the pres-

---

32 ENDRES, Biblical Interpretation, 133, f.n. 39.
33 Jub 30:9-10 connect this law with the testimony from the heavenly tablets, and decree that it has no time limitation.
34 Cf. ENDRES, Biblical Interpretation, 135. In Jub 30:10b the writer proposed this as "the proper interpretation of Lev 18:21 and 20:2-4."
35 ANDERSON, Status of Torah before Sinai, 24 f.n. 43 and 26 f.n. 45.

ence reminds Moses "For this reason I have ordered you: Proclaim this testimony to Israel: See how it turned out for the Shechemites ..." (Jub 30:17a) and "I have written the entire message for you and have ordered you to tell the Israelites not to sin ..." (Jub 30:21a). Even if the narrative and halakah do not correspond perfectly, the authority of Scripture, mediated though Moses, is accentuated.

(4) Jubilees recounts the story of Reuben's incest with Bilhah, the concubine of his father Jacob (33:2-9a). The writer expanded a single-verse notice (Gen 35:22) into eight verses, which serve to exculpate Bilhah from guilt.[36] In the halakic section that follows (Jub 33:9b-20) the narrator uses this case of incest ("any man who uncovers the covering of his father" 33:9b, "a man is not to lie with his father's wife" 33:10; they should die, as punishment) to address the wider issue of sexual impurity (Jub 33:10, 11, 13, 20) forbidden to this holy people, "a priestly nation" (Jub 33:20). The issue of purity is paramount in Jubilees' exposition of this story, and the grave nature of the issue is highlighted by fact that the angel of the presence twice tells Moses to communicate to the Israelites the gravity of this offense. In Jub 33:13 he tells Moses to "order the Israelites to observe this command because it is a capital offense and it is an impure thing", and he explains that after this law is revealed it will have no end-time (Jub 33:17), and it cannot be forgiven. In Jub 33:18 he says "Now you, Moses, write for Israel so that they keep it and do not act like this and do not stray into a capital offense" because God is a just and impartial judge.

To underscore that the revelation of the law comes from highest authority, he writes: "for this reason it is written and ordained on the heavenly tablets" (Jub 33:10a). The order is repeated in Jub 33:12 and all of the Lord's "holy ones" affirm it, saying "So be it, so be it" (Jub 33:12b). Again, the combination of rewritten story and halakic application (connected to the story but drawing on multiple Pentateuchal sources/ texts) demonstrates Jubilees' concern to invoke scriptural authority for his revealed Book of Jubilees.

(5) The writer discusses many aspects of the Festivals of Pesah and Massot in Jub 49:1-23. He draws together and clarifies a number of conflicting details in Exodus 12-13 and other places in the Scriptures, attempting to create a more orderly composite for the community of his generation.[37] Unlike Exodus, where the Passover is to be celebrated in family units (homes), Jub 49:16-21 follows the deuteronomic prescrip-

---

36 ENDRES, Biblical Interpretation, 169, f.n. 22.
37 HALPERN-AMARU, Pesah and Massot in Jubilees, 321-322. Her article carefully considers various scriptural references to these festivals which the author of Jubilees attempts to integrate and harmonize in his account.

tion to celebrate it at the temple in Jerusalem (Deut 16:2), which is also reflected in the Books of Chronicles, especially the Passover celebration of Josiah (2 Chronicles 35).[38] Within these regulations Moses is told to order the Israelites to keep the passover statutes (49:22-23). They must celebrate it annually, and on the correct days of the year, and forever. This eternal statute is "engraved on the heavenly tablets regarding the Israelites" (49:8). Then Moses is addressed specifically:

> 49:22 Now you, Moses, order the Israelites to keep the statute of the passover as it was commanded to you so that you may tell them its year each year, the time of the days, and the festival of unleavened bread so that they may eat unleavened bread for seven days to celebrate its festival, to bring its sacrifice before the Lord on the altar of your God each day during those seven joyful days.

Here again Moses serves as recipient of the revelation from the heavenly tablets; it specifies the date on which the Israelites must celebrate it (Jub 49:8). In this chapter Segal identifies six verses which contain typical legal expressions that characterize so much of Jubilees: vv. 7, 8, 14, 15, 17, and 22.[39] Each of the verses he singles out concern transmission of revelation from the heavenly tablets, and all but v.17 explicitly focus on the issue of the correct calendar. This focus on the transmission of knowledge from the heavenly tablets to Moses further strengthens his position as recipient and proclaimer of revelation, and the rewriting of disparate and sometimes conflicting scriptural references to Pesah demonstrate his ability as interpreter of the (scriptural) tradition. Through these strategic moves the writer of Jubilees continues to make gestures indicating the authority of Scripture for his work.

These five incidents contain the totality of the explicit orders to Moses. Two of them were connected directly with the course of events in Jubilees. Two of them connect laws regarding sexual activities with biblically based events, and a fifth text grounds and explains the obligation of passover observance on the correct date. All these communications to Moses seem to come from the angel of presence. From the framework in 1:27, 29, it seems that the angel of presence dictates all the rest of the Book of Jubilees to Moses. So the same revelatory scheme would authorize additional events with embedded laws, which would offer a broader range of the ways that the figure of Moses gives authority to practices transmitted by the angel of presence, including some

---

38 SEGAL, Jubilees, 197.
39 SEGAL, Jubilees, 227. His discussion of Jubilees 49, including a very helpful close reading of its rewriting of Exodus 12 in pages 223-227, is devoted mostly to demonstrating significant differences from similar material in Jubilees 48, in order to support his thesis of different compositional levels in the book.

worship and ritual practices, especially Sabbath, the Feast of Shavuot/Weeks, the Passover and the circumcision of male Israelites.

Implicit attributions to Moses

(1) Sabbath observance held very high priority for this author. Laws concerning Sabbath appear both at the beginning of the book (Jub 2:1, 17-33) and at the end (Jub 50:1-13). As VanderKam suggests, these sabbath sections "surround all of the history after creation".[40] In Jub 2:1 the angel of the presence relates in his revelation to Moses that the Lord God observes sabbath on the seventh day. God "sanctified it [Sabbath] for all ages and set it as a sign for all his works." Sabbath observance is thus embedded in the very structure of creation.

God finished his work on the sixth day (Jub 2:16; Exod 20:11; but in Gen 2:2, on the seventh day). Then God transmitted the sign to the angels, to work six days but rest from all work on the seventh (Jub 2:17); so the angels (the angels of presence and the angels of holiness) are commanded to keep sabbath with God, in the heavens and on the earth (Jub 2:18). In vv 19-22 the angel of presence informs Moses that God told these angels his intention to separate a people for himself and to give them the sabbath day in order to sanctify[41] and bless them – just like the sabbath day. Further, this people will become God's people, and he their God – clearly covenantal language. Moreover, these descendants of Jacob are his firstborn, so he will inform them about sabbath days and how to observe them (Jub 2: 20). On sabbath, the seventh day, the chosen people are "eat, drink, and bless the creator of all as he had blessed them and sanctified them for himself," together with the angels. The angel also gives a theology and *raison d'etre* for the sabbath day and its stipulations in force in his day. The Lord gave "a festal day to all his creation", and every person who observes sabbath "will be holy and blessed throughout all times like us", i.e. like the angels (Jub 2:28).

At the end of the book, in Jub 50:1-13, the angel of the presence reminds Moses of everything that he made known to him about sabbaths, repeating much information from Jubilees 2. The only allowable work on sabbath is burning incense and bringing sacrifices (as in v. 10), which make atonement for Israel and serve as a memorial day. The angel of the presence characterizes the sabbath as gift of God for a fes-

---

40 VANDERKAM, Jubilees 2001, 84.
41 In Jub 2:23-24 the angel highlights the notion of 22 "kinds of works" made until the seventh day, corresponding with 22 "leaders of humanity." The author seems to conjoin notions of the holiness and blessing of the Israelites with the sanctity of sabbath law.

tival day, for eating and drinking and also bringing sacrifices (Jub 50:9b-10). This law was "written on the tablets" which God placed in his [the angel's] hands so that he could write the laws of the divisions of times (Jub 50:13). So this law is eternal.

The significance of Sabbath cannot be overestimated. The angel of the presence brought it to Moses' attention twice (Jubilees 2, 50). As VanderKam argued, this text looks backwards (historically) and forwards (eschatologically) to a time of fulfillment.[42] This literary *inclusio* of sabbath legislation empowers Moses to pass on to the Israelites this crown of their worship life together, the observance of Sabbath. Jubilees' rewriting of these texts ensures that the scriptural presentation of sabbath in Gen 2:2-3 is connected with the Sinai command to observe sabbath (Exod 20:8-11; Deut 5:12-15). These Torah texts stand behind the revealed messages about sabbath in Jubilees, and they lend it the authority of Moses.

(2) The feast of Weeks, observed on III/15 (Jub 6:10-22), is the most important Israelite festival in Jubilees' calendar. Although Moses is not named, it seems clear in vv. 17 and 20 that the angel of the presence addressed him. The festival was so ancient that it was celebrated "in heaven from the time of creation until the lifetime of Noah" (6:18). Noah and his sons observed the feast during Noah's lifetime, but after his death the sons ignored it, by eating blood. The feast fell out of practice until the time of Abraham; Abraham, Isaac and Jacob celebrated it, but it had been forgotten during Moses' time: that is the reason God renewed the covenant at the mountain, in his time. This renewal had occurred on the previous day (III/15), the day before this theophany of God at Sinai (Jub 1:1).

The obligation to celebrate the feast of Weeks has been "ordained and written on the heavenly tablets" (Jub 6:17) so it dates back to the time of creation (Jub 6:18). The association with Noah, of course, is contained in the heavenly tablets, though temporally it came later. Israelites should celebrate it one day each year, and the angel notes that this festival has a double significance: festival of weeks and festival of firstfruits (Jub 6:21). But its connection to the covenant with God is

---

42 According to VANDERKAM, Jubilees 2001, 84, the most significant aspect of this chapter occurs in vv 2-4, the calculation of this present date according to his scheme. Now there have passed since the time of Adam forty-nine jubilees (= 2401 years) and one week and two days, bringing to date 2410 A.M. Forty years yet remain, for learning the "Lord's commandments" before he leads them across the river into the land of Canaan (v 4). Now, 2410, is the time of the exodus from slavery in Egypt and 2450 will be the date of the entry into the land. 50:1-13:

crucial, providing a rationale why it must be maintained with its sacrifice, and also on its proper date.

Moreover, for this reason the Israelites must observe the (solar) calendar properly (6:32-38); to err from it would mean that festival worship would be improper (Jub 6:33-34). But the critical point is the source of this prescribed calendar, the heavenly tablets:

> 6:35 For I know and from now on will inform you – not from my own mind because this is the way the book is written in front of me, and the divisions of times are ordained on the heavenly tablets, lest they forget the covenantal festivals and walk in the festivals of the nations, after their error and after their ignorance.

In c. 6 the author packages together two basic obligations for the Israelites: to celebrate the feast of Weeks and according to the solar calendar. So Moses becomes the publicist of the feast and calendar, though he is not their originator, for their origins lie deep within the created structures of the cosmos.

(3) Circumcision of Israelite males on the eighth day receives great attention (Jubilees 15). Based on the Abraham story in Genesis 17, this author commands circumcision for Israelites as sign of the covenant; note that Jub 15:1 dates this event at the time of "the festival of the first fruits of the wheat harvest", i.e. the covenantal feast of Weeks. In this telling there is no angel of the presence, but the law still comes from the heavenly tablets:

> 15:25 This law is (valid) for all history forever. There is no circumcising of days, nor omitting any day of the eight days because it is an eternal ordinance ordained and written on the heavenly tablets.

Even though Moses has not been mentioned, there is no reason to doubt that the story forms part of the revelation to him. Moses should address this law to the Israelites, that they should keep this sign of their sanctity before all the angels, by practicing circumcision on the eighth day as the sign of the covenant (Jub 15:28).

> 15:28 Now you command the Israelites to keep the sign of this covenant throughout their history as an eternal ordinance so that they may not be uprooted from the earth
>
> 15:29 because the command has been ordained as a covenant so that they should keep it forever on all the Israelites.

The obligation to circumcise on the eighth day "is an eternal ordinance ordained and written on the heavenly tablets" (15:25). So Jubilees' story of Abraham's circumcision includes its meaning for Israel, specifying it through the revelation to Moses by the angel of presence. Here again, according to Jubilees, Moses is not to proclaim a new law, but to give the deeper significance of its history, especially as it specifies the covenant with the Israelites, chosen as the holy people. Here again Moses, the mediator of the first and the second law, brings the authority of the Scriptures to a more conscious level.

Conclusion

To conclude this section on Moses as Mediator, we have observed the Sinai theophany as an authorizing factor for the writer of Jubilees, for the integration of story and its laws. In five scenes the angel of the presence explicitly commanded Moses what to do. In four more instances, Moses is understood to be the addressee, even though not explicitly named. All the events follow upon or expand the view in Jub 1:29, that the angel of the presence took the heavenly tablets (of the Testimony) in front of all the rest. God remains the ultimate source of all the Torah and Testimony in Jubilees, but always through the mediation of the angel of the presence. Where does this leave Moses? Moses represents the human, prophetic mediator between God, heavenly beings, and humans.

According to the tradition of the Torah, all its laws were revealed through Moses to Israel (Exodus, Leviticus, Deuteronomy); now, according to Jubilees, the angel of the presence reveals to Moses aspects of some previously unknown laws. The history makes more sense when these important laws are known in conjunction with their originating events. The audience of Jubilees can be encouraged by knowing these pre-Sinai-era laws, and the unfolding of events (testimony) from pre-creation to new creation times.

These special revelations to Moses from the heavenly tablets reflect an overall concern that the community understand and celebrate its important signs of holiness and attachment to God in the covenant: Passover, feast of Weeks, and the Sabbath. Circumcision also marks the people as holy, and offers them a specific identity marker. The sexual sins highlighted in this book concern issues of identity, particularly by the prohibition of exogamy. Israel now realizes that its earliest ancestors were not deficient and ignorant, as some might claim.[43] This author demonstrates through Moses that they possessed from the earliest times a deep sense of the calendar ordained by God for their life, wor-

---

43 BICKERMAN, The Jews in the Greek Age, 294, comments that some Jews in the Hellenistic age began comparing their origins in Torah to important lawgivers of other nations, and it became painfully clear that Mosaic Law, though useful for part of their story, was "unknown at the beginning of the world and the beginning of the nation" and thus did not possess "eternal value."

ship and festivals. Their ancestors were not uncivilized brutes, but rather possessed a God-given set of laws to govern their lives.

Almost all of these embellishments to the scriptural tradition come from what is written and engraved on the heavenly tablets; they should enjoy great respect. García Martínez' important study of the heavenly tablets concluded that its content "is complex and diverse" and related to Enoch literature, but most important that they "constitute a hermeneutical recourse which permits the presentation of the 'correct' interpretation of the Law, adapting it to the changing situations of life."[44] In their interpretive function they might resemble what the rabbis call the Torah be-al-peh, "oral Torah".[45] Najman considered the suggestions of García Martínez and concluded that the "heavenly tablets" aid the self-authorization of the writer of Jubilees.[46] Boccaccini recalls that in Jubilees, Moses was the central mediator, Sinai was the privileged place of revelation, and Jubilees the content of the heavenly tablets. On Mt. Sinai Moses became "the repository of both the Pentateuch and Jubilees. Moses (not Enoch) is the *trait d'union* of both traditions." But then he adds that the "exaltation of Moses" is problematic, since for him the Enochic revelation is more important.[47] Himmelfarb's study sees heavenly tablets "as an archive of divine knowledge," containing the contents of both Torah and Jubilees.[48] VanderKam synthesizes these views with the simple claim that "these tablets are a written, unchangeable, permanent depository of information under God's control."[49]

For the audience of Jubilees the authorizing factor is the theophany at Sinai to Moses, with which the book begins. The Torah, i.e. Pentateuch as a written document, is not the authorizing factor for the author of Jubilees; thus we may conceive of it being re-imagined, re-told, interpreted. Nor is it possible to elevate any "Enochic traditions" – such as the notions of calendar and festivals – into the position of highest authority, though each of them plays a crucial role in the religious and imaginative landscape of Jubilees. Rather at the centre of our horizon (as readers of Jubilees) stands Moses, on Mt. Sinai. He experienced the angel of the presence dictate to him from the heavenly tablets the law

---

44　García Martínez, Heavenly Tablets in Jubilees, 258.
45　García Martínez, Heavenly Tablets in Jubilees, 258.
46　Najman, Jubilees and Its Authority Conferring Strategies, 40-59.
47　Boccaccini, Heavenly Tablets, 193-210.
48　Himmelfarb, Torah, Testimony and Heavenly Tablets, 27-29. Regarding the authority of the Torah, she argues that "the existence of a heavenly prototype of the Torah serves not to strengthen the authority of the Torah but to relativize it", 27. It seems in this argument that an authoritative document would be one without a source or a parallel.
49　VanderKam, Moses Trumping Moses, 32.

and the Testimony (Jubilees 2-50), including all the new interpretive material: the covenant before Moses, the obligation of circumcision (even practiced by the angels), the covenant festival dated to III/15 (all 'versions' of the same covenant), a theophany on III/16 ... the day after covenant (renewal). It seems then that Moses in Jubilees, like Moses in Deuteronomy, fills the role of prophetic interpreter of the full revelation from God, engaging in an extended 'Mosaic Discourse' for a people whose vision of Moses needed to be developed and expanded. For Jews of the era when Jubilees was written, even though Zion or Jerusalem are part of their self-understanding, Moses at Sinai still stands clearly on their horizon.

Bibliography

ANDERSON, Gary A., The Status of the Torah Before Sinai: The Retelling of the Bible in the Damascus Covenant and the Book of Jubilees, in: DSD 1 (1994), 1-29.

BERNSTEIN, Moshe, 'Rewritten Bible': A Generic Category which has Outlived its Usefulness?, in: Textus 22 (2005), 169-196.

BICKERMAN, Elias, The Jews in the Greek Age, Cambridge 1988.

BOCCACCINI, Gabriele, From a Movement of Dissent to a Distinct Form of Judaism: The Heavenly Tablets in Jubilees as the Foundation of a Competing Halakah, in: Boccaccini, Gabriele/Ibba, Giovanni (eds.), Enoch and the Mosaic Torah: The Evidence of Jubilees, Grand Rapids/Cambridge 2009, 193-210.

CHARLES, Robert Henry, The Book of Jubilees or the Little Genesis, Translated from the Editor's Ethiopic Text, and Edited with Introduction, Notes, and Indices, London 1902.

CRAWFORD, Sidnie, Rewriting Scripture in Second Temple Times, Grand Rapids 2008.

ENDRES, John, Biblical Interpretation in the Book of Jubilees, CBQ.MS 18, Washington 1987.

ENDRES, John, Eschatological Impulses on Jubilees, in: Boccaccini, Gabriele/Ibba, Giovanni (eds.), Enoch and the Mosaic Torah: The Evidence of Jubilees, Grand Rapids/Cambridge 2009, 323-337.

GARCÍA MARTÍNEZ, Florentino, Heavenly Tablets in the Book of Jubilees, in: Albani, Matthias/Frey, Jörg/ Lang, Armin (eds.), Studies in the Book of Jubilees (TSAJ 65), Tübingen, 1997, 243-260.

HALPERN-AMARU, Betsy, The Festivals of Pesah and Massot in the Book of Jubilees, in: Boccaccini, Gabriele/Ibba, Giovanni (eds.), Enoch and the Mosaic Torah: The Evidence of Jubilees, Grand Rapids/Cambridge 2009, 309-322.

HIMMELFARB, Martha, Torah, Testimony, and Heavenly Tablets: The Claim to Authority in the *Book of Jubilees*, in: Wright, Benjamin G. (ed.), A Multiform Heritage: Studies on Early Judaism and Christianity in Honor of Robert A. Kraft, Atlanta 1999, 19-29.

KNIBB, Michael, *Jubilees* and the Origins of the Qumran Community, in: Knibb, Michael, Essays on the Book of Enoch and Other Early Jewish Texts and Traditions (StVTP 22), Leiden/Boston 2009, 232-254.

KUGEL, James, The Jubilees Apocalypse, in: DSD 1:3 (1994), 322-337.

KUGEL, James, Traditions of the Bible: A Guide to the Bible as it Was at the Start of the Common Era, Cambridge/London 1998.

LOADER, William, Enoch, Levi, and Jubilees on Sexuality: Attitudes toward Sexuality in the Early Enoch Literature, the Aramaic Levi Document, and the Book of Jubilees, Grand Rapids 2007.

NAJMAN, Hindy, Seconding Sinai: The Development of Mosaic Discourse in Second Temple Judaism (JSJ.S 77), Leiden/Boston 2003.

NAJMAN, Hindy, Reconsidering Jubilees: Prophecy and Exemplarity, in: Boccaccini, Gabriele/Ibba, Giovanni (eds.), Enoch and the Mosaic Torah: The Evidence of Jubilees, Grand Rapids/Cambridge 2009, 229-243.

NAJMAN, Hindy, Interpretation as Primordial Writing: Jubilees and Its Authority Conferring Strategies, in: JSJ 30 (1999), 379-410.

SCHIFFMAN, Lawrence H., The Book of Jubilees and the Temple Scroll, in: Boccaccini, Gabriele/Ibba, Giovanni (eds.), Enoch and the Mosaic Torah: The Evidence of Jubilees, Grand Rapids/Cambridge 2009, 99-115.

SEGAL, Michael, Between Bible and Rewritten Bible, in: Henze, Matthias (ed.), Biblical Interpretation at Qumran, Grand Rapids 2005, 10-29.

VANDERKAM, James C., Textual and Historical Studies in the Book of Jubilees (Harvard Semitic Monographs 14), Missoula 1977.

VANDERKAM, James C., The Putative Author of the Book of Jubilees, in: JSS 26 (1981), 209-217.

VANDERKAM, James C., The Book of Jubilees. Translated by James C. VanderKam (CSCO511; SA88), Louvain 1989.

VANDERKAM, James C., The Book of Jubilees, Sheffield 2001.

VANDERKAM, James C., The Manuscript Tradition of Jubilees, in: Boccaccini, Gabriele/Ibba, Giovanni (eds.), Enoch and the Mosaic Torah: The Evidence of Jubilees, Grand Rapids/Cambridge 2009, 3-21.

VANDERKAM, James C., Moses Trumping Moses: Making the Book of *Jubilees*, in: Metso, Sariana/Najman, Hindy/Schuller, Eileen (eds.), The Dead Sea Scrolls: Transmission of Traditions and Production of Texts (STDJ 92), Leiden 2010, 225-244.

VAN RUITEN, Jaques T. A. G. M., Primaeval History Interpreted: The Rewriting of Genesis 1-11 in the Book of Jubilees (JSJ.S 66), Leiden 2000.

VERMES, Géza, Scripture and Tradition in Judaism: Haggadic Stories (StPB 4), Leiden repr. 1973.

WACHOLDER, Ben Zion, The Relationship between 11Q Torah (the Temple Scroll) and the Book of Jubilees: One Single or Two Independent Compositions?, in: SBL.SP 24 (1985), 205-216.

WACHOLDER, Ben Zion, *Jubilees* as the Super-Canon: Torah Admonition Versus Torah-Commandment, in: Bernstein, Moshe/García Martínez, Florentino/Kampen, John (eds.), Legal Texts and Legal Issues: Proceedings for the Second Meeting of the International Organization for Qumran Studies, Cambridge 1995, Published in Honor of Joseph M. Baumgarten (STDJ 23), Leiden 1997, 195-211.

WERMAN, C., Jubilees in the Hellenistic Context, in: LiDonnici, Lynn/Lieber, Andrea (eds.), Heavenly Tablets: Interpretation, Identity, and Tradition in Ancient Judaism (JSJ.S 119), Leiden 2007, 133-158.

Die geheime Offenbarung –
Zur Autorität der Schrift im IV Esra

PAUL METZGER

Mehrere Begriffe des Titels sind in der theologischen Diskussion in so vielen Kontexten gebräuchlich, dass ihre Bedeutung zuweilen unscharf erscheint. Der Begriff der Autorität wird dabei vor allem erstens im Rahmen von Fragen von Verfassung und Recht der Kirche und zweitens im fundamentaltheologischen Kontext gebraucht. Dort geht es um die Frage des Stellenwertes von Schrift und Tradition im Rahmen der theologischen Erkenntnisbildung und Normierung von Interpretation. Dieser Horizont wird im vorliegenden Zusammenhang in die Diskussion einbezogen. Der zweite Begriff „Schrift" gehört gleichsam in diesen Kontext. Beide Begriffe und die Probleme, die mit ihnen zusammenhängen, sollen zunächst kurz umrissen werden.

1. Die Frage der Autorität

Die Frage nach Autorität in einer Religionsgemeinschaft ist nicht per se heikel. Manche dieser Gemeinschaften beruhen geradezu auf der Autorität ihrer Gründungsfiguren und/oder Anführer. Im Judentum und Christentum ist die Frage nach der Autorität schwierig zu beantworten. Hier müssen erstens verschiedene Ausprägungen der Religion betrachtet und zweitens verschiedene Ebenen der Fragestellung beachtet werden. Im Rahmen des Christentums differenziert sich die Frage nach Konfessionen und theologischen Grundüberzeugungen aus. Es lässt sich aber über alle Konfessionsgrenzen hinweg festhalten, dass die Bibel eine maßgebliche Autorität für die Gemeinschaft darstellt. Wie diese Autorität im Einzelnen dann konkret zum Tragen kommt, ist eine andere Frage, die vor allem im ökumenischen Dialog zwischen römisch-katholischer und protestantischer Konfession wichtig ist. Dabei ist eigentlich nicht die zentrale Stellung der Schrift das kontroverse Thema, um das gerungen wird, sondern deren Interpretation bzw. die Frage, ob es eine Autorität gibt, die das Recht hat, die richtige Interpretation der Bibel zu bestimmen. „Die richtige Interpretation der Hl. Schrift [ist demnach] ein ökumenisch bislang noch nicht gelöstes Problem, denn dieselben wissenschaftlichen Methoden führen zwar zu ähnlichen exegetischen Ergebnissen, die jedoch nicht selten in unterschiedliche, teils unvereinbare Positionen münden (...), was wiederum mit einem unterschiedlichen Vorverständnis bzw. einer unterschiedlichen Verhältnisbestimmung von historisch-kritischer und dogmatischer Interpretation zusammenhängt."[1] Während in der römisch-katholischen Theologie klar ist, dass dem Lehramt der Kirche die Autorität zugebilligt wird, in letzter Instanz und verbindlich über die Schriftauslegung zu entscheiden,[2] hat der Protestantismus aufgrund seines „Schriftprinzips" an dieser Stelle keine überzeugende Antwort.[3] Indem Luther der Schrift zutraut, sich selbst auszulegen, verzichtet er programmatisch auf eine menschliche Instanz, der er diese lehramtliche Autorität zugestehen will. Eine normative Schriftinterpretation ist deshalb im Protestantismus schwierig, da die Schrift selbst ihre richtige Interpretation erweisen, dies aber immer von Menschen gezeigt werden muss. Die Interpretation braucht deshalb eine Methode, die eine intersubjektive Überprüfung der Interpretationsergebnisse ermöglicht. Damit hängt aber die weitere Frage nach der Verhältnisbestimmung zwischen der Bibel als Wort Gottes und ihrer Interpretation als rein menschlichem Vorgang zusammen. Hier offenbart sich eine grundlegende Aporie. Auf der einen Seite steht die Begrenztheit der Methode als menschlichem Unternehmen: Es „wird wohl kaum jemand behaupten wollen, daß ein überzeugendes Gesamtkonzept gefunden sei, das den unwiderruflichen Erkenntnissen der historischen Methode Rechnung trägt, zugleich aber ihre Begrenzungen überwindet und sie in eine sachgemäße Hermeneutik hinein öffnet."[4] Auf der anderen Seite steht die Überzeugung, in der Bibel das Wort Gottes zu sehen, dem eine menschliche Methode nicht gerecht werden kann. Daraus folgt: „Das letztlich entscheidende Problem in der Verhältnisbestimmung von Prinzip und Methode ist die Spannung zwischen der unverfügbaren Selbsterschließung Gottes durch die biblischen Schriften und dem durch einen methodischen Zugriff ermöglichten Verstehen der Texte."[5] Letztlich führt diese Problemlage dann doch auf die Frage zurück, mit welchem Recht die Bibel autoritative Grundlage des Christentums sein

---

1 BÖTTIGHEIMER, Lehrbuch, 164.
2 Vgl. die Apostolische Konstitution des II. Vaticanum „Dei Verbum": „Die Aufgabe aber, das geschriebene oder überlieferte Wort Gottes verbindlich zu erklären, ist nur dem lebendigen Lehramt der Kirche anvertraut, dessen Vollmacht im Namen Jesu Christi ausgeübt wird." (DV 10)
3 Vgl. LAUSTER, Prinzip, 11-13.
4 RATZINGER, Schriftauslegung, 90.
5 LAUSTER, Prinzip, 468.

kann. Ist sie es aufgrund ihrer Herkunft, also entweder weil sie von Gott stammt oder weil sie Produkt der Autorität beanspruchenden Kirche ist? Oder ist sie es aufgrund ihres Inhaltes? Beinhaltet sie göttliche Offenbarung von sich aus oder nur dann, wenn der Mensch, der sie liest, selbst von Gott dazu befähigt wird, Offenbarung zu empfangen, sei es durch die individuelle Inspiration des Lesers, die traditionell als das innere Zeugnis des Heiligen Geistes aufgefasst wurde,[6] oder durch den Glauben der Kirche.[7] Wodurch erlangt die Bibel also Autorität für das Christentum bzw. allgemeiner gefasst: woher bezieht eine Schrift Autorität für eine Religionsgemeinschaft?

Die zweite Schwierigkeit, die geklärt werden muss, betrifft die inhaltliche Füllung des Begriffs „Schrift" im vorliegenden Zusammenhang.

2. Die Schrift im IV Esr

Bislang war die christliche Bibel in ihren jeweiligen konfessionellen Ausprägungen gemeint, wenn von „Schrift" die Rede war. Jetzt verengt sich der Begriff und muss definiert werden. Was soll untersucht werden, wenn es um die Autorität einer oder mehrerer „Schriften" im IV Esr[8] geht?

Hier lassen sich drei verschiedene Ansätze benennen. Zunächst kann der Inhalt von Texten als Bezugsrahmen verstanden werden. Im IV Esr scheint die Geschichte Israels, wie sie in der hebräischen Bibel niedergelegt ist, ein geläufiger Argumentationsrahmen zu sein. Dieser Eindruck muss in einem ersten Schritt in den Blick genommen werden. Dann kann ein bestimmter Begriff in den Mittelpunkt der Untersuchung treten, der als Titel, Zusammenfassung o.ä. einer Schrift aufgefasst werden kann. Hier dürfte vor allem der Begriff „Gesetz" von Interesse sein, wobei näher zu untersuchen sein wird, wie das semantische Potential des Begriffs im IV Esr verstanden und ob damit in signifikanter Weise die Tora bezeichnet wird. Dies wird in einem zweiten Schritt angegangen. Schließlich kann unter „Schrift" ein Buch bzw. eine Sammlung, ein Kanon von Schriften verstanden werden. Im vorliegen-

---

6 Vgl. SCHNEIDER-FLUME, Grundkurs, 81: „Die Wahrheit der Schrift bewahrheitet sich durch die Kraft der lebendigen Beziehung auf Gott, die Geist genannt zu werden verdient." In rezeptionsästhetischer Perspektive spricht KÖRTNER, Inspirierter Leser, 112, deshalb von einem „inspirierten Leser".

7 So RATZINGER, Frage des Traditionsbegriffs, 47-48.

8 Der IV Esr wird zitiert nach SCHREINER, 4 Esra, 289-412. Dort finden sich auch wichtige Hinweise zur Textüberlieferung und weiteren Einleitungsfragen. Dafür siehe auch OEGEMA, Apokalypsen; STONE, Fourth Ezra.

den Zusammenhang scheint vor allem die dritte Frageperspektive besonders sinnvoll und interessant zu sein. Diese Fragestellung ist gerechtfertigt, da die Entstehungszeit des IV Esr, ca. 100 n. Chr., ein wichtiges Datum für den Kanonisierungsprozess der hebräischen und auch bereits der christlichen Bibel darstellt. In diesem Kontext lässt sich der IV Esr als ein Diskussionsbeitrag um den Kanon der hebräischen Bibel verstehen.[9] Deshalb lohnt es sich, danach zu fragen, welche Schrift der IV Esr im Blick hat, welchen Stellenwert er dem Konzept einer autoritativen Schriftensammlung zumisst und woher das, was er unter Schrift versteht, Autorität erlangt. Dass die Fragestellung ein wenig anachronistisch anmutet, weil der Kanon noch nicht geschlossen vorliegt und die damit verbundene Problematik von Begründung und richtiger Interpretation noch nicht in ihrer ganzen Tragweite vor Augen steht, lässt sich zwar nur schlecht bestreiten, verdeckt aber auch nicht die Relevanz, die diese Fragestellung schon beim IV Esr hat.

In drei Durchgängen muss die Frage nach der Schrift im IV Esr also behandelt werden.

3. Die Geschichte Israel als Horizont der Argumentation

Das Grundproblem des IV Esr dreht sich um die Deutung der Wirklichkeit.[10] Die Katastrophe der Tempelzerstörung wirft Fragen auf, die sich mit herkömmlichen theologischen Überzeugungen nur unzureichend verstehen lassen. Das Sachproblem des IV Esr „besteht in dem Auseinanderklaffen zwischen Glaube und Bekenntnis im Rahmen bisheriger Weltorientierung und der demgegenüber kritisch reflektierten Erfahrung der Wirklichkeit der Welt".[11] Die Frage nach Israel und seinem Schicksal angesichts der militärischen Niederlage bestimmt die Diskussion zwischen Esra und seinem Angelus Interpres Uriel. Es geht Esra darum, „die Frage nach der Gerechtigkeit zu beantworten angesichts der Welterfahrung."[12] Ihn treibt seine Einsicht um, dass er die Wege des Herrn nicht verstehen kann (IV Esr 4,12). Er versteht nicht, warum Gott den Menschen mit einem bösen Herzen erschaffen hat (IV Esr 3,19ff) und ihn so aus Esras beschränkter Sicht zum Tod verdammt hat (IV Esr 3,7). Letztlich geht es im IV Esr also grundlegend nicht nur um die Verarbeitung der Zerstörung Israels, sondern Esra geht noch

---

9   Vgl. dazu grundlegend BECKER, Grenzziehungen.
10 Vgl. METZGER, Katechon, 190-192.
11 BRANDENBURGER, Verborgenheit, 164. Vgl. ESLER, Social Function, 108.
12 LUCK, Weltverständnis, 294.

einen Schritt weiter und fragt nach Gottes Verantwortlichkeit für das böse Herz des Menschen.[13]

Als Horizont dieser Frage dient die Geschichte Israels. Mehrfach rekurriert Esra auf die Vorkommnisse und Erfahrungen, die Israel mit seinem Gott in Verbindung bringt. Bereits das 1. Gebet Esras (IV Esr 3,4ff) stellt eine Zusammenfassung der Heilsgeschichte dar. Über Adam und dessen Vertreibung aus dem Paradies läuft eine Linie über die Erzväter bis zu David und dem babylonischen Exil. Weiter kann der Autor des IV Esr nicht gehen, da er sonst die Fiktion zerstören würde, die in IV Esr 3,1f etabliert wird, nämlich aus der Situation des Exils heraus zu schreiben. Das babylonische Exil wird mit der herkömmlichen Methode des Tun-Ergehen-Zusammenhangs erklärt, weist also Spuren des sog. deuteronomistischen Geschichtsbilds auf.[14] Die Bewohner Jerusalems sündigen gegen Gott und deshalb werden sie in die Hände der Feinde Israels gegeben (IV Esr 3,25-27). Babylon wird zum Strafinstrument Gottes. Diese Erklärung des Exils zerbricht aber, als Esra selbst die Sünden Babylons sieht und darum nicht mehr akzeptieren kann, dass es den Feinden Israels besser gehen soll als dem vermeintlich erwählten Volk (IV Esr 3,30f).[15] Eine ähnliche Argumentationslinie findet sich in IV Esr 14,27-36, wo das gleiche Muster von Güte, Abfall und Gericht aufgezeigt wird. Allerdings reicht diese „alte" Erklärung auch hier nicht mehr aus.

Es zeigt sich also, dass die Erklärung des Exilschicksals, die im Rahmen des deuteronomistischen Geschichtswerks überzeugen konnte, für Esra zerbrochen ist. Die Geschichte an sich, die sich deutlich an die Darstellung der hebräischen Bibel anschließt, steht aber nicht in Frage und damit die Schriften, die diese Geschichte überliefern auch nicht.

Noch deutlicher wird der Bezug zur hebräischen Bibel im Detail der Geschichtserinnerungen Esras. Vor allem IV Esr 6,38ff zeigen deutliche Bezüge zum priesterschriftlichen Schöpfungsbericht (Gen 1,1-2,4a). Die inhaltliche Bezugnahme zeigt wieder, dass der Text der Genesis nicht nur bekannt gewesen sein muss, sondern dass er die Grundlage für die Argumentation bieten kann. Das bedeutet für die vorliegende Fragestellung, dass der Text als Autorität akzeptiert worden zu sein scheint. Falls es anders gewesen sein sollte, wäre unverständlich, dass sich Esra zur Vorbereitung seiner Klage an Gott, auf diesen Text uneingeschränkt zurückziehen durfte. In keiner Weise zeigt der IV Esr,

---

13 Vgl. dazu ausführlich METZGER, Böses Herz.
14 Vgl. HOFMANN, Rezeption, 334.
15 Vgl. HALLBÄCK, Fall of Zion, 265: „Why Israel, which after all has sinned the less, is to be punished by Babylon, the greater sinner, – this is the question that torments Ezra."

dass diese Bezüge nicht hergestellt werden dürfen. Folglich scheint der Text selbst inhaltlich voll akzeptiert.

Ein weiterer Beleg für die Akzeptanz eines Textes ist die Aufnahme als Zitat. Ein Zitat findet sich in IV Esr 7,129 als Aufnahme von Dtn 30,19.[16] Es wird als ein Zitat des Mose eingeführt, was darauf schließen lässt, dass die Fiktion des Dtn, wonach es eine Rede des Mose sein will, an dieser Stelle verfängt. Das Dtn wird vom IV Esr demnach in seine Argumentation als autoritativer Ausspruch des Mose eingebaut. Uriel geht auf Esras Frage nach dem Sinn des menschlichen Lebens ein und antwortet ihm de facto mit einem „Schriftzitat": „Wähle das Leben, damit du lebst." Der IV Esr unterscheidet hier nicht zwischen der Autorität des Mose und der Autorität des Dtn. Beide fallen für ihn in eins zusammen. Dass aber ausdrücklich gesagt wird, dass Mose nicht mehr lebt, zeigt, dass dessen Autorität auf das Dtn übergangen ist. Nimmt man die weiteren Beobachtungen hinzu, wonach andere Schriften ebenfalls im Horizont des IV Esr benutzt werden, scheint die Annahme berechtigt, dass der IV Esr eine ähnliche Verlagerung der Autorität auch an anderen Orten akzeptiert. So wie er anerkennt, dass die Schrift des Mose, wahrscheinlich die gesamte Tora, seine Autorität auch nach seinem Tod trägt, lässt sich vermuten, dass dies auch für Schriften gilt, die z.B. von David berichten. Blickt man auf IV Esr 14 und die Nennung von 24 Schriften, lässt sich bereits hier vermuten, dass der IV Esr durchaus Schriften als autoritativ anerkennt.

Zunächst kann jedoch festgehalten werden, dass die Schriften, die die Geschichte Israels in der Gegenwart des IV Esr bereitstellen, den argumentativen Horizont des Textes darstellen und insofern eine gewisse Autorität beanspruchen. In einem nächsten Schritt muss die spezielle Frage nach dem Gesetz beantwortet werden.

4. Das Gesetz im IV Esr

Da der IV Esr nur in Übersetzungen überliefert ist, muss eine begriffliche Untersuchung immer in ganz besonderer Weise mit dieser Problematik umgehen. Um die Frage nach einer speziellen Autorität des Gesetzes im IV Esr zu beantworten, ist es deshalb nötig, zunächst zu klären, was mit „Gesetz" im IV Esr gemeint ist. Konkret steht die Alternative zur Debatte, ob „Gesetz" die Tora bezeichnet oder ob der Begriff ein weiteres semantisches Potential besitzt.[17] Überblickt man die einzelnen Stellen, an denen das „Gesetz" eine Rolle spielt, so wird es

---

16 Vgl. OEGEMA, Apokalypsen, 106.
17 Vgl. HOGAN, Tora, 530-552.

weithin offensichtlich als bekannte Größe verstanden. Das Gesetz kann verachtet und verschmäht oder gelehrt und gehalten werden (IV Esr 7,39; 9,11; 8,29; 7,94). Es ist in das Herz des Menschen geschrieben und wird doch durch die Wurzel des Bösen übertreten (IV Esr 3,22). Das Gesetz soll dem Menschen helfen, das böse Herz zu überwinden (IV Esr 9,31),[18] da er durch dessen Befolgung das ewige Leben gewinnen kann (IV Esr 3,19; 14,22.34). Diese Belege lassen nun keine eindeutige Entscheidung zu, was mit „Gesetz" gemeint sein dürfte. Allerdings lassen sich weitere Hinweise finden, die eine nähere Bestimmung doch möglich machen. Zunächst fällt die Rede Esras in IV Esr 14,20ff ins Auge. Esra klagt hier darüber, dass das Gesetz Gottes verbrannt ist. Da das Gesetz aber nötig ist, um das ewige Leben zu erlangen, scheint die Lage derjenigen, die Esras Lehre nicht mehr persönlich hören können aussichtslos. Die ganze Geschichte Israels mit seinem Gott ist verloren, weil das Gesetz nicht mehr da ist. Esra möchte deshalb das Gesetz wieder aufschreiben. Dies zeigt, dass mit „Gesetz" an dieser Stelle eindeutig ein Text gemeint sein muss. Dieser Text führt den Menschen auf den Weg des Lebens. In ihm ist aufgezeichnet, „was in der Welt von Anfang an geschehen ist". Dieser Text existierte in der Fiktion des IV Esr vor dem Exil und ist durch die Babylonier vernichtet worden. Setzt man diese eindeutige Bezugnahme von „Gesetz" auf einen Text in Beziehung zu IV Esr 3,19; 14,3ff dann wird deutlich, dass Gott Israel das Gesetz durch Mose gegeben hat. Von daher kann als Antwort gesagt werden, dass „Gesetz" sicherlich mit dem Textkorpus der Tora identifiziert werden kann. Dies harmoniert mit der sonstigen Hochschätzung von Texten, die der IV Esr erkennen lässt. Erstens indem er bereits in IV Esr 12,37 seinem Protagonisten den Befehl erteilt, ein Buch zu schreiben, zweitens indem er dies in IV Esr 14,20ff breit durchführt und drittens indem er nicht zufällig Esra als Pseudonym seines Werkes benutzt. Ist dieser doch in der Tradition als „der Schreiber" Israels gekennzeichnet, der als „ein kundiger Schriftgelehrter im Gesetz des Mose, das der Herr, der Gott Israels, gegeben hatte" (Esr 7,6) ausgewiesen ist.[19] Von daher dürfte es schwer fallen, „Gesetz" nicht mit der Tora in Verbindung zu bringen.

Einen scheinbaren Widerspruch innerhalb des IV Esr scheint diese Begriffsbestimmung aber auszulösen. Wenn Esra in IV Esr 9,37, davon spricht, dass das Gesetz nicht vergeht, sondern in seiner Herrlichkeit bleibt, dann ist es doch zweifelhaft, wie es dann verbrennen kann (IV Esr 14,21). Zeigt sich an diesem Widerspruch, dass „Gesetz" doch wei-

---

18 Vgl. REISER, Gerichtspredigt, 103.
19 Vgl. METZGER, Esra.

ter zu verstehen ist als bislang vorgeschlagen? Betrachtet man z.B. IV Esr 7,21, dann scheint die Anklage Uriels, wonach Gott „den Kommenden" auch geboten habe, was sie tun sollen, eine universale Perspektive anzunehmen. Diesen wird in IV Esr 7,24 vorgeworfen, das „Gesetz" zu verachten. Worauf bezieht sich die Rede von den „Kommenden" konkret? Die gleiche Frage entspringt IV Esr 7,72, wenn dort von denen gesprochen wird, „die auf der Erde weilen" und das Gesetz nicht gehalten haben. Wer ist damit gemeint? Generell scheint IV Esr 7,127 den Weg zu weisen. Hier liegt eine theologische Sinndeutung der existentiellen Frage des IV Esr vor. Der Sinn seiner Gegenwart liegt für ihn darin, dass der Mensch geprüft wird und um das Paradies gegen sein böses Herz kämpfen muss. Mit dieser allgemeinen Aussage scheint die universale Deutung der eben gestellten Fragen plausibel. Allerdings ist hier eine feine Unterscheidung zu treffen. Wie gesehen argumentiert der IV Esr betont aus der Perspektive Israels heraus.[20] Seine ganze Argumentation verfängt nur auf dem heilsgeschichtlichen Hintergrund, den Israel für sich als identifikationsstiftend akzeptiert. In der Mehrzahl der Belege lässt sich unter „Gesetz" entsprechend als Tora bestimmen. Es fällt daher insgesamt nicht leicht, dem Werk eine universale Perspektive zu konstatieren und ihm deshalb als Problem eine systematische Aufarbeitung der Theodizeefrage zuzugestehen.[21] Von daher muss letztlich die Frage nach dem Bezug von „Mensch", den „Kommenden", denen, „die auf der Erde weilen", offen bleiben. Es kann sein, dass der IV Esr immer nur aus der Binnenperspektive argumentiert und nur Israel im Blick hat. Das semantische Potential des Begriffs „Gesetz" unter diesen Umständen auch auf den „gesunden Menschenverstand" („Common sense") oder das „Naturrecht" auszuweiten, scheint lediglich möglich.[22] Immerhin widerspricht die Rede von dem ewigen Bleiben des Gesetzes nicht der Beobachtung, dass „Gesetz" hier mit der Tora gleichgesetzt werden und dieses als Text auch verbrennen kann. Da nämlich das Gesetz von Gott gegeben und bei ihm vorhanden ist, kann es zwar in menschlicher Verfügungsgewalt als Ansammlung von Zeichen auf Papier durchaus verbrennen und vernichtet werden, sein eigentliches – „himmlisches" – Wesen

---

20 Auch BRANDENBURGER, Verborgenheit, 186, sieht den IV Esr vor allem mit Problemen seiner engeren Umgebung befasst: „Der Verfasser begegnet mit seinem Werk einer tiefgreifenden Krisensituation in seinem engeren Lebenskreis, der jüdischen Gemeinde."
21 Vgl. HOFFMANN, Gesetz, 222. Auch MAIER, Theodizee, 219, gesteht dem IV Esr allenfalls einen „Ansatz zu systematischen Überlegungen" zum Thema Theodizee zu.
22 So der Vorschlag von HOGAN, Tora, 551. Diesem Vorschlag folgt BECKER, Rewriting, 93.

bleibt aber davon unberührt.²³ Man muss demnach keine Ausweitung des Begriffspotentials allein aufgrund dieser Stelle vornehmen.

Zwar drängt sich durchaus der Eindruck auf, dass mit „Gesetz" nicht immer nur die Tora gemeint sein dürfte, doch ist lediglich sicher, – und für den vorliegenden Zusammenhang wesentlicher – das „Gesetz" zuweilen durchaus mit der Tora in eins gesetzt werden kann und dass es schließlich als Text bekannt war, der für den IV Esr eine Autorität darstellt. Insofern kennt der IV Esr eine gewisse Form von Schriftautorität. Gleichzeitig ist deutlich, dass der IV Esr auch noch andere Texte als „Schrift" akzeptiert. Einen klar bestimmten Begriff der „Schrift" kennt er nicht. „Schrift" ist für ihn auf jeden Fall mehr als „Gesetz", allerdings erkennt er dem „Gesetz" eine besondere Autorität zu. Welches spezielle Konzept von „Schriftautorität" er in dieser Hinsicht entwickelt, muss im nächsten Abschnitt untersucht werden.

5. Die Bedeutung der Schrift im IV Esr

Bislang wurde deutlich, dass die Geschichte Israels den Argumentationshorizont bildet, in dem sich der IV Esr bewegt. Damit ist ersichtlich, dass auch die Schriften, die diese Geschichte überliefern, für ihn eine gewisse Autorität haben. Besonders interessant wird diese Feststellung, wenn nach dem Verhältnis von Schrift und neuer Offenbarung gefragt und dies im historischen Rahmen der Kanonisierung betrachtet wird.

Da in der Regel eine apokalyptische Schrift beansprucht, ihren Lesern neues Wissen zu vermitteln und darauf angewiesen ist, dass dieses Wissen als Offenbarung Gottes von den Lesern akzeptiert wird, muss der IV Esr zwangsläufig eine Balance finden zwischen der Autorität überkommener Schriften und seinem eigenen Anspruch, neue Offenbarung zu verkünden.²⁴ Da das alte Wissen nicht mehr überzeugend zur Deutung der Gegenwart ausreicht, muss der IV Esr seine eigenen theologischen Deutungen seinen Lesern so vermitteln, dass einerseits die Schriftautorität, auf die er sich beruft, nicht beschädigt wird, dass andererseits die Schrift aber auch nicht so dominant wird, dass er sein eigenes Anliegen nicht mehr überzeugend zum Tragen bringen kann. Diese Ausgangslage bestimmt sein Verhältnis zur Autorität der Schrift.

An dieser Stelle scheint es angebracht, zunächst den Prozess der Kanonisierung der hebräischen Bibel kurz in den Blick zu nehmen und zu konstatieren, dass dieser bereits in vollem Gang zu sein scheint.

---

23 Vgl. STONE, Forth Ezra, 307-308.
24 Vgl. METZGER, Esra, 263-265.

Hierauf deutet die Zahl der Bücher hin, die Esra öffentlich zugänglich machen soll. Die in IV Esr 14,45 genannten 24 Bücher dürften wohl kaum zufällig den hebräischen Kanon abbilden.[25] Von daher scheint der Kanonisierungsprozess der hebräischen Bibel im IV Esr so weit gediehen zu sein, dass der Kanon relativ fest umrissen war und sich mit späteren Kanonlisten deckt.[26] Die Existenz eines solchen Kanons macht die eben beschriebene Problematik nochmals dringlicher: Wie soll der IV Esr seine eigene Theologie glaubwürdig einbringen, wenn er sich einem sich immer mehr verfestigenden Kanon gegenübersteht? Und wie bemisst er angesichts dieser Problemstellung die Autorität des sich abzeichnenden Kanons?

Zunächst ist die Wahl des Pseudonyms sprechend.[27] Indem der IV Esr – wie bereits erwähnt – Esra, den „Schreiber" zu seinem Protagonisten macht, versucht er an dessen Autorität und der Autorität des Werkes, das Esra zugeschrieben wird, zu partizipieren. Er gewinnt dadurch Anschluss an die rabbinische Überlieferung (t.Sanh 4,7; b.Sanh 21b), wonach Esra die Tora von Babylon nach Israel mitbringt.[28] Esra ist demnach prädestiniert, die Schrift aufzuzeichnen.

Einen Kunstgriff der Fiktionalität greift der IV Esr in IV Esr 12,37 auf. Dort wird Esra gesagt, dass er die Vision von Löwe und Adler und deren Deutung aufschreiben, aber nicht veröffentlichen soll. Damit kreiert der IV Esr die Fiktion, wonach Esra etwas aufgeschrieben, aber zu seiner Zeit auf göttlichen Befehl hin nicht veröffentlicht hat. Damit wird behauptet, dass es zur Zeit des IV Esr neben der bekannten Schrift noch andere Überlieferungen gibt, die aus derselben Quelle stammen. Es ist offensichtlich, dass der IV Esr damit vor allem sein eigenes Werk meint und ihm mit dem Hinweis auf Gottes Befehl einerseits die selbe Autorität zukommen lassen will wie der Schrift und andererseits gleichzeitig erklären kann, warum der „neue" Text in Wirklichkeit „alte" Offenbarung enthält und lange verborgen bleiben musste. Interessant ist der Hinweis, dass Esra die Vision sehr wohl „den Weisen" seines Volkes lehren darf. Es geht hier also nicht um absolute Geheimhaltung, sondern der IV Esr akzeptiert wohl grundsätzlich eine autoritative mündliche Überlieferung.[29] Bezieht man allerdings den fiktionalen Charakter des Textes in diese Fragestellung ein, dann zeigt sich, dass es sich hier nur scheinbar um eine Akzeptanz mündlicher Überlie-

---

25 Vgl. STONE, Forth Ezra, 439: „This is clearly a reference to the twenty-four books of the Hebrew Bible."
26 Vgl. BECKER, Rewriting, 97.
27 Vgl. METZGER, Esra, 263-265.
28 Vgl. STONE, Forth Ezra, 411.
29 Vgl. BECKER, Grenzziehungen, 247.

ferung handeln kann. Denn da erst der „verborgene" Text (des IV Esr!) die neue Erkenntnis bringt, zeigt sich, dass die Weisen des Volkes, diese Offenbarung augenscheinlich nicht weiter gegeben haben oder immer noch geheim halten. Von daher kann die Stelle die Frage nach dem Verhältnis von Schrift und mündlicher Überlieferung nicht endgültig beantworten. Immerhin bleibt zu notieren, dass das Konzept nicht deutlich abgelehnt wird.

In erster Linie muss die Frage der Schriftautorität auf dem Hintergrund von IV Esr 14 beantwortet werden. Die Symbolik des Anfangs zeigt bereits an, dass es sich in diesem Kapitel um den Empfang der Schrift gehen wird. Esra sitzt unter einer Eiche, was an den Besuch Gottes bei Abraham in Gen 18,1 erinnert, und hört eine Stimme aus einem Dornbusch, was die Begegnung des Mose mit Gott in Ex 3,2 in den Sinnzusammenhang des Textes hinein holt. Auch die Zeitangabe des dritten Tages deutet in diese Richtung.[30] Esra wird bei seinem Namen gerufen, was ein Trostmoment darstellt (vgl. Jes 43,1), und ihn gleichzeitig auszeichnet. Gott spricht hier direkt mit Esra, während der Deuteengel verschwunden ist. Ein heilsgeschichtlicher Abriss folgt, der Esra in eine direkte Parallele zu Mose setzt.[31] Deutlich wird auf die Vorstellung von Ex 20ff rekurriert, wonach Mose die Tora auf dem Sinai von Gott empfängt. Allerdings baut der IV Esr in diesen Rückblick ein folgenschweres Detail ein, das sich nicht in der Sinaiperikope des Exodusbuches findet. Laut IV Esr 14,5f hat Gott Mose noch mehr mitgeteilt, als bislang bekannt wurde. Damit ist aber nicht an das rabbinische Modell von schriftlicher und mündlicher Überlieferung gedacht,[32] sondern es wird auf das verwiesen, was im IV Esr „offenbart" wurde. Allerdings durfte Mose – genau wie Esra nun auch – nicht alles veröffentlichen, sondern musste einige Dinge, eben den Inhalt des IV Esr, verheimlichen. Diese Geheimhaltungsanweisung ist – wie gesehen – bereits in IV Esr 12,37 vorbereitet und kommt jetzt voll zum Tragen. Gott enthüllt Esra dessen persönliche Zukunft, er wird entrückt werden, und befiehlt ihm, sein Haus zu bestellen (IV Esr 14,13). Die rasch verrinnende Weltzeit wird nochmals betont (IV Esr 14,10) und so auf der historischen Ebene des IV Esr seinen Lesern Trost gespendet. Im vorliegenden Zusammenhang ist die Antwort Esras auf Gottes Enthüllung wichtig. Wie bereits im vorhergehenden Abschnitt kurz angerissen, fragt Esra stellvertretend für die Leser des IV Esr. Wie sollen diese das Leben gewinnen, wenn die Schrift verbrannt ist? Da an dieser Stelle offensichtlich die Tora gemeint ist, lässt sich zuerst erkennen, dass der

---

30 Vgl. BECKER, Rewriting, 89.
31 Vgl. BECKER, Grenzziehungen, 245.
32 Vgl. BECKER, Rewriting, 92.

IV Esr zwar eine Vorform des Kanons der hebräischen Bibel kennen mag,[33] dass er aber die Tora als die zentrale Schrift ansieht. Die Tora ist nämlich verbrannt (IV Esr 14,21) und deshalb gibt es kein Licht mehr in der Welt. Eine trennscharfe Begrifflichkeit im Hinblick auf die Schrift lässt sich demnach beim IV Esr nicht ersehen. Autorität haben sowohl die 24 Bücher des Kanons, eine besondere Stellung genießt aber die Tora. Zweitens ist zu bemerken, dass Esra an dieser Stelle funktional argumentiert. Die Schrift, hier synonym mit Tora verstanden, ist nicht an sich in einem sakrosankten Status, sondern sie wird gebraucht, um die künftigen Generation zu unterrichten. Wenn Esra darum bittet, dass er das Gesetz, faktisch dann die 24 Bücher des Kanons plus weitere 70 Schriften, aufzeichnen darf, dann zeigt er sich eher distanziert von weisheitlichen (vgl. Prov 8,22-31) bzw. rabbinischen (vgl. BerR 1,4) Überzeugungen, wonach die Tora quasi eine mythische Größe darstellt.[34] Zwar kennt auch er – wie gesehen – eine himmlische Analogie zur Tora (IV Esr 9,36f), allerdings tritt die Funktion, die die Schrift erfüllt, doch deutlich in den Vordergrund. So argumentiert der IV Esr vor allem mit dem Nutzwert der Tora. Man braucht die Tora, „damit die Menschen den Weg finden können und die, welche leben wollen, in der Endzeit das Leben erlangen." (IV Esr 14,22). Dies ist die zentrale Begründung für die Autorität der Tora bzw. der ganzen Schrift im IV Esr. Weil Gottes Wille sich in der Tora offenbart, ist sie der Weg, der trotz des bösen Herzens zum ewigen Leben führt: „Wenn ihr also euren Sinn beherrscht und euer Herz in Zucht nehmt, werdet ihr am Leben erhalten werden und nach dem Tod Erbarmen erlangen." (IV Esr 14,34) Die Tora ist „das Gesetz des Lebens" (IV Esr 14,28).

Gott geht auf die Argumentation Esras ein (IV Esr 14,23ff) und gibt Anweisungen, wie die Neuaufzeichnung des Gesetzes und der anderen Schriften vor sich gehen soll. Esra entspricht den Anweisungen, nimmt sich viel Schreibwerkzeug und fünf Männer mit, die schnell schreiben können (IV Esr 14,24.37), und geht zum Ort des Geschehens. Der Text wird nun recht anschaulich. Nachdem Esra in IV Esr 14,22 ausdrücklich um die Gabe des Heiligen Geistes gebeten hatte, wird nun symbolisch diese Bitte erfüllt. Esra bekommt „Feuerwasser" zu trinken, sein Herz wird verständig und sein Mund geht über.[35] Damit ist der Vorgang der

---

33 Vgl. BECKER, Grenzziehungen, 246-247.
34 Vgl. GRÖZINGER, Jüdisches Denken, 171: „Die Tora wird nun als eine ontologische Größe gesehen, eine die Schöpfung durchwaltende Macht, ewiger Ursprung des Werdens." Laut SCHIMANOWSKI, Weisheit, 208, ist die Präexistenzvorstellung der Tora „zu einem nicht mehr wegzudenkenden Baustein in der jüdischen theologischen Tradition geworden."
35 Vgl. BECKER, Rewriting, 96.

Inspiration Esras beschrieben. Auch die Schreiber, denen Esra 40 Tage lang diktiert, werden vom Geist Gottes mit Einsicht beschenkt und können so wortgetreu aufschreiben, was Esra von Gott eingegeben bekommt. Aufschlussreich sind an dieser Schilderung mehrere Details. Da Esra nur sprechen kann, weil er zuvor von Gott mit Weisheit „gefüllt" wurde, bedeutet dies für den Text, dass sein Autor inspiriert wurde. Da die Inspiration eines Textes ins Feld geführt wird, wenn es um dessen Autorität geht, zeigt die Erzählung an dieser Stelle einen besonderen Nachdruck. Nicht nur dass Esra zweimal auf den Geist Gottes Wert legt (IV Esr 14,22.40), sondern dass auch die eigentlichen Schreiber Einsicht von Gott bekommen, zeigt den Wert der Schrift. Ohne menschliches Zutun entstehen die autoritativen Schriften Israels, weil Gott selbst sie Esra eingibt und weil diejenigen, die sie aufzeichnen, keine Autoren, sondern lediglich Schreiber sind. Auch die Zahl „vierzig" symbolisiert mit ihrem Verweispotential auf die Zeit der Wüste den Neuanfang, der jetzt durch die Hilfe Esras möglich gemacht wird.

Nachdem die 40 Tage vergangen und die Produktion von 94 Büchern abgeschlossen ist, ergeht an Esra ein besonderer Befehl. „Die ersten Bücher, die du geschrieben hast, leg offen hin. Würdige und Unwürdige mögen sie lesen. Die letzten siebzig aber sollst du verwahren, um sie den Weisen aus deinem Volk zu übergeben. Denn in ihnen fließt die Quellader der Einsicht, die Quelle der Weisheit und der Strom des Wissens." (IV Esr 14,45-47) Damit gewinnt die Frage nach der Schriftautorität eine ganz neue Facette. Vorbereitet ist dies – wie bereits erwähnt – durch den Rekurs auf die Sinaioffenbarung des Mose in IV Esr 14,5, wo in direkter Analogie gesagt wird, dass auch Mose nicht alle Worte öffentlich machte, die er von Gott gesagt bekam. Der IV Esr behauptet demnach, dass von Anfang der Schrift an nicht die ganze Offenbarung Gottes in ihr enthalten ist. Wenn schon Mose nicht sein ganzes Offenbarungswissen in die Schrift, hier wohl die Tora, gelegt hat, dann ist verständlich, dass auch Esra dies nicht tun kann. Der IV Esr unterscheidet also zwischen einer Offenbarung, die in der Schrift überliefert ist, und einer geheimen Offenbarung, die zwar von Gott empfangen, aber nicht in der Schrift enthalten ist. Deutlich kennzeichnet der IV Esr, dass die geheime Offenbarung wertvoller ist als die Schrift. Dies führt zu der paradox anmutenden Einsicht, dass die Schrift bzw. das Gesetz zwar für die Rettung des Menschen hinreichend ist (IV Esr 14,34), trotzdem aber nicht Gottes letztes Wort darstellt. Der IV Esr hält die Offenbarung Gottes offen, indem er in der Fiktion 70 weitere Schriften produzieren lässt, welche zugleich die eigentliche „Quelle der Weisheit" enthalten. Damit bringt der IV Esr einen dezidiert esoterischen Zug in seine Argumentation und verweist durch die symbolische Zahl „siebzig" auf die Universalität dieser Schriften (vgl. Gen 10; 46,27; Num 11,16). In ihnen liegt die ganze Offenbarung Gottes vor.[36]

Der IV Esr gewinnt mit dem Hinweis auf die verborgenen Schriften die Autorität, sein eigenes Werk in diesen „Strom des Wissens" einzureihen.[37] Wenn nämlich in den 24 Schriften, die jedermann, also „Würdige und Unwürdige", lesen dürfen, die ganze Autorität Gottes läge, wäre es für den IV Esr schwer, seinen eigenen Text als Offenbarung Gottes auszugeben. Darum dürfen in seiner Konzeption diese 24 Schriften nicht die ganze Offenbarung Gottes enthalten, da sonst für seine Offenbarung keine Autorität zur Verfügung stünde. So gewinnt er durch die Wahl des Pseudonyms „Esra" die Möglichkeit, dem anerkannten Schreiber des Gesetzes in der Fiktion weitere Schriften mit göttlicher Offenbarung zuzuschreiben. Indem er sich selbst als Esra ausgibt und diesen weitere, bislang geheime Bücher schreiben lässt, kann er seinen eigenen Text als ein „geheimes", erst jetzt in seiner Gegenwart gefundenes Buch ausgeben. Dieser Text kann dann auch angesichts eines sich verfestigenden Kanons göttliche Autorität beanspruchen und so autoritativ die eigene Gegenwart durch neues Wissen deuten. Angesichts der Problemlage, die der IV Esr bearbeitet, ist es auch verständlich, warum das geheime Wissen, das jetzt ans Tageslicht kommt, wertvoller als die „alte" Schrift sein muss. Denn auf mit dem von der Schrift bereitgestellten Wissen und Deutungspotential gelingt eine überzeugende Gegenwartsbewältigung gerade nicht mehr. Deshalb braucht der IV Esr neue Offenbarung und die Autorität, diese Offenbarung glaubhaft zu machen. Unzweifelhaft ist also, dass der IV Esr bislang geheim gehaltene Schriften als Bedingung der Möglichkeit seiner eigenen Autorität ins Feld führt und diese gleichzeitig als der Schrift überlegenes Wissen darstellt. Obwohl der IV Esr nicht dezidiert beansprucht, eine der 70 Schriften, die Esra in der Fiktion des Textes diktiert, zu sein, ist es deutlich, dass er seinen Text zu diesen geheimen

---

36 Ob mit den 70 Schriften „jegliche apokryphe Literatur gemeint sein dürfte" (HOFMANN, Rezeption, 335), scheint fraglich, erklärte doch dann der IV Esr Texte, die nicht von ihm stammen und zum Teil andere theologische Positionen beziehen, zur „Quelle der Weisheit". Es scheint plausibler, dass der IV Esr hier keine konkreten Schriften im Blick hat, sondern lediglich seinen eigenen Text in diesem Zuge verstanden sehen will.

37 Ob der IV Esr tatsächlich seinen eigenen Text in den sich abzeichnenden Kanon der hebräischen Bibel bringen will (vgl. BECKER, Grenzziehungen, 247-248; BECKER, Rewriting, 99), scheint möglich, ist aber schwierig, da er das Konzept eines geschlossenen Kanons durch seine geheimen Offenbarungen prinzipiell erschwert. Sicherlich ist die Schlussfolgerung von BECKER, Rewriting, 100, zum Verhältnis von „Schrift" und IV Esr treffend: „Only a Torah completed by the apocalyptic tradition can help in getting access to the coming aeon."

Schriften rechnet und damit seinen Lesern erklärt, warum der Text erst jetzt ihnen bekannt wird.[38] Auf göttlichem Befehl hin durfte dieser Text nicht von Esra sofort veröffentlicht werden. Die „Weisen aus dem Volk" haben diesen Text für die Zeit seiner Veröffentlichung aufgehoben.

Das Aufregende an dieser Konzeption besteht nun nicht unbedingt daran, dass eine Schrift sich mit Hilfe eines literarischen Tricks Autorität verschafft, sondern dass durch diese Konzeption weitere Schriften vorbereitet sind. Die Offenbarung Gottes kann damit potentiell weiter gehen. Durch das Konzept einer geheimen Offenbarung, die aber trotzdem schriftlich niedergelegt ist, können von den „Weisen des Volkes" immer weitere Schriften produziert und aufgrund dieser Konzeption veröffentlicht werden. Der IV Esr gewinnt dadurch eine gewisse Flexibilität hinsichtlich der Offenbarung Gottes. Während ein geschlossener Kanon das Problem hat, das er immer weiter in die fortschreitende Zeit mit Hilfe von Kommentierungen entwickelt werden muss, umgeht der IV Esr dieses Problem, indem er einen verbindlichen Kanon durch seine Esoterik aushebelt. Ein Kanon von Schriften, der gerade die Varianz der Überlieferung bändigen und die Möglichkeit immer neuer Gottesoffenbarung abwehren soll,[39] wird durch das Konzept einer geheimen Offenbarung unmöglich gemacht. Es ist fraglich, ob der IV Esr die Tragweite seiner Esoterik überblickt, da er der Tora doch eine hohe Autorität zuweist. Weiter bleibt fraglich, ob der IV Esr daran gedacht hat, weitere Texte zu produzieren und sie als Texte dieser geheimen Offenbarung auszugeben. Im IV Esr lässt sich eine solche Absicht zwar eher nicht erkennen, doch ist deutlich, dass der IV Esr zumindest den ihm bekannten Kanon von autoritativen Schriften erweitern will.[40] Deshalb erscheint es plausibel, dass der IV Esr keine grundlegenden Einwände gegen die Verfestigung der autoritativen Schrift hat, sondern lediglich seinen Text mit Autorität versehen wollte. Da er nicht einmal explizit den Anspruch erhebt, dass sein eigener Text einer dieser geheimen Texte darstellt, scheint er vor allem zum Ausdruck bringen zu wollen, dass die Offenbarung Gottes trotz aufkommendem Kanon nicht zu Ende ist. Damit schafft er auf der einen Seite die Möglichkeit eines sich immer neu artikulierenden Gottes, auf der anderen Seite liegt aber in seiner Konzeption die Möglichkeit vor, einen jeglichen Kanon zu entwerten.

---

38 Vgl. STONE, Forth Ezra, 439.
39 Vgl. ASSMANN, Kulturelles Gedächtnis, 122-123.
40 Vgl. BECKER, Rewriting, 100: „With his own model he advocates an expansion of a canon of authoritative Scripure."

6. Die geheime Offenbarung – Resümee

Der IV Esr akzeptiert die Autorität der „Schrift" und versteht darunter einen 24-Schriften-Kanon. Er kennzeichnet damit eine Stufe auf dem Weg zur endgültigen Kanonisierung der hebräischen Bibel. Eine besondere Hochschätzung erfährt in seinem Denken das Gesetz, die Tora, die zwar eine himmlische Analogie hat, dennoch aber nicht in den Rang erhoben wird, den das weisheitliche bzw. rabbinische Denken ihr zubilligen. Die Autorität des Gesetzes wird demnach im IV Esr nicht in erster Linie ontologisch begründet, sondern funktional. Doch ist weder mit Gesetz noch mit der das Gesetz umgreifenden Schrift die Offenbarung Gottes gegeben. Diese übersteigt beide und liegt partiell auch im IV Esr vor. Der IV Esr beansprucht demnach Autorität und nimmt dabei in Kauf, dass das Konzept eines autoritativen Kanons desavouiert wird.

Für die Frage nach der Autorität der Schrift, also eines Kanons, im Rahmen einer Religionsgemeinschaft lassen sich zwei grundlegende Aspekte im IV Esr beobachten. Zunächst geht es um die Begründung einer Schriftautorität, dann um die Problematik eines Kanons.

Wie gezeigt, begründet der IV Esr die Autorität der Textsammlung, die er als „Schrift" kennt, vor allem die der Tora, mit ihrer Funktion. Der Schrift kommt Autorität zuerst aufgrund ihres Inhalts zu. Sie bildet den Rahmen der Gespräche Esras mit Uriel bzw. Gott. Auf ihrem Hintergrund versucht Esra seine Gegenwart zu verstehen. Indem sie die Geschichte Israels mit Gott überliefert, bildet die Schrift die Grundlage der religiösen Identität des IV Esr. Das ist ihre basale Funktion. In einem zweiten Schritt leuchtet eine heilsrelevante Funktion auf. Da die Schrift dazu gebraucht wird, um den Weg des Heils allen Menschen zu zeigen, an die der IV Esr denkt, ist sie in der Gegenwart des IV Esr heilsnotwendig. Das böse Herz kann nur mit ihrer Hilfe in Zaum gehalten werden und der Mensch so zum ewigen Leben geführt werden. Die Schrift bildet also die Identität Israels aus und weist den Weg, auf dem Israel das böse Herz des Menschen bezwingen und seine Erwählung gewinnen kann. Aufgrund beider Funktionen erkennt der IV Esr der Schrift Autorität zu.

Gleichzeitig problematisiert er – ob bewusst oder unbewusst, gewollt oder nicht – das Problem des sich verfestigenden Kanons. Indem er darum bemüht ist, seine eigene Autorität abzusichern, spricht er der Schrift ab, die ganze Offenbarung Gottes zu enthalten. Die Schrift ist demnach für den IV Esr im Hinblick auf das Heil Israels nicht suffizient. Sie bedarf der Ergänzung durch das Wissen, das in den 70 geheimen Büchern verborgen liegt bzw. sie bedarf der Ergänzung durch den IV Esr. Mit diesem Konzept einer geheimen und erst jetzt veröffentlichen Offenbarung gewinnt der IV Esr einen dynamischen Offenbarungsbegriff. Allerdings klärt der IV Esr nicht grundsätzlich, wer dazu berechtigt ist, neue Offenbarung zu verkünden. Ihm genügt es, seinen eigenen Text als Offenbarung ausweisen zu können. Eine grundsätzliche Autorität neben der Schrift etabliert er daher nicht, sondern hält nur eine Leerstelle offen, die es ihm erlaubt, durch seinen eigenen Text neue Offenbarung zu bringen.

Durchdenkt man dieses Konzept aber grundsätzlich, dann zeigt sich ein Problem. Wenn eine Schrift zwar als autoritative Grundlage einer Religionsgemeinschaft angenommen wird, gleichzeitig diese aber für nicht suffizient erklärt wird, dann stellt sich die Frage, wer oder was dazu berechtigt ist, die Schriftbasis in autoritativer Weise zu ergänzen. Das Konzept der geheimen Offenbarung bringt es mit sich, die Autorität der Schrift geschmälert und das Autoritätsproblem verschoben zu sehen.

Bibliographie

ASSMANN, Jan, Das kulturelle Gedächtnis. Schrift, Erinnerung und politische Identität in frühen Hochkulturen, München ⁶2007.

BECKER, Michael, Grenzziehungen des Kanons im frühen Judentum und die Neuschrift der Bibel nach dem 4. Buch Esra, in: Becker, Michael/Frey, Jörg (Hg.), Qumran und der biblische Kanon (BThS 92), Neukirchen-Vluyn 2007, 195-253.

BECKER, Michael, Rewriting the Bible: 4 Ezra and Canonization of Scripture, in: Laato, Antti/ van Ruiten, Jacques (eds.), Rewritten Bible reconsidered, Turku 2008, 79-101.

BÖTTIGHEIMER, Christoph, Lehrbuch der Fundamentaltheologie, Freiburg 2009.

BRANDENBURGER, Egon, Die Verborgenheit Gottes im Weltgeschehen. Das literarische und theologische Problem des 4. Esrabuches (AThANT 68), Zürich 1981.

ESLER, Philip F., The social Function of 4 Ezra, in: JSNT 53 (1994), 99-123.

GRÖZINGER, Karl-Erich, Jüdisches Denken. Theologie, Philosophie, Mystik I, Frankfurt a.M. 2004.

HALLBÄCK, Geert, The Fall of Zion and the Revelation of the Law. An Interpretation of 4 Ezra, in: SJOT (1992), 263-292.

HOFFMANN, Heinrich, Das Gesetz in der frühjüdischen Apokalyptik (StUNT 23), Göttingen 1995.

HOFMANN, Norbert J., Die Rezeption des Dtn im Buch Tobit, in der Assumptio Mosis und im 4. Esrabuch, in: Braulik, Georg, Das Deuteronomium, Frankfurt a.M. 2003, 311-342.

HOGAN, Karina M., The meanings of „tora" in 4 Ezra, in: JSJ 38 (2007), 530-552.

KÖRTNER, Ulrich H.J., Der inspirierte Leser. Zentrale Aspekte biblischer Hermeneutik, Göttingen 1994.

LAUSTER, Jörg, Prinzip und Methode. Die Transformation des protestantischen Schriftprinzips durch die historische Kritik von Schleiermacher bis zur Gegenwart (HUTh 46), Tübingen 2004.

LUCK, Ulrich, Das Weltverständnis in der jüdischen Apokalyptik dargestellt am äthiopischen Henoch und am 4. Esra, in: ZThK 73 (1976), 283-305.

MAIER, Johann, Theodizee III. Judentum, in: TRE 33 (2002), 218-222.

METZGER, Paul, Das böse Herz. Der Mensch als Schicksal der Schöpfung im IV Esr, in: Nicklas, Tobias/Zamir, Korinna (Hg.), Theologies of Creation in Early Judaism and Ancient Christianity (DCLS 6), Berlin/New York 2010, 225-251.

METZGER, Paul, Esra und das vierte Esra-Buch. Die Bedeutung des Pseudonyms für die Interpretation einer apokalyptischen Schrift, in: Wolter, Michael/Horn, Friedrich Wilhelm (Hg.), Studien zur Johannesoffenbarung und ihrer Auslegung, FS Otto Böcher, Neukirchen-Vluyn 2005, 263-290.

METZGER, Paul, Katechon. II Thess 2,1-12 im Horizont apokalyptischen Denkens (BZNW 135), Berlin/New York 2005.

OEGEMA, Gebern S., Apokalypsen (JShrZ VI,1), Gütersloh 2001.

RATZINGER, Joseph, Ein Versuch zur Frage des Traditionsbegriffs, in: Ders./Hünermann, Peter/Söding, Thomas (Hg.), Wort Gottes. Schrift – Tradition – Amt, Freiburg i.B. 2005, 37-81.

RATZINGER, Joseph, Schriftauslegung im Widerstreit. Zur Frage nach Grundlagen und Weg der Exegese heute (1989), in: Ders./Hünermann, Peter/Söding, Thomas (Hg.), Wort Gottes. Schrift – Tradition – Amt, Freiburg i.B. 2005, 83-116.

REISER, Marius, Die Gerichtspredigt Jesu. Eine Untersuchung zur eschatologischen Verkündigung Jesu und ihrem frühjüdischen Hintergrund (NTA NF 23), Münster 1990.

SCHIMANOWSKI, Gottfried, Weisheit und Messias (WUNT II 17), Tübingen 1985.

SCHNEIDER-FLUME, Gunda, Grundkurs Dogmatik, Göttingen ²2008.

SCHREINER, Josef, Das 4. Buch Esra (JShrZ V/4), Gütersloh 1981.

STONE, Michael E., Fourth Ezra. A Commentary on the Book of Fourth Ezra (Hermeneia), Minneapolis 1990.

The Sources of Authority in Second Baruch

BALÁZS TAMÁSI

Introduction

Since 1855, when Antonio M. Ceriani discovered a Syriac witness to 2 Baruch in the Ambrosian Library, different assumptions and hypotheses have appeared in the scholarship regarding the date, provenance, transmission and structure of the composition. I do not intend to go into details regarding these more or less unresolved questions in connection with 2 Baruch; I will only briefly touch upon them to the extent that they relate to the topic of my article. First I will discuss the manuscripts which have preserved parts or the entire text of the composition of 2 Baruch. Then I will turn to the main issue of this study, namely, what kind of self-authorization strategy can be detected in the composition, and what the sources of authority for the early Jewish readers of the time may have been.[1]

The Codex Ambrosianus (7a1 or B. 21 Inf.), which dates from the sixth or seventh century CE represents the oldest complete text-witness to the Syriac Old Testament and includes the earliest complete text extant of 2 Baruch as well (fols. 257 recto – 267 recto). The manuscript, containing Estrangela handwriting, was published by its discoverer in transcription in 1868, and later it was edited in facsimile in 1876.[2] The Codex Ambrosianus has also preserved the Epistle of Baruch in two different versions. One of them constitutes an integral part of 2 Baruch (chapters 78-87) and the other, placed between the Epistle of Jeremiah and the Book of Baruch, appears as a separate text.[3] According to the recently prevailing opinion, scholars consider the two parts (Apocalypse of and the Epistle of Baruch) in unity.[4] In accordance with this

---

1   See POPOVIĆ, Introducing Authoritative Scriptures, 1-17.
2   See CERIANI, Monumenta Sacra, 113-180, and CERIANI, Translatio Syra Pescitto, 533-553.
3   The position of the two letters in the Codex Ambrosianus is fols. 265 verso – 267 recto and fols. 176 verso – 177 verso, see CERIANI, Translatio Syra Pescitto, 550-553 and 364-366.
4   See HENZE, Jewish Apocalypticism, 43; LIED, Other Lands, 24-25 and WHITTERS, Epistle, 34, 65, 114, 126.

scholarly view, my study also presupposes that 2 Baruch is a unified and coherent writing.

This approach was introduced by German-Language scholars of the late nineteenth and early twentieth centuries[5] and was supported by Bogaert's magna opus (1969). Bogaert argued for the fundamental unity of the composition and concluded that the independence of the Epistle is just a secondary phenomenon.[6] Nevertheless, the transmission of the independent Epistle from the sixth to the nineteenth century CE can be proved by the thirty-eight Syriac manuscripts of the Epistle which have been preserved all throughout this period.[7] In contrast, the textual transmission of a complex 2 Baruch was less successful. Besides the so-called Ambrosianus, we know just one other "complete" text of 2 Baruch. The Arabic translation of 2 Baruch (chapters 3-86) from the tenth or eleventh century CE, which was discovered in 1974 in the archive of the St. Catherine Monastery, testifies the existence of a partly different version of the Syriac 2 Baruch.[8] The later medieval reception of 2 Baruch (44:9-15, 72:1-73:2) was recorded in three Jacobite lectionaries dating from the thirteenth and fifteenth centuries CE.[9] However, the complete work of 2 Baruch was transmitted by early Christians who presumably preserved its content and thus it can be analyzed in the context of the early Jewish history and literature. Parts of the text were re-contextualized in Christian lectionaries and they consequently may be interpreted in the context of the Syriac Christian Liturgy.

The earlier existence of the Greek version is proven by the Greek fragment of 2 Baruch (12:1-13:2; 13:11-14:3) which was discovered by Grenfell and Hunt among the Oxyrhynchus Papyri. The papyrus which dates from the fourth or fifth century CE was published by the two scholars in 1903.[10] The find of the tiny Greek fragment reinforced the 'The Book of the Apocalypse of Baruch bar Neria, translated from Greek into Syriac'.[11]

---

5   See CLEMEN, Zusammensetzung, 211-246; VIOLET, Apokalypsen, lxxiv.
6   BOGAERT, Apocalypse de Baruch I, 78.
7   To the list of the manuscripts, see BOGAERT, Apocalypse de Baruch I, 43-45.
8   To the publication of the Arabic text, see LEEMHUIS/KLIJN/GELDER, Arabic Text.
9   BAARS, Neue Textzeugen, 476-478; DEDERING, Old Testament, iii.
10 Pap. Oxyrh. 403, see GRENFELL/HUNT, Oxyrhynchus, 3-7; CHARLES, Apocalypse of Baruch (APOT), 487-490, and BOGAERT, Apocalypse de Baruch I, 40-43.
11 See DEDERING, Old Testament, 1. For the translation of the Syriac text I used this recent text edition of the Apocalypse of Baruch which contains chapters 1-77 but does not include the Epistle of Baruch (78-87). For the Syriac text of the epistle I

It is probable that the Greek version of 2 Baruch was translated from a Semitic language. This has often been assumed since in 1896 R. H. Charles first suggested that the original language of the writing was Hebrew.[12] Owing to the linguistic evidence, this assumption has prevailed until recently.[13] However, Bogaert argued for the Greek Vorlage of 2 Baruch on the basis of the philological analysis of the text (e.g. the utilization of the Septuagint (LXX) by the author) and he supposed that the original language may have been Koiné with Hebraisms.[14] Nevertheless, in few cases the re-contextualized scriptural verses reflect the LXX (e.g., Jer 1:18)[15] but their origin is elusive because both these verses and the Koiné Greek words of the text may be attributed either to the author or the translator.

Turning to the date of the composition, despite the uncertainties of evidence the modern consensus is that 2 Baruch was composed around the turn of first century CE, after the Fall of Jerusalem. The author, in the narrative part of 2 Baruch, retells the story of the first fall of the Temple as a reflection on the Roman destruction of Jerusalem and the Sanctuary in 70 CE. Consequently, through the authoritative voice of Baruch he tries to give an answer to the burning question why God allowed his temple to be destroyed again and what can be the guarantees for the future life of the Jewish people or for the author's own community. The apocalyptic writer of 2 Baruch reinterprets the shocking event by means of historical visions and their interpretations of Israel's past, present and future.

My thesis is that the author of 2 Baruch already had or claimed to have had the personal respect of his followers or readers in late first century Israel. Through the different contemporary "authority-coffering strategies"[16] he intended to create an authoritative writing for both his community and his possible disciples. It would be anachronistic to label the anonymous author a pseudo-prophet or to designate the composition a pseudepigraphic writing. I concur with Hindy Najman, who said that we should not presuppose that these texts or their authors

---

   turned to CERIANI, Monumenta Sacra, 167-180 and CHARLES, Apocalypse of Baruch (1896).
12 See CHARLES, Apocalypse of Baruch (1896), xliv-liii.; RYSSEL, Syrische, 410-411; GINZBERG, Apocalypse, 555; VIOLET, Apokalypsen, lxxiii; KLIJN, 2 Baruch, 616.
13 See HENZE, Jewish Apocalypticism, 23-25.
14 BOGAERT, Apocalypse de Baruch I, 353-380; cf. PERDUE, Mantic Sages, 160.
15 See BOGAERT, Apocalypse de Baruch I, 360.
16 I take this exact term from Hindy Najman, see NAJMAN, Interpretation, 379-410. I would like to thank Hindy Najman for her invaluable advice on this project (Sixth Enoch Seminar in Milan, June 26-30, 2011).

aspired to replace an older authentic biblical tradition with a new version.[17]

In the following I discern three main possible sources of authority in 2 Baruch and at the same time I focus on the authority-conferring strategies presumably employed by the author.

1) The first is the presentation of the *authoritative figure of Baruch and his prophetic voice,* as these are elaborated in 2 Baruch.

2) The second is the use of the *authoritative literary genres* and *techniques* as forms of modern "prophetic" communication at the end of the Second Temple Jewish Literature.

3) The third source is constituted by the *themes* and *motifs* in the writing which will be discussed along with the two aforementioned.
Nevertheless, all the three are interconnected in the whole composition. Several important questions may arise concerning the sources of authority in the text. Why did the author of 2 Baruch choose this character? Why did these genres, the apocalypse, the letter and the testament attract the author? What guided the author of 2 Baruch in the selection of themes?

In order answer to these salient questions, I make an attempt to detect the possible sources of authority in 2 Baruch at that time and in early Jewish context; however, I do not intend to discuss in detail the question of the later authority of either 2 Baruch or the Epistle of Baruch among the Syrian Christians.

1. Authoritative figures and attributes behind Baruch (Jeremiah, Moses and Others)

1.1 Baruch and Jeremiah

A common feature of the early Jewish and Christian writings is that they are attributed to ancestral authors like patriarchs, prophetic or scribal figures whose characters were elaborated more or less in the Scriptures. The author of 2 Baruch also writes in the name of a scriptural figure, namely Baruch, in order to make his writing respected and authoritative. Throughout the description of Baruch in the composition, this figure claims to possess different attributes of scriptural prophetic figures. We can learn from early Jewish and Christian writings attributed to or related to Baruch – Book of Baruch, 2 Baruch, Epistle of Baruch, 3 Baruch, Paralipomena Jeremiou – that the ancient authors often

---

17 NAJMAN, Seconding Sinai, 7.

reshaped the Jeremiah-Baruch traditions in accordance with their own interest.

Again, the question arises: Why did the author of 2 Baruch choose this character? My preliminary assumption is that both the similarity of the historical situations, namely the destruction of the First and the Second Sanctuary, and the existence of a developing Jeremiah–Baruch tradition in the late Second Temple Period may explain this phenomenon.

It is intriguing to see how the figure of Baruch takes a colorful shape in 2 Baruch, with special regard to the claim to self-authorization by the text and its author. Baruch in his Syriac apocalypse is depicted as the prophetic figure and seer who receives the attributes of Jeremiah. For connecting Baruch with the scripture-like prophecies, the author uses the standard scriptural formula to introduce the divine speeches addressed to Baruch:[18] 'And it happened in the twenty-fifth year of Jeconia, the king of Judah, that the word of the Lord came to Baruch, the son of Neria, and said to him" (1:1-2).[19]

Adapting this revelatory formula, the author recalls and re-contextualizes similar sections of the scriptural Jeremiah (especially Jer 1:1, 36:1; cf. 25:1; 26:1; 27:1; 32:1, cf. Ez 1:1) and introduces his claim to authority for the composition and its protagonist.

It is visible by the first verse of 2 Baruch and it may be observed throughout the composition that the author is intimately familiar with the Jewish Scripture(s) and often speaks in biblical idioms.[20] The *divine speech* formulas, e.g. "And the Lord answered and said to me",[21] express the author's claim to the divine and prophetic authority of the apocalypse throughout 2 Baruch (mainly in 2 Bar 1-77). Other general authorization strategies in the writing are both the use of the *authorial voice* of Baruch and the *re-contextualization* of different scriptural prophecies. An example of the latter appears at the beginning of the text, where 2 Baruch adapts the divine words revealed to Jeremiah[22] in the Book of Jeremiah as a revelation to Baruch. According to the scriptural version the Lord said to Jeremiah: "And I for my part have made you today a fortified city (עיר מבצר), an *iron pillar* (עמוד ברזל), and a bronze wall (חמות נחשת), against the whole land – against the kings of

---

18 WRIGHT, Baruch, 87.
19 ܘܗܘܐ ܒܫܢܬ ܥܣܪܝܢ ܘܚܡܫ ܕܝܟܘܢܝܐ ܡܠܟܐ ܕܝܗܘܕܐ ܗܘܐ ܦܬܓܡܗ ܕܡܪܝܐ ܥܠ ܒܪܘܟ ܒܪ ܢܪܝܐ ܘܐܡܪ ܠܗ
20 HENZE, Qohelet, 29.
21 See 2 Bar 4:1; 5:2; 15:1; 17:1; 19:1; 22:1; 23:2; 25:1; 27:1; 29:1; 39:1; 42:1; 48:26; 50:1; 76:1.
22 See BOGAERT, Apocalypse de Baruch I, 359-360; LIED, Other Lands, 138-139.

Judah, its princes, its priests, and the people of the land" (Jer 1:18),[23] while Baruch in his apocalypse receives the revelation from God that: "For I have said to you that you may speak with Jeremiah and all those who are like you that you may retire from this city. For your works are for this city (ܠܡܕܝܢܬܐ ܗܕܐ) like the firm pillar (ܥܡܘܕܐ ܫܪܝܪܐ), and your prayers as the strong wall (ܫܘܪܐ ܚܣܝܢܐ)" (2 Bar 2:1-2).

First of all we learn from this part of 2 Baruch that Baruch is a prophetic figure who receives the revelation that Jerusalem will be destroyed. Secondly, the firmness of Jeremiah, which protects the prophet against the Judeans according to the Scripture, becomes the common attribute of Baruch, Jeremiah and the nobles which protects the city against the Babylonians. Subsequently, Baruch's task is to inform Jeremiah and the honorable men of the people about the coming event, and he leads them out of Jerusalem to the Kidron valley (2 Bar 5:5-6) before the city was destroyed. Shortly after the re-contextualized verse of Jeremiah, the text continues with another reinterpretation of a scriptural prophecy.

This verse from Isaiah (49:16) originally contains a consolation of God for the captives in Babylonia at the time when Cyrus conquered it. The consolation emphasizes that He never forgot Israel thus the exiles will be gathered soon and Jerusalem will be rebuilt in its earthly physical form: "See, I have inscribed you on the palms of my hands; your walls are continually before me". But the author of 2 Baruch reinterprets this divine promise according to the new historical situation, namely the fall of the Second Temple: "Or do you think that this is the city of which I said: 'On the palms of my hands have I graven you?'" (2 Bar 4:2). Then the divinely revealed interpretation immediately continues, stating that besides the earthly Jerusalem there is another, a pre-existing heavenly Jerusalem[24], which was created by God before his counsel to create the Paradise and shown to Adam, Abraham and Moses (2 Bar 4:3-6). The authority of the author's response to the contemporary question of the destruction of the Second Temple may have derived from three sources, namely the direct quotation of Isaiah[25] and its scriptural authority, the prophetic voice of Baruch as the narrator of the whole composition, and the actuality of the scriptural prophecy. The meaning of this section is not clear enough, thus the scholars inter-

---

23 See The *New Revised Standard Version Bible* (NRSV) which I quote all through my paper.
24 See MURPHY, Structure, 86-87.
25 2 Bar 4:2 contains the exact quotation of Isaiah 49:16 from the Peshitta which slightly differs from the MT and LXX versions ("on my hands"), because the Syriac writes "On the palms of my hands". See CHARLES, Apocalypse of Baruch (APOT), 482, note to iv, 2.

pret it in different ways. According to the prevailing opinion the author comforts his audience that God's promise, expressed in Isaiah's prophecy, refers to the heavenly Jerusalem and the eternal sanctuary but no longer to the earthly one. The other view is that the author had no more interest in the future of the earthly or heavenly Jerusalem.[26] This might be explained by the fact that Baruch's temple comes into being on a totally different axis of time and space, when seen in comparison with Jeremiah's restoration theology.[27]

The writing continues with a narrative (chaps. 6-10), which retells the destruction of the first Sanctuary. The author rewrites the scriptural stories of the devastation of the city (Jer 39-44; 52, cf. 2 Macc 2:1-12). He also employs haggadic materials that we know from early Jewish and Rabbinical writings as well.[28] We do not have definite answers about the exact sources of these stories in 2 Baruch and how authoritatively they were regarded by the followers of the author. We assume that these traditions were available at that time and the haggadic tales simply made the main messages of the writing complete. In chapter 6, Baruch as a seer is lifted up by a strong spirit above the wall of Jerusalem in the moment of the destruction. God allows him to see in an awakened vision how the four archangels command the Earth to swallow the objects of the Sanctuary and how they destroy the city's walls. This entire scene, as Matthias Henze notes, "is modeled closely after Ezekiel's second vision, in which the prophet sees how Israel violates the covenantal relationship and how God, abhorred by Israel's offences, abandons the temple (8:1-11:25)".[29]

At the end of the frame-story, in chapter 10, God commands Baruch to send Jeremiah unto Babylon to support the captives (10:1-2). With this event Jeremiah disappears from the story and Baruch remains the only prophetic figure. If we carefully read this narrative section of 2 Baruch we can recognize that Jeremiah remains a passive and silent companion of Baruch till his departure: he wept and fasted together with Baruch and the nobles after they left Jerusalem to let it be destroyed (5:5-6) then he mourned and fasted again for seven days with

---

26 For the different viewpoints, see NIR, Destruction, 21.
27 WHITTERS, Epistle, 120.
28 For a detailed study on the different traditions of the hiding temple vessels and the abandonment of the Sanctuary which were preserved in the early Jewish, Christian and the Rabbinic Literature, see NIR, Destruction, 43-117.
29 HENZE, Jewish Apocalypticism, 101. Matthias Henze points out that: "the visionary materials in particular made the book of Ezekiel a fertile ground for 2Bar's religious immagination" and "the most striking adaption, no doubt, is found in the narrative frame of 2Bar, where we read of the Babylonian invasion of Jerusalem" (Ezek 8:1-11:25 and 2Bar 5:5-9:1). See HENZE, Jewish Apocalypticism, 101-102.

Baruch when the Chaldeans seized the Sanctuary and the people were led into captivity (9:1). His deeds and prayers were reckoned as a strong wall for the city (2:1) and his heart was found pure (9:1). It is obvious throughout the whole composition that Baruch is the protagonist and the authoritative speaker in the evoked historical situation. In addition, the transmission of the prophetic task from Jeremiah to Baruch is most explicitly declared in the context of Baruch's speech with the people (2 Bar 33:1-3). While Baruch prepares the people for his coming leaving, the people admonishes him: "These are the commands which your companion, Jeremiah the prophet, commended you and said to you: "Look to this people until I go and prepare the rest of our brothers in Babylon against whom has gone forth the sentence that they should be carried into captivity!" Three authoritative voices are employed here in unity, namely Baruch as the narrator of the whole apocalypse recounting the speech of the people which echoes the non-scriptural words of Jeremiah.

To further explore Baruch's character, I will briefly deal with both the scriptural attributes of Jeremiah and Baruch, and their interaction. We may ask first whether we should aim to identify the evolution of the scribal Baruch to the prophetic one at the end of the late Second Temple period and regard 2 Baruch as the result of it, or whether we should presume the reverse process behind these characters, namely that 2 Baruch should be placed in the scribalizing process of the religion and be reckoned among the elevated scribal characters of the time. Should we regard the scribal Baruch of the Hebrew Scripture as the authoritative character for 2 Baruch? The inconsequent naming of Baruch in the Scriptures (MT, LXX, Peshitta) and in the Baruch literature can probably be perceived as a marker of the uncertain and/or manifold status of this character. As Matthias Henze has recently observed, "While in biblical Jeremiah Baruch is an ideal scribe, the title 'scribe' is conspicuous for its absence from 2 Baruch".[30] In agreement with this I would like to point out another interesting phenomenon, namely that in a few versions the independent Epistle of Baruch names him "Baruch the scribe" (ܒܪܘܟ ܣܦܪܐ).[31]

Focusing on the possible scriptural background I first turn to the Hebrew Jeremiah. In the Masoretic version Baruch is not a prophetic but a scribal character. The prophet Jeremiah dictates to "Baruch, the

---

30 HENZE, From Jeremiah, 163.
31 It appears both in the inscription and subscription of the independent Epistle of Baruch (c) in the Codex Ambrosianus (176 v, 177 v), see CERIANI, Translatio Syra Pescitto, 364, 366. It can be found also in other manuscripts of the epistles (b, g, h), see CHARLES, Apocalypse of Baruch (1896), 125.

son of Neriahu, the scribe/ברוך בן נריהו הספר" (Jer 36:32, cf. 36:26) all the prophetic messages which God said to him as well as his own admonitions.

It is also undoubted that Baruch's scriptural role is to record, transmit and read out Jeremiah's prophecy before the public, e.g. during the fast day in the Sanctuary, because the prophet was imprisoned by the king (36:5-8).[32] When in the Book of Jeremiah King Jehoiakim finally burns the scroll with the prophecies of Jeremiah, the Lord again commands Jeremiah to have Baruch the scribe write another scroll, completing it with new prophecies about the destruction of Jerusalem (36:27-32). Jeremiah 36 contains most of the details on Baruch's scriptural activities which are incorporated into the larger narrative of the Babylonian conquest of Jerusalem and the events afterwards (Jer 39-44, 52). Henceforth, in Jeremiah the remaining group of Judeans flees to Egypt, although Jeremiah preached "Do not go to Egypt" (42:19). In this part of the text, the people accused Baruch of attempting to mislead them with his agitations for remaining in Judea. Baruch's activities reinforce that Jeremiah remains in a distance from the people and Baruch becomes a mediator between the prophet and the people. It is probable that this latter scriptural attribute may lie behind Baruch's community leadership role in 2 Baruch.

If we compare the two narratives, those of Jeremiah and 2 Baruch, it is conspicuous that only the mediator activity of Baruch receives greater attention in 2 Baruch. Other scriptural events concerning Baruch are neither echoed in 2 Baruch and his scribal activity nor emphasized in the apocalypse. Probably his letter-writing activity (2 Bar 77:12, 19; 87:1; cf. 4 Bar 6:11-13) could be understood as a scribal function, but prophet Jeremiah also writes letters in his scriptural and early Jewish traditions (Jer 29:1-23; Epistle of Jeremiah).

The Book of Jeremiah in the LXX attributes a more important role to Baruch than the MT. This becomes obvious if we compare the place of the prophecy on Baruch's future in the MT (ch. 45) with its place in the LXX (ch. 52). Additionally, in the LXX this oracle is the conjunctive chapter between the Book of Jeremiah and the text of the Book of Baruch. In the light of these we may say that the author presumably intended to portray Baruch as the successor of the prophet Jeremiah in the Greek version of Jeremiah.[33] Nevertheless, Baruch appears as a scribal figure in the LXX similar to the MT. On the other hand, the Greek Jeremiah (43:27, 32) does not contain the title "the scribe" (ὁ

---

32 HENZE, From Jeremiah, 162.
33 WRIGHT, Baruch, 37.

γραμματεύς),[34] just as Baruch has no title in 2 Baruch. Without simplifying the problem, we can assume that the developed character of Baruch in the Septuagint may have been more authoritative for the author of 2 Baruch (and his community).[35]

In summary, Baruch in 2 Baruch – with the claim of becoming an authoritative character – takes from the books of Jeremiah both his scribal authority and the ideas of the prophetic succession that show a more developed shape in the LXX than in the MT. Moreover, 2 Baruch borrowed the prophetic mantle of Jeremiah,[36] transforming the character into an apocalyptic seer. On the other hand we can observe the developing figure and tradition of Jeremiah in the LXX and in the non-scriptural writings, e.g. in 4QApJer C[37] from Qumran. This rich Jeremiah tradition with its other features and motifs might have influenced the author of 2 Baruch, or at least the earlier Baruch tradition which our author probably inherited. The Septuagint in 2 Maccabees (2:1-12) contains a short narrative in connection with Jeremiah. This says that Jeremiah handed over the Law of Moses to the deportees; he exhorted them to observe it and hide the vessels in a cave at Mount Nebo. He is portrayed as a second Moses who looked down from the top of Nebo into the Promised Land before his death. Probably the author of 2 Maccabbees tried to authorize his short narrative on Jeremiah by both the introductory line that: "One finds in the records that prophet Jeremiah" and the later reference that: "It was also in the same document that the prophet". The three new features of Jeremiah in 2 Maccabees – namely the exhortation to keep the Torah, the hiding of the temple vessels and his Mosaic deeds – all recurs in 2 Baruch in an elaborated form, in connection with Baruch. The other important attribution to Jeremiah in the Septuagint is his lamentation over the destruction of Jerusalem. While in the Hebrew Scripture and especially in

---

34 RAHLFS/HANHART, Septuaginta.
35 Here I just remark that the earliest Peshitta manuscript, the Codex Ambrosianus, has preserved the scribal title of Baruch in the relevant verses of Jeremiah (36:27, 32).
36 HENZE, From Jeremiah, 166.
37 The fragments of 4QApJer C which were reconstructed and published by D. Dimant dates from the first century CE. These fragments contain epitomized and recontextualized narratives from Jeremiah which are in the heart of a longer historical prophecy on Israel's past, present (i.e. Jeremiah's time) and future (post-exilic period). According to frg. 4Q385a 18 i-ii, Jeremiah escorts the captives unto an unknown river, he exhorts the people to keep the Law and laments for the catastrophe as well (cf. 4Q383 1:1). In another fragment of the writing (4Q389 1) we find the public reading of Jeramiah's prophecies in the captivity which is situated near to the river Sour. However, the name of Baruch has not been preserved in the fragment, although it re-echoes the first verses of Book of Baruch. See DIMANT, DJD 30, 117-119, 159-166, 219-223.

the Lamentations there is no such reference to Jeremiah (or Baruch), the headline of the LXX and the Peshitta (see, 7a1, 174 v.) preserved this attribution of lamentation to the prophet. However, in 2 Baruch it is again Baruch and not Jeremiah who utters his lamentations over the devastated city (chaps 10-12, 35, cf. 81:2)[38]: "And he (Jeremiah) indeed departed with the people, but I Baruch returned, and sat before the gates of the Sanctuary, and I lamented with this *lamentation* (ܐܘܠܝܬܐ) over Zion and said:" (2 Bar 10:5).

In the preceding paragraphs I have taken Baruch in 2 Baruch as a prophetic successor of Jeremiah and I also tried to find what kind of scriptural features are employed in the book. Thus we can easily recognize that the different traditions of Jeremiah and Baruch lived together in the same period, that of the late Second Temple Literature. I believe that the author of 2 Baruch may have been able to use these well-known ideas to make Baruch an authoritative character.

Nevertheless, the question remains why Baruch has not got the title of "the prophet" in 2 Baruch and in the later writings of the Second Temple Literature, while he does have this designation in the Rabbinic Literature[39] and in Christian Literature[40] at the end of the late antiquity. This is a highly relevant question, as Baruch meets all the requirements of the new prophets of Second Temple Judaism, [41] just as Henoch, Daniel and Ezra does. It is obvious that other scribal characters as

---

38 On the lamentations in 2 Bar and in the later Jewish tradition see BOGAERT, Apocalypse de Baruch I, 127-176.
39 The Seder Olam Rabbah, the third-century CE Hebrew language chronology, gives the dates of biblical events in detail from the Creation to the Bar Kochba Revolt. The author of the SOR reckons Baruch among the prophets (20:48-52). Rabbi Eliezer says in the Sifre Bamidbar (Be-ha'alotecha, 78) which is dated to the tannaitic period that Baruch ben Neriah was a prophet. In accordance with this tradition, in the Babylonian Talmud (BT) Baruch ben Neriah is reckoned among the "eight prophets who were also priests" (Meg. 14b). R. Nahman, also in the BT (Meg. 15a) says that "Baruch the son of Neriah, and Seraiah the son of Mahseiah and Daniel and Mordecai, Bilshan, Haggai, Zechariah and Malachi all prophesied in the second year of Darius". Malachi is identified with Ezra immediately after this talmudic saying, while Ezra is presented elsewhere in the Talmud and the Midrash as the pupil of Baruch and the last prophet. In haggadic materials they appear as prophetic master and his prophetic pupil who lived in Babylon (BT Meg. 16b, Shir ha-Shirim Rabbah 5:5). See BOGAERT, Apocalypse de Baruch I, 104-119.
40 E.g. Eusebius (c. 263-339 CE) in his Praeparatio Evangelica (10.14.6) mentions that Jeremiah and Baruch prophesied in the time of Josiah. It seems to be obvious that Baruch's later prophetic status in the Christian thought was connected to the separation and canonic status of the Book of Baruch within the LXX.
41 To the convincing typology of the three possible sources and features of the prophecies in the Second Temple Literature, see GRABBE, Poets, 209.

Enoch and Ezra also "receive" apocalyptic revelations and gain prophet-like status in the late Second Temple Judaism (e.g., 1 Enoch, 4 Ezra).

The new language of prophecy which emerged in the Second Temple period affected the development of the scriptural characters both within and beyond the Scriptural writings. Some of these characters (e.g. Levi, Daniel, and Ezra) who were given the role of an apocalyptic seer received the prophetic title. For instance, Daniel received the prophet title in Qumran,[42] and Josephus writes that Daniel was able to prophesy future events, just as the other prophets (see Ant 10.267-269, 10.245-246, 249). Nevertheless, Josephus reflects this phenomenon when he introduces the biblical prophets with the term "prophets", while the contemporary prophets are referred to by the term "mantis" (mantic). Josephus emphasizes that there is a qualitative difference between prophecy before and after Artaxerxes. He states also that "the exact succession of the prophets" ceased after the time of Artaxerxes (Apion 1.8. 40-41). The later rabbinical concept that the age of the prophets endured from Moses to Ezra[43] is also in harmony with the aforementioned view of Josephus. Therefore it might have not been incidental that the authors of the new prophecies chose their scriptural characters from among the patriarchs, prophets and scribes until the time of Ezra. Our author's choice regarding Baruch fits well into this picture.

The models of the new divine revelations and prophecies are delivered through 1) reading, writing and interpreting the scriptural text, 2) dreams and visions, and 3) the cultivation of the wisdom.[44] I assume that all these "trends" had influences on the author of 2 Baruch and were used to construct the authority of both his character and the writing. All three of them can be recognized in scriptural and non-scriptural Jewish writings from the Persian and Hellenistic period. Here I mention that Baruch meets the three requirements. He is (1) a Torah-sage, (2) a divinely inspired interpreter of the Law, and last but not least (3) an apocalyptic seer. Accordingly, he is also closely interconnected with wisdom. The word "wisdom" (ܚܟܡܬܐ) appears 13 times in the poetical parts of the writings. These wisdom-related texts can be found mainly in Baruch's lamentations and in the direct speeches between Baruch and God. These meditations about the greatness of creation and the mightiness of God call the Book of Job or Ben

---

42 See 4Q174 1–3 ii 3 (cf. 11Q13 2:18).
43 See Shir. Rab. 8.9-10; Num. Rab. 15.10; BT. Yoma 9b, 21b; Tosefta Sota 13.2; JT. Bava Bathra 14b-15c.
44 JASSEN, Mediating the Divine, 202.

Sira and Qohelet to our mind.⁴⁵ Moreover, Baruch is depicted exactly as a Torah-sage and an inspired interpreter of the Torah.⁴⁶ This is affirmed by a scene in which Baruch tells the people that he was about to leave them in order to speak with God. The elders answered: "Then we shall truly be in darkness! There will be no light for the people who are left! Where shall we again investigate the Torah, or who will distinguish between death and life for us?" (46:1-6). Through the voice of the elders and people 2 Baruch depicts his character as an appropriate reader and interpreter of the Torah. Thus Baruch's subsequent answer to them in the dialogue is the author's response to his own followers: "But only prepare your hearts that you may obey the Law, and be subject to those who in fear are wise and understanding." It is clear that 2 Baruch promotes his authority as a community leader.

1.2 Baruch and Ezra

In the following I will point out a few parallels between Ezra and Baruch⁴⁷ which may represent similar authoritative features in the two characters. Their figures show even closer connections in later apocalyptic writings (4 Ezra, 2 Baruch). However, while both Baruch and Ezra appear in the Scriptures as scribes, only Ezra meets the requirements of scribe skilled in the Torah of Moses (Ezra 7:6). Contrary to Baruch, Ezra is both an outstanding priest and a community leader whose authority is established by his deep knowledge in the Torah. Nehemiah (Ezra 8:1-8) recounts Ezra's symbolic deed about the time he read and interpreted the Torah in the presence of the returnees immediately after the rebuilding of the Sanctuary.

Since the author presents Ezra as the first to read the Torah of Moses in Jerusalem after returning from exile, it also places Ezra firmly in line with the pre-exilic past, specifically with Moses, the first Lawgiver.⁴⁸ The parallels between the scriptural Ezra and Baruch may be assumed if we recall the picture of their public readings and other community activities. Their characteristic similarities become more visible if we compare them in 4 Ezra and 2 Baruch (certainly, the scriptural Ezra and 2 Baruch could also be comparable). Significantly, the later careers of Ezra and Baruch start in the apocalyptic writings after

---

45 On the presence of Qohelet in 2 Baruch and the impact of wisdom on the apocalypticizm, see HENZE, Qohelet, 28-43.
46 WRIGHT, Baruch, 38-39, 41-69, 82, 89-90, 111-112; 124.
47 On this theme M. Henze has already wrote extensively in his article. See HENZE, From Jeremiah, 162-164.
48 HENZE, From Jeremiah, 162.

the destruction of the Second Temple, in similar historical situations, which evoked more or less similar responses by the two authors in their apocalypses. Both Ezra in 4 Ezra and Baruch in 2 Baruch appear as prophetic seers who receive revelations in the form of visions about Israel's past and future, in order to instruct the people. Like Ezra, Baruch is portrayed as Moses redivivus as well.[49] The authors utilized these mosaic features and attributes as parts of an authorizing strategy which was a general phenomenon in the Second Temple Period. That is, by means of the mosaic overtone, the writings of 4 Ezra and 2 Baruch claimed prophetic and revelatory authority to these characters.

1.3 Baruch as Moses Redivivus

In the following I shall show how 2 Baruch attempts to further legitimize and make Baruch more authoritative by linking him with Moses, the prophet *par excellence*.[50]

Like Moses, Baruch also exhorts the people to follow the Torah (38:2, 77:3, 84:2-11). Consequently, we may also assume that the author of 2 Baruch exhorts his contemporaries and readers to keep the Law.

God reports to Baruch in his speech that He showed this heavenly sanctuary with its vessels to Adam, Abraham and also to Moses, but not to him (4:3-7). The showing of the Sanctuary to Moses appears again when Ramael/Remiel interprets the *Vision of the Fourth Bright Waters* (chaps. 56-74). Among the others revealed to Moses two things appear which were also revealed to Baruch: "many admonitions together with the rules of the Law and the consummation of the time, as also to you" (59:4). The author refers here to Baruch purposely: First, he claims to associate again Baruch with Moses, and second, he emphasizes Baruch's two prophetic features, the outstanding knowledge of the Law and the ability to understand the eschatological revelation. It is indirectly and immanently said that the esoteric knowledge of the secrets of the universe was not revealed to Baruch (as it was acquired by Enoch in 1 Enoch or Ezra in 4 Ezra). In contrast the "Most High" showed Moses the measures of fire, the depths of the abyss, the weight of the winds, the number of the raindrops, etc. (59:5-12). This knowledge includes the cognition of the heavens and the heavenly Zion.

Just as Moses addresses the people "Hear, O Israel" in the Deuteronomy (5:1; 9:1), so Baruch addresses them (31:3; cf. 77).[51] The parallel

---

49 HENZE, From Jeremiah, 162, 165.
50 The importance of the Moses-Baruch typology used throughout 2 Bar is often emphasized by the scholars, see, HARNISCH, Verhängnis, 202, 208; MURPHY, Structure, 128-130; WRIGHT, Baruch, 87-94., HENZE, From Jeremiah, 165, 168-170.

between Baruch and Moses is further sharpened in chapter 76: as in Deuteronomy 34, Moses is told to ascend the mountain to look at the Promise Land before his death, so is Baruch told to ascend before his passing.

Probably the most striking link between Moses and Baruch can be found in chapter 84:1-7. This chapter forms part of the Epistle which Baruch writes to the nine and a half tribes (chaps. 78-87). Here both Baruch's previous exhortations/instructions to the people, which are recurring throughout the whole Apocalypse (chaps. 31-34, 44-46, 77), and his letter are compared with Moses' work in establishing the covenant.[52] Below, I quote further these verses as these include important authority-conferring strategies:

> "(1) I have therefore instructed you while I am still alive, for I said that you should especially learn the commandments of the Almighty who admonished you. I will briefly set before you some of the commandments of his judgment before I die. (2) Remember that once Moses indeed invoked heaven and earth to witness against you, and said: 'If you transgress the Law, you shall be dispersed. But if you keep it, you shall be kept.' (3) Also he said other things to you when you where together, the twelve tribes in the desert. (4) And after his death you cast them away from you, and on this account, there came upon you what had been predicted. (5) And now Moses spoke to you beforehand so that it might not happen to you, and lo, it has happened to you. For you abandoned the Law. (6) Lo! I also say to you after you have suffered that if you obey those things that were said to you, you will receive from the Almighty everything ordain and reserved for you. (7) Let then this letter be a witness between you and me that you may remember the commandments of the Almighty, and that also there may be for me a defense before Him who sent me. " (84:1-7).[53]

The main question for the author was how his claim to revelation and authority relate to the already established authority of Mosaic revelation.[54] As I have presented above the author reshaped the biblical figure of Baruch: on the one hand he borrowed from and developed the character of Jeremiah, on the other hand Baruch was portrayed as a Moses, the "second lawgiver"[55].

It is clearly recognizable that the author has a direct claim to the Mosaic authority. He evokes Moses' authority and adopts a similar rhetoric. His final words in chapter 84 are strikingly similar to the final

---

51 MURPHY, Structure, 128; HENZE, Jewish Apocalypticism, 192.
52 MURPHY, Structure, 128.
53 Here I adapt the careful translation of this passage from Whitters, see, WHITTERS, Epistle, 160. I intensively consulted the text edition of Charles, see, CHARLES, Apocalypse of Baruch (1896), 148-153.
54 HENZE, From Jeremiah, 169., HENZE, Jewish Apocalypticism, 103.
55 HENZE, From Jeremiah, 165.

address of Moses' in Deut 30.[56] The saying "If you transgress the Law, you shall be dispersed. But if you keep it, you shall be kept." (84:2) as a quotation from Moses imitates the conditional sentences in the Deuteronomy.

This kind of conditional form often recurs throughout 2 Baruch, mainly in the context of exhortations which constitute the essence of the public speeches (32:1; 44:7; 46:5; 46:6; 75:7; 75:8; 77:6; 77:16; 78:6; 78:7; 84:2; 84:6; 85:4). The structure of the exhortations in 2 Baruch is the same as in the Deuteronomy because both use the promise of future blessings to motivate the people to keep the Law. But the two distinct authors adapt these forms in two different historical situations with their diverse problems.[57]

By means of this form Baruch reminds his readers of the reasons of their actual suffering and he also recalls his similar admonitions regarding the Law. So he clearly attempts to identify his teaching with the divine revelations to Moses. The deuteronomic scene of this public speech evokes the multifold situation of the departing prophet or community leader who transmits his testament in the form of a letter which is a witness of a renewed covenant between God and the people or the contemporary reader of 2 Baruch.

2. Authoritative literary genres in 2 Baruch (apocalypse, letter, testament)

In the following I will focus on the different authoritative literary genres which are employed in 2 Baruch, primarily on the genres of the apocalypse, the letter and the testament. We may add to them other literary forms like the speeches of Baruch, prayers and lamentations, and the narrative framework of the composition that make up the whole Apocalypse of Baruch. I assume that the author used and combined these genres or literary form with the claim to authority. Firstly, I consider apocalypse as one of the authoritative revelatory forms. The other revelatory technique is the interpretative revelation that I have discussed above as an authoritative and prophetic feature of Baruch (cf. 2 Bar 46:1-6). Beside the literary attributions to Baruch, the interpretative revelation, namely the re-contextualization of the scriptural prophetic verses, is also employed by the author as an authorizing strategy several times (e.g., 2 Bar 2:1-2; 4:1-6).[58] Nevertheless, the visions and their interpretations may also be discussed along with the public

---

56 WHITTERS, Epistle, 84.
57 MURPHY, Structure, 123-124.
58 For my discussion on these examples, see in the present article (1.1.).

speeches, since they gain authority from the apocalyptic visions that Baruch experienced.[59]

2.1 The Apocalypse and Its Authoritative Visions

Turning to the authoritativeness of the concrete visions, we should touch upon the themes employed in them and their place in the structure of the whole Apocalypse. The author's apocalyptic heritage dates from the period of the late Second Temple Literature. The book takes the form of an extended dialogue between God and Baruch, which includes several visions on history and the coming eschatological time. Baruch is depicted as a typical seer who fasts, prays, and receives visionary revelations and interpretations. The fasts and prayers are not only important structural devices in the text, but also hint at actual visionary practices.[60] In response to historical reality, the author offers two main conflating "solutions", namely the obedience to the Torah and the eschatological expectations.[61] The first is the central topic of Baruch's public speeches; the latter is explicitly expressed in the form of historical visions throughout the writing. At the beginning of 2 Baruch, in the first narrative section, Baruch sees a waking vision about the miraculous hiding of the temple objects (6:3-8:2). A strong spirit raised Baruch "aloft over the wall of Jerusalem", then he saw and heard the angels. The *par excellence* historical visions appear in the three dream visions of Baruch: 'The Vision of the Twelve Calamities', 'The Vision of the Forest' and 'The Vision of the Dark and Bright Waters' (27:1-15; 35-41; 53, 56-74). While the interpretations of the first two come directly from God, in the last and lengthiest vision of the history and the Messianic Age Ramael/Remiel, the *angelus interpres* appears. The hoped-for authority of these visions was guaranteed by the divine. If we observe the themes of these visions we find that they utilize the modern symbolic language of the time.

The first historical vision in 2 Baruch is 'The Vision of the Twelve Calamities' (27:1-15). The twelve periods of history preceding the End Time and the Messianic Age (with the Anointed One), are depicted by wars, death, famine, thirst, earthquakes, terrors, ghosts and demons, fire, rape and violence, injustice and unchastity, disorder and the com-

---

59　WHITTERS, Epistle, 51.
60　WRIGHT, Baruch, 81.
61　M. Henze has pointed out that the author of 2 Baruch manages to harmonize two distinct strands of early Jewish thought, the Deuteronomic promise and the apocalyptic promise, and he himself conflated the two central themes, the Torah and the Eschatology, in one coherent book as well. See HENZE, Torah, 204.

bination of all these. The events depicting the last epoch of the twelve periods are too general to identify them with real historical events or to see them an exact computation of time. Regarding this division of time a close link appears between the two contemporaries, 2 Baruch and 4 Ezra. In the vision of Ezra (11-12) the eagle's twelve wings may represent the Roman rulers or other short periods. The pre-supposed authority of this symbolic language can be supported by the fact that it was adopted by the authors of both 2 Baruch and 4 Ezra.

In the second vision (35-41) Baruch sits on the ruins of the Sanctuary and weeps. Then he falls asleep and dreams of a forest planted in a valley surrounded by mountains. Opposite the forest there is a vine, below which flows a spring. Rising to a mighty stream, the fountain overturns the forest, leaving only a cedar standing. Shortly after the cedar also falls down, and the vine predicts its final destruction in the near future. The interpretation following the vision comes directly from God, and the *angelus interpres* is not present. The mountains and the forest represent four future kingdoms, of which the cedar is the fourth; the spring represents the Messianic Age; the vine is the Messiah. It is generally agreed that this picture of the four empires is based on the vision of Daniel (6-7) who alludes by the fourth animal to the Hellenistic powers. 2 Baruch logically identifies the fourth empire with Rome because the identification of the fourth kingdom with the Roman Empire in Daniel was common at the time of Josephus (Ant. 10.276). Examining these symbols, it seems that the author of 2 Baruch uses the popular and presumably authoritative motifs of his time. Each symbol has scriptural antecedents and may come from non-biblical sources as well. The symbolic meaning of the tree has been transmitted by Daniel in which the angel commands to cut it down in Nebuchadnezzar's dream (4:10-11, 20). In all probability the two apocalyptic ideas are conflated in the so-called 4QFour Kingdoms text (4Q552-553),[62] the fragments of an Aramaic writing discovered in Qumran. The first idea appearing in the text is the division of the post-exilic period into four epochs (cf. 1 Enoch, Daniel, Josephus), while the second idea contains the trees which stand for the great empires. The fourth tree of the vision is higher than all the others since it represents a mighty power of the author's time, which is presumably identifiable with Rome.[63] A very similar picture appears in the interpretative part of Baruch's vision: "And after these things a fourth kingdom will arise whose power is harsher and more evil than those which were before it..."[64] Finally the tree as a

---

62 See PUECH, DJD 37.
63 COLLINS, Apocalypticism, 415-417; FLINT, Daniel, 363.
64 See KLIJN, 2 Baruch, and CHARLES, Apocalypse of Baruch (APOT).

symbol appears in the same context in another fragmentary text from Qumran. The 4QNarrative (4Q458)[65] writes about the 'tree of wickedness', which would be destroyed (Frag. 1, 9), and there appears a messianic figure anointed with the oil of kingship (Frag. 2 coll. 2). Besides the parallelism of 'the burning/killing of the cedar tree' in 2 Baruch, the author of 2 Baruch depicts the messianic idea with the dominion of the Anointed One (39:7). To conclude, the use of authoritative symbols of the second vision in 2 Baruch is justified by other nearby contemporary sources like Daniel, 4QFour Kingdoms and 4Q458.

The third vision is introduced by the divine announcement that the departure of Baruch from the earthly world is imminent (43: 2, cf. 76: 2). With all probability the next chapters, which constitute Baruch's second public speech, form the central core of the work (chaps. 44–46).[66] The speech contains many ideas which reappear in the Epistle,[67] and from this point Baruch starts preparing the people for his departure and to all consequences that go together with it. Further, after his third and most symbolic vision, he gathers the people to speak to them for the third time, telling them that he has 40 days left to instruct them (76:1-5).

The third historical vision in 2 Baruch, the 'Vision of the Dark Waters and Bright Waters' (53, 56-74) is also the most challenging one for the modern interpreters. To the best of my knowledge its symbolic periodization of history is unparalleled in the early Jewish Literature, as it divides history into thirteen (and twelve) dark and bright epochs running from Adam's time to the End Time. This vision together with the others creates the historical framework of the contemporary crisis by means of concluding the sequence of the epochs into the final, eschatological age. As the central theme of the work is eschatology; 2 Baruch was not reckoned by the Jews authoritative enough for transmission, hence it was transmitted by early Christians.

While the third vision could be discussed alone in another study, it is intriguing to look at the protagonists of the presented historical ages, with special regard to the periods of the bright waters (Abraham, Moses,[68] David and Solomon,[69] Hezekiah and Josiah). It is not surpris-

---

65 LARSON, DJD 36, 353.
66 WHITTERS, Epistle, 44.
67 WHITTERS, Epistle, 45.
68 For the description of his time, see 2 Bar 59:2: „For at that time the lamp of the eternal law shone on all those who sat in darkness, which announced to them that believe the promise of their reward, and to them that deny, the torment of fire which is reserved for them"; see also CHARLES, Apocalypse of Baruch (APOT).
69 2 Baruch portrays their period with these words: „And wisdom was heard in the assembly: And the riches of understanding were magnified in the congregations" (2 Bar 61:4). See CHARLES, Apocalypse of Baruch (APOT).

ing that he chose the most outstanding leaders from Israel's past, because community leadership is an emphasized theme of 2 Baruch.[70] Two of them, Abraham and Moses, were especially respected. Thus while they are depicted as the leader figures of their own bright epochs, their figures amalgamate with Baruch's character. Beside all this, Baruch is portrayed also as a second Moses as I have pointed out above, and he acts as Abraham as well, when he moves from the Kidron valley to Hebron (47-77).

This public speech of Baruch with the elders (chaps. 31-34) which is delivered in the Kidron valley, together with the two others (chaps. 44-46, 78-87), constitute the turning-points of the composition. In these speeches the author claims to communicate directly with his addressees and to establish the authority of his message. This message, namely keeping the Law and the covenant, the former symbolizing life and understanding, are at the heart of these speeches.[71]

In 2 Baruch there are three passages, two of them as parts of Baruch's speeches, which reveal the burning question of the author and accordingly, the anxiousness of his addressees (46:1-3; 77:13-16 and 85:1-5): how will the people be able to survive without such leaders as the biblical prophets and their prophetic successors like Baruch? Here Baruch's (and probably the author's) leadership and authority are emphasized by means of these questions. These allegoric verses illustrate the point well: "And the whole people answered and said to me: ...For the shepherds of Israel have perished, and the lamps which gave light are extinguished". The author answers this question in the name of Baruch: "Shepherds and lamps and springs come from the Torah, even though we pass away, the Torah abides." Baruch is depicted in the three speeches as the successor of the prophets who is able to transmit his duties as a leader to his first-born son (44:1-3).[72] The idea of the cessation of the prophets does not stand alone in the Second Temple Literature; we may refer, for example, to the contemporaneous 4 Ezra (12:41-42),[73] Josephus (Apion 1.41), or 1 Maccabees (1 Macc 9:27), Prayer of Azariah (15), as well as many passages in later Rabbinic Literature.[74]

---

70 WRIGHT, Baruch, 38-39.
71 See WHITTERS, Epistle, 42-48, esp. 47.
72 LIED, Other Lands, 134-138.
73 "How have we offended you, and what harm have we done to you that you have forsaken us and sit in this place? For of all the prophets you alone are left to us, like a cluster of grapes from the vintage, and like a lamp in a dark place, and like a haven for a ship saved from a storm" (4 Ezra 12:41-42), see the *Revised Standard Version* of the Bible.
74 See SOR 30, T. Sot. 13:2-3, TB Sanh. 11a, TB Yoma 9b, TB Sot. 48b, Shir. R. 8:9 3.

2.2 The Epistle of Baruch: the Testimonial Letter as an Authoritative Genre

In the following I will again address the question of the literary genres and their authoritative function in the text. Reading 2 Baruch we can easily observe that there is a letter at the end of the writing (chaps. 78-87).[75] Following the prevailing opinion, in discussing the authority question I regard the Epistle as an integral part of 2 Baruch (1-87). Nevertheless, the Epistle may have its independent claim to authority. This letter-writing of Baruch is reminiscent how Jeremiah writes and sends letters in the scriptural and early Jewish literature (Jer 29:1-23; EpJer of LXX, Par. Jer 7:23-29). Thus Baruch is not only the prophetic successor and fellow of Jeremiah but they are both letter-writers and pen-friends as well (cf. Par. Jer 6:17-23, 7:23-29).[76] This coexistence is justified in one codex, namely the Codex Ambrosianus in which after the Lamentations of Jeremiah come the "Epistles of Jeremiah and Baruch", according to its heading.[77]

If we compare the Epistle of Baruch (78-87) to the Apocalypse (1-77) we can recognize that the Epistle is not introduced with a divine or revelatory idiom (e.g. "thus said the Lord") and neither has a claim to be divine speech.[78] Thus, the letter begins with the messenger formula of "Thus said Baruch, son of Neria" (78:2) which alludes to the divine voice ("thus said the Lord") but here identifies Baruch, not God, as the authorial voice of the letter.[79] In the closing lines of the Apocalypse the people (the remnant of Israel) requests Baruch to write a letter to the captives in Babylon: "Nevertheless, do this for us your people: write also to our brothers in Babylon an epistle of doctrine and a scroll of hope, that you may confirm them also before you depart from us" (77:12). This quotation refers to the initiative of letter-writing, related to Baruch's imminent departure, as announced by God after the last revelation (76:1-4). In like manner, Baruch writes both consolations to the captives and a testament with his instructions. Throughout the whole composition the reader is informed many times that Baruch's earthly existence is going to end.[80] The testament formula will culminate in chapter 84 (see above) where his letter, the Epistle, is explicitly identified as Baruch's testimony and a renewed covenant. But before discuss-

---

75 To the letter problem see the Introduction of the present article, page 1.
76 DOERING, Reading, 62.
77 CERIANI, Translatio Syra Pescitto, 363 (176 recto).
78 DOERING, Reading, 58.
79 See HENZE, Jewish Apocalypticism, 357.
80 See 2 Bar 13:3; 25:1; 43:2; 44:2; 46:7; 48:30; 76:2, and WHITTERS, Epistle, 160.

ing the testamentary form, I will look at the authorizing strategies of the whole Epistle. According to the introductory narrative (77:11-26), in addition to the first letter Baruch initiates another to the nine and a half tribes who were led into captivity before the Judeans. Baruch writes the two letters in Hebron, sitting under the branches of an oak tree. Thereafter we learn from the text that he wrote the letters and sent the first by three men to the two tribes, while the other was conveyed by an eagle to the nine and a half tribes.[81] There are a few motifs which might represent the self-authorization of 2 Baruch and the Epistle of Baruch, too. By narrative action, the author claimed to reach a significantly larger audience, namely all the tribes of Israel/the whole Jewish Diaspora. Through the place of the letter-writing, Hebron, also where Baruch received the third vision, and the oak, the author evokes the scene where God made covenant with Abraham (Gen 18: 1), and adapts it for Baruch's character (cf. 84:1-7).[82] The motif of the eagle enables to deliver the written material in a supernatural way, and this transmission also becomes the possible source of authority.[83] The closing formula of the Epistle of Baruch repeats that the letter was carefully sealed, bound to the neck of the eagle and sent. This version has survived only in the Epistle of Baruch which constitutes a part of 2 Baruch, but the independent versions of the Epistle have not preserved this authoritative story on the transmission of the writing.[84] Following this part, a very short narration appears about the Destruction of the Sanctuary and the Hiding of the Vessels (ch. 80). However, the visions are missing from the text, only an epitomized description appears in the chapter 81: "And He showed me the visions that I should not again endure anguish, and He made known to me the mysteries of the times, and the advent of the hours He showed me" (81:4). Nevertheless, Baruch in his Epistle derives his authority from the allusion that God has revealed these visions to him.[85] The Epistle comprises the themes of consolation, Torah paraenesis and the final judgment.[86] The exhortations of the Torah constitute his public speeches throughout his Apocalypse. This central message is included into chapter 84 which constitutes the heart of the testimonial letter: here Baruch as a Second Moses transmits his paraenetical teaching to his followers, thus renewing the covenant be-

---

81 At the end of the introductory part, 2 Baruch invokes the good memories of Noah (with the dove), Elijah (with the ravens) and Solomon (with a bird). See 2 Bar 77:23-24.
82 WHITTERS, Epistle, 166.
83 WHITTERS, Epistle, 51.
84 CHARLES, Apocalypse of Baruch (1896), 166.
85 HENZE, Jewish Apocalypticism, 352.
86 BOGAERT, Apocalypse de Baruch I, 334; see more in DOERING, Reading, 62.

fore his departure, saying: "Deliver you this letter and the traditions of the Law to your sons after you, as also your fathers delivered (them) to you". If we look at the structure and the themes of the Epistle of Baruch we may conclude that it more or less summarizes the whole Apocalypse (1-77). Besides the successful summary, there are two important authoritative elements which are strikingly missing from the testimonial letter: the authoritative character of Baruch as Second Jeremiah and his visions. At the same time it is notable that in the Epistle the character of Baruch is more scribal-like and the emphasis is on the written letters and the scroll of hope instead of the prophetic praxis of the sage and seer. We can witness a very effective characterization of Baruch as Second Moses and a convincing adaptation of the deuteronomic scene. In summary, the testament form of the Epistle, one of the self-authorization strategies, builds a literary bridge between the scriptural testament of Moses and the last words of 2 Baruch.[87]

3. Conclusions

In the course of the analysis I focused on the different sources of authority in 2 Baruch, with special regard to the authoritative scriptural characters, literary genres, and the self-authorizing themes and motifs in the composition.

Starting with the characters, I have found a strikingly different Baruch in 2 Baruch in comparison with his scriptural antecedent. He is introduced in the narrative part as a Second Jeremiah who receives several authoritative prophetic attributes. In this context he directly receives the divine speech that Jerusalem will be destroyed, he becomes community leader of the survivors and he is the *last prophet*, because the Lord sends Jeremiah to Babylon.

Three historical visions are revealed to Baruch and as a *seer* he gets acquainted with the Eschatology and the commandments: these are strong claims of the author to the *apocalyptic authority*. The author has claim to the already established *mosaic authority* as well.[88] As a result, 2 Baruch depicts Baruch as a Second Moses and adapts the deuteronomic schema of sin and repentance. As a *Torah-sage*, he admonishes the people to keep the Law. He is declared by the elders/people as an *authoritative interpreter* of the Law. The author of 2 Baruch may be an

---

[87] See WHITTERS, Testament, 157 and 163; cf. BOGAERT, Apocalypse de Baruch I, 120-126.
[88] I concur with Matthias Henze who says that there is no conflict between the apocalyptic and mosaic authority because the first incorporates the latter. See HENZE, Jewish Apocalypticism, 103.

authoritative *community leader* as well. Thus he exhorted his community through Baruch's three public speeches after his historical visions.

In summary, I have demonstrated that author's claims to authority derive from the following: 1) Baruch's scriptural name and its tradition, 2) non-scriptural Jeremiah–Baruch traditions (LXX-like and rabbinical), 3) the figure of Baruch, as it is depicted in 2 Baruch (New Moses and New Jeremiah), 4) Baruch's main attributes in 2 Baruch (literary prophet, seer, Torah-sage, authentic interpreter of the Torah, and community leader), 5) authoritative literary genres and their motifs.

The three main authoritative literary genres that I discuss are the apocalypse, the letter and the testament. I add to them the techniques of re-contextualization/reinterpretations of prophetic verses, the public speeches and the prayers/lamentations.[89] The apocalypses had claim to authority on the basis of the divine revelations and by using the authoritative symbolic language. The testament and the letter as contemporary authoritative genres were often attached to longer writings to promote their message and authority. Nevertheless, one of the few which combines all three authoritative genres is 2 Baruch. On the one hand, in the Apocalypse (1-77) the author employs the divine/prophetic authority and he seems to ignore Baruch's scribal authority. On the other hand, the Epistle of Baruch (78-87), which offers a summary of the composition, claims to establish its authority by written "letter and traditions (of the Law)" without any divine initiative. Only referring to the visions without the Messiah, the author omits Jeremiah and the seer image of Baruch. Moreover, the letter-writing of Baruch causes the reader to recall both his scribal character in the Book of Jeremiah and the epistles of Jeremiah in the scriptural and early Jewish literature (Jer 29:1-23; EpJer of LXX, Par. Jer 7:23-29). It is probable that these differences made the Apocalypse of Baruch and the Epistle of Baruch too divergent to receive the same authority which may also explain their later separation.

Bibliography

BOGAERT, Pierre-Maurice, L' Apocalypse syriaque de Baruch. Introduction, traduction du syriaque et commentaire (Sources chrétiennes 144-145), Paris 1969, I-II.

BAARS, William, Neue Textzeugen der syrischen Baruchapokalypse, in: VT 13 (1963), 476-478.

CERIANI, Antonio M., Monumenta Sacra et Profana, Mediolani 1868, Tom. V, fasc. 2.

---

89 I have finally decided not to discuss this genre or literary form in my paper because of its complexity.

CERIANI, Antonio M., Translatio Syra Pescitto Veteris Testamenti ex codice Ambrosiano sec. fere VI photolitographice edita, in: Monumenta Sacra et Profana VI, Mediolani 1876, 533-553.

CHARLES, Robert H., The Apocalypse of Baruch, Translated from Syriac, Chapters I-LXXVII from the Sixth Cent. MS in the Ambrosian Library of Milan, and Chapters LXXVII-LXXXVII – the Epistle of Baruch – from a New and Critical Text Based on Ten MSS and Published Herewith, London 1896.

CHARLES, Robert H., The Apocalypse of Baruch Translated from Syriac, in: APOT 2, 470-526, Oxford 1913.

CLEMEN, C., Die Zusammensetzung des Buches Henoch, der Apokalypse des Baruch und des vierten Buches Esra, in: TSK 11 (1898), 211-246.

COLLINS, John J., Apocalypticism and Literary Genre in the Dead Sea Scrolls, in: Flint, Peter W./VanderKam, James C. (eds.), The Dead Sea Scrolls after Fifty Years: A Comprehensive Assessment, Leiden 1998-1999, 2:403-430.

DEDERING, S. (ed.), The Old Testament in Syriac According to the Peshitta Version, Part IV, fasc. 3: ApBar, 4 Esr, Leiden 1973.

DIMANT, Devorah (ed.), Qumran Cave 4. XXI; Parabiblical Texts, Part 4: Pseudo-Prophetic Texts (DJD 30), Oxford 2001.

DOERING, Lutz, Jeremiah and the "Diaspora Epistles" in Ancient Judaism: Epistolary Communication with the Golah as medium for Dealing with Present, in: De Troyer, Kristin/Lange, Armin (eds.), Reading the Present in the Qumran Library (SBLSS 30), Atlanta 2005, 43-72.

ELLINGER, Karl/RUDOLPH, Wilhelm (eds.), Biblia Hebraica Stuttgartiensia (BHS), standard edition, Stuttgart 1977.

FLINT, Peter W., The Daniel Tradition at Qumran, in: Evans, Craig A./Flint Peter W., (eds.), Eschatology, Messianism, and the Dead Sea Scrolls, Michigan 1997, 41-60.

GINZBERG, L., Apocalypse of Baruch (Syriac), in: The Jewish Encyclopedia, New York 1902, II. 551-556.

GRABBE, Lester L., Poets, Scribes or Preachers? The Reality of Prophecy in the Second Temple Period, in: Grabbe, Lester L./Haak, Robert D., (eds.), Knowing the End from the Beginning: the Prophetic, the Apocalyptic and their Relationships, London 2003, 192-214.

GRENFELL, Bernhard P./HUNT, Arthur S. (eds.), The Oxyrhynchus Papyri (III), London 1903.

HARNISCH, Wolfgang, Verhängnis und Verheißung der Geschichte: Untersuchungen zum Zeit- und Geschichtsverständnis im 4. Buch der Esra und der syr. Baruchapokalypse (FRLANT 97), Göttingen 1969.

HENZE, Matthias, From Jeremiah to Baruch: Pseudepigraphy in the Syriac Apocalypse of Baruch, in: Hempel, Charlotte/Lieu, Judith M. (eds.), Biblical Traditions in Transmission. Essays in Honour of Michael A. Knibb (SJSJ 111), Leiden 2006, 157-177.

HENZE, Matthias, Torah and Eschatology in the Syriac Apocalypse of Baruch, in: Brooke, George J./Najman, Hindi/Stuckenbruck, Loren T. (eds.), The significance of Sinai. Traditions about Sinai and Divine Revelation in Judaism and Christianity, Leiden 2008, 201-215.

HENZE, Matthias, Qohelet and the Syriac Apocalypse of Baruch, in: VT 58 (2008), 28-43.

HENZE, Matthias, Jewish Apocalypticism in Late First Century Israel. Reading Second Baruch in Context (TSAJ 142), Tübingen 2011.

JASSEN, Alex P., Mediating the Divine: Prophecy and revelation in the Dead Sea Scrolls and Second Temple Literature (STDJ 68), Leiden 2007.

KLIJN, Albertus F. J. (transl. by), 2 (Syriac Apocalyse of) Baruch, in: Charlesworth, James H. (ed.), The Old Testament Pseudepigrapha: Apocalyptic Literature & Testaments, (Vol. 1), New York 1983, 615-652.

LEEMHUIS, Frederik/KLIJN, Albertus F. J./VAN GELDER, Gert Jan H., The Arabic Text of The Apocalypse of Baruch: Edited and Translated with a Parallel Translation of The Syriac Text, Leiden 1986.

LIED, Liv I., The Other Lands of Israel, Imaginations of the Land in 2 Baruch (JSJS 129), Leiden 2008.

MURPHY, Frederik J., The Structure and Meaning of Second Baruch (SBLDS 78), Atlanta 1985.

NAJMAN, Hindi, Interpretation as Primordial Writing: Jubilees and its Authority Conferring Strategies, in: JSJ 30 (1999), 379-410.

NAJMAN, Hindi, Seconding Sinai: The Development of Mosaic Discourse in Second Temple Judaism (SJSJ 77), Leiden 2003.

NIR, Rivkah, Destruction of Jerusalem and the Idea of Redemption in the Syriac Apocalypse of Baruch (SBL EJIL 20), Leiden 2003.

PERDUE, Leo G., Mantic Sages in the Ancient Near East, Israel, Judaism, and the Dead Sea Scrolls, in: De Troyer, Kristin/Lange, Armin (eds.), Prophecy after the Prophets? – The Contribution of the Dead Sea Scrolls to the Understanding of Biblical and Extra-Biblical Prophecy, Leuven 2009, 133-192.

POPOVIĆ, Mladen, Introducing Authoritative Scriptures in Ancient Judaism, in: Popović, Mladen, (ed.), Authoritative Scriptures in Ancient Judaism (JSJS 141), Leiden 2010, 1-18.

PUECH, Émile (ed.), Qumran Grotte 4.XXVII: Textes en Arameen, deuxieme partie (DJD 37), Oxford 2008.

RAHLFS, Alfred/HANHART, Robert, (eds.), Septuaginta: editio altera, Stuttgart 2006.

RYSSEL, Victor, Die syrische Baruchapokalypse, in: Kautzsch, Emil (ed.), Die Apocryphen und Pseudepigraphen des Alten Testaments, Tübingen 1900, 404-446.

VIOLET, Bruno, Die Apokalypsen des Esra und des Baruch in deutscher Gestalt (GCS 32), Leipzig 1924.

WHITTERS, Mark F., Testament and Canon in the Epistle of Second Baruch (2 Baruch 78-87), in: JSP 12/2 (2001), 149-163.

WHITTERS, Mark F., The Epistle of Second Baruch (JSPS 42), Sheffield 2003.

WRIGHT, Edward J., Baruch ben Neriah: From Biblical Scribe to Apocalyptic Seer, Columbia 2003.

Writing Scripturally in the Testament of Job

Advancing Our Notions of Scripture and Authority in Judean Literature of the Early Roman Era

Rob Kugler

No one disputes that the *Testament of Job* interpreted and reused the Book of Job and considered it somehow to be "scripture" and to have "authority" as such. Beyond that, though, Job's valedictory speech is generally thought to have relied very little if at all on other texts that had begun to attain scriptural status among Judeans. My contention is that dismissing the possibility of greater influence of the Hebrew Scriptures on the *Testament of Job* leads us to overlook the very subtle uses of scripture that are present in the work, products of what I call "writing scripturally."[1] Furthermore, in neglecting these intriguing echoes of scripture we also fail to appreciate the intensity of the authority scripture had for ancient Judean writers.[2] The following essay begins to remedy this lacuna in the study of the *Testament of Job* and offers concluding reflections on what lies ahead in discovering this "hidden authority" of the scriptures in the production of Judean literature in the Greco-Roman period.[3]

---

1   For this adverbial use of "scripture," see SMITH, What Is Scripture? For Smith, the noun "scripture" named the symbol that mediates between the human and the transcendent. As such, a verbal use of the word can refer to the process by which such an encounter takes place, and an adverbial use refers to the rhetoric and language in which the encounter takes place. Adapting Smith's elegantly simple insight to the study of Judean texts of the Greco-Roman era, one can say that writing "scripturally" among such authors was to use the rhetoric and language of the emerging Judean scriptures to inform and shape their own works.

2   Throughout this essay it will be my practice to eschew the terms "Jew" and "Judaism" and related words in favor of the term "Judeans" to denote the members of an ἔθνος that hailed from Judea and that derives its customs, laws, and God from the practices of that place, but dwelt throughout the Mediterranean and Aegean world. For a strong articulation of the reasons for this change in terminology regarding Judeans in the Greco-Roman period (at least to around 200 CE), see MASON, Jews, Judaeans, Judaizing, Judaism.

3   To be sure, scholars have already devoted considerable attention to the "echoes" of scripture in the other major exemplar of testamentary literature from Greco-Roman

The Testament of Job: A Summary of its Contents, Date and Provenance

The *Testament* is Job's deathbed speech to his children born from a marriage to Dinah, daughter of Jacob. Job tells his children that he lost everything – his possessions, his children, his first wife, and his health – earlier in life because he destroyed a local temple to save his neighbors from unwittingly worshipping Satan. As a consequence Satan gained charge over his fate, but an angel from God promised Job a throne in heaven, a name of renown, twice all he lost back, and participation in the resurrection if he patiently endured Satan's onslaught (chapters 1-5). Before attacking Job, Satan visited his home disguised as a beggar to mockingly take advantage of Job's generosity. Although Job's maidservant failed to recognize Satan, Job knew the visitor's identity and instructed the (disobedient) servant to send Satan away empty-handed (chapters 6-8). Chapters 9-15 describe Job's enormous wealth and generosity as a measure of his losses to Satan while chapters 16-26 narrate the destruction of his fortune, honor, and children, and the humiliation of his wife, Sitidos. In chapter 27 Job relates his face-to-face meeting with Satan and Satan's defeat in the ensuing agonistic encounter. Only then did Job's fellow kings, Baldad, Eliphaz, Sophar, and Elihu appear to lament his losses, focusing in particular on his wealth and honor. They tested his sanity and offered him their royal physicians, to which Job replied that his reward, restoration, and vindication would come from God in due time (chapters 28-38). Sitidos, Job's wife, then reappeared to seek burial for her children, only to discover that they were already rejoicing in heaven. She then died a lonely death to be mourned nonetheless by those who had benefited from her husband's largesse in better days (and by the beasts with which she shared a stall as her living quarters at the end; chapters 39-40). Next Elihu spoke against Job and God rewarded Job's patience by restoring to him twofold of all that he lost. God forgave the kings (save Elihu) for their mistaken reading of Job's condition and Job recovered. Having completed his story Job distributes his inheritance to his sons (chapters 41-45). Job's daughters then plead for an inheritance and he gives to them the magical sashes

---

era Judean writers that lends itself to such analysis, the *Testaments of the Twelve Patriarchs* (because it survives in a single manuscript that is a translation of a translation, the *Testament of Moses* discourages efforts to hear echoes of scripture in it); see my work in KUGLER, The Testaments of the Twelve Patriarchs, 88-99; from a different perspective, see KUGEL, Some Translation. Neither of us, though, has begun to explore sufficiently the implications of the subtle echoing of scripture we both discern in the *Testaments* for notions of scripture and authority.

God gave him to gird himself (Job 38:3); these transform the daughters into a tongue-speaking choir of quasi-heavenly beings, Job's brother eulogizes Job, Job's soul ascends to God in a heavenly chariot, and his survivors bury his body with proper lamentations (chapters 46-53).

Although consensus on the *Testament*'s date and provenance eludes the scholarly community, the weight of the evidence and the greatest number of observers favor dating the testament to the second half of the first century CE and assigning it to Egyptian Judeans contending with the abrupt transition from Ptolemaic rule and the privileges it permitted them to Roman rule and its much more restrictive policies vis-à-vis non-Roman inhabitants in their lands.[4] It is especially pertinent to the focus of the present article to note that in this context we can expect Judeans to have had a close acquaintance with the Greek translation of the Hebrew Scriptures, the LXX. That is in any case certain for the author of the *Testament* inasmuch as his reliance on LXX Job is abundantly clear.[5]

Echoing Judean Legal Norms: Lev 19:13 and T. Job 12:4

While there is a general reluctance to assign to the author of the *Testament of Job* much subtlety in the use of Hebrew Scriptures, there is even greater hesitation to grant that he had any concern for elaborating on and promoting Judean law as it was articulated in the Torah.[6] Yet there is reason to question this stance. I cite here only the example of T. Job 12:4 and Lev 19:13.

In the context of elaborating the measure of his losses to Satan after destroying his temple Job makes a seemingly out-of-place remark about not withholding the wages of a worker. As one of the measures of his great charity to others, in chapters 11-12 Job tells how he aided others

---

4   For literature on the testament, see, among others: CHESNUTT, Revelatory Experiences; COLLINS, Structure and Meaning in the Testament of Job; DELCOR, Le Testament de Job; GARRETT, The 'Weaker Sex' in the *Testament of Job*; GRAY, Points and Lines; GRUEN, Seeking a Context for the *Testament of Job*; HAAS, Job's Perseverance; VAN DER HORST, Images of Women; JACOBS, Literary Motifs; KEE, Satan, Magic and Salvation; KIERKE-GAARD, Satan in the *Testament of Job*; KLANCHER, The Male Soul in Drag; KUGLER, On Anthropology and Honor; KUGLER/ROHRBAUGH, On Women and Honor; LEGASPI, Job's Wives; LESSES, Amulets and Angels; MACHINIST, Job's Daughters; PHILONENKO, Le *Testament de Job* et les Thérapeutes; IDEM, Le Testament de Job: Introduction, traduction et notes; RAHNENFÜHRER, Das Testament des Hiob und das Neue Testament; SCHALLER, Das Testament Hiobs; IDEM, Zur Komposition und Konzeption des Testaments Hiobs; SPITTLER, Testament of Job; IDEM, The Testament of Job: A History of Research; WAHL, Elihu, Frevler oder Frommer?; YOSHIKO REED, Job as Jobab.

5   On this see especially SCHALLER, Das Testament Hiobs, *passim*.

6   For most readers there is only his admonition to his sons in T. Job 45:3 not to marry foreign women which may reflect an expansive reading of Deut 7:3.

who wanted to do good to their neighbors but lacked the personal wealth necessary to do so. So he would provide some with the means to act independently (chapter 11), and others he allowed to volunteer in his own charitable operations (chapter 12). At the end of chapter 12, Job remarks that he even went so far as to pay the volunteers for their trouble, enriching them in ways they did not expect and insisting that they take the "wage" for their own acts of beneficence (12:1-3). Then in 12:4 Job adds a final comment that seems quite beside the point in the context of an account of "gifting" payment to volunteers as an extended act of charity: καὶ οὐκ ἔων μισθὸν μισθωτοῦ ἀπομέ-νειν παρ' ἐμοί ἐν τῇ οἰκίᾳ μου, "And I did not allow the wage earner's <pay> to remain behind with me in my house."[7] Compounding the peculiarity of the statment is the fact that this is the only time in the book that the term ὁ μισθωτής appears, and it occurs just after Job has referred to the volunteer he pays out of extended charity as ὁ ἐργάτης (12:3). What explains this curious interjection?

Testament of Job 12:4 is surely an instance of the author writing scripturally, in this case invoking Lev 19:13. The Leviticus text reads, οὐκ ἀδικήσεις τὸν πλησίον καὶ οὐχ ἁρπάσεις καὶ οὐ μὴ κοιμηθήσεται ὁ μισθὸς τοῦ μισθωτοῦ παρὰ σοὶ ἕως πρωί, "You shall not defraud your neighbor; you shall not steal; *and you shall not keep for yourself the wages of a laborer until morning.*" Indicative of the influence of LXX Leviticus on the author's imagination are two of the lexical choices in the *Testament*'s verse. Surely μισθὸν μισθωτοῦ reflects the influence of ὁ μισθὸς τοῦ μισθωτοῦ in Leviticus, as does the παρ' ἐμοί of the testament echo the παρὰ σοί in Leviticus.

Was this a conscious or unconscious use of Lev 19:13? There is good reason to believe the former to be the case. The LXX uses the unusual construction οὐ μὴ κοιμηθήσεται ... ἕως πρωί, "And do not let remain overnight . . . until morning" (to translate לא תלין ... עד בקר). Of the remaining 194 occurrences of κοιμάομαι in the LXX, fewer than 20 take the meaning "to remain overnight," and where the verb occurs otherwise in the *Testament of Job* it also has the more conventional meaning of "to sleep" (3:1, where Job's sleep is interrupted by the visit from the heavenly messenger; 40:6, where Sitidos is said to sleep near a trough on the night of her death). It appears that the author of the testament, though intent on asserting Job's piety vis-à-vis the law regarding payment of wages to day-laborers, was puzzled by the unusual verb in LXX Lev 19:13 and worked to replace it with a meaning that was clea-

---

[7] The text and translation of the *Testament of Job* used here is KRAFT, The Testament of Job According to the SV Text.

rer to him and his readers, yet in keeping with the general idea of the biblical verse. It is even possible that the author's strategy for doing so was to borrow from the language and the very letters and sounds of the biblical text to construct his own language, letters and sounds. The elements οὐκ ἔων ... ἀπομένειν ... ἐν τῇ οἰκίᾳ μου clearly convey the meaning of the phrase οὐ μὴ κοιμηθήσεται ... ἕως πρωί of the biblical verse, but without replicating the strange verb while preserving its meaning all the same, and doing so through the use of Greek words, sounds and letters that build from ἕως πρωί of the same portion of text (cf. ἔων ... ἀπομένειν). This looks very much like a conscious adaptation of Lev 19:13 in *T. Job* 12:4. It appears, contrary to the general consensus, that of our author wrote scripturally, and subtly so.

Echoing Judean Narrative Traditions: Lev 4:21 and T. Job 14:1-5

As Job recounts for his children his generosity and magnanimous nature in the old days he tells them that he even played music for the widows and his maidservants to put them in mind of God and calm them when they were stressed.

> 14:1 εἶχον δὲ ἓξ ψαλμοὺς καὶ δεκάχορδον κιθάραν. 14:2 καὶ διεγειρόμην τὸ καθ' ἡμέραν μετὰ τὸ τρέφεσθαι τὰς χήρας καὶ ἐλάμβανον τὴν κιθάραν ἔψαλλον αὐτοῖς καὶ αὐταὶ ὕμνουν. 14:3 καὶ ἐκ τοῦ ψαλτηρίου ἀνεμιμνῄσκον αὐτὰς τοῦ θεοῦ ἵνα δοξάσωσιν τὸν κύριον. 14:4 καὶ εἴ ποτε ἐγόγγυζον αἱ θεράπαιναί μου ἐλάμβανον τὸ ψαλτήριον καὶ τὸν μισθὸν τῆς ἀνταποδόσιας ἔψαλλον αὐταῖς· 14:5 καὶ κατέπαυον αὐτὰς τῆς ὀλιγωρίας τοῦ γογγυσμοῦ.

And I used to have six psalms and a ten-stringed lyre. And I would arise daily after the widows were fed and would take the lyre and play for them [the servants], and they [the widows] would chant. And by means of the psalterion I would remind them [the widows] of God so that they might glorify the Lord. And if my maidservants ever began murmuring, I would take up the psalterion and play for the payment of recompense. And I would make them stop murmuring in contempt.

The connection between this passage and a motif of psalterions or harps and lyres in the canonical Book of Job has been noted by Marc Philonenko, although somewhat incompletely. In connection with the passage he cites LXX Job 30:31, ἀπέβη δὲ εἰς πάθος μου ἡ κιθάρα ὁ δὲ ψαλμός μου εἰς κλαυθμὸν ἐμοί, "My lyre has been turned into mourning and my melody into weeping for me," a line from Job's lament over his vastly diminished circumstances.[8] There are, in fact, two further verses

---

8 PHILONENKO, Le Testament de Job: Introduction, traduction et notes, 33.

in the Book of Job that resonate with *T. Job* 14:1-5, one of which bears the greatest resemblance to the testament's language. First, LXX Job 30:9 reads, νυνὶ δὲ κιθάρα ἐγώ εἰμι αὐτῶν καὶ ἐμὲ θρύλημα ἔχουσιν, "But now I am their lyre and they have me as a byword," another declamation from Job's lament over his poor circumstances. Second, LXX Job 21:11-12 reads, τὰ [δὲ] παιδία αὐτῶν προσπαίζουσιν ἀναλαβόντες ψαλτήριον καὶ κιθάραν καὶ εὐφραίνονται φωνῇ ψαλμοῦ, "Their children play about when they take up the harp and lyre and make merry to the sound of a melody," as a commentary on how the impious prosper even as he suffers. The last verse has the strongest echo in the testament text, using three of the key words that reappear there: τὸ ψαλτήριον, ἡ κιθάρα, and ὁ ψαλμός. Still, the references in the Book of Job to these musical instruments and to psalmody are never particularly appropriate for the more positive use that Job puts them to in *T. Job* 14:1-5. Is there a better source in the biblical tradition for this curious claim regarding Job's musical sensibilities?

As it turns out LXX Gen 4:20-21 is a better source. It reads, καὶ ἔτεκεν Αδα τὸν Ιωβελ οὗτος ἦν ὁ πατὴρ οἰκούντων ἐν σκηναῖς κτηνοτρόφων, καὶ ὄνομα τῷ ἀδελφῷ αὐτοῦ Ιουβαλ οὗτος ἦν ὁ καταδείξας ψαλτήριον καὶ κιθάραν, "And Ada bore Iobel; he was the ancestor of the cattle-raisers living in tents. And his brother's name was Ioubal; he was the one who introduced the harp and lyre." The passage is from the genealogy of Enoch. Especially verse 21 obviously links handsomely – and positively – with the theme of *T. Job* 14:1-5, as well as its vocabulary (cf. τὸ ψαλτήριον and ἡ κιθάρα, a pairing that appears otherwise in the LXX only in Ps 32:2; 56:9; 80:3; 91:4; 107:3; 150:3; Is 5:12; Dan 3:5, and Job 21:12, as noted above).

What makes the connection between *T. Job* 14:1-5 and Gen 4:20-21 much more intriguing is the assonant play between the names of the two descendants of Enoch named in vv. 20-21 and the name Job had before God renamed him Job, as well as the links between the two biblical figures' culture-bringing roles and Job's possessions and passions. Regarding the names, *T. Job* 1:1 introduces the book with the words, Βίβλος Ἰὼβ τοῦ καλουμένου Ἰωβάβ, "[The] book of Job, the one called Jobab." The name Jobab appears again in 2:1 where Job explains that God changed his name from Jobab to Job, apparently after the night vision in which he was warned of the consequences of destroying Satan's temple (see also 3:1, where the name appears in the call of the heavenly messenger to Job at the start of the vision; it is also used by Satan of Job in 17:3, and by his fellow kings in 28:7; 29:2). The assonance of Ἰωβάβ with Ιωβελ and Ιουβαλ could be thought to be merely accidental. But when one takes into account Job's possessions and passions – his inflated fame in the testament for owning livestock (*T. Job* 9:1-6) and his musical inclination with the harp and the lyre – it is difficult to dismiss the assonance as mere happenstance. It seems evident that the author of the testament sought to invoke, scripturally as it were, an association between Job and Iobel and Ioubal, descendants of Enoch.

The question, of course, is why the author would have wanted to prompt readers to connect Job with descendants of Enoch. Considering the length to which the author went to place him through marriage and obedience to God within the people of Israel, it is not surprising that he might also have sought to link him also with Enoch, a great hero of the ante-diluvian, pre-ancestral period. The assonance of his name and the resonance of his possessions and passions in life with the aspects of culture authored by the great-great-great-grandsons of Enoch had to be worth something.[9]

Some Concluding Remarks on the Scripture and Authority in the Testament of Job

The foregoing two brief probes into the subtle uses of the Hebrew Scriptures in Greek translation in the *Testament of Job* are but the tip of an iceberg. Further work will show that the author of the *Testament* wrote scripturally more than just these two times. That evidence will provoke in turn some significant questions: What does this stance vis-à-vis the texts that in time became the canonical scriptures of Judaism and Christianity indicate about their authority for this author, and to be sure many other Judean authors of the Greco-Roman period who also wrote "scripturally"? What does this level of facility with the details and subtleties of those earlier texts and traditions indicate about the authors' familiarity with them, let alone about their audiences' sensitivity to the language and rhetoric of those texts and traditions? My own view, to be tested in the work that lies ahead on the *Testament of Job* and still other early Judean literature, is that all of this means we have underestimated the degree and kind of authority these writers attached to the emerging scriptures of their likewise emerging religious identity. A

---

9   See REED, Job as Jobab, *passim*, for a sophisticated discussion of the background and purpose of the appendix in LXX Job 42:17b-e that provides the name Jobab in the first place. Note well that my argument here is not that the name had its origins in the play on Gen 4:20-21; rather it is only that in *T. Job* 14:5 the author took an opportunity to link the name with Enoch and so give Job this additional claim to good positioning vis-à-vis the God of Israel.

new, exciting story remains to be told, one that begins though with the small stories of texts within texts like those recounted here.

Bibliography

CHESNUTT, Randall, Revelatory Experiences Attributed to Biblical Women in Early Jewish Literature, in: Levine, Amy-Jill (ed.), "Women Like This:" New Perspectives on Jewish Women in the Greco-Roman World (SBLEJL 01), Atlanta 1991, 107-125.

COLLINS, John J., Structure and Meaning in the Testament of Job, Society of Biblical Literature: 1974 Seminar Papers, 2 vols., Cambridge 1974, 1.35-52.

DELCOR, Mathias, Le Testament de Job, la prière de Nabonide et les traditions targoumiques, in: Wagner, Siegfried (ed.), Bibel und Qumran: Beiträge zu Erforschung der Beziehungen zwischen Bilbel- und Qumranwissenschaft, Berlin 1968, 57–74.

GARRETT, Susan, The 'Weaker Sex' in the *Testament of Job*, in: JBL 112 (1993), 55-70.

GRAY, Patrick, Points and Lines: Thematic Parallelism in the Letter of James and the *Testament of Job*, in: NTS 50 (2004), 406-424.

GRUEN, William, Seeking a Context for the *Testament of Job*, in: JSP 18 (2009), 163-179.

HAAS, Cees, Job's Perseverance in the Testament of Job, in: Knibb, Michael A./van der Horst, Pieter W. (eds.), Studies on the Testament of Job, Cambridge 1989, 117-154.

JACOBS, Irving, Literary Motifs in the Testament of Job, in: JJS 21 (1970), 1-10.

KEE, Howard Clark, Satan, Magic and Salvation in the Testament of Job, Society of Biblical Literature: 1974 Seminar Papers, 2 vols., Cambridge 1974, 1.53-76.

KIERKEGAARD, Bradford, Satan in the *Testament of Job*: A Literary Analysis, in: Evans, Craig (ed.), Of Scribes and Sages: Early Jewish Interpretation and Transmission of Scripture, 2 vols., London 2004), 2.4-19.

KLANCHER, Nancy, The Male Soul in Drag: Women-as-Job in the *Testament of Job*, in: JSP 19 (2010), 225-245.

KRAFT, Robert A. (ed.), The Testament of Job According to the SV Text: Greek Text and Translation (Texts and Translations 5/Pseudepigrapha Series 4), Missoula 1974.

KUGEL, James L., Some Translation and Copying Mistakes from the Original Hebrew of the *Testaments of the Twelve Patriarchs*, in: Metso, Sarianna/Najman, Hindy/Schuller, Eileen (ed.), The Dead Sea Scrolls: Transmission of Traditions and Production of Texts (STDJ 92), Leiden 2010, 45-56.

KUGLER, Robert, On Anthropology and Honor in the *Testament of Job*, forthcoming.

KUGLER, Robert, The Testaments of the Twelve Patriarchs, Sheffield 2001.

KUGLER, Robert/ROHRBAUGH, Richard, On Women and Honor in the *Testament of Job*, in: JSP 14 (2004), 43-62.

LEGASPI, Michael C., Job's Wives in the *Testament of Job*: A Note on the Synthesis of Two Traditions, in: JBL 127 (2008), 71-79.

LESSES, Rebecca, Amulets and Angels: Visionary Experiences in the *Testament of Job* and the Hekhalot Literature, in: Lidonnici, Lynn R./Lieber, Andrea (eds.), Heavenly Tablets: Interpretation, Identity and Tradition in Ancient Judaism (SJSJ 119), Leiden 2007, 50-74.

MACHINIST, Peter, Job's Daughters and their Inheritance in the Testament of Job and its Biblical Congeners, in: Dever, William/Wright, J. Edward (eds.), The Echoes of Many Texts: Reflections on Jewish and Christian Traditions, Essays in Honor of Lou H. Silberman (BJS 313), Atlanta 1997, 67-80

MASON, Steve, Jews, Judaeans, Judaizing, Judaism: Problems of Categorization in Ancient History, in: JSJ 38 (2007), 457-512.

PHILONENKO, Marc, Le *Testament de Job* et les Thérapeutes, in: Sem 8 (1958), 41-53.

PHILONENKO, Marc, Le Testament de Job: Introduction, traduction et notes, in: Sem 18 (1968), 1-75.

RAHNENFÜHRER, D., Das Testament des Hiob und das Neue Testament, in: ZNW 62 (1971), 68-93.

SCHALLER, Berndt, Das Testament Hiobs und die Septuaginta Übersetzung, des Buches Hiob, in: *Bib* 61 (1980), 377-406.

SCHALLER, Berndt, Zur Komposition und Konzeption des Testaments Hiobs, in: Knibb, Michael A./van der Horst, Pieter W. (eds.), Studies on the Testament of Job, Cambridge 1989, 46-92..

SMITH, Wilfred Cantwell, What Is Scripture? A Comparative Approach, Minneapolis 1993.

SPITTLER, Russell, Testament of Job: A New Translation and Introduction, in: *OTP*, 1.829-68.

SPITTLER, Russell, The Testament of Job: A History of Research, in Knibb, Michael A./van der Horst, Pieter W. (eds.), Studies on the Testament of Job, Cambridge 1989, 7-32.

VAN DER HORST, Pieter W., Images of Women in the Testament of Job, in: Knibb, Michael A./van der Horst (eds.), Pieter W., Studies on the Testament of Job, Cambridge 1989, 93-116.

WAHL, Harald M., Elihu, Frevler oder Frommer? Die Auslegung des Hiobbuches (Hi 32-37) durch ein Pseudepigraphon (TestHi 41-43), in: JSJ 25 (1994), 1-17.

YOSHIKO REED, Annette, Job as Jobab: The Interpretation of Job in LXX Job 42:17b-e, in: JBL 120 (2001), 31-55.

Authority of a Forgiven King:
David's Psalms in the Letter to the Romans

LEVENTE B. MARTOS

Writing a letter is a way of exerting authority. The one who communicates by writing a letter, builds his or her personal authority by means of his or her letter. The manner which an individual structures and builds up his or her letter is also a sign of his or her personality. In this paper I am going to argue for Paul as the writer of the letter to the Romans, who built his letter and therefore his authority on many quotations from the Old Testament and, among others, also on quotations from the psalms. I would like to look at the psalm quotations in the letter to the Romans as they reflect their author of tradition, David, and as they construct the letter itself and the authority of its author, Paul.

Old Testament quotations and allusions abound in the letter to the Romans, and whereas scholars rejoice in describing meticulously the different nuances of these texts, readers are often troubled with their meaning. Quotations should make the understanding of the point easy – but in many ancient texts the opposite is true. Scholars should find a simple theory, which helps to understand the line of thought. The best theories are always simple, understandable, and very realistic in the sense that even ancient writers could think in that easy way.

But how can we get a rather simple picture of the many different texts which were interwoven by Paul to form the Letter to the Romans? How can we understand the way, that these different texts "worked" in the process of communication between Paul and his adressees, assuming that even these adressees were of various origin, background, and cultural niveau, and that a conscious writer in the person of Paul, who knew his adressees and their problems very well despite great distance?[1] The picture we get about the Old Testament quotations cannot

---

1   The use of Scripture in the Pauline epistles shows practically all possible types of questions to be made about texts in general. AAGESON, Written, 152, gives a helpful category in five: 1. textual traditions and textual manipulations; 2. comparison of Paul's use of Scripture with other Jewish interpreters; 3. the question whether Paul used or not earlier christian *testimonia* or *excerpta*, and how these could influence his interpretation; 4. the question how the original context of the rather short quotations

be independent of the picture of the whole communication between Paul and his readers, a communication which by no means should be considered simple. But once these difficulties are solved, at least to a certain degree, the actual readers will be better prepared to view the text as if it was addressing to themselves.

It seems obvious that word by word quotations introduced by an introductory formula can assume the function that a modern reader most usually associates with quotations: as an introduction or as a powerful closure of a section, like the quotations and allusions in Rom 1:17; 3:10-18; 9:33; 10:18-21; 11:33-36; 15:9-12. Nowadays, it should not cause great surprise if an authoritative text is commented or explained. Neither should it cause any surprise if words of an authoritative figure or a person with historical importance are reported. These phenomena are also to be found in the letter to the Romans. There is scholarly consense about the fact that the key passages from the Book of Isaiah and Deuteronomy were of preliminary importance not only for shorter sections of Romans but also for the way Paul understood the history of salvation and the history and aim of his own mission. For example, with regard to Rom 9-11, Richard B. Hays said that "Deuteronomy 32 *contains* Romans in nuce".[2] Further, about the role of Isaiah in the same chapters, J. Ross Wagner concluded:[3]

> "Paul finds in Isaiah a fellow preacher of the gospel, the message that reveals God's righteousness for all who believe, for the Jew first and also for the Greek. He uncovers in Isaiahs heralds a veild prefiguration of his own mission to proclaim the good news to those among the Gentiles who have not yet heard news of the victory of Israel's God. (...) Through adopting as his own the stories Isaiah and his fellow scriptural witnesses tell about God's unquenchable love for his people, Paul finds assurance that God will be faithfull to redeem and restore his covenant people Israel, so that Jew and Gentile together can sing the glories of God's name."

Neither Deut 32 nor Deutero- and Trito-Isaiah are narrative texts, but they suppose and belong to the great narrative of the story of God with his people. This is a story that, according to Paul, is in some way renewed and drawn further in the story of the Christians. Paul had a high esteem, not only for the *words* of Isaiah, but also for his personal mis-

---

influenced Paul and the interpretation of his text; 5. "the character of intertextuality and inner biblical exegesis".

2   Coursive is mine. So HAYS, Echoes of Scripture, 164. Cited approving by ALETTI, Romains 11, 221.

3   WAGNER, Heralds of the Good News, 356. Wagner was not the very first with this idea: In his 1998 dissertation and some subsequent articles Florian Wilk drew a picture of Paul, according to which the apostle saw himself as the prophet foretold by Isaiah 52,15, a prophet for the (pagan) nations – see WILK, Die Bedeutung des Jesajabuches für Paulus.

sion to be "a herald of the good news". The stories told by Isaiah continue in the story of the gospel, the mission of the prophet continues in the mission of Paul.[4] The actual authority of Paul – meaning the complex relationships of Paul to the community which he is addressing, his liberty of action in front of the community – is being enriched by his "co-identity" in Isaiah. This too is a simple way of explaining why one quotes a definite person: the story of that person and the story that the actual speaker belongs to, are in some way parallel. The words of the quoted person recall the story of that person, they move the actual reader in that story. In our case, the two stories are not only "parallel" or function like similars, but the second is the continuation and fulfilling of the first, in the eyes of Paul.

This type of quotation then has at least two important features. First, there must be a person, to whom the cited words are to be bound. Second, the words and their author must have a recognisable and recallable story. The rhetorical impact of such a quotation will depend on the actual validity, the actual realization of these elements. To understand these quotations means to have present the person and story in case and to find its present equivalents – person and story. The study of these quotations follows the two narratives, their actual and potential connections, and the function of the figures which connect them.

What about Paul and the letter to the Romans? Does Paul have an interest for the people who stand behind the quotations? In none of his other letters, where Paul cites the Scripture, does he introduce the quotations by the name of the traditional author's name, as he does here – e.g. Moses (Rom 10:5.19), Isaiah (Rom 9:27.29; 10:16.20; 15:12), David (Rom 4:6; 11:9) or Hosea (Rom 9:25).[5] The story and person of Elijah is recalled in a most powerful way in Rom 11:2-4 and its actual meaning (οὕτως οὖν καὶ ἐν τῷ νῦν καιρῷ) is without delay explained in 11:5-6. These passages are almost exclusively from Rom 9-11, where quotations of the book of Isaiah abound, and they are always references to prophets – David included, as we will see. The density of the quotations gives hint to the reader that he should recall the story of Israel and the words of the prophets, and he should understand the parallel mission of Paul and the situation of the Christian community respectively.

Faced with the great value of quotations in chapters 9-11 of the letter, we ask ourselves whether this practice is prepared in some way in former sections of the letter and whether it is used by what stands be-

---

4 See also NICKLAS, Apostel.
5 The Scripture speaks in Rom 4:3; 9:17; 10:11; 11:2 and Gal 4:30. See KOCH, Schrift als Zeuge, 25, n. 5.

hind. Do the scriptural references have a similar function in the earlier and latter sections of the letter?[6] In chapters 2-4 of Romans, but not only there, psalms of David play a very significant role. Do the quotations from the psalms have a similar function as those of Isaiah? Is there a story and is there a person behind them which they allude to? Do they have a recognisable reference in the communication between Paul and the Romans? And if these questions are to be answered with a simple yes, how much is the value of this reference? How much do the story of David and the story of the psalms fit the story of Paul and the Roman Christians?

In light of what has been told, I would like to give a short presentation of the psalms as story, and we ask for their presence and literal function in the story of Paul and the Roman Christians.

1. Psalms as Story

Psalms are poetic texts, yet they function as stories on at least two levels: as individual psalms and as part of the Psalter as a whole. Behind the majority of the individual psalms there is a clearly recognisable story. The psalms themselves are often articulated as pleas for liberation from a (shortly explained) bad situation of an individual or of the whole people of Israel, or on the other hand, as thanksgiving for a certain grace received from God. Psalms are relatively closed, independent texts. Their stories are also rather unified and finished. Sadness and description of the bad situation gives way to the gratitude over the received graces. But there is a second level, too. In the early history of their interpretation, already in biblical times, psalms were connected more and more to the person and story of David. One of the ideas which led the redaction of the whole Psalter was the connection of the individual psalms to events of the story of David. The individual psalms were rarely changed but psalms were added at significant points of the Psalter. Some of the psalm headings are also linked to the story of David as told in the books of Samuel, Kings and Chronicles.[7] The psalms connected to the person of David are mostly individual

---

6 If we take a look on the letter to the Romans, we see how much certain scriptural witnesses are bound to specific sections of the letter. In the first 8 chapters we find the famous quotation of Hab 2:4 (Rom 1:17), Isaiah only twice (Isa 52:5 – Rom 2:24; Isa 59:7-8 – Rom 3:15-17, in a „chain-quotation"), four times in chapter 4 the story of Abraham from Genesis (Rom 4:3.17.18.23 – Gen 15:6; 17:5; 15:5; 15:6).

7 See: HOSSFELD, David als exemplarischer Mensch, 243-255; DIETRICH, Prophet und Gesalbter, 25-29. Walter Dietrich does not only give a short presentation of the way the Psalter is brought near to David and than David to Jesus, he shows also how already in New Testament times their differences were also underlined.

laments, so they offer a possibility of identification for the reader who is in trouble. Scholars agree to find David's person in the psalms as a kind of "example of Israelites": "as David so every man". Further, as individual psalms go from trouble to thank and praise, so the whole Psalter too is meant to bring its pious readers from lament to praise and hymns.[8]

By the time of Paul the "Davidisierung" of the Psalter had already been complete. Not only much of the New Testament but also the writings of Josephus Flavius and the Qumran literature are filled with David's image as author of the psalms. So in general terms we can say that the Psalter was connected to the person and story of David and it was possible that Paul and his readers read psalms as texts from and about David.

2. Psalm Quotations in Romans and the Story of the Psalms

The question is now, whether the psalm quotations in Romans allude to the stories which lay behind the text – whether they report the story of the individual psalms and, as a separate issue, the person and story of David. We adress now the first of these questions by presenting a short evaluation of the explicit psalm quotations in Romans.[9]

Rom 3:4 – Ps 50:6 LXX

We find the first explicit quotation from psalms in Rom 3:4b. It is a quotation of Ps 50:6 LXX, a psalm of repentance of an individual sinner in front of God, the famous "Miserere". The psalm has the structure "repentance – forgiveness – new creation – praise – offering". The psalmist pleas for God's mercy, who may cleanse him from sin by judging mercifully and by creating in him a new heart. The psalm departs from the confession of the sinner but arrives to the vow of praise and even to the well being of Zion and the altar of God in Jerusalem. Psalm 50 LXX is introduced in its heading (both in the Hebrew and Greek

---

8 On the possibility of a Pauline exegesis of not only psalms but also of the Psalter as a whole, cf. also POPKES, Und David spricht, 334.

9 In this paper I only deal with quotations which are clearly recognisable as such, mainly through an introductory formula. It has to be admitted, however, that the so called explicit quotations are somewhat like the peak of an iceberg, allusions or use of biblical language often go together with them, sometimes giving even much more strength and deepness to the effects of combining an existing text with a new one. Explicit quotations remain always firm points for further investigation, but we will point to allusions too, if they are clearly combined with the explicit quotations.

version) by pointing to the sin of David with Batsheba and against her man Uriah (cf. 1 Sam 11-12). So it has an early and common connection with the story of David as told in the biblical narrative.

Paul has to maintain in the first section of Romans (1:18-3:20) two positions which at first sight might be mutually exclusive: all humanity is under sin, Jew and Gentile alike, but God is righteous in judging, when he declares the sinner innocent. Rom 3:4 and the quotation of Ps 50 LXX belongs to Section 2:1-3:20 and more precisely 3:1-8 where Paul responds to possible interlocutions about the situation of Jewish believers.[10] The quotation says with the words of the psalmist: God's words prove to be right and God proves to be right in them – even in the unfaithfulness of his believers, in the unfaithfulness of some Jews, even in "my" or "our" unfaithfulness (cf. the speaker of the psalm and 3:5). As in the psalm, it is also in the text of Paul the faithfulness and righteousness of God which makes possible a new beginning. The psalmist will speak about new creation, new offering and praise, because he hopes to find mercy in the eyes of God, and Paul will explain the realization of God's mercy through Jesus Christ first in Rom 3:21-26, and later on in the whole letter.

Paul actually speaks of the situation of the Jews, but he will sum up shortly (3:9.19-20.23) the sinfullness of all humanity. The theme of the "words of God" not only connects the quotation to the immediate context (3:2), but also shows its importance in the rhetorical structure of the whole letter (cf. 9:6; 3:31). The argumentation about the wickedness of the Gentiles and of the Jews is an "a fortiori" argumentation. The wickedness of the Jewish people is a stronger case of the sinfulness of humanity, and gives therefore even more weight to the mercy of God.

The text of Psalm 50 LXX (vv. 16-21) is probably also alluded to in Rom 2:20. The vow of praise taken by the sinner at the end of the psalm becomes a sign of inconvenient proudness of a Jewish-Christian believer. The quotation and the allusion to the beginning and the end of the same text prove that Paul has in mind the whole text of the psalm. At the beginning of the paraenetic section, in Rom 12:1 Paul "appells" the community "by the mercies of God". This appell can be evaluated again as an allusion to Ps 50:3 LXX. Paul, who associated himself first to the sinner in appelling God's mercy, now "by the mercies of God" is a reminder of that mercy and its practical consequences.

---

10 Cf. FITZMYER, Romans, 296-297 and HOFIUS, Der Psalter als Zeuge des Evangeliums, 72-74. Both operate with a slightly different structure of the text, but their opinion regarding the place of 3,1-8 and 3,9-20 in it does not differ fundamentally.

Rom 3:10-18

In Rom 3:10-18 we find a catena, the longest combined citation in the pauline letters, which is built on two major texts, Ps 13:1-3 LXX and Isa 59,7-8, and combined with Pss 5:10; 139:4; 9:28; 35:2 LXX. All these psalms are laments of righteous sufferers against enemies. They represent the "darkest point" in the letter: humankind itself is totally corrupt and worthy of God's wrath in its wickedness.

In this case there are so many texts interwoven that we cannot assume a specific understanding of each psalm alluded to. Paul uses this catena[11] in order to underline the total uselessness of every human's "boasting". The speaker of the text is in this case not confessing his own sins, but speaking of others'. Is Paul excluding himself from the wickedness, which the psalmist and Isaiah cry about? No, at this point of the letter he is not present explicitly, only in the "voice" of his words. He does not specify his personal relationship with what he presents as the universal state of affairs.

Rom 4:7-8 – Ps 31:1-2a LXX

In Rom 4:7-8 Paul inserted Ps 31:1-2a LXX, the first time naming also David as author of the text. Paul cited the beginning of the psalm but left out the second half of v. 2.[12] The psalm itself is a wisdom text, praising the man whose sins are forgiven to be "happy" and praying for God's forgiveness and teaching about it. Chapter 4 of the letter to the Romans is one of the most skillfully realized explication or even commentary to a scriptural text in the Pauline literature – Gen 15:6 is cited first in Rom 4:3, but it is then alluded to in vv. 9 and 22, and repeated partially in v. 23. Paul develops his teaching about the justification by faith explaining the story of Abraham, in this case as father of the uncircumcised, and quoting words of David, who represents the Jews.[13]

---

11 There is scholarly debate on whether this text would be or not part of a Pre-Pauline florilegium. The parallels presented in favour of such a hypothesis seem often quite indefinite, therefore far from convincing. Although it is very probable, that the catena was constructed prior to the writing of the letter, we can assume, that Paul composed it.

12 Cf. STANLEY, Paul and the language of Scripture, 101: „Indeed, the parallel that it presents between the maintaining a pure mouth (v. 2b) and having one's sin overlooked by the Lord (v. 2a) might have suggested to some exactly the kind of 'work-righteousness' that Paul is at such pains to root out."

13 HOFIUS, Der Psalter als Zeuge des Evangeliums, 88-89, speaks about Abraham as a „pagan", justificated by God, and of David as an „Israelite sinner", forgiven and justificated by God.

The intentional choice of a still "Gentile" Abraham and of the Jew, David, becomes more evident, if we hold present the theme of chapters 2-3, where both Gentiles and Jews prove to need God's mercy.

The psalm quotation, that is the reference to the "story of the psalm" has only an explicative role as to the story of Abraham. The introduction and short explanation of Paul before and after the quotation limitates also the use of the psalm to its beginning, the *makarismos*. There are however some interesting resonances of the original context. The psalm depicts the moment of an inner conversion, which leads to the confession of sins and thereafter to the inner healing. The theme of "boasting" appears frequently in the letter (Rom 2:23; 3:27; 4:2), and it is part of the final exhortation of the psalm text, too (Ps 31:11 LXX). Ps 31:2b LXX, which was dropped out of the quotation, is linked thematically to the catena of Rom 3:10-18 by the expressions "deceit" and "mouth" (cf. Rom 3:13-14). Ps 31:10 LXX gives trust to the righteous by naming God's "mercy", which will be so important in the letter to the Romans too.

Rom 8:36 – Ps 43:23 LXX

In Rom 8:36 we read a verse from Ps 43:23 LXX. This is the first community lament psalm quoted in the letter. It gives a slightly different meaning to the rhetorical climax of chapter 8 which without this quotation could be even misunderstood in way of unrealistic happiness or triumphalism. Sylvia C. Keesmat showed the lexical and conceptual similarities between the psalm and the letter.[14] They belong to the lament of Israel about foreign dominion and to the lament of the Christian community about the power of the Roman Imperium respectively. Paul gives hope to the Roman Christians by pointing to the work of the Spirit and new childhood of God Father, and to redemption in Jesus. After speaking about the inner enemies of the faith, the power of sin, law and death, now he looks also to the increasingly threatening persecution and political oppression. The psalmist's faith and trust even in

---

14 KEESMAT, The Psalms in Romans and Galatians, 149-152. Besides more generic allusions to the language of community lament psalms we find: oppression – Ps 43:8.25 LXX; Rom 8:35; shame – Ps 43:8.10.16; Rom 5:5; 10:11; hope – Ps 43:7 LXX; Rom 8:24; heart – Ps 43:19 LXX; Rom 8:27. Keesmat emphasizes the presence of community lament psalms among those cited by Paul and describes how these prayers become the expression of the faith of the Roman Christian community, which lives in the shadow of the Roman Empire. By quoting these lament psalms Paul would then communicate with the more or less unexpressed fear of the Roman community. On the one hand he shows a deep understanding of their worry, but on the other hand he would offer the key to the solution.

bad times as well as his cry for help in a difficult situation fit very well the new, pauline context and rhetorical aim.

The quotation of Ps 43:23 LXX in Rom 8:36 expresses the suffering of the community of the oppressed. But the same psalm text has some resonances with Isa 53:7. The psalm and its quotation has ἐλογίσθημεν ὡς πρόβατα σφαγῆς, and Isa 53:7 reads ὡς πρόβατον ἐπὶ σφαγὴν ἤχθη, the difference being the number and the person. Isa 53:7 is again quoted in Acts 8:32, with clear reference to Jesus and his redeming fate. How should we then understand the overlap of the two narratives – the one of the psalmist and the one of the Christians? The "we" of the psalm gives Paul the opportunity to identify himself with the sufferer Christians, but he is in fact able to connect the suffering with redemption and hope, because of his faith in Jesus Christ, as expressed in Rom 8:31-39 and as witnessed by Isa 53:7 and Ps 43:23 LXX.

Rom 10:18 – Ps 18:5 LXX

Rom 10:18 does not have any introductory formula, but is clearly recognisable as a quotation by the change of style and syntax. It is a word by word quotation of Ps 18:5 LXX, a hymn about God's word in creation and law. In this text again we are faced with numerous lexical connections to the whole of chapter 10 in Romans. The first word of Ps 18 LXX is "heaven", which figures also in Dtn 30:12, quoted by Paul in Rom 10:7. Rom 10:4-5 concentrates on the "law", which governs the text of the psalm from v. 8 onwards. According to the psalmist the precepts of the Lord rejoice the heart (v. 8), which shelters the faith in Christ according to Paul in Rom 10:9. The "word" is also central in the psalm (v. 3) and in Rom 10:8 (twice) and 10:17. We can say, therefore, that at the moment of its direct quoting in Rom 10:18 Paul had already passed the way of the psalm. No wonder then, when the church fathers of the II-IV centuries identify the risen Christ with the rising sun (sometimes quoting Ps 18 LXX, sometimes not)[15] – they reuse the concept established already by Paul in Rom 10:6-9: Christ is risen, he is already in heaven, and he is also with us, near us, as the new, living and life-giving law.

---

15 Cf. IRENAEUS, *Epideixis* 86; Fontes Christiani 8/1; AUGUSTINUS, *Enarr. in Psalmos* 18,I,6-7 and 18,II,2; PL 36,155 and 156-157.

Rom 11:9-10 – Ps 68:23-24 LXX and Rom 15:3 – Ps 68:10 LXX

Rom 11:9-10 Ps 68:23-24 LXX is quoted. This quotation parallels the combined quotation of Deut 29:3 and Isa 29:10 in the former verses. The text of the quotation fits the context of the other quotations because of its vocabulary of "darkening of the eyes" and "being scandalised". The psalm quotation mentioning the name of David explicits and reinforces the authority of Scripture, but this is not its only function here.

Psalm 68 LXX is a lament of a righteous sufferer. Whereas this time it says a curse against the enemies, the other verse of Rom 15:3 (68:10 LXX) emphasizes the humble attitude of the sufferer in front of God's will and gives an example of how Christians should imitate Christ in suffering patiently. Is this twofold use of the psalm against our theory of the "story of the psalm"? At first sight, definitely. Strictly speaking, we should attend that the verses of the psalm would be quoted in the original sequence, and here the opposite is the case. The two textual elements seem to propose an opposite moral attitude: to say a curse against the enemies who cause suffering – or to bear humbly the sufferings with regard to God.

This question can be solved by a more precise interpretation of the text of Romans and by pointing to the special features of the Psalter, as much as its "subject", its leading personality is concerned. Rom 11:9-10 does not form a curse against Jews, who did not converse to the Gospel of Christ – although it was indeed a curse, spoken against the enemies of the psalmist. What was a curse, a deadly threat, is now part of God's mysterious plan, who seeks to convert his people again. So in fact the same logic comes true: the humbling suffering brings salvation in both cases – Christ, the innocent brings salvation through his suffering (15:3) and those who "stumbled", although they "stumbled", receive salvation (11:9-11). In both cases unjust suffering is revolved into justice of God.

As Enno E. Popkes convincingly showed, the quotation of Ps 68:23-24 in Rom 11:9-10 corresponds to the original context of the whole psalm: a sufferer pleas to God, because he has become alien from his own people.[16] This context is then applicable to Paul, who from the beginning of chapter 11 speaks about his own example, citing scriptural texts about Elija, and then citing David. As Elija, persecuted by his own people, flees to God, so in this psalm "David" trusts God alone, and by the end of the psalm his trust adds to the salvation of the whole community.

---

16 POPKES, Und David spricht, 331-332.

Mary T. Brien spoke[17] about the psalms as "familiar site of Israel's identity", "dependable sites where alternatives can be considered." In the twofold quotation of Ps 68 LXX, we can observe this alternative reading. In order to reach a correct understanding of the psalms, we have to serve the unity of the psalm and the possibly different figures, who belong to the same story, namely to God's salvational actions.

Rom 15:9.11

The last two quotations form part of the catena, which closes the argumentative section of Romans (15:9-12). Rom 15:9 quotes Ps 17:50 LXX, and Rom 15:11 Ps 116:1 LXX. Both are hymns. All four quotations of vv. 9-12 speak about the "nations", inviting God's elected to accept his intention, his willingness to share his grace also to the nations. The original story of Ps 17 LXX is thanksgiving of a victorious king, who was saved from a difficult situation. Ps 116 LXX does not have a real story, since it is only two verses long, inviting all nations to praise the Lord because of his mercy and righteousness. At the end of his argumentation Paul sums up his call for unity and praise in the community, founded in the salvific plan of God's mercy, proclaimed and pretold by the prophets who had experienced God's grace.

Our first observation is that the letter to the Romans moves from lament (over a sinful humanity) to the hymn of God's grace. In this sense the structure of the letter reflects the overall structure of the Psalter which moves from lament to praise. The lament over a sinful humankind culminates in Rom 3:10-18 which is mainly composed of psalm verses. The praise finds its expression in Rom 11:33-36 using words of Isaiah and 15:9-12 again with psalm quotations. As far as the psalms quoted in the letter are concerned, it is Ps 50 LXX which expresses the most theological structure of the letter.

As we have seen, in most cases of direct quotations the original story of the psalm and the new story, the new context formed in the letter of Paul are bound to each other. In some cases, such as Ps 50 LXX in Rom 3:4 or Ps 18 in Rom 10:18, even the structure of the letter seems to reflect the structure of the psalm. The lexicografical similarities are not in every case very strong: we observe a more general parallelity as for Ps 43 LXX and the community lament psalms in Rom 8:36.

---

17 BRIEN, The Psalter at Work, 486. I find the suggestion by Brien to find an „alternative" reading in the psalms very useful. I would call it the dialogic character of the psalms. These texts invite every reader to be in dialogue with God and to hear also the inner dialogue of biblical texts in general but especially the inner dialogue of the psalms themselves.

The above observations do not say anything about how much Paul thought of his audiences' scriptural knowledge. In a long letter we would have found it natural for Paul to make a clear sign of his intention to broaden the scriptural knowledge of his adressees. Paul might have had in mind the possibility that the Roman community would know or even check his scriptural quotations, but we cannot be sure about this.[18] Paul creates his own text, and not a comment to certain scriptural texts, which should be known first. We do have the impression, however, that Paul did know very well the original context, even if we do not really know how much he could think about his audiences' competence.

What is then the impression we get after seeing the similarities between the old and the new stories? These similarities are in my opinion best explained as the way *Paul* came to quote these psalms and not others. As someone who knew the Scripture well, he could even unintentionally choose texts which matched very well what he said in his letter. It is not true, that Paul would have had in mind only the verse of the psalm he quoted. It is not provable, on the other hand, that he intended the whole psalm, from which he quoted one or two verses. But it is probably true, that he himself – intentionally or not – built his text from scriptural texts, which were not alien to his own line of thinking.

3. The Story of David and the Story of Romans

After reading the quotations of the psalms in the letter to the Romans we are now prepared to respond to the second question: do the quotations of Paul build a story with the main character of the Psalter, King David? Tradition made David the main figure of the Psalter. His sufferings, his sins and his praise to the Lord is unifying the originally different songs of Israel. How is David present in the letter to the Romans? Do the psalm quotations form a distinct image of David in the letter?

We find David's name mentioned in the letter three times. The first occurrence happens in the famous early Christian creed of Rom 1:3-4, where Jesus is called "born of the seed of David". This verse is probably echoed by the closing section of the argumentation of the letter,

---

18 BRIEN, The Psalter at Work, 485-486 states that especially quotations of the first line of psalms were also meant to pick up the whole text of the psalm in the mind of the audience: „Paul wrote with an audience in mind. His awareness that his Letter would be read aloud in congregations may have influenced his choice of psalm and his prevalent choice of initial verses of psalms. To a knowing audience this would have had an effect much like mentioning a song's title or the first lines of a song today."

namely to Rom 15:12, where Paul mentions the "offspring of Jesse", citing Isa 11:10 LXX.[19] There is for sure scholarly debate about the exact weight and meaning of this early Christian creed. For our purposes it seems sufficient that we notice the bondage of David to Jesus in a text, which is identified as traditional in the first Christian century. We should also notice the fact that both the beginning and the end of the argumentative section are structurally relevant.

As we have already seen, Paul introduced two of his psalm quotations by naming also their author of tradition, David (4:6-8; 11:9). This is however a smaller percentage than with Isaiah, where we find five times his name in the letter and 10 quotations all together.

Why does Paul mention the *name* of David in Rom 4:6, which introduces the quotation of Ps 31 LXX? After the beginning of the psalm by a *makarismos*, the speaker of the psalm shifts from third person to first person singular. The prospective of his speech is therefore open to convey his own experience of repentance.[20] David the Jew testifies the blessedness of Gentile Abraham, while by the text of the psalm he admits to having had the same experience. So the quotation of Psalm 31 LXX in Rom 4 sums up the former teaching of God's just wrath and yet justification as forgiveness offered in Christ Jesus in a very personal way. For an attentive reader this quotation could be a link to the former cluster of psalm quotations in chapter 3 of the letter.

Until this point, David – an author of the tradition of the psalms – was a witness of God's just wrath against all mankind. Here he is a prophet, speaking in the words of the psalm about his own experience of being forgiven.[21] The *makarismos* of Psalm 31 LXX introduced in the original a story ending with thanks to the Lord. In the immediate context Paul uses it as a parallel to the story of Abraham, but in the broader context it is also a fulfillment of the vow of praise, which

---

19 Cf. WILCKENS, An die Römer III., 108: „Die prophetische Ankündigung des kommenden Davididen, der 'sich erheben wird, um über die Völker zu herrschen', hat sich in Christus erfüllt: Er ist der Sohn Davids, der als Auferstandener in die Machtstellung des Sohnes Gottes eingesetzt ist (1,3f), dessen Herrschaft kosmischuniversal (1 Kor 15,25) und dessen Macht die der göttlichen Liebe ist, in der alle, die sich im Glauben hoffend auf ihn verlassen, zeitlich und räumlich universal geborgen sind (8,35ff)."

20 HOFIUS, Der Psalter als Zeuge des Evangeliums, 89 connects the quotation of Ps 31:1-2a LXX in Rom 4:7-8 to the sin of David with Batseba, but does not combine it with the former Rom 3:4, where Ps 50 LXX is quoted.

21 The figure of David in contemporary Jewish writings however is in fact associated – among many others – with the concept of forgiveness. For the examples see MIURA, David in Luke-Acts, 47-48 (Sir 47:11); 76-77 (CD 5:1-6); 96 (Ant 7,130-158); 124: „Due to the virtue of his confession of sins, David, a sinner, becomes a model for every ordinary Israelite, not only leaders of Israel."

would end Psalm 50 LXX, quoted earlier in the letter (Rom 3:4), and it is an answer to the dark lament of the psalmist quoted by Paul in a cluster of quotations in 3:10-18.

The other case mentioning David explicitly as the speaker of the Psalms is Rom 11:9. As we have already seen, the original and the new context, the original and the new story are bound together by the comparison of David and Paul. Paul and his message scandalize many of his contemporary Jews, but this scandalization brings salvation to others and at the end to many. David is here again understood as a prophet.[22] His words – which in their original context were words of a curse – become words of hope. David is like a "suffering prophet", who testifies to God's way that surpasses all human expectations. God's grace revolves human history of sin and negation into a history of salvation.

Therefore, we can say that David's prophetic role in Romans is one of a sinner, who attests the forgiving mercy of the Lord, experienced in his own life and one of a just man who is suffering for his faithfulness to the Lord. All this is realized in reading the psalms in dialogue with each other. Ps 50 LXX together with Ps 31:1-2 in Rom 4:7-8 form the one side of the dialogue, whereas the catena in Rom 3:10-20 and the quotation of Ps 43:23 LXX in Rom 8:36 and Ps 68:23-24 LXX in Rom 11:9 form the other side. It is a dialogue between the sinner who is conscious of his sins and hopes for forgiveness, and between a righteous sufferer who has a case against his enemies and hopes for salvation from God. By the end of the letter both requests have been heard and the sinner and sufferer praise together the Lord for salvation which is forgiveness and justification.

Now we come back to our initial question: does Paul consciously construct by means of the quotations an image of David? Can we say that the person of David had an impact on Paul similar to that of Isaiah?

The evidence we have in the letter commands caution. The number of quotations and the number how often Paul named David is not so high as in the case of Isaiah. Even if it seems that Paul consciously collected his psalms for the letter and he followed their way of thinking and praying, we cannot say that he wanted to design an image of David in the letter. But on the other hand it is certain that the psalm

---

22 Cf. POPKES, Und David spricht, 325: „Diese zusätzliche Einleitung dokumentiert eine Vorstellung, die Paulus mit verschiedenen frühjüdischen und frühchristlichen Auslegungstraditionen verbindet, nämlich die Vorstellung, dass der Psalmendichtung Davids eine prophetische Dignität zukommt." See further SUBRAMANIAN, The Synoptic Gospels, 19-29.

quotations play a significant role in the argumentation. So first we can speak about the impact of the psalm's message on the letter. Second, the message of the psalms is related to the story and personality of David. Whereas the words and personality of Isaiah function as a prefiguration of Paul's mission, the story, the prophetic words and, in a "cumulative" sense, the "personality" of David unify multiple aspects: the personality of David combines the possibility of messianism and popularism. David can stand for the Messiah and also Israel. It is Paul who speaks,[23] but his words integrate the authority of Scripture and its different characters: God's power and possibilities, the experience and faith of the prophets, the voice of Israel, whose hope is in the Lord, and the Christian community which is enriched by the experience of this dialog in faith.

David as Messiah takes us in the letter to the Romans to the relation of David and Jesus Christ. This identification begins with the introductory section of the letter (Rom 1:3-4), with the already mentioned "paulinised version" of an early Christian creed formula. The identification of David with Israel suffering under foreign rulers in Romans brings us to the relation of David and the Christian community. It is this community conceived in a very realistic and also eschatological sense, which praises the Lord for his salvation as forgiveness and justification. It is a community which needs courage to look forward to persecution and multiple hardships (cf. Ps 43 LXX in Rom 8:36) In all this, they also find the example of Jesus as sufferer (Rom 8:36; 15:3).

---

23 HAYS, Christ Prays the Psalms, 101-118 formed the hypothesis of a symbolic identification of „David – Israel – Messiah" in the early church. His concept was built on the quotation of Ps 68:10 of the Septuagint in Rom 15:3, where the speaker of the psalm in the citation had to be the suffering Jesus. It is, however, less convincing to „hear the voice of Jesus" in 2 Cor 4:13 (Ps 115:1 LXX) or Rom 15:9 (Ps 17:50 LXX), which Hays argues for. There is no doubt that 2 Cor 4:13 parallels the sufferings of Paul and the sufferings of Jesus. The vocabulary of the text, however, does not demonstrate any reference to the text of the psalm, which would be then a direct sign of its primitive Christian use regarding the fate of Jesus. The reference to the hardships of Paul at the beginning of the section (2 Cor 4:8-9) and the theme of speaking – that is testifying to the faith – explain very well the use of this psalm of thanksgiving. Moreover, there is an other text, where the influence of Ps 115:2 is generally admitted, Rom 3:4 – and the context offers no real possibility of Jesus' use. Rom 15:9 is another verse where Hays thinks Christ was actually intended as the speaker of Psalm 17:50 LXX by Paul. Taken together the four quotations in vv. 9-12 I would argue here too for Paul as the actual speaker of the quotations. The reference to the „offspring of Iesse" from Isa 11:10 LXX in v. 12 is the climax of the whole cluster of quotations. It is seems difficult to have Christ the speaker and addressee of the text at the same time. The Psalm quotations in the first sections of the letter to the Romans, where Paul cites several times psalms of repentance, do not correspond the idea of Richard Hays. See also LAMBRECHT, A Matter of Method, 441-448. Lambrecht speaks about simple „comparison" between the psalmist and Paul.

4. Authority of David and Authority of Paul

The identification of David with Paul brings us to the rhetoric of the letter – how is Paul using the authority of David? How does the authority of David and the authority of Scripture reinforce the authority of Paul?

Although Romans remains the letter of Paul, where he apparently withdraws himself more than in his other writings, he speaks about himself in the letter in positive terms. The service of Paul is characterized significantly at the beginning (1:1-17) and at the end of the letter (15:14-21).[24] He presents himself in the letter as a "servant of Christ Jesus" and an "invited apostle" (1:1), who was bestowed grace and who served God by preaching the Gospel of Jesus (1:5.9). In the end the readers recognise him as a priest, who gives God the gentiles as an offering (15:16). Paul's personal notes to the content of the gospel, which he is describing in the letter, appear almost exclusively with regard to his Jewish identity and the salvation of Israel (9:1-5; 10:1-2; 11:1). He leaves wide place to imaginary speakers and interlocutors, and creates also an inner dialogue by means of his scriptural quotations.[25]

Paul is giving new insights to the readers. That is authority and liberty of action. He did not have any personal contact with the Roman Christian Community earlier, so he does not have any problems of authority of his own. He makes an effort to establish his authority by writing the letter.[26] The Letter to the Romans is in fact a foundational act of the relationship between Paul and the Romans. The reader could be rather surprised by how Paul gives straightforward admonitions to the Roman Christians, although he has not had any real contact with the whole community yet. He was probably considered to have already been known to them and he also showed his Christian competence in the letter.

What is, then, the rhetorical impact of the psalms in the letter to the Romans? Paul uses psalms in the first section of the letter in order to express the sinfulness of the world. That is a rather prophetic way. The proclamation of the divine mercy begins with the proclamation of human sins. By means of his psalm quotations, by means of words of David, the forgiven, Paul is able to speak about sins not only as a prophet or as a judge, he can identify himself with the sinner. Paul did

---

[24] See HORN, Selbstverständnis, 225-246.
[25] The best example being the unity of Rom 11:1-10.
[26] For the view that Paul had a serious influence and possibly also leading function later in Rome see BARENTSEN, Pre-Pauline Leadership, 595-616.

not introduce himself to the Romans as a sinner, in a self-diminishing way, although that would have not been unthinkable for him (see e.g. 1 Cor 15:8-9; see also 1 Tim 1:12-14). Here he remains an authorized leader of the community, but at the same time, a prophet and a sinner praying for mercy.

Because of their multiple functions, psalms are very useful for Paul to be at the same time on the side of the suffering community and show himself as the righteous one who has the right to admonish others. He can plea to God but he can also praise God for his glory. By quoting the psalms, Paul can represent the sufferings of Jesus and associate himself with the Romans to Jesus. This time the adjective "prophetic" says no more than the prophetic utterance, but rather the conjunction of the past and the future in David and in Jesus.

By means of the psalms the authority of Paul is based on empathy and aims to define his relationship with the community and redefine inner relationships in the community (Jews and Gentiles, cf. the paraenetic section and its ending in Rom 15:9-12). Forgiveness and justification by faith become occasion of peace and praise. David is offered as a model in Christ for the Christians who suffer. In his quotations Paul identifies himself with David, who is a prophet and also a sinner in the second line. Moreover, he identifies David with Jesus, who encompasses and redefines all in a new humanity. Paul realizes what the psalm of David promises in case of the forgiveness experienced: *I will praise You among the gentiles and I will teach them your ways*. And he gives the right offering also promised in the psalm (Rom 15:16).

The "concert" of Isaiah and Paul (Ross Wagner) cannot take place without the divine Psalmist, David. His melody is perhaps not the first or the loudest, but it is an integral part of the message in the letter to the Romans and of Paul's authority.

Bibliography

AAGESON, James W., Written also for Our Sake: Paul's Use of Scripture in the Four Major Epistles, with a Study of 1 Corinthians 10, in: Porter, Stanley E. (ed.), Hearing the Old Testament in the New Testament, Grand Rapids, Michigan/Cambridge U.K. 2006, 152-181.

ALETTI, Jean-Noel, Romains 11. Le développement de l'argumentation et ses enjeux exégético-théologiques, in: Schnelle, Udo (ed.), The Letter to the Romans (BETL 226), Leuven 2009, 197-223.

BARENTSEN, Jack, Pre-Pauline Leadership and Pauline Constitution in the Roman Church. An Alternative Interpretation of Romans 12 and 16, in: Schnelle, Udo (ed.), The Letter to the Romans (BETL 226), Leuven 2009, 595-616.

BRIEN, Mary T., The Psalter at Work in Paul's Letter to the Romans, in: Schnelle, Udo (ed.), The Letter to the Romans (BETL 226), Leuven 2009, 475-486.

DIETRICH, Walter, Prophet und Gesalbter. König David im Neuen Testament, in: BiKi 66 (2011) 25-29.

FITZMYER, Joseph A., Romans. A New Translation with Introduction and Commentary (AB 33), Doubleday 1993.

HAYS, Richard B., Christ Prays the Psalms: Israel's Psalter as Matrix of Early Christology, in: Id., The Conversion of the Imagination. Paul as Interpreter of Israel's Scripture, Grand Rapids, Michigan/Cambridge 2006, 101-118.

HOFIUS, Otfried, Der Psalter als Zeuge des Evangeliums. Die Verwendung der Septuaginta-Psalmen in den ersten beiden Hauptteilen des Römerbriefes, in: Reventlow, Henning Graf (Hrsg.), Theologische Probleme der Septuaginta und der hellenistischen Hermeneutik, Gütersloh 1997, 72-90.

HORN, Friedrich W., Das apostolische Selbstverständnis des Paulus nach Römer 15, in: Schnelle, Udo (ed.), The Letter to the Romans (BETL 226), Leuven 2009, 225-246.

HOSSFELD, Frank-Lothar, David als exemplarischer Mensch. Literarische Biographie und Anthropologie am Beispiel Davids, in: Frevel, Christian (Hrsg.), Biblische Anthropologie. Neue Einsichten aus dem Alten Testament (QD 237), Freiburg 2010, 243-255.

KEESMAAT, Sylvia C., The Psalms in Romans and Galatians, in: Moyise, Stephen/Menken, Marten J. J. (eds.), The Psalms in the New Testament, London/New York 2004, 139-162.

KOCH, Dietrich-Alexander, Die Schrift als Zeuge des Evangeliums. Untersuchungen zur Verwendung und zum Verständnis der Schrift bei Paulus (Beiträge zur historischen Theologie 69), Tübingen 1986.

LAMBRECHT, Jan, A Matter of Method (II) 2 Cor 4,13 and the Recent Studies of Schenk and Campbell, in: ETL 86 (2010) 441-448.

MIURA, Yuzuru, David in Luke-Acts. His Portrayal in the Light of Early Judaism (WUNT 2,232), Tübingen 2007.

NICKLAS, Tobias, Paulus – der Apostel als Prophet, in: Nicklas, Tobias/Verheyden, Joseph/Zamfir, Korinna (eds.), Prophets and Prophecy in Jewish and Early Christian Literature (WUNT II 286), Tübingen 2010, 77-104.

POPKES, Enno E., Und David spricht ... Zur Rezeption von Ps LXX 68,23f. im Kontext von Röm 11,1-10, in: Wilk, Florian (ed.), Between Gospel and Election. Explorations in the Interpretation of Romans 9-11 (WUNT 257), Tübingen 2010, 321-337.

SUBRAMANIAN, J. Samuel, The Synoptic Gospels and the Psalms as Prophecy (LNTS 351), London 2007.

STANLEY, Christopher D., Paul and the language of Scripture: Citation Technique in the Pauline Epistles and contemporary literature (SNTSMS 69), Cambridge 1992.

STANLEY, Christopher D., Paul's "Use" of Scripture. Why the Audience Matters, in: Porter, Stanley E./Stanley, Christopher D. (eds.), As it is Written. Studying Paul's Use of Scripture (SBL Symposium Series 50), Atlanta 2008, 125-155.

WAGNER, J. Ross, Heralds of the Good News. Isaiah and Paul 'in Concert' in the Letter to the Romans (NovTS 101), Leiden/Boston/Köln 2002.

WILCKENS, Ulrich, Der Brief an die Römer (Röm 12-16) (EKK VI/3), Neukirchen-Vluyn ²1989.

WILK, Florian, Die Bedeutung des Jesajabuches für Paulus (FRLANT 179), Göttingen 1998.

Scriptural Authority in Q

PAUL FOSTER

1. Introduction

The devil quotes the longest single passage of scripture in Q (Q 4.10-11//LXX Ps 90.11-12).¹ Can anything be inferred from this fact for determining the attitude to scripture in the Q document? Since this is the only example where scripture is cited from a perspective opposed to that of the Jesus of Q, or contrary to the comments of the narrator or other characters aligned with the author's point of view, it is certainly not the case that scripture should seen as a 'weapon' used solely by opponents. In total, Q contains approximately ten passages that might be counted as citations of scripture. While these passages represent some of the most important data for analyzing the attitude exhibited in Q to scripture, there are other important ways in which Q draws upon Jewish sacred texts. These include references to scriptural personages, the mention of places that occur in the biblical text, and use of supernatural characters shared with scriptural writings.² The categories of allusions and echoes remain nebulous and ill-defined.³ There are certainly some places where Q shares earlier biblical language or expressions. However, it is difficult to tell whether such shared language represents a conscious attempt to draw upon biblical motifs to exploit

---

1   Strictly speaking the Q passage parallels LXX Ps 90.11a, 12, since the second half of Ps 90.11 is omitted by Q. As Fleddermann observes, 'In Psalm 90 the second half of v. 11 describes God's day-to-day care of the person of faith, and so it did not fit the extraordinary circumstances of Jesus casting himself down from the pinnacle of the temple. FLEDDERMANN, Q: A Reconstruction and Commentary, 247.
2   ALISON, Intertextual Jesus, 6-7.
3   Perhaps the clearest and most helpful attempt to define the conditions under which an echo might be identified remains the seven criteria suggested by Richard Hays. However, this list of criteria is not unproblematic. In particular it is worth noting how Hays downplays the criterion concerning the history of interpretation, saying this is the least important of the seven. However, one wonder if an 'echo' has not been detected for two millennia whether it ever actually existed, or if its 'detection' is not due more to modern biblical software rather than stemming from authorial intent! HAYS, Echoes of Scripture.

the wider contextual themes of the passage from which the shared language may be drawn, or if such language permeated the thought-world of the Q tradents to such an extent that it simply became a standard mode of discourse without any reference to the original context. Since the points of contact are often slight, sometimes with multiple possible sources for the base text, it appears to be highly speculative to derive anything more form these loose word associations, other than the general observation that the Q source is indebted to the language and expressions of the Jewish scriptures.

2. Scriptural Citations in Q

The extent of the Q material is a highly contested issue, with major reconstructions varying in their assessments of the amount of material contained in Q, from between 193 Lukan verses in Harnack's classical attempt to list the contents of Q,[4] to a much larger Q with 292 Lukan verses in Burkett's recent study.[5] While an enlarged Q, containing various *Sondergut* tradition from either Matthew or Luke may also increase the number of scriptural citations, the approach here draws upon passages that are strictly double tradition parallels in order to avoid the possibility of considering non-Q material. Given both the upper and lower estimates for the number of verses contained in Q, and taking 11 verses in Q to contain scriptural citations (the ten citations occupy 11 verses cf. Q 4.10-11//LXX Ps 90.11-12), it can be calculated that direct citations of the Jewish scripture occur in only between 3.8-5.7% of Q verses. While this may not appear to be a particularly striking statistic, two factor need to be considered. First, Q is not a compendium or *testimonia* collection of Jewish scriptures, but rather it seeks to present sayings of Jesus. Secondly, Mark's gospel contains 661 verses,[6] of which 32 contain direct citations of the Jewish scriptures.[7] That is a percentage of 4.8%, which falls within the possible range for the Q rate of citation. This shows that Q is not doing anything out of the ordinary in terms of its rate of use of Jewish scriptures in recounting Jesus traditions of a

---

4   HARNACK, Sayings of Jesus, 182.
5   BURKETT, Rethinking, 77 and appendix 1.
6   This total is obtained by taking only the first eight verses of Mk 16 as authentic, and also excluding the following verses from the count: Mk 7.16; 9.44, 46; 11.26; 15.28. This total of 661 agrees with the count of Streeter, who states '[t]he authentic text of Mark contains 661 verses.' STREETER, Four Gospels, 159.
7   Mark's Gospel has been chosen because it does not contain double tradition material, and consequently provides a fully independent sample for comparative purposes.

synoptic type. Having made these general observations, it is now helpful to turn to the individual citations in Q. Since at times these occur in clusters, some of these will be treated together rather than individually.

2.1 The Temptation Story (Q 4.1-13)

This second major block of Q material contains the most concentrated use of scripture in this source, with four citations found in the material contained in Q 4.1-13. The narrative form of the temptation story has been considered by some to be so discordant with the general character of Q, seen as a collection of short sayings of Jesus, that it has been suggested that it is not part of the Q material. Thus Lührmann argued that, '[t]he temptation story ... falls so far outside the scope of the remaining Q material, that I would suggest that Matthew and Luke independently of each other took it over from another tradition.'[8] This position appears to require far too high a level of generic consistency for a set of traditions that had in fact not been assembled because of their formal coherence, but because of their utility for members of a fledgling religious movement. Others have suggested that the pericope is part of Q, but that it was one of the latest elements to be incorporated into the document. Apart from the difficulties that attend tracing the redactional layers of Q, Kloppenborg comes to this position both on the basis of the 'paradigmatic and aetiological significance [the story had] for the rest of Q', and perhaps more importantly for this discussion because,

> the septuagintal character of the biblical quotations and the presence of non-Semitizing Greek make it unlikely that the account belonged to a Palestinian sphere. On the contrary, it was formulated in a Greek-speaking milieu where Palestinian politics are not likely to have occupied centre stage.[9]

Thus the first important observation to be made is that textual character of all the quotations in this unit appears to be broadly septuagintal.

Following the Matthean order,[10] the first citation is drawn from Deut 8.3. The relevant textual data is as follows:

---

8   LÜHRMAN, Redaktion, 56. Here the translation is drawn from KLOPPENBORG, Formation of Q, 247.
9   KLOPPENBORG, Formation of Q, 256.
10 Whilst in general most commentators feel the Lukan order and arrangement of material in individual units of double tradition material more faithfully preserves the order of Q, in relation to the temptation narrative the majority opinion is that Luke reversed the order of the final two temptations to create a climax that takes place in Jerusalem. See HEIL, Temptations, 148-184. Davies and Allison offer a summary of the major reasons for preferring the Matthean order: '(1) in Matthew the two Son of God temptations are together and this seems original; (2) the most blatant

Matt 4.4 οὐκ ἐπ' ἄρτῳ μόνῳ ζήσεται ὁ ἄνθρωπος, ἀλλ' ἐπὶ παντὶ ῥήματι ἐκπορευομένῳ διὰ στόματος θεοῦ

Lk 4.4 οὐκ ἐπ' ἄρτῳ μόνῳ ζήσεται ὁ ἄνθρωπος

LXX Deut 8.3 οὐκ ἐπ' ἄρτῳ μόνῳ ζήσεται ὁ ἄνθρωπος ἀλλ' ἐπὶ παντὶ ῥήματι τῷ ἐκπορευομένῳ διὰ στόματος θεοῦ ζήσεται ὁ ἄνθρωπος

Where these passages overlap the correspondence is identical, the difference arises in the amount of text they cite. The Lukan form is the most abbreviated, citing only Deut 8.3a. By contrast, while Matthew (like Luke) reproduces Deut 8.3a LXX exactly, he also includes a truncated form of the following phrase. Matthew probably abbreviated Deut 8.3b to avoid the duplication of the subject and finite verb, ζήσεται ὁ ἄνθρωπος, that is repeated in both halves of LXX Deut 8.3. Comparing the septuagintal form with the Hebrew of the MT, the most importance difference is that the term ῥήματι, contained in the phrase ἀλλ' ἐπὶ παντὶ ῥήματι τῷ ἐκπορευομένῳ διὰ στόματος θεοῦ ζήσεται ὁ ἄνθρωπος, is an epexegetical gloss on the Hebrew phrase (MT Deut 8.3). The correspondence of the Matthean and Lukan forms to the LXX form of Deut 8.3 strongly suggests the dependence of Q on a septuaginual text form at this point in the tradition. Whether one automatically is forced to accept Kloppenborg's argument that this shows the temptation narrative is a later element in Q is debatable. His conclusion arises from the prior decision to view Q as a document composed in Greek, but originating in a Galilean milieu, reflecting a Jewish scribal origin yet without strong allegiance to Torah. He suggests that it 'is perhaps significant that neither Moses nor David – associated with Torah learning and kingship – appears in Q's list of heroes.'[11] While not wanting to propose anything definite about the stratigraphy of Q, if one resists the tendency to separate the document into discrete layers then not only is the form of the citation suggestive of a Greek speaking origin for the document's use of scripture, it perhaps calls into question the notion that in its earliest stages it was either intentionally or unintentionally unconcerned with Torah as an authority source.

In Matthean order, the second temptation, which challenges Jesus' to cast himself down from the pinnacle of the temple, is accompanied by the supporting citation of Ps 91.11a, 12 (LXX Ps 90.11a, 12). Both the Lukan and Matthean forms of the citation replicate the septuagintal

---

temptation ('worship me') is most naturally put off until the end, where it has the most dramatic effect; (3) Luke's interest in the temple and Jerusalem could have moved him to turn the scene in the temple into the climax.' DAVIES/ALLISON, Matthew vol. 1, 364.

11 KLOPPENBORG, Excavating Q, 203.

text. Luke, however, gives a slightly longer form of the quotation by citing the first three words of LXX Ps 90.11b, τοῦ διαφυλάξαι σε. In the citations of Matthew and Luke the only alteration to the septuagintal form is the introduction of a conjunctive term (καί, so Matthew), or phrase (καί ὅτι, so Luke), which creates a smoother link between the truncated first part of the citation (90.11a), and the continuation of the quotation (90.12). Here again, the form follows the Greek translation of the passage from the Psalm, and its purpose is to portray an attempt by the devil to employ scripture to legitimate the validity of his own challenge to Jesus. As Marshall suggests, '[t]he temptation is, therefore, to prove the truth of God's promise by putting it to the test.'[12] Jesus once more answers the devil's challenge by citing a short snatch of scripture drawn from Deut 6.16, οὐκ ἐκπειράσεις κύριον τὸν θεόν σου. The correspondence between the Matthean, Lukan and septuagintal forms is identical.

The third temptation in Matthean sequence is a call for Jesus to pay homage to the devil. In line with the pattern established, the devil is rebuffed with a third citation from Deuteronomy. The form of Deut 6.13 cited in Matt 4.10//Lk 4.8 may initially be seen as problematic because it appear to deviate from both the MT and the LXX.

Matt 4.10//Lk 4.8 κύριον τὸν θεόν σου προσκυνήσεις καὶ αὐτῷ μόνῳ λατρεύσεις

LXX Deut 8.3   κύριον τὸν θεόν σου φοβηθήσῃ καὶ αὐτῷ λατρεύσεις

There are two differences between the Q form and that of the form of the LXX cited above. First, Matthew and Luke insert the addition word μόνῳ. Whether this is simply to emphasize the original meaning, which is particularly apposite to this context, or if this reflects a now no longer extant form of a Greek text of Deut 8.3 cannot be determined with certainty. The second difference is that of Matthew and Luke agreeing in the use of προσκυνήσῃς against the term φοβηθήσῃ as used in the LXX, which is a more natural synonym for תַּעֲבֹד, used in the MT. However, in Codex Alexandrinus προσκυνήσῃς is used in Deut 6.13. Admittedly, it would be possible to argue that the reading in Alexandrinus has been altered to confirm to the textual form contained in the temptation narrative.[13] This, however, is less likely than the simpler suggestion that Q knew a form of the Greek OT that used προσκυνήσῃς, and hence cited that form of the text. In many ways προσκυνήσῃς is a more dynamic translation, intended to communicate the underlying meaning of the Hebrew term, rather than rendering it with the more precisely equiva-

---

12   MARSHALL, Gospel of Luke, 173.
13   See HOLTZ, Untersuchungen, 62.

lent term φοβητήση. This may suggest that the version of the Greek OT used by the Q tradents, was one that made more concessions for a Greek speaking audience for whom the concept 'fear of the Lord' might be somewhat difficult to apprehend. Whether this implies anything about the ethnic make-up of the audience of Q is debatable; it may simply reflect the form of the septuagintal text which was most readily available.

There can be little doubt that in the temptation account scripture functions in an authoritative manner. However, one is still left with the specific question concerning the nature of its authority. The fact that Jesus himself is challenged with scripture in the second temptation, suggests that what actually carries authority for Q is scripture combined with dominical interpretation. Thus, incorrect use of the biblical text is countered by another scriptural citation wherein Jesus reveals himself not only as skilled in the deployment of biblical texts, but shows that unlike Israel, which provoked God in the wilderness by putting him to the test, Jesus is truly the son of God because he does not put God to the test. Here both Jesus' filial obedience and his correct interpretation of the biblical text establish the authority claims for Q. That authority base is not scriptural alone, but emerges from the understanding of scripture mediated through Jesus' understanding of it.[14]

2.2 John's Question (Q 7.18-19, 22-28, 31-35)

The next complex of material in Q to employ scriptural citations is found in the traditions contained in Lk 7.18-19, 22-28, 31-35//Matt 11.2-11, 16-19. While there are some differences in the various reconstructions of the Q text, many agree in terms of the broad contents.[15] Fortunately, the high level of verbatim agreement between the parallels for the two citations drawn from the Jewish scriptures makes reconstruction of the source text relatively straightforward at these two specific points in the tradition.

While the base form of the first Q quotation (Matt 11.5//Lk 7.22b) might be relatively simple to reconstruct, the process by which the composite citation was assembled is probably not recoverable. In response to the question posed by John's messengers concerning his identity, the Jesus of Q provides a list of six signs that they are to report to John, and from which inferences may be drawn concerning Jesus'

---

[14] For further discussion of critical issues surrounding this passage see ROBBINS, Testing of Jesus in Q.

[15] ROBINSON/HOFFMANN/KLOPPENBORG, Critical Edition of Q, 118-149; NEIRYNCK, Q-Parallels, 22-25; FLEDDERMANN, Q: A Reconstruction and Commentary, 353-369.

identity. Only four of the items in the list have a possible parallel to a textual element in Isaiah. The six items with possible Isaianic parallels are:

τυφλοὶ ἀναβλέπουσιν	(Isa 29.18; 35.5; 42.18)
χωλοὶ περιπατοῦσιν	
λεπροὶ καθαρίζονται	
καὶ κωφοὶ ἀκούουσιν	(Isa 29.18; 35.5; 42.18)
νεκροὶ ἐγείρονται	(Isa 26.19)
πτωχοὶ εὐαγγελίζονται	(Isa 61.1)

The short florilegium of Isaianic elements mixed with two items that 'are not related to any promises of the OT'[16] results in a curious list, the function of which is not altogether transparent. The author of this tradition may have wished to exploit the idea of the fulfilment of scripture in some generalized manner, but appears more concerned to describe the types of blessings brought about by Jesus which are seen as indications of his identity. The fact that four of the elements have Isaianic parallels, may point to an understanding of Jesus framed in prophetic terms. For Kloppenborg, this prophetic perspective is an important aspect of the depiction of both Jesus and John in Q.

> Once the Elijianic expectations are engaged, the question of Q 7:19-20 and its answer in 7:22 are less unnatural, since 7:22 also evokes qualities associated with Elijah. ... The interplay between various expectations associated with Elijah allows Q to distribute these qualities between John and Jesus and thus to negotiate the relationship between these two figures. John proclaims repentance and is the Elijianic messenger; Jesus is the Coming one who emulates Elijah's restorative ministry; both are children of Sophia.[17]

Therefore, this composite citation formed out of Isaianic and non-scriptural elements may be designed by the framer of this tradition to ascribe prophetic authority to Jesus. This may also be the function of the unique Lukan tradition (Lk 4.18-19a), which overlaps with two of the elements in Q 7.22.[18] Hence it appears that it is not scriptural authority *per se* that is attributed to Jesus in this passage, but that scripture testifies to Jesus' authoritative prophetic actions and identity.

The second citation in this unit also draws upon prophetic tropes and texts, but here applies them to John rather than Jesus. Yet, as the text explicitly states, the point is to identify John as *more* than a prophet. The citation is intended to emphasize this point. 'The scripture quota-

---

16   FITZMYER, Gospel according to Luke I-IX, 668.
17   KLOPPENBORG, Excavating Q, 123-124.
18   See FITZMYER, Gospel according to Luke I-IX, 668.

tion spells out the "more." John is the messenger sent to prepare Jesus' way. As the last and greatest prophet he prepares for the one who brings the old order to an end.'[19] This Q text (Matt 11.10//Lk 7.27; cf. Mk 1.2) combines Ex 23.20a and Mal 3.1a, again apparently in septuagintal form. The similarity between the openings of these two texts has resulted in the conflation of these two traditions.

> LXX Ex 23.20 καὶ ἰδοὺ ἐγὼ ἀποστέλλω τὸν ἄγγελόν μου πρὸ προσώπου σου ἵνα φυλάξῃ σε ἐν τῇ ὁδῷ
>
> LXX Mal 3.1a ἰδοὺ ἐγὼ ἐξαποστέλλω τὸν ἄγγελόν μου καὶ ἐπιβλέψεται ὁδὸν πρὸ προσώπου μου
>
> Q 7.27 b-c καὶ ἰδοὺ ἀποστέλλω τὸν ἄγγελόν μου πρὸ προσώπου σου, ὃς κατασκευάσει τὴν ὁδόν σου ἔμπροσθέν σου

There has been considerable freedom employed to adapt the biblical tradition to the meaning for which the author wishes to derive support. Scripture is a source of establishing authority in Q, but the primary conviction is that of allegiance to the perspectives and interpretations of Jesus. Textual tradition is made subservient to this agenda, and traditions are reshaped to emphasize that Jesus' declaration concerning John as greater than the prophets is not only attested by Jesus, but also has scriptural warrant.

2.3 Family Divisions (Q 12.51-53)

It is uncertain whether a direct parallel exists between Q 12.53 and Mic 7.6, or if the slight points of contact with the Jewish text reflects a saying that has evolved into a proverbial maxim, or even if the shared terminology is simple due to the coincidental use of reasonably common terminology. What is, however, more likely is that Matthew has recognized the potential resonance between the Q tradition and Mic 7.6, and made his form of the tradition a fairly unmistakable reference to the Micah text by adding a modified version of the last phrase of Mic 7.6.

> Mic 7.6d ἐχθροὶ ἀνδρὸς πάντες οἱ ἄνδρες οἱ ἐν τῷ οἴκῳ αὐτοῦ
>
> Matt 10.36 καὶ ἐχθροὶ τοῦ ἀνθρώπου οἱ οἰκιακοὶ αὐτοῦ

However, this parallel is Matthean *Sondergut* material and does not reflect the handling of scripture in Q. Somewhat curiously, Burkett argues that Matt 10.36 was part of the material that 'came to both Mat-

---

19 FLEDDERMANN, Q: A Reconstruction and Commentary, 382.

thew and Luke as pre-existing unit.'[20] However, he goes on to argue that this tradition, which is taken as best preserved in Matt 10.24-39, does not come from Q, but 'from a different source than the material we have identified as Q. It may have circulated independently as a short discourse or tract of prophetic exhortation.'[21]

It is perhaps helpful to classify this material as exhortation of a prophetic type, and this is supported by the resonance with ideas in Mic 7.6, which Matthew has made explicit through incorporating a direct citation of material from this prophetic text. Fleddermann, however, sees Matt 10.36 as part of the Q text although his reasons are not totally clear. Part of the reasoning appears to be that he feels much Lukan reworking has taken place with this tradition. Thus he states, '[i]t might seem that Luke preserves the original Q wording and that Matthew conformed the text to the Septuagint. But neither Matthew or Luke are close to the Septuagint, and the wording of Luke 12,52 suggests that the verse is a Lucan redactional formulation.'[22]

Given the uncertainty concerning the form of the Q saying behind Matt 10.34-34//Lk 12.51-53, whether Matt 10.36 was ever part of the Q source, and most significantly if Matt 10.36 was part of Q whether there is a trace of an allusion to LXX Mic 7.6, it appears best not to place too much weight on this material for determining the attitude to scripture in Q. At most, it shows that in the double tradition the prophetic-like message of Jesus had an expectation of disharmony and painful divisions. As such this might have brought some degree of comfort to those among whom this tradition circulated, for it both assures hearers that the experience of family rejection was not unexpected, and in the wider perspective of Q the life of discipleship is seen as providing a replacement kinship network.

2.4 The Parable of the Mustard Seed (Q 13.18-19)

This parable is one of the so-called Mark-Q overlap texts.[23] Kloppenborg states the case for the existence of two separate versions of the tradition in the following terms: 'the parable of the mustard seed (Q 13:18-21) existed in both Mark and Q, for there are significant Matthew-Luke agreements against Mark, and in each instance Matthew and

---

20 BURKETT, Rethinking, vol. 2, The Unity and Plurality of Q, 66.
21 BURKETT, Rethinking, vol. 2, The Unity and Plurality of Q, 67.
22 FLEDDERMANN, Q: A Reconstruction and Commentary, 643.
23 On Mark-Q overlaps in general see FLEDDERMANN, Mark and Q. For the parable of the mustard seed, see 90-99.

Luke have a much longer version than the Markan account.'[24] Actually, contrary to Kloppenborg's versification, the Mustard seed is contained in Q 13.18-19, with the parable of the leaven in Q 13.20-21. These two parables form a thematically related pairing, and the fact that this combination is preserved by both Matthew and Luke also suggests that this pairing stood together in Q. Matthew (Matt 13.31-32) has, however, conflated the Q form of the mustard seed with the Markan version (Mk 4.30-32). Furthermore, both Matthew and Luke appear to have produced redactional introductions to this pair of parables. Overall the Lukan form is usually adjudged to be closer to the putative underlying Q form.[25]

A possible reference to a scriptural text occurs at the conclusion to the parable in both the Markan and Q forms.

Matt 13.32 ὥστε ἐλθεῖν τὰ πετεινὰ τοῦ οὐρανοῦ καὶ κατασκηνοῦν ἐν τοῖς κλάδοις αὐτοῦ

Lk 13.19 καὶ τὰ πετεινὰ τοῦ οὐρανοῦ κατεσκήνωσεν ἐν τοῖς κλάδοις αὐτοῦ

Mk 4.32 ὥστε δύνασθαι ὑπὸ τὴν σκιὰν αὐτοῦ τὰ πετεινὰ τοῦ οὐρανοῦ κατασκηνοῦν

LXX Ps 103.12 ἐπ' αὐτὰ τὰ πετεινὰ τοῦ οὐρανοῦ κατασκηνώσει ἐκ μέσου τῶν πετρῶν δώσουσιν φωνήν

The correspondence between the Q version and LXX Ps 103.12 involves two elements the phrase τὰ πετεινὰ τοῦ οὐρανοῦ and differing verbal forms of κατασκηνόω. However, there are important differences, in particular the birds do not live in the 'branches' (or 'shade', cf. Mk 4.32) of the mustard tree 'but among the rocks', ἐκ μέσου τῶν πετρῶν. The parallel is closer with the MT, which speaks of the birds having their habitations among branches (MT Ps 104.12). The use of this scriptural resonance in the synoptic tradition makes no explicit reference to its wider biblical context or origin. There is no attempt to derive any authoritative support for the sentiments expressed in the parable from the textual allusion. This raises the question whether the possible allusion is an intentional biblical reference, or whether the phrase has simply entered the wider cultural vocabulary without any ongoing connection to its possible origin. Again, the possible use of scripture is not a factor that is particularly significant for the meaning or authority of this dominical pronouncement. It may simply function to provide a scriptural assonance to the tone of language employed by the Jesus of Q. This

---

24 KLOPPENBORG, Excavating Q, 92.
25 FLEDDERMANN, Q: A Reconstruction and Commentary, 658.

idea of Q exploiting the tone of common biblical language is reinforced by the fact that similar language also occurs in Ezekiel:

LXX Ezek 17.23 καὶ πᾶν πετεινὸν ὑπὸ τὴν σκιὰν αὐτοῦ ἀναπαύσεται τὰ κλήματα αὐτοῦ ἀποκατασταθήσεται

Furthermore, the Markan phrase ὑπὸ τὴν σκιὰν αὐτοῦ finds an exact parallel in the Theodotianic version of Dan 4.21. This traditional element contained in the parable of the mustard seed reflects biblical language, but does not directly cite or draw upon the wider context of the scriptural language employed.

2.5 Those who do not know the Lord (Q 13.25-27)

Rejection is the promised fate of those who find the door of the kingdom shut to them (Q 13.25), or who cry to the Lord without knowing him (Q 13.26). The Lord's response to these plaintive and hollow calls is narrated in Q 13.27, which consists of three elements: a short phrase introducing speech, the first part of a dominical pronouncement of rejection stating 'I do not know from where you are', and the citation of a scriptural text sending the reject people away. It is this final element that provides further evidence for the deployment of scriptural language in Q.

Lk 13.27c   ἀπόστητε ἀπ' ἐμοῦ πάντες ἐργάται ἀδικίας
Matt 7.23c   ἀποχωρεῖτε ἀπ' ἐμοῦ οἱ ἐργαζόμενοι τὴν ἀνομίαν
LXX Ps 6.9a ἀπόστητε ἀπ' ἐμοῦ πάντες οἱ ἐργαζόμενοι τὴν ἀνομίαν

While it is obvious that LXX Ps 6.9a stands behind the Q form of wording, it is the determination of the details of the reconstruction of the Q tradition that is problematic, since Matthew and Luke differ from the septuagintal form in different ways. It is difficult to determine whether Matthew and Luke have each independently modified the Q form to make it correspond to the scriptural citation more closely, or have altered it so it varies from the biblical text to a greater extent but reflects the theological agendas of the evangelists to a greater extent.[26]

The purpose of the citation is to highlight the theme of rejection. Pao and Schnabel argue that the Psalm is quoted 'to emphasize not

---

[26] Fleddermann suggests that the evangelists have redacted their respective versions in ways that reduce the higher degree of correspondence with LXX Ps 6.a in the Q text. Thus, it is argued that Luke 'preserves the original expression ἀπόστητε', since Matthew doesn't like ἀπίσθημι, a word he never uses.' FLEDDERMANN, Q: A Reconstruction and Commentary, 685.

only that Jesus does not know them, but also that he positively excludes them.'²⁷ Furthermore, they raise the following possibility:

> Unless Jesus uses the words of Ps. 6:8 only to add solemnity, we note that in Ps. 6 the speaker is someone who suffers and is subsequently vindicated by God, and that in 13.27-28 he refers to weeping and gnashing of teeth. This suggests that Jesus may have used the language of Ps. 6:8 in order to describe himself as the one who has suffered at the hands of hostile opponents and will pronounce judgment against those who heard but opposed his message to be excluded from the heavenly banquet.²⁸

Attributing such a pivotal role to LXX Ps 6.9a in generating this meaning appears to over-theologize the significance of the scriptural citation. The exclusion of opponents is present in the pericope without an allusion to from the context of the Psalm as the basis for representing Jesus as a vindicated sufferer. Therefore it does indeed appear that the words of the Psalm are used simply to emphasize the key point of the pericope by solemnizing its sentiments with language that has a scriptural tone.

2.6 Lament over Jerusalem (Q 13.34-35)

This lament uttered by Jesus, again places him in the prophetic tradition. Such pronouncements against Jerusalem are found in the Jewish scriptures in passages such as Isa 3.8; 51.17; Jer 6.8. For those who heard this saying in a post-Easter context the irony of Jesus declaring Jerusalem as the 'city that murders prophets' would not be read simple a reference to the distant history of the fate of the prophets, but also as prediction from the recent past that portrayed Jesus' own death as aligning with the murdered prophets. The conclusion to this lament corresponds exactly to the text of the citation from Ps 118.26 = LXX Ps 117.26:

LXX Ps 117.26 εὐλογημένος ὁ ἐρχόμενος ἐν ὀνόματι κυρίου

This may lead to the supposition that this tradition sought to echo the text of the Psalm, and perhaps for readers to draw on the wider context of the citation to inform an understanding of its intended meaning. Such is the opinion of Pao and Schnabel, who in relation to the Lukan usage state that '[i]t is unlikely that Luke did not recognize these words as a quotation from Ps. 118.'²⁹ Although this Psalm is an individual thanksgiving, given its connections with military victory and kingly triumphs, others have seen it as a royal Psalm. Given this interpreta-

---

27 PAO/SCHNABEL, 'Luke', 335.
28 PAO/SCHNABEL, 'Luke', 335.
29 PAO/SCHNABEL, 'Luke', 337.

tion, the use of the Psalm in the Lukan context is sometimes understood as signalling the Lord's salvific purpose, combined with messianic overtones.[30] Notwithstanding such interpretations, this phrase from Psalm 118 was used as a Passover greeting chanted to pilgrims arriving in Jerusalem. This is documented from a variety of Rabbinic sources.[31] Given the wide currency of this verse as a free-floating element as part of the Passover festival, it may well be the case that it was employed in Q without consideration of its original context in the Psalm.

Unlike the use of this citation in the Lukan narrative, where the prediction finds its fulfillment at the triumphal entry into Jerusalem (Lk 19.38), the usage in Q leaves open the conditions of fulfillment. It is not possible to tell whether it envisages the possibility of repentance before the parousia, or if it sees a begrudging acknowledgment of Jesus' status at his second coming by those who will pronounce such sentiments when it is too late.[32] Thus certainty is not possible, and it is difficult to determine whether final judgment or the possibility of a delayed repentance is the purpose of the citation. However, it may simply be the case that this widely-known formula is cited here because it is a standard greeting for non-residents arriving at the city of Jerusalem.

3. References to Biblical Characters in Q

At various points in Q and for differing purposes a range of Old Testament characters are mentioned. However, what is perhaps striking is the fact that there is no mention of Moses in Q. This may be coincidental, or it may reflect a bias towards the prophetic strand of Jewish religious heritage. Combined with repeated references to prophetic figures this does reveal a strong indebtedness to the voice of the prophets, although it is not possible to infer that a diminution in allegiance to Torah is necessarily intended.

3.1 Abraham and other Patriarchs

The first character from the Jewish scriptures mentioned in Q is Abraham. There are two references to the patriarch. In the context of John's preaching, he warns those addressed as a 'brood of vipers' not to place their confidence in Abraham as their father (Q 3.8). Here John juxta-

---

30   See GREEN, Gospel of Luke, 538, 709. See also, PAO/SCHNABEL, 'Luke', 337.
31   STRACK/BILLERBECK, Kommentar, 845-850.
32   FLEDDERMANN, Q: A Reconstruction and Commentary, 706.

poses false reliance on descent from Abraham, with the imperative of producing fruit worthy of repentance. As Manson comments, 'John addresses his audience as "offspring of vipers" is sharp contrast to their own thought of themselves as children of Abraham.'[33] It would be going too far to read an implied criticism of Abraham here, although the attitude toward him is ambiguous. Rather, the explicit critique is against those who derive religious confidence on the basis of physical descent from the patriarch. Some commentators have also seen a critique of the sentiments expressed in Isa 51.1-2 being encapsulated in this verse. The text counsels its hearers to 'look to the rock from which you were hewn, and to the quarry from which you were dug. Look to Abraham your father and to Sarah who bore you' (Isa 51.1-2a). If this reference to the Isaianic passage is intended by Q, then its purpose appears to be an inversion of the perspective that this text presents. As Alison observes, if the allusion were intended the relationship would then be antithetical. 'Although Isa 51:1-2 holds out hope that Israel will be restored because of the promises to Abraham, John declares that descent from the patriarch does not necessarily mean inclusion in Israel.'[34]

The second reference to Abraham occurs in the formulaic expression 'Abraham and Isaac and Jacob' (Q 13.28). Here the promise given is that many will share in the eschatological banquet with the three patriarchs. While the three figures feature prominently in Genesis and other sections of the Hebrew bible, there is no depiction of the three reclining at an eschatological banquet.[35] Green wishes to link the two Abrahamic references contained in Q. He states 'some who claim Abraham as father will be forbidden access to Abraham's table, not because they have miscalculated their family tree but because status among those being saved is not inherited.'[36] However, such an interpretative link is not suggested by Q. Thus, the two references to Abraham contained in the text of Q occur in an *ad hoc* manner, and the identity of the patriarch is subsidiary to the main point being made in the two pericopae. Hence the figure of Abraham is not tightly linked to any particular scriptural text, nor does Q derive any authority for its message from the references to Abraham.

---

33 MANSON, The Sayings of Jesus, first published as part II of The Mission and Message of Jesus, 40.
34 ALISON, Intertextual Jesus, 103.
35 There are references to a future banquet Isa 25.6; 55.1-2; 65.13-14; Zeph 1.7, but without mentioning any of the patriarchs.
36 GREEN, Gospel of Luke, 532.

3.2 The Prophets

A more prominent group in the text of Q is the prophets, Q 6.23; 11.47, 49, 50; 13.34; 16.16; and in the combined phrase 'prophets and kings/righteous' 10.24. The first reference is a generic description of the persecution of such figures, 'for thus they persecuted the prophets before you' (Q 6.23).[37] While there are references to prophets being persecuted in various scriptural texts, and although this theme is developed in various writings that emerged in the intertestamental period, the Q text is not indebted to any specific textual reference for its maxim concerning persecuted prophets. Rather, this motif is deployed as a generally received truism, and in particular one that resonates with the values of the hearers of Q. As Bovon notes '[t]he Q community clarifies its self-understanding in v.23c: its role within Israel is a prophetic one, and its persecution confirms this understanding.'[38]

The second reference to prophets in Q comes as the culmination of a pericope that described the privileged revelatory position of believers in Jesus (Q 10.21-24). In the double tradition 'prophets' are paired 'righteous' in the Matthean form of the saying (Matt 13.17) and with 'kings' in Luke (Lk 10.24). Given that δικαι- 'righteousness' terminology is Matthean redactionally favoured language, a strong case can be mounted for the originality of the Lukan pairing 'prophets and kings'.[39] Such a combination does not have an antecedent in the Jewish scriptures.[40] Therefore, at this point the Q text draws upon the general concept of 'prophets', without alluding to any specific scriptural tradition. The sentiment of the addressees of the Q text being in a privileged position in comparison with even the prophets of former generations, reflects the same idea that surrounds the present generation's status in regard to John (cf. Q 7.28).

The series of woes (Q 11.39-52) contains three references to 'the prophets' (Q 11.47, 49, 50). In each of these woes, the prophets are held up as exemplary figures whose behaviour highlights the hypocrisy of

---

[37] The reconstruction of the text of Q is not entirely secure at this point. The verb may be either 'persecute' (cf. Matt 5.12), or 'do to' (cf. Lk 6.23). If the Lukan text is the original reading the meaning is not radically altered since the verb refers back to the actions depicted in 6.22 were community members experience 'rejection and revulsion', which are forms of social persecution.

[38] BOVON, Luke 1, 228.

[39] As reflected by both the IQP and the Critical Edition of Q. See NEIRYNCK, Q-Parallels, 84-85.

[40] There are some verses that contain both terms in close proximity, 2 Kgs 3.13; Neh 9.32; Jer 2.26; 8.1; 13.13; 32.32; Dan 9.6, but in none of these do the two terms occur as a co-ordinated pair.

'the Pharisees' (Q 11.39, 42), who are accused of being punctilious with halakhic minutiae. Here the prophets are claimed by the framers of Q as aligning with their own perspectives, which they view as representing the core religious requirements to practice justice and mercy (Q 11.42). This has echoes with the prophetic call to align one's practices with the major themes of the law (Mic 6.8).[41] This conceptual background sets up the transition in the woes sequence to more direct references to the prophets. The first explicit use of the term 'prophets' accuses opponents of building up the tombs of the prophet (Q 11.47). The bitter irony for Q stems from the fact that it sees its foundational figure and its ongoing religious commitments as aligning with prophetic perspectives, which opponents are attempting to suppress even though they superficially (from the perspective of Q) honour the historic prophets. As Manson comments,

> In the second woe the attitude of the scribes to prophecy is challenged. Put in a word the criticism is: The only prophet you honour is a dead prophet. … The reference to the building of tombs for the prophets may be bitter irony. … It is possible that here Jesus is hitting at the absolute supremacy given by the scribes to the Law. … in the scribal view the Law was supreme. Prophecy could confirm, but could not reform it.[42]

In contrast with the veneration shown to dead prophets, Q accuses the ancestors of its opponents of slaughtering the prophets that were sent to them (Q 11.49-50). From this perspective, the persecution experienced by the prophets in the past becomes paradigmatic as an explanation for why Q adherents experience rejection and persecution in their contemporary situation, namely because they stand in the prophetic tradition.[43]

In the lament over Jerusalem (Q 13.34) the inhabitants of that city are accused of killing prophets and those sent there (cf. the combination of 'prophets and apostles' in Q 11.50). The language of extreme persecution raises the question of whether any were known to the compilers of Q who had been executed or murdered. It appears that the pattern of

---

41 Although Q does not explicitly cite Mic 6.8, if the Matthean form (Matt 23.23) of the saying in Q 11.42 is closer to the original wording, then the pairing of 'justice and mercy' may be a resonance with Micah's prophetic plea for ethically motivated religious attitude.
42 MANSON, Sayings of Jesus, 101.
43 The applicability of this saying to the contemporary circumstances of those hearers of Q may have been increased if they saw the term 'prophets' as also being a reference to such figures in their own communities. While the context demands that the priority given to prophets in the expression 'prophets and apostles' suggests these as the historic prophets of the Jewish scriptures, as Marshall notes, '[i]t is possible, however, that the early church saw here an allusion to Christian prophets.' MARSHALL, Gospel of Luke, 504.

persecuted prophets is viewed as applying to the contemporary situation because of rejection of its proclamation concerning Jesus, rather than stemming from the experience of extreme physical persecution. Tuckett understands the intense polemic in Q to be a rhetorical device, and in relation to this passage in the following terms.

> There is, however, no need to assume that the killings and stonings reflect the present experience of Q Christians. ... Given the nature of the audience elsewhere in Q, which all seems to indicate that any physical violence related to the past and the present is characterized by a situation of at most verbal animosity and insulting gestures, it would seem best to interpret 13:34f. in the same way. The speaker is looking back at the past, and sees past examples of prophetic deaths (or perhaps better, refers to such a standard topos). But this does not necessarily say anything about the present.[44]

Once again, Q is not alluding to any specific text about the prophets, but is rather is drawing upon a wider pattern of thought that sees prophets as examples of those murdered and persecuted for their religious message.

The final reference to prophets in Q, occurs in the stock phrase 'the law and the prophets' (Q 16.16, but cf. Matt 11.13 'the prophets and the law'). The sentiment that 'the law and the prophets were until John', places some type of temporal limitation on the validity of this pairing as an authority source at least from the stand-point of Q. This insight is often softened, by referring to the 'salvation history' perspective of the text. Such a description may blunt they radical stance enshrined in this statement. The meaning of the term 'the law and the prophets' may need to be understood in a fuller way, so it is not taken as a simple circumlocution for Hebrew Bible revelatory texts. Drawing attention to the contrast with the phrase 'kingdom of God' is the second half of the clause which refers both to a new revelation and the community which safeguards that teaching, Fleddermann suggest that 'we need to interpret "the Law and the prophets" as both the OT revelation and the community it called into existence.'[45] Here it is possible to see, in the vision Q, the belief that those who hold to the teaching of Jesus as being a new prophetic community transmitting his new teaching.

3.3 Jonah and the Ninevites

After the Beelzebul controversy (Q 11.14-15, 17-26), another Mk-Q overlap text occurs in the Lukan order of double tradition material (Q 11.16, 29-32), whereas in Matthew the demand for a sign (Matt 12.38-42) is

---

44 TUCKETT, Q and the History of Early Christianity, 314.
45 FLEDDERMANN, Q: A Reconstruction and Commentary, 790.

embedded within the Beelzebul narrative (Matt 12.22-30, 43-45).[46] Here Q reveals knowledge of only two details of the Jonah story, namely that Jonah was a sign to the Ninevites (Q 11.29-30) and that when he preached to the inhabitants of Ninevah they repented (Q 11.32; cf. Jon 3.5-9). While the text of Jonah does not describe Jonah as 'a sign' to the Ninevites, it is not a huge interpretative leap to represent Jonah in this way. In fact the term 'sign' may be part of the Q redaction, which suggested linking the Beelzebul tradition with that of Jesus' reference to Jonah. In Q, no explanation is given as to what constitutes 'the sign of Jonah', although the Matthean gloss on the Q form of the tradition explicates the sign as Jonah's three day interment in the sea-monster which then is seen as proleptically pointing to the Son of Man being in the earth for the same period (Matt 12.40).

Edwards has argued that the saying concerning the refusal of a sign is a pre-Markan tradition, to which Q added the exceptive clause referring to the sign of Jonah.[47] The sign of Jonah is illustrative of repentance as a response to prophetic preaching. Edwards goes further than this and suggests there are two important features present in the mind of the Q community concerning this prophetic figure. 'Jonah is the one who escapes death and is raised by God to become the preacher to the Gentiles. Jonah is the one who preaches judgment and warning to the Ninevites, who demands that they prepare for an imminent judgment.'[48] While the first element is present in the text of Jonah, it is not exploited in the Q reference, which rather appears simply to confront those with supposed nationalistic privileges with the examples of those who repent without the background in Judaism. However, this should not be overplayed as being a mandate for Gentile mission. The second point may be closer to the Q emphasis, which appears to be that the sign of Jonah is the repentance produced in those who receive his message. Therefore Q does not derive its authority for its self-understanding as a prophetic community, calling fellow Jews to repentance from the scriptural text itself. Instead, having first come to the self-understanding that its message of repentance is correct and in line with prophetic proclamations it finds convenient support for this position in the story of Jonah's preaching to the Ninevites.

---

46 On the relationship between between the versions of the 'Demand for a Sign' pericope in Q (Q 11.16, 29-32) and in Mark (8.11-13), see FLEDDERMANN, Mark and Q, 126-134.
47 EDWARDS, Sign of Jonah, 55-58, 80.
48 EDWARDS, Sign of Jonah, 57.

3.4 Solomon and the Queen of the South (Q 11.31)

Embedded within the pericope concerning the sign of Jonah, there is a second example that also draws support from a scriptural text. Like the Ninevites who will rise up to judge the current generation, the Queen of the South will do the same, according to Q, because the present generation have the opportunity to respond to a wisdom greater than even that of Solomon. The intertext for this scriptural reference is 1 Kgs 10.1-10, where the Queen of Sheba visits Solomon, and all of her questions were answered (1 Kgs 10.3). The editorial comment that follows is that 'the Queen of Sheba perceived all the wisdom of Solomon' (1 Kgs 10.4). Beyond the name of the two main protagonists, the visit of the Queen of Sheba, and the motif of wisdom there is no detailed use of the text of the story. Again the Q handling of this tradition does not place undue weight on the fact that the Queen of the South was a Gentile, although combined with other statements in Q regarding Gentiles it may reflect a positive attitude to inclusion of non-Jews as recipients of Jesus' teaching.[49] The purpose falls on emphasizing those who seek wisdom, as a contrast to the current generation, which rejects even greater wisdom when it is presented directly to it. Fleddermann comments on this antithetical depiction. 'In contrast, "this generation" does not accept Jesus' wisdom when it is offered to them, and they do not heed his call to repentance. The term "this generation" is a technical term that refers to the people Israel in its sinfulness.'[50]

The example of the Queen of the South is closely paralleled with the repentance displayed by the Ninevites.[51] Both illustrations are based on stories derived from the Jewish scriptures. They are not the primary authority source for Q in pronouncing its message of repentance. That primary authority is found in the person of Jesus, whom Q describes as greater than Jonah (Q 11.32), and greater than the wisdom of Solomon (Q 11.31). However, Q does derive a kind of secondary authority from the scripture, which does serve not as the basis for the convictions that are held, but instead legitimates such prior convictions by showing that they actually align with certain typological examples contained in the Hebrew Bible.

---

49 This point is made by Tuckett, who observes that this 'is however not an isolated reference to Gentiles in such a context in Q and may have some significance for determining the attitude of Q to Gentiles.' TUCKETT, Q and the History of Early Christianity, 189.
50 FLEDDERMANN, Q: A Reconstruction and Commentary, 512.
51 MANSON, Sayings of Jesus, 91.

3.5 Abel and Zechariah (Q 11.51)

The polemic against this generation in Q 11 finds bitter vent in the accusation that not only the blood of the prophets (Q11.50), but all blood shed from the time of Abel to that of Zechariah 'shall be required of this generation' (Q 11.51). While the identity of Abel is self-evident, that of Zechariah is less obvious. In Matthew the ambiguous double tradition designation 'Zechariah' is clarified with the explanatory note 'the son of Berechiah' (Matt 23.35). If this interpretation correctly reflects the character designated by Q then the intention is to charge 'this generation' with the blood of all victims of murder recorded in scripture, from the first case, Abel, to what many have seen as the last example, namely Zechariah son of Berechiah (2 Chr 24.21). This interpretation may make sense for Matthew,[52] and it may be the one intended by Q, although certainty is not possible.[53] It may not be insignificant, given the interest in prophets in Q, that a strand of Jewish tradition portrayed Zechariah son of Berechiah as a prophet (cf. Josephus, *Ant.* 9.169; and perhaps also Lam 2.20, 2 Chr 24.20, *b.San.* 96b)

Regardless of the identity of the Zechariah denoted by Q, the intention of this text is to heighten the polemic against those who reject the proclamation of the message of Jesus, by attributing to them all the blood of the righteous shed from the time of Abel to that of Zechariah. The details of these characters known from biblical traditions (if Zechariah is a biblical figure) are unimportant for the compositors of Q. Rather they are used as well-known tropes for victims of murder who are considered innocent and righteous. Thus the charges laid against

---

52 Davies and Alison style the murder of Zechariah as the last murder recorded in the bible. The state, '[b]y "last" we refer to a literary, not chronological fact. (Jer 26.20-3 records a later martyrdom.) – Today Chronicles concludes the Hebrew Bible and presumably it already did in some first-century collections; see *b. B. Bat.* 14b.' DAVIES/ALLISON, Gospel according to Saint Matthew, 319, n.50. However, the supposition that there was fixed canonical order, especially as the Jewish scriptures were not gathered together in a codex, may detract slightly from this theory.

53 Fitzmyer notes an exegetical preference for seeing the Zechariah mentioned in Lk 11.51 as the son of Berechiah because he is the last named person to be murdered in the final book of the Hebrew canon. However, he immediately raises the various problems that attend this interpretation. 'But was the so-called Hebrew canon closed or formed at the time that this saying of Jesus was fashioned (or recorded in "Q")? What guarantee is there that the order of books was the same then as it is today in the MT. Indeed, one might argue from this reference that it was. But that really has to be established independently of this reference in order to make certain the identity of Zechariah here. In deed in codex L of the Hebrew OT, Chronicles stands at the head of the "Writings".' FITZMYER, Gospel according to Luke X-XXIV, 951. Notwithstanding these comments, somewhat idiosyncratically, Fitzmyer argues that the phrase 'son of Berechiah' stood in Q.

this generation are inflated from responsibility for the blood of the prophets (Q 11.50) of whom Q followers see themselves as the continuing representatives of the prophetic tradition, into the outlandish claim that all righteous blood shed will be attributed against those who reject the message that Q announces.

3.6 Noah (Q 17.26-27)

The reconstruction of the apocalyptic discourse, which includes some of the material in Lk 17.22-37, is problematic. Many older reconstructions included all of Lk 17.22-37 as a block of Q material.[54] Streeter appreciated the difficulties, but was optimistic in his maximalistic attribution of the entire section to Q. He answers the question he frames in the following terms. 'Can we, in spite of considerable verbal differences, hold that the whole section, Lk xvii. 22-37, which has been described as "the Apocalypse of Q" has been legitimately named? I think so.'[55] If Streeter were correct, then apart from the reference to the biblical figure of Noah (Lk 17.26-27), Q would also make use of the figures of Lot (Lk 17.28-29) and his wife (Lk 17.32). Alison accepts Lk 17.28-29 as Q material, although he is more cautious about Lk 17.32. Concerning Lk 17.28-29 he states, 'Luke continues with a parallel passage about Lot. It should probably be assigned to Q: the language is not especially Lukan, Q is fond of co-ordinated sayings, Noah and Lot and their generations were traditionally paired.'[56] Whereas for Lk 17.31-32 he simply states '[t]his is sometimes assigned to Q.'[57] Consequently, he discusses these two figures as part of the use of scripture by Q.[58] However, most recent reconstructions omit Lk 17.31-32, and many do not include Lk 17.28-29. The IQP reconstructs the Q material as 'Q 17,?20-21?.23-24.37.26.27.30.34-35', with 'Q 17,33 after 14,27'.[59] This is followed by *The Critical Edition of Q*, but with verses 28-29 included between question marks, which shows their presence is doubtful.[60] Fleddermann's reconstruction is nearly identical to the IQP, but with verses 20-21 omitted,

---

54 For instance see STREETER, Four Gospels, 271-294; MANSON, Sayings of Jesus, 16.
55 STREETER, Four Gospels, 287.
56 ALISON, Intertextual Jesus, 95.
57 ALISON, Intertextual Jesus, 97.
58 ALISON, Intertextual Jesus, 6, 95-100.
59 For a convenient display of the IQP reconstruction see NEIRYNCK, Q-Parallels, 84-85.
60 ROBINSON/HOFFMANN/KLOPPENBORG, Critical Edition of Q, 512-521. Although Kloppenborg's own opinion is that the inclusion of Lk 17.28-29 in Q is 'probable'; see KLOPPENBORG, Excavating Q, 100.

and not even marked as doubtful.⁶¹ Among older reconstructions, Harnack also omitted the material in Lk 17.28-29, 31-31 from his listing of Q material.⁶² Therefore, because the references concerning Lot and his wife occur in Lukan *Sondergut* passages, and Luke can at times supplement Q material with thematically related traditions (consider the triad of parables in Lk 15.3-32),⁶³ the most secure approach to discussing Q material would appear not to discuss the figures of Lot and his wife since there inclusion in Q is doubtful.

The figure of Noah is utilized in Q to illustrate the foolish actions of the majority of people in contrast to the righteous few who prepare for coming judgment. The story of Noah is narrated in considerable detail in the biblical account (Gen 5.28-9.29). However, Q is concerned with only a few details of the story. The period of this antediluvian character is simple described as 'the days of Noah' (Q 17.26a, cf. 17.27b). This language is important since it allows the framers of Q to set up the contrast with 'the day of the Son of Man'. While the phrase 'the days of Noah' is part of the Genesis account (Gen 9.29), in that context it has no eschatological overtones, but is used in the formulaic expression that occurs at the end of the life of characters described in Genesis 1-11 to report the duration of lifespan. The second detail is the description that the majority of people 'were eating and drinking, marrying and being given in marriage' (Q 17.27a). Again there is no direct citation of scripture here, although the general idea is present in the Genesis account (cf. Gen 6.1-6, 11-13). The story of the Nephalim (Gen 6.1-4) may inform the depiction of 'marrying and being given in marriage', perhaps with the passive expression picking up the sentiment in Gen 6.2 that the sons of God 'took' the daughters of men. Given the fascination that surrounded Gen 6.1-4 in intertestamental literature as seen in the expansive rewritings of this tradition it may have been in the mind of those who created or transmitted this apocalyptic discourse. However, it is equally possible that the pairing 'marrying and being given in marriage' is simply structured to balance the previous double clause of 'eating and drinking' (Q 17.27a). The Q account also mentions Noah's entrance into the ark (Q 17.27b), but not the fact he was accompanied by other members of his family (cf. Gen 7.1, 7, 13). Finally the destruction of those who were not in the ark is mentioned by Q (Q 17.27c), which is a detail described in greater detail in the Genesis narrative (Gen 7.21-23).

---

61 FLEDDERMANN, Q: A Reconstruction and Commentary, 827.
62 HARNACK, Sayings of Jesus, 145-146.
63 This assessment holds regardless of whether one attributes the second parable, that of the lost coin, to Q or to Lukan special tradition.

The purpose of Q in recalling the story of Noah in such general terms is to create an 'expanded comparison between the days of Noah and the day of the Son of Man.'[64] The figure of Noah is particularly apposite to the understanding of the coming eschatological judgment contained in Q. In contrast to Markan view of a series of apocalyptic portents that lead to the eschaton (Mk 13.5-31), in Q, the phrase 'as in the time of Noah', is utilized to emphasize that normality characterizes the period before impending judgment.[65] Therefore, the Lukan preamble to this Q material correctly understands the eschatological perspective of Q when it states 'the kingdom of God is not coming with observation' (Lk 17.20). Once again, scripture is quarried by those that assembled this apocalyptic material, in order to find biblical support for their view of the eschaton. The biblical example of Noah corroborates the prior theological understanding of the community. Consequently it provides a further authoritative warrant for a view already held. For this reason only, those sparse details of the Noah story that support this perspective are included, while the bulk of the story is irrelevant to the purpose of Q in this apocalyptic discourse.

4. Scriptural Locations and Supernatural Figures[66]

The geography of the bible also impinges on the Q document. This is unsurprising, since the location for the events described in Q overlaps at points with those contained in the Jewish scriptures. There is a strong typological patterning between the wilderness in the Exodus account, and the depiction of Jesus' temptations in the wilderness (Q 4.1-13). In this pericope scriptural traditions heavily shape the account of the testing of Jesus. Other references to places are less indebted to the traditions that accompany the same locations in the scriptures. Perhaps Jerusalem as a place where prophets are murdered (Q 13.34) may echo ideas about their abuse in that city, but those sentiments may reflect a general conceptual topos, rather than a specific biblical text.[67] Other places referred to in Q which are also mentioned in the Jewish scriptures include 'the temple' = 'your house' (Q 4.9; 13.35), Sodom (Q 10.12), Hades (Q 10.15), Genenna (Q 12.5). Also heaven has numerous references (Q 6.23; 10.15, 21; 11.13, 16; 12.33; 16.17). However, these are

---

64 FLEDDERMANN, Q: A Reconstruction and Commentary, 834.
65 See MANSON, Sayings of Jesus, 143.
66 Here use has been made of the lists supplied by Dale Alison. See ALISON, Intertextual Jesus, 6.
67 As Manson states '[t]he reputation of Jerusalem as a place where the prophets are murdered is hard to understand.' MANSON, Sayings of Jesus, 126-127.

more likely to reflect wider religious and cultural usage, rather than being indebted to any specific biblical texts.

In Q there are multiple references to God, or to the term κύριος as an equivalent. The term θεός occurs at least nine times.[68] The Spirit is referenced on at least three occasions (Q 3.16; 4; 12.10), and heavenly beings such as angels are mentioned twice (Q 4.10; 12.8-9). Q also has an interest in demonic figures: demons (Q 7.33; 11.14, 15, 19, 20; Beelzebul (Q 11.15, 19); Satan (Q 11.18), and the devil (Q 4.2, 3, 5, 13). While the wider conceptual background for each of these characters is informed by the Jewish scriptures, there is not a direct or exclusive relationship between the portrayal in Q and that of any specific biblical text.

5. Conclusions

To speak of 'scriptural authority' in Q, may fundamentally obscure a correct understanding of how scripture and scriptural traditions are used in the document. The biblical text is not understood as the primary source of authority in Q, rather that role is given to Jesus, his words, and his proclamation of the kingdom. Scripture plays a supporting role in Q. It functions to legitimate the teachings and perspectives of the Jesus of Q. In one pericope it does play a noticeably different role. In the temptation narrative, scripture is used as a weapon in a spiritual joust. Yet, the citation of scripture does more than defend Jesus from the assault of his opponent, it portrays Jesus as God's faithful son. Thus Green notes,

> The deployment of these scriptural texts in the production of this new text opens the door to a particularly fertile discursive play; we hear a virtual choir of voices telling this story and giving it significance. The similarities are sufficient in scope and quantity to show that the narrator has drawn attention deliberately to Jesus in his representative role as Israel, God's son.[69]

The striking differences in this pericope from other Q passages, both in its use of scripture and in its narrative genre, have led some to suggest that it is a late addition to the core of the Q material.[70] This may be the case, although it is not impossible that disparate materials were gathered into Q at its inception as a collection of preformed traditions.

---

68 See the concordance to Q in The Critical Edition. The difficulty with providing firm figures is a reflection of the varying reconstructions of the document. See ROBINSON/HOFFMANN/KLOPPENBORG, Critical Edition of Q, 563-581.
69 GREEN, Gospel of Luke, 193.
70 Kloppenborg sees Q 4.1-13 as the most substantial addition to the Q text in its final redaction – his so-called Q3 layer; the other elements being Q 11.42c and Q 16.17. KLOPPENBORG, Formation of Q, 212-213.

Notwithstanding the slightly anomalous use of scripture in the temptation narrative, in the other Q pericopae a more consistent attitude towards scripture emerges. Biblical texts and imagery appear to have a secondary authority, that is they reinforces views that are already entrenched in the theology of Q. There is also a strong commitment to the prophetic tradition in a generalized form, which may reflect the view Q adherents held concerning their foundational figure and their own ongoing role in the salvific plan. Like the prophets, they were calling those who had not received the message of Jesus to repentance, and moreover they were pronouncing sudden and unexpected judgment on those who rejected the reform agenda that they promoted. Acts of persecution in the form of rejection or being reviled were seen as proofs that the Q kerygma functioned in the same way as the prophetic voice was recorded as often having been received in scriptural texts. Such a reforming outlook may have made Q at the least ambivalent to strict halakhic interpretations of scripture, which may have been seen as ossifying religious observance into a stream of punctilious details. Thus for Q, it message and core commitments did not gain their authority from scripture, but scripture gained its ongoing utility at those points where its broad details aligned with the beliefs espoused by Q.

Bibliography

ALLISON, Dale. C., The Intertextual Jesus: Scripture in Q, Harrisburg 2000.

BOVON, François, Luke 1: A Commentary on Luke 1:1-9.50 (Hermeneia), Minneapolis 2002.

BURKETT, Delbert Royce, Rethinking the Gospel Sources, vol. 2, The Unity and Plurality of Q, Atlanta 2009.

DAVIES, William David/ALLISON, Dale C., A Critical and Exegetical Commentary on the Gospel according to Saint Matthew, vol. 1 (ICC), Edinburgh 1988.

DAVIES, William David/ALLISON, Dale C., A Critical and Exegetical Commentary on the Gospel according to Saint Matthew, vol. 3 (ICC), Edinburgh 1997.

EDWARDS, Richard Alan, The Sign of Jonah, London 1971.

FITZMYER, Joseph A., The Gospel according to Luke I-IX (AB 28), New York 1981.

FLEDDERMANN, Harry T., Mark and Q: A Study of the Overlap Texts. With an Assessment by Frans Neirynck (BETL 122), Leuven 1995.

FLEDDERMANN, Harry T., Q: A Reconstruction and Commentary, Leuven 2005.

GREEN, Joel B., The Gospel of Luke (NICNT), Grand Rapids 1997.

HARNACK, Adolf, The Sayings of Jesus: The Second Source of St Matthew and St Luke (New Testament Studies, vol. 2), London/New York 1908.

HAYS, Richard B., Echoes of Scripture in the Letters of Paul, Yale 1993.

HEIL, Christoph, Q 4:1-13, 16 The Temptations of Jesus Nazara, Leuven 1996.

HOLTZ, Traugott, Untersuchungen über die alttestamentlichen Zitate bei Lukas (TU 104), Berlin 1968.

KLOPPENBORG, John S., Excavating Q: The History and Setting of the Sayings Source Gospel, Edinburgh 2000.

KLOPPENBORG, John S., The Formation of Q: Trajectories in Ancient Wisdom Collections, Philadelphia 1987.

LÜHRMANN, Dieter, Die Redaktion der Logienquelle (WMANT 33), Neukirchen-Vluyn 1969.

MANSON, Thomas Walter, The Sayings of Jesus, London 1949 (first published as part II of The Mission and Message of Jesus, London 1937).

MARSHALL, Ian H., The Gospel of Luke: A Commentary on the Greek Text (NIGNT), Exeter 1978.

NEIRYNCK, Frans, Q-Parallels: Q-Synopsis and IQP/CritEd Parallels, Leuven 2001.

PAO, David W./SCHNABEL, Eckhard J., 'Luke', in: Beale, G.K./Carson, D.A. (eds.), Commentary on the New Testament Use of the Old Testament, Nottingham 2007, 251-415.

ROBBINS, C. Michael, The Testing of Jesus in Q (SBL 108), New York/Frankfurt a. M. 2007.

ROBINSON, James McConkey/HOFFMANN, Paul/KLOPPENBORG, John S. (eds.), The Critical Edition of Q, Minneapolis/Leuven 2000.

STRACK, Hermann L./BILLERBECK, Paul, Kommentar zum Neuen Testament aus Talmud und Midrasch, 1. Das Evangelium nach Matthäus, München 1926.

STREETER, Burnett Hillman, The Four Gospels: A Study in Origins, London 1924.

TUCKETT, Christopher M., Q and the History of Early Christianity: Studies on Q, Edinburgh 1996.

Schriftgebrauch in der Stephanusepisode Apg 6,1-8,3

HEIKE HÖTZINGER

1. Einführende Vorüberlegungen

Bereits eine erste Lektüre der Stephanusepisode Apg 6,1-8,3 zeigt deutliche Anspielungen auf alttestamentliche Texte, so dass Schriftgebrauch als prägendes Element dieses Textes erscheint. Demnach spiegelt sich in Apg 6,1-8,3 ein Charakteristikum, das in der Apostelgeschichte[1] häufig beobachtet werden kann und in der Actaforschung als „Septuaginta-Mimesis"[2] bezeichnet wird. Dieses Phänomen versuchte man zunächst mit quellentheoretischen bzw. -kritischen Untersuchungen zu erklären,[3] weiterhin mit redaktionskritischen Überlegungen,[4] und mit zunehmender Betrachtung des lukanischen Doppelwerks als literarisches Werk wird häufiger über die Funktion des Schriftgebrauchs nachgedacht.[5] Ähnlich verhält es sich bei Untersuchungen zur Verwendung der Schrift in der Stephanusepisode und insbesondere in der Stephanusrede Apg 7,2-53.[6] Mit steigendem Interesse an Apg 6,1-8,3 als literarischer und theologischer Text werden vermehrt zentrale theologische Themen herausgearbeitet.[7] Dabei wird auch verstärkt mithilfe literaturwissenschaftlicher Methoden nach der Funktion des Schriftgebrauchs in der Stephanusepisode hinsichtlich der als zentral erachte-

---

1 Auch im Lukasevangelium wird Septuaginta-Mimesis festgestellt. Vgl. RUSAM, Das Alte Testament bei Lukas, 2-3.
2 Vgl. etwa PLÜMACHER, Apostelgeschichte, 490. Eine Häufung des Schriftgebrauchs falle zum einen am Anfang und am Ende des Lukasevangeliums, zum anderen in den Reden Apg 2,14-39; 7,2-53; 13,16-47 auf.
3 Vgl. PLÜMACHER, Apostelgeschichte, 492. RUSAM, Das Alte Testament bei Lukas, 6.
4 Vgl. RUSAM, Das Alte Testament, 15-20.
5 Vgl. RUSAM, Das Alte Testament, 20-26.
6 Ein Überblick über die Forschungslage zur Stephanusepisode findet sich in BRAUN, Geschichte des Gottesvolkes, 6-32, und dort angegebener Literatur.
7 So werden z.B. folgende Themen als zentral erachtet: heilsgeschichtliche Kontinuität zwischen Israel und der Kirche, Distanzierung vom Judentum, Kritik an der jüdischen Führerschaft, besondere Sicht der Geschichte Israels, Rolle des Tempels.

ten Themen oder aber im Hinblick auf theologische Grundzüge des lukanischen Doppelwerks gefragt.⁸

So werden in Anknüpfung an literaturwissenschaftlich orientierte Forschungsansätze in diesem Beitrag folgende Fragen gestellt:
1. Wie wird ‚Schrift' in Apg 6,1-8,3 verwendet?
2. Welche Funktion hat der Schriftgebrauch in der Stephanusepisode Apg 6,1-8,3?
3. Wie formt die Art und Weise des Schriftgebrauchs in Apg 6,1-8,3 die Bedeutung der Stephanusepisode innerhalb der Apostelgeschichte und des lukanischen Doppelwerks mit?

Wegen der dichten Vernetzung des Textes Apg 6,1-8,3 mit seinem näheren Kontext ‚lukanisches Doppelwerk' und mit seinem weiten Kontext ‚christliche Bibel' wird als methodisch-hermeneutischer Zugang für die folgenden Untersuchungen exemplarischer Textpassagen der Zugang „kanonisch-intertextuelle Auslegung"⁹ verwendet. Diesem Ansatz zufolge wird die Stephanusepisode als literarischer Text bzw. als eine ‚Erzählung'¹⁰ betrachtet, die einen Teil ihres Kontextes ‚Apostelgeschichte' bzw. ‚lukanisches Doppelwerk' bildet und dieses mitgestaltet. Daher sind folgende Vorüberlegungen von Bedeutung:

(1) In breitem Konsens wird das lukanische Doppelwerk (insbesondere die Apostelgeschichte) in die antik-jüdische Geschichtsschreibung eingeordnet,¹¹ die darauf abzielt, im Ringen um das Zusammenleben mit der dominanten hellenistischen Kultur jüdisches Selbstverständnis zu formulieren.¹² Dementsprechend dient auch die Apostelgeschichte der Selbstvergewisserung und Identitätssicherung der entstehenden christlichen Gemeinschaft, die sich in ihrer heidnischen Umwelt verorten muss.

(2) Analog zu antik-jüdischer Geschichtsschreibung bildet die Geschichte Gottes mit Israel den zentralen inhaltlichen Gegenstand des

---

8   Vgl. etwa RUSAM, Das Alte Testament bei Lukas. SCHIFFNER, Lukas liest Exodus. PENNER, Praise.
9   Dieses Konzept wurde von Georg STEINS geprägt. Besonders wichtig: STEINS, Bindung Isaaks. DERS., Der Bibelkanon als Denkmal. Nahezu denselben Ansatz bezeichnet Christoph DOHMEN mit dem Begriff „biblische Auslegung". Vgl. insbesondere: DOHMEN, Biblische Auslegung, 174-191.
10 In Anlehnung an SCHNELLE, Historische Anschlussfähigkeit, 57, Anm. 51, wird hier ein weiter Erzählbegriff vorausgesetzt, der nicht auf bestimmte literarische Gattungen fixiert ist. Erzählung wird „als eine bedeutungs- oder sinnhafte bzw. Bedeutung oder Sinn stiftende Sprachform" aufgefasst. Vgl. auch EISEN, Poetik, 40.
11 Vgl. BACKHAUS, Historiographie, 31. PENNER, Praise. BREYTENBACH/SCHRÖTER,/DU TOIT, Hellenistische Geschichtsschreibung, u.a.
12 Vgl. BACKHAUS, Historiographie, 31, 34. HAGENE, Zeiten, 53-58.

lukanischen Doppelwerks.[13] Dessen theologisches Konzept kann folglich nach HANS KLEIN mit der Wendung *"Weg des Heils"*[14] beschrieben werden. Inhaltlich umschreibt der „Weg des Heils" sowohl eine Botschaft als auch einen Lebenswandel und deutet darauf hin, dass Heil nur auf einem Weg zu erreichen ist, der den Weg Jesu nachahmt.[15]

(3) Die Apostelgeschichte erweist sich zu Beginn mit einer Zusammenfassung des Lukasevangeliums (Apg 1,1-2) als Fortsetzung des Weges Jesu. Denn sie setzt nicht nur zeitlich (Erscheinung des Auferstandenen und Himmelfahrt) und örtlich (Jerusalem) am Ende des Lukasevangeliums an, sondern auch inhaltlich.[16] Als Zentrum und Ziel der Apostelgeschichte formuliert nämlich der Auftrag des Auferstandenen in Apg 1,8 die Bezeugung Jesu Christi und damit verbunden der Königsherrschaft Gottes in Jerusalem, in ganz Judäa und Samaria und bis ans »Ende der Erde«[17]. Damit wird nicht nur ein geographisches Programm des weiteren „Weges des Heils" formuliert, sondern zugleich ein ethnisches. Es geht also um die *Überschreitung* von geographischen und ethnischen, implizit auch religiösen *Grenzen*.[18]

Entsprechend der in Apg 1,8 vorgegebenen geographischen Struktur werden in der Apostelgeschichte folgende Etappen des „Weges des Heils" erzählt: Apg 1,4-8,3 umfasst die Verkündigung des Evangeliums in Jerusalem, wobei die Anfänge der Jerusalemer Gemeinde tendenziell als Idealbild voller Harmonie dargestellt werden. Die Stephanusepisode Apg 6,1-8,3 bildet dann das Ende der Jerusalemer Zeit, denn die Steinigung des Stephanus zieht eine große Verfolgung und Zerstreuung der Jerusalemer Gemeinde nach sich (Apg 8,1b.3), durch die geographisch gesehen die Schwelle zur nächsten Etappe überschritten wird. Apg 8,4-11,18 enthält nämlich die Verkündigung des Evangeliums in ganz Judäa und Samarien, wobei es auch zur Überschreitung von ethnischen Grenzen kommt und der Prozess der (religiösen) Ordnungstransformation[19] voranschreitet. In der dritten Etappe Apg 11,19-28,31 findet vor allem die Verkündigung des Evangeliums unter den „Völkern" durch Paulus bis nach Rom statt.

---

13 Für weitere Kennzeichen anitk-jüdischer Geschichtsschreibung vgl. ZMIJEWSKI, Apg, 24-30. HAGENE, Zeiten, 55. BACKHAUS, Historiographie, 30-35.
14 Ausschließlich in Apg 16,17 ist die Wortkombination ὁδὸς σωτηρίας zu finden. Damit wird dort das Geschehen, das im lkn Doppelwerk erzählt wird, prägnant zusammengefasst. Vgl. KLEIN, Lukasstudien, 106, 111. DERS., Lukasevangelium, 53.
15 Vgl. KLEIN, Lukasstudien, 111.
16 Vgl. BACKHAUS, Historiographie, 43. EISEN, Poetik, 222.
17 Vgl. EISEN, Poetik, 144-145, 221.
18 Vgl. EISEN, Poetik, 165, 169.
19 Vgl. EISEN, Poetik, 226. Beispielsweise markiert die Taufe des Gottesfürchtigen Kornelius (Apg 10,1-11,18) einen Schritt im Prozess der Ordnungstransformation.

2. Szenische und thematische Rahmenbedingungen
Apg 6,1-7,1

In den beiden ersten Abschnitten[20] der Stephanusepisode Apg 6,1-7 und Apg 6,8-7,1 sind ein paar unterschwellige Anspielungen auf die Schrift zu finden. Mit denen primär ein Bild von der Jerusalemer Gemeinde und von der Gestalt des Stephanus entworfen wird.

Mit der Situationsangabe, dass in der wachsenden Jerusalemer Gemeinde eine mangelhafte Versorgung der bedürftigen hellenistischen Witwen Unmut erregt, ordnet Apg 6,1 die Szene in das von Apg 1-5 gezeichnete Bild der Jerusalemer Gemeinde ein. Diese befindet sich aufgrund der Verkündigung des Wortes durch die Apostel in einem stetigen Wachstumsprozess, wird aber auch mit Konflikten mit den Jerusalemer Autoritäten (Apg 4,1-3.17-19; 5,17-18.21-42) und mit einzelnen Gemeindemitgliedern (Apg 5,1-11) konfrontiert. Die Problemsituation, die in Apg 6,1 mit »Murren« (γογγυσμός) der Hellenisten gegen die Hebräer beschrieben wird, scheint nun ein Konflikt mit gesteigertem Ausmaß auf der Gemeindeebene zu sein. Dabei wird die nicht genauer geschilderte Witwenproblematik vor allem auf dem Hintergrund der Kontrastfolie der idealen Jerusalemer Gemeinde sowie Gott und Jesus als Idealvorbildern der Witwenversorgung greifbar. Die Notiz von einer mangelhaften Versorgung der Witwen stellt nämlich einen Kontrast zur Aufforderung in den Gesetzes- und Prophetenbüchern, für Witwen in ihrem Los besonders tiefer Armut zu sorgen (vgl. Dtn 14,29; 24,17; 26,12; Jes 1,23; 10,2; Jer 7,6; 22,3; Mal 3,5) dar.[21] In Fortsetzung der dort gezeichneten Rolle Gottes als Beschützer der Witwen, ist es im Lukasevangelium Jesus, der die Witwen unterstützt (vgl. Lk 18,1-8; 20,45-47; 21,1-6).[22] Dass der mit γογγυσμός bezeichnete Konflikt neben einer sozialen auch eine theologische Dimension enthält, zeigt außerdem die Anspielung auf das Murren Israels gegen Gott im Kontext des Mannawunders Ex 16. In diesem Text wird nämlich verschiedentlich deutlich, dass mit γογγυσμός eigentlich ein Fehlverhalten des Volkes gegenüber Gott bezeichnet wird (vgl. etwa Ex 16,8.16b).[23] Befindet sich ein Teil der Jerusalemer Gemeinde ebenfalls in einer Versor-

---

20 Die Stephanusepisode kann grob in drei Teile untergliedert werden: I) Szenische und thematische Rahmenbedingungen (Apg 6,1-7 und 6,8-7,1), II) Stephanusrede (Apg 7,2-53), III) Folgen der Stephanusrede (Apg 7,54-8,3). Eine Strukturanalyse findet sich in BRAUN, Geschichte des Gottesvolkes, 78-83.
21 Vgl. FITZMYER, Acts, 345. JERVELL, Apg, 216.
22 Vgl. SPENCER, Acts, 65.
23 Ähnlich in Dtn 1,27; Num 14,2.36; Jos 9,18; 17; Weish 1,11. Vgl. SCHNEIDER, Apg, 423, Anm. 18.

gungsnotlage und reagiert darauf mit Murren – ähnlich wie Israel in der Wüste –, kann vor dem Hintergrund des Mannakonflikts mit einer ähnlichen Notsituation gerechnet werden, in der das Verhältnis zu Gott und seinen Weisungen berührt ist. In Apg 6,1 deutet sich also insofern eine ‚theologische' Dimension des Konflikts an als es – in Nachahmung der Fürsorge Gottes für Israel in der Wüste – dem Idealbild der Jerusalemer Gemeinde entspricht, dass innerhalb des harmonischen Wachstumsprozesses jeder gemäß seines täglichen Bedarfs versorgt ist (vgl. Apg 2,44-46; 4,32-35).

Nach dieser relativ vagen Konfliktbeschreibung handelt Apg 6,2-6 von einem Lösungsversuch, der von den Zwölf initiiert wird: Die gesamte Gemeinde soll aus ihren eigenen Reihen sieben Männer[24] wählen, die primär für den Witwendienst zuständig sein sollen. Dieser Vorschlag in Apg 6,2-3 zeigt Ähnlichkeiten mit Num 11,13-17,[25] wo Israel im Zusammenhang des Mannawunders gegen Gott murrt, weil es kein Fleisch zu essen hat. Da Mose mit dieser Angelegenheit überfordert ist, weist ihn Gott an, den Konflikt mithilfe einer Gruppe von Repräsentanten des Volkes zu lösen (vgl. Num 11,16b). Gemeinsam[26] ist beiden Texten, dass die auszuwählenden Männer jeweils von besonderen Qualitäten gekennzeichnet sind. Besonders signifikant ist dabei die Geistbegabung (Apg 6,3), die in Num 11,17 ausdrücklich auf Gott zurückgeht und offensichtlich im Zusammenhang mit der Unterstützung für Mose steht. Analog dazu dürfte die Geistbegabung der Sieben ebenfalls mit ihrer Aufgabe, die zur Unterstützung der Zwölf und damit zur Konfliktlösung dient, verbunden sein.[27]

Die Anspielungen auf die genannten Intertexte über nachträglich gewählte Anführer des Volkes Israel zur Unterstützung für Mose mithilfe von Stichwortverbindungen, kontextuelle oder motivische Analogien machen also deutlich, dass die in Apg 6,2-3 skizzierte Konfliktlösung Ähnlichkeiten mit einem bestimmten Muster hat, das aus der Geschichte des Volkes Israel bekannt ist und dort sogar von Gott selbst

---

24 Eventuell weist die Sieben-Zahl auf ein Gremium mit einer besonderen Funktion in der Gemeinde hin, da jüdische Kollegien häufig aus sieben Mitgliedern bestanden (vgl. Jos 6,4; Est 1,14; Jer 52,25) und in Apg 21,8 »die Sieben« als feste Bezeichnung dieser Männer gebraucht wird. Vgl. GAVENTA, Acts, 114. Zur Diskussion um die Sieben-Zahl vgl. ZMIJEWSKI, Apg, 285. PESCH, Apg, 228. BARRETT, Acts, 312 u.a.
25 Vgl. PENNER, Praise, 266.
26 Allerdings ist auch der Unterschied zu bemerken, dass in Num 11,16b Mose allein seine Helfer auswählt, während in Apg 6,2-3 das ganze Volk die Sieben wählt.
27 Diese Verbindung zwischen den Auswahlkriterien für die Sieben und ihrer Aufgabe wird durch die Anspielung auf Dtn 1,13-15 noch deutlicher. In beiden Texten ist nämlich die gesamte Gemeinde an der Konfliktlösung beteiligt, und die Kandidaten unter anderem durch Weisheit auszeichnen. Vgl. PENNER, Praise, 266.

vorgeschlagen wird.²⁸ Auf diese Weise wird die Konfliktlösung idealisiert und erneut das Bild einer gut funktionierenden und in einer Art Arbeitsteilung zusammenwirkenden Gemeinde wiederhergestellt.²⁹

Neben der Darstellung der Jerusalemer Gemeinde liegt ein weiterer Schwerpunkt der erzählenden Rahmenstücke Apg 6,1-7; 6,8-7,1 in der Vorstellung des Stephanus. So wird er aus dem Siebenerkreis besonders hervorgehoben, indem er als erster der Sieben genannt und zugleich als ἄνδρα πλήρης πίστεως καὶ πνεύματος ἁγίου (Apg 6,5) charakterisiert wird. Damit wird nicht nur betont, dass er die geforderten Wahlkriterien vollkommen erfüllt,³⁰ sondern Stephanus wird auch mit Zügen einer prophetischen Gestalt und in Analogie zum lukanischen Jesus vorgestellt (Apg 6,5).³¹ Dies bestätigt sich in Apg 6,8-15, denn Vers 8 hält erneut seine besondere Erfüllung mit Gnade und Kraft, die sich in seinem Wunderwirken im Volk ausdrückt, fest und zeigt somit eine Parallele zur Darstellung Jesu als Prophet (Lk 4,14-30) auf.³² Damit geht zugleich einher, dass Stephanus – gemäß dem typischen Geschick der Propheten Israels und Jesu – Ablehnung erfährt, wie Apg 6,9-14 schildert: So erzählt Apg 6,9-12 von sich steigernden Angriffen gegen Stephanus durch verschiedene Personengruppen. Dabei wird ihm zunächst der schwerwiegende Vorwurf der Blasphemie gemacht (Apg 6,11). Die Hetzkampagne gegen Stephanus mündet schließlich in einer offiziellen Gerichtsverhandlung vor dem Synedrium (ab Apg 6,12b), wo Falschzeugen folgende Anklagen gegen ihn vorbringen: Er kritisiere Tempel und Gesetz (Apg 6,13) und behaupte, Jesus, der Nazoräer, wollte den Tempel und das Gesetz auflösen (Apg 6,14). Zum einen wird Stephanus hier mit Jesus parallelisiert, da diese Anklagen motivisch weitgehend denen gegen Jesus (Mk 14,55-65) entsprechen.³³ Zum anderen wird Stephanus als prophetischer Verkündiger des Tempelwortes Jesu (Apg 6,14a) in Analogie zu prophetischer Unheilsverkün-

---

28 Ähnlich PENNER, Praise, 266. TALBERT, Reading Acts, 73, sieht darin ein Spiegelbild alttestamentlicher Formen der Wahl nachträglicher Führer.
29 Dieses Bild wird durch die sofortige Umsetzung dieses Vorschlags durch die Gemeinde (Apg 6,5-6) und durch die summarische Notiz von einem weiteren, sogar gesteigerten Wachstum der Jerusalemer Gemeinde (Apg 6,7) unterstrichen. Zu Apg 6,4-7 vgl. BRAUN, Geschichte des Gottesvolkes, 115-129.
30 Vgl. FITZMYER, Acts, 350. ZMIJEWSKI, Apg, 153-154.
31 Zur Darstellung des Stephanus in Apg 6,5.8.10 mit prophetischen Zügen in Analogie zu Jesus vgl. BRAUN, Geschichte des Gottesvolkes, 118-119, 133-136, 139-140.
32 Auch Apg 6,10 intensiviert die Analogie zu Jesus, denn dort erfüllt sich Lk 21,15. Vgl. dazu BRAUN, Geschichte des Gottesvolkes, 139.
33 Für einen Vergleich von Apg 6,11.13-14 mit Mk 14,55-65 vgl. BRAUN, Geschichte des Gottesvolkes, 141-142, 148-149, 152-155.

digung, wie z.B. Jer 7,3.7.12.14 u.a., dargestellt.[34] So werden mithilfe dieser Anklagen zentrale Themen aufgeworfen, die auch von Propheten Israels behandelt wurden: die Haltung zu Gott, zum Gesetz und zum Tempel als Ort der Anwesenheit Gottes und damit identitätsstiftendes Zentrum Israels.

Bevor Stephanus sich in der Rede Apg 7,2-53 dazu äußert, wird die Gerichtsverhandlung gewissermaßen unterbrochen, wenn Apg 6,15 Stephanus in der außergewöhnlichen Erscheinung eines engelsgleichen Gesichts (εἶδον τὸ πρόσωπον αὐτοῦ ὡσεὶ πρόσωπον ἀγγέλου) beschreibt. Damit bestätigt sich, dass Stephanus als prophetische Gestalt gezeichnet wird,[35] was sich vor allem aufgrund von Ex 34,29b nahe legt, wo das Gesicht des Mose, der mit den Gesetzestafeln vom Sinai heruntersteigt, ein verändertes Aussehen von Moses Gesicht notiert wird: Μωυσῆς οὐκ ᾔδει ὅτι δεδόξασται ἡ ὄψις τοῦ χρώματος τοῦ προσώπου αὐτοῦ ἐν τῷ λαλεῖν αὐτὸν αὐτῷ. Die Beschreibung von Moses Gesicht mit dem Verb δοξάζω weist darauf hin, dass die Herrlichkeit Gottes (δόξα) von seinem Angesicht zurückstrahlt, „so dass die Israeliten im Strahlen des Angesichts des Mose Gottes Nähe sozusagen ‚sehen' können."[36] Ursache für dieses strahlende Gesicht ist also die Nähe Gottes mit seiner Herrlichkeit zum Offenbarungsmittler Mose, der dadurch in dieser Funktion bekräftigt wird. Vor diesem Hintergrund dürfte auch das veränderte Gesicht des Stephanus seine Ursache in Gott selbst haben, der ihn wie Mose als einen Propheten mit einer besonderen Mittlerfunktion[37] bestätigt. Analog zu Mose ist diese Erscheinung des geistbegabten Stephanus (Apg 6,5.8.10) wohl auch Zeichen besonderer Nähe Gottes, als deren Ausdruck das engelsgleiche Gesicht des Stephanus Gottes Herrlichkeit sehen lässt.

Insgesamt wird die Schrift in den Erzählabschnitten Apg 6,1-7 und Apg 6,8-7,1 also eher unterschwellig verwendet. Dabei zeigt sich allerdings, dass mithilfe von intertextuellen Referenzen durch kontextuelle bzw. motivische Analogien oder Stichwortverknüpfungen ein besonderes Bild der Jerusalemer Gemeinde und das Profil der Gestalt des Stephanus skizziert werden.

---

34 Vgl. GANSER-KERPERIN, Tempel, 44. BRAUN, Geschichte des Gottesvolkes, 154-155.
35 Darauf weisen auch sprachliche und kontextuelle Analogien zur Antrittsrede Jesu Lk 4,20 hin. Ähnlich wie dort, dient auch Apg 6,15 als retardierendes Moment. Vgl. WOLTER, Lukasevangelium, 193.
36 DOHMEN, Exodus, 374.
37 Vgl. SCHIFFNER, Lukas liest Exodus, 352. Als göttliche Bestätigung kann Apg 6,15 auch aufgrund von Anspielungen auf die Verklärung Jesu Lk 9,28-36 (bes. 9,29.35) verstanden werden. Vgl. ZMIJEWSKI, Apg, 303. SCHNEIDER, Apg 440.

3. Die Stephanusrede Apg 7,2-53

Auf unterschiedlichen Ebenen erfolgt in der Stephanusrede Verwendung von Schrift, angefangen von subtilen Anspielungen bis hin zu sehr offensichtlichen Referenzen oder sogar wörtlicher Wiedergabe von Subtexten.

3.1 Entscheidende Basis der Geschichtserzählung Apg 7,2-8

Die ersten Worte der Stephanusrede ὁ θεὸς τῆς δόξης ὤφθη τῷ πατρὶ ἡμῶν ᾽Αβραάμ (Apg 7,2), die überschriftartig das Thema dieses Redeabschnittes bzw. sogar der gesamten Rede – wie sich im Lektüreverlauf zeigen wird – benennen, spielen auf Ps 28,3 LXX an:[38] φωνὴ κυρίου ἐπὶ τῶν ὑδάτων ὁ θεὸς τῆς δόξης ἐβρόντησεν κύριος ἐπὶ ὑδάτων πολλῶν.

Diese Referenz auf den so genannten „Theophaniehymnus"[39] verdeutlicht einige Implikationen der Rede vom »Gott der Herrlichkeit«: Es handelt sich um den mächtigen Schöpfergott (er bändigt nämlich die Chaoswasser; vgl. Ps 28,4 LXX), der durch seine Herrlichkeit in Beziehung zu den Menschen tritt, indem er seine δόξα bzw. sich in der δόξα offenbart. Die Rede von der δόξα drückt also einerseits Gottes Transzendenz aus, andererseits Gottes Wirken in der Welt.[40] Mithilfe dieser Worte aus Ps 28,3 LXX, die die grundlegende Offenbarung Gottes in seiner herrlichen Schöpfermacht implizieren, formuliert Apg 7,2 programmatisch das Thema der nun folgenden Rede: Es geht um eine bestimmte Vorstellung von Gott und zwar um den grundsätzlich transzendenten Gott, der sich in seinem schöpferischen, heilvollen und richterlichen Wirken in der Geschichte offenbart, und dem seiner Herrlichkeit entsprechende Ehre dargebracht werden soll (vgl. Ps 28,1-2).[41]

---

38 Die Wendung ὁ θεὸς τῆς δόξης findet sich in exakt dieser Form nur in Apg 7,2 und Ps 28,3 LXX. Dies fällt besonders angesichts des häufigen Vorkommens des δόξα-Begriffs innerhalb der christlichen Bibel auf. Vgl. LANGER, Herrlichkeit, 21. Eine Anspielung auf Ps 28,3 beobachten z.B. FITZMYER, Acts, 369. JERVELL, Apg, 232.

39 ZENGER, Psalmen 3, 118. Zur Auslegung von Ps 28 insgesamt vgl. EBD., 113-120. Zu כבוד in den Psalmen vgl. auch LANGER, Herrlichkeit, 47-55.

40 Vgl. CHIBICI-REVNEANU, Herrlichkeit, 425, 458, 462 u.a. Darüber hinaus enthält der δόξα-Begriff eine kultische Dimension, wie nicht nur Ps 28,1-2.9-11 zeigt, sondern auch die Bewertung des Tempels bzw. Zions oder Jerusalems als Wohnstätte der Gottesherrlichkeit und zentralem Ort der kultisch gestalteten δόξα-Beziehung zwischen Gott und Menschen (vgl. auch DOHMEN, Exodus, 247-248, 398-402. LANGER, Herrlichkeit, 33-34). CHIBICI-REVNEANU, Herrlichkeit, 461, erkennt auch eine soteriologische und eschatologische Dimension der δόξα Gottes.

41 Vgl. ZENGER, Psalmen 3, 115-116. In Ps 28,1-2 werden die Gottessöhne aufgefordert, dem Herrn Ehre und Ehrfurcht (δόξαν καὶ τιμήν) und dem Namen des Herrn δόξα darzubringen und sich vor ihm niederzuwerfen (προσκυνέω).

Mit der Rede von diesem »Gott der Herrlichkeit« geht es also zugleich um eine Geschichte der Gottesbegegnung und -beziehung.

Die nun folgenden Ausführungen darüber, inwiefern sich der Gott der Herrlichkeit offenbart, arbeiten in vielfältiger Weise mit den Abrahamserzählungen aus dem Buch Genesis, etwa durch die Aufnahme von Wörtern oder Wendungen, Motivverknüpfungen, Struktur- oder Kontextanalogien.[42] Durch subtile Veränderungen dieser Subtexte erhält die Erzählung der Erscheinung Gottes vor Abraham in Apg 7,2-8 allerdings ein eigenes Profil, was an einigen Beispielen verdeutlicht werden soll:

(1) Die Konstatierung der Erscheinung Gottes vor Abraham in Apg 7,2c unterscheidet sich von der Notiz dieses Ereignisses in den Genesistexten hinsichtlich der Ortsangabe. Laut Gen 11,31 und Gen 12,4 erscheint Gott Abraham nämlich, während dieser sich zusammen mit seiner Familie in Charran, einer Zwischenstation auf dem Weg nach Kanaan, befindet. In Apg 7,2c dagegen wird dieses Ereignis ausdrücklich vor Abrahams Aufenthalt in Charran angesetzt, nämlich in Mesopotamien. Indem es also im Vergleich zur Genesisdarstellung um eine Station auf dem Weg Abrahams nach vorne in seine Heimat verlegt (Gen 11,28)[43] wird, wird akzentuiert, dass Gott Abraham von seinem Ursprung an herausgerufen und geführt hat. Diese ursprüngliche Initiative Gottes für den Weg Abrahams gilt implizit auch für den der Zuhörer selbst wie die Anrede ("Ἄνδρες ἀδελφοὶ καὶ πατέρες) und die Einführung Abrahams (ὁ πατὴρ ἡμῶν 'Ἀβραάμ) ausdrücken. Außerdem deutet die Situierung der Erscheinung Gottes vor Abraham in Apg 7,2c darauf hin, dass das Thema ‚Land' fokussiert wird. Dieser Akzent wird auch durch einen Vergleich mit der Einführung Abrahams in Gen 11,26-32 deutlich: Während er dort in die Genealogie Terachs eingebettet wird, also die familiäre Abstammung und Situation im Vordergrund steht,[44] wird Abraham in Apg 7,2 ausschließlich mit seinem Herkunftsland verbunden. Durch diese Gestaltung des Rekurses auf Abraham wird weiterhin im Hinblick auf das Thema der Offenbarung Gottes (ὁ θεὸς τῆς δόξης ὤφθη) gezeigt, dass Gotteserscheinung bzw.

---

42 Schon die Formulierung der Erscheinung mit ὤφθη ähnelt den Offenbarungsgeschehen in Gen 17,1; 26,24 oder Ex 3,1. Vgl. ZMIJEWSKI, Apg, 313. FITZMYER, Acts, 369.
43 Gen 11,28 nennt das Land der Chaldäer in Mesopotamien als Heimat Abrahams und seiner Familie. FITZMYER, Acts, 370, erklärt die unterschiedlichen Bezeichnungen der Herkunft Abrahams im hebräischen Text (Ur) und in der LXX χώρα τῶν Χαλδαίων.
44 Vgl. HIEKE, Genealogie, 138.

-präsenz auch, ja sogar ursprünglich, außerhalb des verheißenen Landes möglich ist.⁴⁵

(2) Das eigentliche Offenbarungsgeschehen wird in Apg 7,3b.c in direkter Rede Gottes an Abraham formuliert: ἔξελθε ἐκ τῆς γῆς σου καὶ [ἐκ] τῆς συγγενείας σου καὶ δεῦρο εἰς τὴν γῆν ἣν ἄν σοι δείξω. »Geh weg aus deinem Land und aus deiner Verwandtschaft, und hierher in das Land, das ich dir zeigen werde.« Fast wörtlich wird hier aus Gen 12,1-3 die Aufforderung an Abraham, sein Land und seine Verwandtschaft zu verlassen (ἔξελθε ἐκ τῆς γῆς σου), sowie die Bezeichnung des Ziellandes (εἰς τὴν γῆν ἣν ἄν σοι δείξω) wiedergegeben. Es fehlt allerdings aus Gen 12,1 die Aufforderung, das Haus des Vaters zu verlassen, was erneut zur Fokussierung de Themas ‚Land' auf Kosten des Aspektes der Familie beiträgt. Das Zurücktreten des Themas ‚Verwandtschaft' in Apg 7,3 zeigt sich auch daran, dass die ausführliche Zusage von Nachkommenschaft und Segen, die Gen 12,2-3 bietet, fehlt. Dadurch werden in Apg 7,3 nicht nur der Aufforderungscharakter der Gottesrede (vgl. auch δεῦρο) und die Ungewissheit des Verlassens von Vertrautem betont, sondern zugleich das Zielland. Indem es durch die Wendung ἡ γῆ ἣ ἄν σοι δείξω umschrieben wird, steht außerdem das aktive Handeln Gottes im Vordergrund.⁴⁶

(3) Die als Zeitangabe formulierte Notiz über den Tod von Abrahams Vater (Apg 7,4b) fungiert als eine Art Abschluss und Überleitung. Analog zur Nachricht von Terachs Tod in Gen 11,32,⁴⁷ die dazu dient den Toledot-Abschnitt abzuschließen und einen neuen Spannungsbogen zu eröffnen,⁴⁸ markiert auch Apg 7,4b das Ende des Aufenthalts in der Durchgangsstation Charran und stellt damit den Ausgangspunkt dafür dar, dass und wie Abraham in das Land gelangt, in dem auch seine Nachkommen leben: μετῴκισεν αὐτὸν εἰς τὴν γῆν ταύτην εἰς ἣν ὑμεῖς νῦν κατοικεῖτε. Dieser Neubeginn innerhalb der Geschichte Abrahams enthält einen Subjektwechsel gegenüber Apg 7,4a, denn hinter μετῴκισεν⁴⁹ steht Gott, dessen Initiative hier erneut betont wird.

---

45 Vgl. JESKA, Geschichte Israels, 156. Dies unterstreicht auch Apg 7,4, in der die Orts- und Zeitangabe von Apg 7,2c aufgenommen wird.
46 Für einen genauen Vergleich von Apg 7,3 mit Gen 12,1-3 vgl. BRAUN, Geschichte des Gottesvolkes, 175-176.
47 Im Vergleich zu Gen 11,32 wird Terach in Apg 7,4b nicht namentlich genannt, sondern nur über Abraham definiert (ὁ πατὴρ αὐτοῦ). Diese Umkehrung gegenüber Gen 11,27-32 verweist erneut auf das betonte Interesse am »Vater Abraham«.
48 Vgl. HIEKE, Genealogien, 243. Zur Nachricht von Terachs Tod in Gen 11,32 vgl. auch SEEBASS, Genesis II, 4. JACOB, Genesis, 330; WESTERMANN, Genesis II, 161-162.
49 μετοικίζω bedeutet wörtlich „einen anderen Wohnsitz anweisen", „umsiedeln", „wegführen". Vgl. BAUER, Wörterbuch, 1041.

Auffälligerweise nennt Apg 7,4c das Land nicht namentlich mit Kanaan wie in Gen 12,5, sondern beschreibt es mit dem Relativsatz εἰς ἣν ὑμεῖς νῦν κατοικεῖτε »in dem ihr jetzt wohnt«. Dadurch wird es explizit in Bezug zur gegenwärtigen Zuhörerschaft gestellt: Als Nachkommen ihres »Vaters Abraham« (Apg 7,2c) sind letztlich auch sie durch Gott in dieses Land gekommen.[50] So verdeutlicht diese „Kurzaktualisierung"[51], dass die bisherige Geschichtserzählung auch für die Hörer der Stephanusrede relevant ist.[52] Überraschenderweise spricht Stephanus in diesem aktualisierenden Zusammenhang davon, dass seine Zuhörer (ὑμεῖς) dort wohnen, und distanziert sich damit von ihnen, obwohl er in der Anrede ἄνδρες ἀδελφοὶ καὶ πατέρες (7,2b) und im Rekurs auf Abraham als ὁ πατὴρ ἡμῶν (7,2c) seine Verbindung mit ihnen ausdrückt.

(4) Nach dieser aktualisierenden Notiz blickt Apg 7,5 wieder in die Geschichte Abrahams zurück und spricht erneut das Thema ‚Land' an. Dabei wird zum einen deutlich, dass Gott bleibend das Verhältnis zwischen dem Land und Abraham bzw. seinen Nachkommen bestimmt.[53] Zum anderen wird mithilfe von Anspielungen auf die Landverheißungen in Gen 17,8 und Gen 15,8 der Verheißungscharakter des Landes betont. Damit geht zugleich eine Relativierung der Bedeutung des verheißenen Landes einher.[54]

(5) Die Verse 6 und 7 werden als Worte Gottes ausgewiesen, deren Adressat aufgrund des Kontextes implizit Abraham ist, aber nicht explizit genannt wird, so dass diese Gottesworte allgemeinen Charakter erhalten. Inhaltlich handelt es sich um eine Zukunftsansage – ausschließlich für die Nachkommen Abrahams (τὸ σπέρμα αὐτοῦ) –, die in Form von drei negativen Ankündigungen formuliert wird: Nach der Betonung des Fremdseins (πάροικος) in Apg 7,6b unterstreichen die sehr unspezifisch wirkende zweite und dritte Ankündigung, die Nachkommenschaft werde versklavt (καὶ δουλώσουσιν αὐτό) und dabei

---

50 Unterstrichen wird diese Kontinuität durch das Wortfeld ‚wohnen': So wie Abraham in Charran wohnt (κατοικέω), wohnen (κατοικέω) die Hörer in diesem Land, in das Gott Abraham umgesiedelt hat (μετοικίζω). Vgl. FITZMYER, Acts, 370-371. JERVELL, Apg, 233.
51 JESKA, Geschichte Israels, 142. Zur Funktion von „Aktualisierungen" innerhalb von Summarien der Geschichte Israel vgl. EBD., 86-94, 142-148.
52 Die Verheißung des Landes an Abraham ist für sie in Erfüllung gegangen. Vgl. ZMIJEWSKI, Apg, 314.
53 Das wird zum einen durch die Wortwahl (κληρονομία bedeutet hier „Eigentum"; κατάσχεσις verweist auf temporären Besitz) ausgedrückt, zum anderen durch die Einspielung von Dtn 2,5, wonach Gott bleibender Eigentümer des Landes ist. Vgl. BRAUN, Geschichte des Gottesvolkes, 183, und dort angegebene Literatur.
54 Für einen ausführlichen Vergleich von Apg 7,5 mit Gen 17,8 und Gen 15,8 vgl. BRAUN, Geschichte des Gottesvolkes, 184-187, und die dort angegebene Literatur.

schlecht behandelt werden (καὶ κακώσουσιν), die Bedrohlichkeit der Situation für die Nachkommenschaft Abrahams. Vers 7a konkretisiert, dass die Nachkommenschaft Abrahams nicht näher benannten Nicht-Israeliten (τὸ ἔθνος) als Sklaven dienen werde (δουλεύσουσιν). Bei der Schilderung dieses Tiefpunkts wird aber zugleich eine Wende (κρινῶ ἐγώ) formuliert, die Gott durch das Richten dieses Volkes (τὸ ἔθνος) selbst initiiert.[55] Als positive Konsequenzen davon kündigen Apg 7,7c-d Folgendes an: Erstens werden Abrahams Nachkommen »herausgehen« (ἐξ-έρχομαι).[56] Selbst wenn dabei das Ziel offen bleibt, stellt der Rekurs auf Abraham durch Aufnahme von Apg 7,3b-4 (ἐξέρχομαι) das verheißene Land als Möglichkeit vor Augen. Als zweite positive Folge des Gerichts nennt Apg 7,7d den Gottesdienst und deutet damit an, dass die von Gott initiierte positive Beziehung zu den Nachkommen Abrahams von diesen angemessen beantwortet wird.

Apg 7,6-7 nimmt fast wörtlich die Ankündigungen Gottes an Abraham von Gen 15,13-14 auf:

Gen 15,13-14		Apg 7,6-7
13 καὶ ἐρρέθη πρὸς Αβραμ γινώσκων γνώσῃ ὅτι πάροικον ἔσται τὸ σπέρμα σου ἐν γῇ οὐκ ἰδίᾳ καὶ δουλώσουσιν αὐτοὺς καὶ κακώσουσιν αὐτοὺς καὶ ταπεινώσουσιν αὐτοὺς τετρακόσια ἔτη	6a	ἐλάλησεν δὲ οὕτως ὁ θεὸς
	b	ὅτι ἔσται τὸ σπέρμα αὐτοῦ πάροικον ἐν γῇ ἀλλοτρίᾳ
	c	καὶ δουλώσουσιν αὐτὸ καὶ κακώσουσιν
		ἔτη τετρακόσια·
14 τὸ δὲ ἔθνος ᾧ ἐὰν δουλεύσωσιν κρινῶ ἐγώ	7a	καὶ τὸ ἔθνος ᾧ ἐὰν δουλεύσουσιν κρινῶ ἐγώ,
	b	ὁ θεὸς εἶπεν,
μετὰ δὲ ταῦτα ἐξελεύσονται ὧδε μετὰ ἀποσκευῆς πολλῆς	c	καὶ μετὰ ταῦτα ἐξελεύσονται
	d	καὶ λατρεύσουσίν μοι ἐν τῷ τόπῳ τούτῳ.

Beide Texte halten grundsätzlich ähnlich die aussichtslose Lage vor Augen, in der sich die Nachkommen Abrahams als Fremde[57] in einem fremden Land[58] befinden werden, und verdeutlichen, dass Gottes Gericht zu einer Wende führt. Apg 7,6-7 akzentuiert allerdings die Initiative Gottes noch etwas stärker (vgl. den Zusatz ὁ θεὸς εἶπεν in Apg

---

55 Dies wird sprachlich unterstrichen: Bei κρινῶ ἐγώ handelt es sich plötzlich um eine direkte Rede Gottes.
56 Zu ergänzen ist wohl ‚aus dem fremden Land der Sklaverei' (Apg 7,6b).
57 In Gen 15,13 steht πάροικος sogar voran. In Apg 7,6 fehlt nur καὶ ταπεινώσουσιν αὐτούς aus Gen 15,13, was inhaltlich keine besonderen Veränderungen nach sich zieht.
58 Die Veränderung von γῇ οὐκ ἰδίᾳ (Gen 15,13) zu γῇ ἀλλοτρίᾳ (Apg 7,6) ist inhaltlich kaum von Bedeutung.

7,7b). Weiterhin zeigt sich eine Fokussierung des Gottesbezugs, denn die Verheißung großen Besitzes, den die Nachkommen bei ihrem Auszug mitnehmen würden (Gen 15,14: μετὰ ἀποσκευῆς πολλῆς) fehlt in Apg 7,7. Stattdessen wird in Apg 7,7d im Vergleich zu Gen 15,14 zusätzlich καὶ λατρεύσουσίν μοι ἐν τῷ τόπῳ τούτῳ als Ziel der Nachkommen Abrahams angekündigt.[59] Damit wird interessanterweise deutlich auf Ex 3,12b angespielt:

εἶπεν δὲ ὁ θεὸς Μωυσεῖ λέγων ὅτι ἔσομαι μετὰ σοῦ καὶ τοῦτό σοι τὸ σημεῖον ὅτι ἐγώ σε ἐξαποστέλλω ἐν τῷ ἐξαγαγεῖν σε τὸν λαόν μου ἐξ Αἰγύπτου καὶ λατρεύσετε τῷ θεῷ ἐν τῷ ὄρει τούτῳ.

Dadurch kann also die negative Verheißung von Apg 7,6 mit Israels Sklaverei in Ägypten in Verbindung gebracht und implizit an das Exodusereignis erinnert werden.[60] Auffälligerweise ändert Apg 7,7d aber die Ortsangabe von Ex 3,12b: Statt den Gottesdienst auf dem Berg Horeb zu lokalisieren (ἐν τῷ ὄρει τούτῳ), ist der Ort des Gottesdienstes in Apg 7,7d nicht eindeutig, denn die Formulierung ἐν τῷ τόπῳ τούτῳ kann mit verschiedenen Inhalten gefüllt werden.[61] Aufgrund des unmittelbaren Kontextes der Verheißungen an Abraham, die mit der Zusage des Landbesitzes in Apg 7,5 beginnen, kann »dieser Ort« zunächst »das Land« bezeichnen. Darüber hinaus kann ἐν τῷ τόπῳ τούτῳ den Tempel meinen, da mit dieser Wendung die Anklagen gegen Stephanus Apg 6,13-14 aufgegriffen werden (οὐ παύεται λαλῶν ῥήματα κατὰ τοῦ τόπου τοῦ ἁγίου [τούτου] ... καταλύσει τὸν τόπον τοῦτον).[62] Die unspezifische Formulierung ἐν τῷ τόπῳ τούτῳ öffnet also grundsätzlich verschiedene Sinnpotentiale für »diesen Ort« des Gottesdienstes.[63]

59　Das Verb λατρεύειν wird auch in Apg 7,42 verwendet, dort aber für den Götzendienst. Somit verweist es schon darauf, dass in der Stephanusrede insgesamt das Thema Gottesdienst von zentraler Bedeutung ist. Im Genesistext dagegen wird primär der erfolgreiche Auszug der Nachkommen verheißen. Vgl. JACOB, Genesis, 399.

60　Vgl. SCHIFFNER, Lukas liest Exodus, 358. Innerhalb Ex 1-15 werde der Dienst für Gott wiederholt als Ziel des Auszugs Israels genannt. Vgl. Ex 7,16.26; 8,16; 9,1.13; 10.3 u.a.

61　Zur Diskussion verschiedener Interpretationsmöglichkeiten vgl. FITZMYER, Acts, 372. Kanaan und Jerusalem nennen u.a. BARRETT, Apg, 345. JESKA, Geschichte Israels, 157. Den Tempel erwähnen ZMIJEWSKI, Apg, 315. SCHNEIDER, Apg, 455 u.a.

62　Insofern demnach der Tempel implizit als von Gott selbst angekündigter Ort des Gottesdienstes vorgestellt wird, ist freilich der Vorwurf, Stephanus rede blasphemisch gegen den Tempel als Ort Gottes, nicht haltbar. Vgl. PENNER, Praise, 308-309. WASSERBERG, Israels Mitte, 246. TANNEHILL, Narrative, 92-93.

63　An dieser Stelle der Rede kann mit Sicherheit nur festgehalten werden, dass das Ziel des verheißenen Auszugs der Dienst für Gott ist. Dieser ist so bedeutend, dass er bereits in die erste Ankündigung des Exodus integriert wird. SCHIFFNER, Lukas liest Exodus, 358, Anm. 104, beobachtet, dass ὁ τόπος οὗτος innerhalb der Exoduserzählung selbst ebenfalls polysem ist (vgl. Ex 7,16; 8,16; 9,1.13; 10,3.7).

(6) Dass die von Gott initiierte Gottesbeziehung in der Stephanusepisode eine entscheidende Bedeutung hat, drückt sich weiterhin in der Notiz über den Beschneidungsbund in Apg 7,8 aus. Gegenüber der durch διαθήκη περιτομῆς[64] eingespielten, sehr stark gerafften Erzählung von Gen 17, wird hier die Qualität des Bundes als Gabe (δίδωμι)[65] betont. Gemeinsam ist beiden Texten, dass Abraham und seine Nachkommen den Bund der Beschneidung einhalten.[66]

Die Aufzählung von Isaak, Jakob und den zwölf Patriarchen, weist nicht nur auf die kontinuierliche Weitergabe des Bundes hin, sondern ähnelt außerdem biblischen Genealogien, wie z.B. Gen 25,19b.[67] Sie dienen häufig in literarischer Hinsicht als Struktursignal und Leseanweisung, haben in der Konstruktion von Identität eine wichtige Bedeutung und transportieren theologische Botschaften.[68] Auch die genealogieartige Aufzählung in Apg 7,8 überbrückt literarisch einen langen Zeitraum (von Abraham bis zu den zwölf Patriarchen) und dient damit der Strukturierung der Stephanusrede, insofern sie die Erzählung über Abraham abschließt und einen neuen Spannungsbogen eröffnet. Dabei wird auch eine Rückbindung alles Folgenden an Abraham bzw. Gott selbst deutlich. Weiterhin kristallisiert sich durch das Herausgreifen bestimmter Namen und das Fehlen anderer, die Linie heraus, die zur Bildung des Volkes Israel führt – ähnlich wie im Buch Genesis.[69] So dienen auch in Apg 7,8 die genannten Personen als „Identitätskonzepte und in Literatur kristallisierte Gotteserfahrungen", die den Hörer bzw. Leser der Rede zu einem „aktuellen Nachvollzug des Geschehens"[70] auffordern.

Insgesamt präsentiert sich die Erzählung von der Erscheinung Gottes vor Abraham in Apg 7,2-8 durch die verschiedenen Arten des Schriftgebrauchs als deutende und aktualisierende Geschichtserzählung. Dabei wird die Abrahamsgeschichte als eine Art Ideal-Anfang der Geschichte Israels dargestellt, insofern sie von Gott außerhalb des

---

64 Vgl. JESKA, Geschichte Israels, 159. Hier liege ein ntl. Hapaxlegomenon vor.
65 Gen 17 lässt mit dem Verb τίθημι eher an eine Art Vertrag denken und ist zusätzlich mit der Landverheißung verknüpft.
66 Zwar fehlt in Apg 7,8 die Charakterisierung als eines »ewigen Bundes« (διαθήκη αἰώνιος), aber die Liste in Apg 7,8b-d impliziert diesen Gedanken. Vgl. BRAUN, Geschichte des Gottesvolkes, 198.
67 Die Geburt Jakobs wird innerhalb der Toledot Isaak erzählt (Gen 25,21-26). Vgl. auch Gen 46,8-27 und Ex 1,1-5.
68 Zur Funktion biblischer Genealogien vgl. HIEKE, Genealogien, 343-352.
69 Vgl. die Erwähnung der zwölf Patriarchen am Ende der Aufzählung von Apg 7,8 und ihre namentliche Nennung in Ex 1,1-5, womit das entstandene Volk Israel umrissen wird. Vgl. JESKA, Geschichte Israels, 159.
70 HIEKE, Genealogien, 352. Ergänzung durch Heike Braun.

Landes mittels ‚anspruchsvoller' Verheißungen auf den Weg gebracht wird, und zwar nicht nur ins verheißene Land, sondern auch an jeden Ort (Apg 7,7d) für unbegrenzte Zeit.[71]

Dieses eigene Profil der Abrahamsgeschichte in Apg 7,2-8 steht allerdings nicht im Widerspruch zur Funktion der Genesistexte. So ist nämlich schon allein Gen 12,1-8 eine grundlegende Erzählung zur Selbstdeutung Israels vor seinem Gott, die zugleich in die Abrahamserzählung einführt. In dieser steht dann primär die Konstitution des Gottesvolkes im Festhalten an der Verheißung Gottes trotz größter Verzögerungen bei deren Realisierung im Zentrum. Auf diese Weise kommt den Abrahamserzählungen im Buch Genesis (insbesondere Gen 12,1-8) eine Zeit überspannende Verbindlichkeit zu, die sich auch in Apg 7,2c-8 spiegelt. Zwar interessieren hier nicht so sehr die Gottesvolk- und Menschheitserschließenden Aspekte der Abrahamserzählungen, sondern vielmehr der Gottesbezug Abrahams und das Verhältnis zum Land. Aber gemeinsam ist Apg 7,2c-8 mit den Genesistexten, dass Erschließung der Wirklichkeit von Geschichte stattfindet, die (universales) Potential für Gegenwart und Zukunft hat.[72] Das zeigt sich z.B. in den kurzen Bezugnahmen zur Hörerschaft (Apg 7,2c.4) und der genealogieartigen Aufzählung von Abraham bis zu den zwölf Patriarchen (Apg 7,8). Auch die Fortsetzung der Stephanusrede entfaltet, inwiefern die Geschichte der Erscheinung des Gottes der Herrlichkeit vor Abraham für Gegenwart und Zukunft wegweisende Bedeutung hat. Denn immer wieder werden die Verheißungen Gottes an Abraham aufgegriffen und deren sukzessive Erfüllung erzählt. Auch die Fokussierung des Themas ‚Land' zieht sich durch die Stephanusrede hindurch. Entsprechend der Relativierung der Bedeutung des Landes für die Begegnung mit Gott, auf die Apg 7,2bc-8 hinweist, wird der polyseme Begriff ὁ τόπος οὗτος (Apg 7,7d) an verschiedenen Stellen der Rede implizit oder explizit mit unterschiedlichen Bedeutungen gefüllt.

So werden in dieser Art Relektüre von Genesisbildern in Apg 7,2-8 entscheidende Grundlagen – sowohl thematische als auch textstrategische – für die weitere Geschichtserzählung in der Stephanusrede gelegt. Deshalb wird in Folgendem an einigen Textpassagen exemplarisch untersucht, wie die Stephanus mithilfe der Schrift Geschichte Israels in besonderer Weise deutet und die bleibende Relevanz darin enthaltener Themen für seine Hörerschaft verdeutlicht.

---

71 Vgl. SCHIFFNER, Lukas liest Exodus, 358-359.
72 Vgl. SEEBASS, Genesis II, 12, 20-21. Ähnlich WESTERMANN, Genesis II, 183.

3.2 Starke Raffungen Apg 7,9-16 und Apg 7,17-19

Der Schriftgebrauch der nächsten beiden Abschnitte der Stephanusrede ist vor allem durch starke Raffungen von Erzählungen der eingespielten Intertexte gekennzeichnet.

Strukturell folgt die *Geschichte Josefs in Apg 7,9-16* zwar weitgehend dem Text von Gen 37-50,[73] spielt aber meist nur kurz wenige Elemente daraus ein, so dass der Leser häufig gefordert ist, ausgelassene Passagen oder ganze Subtexte aus dem Grundplot der Genesiserzählung selbst einzublenden. Nicht nur durch die Kürze der Schilderung, sondern auch durch die eigene Art ihrer Zusammenstellung und die Kombination mit Referenzen auf Subtexte außerhalb der Josefserzählung, werden bestimmte Aspekte daraus in besonderer Weise fokussiert.[74]

Neben dem Hinweis auf einen Kontrast der »Patriarchen« (Apg 7,9), die Josef verkaufen, zu den in Apg 7,8 erwähnten »Patriarchen«, die den Beschneidungsbund vorbildlich einhalten, steht in Fortsetzung der Abrahamserzählung auch in Apg 7,9-16 das Thema der Anwesenheit Gottes auch außerhalb des verheißenen Landes im Zentrum. Indem hier auf verschiedene Weise aufgezeigt wird, wie Gottes Nähe zu Josef im fremden Ägypten sich positiv für das entstehende Volk Israel auswirkt, wird nämlich die Josefsgeschichte hier als Beispiel für die Erscheinung Gottes in der Geschichte (Apg 7,2) präsentiert. Dabei steht zugleich die Frage nach dem Verhältnis des entstehenden Volkes Israel zum verheißenen Land im Hintergrund.[75] So bilden im Kontext der Stephanusrede die Geschichte Abrahams[76] und Josefs die gemeinsame Basis der Verheißungsgeschichte Israels. An ihnen wird illustriert, dass sich das Volk Israel außerhalb des verheißenen Landes konstituiert und dass sich in der Spannung von Nähe und Distanz zum verheißenen Land ein Leben der Gottesnähe vollzieht.[77]

Die kleine Einheit *Apg 7,17-19* nimmt in verschiedener Hinsicht eine *Schwellenfunktion* innerhalb der Stephanusrede ein, zum einen indem verschiedene Abschnitte innerhalb der Stephanusepisode miteinander

---

73 Das wird an einem Vergleich von Apg 7,9-16 mit der groben Gliederung der Josefsgeschichte deutlich. Letztere findet sich in JACOB, Genesis, 693.
74 Für eine Analyse von Apg 7,9-16 und der darin eingespielten Intertexte vgl. BRAUN, Geschichte des Gottesvolkes, 204-233, und die dort angegebene Literatur.
75 Vgl. z.B. die vielen Wege, die in Apg 7,9-16 beschrieben werden oder die Verlagerung des Begräbnisortes der Erzeltern nach Sichem (Apg 7,16).
76 Es fällt auf, dass die Erwähnung Abrahams in Apg 7,2.16 einen Rahmen um beide Abschnitte der Geschichtserzählung bildet.
77 Ähnlich SCHIFFNER, Lukas liest Exodus, 360.

verknüpft werden,[78] zum anderen durch intertextuelle Referenzen auf Passagen aus der Einleitung des Buches Exodus Ex 1,7-22(2,3).

Nachdem Apg 7,17 die Erfüllung der positiven Verheißung, nämlich das Wachstum des Volkes in Ägypten, notiert und betont (besonders durch die Referenz auf Ex 1,7), dass aus dem *Stamm* Jakobs das *Volk* Israel geworden ist, markiert Apg 7,18 die Schwelle zur Erfüllung der negativen Verheißungen. Hier wird nämlich in Aufnahme von Ex 1,8 der »andere« König über Ägypten als Kontrast zum Pharao der Zeit Josefs (Apg 7,10) eingeführt und damit das Ende der positiven Wachstumsphase angekündigt. Dementsprechend berichtet Apg 7,19 mit Bezügen zu Ex 1,9-14.14-22 von der Erfüllung der negativen Verheißungen, die konkret im lebensbedrohlichen Vorgehen des Königs von Ägypten gegen die Säuglinge »unserer Väter« (Apg 7,19b) besteht. Diese Aussage über den Kindermord dient zugleich als Überleitung, denn hier wird implizit durch die Verknüpfung mit Ex 2,3 über das Verb (ἐκ-)τίθημι zur Mosegeschichte hingeführt.

Indem Apg 7,17-19 die in den Exodustexten zum Teil lebendig ausgestalteten Erzählungen auf wenige Worte verkürzt, werden die Kontraste zwischen der lebensfördernden Wachstumssituation und der lebensbedrohenden Knechtschaft, also auch zwischen der positiven und negativen Verheißung akzentuiert. Außerdem wird durch diese Komprimierung ein unbestimmt langer Zeitraum kurz umrissen, so dass die enge Verbindung der einzelnen Geschichtsabschnitte und -ereignisse umso deutlicher hervortritt. Darüber hinaus erhalten die Inhalte der Exoduserzählungen durch diese Verkürzungen tendenziell einen generellen Charakter, wie etwa die Notiz vom Kindermord (Apg 7,19; Ex 1,15-22) zeigt.

Die in Apg 7,17-19 skizzierte Zeit der Erfüllung der Verheißungen Gottes an Abraham präsentiert sich auch als Schwelle zu den Zuhörern der Rede und zu Stephanus selbst. Die ähnlichen Formulierungen der Wachstumsnotizen in Apg 7,17 und Apg 6,1.7 stellen nämlich die Jerusalemer Gemeinde in Kontinuität zum Wachstum des Volkes Israel. Aber auch die Verbindung der negativen Verheißungen zu den Zuhörern wird betont, indem Apg 7,19 von der schlechten Behandlung »unseres Geschlechts« (τὸ γένος ἡμῶν) und »unserer Väter« (οἱ πατέρες ἡμῶν) spricht. Damit erhält die hier erzählte Verheißungsgeschichte bleibende Relevanz für die Adressaten der Rede.

---

78   So spiegelt sich in Apg 7,17-19 die Struktur der unmittelbaren Abfolge der positiven und negativen Verheißungen von Apg 7,5-7 wider. Inhaltlich kann sogar eine Art wechselseitige Ergänzung zwischen Apg 7,5-7 und Apg 7,17-19 beobachtet werden. Für ausführlichere Untersuchungen zu Apg 7,17-19 und dem darin enthaltenen Schriftgebrauch vgl. BRAUN, Geschichte des Gottesvolkes, 233-245.

3.3 Aktualisierende Deutung der Mosegeschichte Apg 7,20-43

Die relativ lange Erzählung der Mosegeschichte in Apg 7,20-43[79] wird bereits durch intratextuelle Referenzen innerhalb der Stephanusrede in besonderer Weise gestaltet. Signifikant dabei ist, dass sie in die Schilderung der »Zeit der Erfüllung der Verheißung Gottes an Abraham« (Apg 7,17) eingeordnet wird.[80] Zur Darstellung der Mosegeschichte tragen aber auch zahlreiche Bezüge zu diversen Intertexten bei, mit denen in unterschiedlicher Weise umgegangen wird.[81] Dabei lässt sich eine große Bandbreite im Umgang mit diesen Texten beobachten:

Beispielsweise bewirken *Verkürzungen* der Subtexte sowie *auffällige Zusätze* zu ihnen, wie sie etwa in der Schilderung von Moses Kindheit und Jugend Apg 7,20-22 zu finden sind, eine unterschwellige Leserlenkung.[82] Denn durch diesen Umgang mit den Intertexten wird die Aufmerksamkeit auf Besonderheiten der Mosedarstellung gerichtet und die Gestalt des Mose in spezieller Weise profiliert. Die auffälligen Abweichungen zu den Exodustexten dienen also dazu, die Aufmerksamkeit auf die Besonderheiten von Mose zu lenken. So wird Mose mithilfe intra- und intertextueller Referenzen von Beginn an als Prophet ausgewiesen und dabei mit Jesus und Stephanus parallelisiert. Dadurch öffnet sich nämlich der Text für eine Erzählung von Moses prophetischer Wirksamkeit, aber auch für eine Erzählung von möglicher Ablehnung entsprechend dem typischen Schicksal eines Propheten.

Aufschlussreich für die Geschichtsdarstellung der Stephanusrede ist weiterhin die Tatsache, dass manche Passagen aus Exodustexten zum Teil fast wörtlich wiedergegeben werden oder nur sehr gering von ihnen abgewichen wird. Das ist etwa in der Schilderung zweier Konflikte in Apg 7,23-29 der Fall,[83] in der sich zeigt, dass hier gedeutete und aktualisierte Geschichtserzählung vorliegt. Indem die beiden exemplarischen Konfliktsituationen ähnlich ausführlich und anschaulich erzählt

---

79 Zur Struktur von Apg 7,20-43 vgl. BRAUN, Geschichte des Gottesvolkes, 246-249.
80 Dies signalisieren die Zeitangaben (Apg 7,20.23.30) sowie etliche motivische oder lexematische Rückgriffe auf die Verheißungen in Apg 7,5-7 und auf die Schwellenpassage Apg 7,17-19. Vgl. dazu BRAUN, Geschichte des Gottesvolkes, 250-251.
81 Im Rahmen dieses Beitrags können nur wenige Passagen daraus angerissen werden, um Besonderheiten des Schriftgebrauchs in Apg 7,20-43 aufzuzeigen. Für exaktere Untersuchungen zu Apg 7,20-43 vgl. BRAUN, Geschichte des Gottesvolkes, 250-327.
82 Apg 7,20-22 folgt dem Grundplot von Ex 2,1-10, spielt aber auch auf Ex 4,10; Lk 24,19 und Apg 6,3.10 an. Für eine Analyse von Apg 7,20-22 vgl. BRAUN, Geschichte des Gottesvolkes, 250-257, und die dort angegebene Literatur.
83 Apg 7,23-24 entfaltet anhand eines Konflikts zwischen einem Ägypter und einem Israeliten (in Analogie zu Ex 2,11-12) Moses besonderen Gottesbezug und seine prophetischen Züge, Apg 7,26-29 setzt dieses Mosebild mithilfe fast wörtlicher Einspielung von Ex 2,13-14 fort. Vgl. dazu BRAUN, Geschichte des Gottesvolkes, 258-276.

werden wie in den Exodustexten (Ex 2,11-12.13-14), wird die hier erzählte Geschichte für die Hörer der Rede gewissermaßen neu lebendig. Durch die Tendenz der Generalisierung dieser Episoden werden sie zugleich transparent für andere, analoge Situationen.[84]

Ein ähnlicher Umgang mit Subtexten findet sich auch im nächsten Abschnitt der Mosegeschichte Apg 7,30-34, der mit ‚Erscheinen Gottes vor Mose in der Wüste des Berges Sinai' (Apg 7,30) überschrieben werden kann und sich an Ex 3,1-10 anlehnt.[85] Die zum Teil nur sehr geringen Unterschiede zu den jeweiligen Subtexten verdeutlichen einige Schwerpunkte der Geschichtsdarstellung.[86] Signifikant ist auch hier eine Tendenz zur Generalisierung im Vergleich zu Ex 3,1-10, die hinsichtlich der Notlage Israels, des Befreiungswillens Gottes und der Sendung von Mose erkennbar ist. Dadurch verstärkt sich erneut der exemplarische Charakter dieser Erzählung vom Heilshandeln Gottes in Apg 7,30-34, so dass sie leichter auf andere Situationen übertragbar wird.[87]

Besonders interessant sind deutende Reflexionen mithilfe der Schrift, die in der Geschichtsdarstellung der Stephanusrede wiederholt zu finden sind. So kommentiert etwa Apg 7,35 die bisherige Mosegeschichte und thematisiert dabei mithilfe von vielfältigen intratextuellen Verknüpfungen die Ablehnung des von Gott erwählten Heilsmittlers Mose durch die Israeliten.[88] Damit wird ein Schema formuliert, das auch die weitere Darstellung des Geschichtsverlaufs prägt.[89] Zentral

---

84 Ein Transfer auf andere Situationen deutet sich bereits innerhalb der Stephanusrede in Apg 7,35 an. Die Abwendung von Mose bzw. Gott wird auch in Apg 7,40 generalisiert. Vgl. BRAUN, Geschichte des Gottesvolkes, 308-311.

85 Vgl. Apg 7,30-31 mit Ex 3,1-4, die Gottesrede in Apg 7,32a mit Ex 3,6b, Moses Reaktion darauf in Apg 7,32b mit Ex 3,6c und die Rede Gottes an Mose in Apg 7,33-34 mit Ex 3,5-10. Vgl. BRAUN, Geschichte des Gottesvolkes, 276-290.

86 Das Zentrum bildet hier die Selbstoffenbarung Gottes als Gott, der in der Geschichte der Väter Israels kontinuierlich wirkt (Apg 7,32a), zugleich aber bleibend transzendent ist. Dem entspricht eine angemessene Gottesfurcht durch Mose (Apg 7,31a.b.32b) und die Qualifizierung des Ortes der Gottesoffenbarung als heilig (Apg 7,33b).

87 Diese Offenheit korrespondiert dem bisherigen Duktus der Stephanusrede, was etwa an der Thematik ‚Ort Gottes' zu sehen ist: Nachdem Apg 7,7d angesichts der Frage nach dem Tempel als einem privilegierten Ort der Anwesenheit Gottes (Apg 6,13-14) andeutet, dass es verschiedene Orte Gottes und des Gottesdienstes gibt, wird dies durch die Gottesrede in Apg 7,33b noch einmal unterstrichen.

88 So wird auf Apg 7,25.27-28 angespielt. Außerdem zeigen sich Referenzen auf Ex 2,14; Lev 25,31.32; Ps 18,15; 77,35. Vgl. BRAUN, Geschichte des Gottesvolkes, 292-293. Daneben verdeutlichen auch lexematische und strukturelle Bezüge zu Apg 3,13-14 den Kontrast zwischen dem Handeln Gottes an Mose und dem Verhalten der Israeliten.

89 Innerhalb der Stephanusepisode kann Apg 7,35 auch als Widerlegung der Anklage, Stephanus rede blasphemisch gegen Mose (Apg 6,11.14) verstanden werden. Vgl. auch BARRETT, Acts, 364. FITZMYER, Acts, 378.

dabei ist demnach das spannungsvolle ‚Dreiecksverhältnis' zwischen Gott, Mose und »unseren Vätern« bzw. dem Volk Israel. Wenn dieses (im Folgenden) anhand einzelner Ereignissen der Wüstenzeit Israels entfaltet wird, stellt sich zugleich durchgehend die zentrale Frage nach Gottes Präsenz und Wirksamkeit.

Dementsprechend wird in Apg 7,36-38 Mose hymnusartig[90] als Heilsmittler Gottes fokussiert und dabei ebenfalls verschiedene Intertexte verwendet (vgl. Apg 7,37 mit Dtn 18,15 und Apg 3,22; Apg 7,38 mit Ex 19,1-2 und Dtn 4,1-10[91]). Ab Apg 7,39 wird auch das Verhalten »unserer Väter«, also des Volkes Israel, mithilfe von Referenzen auf diverse Intertexte eingehend reflektiert (vgl. insbesondere Apg 7,42a mit Dtn 4,16-30[92]).

Die Prophetenworte in Apg 7,42b-43 bündeln abschließend die bisher geschilderte Kontrastgeschichte und das Verhältnis Gott – Mose – Volk Israel. In fast wörtlicher Wiedergabe von Am 5,25-27 wird hier nämlich die Wüstenzeit als Zeit der Abwendung Israels von Gott durch Übertreten des Verbots von Götterbildern und von Götzendienst charakterisiert und die in Apg 7,39-42 dargestellte Dynamik zwischen dem Fehlverhalten Israels und der entsprechenden Strafe Gottes illustriert. Gerade die geringen Unterschiede zu Am 5,25-27 zeigen,[93] dass in Apg 7,42b-43 die Anstößigkeit des Ungehorsams Israels betont[94] und die Strafankündigung Gottes mit einer Anspielung auf das Babylonische Exil sogar einer Übertreffung davon (ἐπέκεινα Βαβυλῶνος) darstellt.[95] Indem die Prophetenworte in Apg 7,43 mit dieser Gerichtsankündigung enden, ohne noch einmal Gott als Sprecher zu erwähnen (Am 5,27), erhalten sie im Kontext der Stephanusrede den Charakter unmittelbarer Aktualität. Damit erweist sich dieses kommentierende Prophetenwort als eine Schwelle zwischen der Geschichte Israels und der Si-

---

90 Vgl. den stereotypen Beginn der Aussagen von Apg 7,36-38 mit οὗτος.

91 Ein Vergleich zwischen Dtn 4,1-40 und Apg 7,38 findet sich bei VAN DE SANDT, Amos, 67-87 und SCHIFFNER, Lukas liest Exodus, 371. Für eine Zusammenfassung dazu vgl. BRAUN, Geschichte des Gottesvolkes, 303-305.

92 Vgl. dazu VAN DE SANDT, Amos, 74-77. Vgl. SCHIFFNER, Lukas liest Exodus, 375, Anm. 191. BRAUN, Geschichte des Gottesvolkes, 314-317.

93 Für eine Gegenüberstellung von Am 5,25-27 und Apg 7,42b-43 vgl. insbesondere RUSAM, Das Alte Testament bei Lukas, 141-144. VAN DE SANDT, Amos, 75, 78, 86-87. SCHIFFNER, Lukas liest Exodus, 376–377. BRAUN, Geschichte des Gottesvolkes, 319-323.

94 Darauf weist etwa folgender Unterschied zum Amostext hin: Während Am 5,26 die Absicht für das Anfertigen der τύποι mit dem Relativsatz οὓς ἐποιήσατε ἑαυτοῖς als ‚Selbstzweck' für die Israeliten beschreibt, liegt diese Absicht laut Apg 7,43 (οὓς ἐποιήσατε προσκυνεῖν αὐτοῖς) ausdrücklich in der Verehrung der τύποι.

95 Apg 7,43b nennt bei der Ankündigung der Strafe für den Götzendienst ἐπέκεινα Βαβυλῶνος als Ort der Umsiedelung statt Damaskus (Am 5,27).

tuation in der Stephanusepisode. Eine Art Scharnierfunktion[96] kommt Apg 7,42b-43 aber auch innerhalb der Stephanusrede zu. Zum einen nimmt es nämlich zentrale Themen der vorangehenden Geschichtsdarstellung auf,[97] zum anderen öffnet es den Abschnitt für die Fortsetzung der Rede, indem es die Frage nach der Umsetzung der angedrohten Verbannung in den Raum stellt sowie Motive und Stichworte bietet, die im Folgenden bedeutend sein werden.

Insgesamt wird in Apg 7,20-43 also die Mosegeschichte durch verschiedene Arten intertextueller Bezüge nicht nur nacherzählt, sondern gedeutet und aktualisiert. Gedeutet wird sie als Geschichte der bereits erfüllten Verheißungen und der noch nicht erfüllten Verheißungen, als Geschichte des Konflikts zwischen Gottes Heilsmittler Mose und dem Volk Israel, also auch als Geschichte des Kontrastes zwischen Mose und dem Volk Israel. Letztlich wird sie sogar als Geschichte der Abwendung von Gott interpretiert, die eine unheilvolle Gerichtsankündigung nach sich zieht. Diesen Deutungen der Mosegeschichte liegt insgesamt die Frage nach der Anwesenheit Gottes in der Geschichte Israels zugrunde. Aktualisiert wird diese Geschichte durch die Offenheit des Textes für verschiedene Kontexte, denn dadurch entsteht für die Adressaten der Rede die Möglichkeit, sich innerhalb des kontrastreichen ‚Dreiecksverhältnisses' zwischen Gott, Mose (Gesetz) und Volk Israel (»unsere Väter«) zu positionieren.

3.4 Effektvolle Kombination von Intertexten Apg 7,44-50

Mit der Einführung des Zeltes des Zeugnisses (ἡ σκηνὴ τοῦ μαρτυρίου)[98] in Apg 7,44 in Anspielung auf Ex 33,7-11[99] wird vor dem Hintergrund des Abfalls Israels von Gott (Apg 7,39-43) die Frage thematisiert, wie Gott trotzdem im Volk Israel anwesend ist.[100] Ein Vergleich mit Ex 33,7-

---

96 RUSAM, Das Alte Testament bei Lukas, 143, spricht von einer „Schlüsselfunktion".
97 Für Verknüpfungen zur gesamten Stephanusepisode vgl. BRAUN, Geschichte des Gottesvolkes, 323-324, 326, und die dort angegebene Literatur.
98 ἡ σκηνὴ τοῦ μαρτυρίου ist in der Regel Terminus für die Stiftshütte, das tragbare Heiligtum in der Wüste. Vgl. BAUER, Wörterbuch, 1508. Laut FITZMYER, Acts, 382, ist dieser Begriff in der LXX eine Übertragung des hebräischen 'ōhel mô'ēd.
99 In Ex 33,7 wird im Anschluss an den Götzendienst Israels, der es dem Herrn unmöglich macht, mit dem »halsstarrigen« Volk ins verheißene Land einzuziehen, das Zelt des Zeugnisses eingeführt. Vgl. DOHMEN, Zelt, 164. VAN DE SANDT, Amos, 70.
100 Dies zeigt sich zum einen an der besonderen Art der Einführung von ἡ σκηνὴ τοῦ μαρτυρίου sowie seiner kontextuellen Einbettung, zum anderen durch die Anspielung auf Ex 33,7-11. Vgl. VAN DE SANDT, Presence, 35. BRAUN, Geschichte des Gottesvolkes, 330-331.

11[101] zeigt, dass die Stephanusrede die Funktion des »Zeltes des Zeugnisses« als Ort der Anwesenheit Gottes trotz der Sünde fokussiert. Es ist nämlich laut Apg 7,44-45 in andauerndem Besitz der Väter Israels während der Wüstenwanderung und zeichnet sich daher auch durch eine grundlegende Mobilität aus, die bei aller Nähe die Transzendenz Gottes wahrt.[102]

In Kontinuität zu diesem tragbaren Zelt als Ort der Präsenz Gottes wird in Apg 7,46 das Gesuch Davids nach einer »Zeltwohnung« vorgestellt: ὃς εὗρεν χάριν ἐνώπιον τοῦ θεοῦ καὶ ᾐτήσατο εὑρεῖν σκήνωμα τῷ οἴκῳ Ἰακώβ. Auch hier wird der Aspekt der Beweglichkeit betont, was sich anhand der Kombination der jeweils fein veränderten Intertexte Ex 33,12-17; 2 Sam 7,1-7 und Ps 131,5 LXX zeigt.[103] Die Phrase zur Charakterisierung Davids in seinem Gottesbezug (ὃς εὗρεν χάριν ἐνώπιον τοῦ θεοῦ) findet sich in identischer oder ähnlicher Form des Öfteren in Ex 33,12-17[104] bezogen auf Mose. Während nach Ex 33,17 Moses Frage, wie Gott im Volk auf dem Weg ins verheißene Land anwesend sein wird, offen bleibt, antwortet Apg 7,45 darauf, indem das Mitführen der σκηνὴ τοῦ μαρτυρίου bis zur Inbesitznahme der Völker und bis zu den Tagen Davids notiert wird.[105] In dieser neuen Situation ist es nicht Mose, der nach Gottes Präsenz im Volk fragt, sondern David, indem er ein σκήνωμα (»Zeltwohnung«) für das Haus Jakob (und im Haus Jakob)[106] sucht. Durch die Parallelisierung von David und Mose über den besonderen Gottesbezug mit der Wendung εὗρεν χάριν ἐνώπιον τοῦ θεοῦ wird auch David als Mittler vorgestellt. Auf dieser Grundlage lässt sich auch Davids Bitte zugunsten Israels, also »für das Haus Jakob« (τῷ οἴκῳ Ἰακώβ), verstehen.[107] Dass es dabei ebenfalls um die Frage nach der Anwesenheit Gottes geht, wird noch deutlicher, insofern mit der Notiz von Davids Bitte 2 Sam 7,1-7 eingespielt wird.[108] Da die Zeitangabe ἕως

---

101 Vgl. BRAUN, Geschichte des Gottesvolkes, 331-336. Gemeinsam ist beiden Texten die Fokussierung auf Mose als Offenbarungsmittler. Dies wird in Apg 7,44 zusätzlich durch die Einspielung von Ex 25,8-9, einer Passage aus den Anweisungen Gottes für das Heiligtum, deutlich.
102 Vgl. GANSER-KERPERIN, Tempel, 250. BRAUN, Geschichte des Gottesvolkes, 336-338.
103 Vgl. VAN DE SANDT, Presence, 46, 51-52.
104 Vgl. VAN DE SANDT, Presence, 52, Anm. 58.
105 Vgl. VAN DE SANDT, Presence, 41-42.
106 Zur Zweideutigkeit des Dativs τῷ οἴκῳ Ἰακώβ vgl. BRAUN, Geschichte des Gottesvolkes, 339. Zur textkritischen Diskussion von τῷ οἴκῳ Ἰακώβ vgl. METZGER, Textual Commentary, 351-353. Die Mehrzahl der Exegeten folgt der Lesart τῷ οἴκῳ Ἰακώβ.
107 Denn ähnlich wie in Ex 33,13 werden hier Ausgangspunkt und Ziel der Bitte jeweils mit dem Verb εὑρίσκω formuliert. Die parallele Darstellung von Davids Gottesbezug zu dem von Mose suggeriert außerdem eine positive Resonanz Gottes auf Davids Bitte (ähnlich wie in Ex 33,12-17). Vgl. VAN DE SANDT, Presence, 52.
108 Auf 2 Sam 7,1-7 verweisen u.a. BARRETT, Acts, 372. SCHNEIDER, Apg, 466.

τῶν ἡμερῶν Δαυίδ (Apg 7,45), die den Abschluss des Mitführens der σκηνὴ τοῦ μαρτυρίου und der Vertreibung der Völker durch Gott markiert, fast wörtlich ἕως τῆς ἡμέρας ταύτης (2 Sam 7,6) aufnimmt, spiegelt sich auch in Apg 7,46 die neue historische Situation der Ruhe vor den Feinden im verheißenen Land von 2 Sam 7,1 wider. In dieser Lage geht es erneut um die Frage nach der Anwesenheit Gottes, ähnlich wie beim Aufbruch vom Sinai nach dem Abfall Israels von Gott. Das deutet sich besonders darin an, dass der Bericht von der Mitnahme des Zeltes als beweglicher Offenbarungsort Gottes bis zu den Tagen Davids (Apg 7,45-46) auf die summarische Darstellung Gottes über seine Anwesenheit im Laufe der Geschichte Israels in einem beweglichen Zelt 2 Sam 7,6-7 (οὐ κατῴκηκα ἐν οἴκῳ ... καὶ ἤμην ἐμπεριπατῶν ἐν καταλύματι καὶ ἐν σκηνῇ) anspielt.[109] Neben dieser Antwort Gottes wird in Apg 7,45-46 auch das Anliegen Davids eingespielt, das implizit in der Zurückweisung Gottes 2 Sam 7,5b (οὐ σὺ οἰκοδομήσεις μοι οἶκον τοῦ κατοικῆσαί με) enthalten ist. Allerdings ist in Davids Bitte in Apg 7,46 nicht vom ‚Bauen' eines ‚Hauses' für Gott in scharfem Kontrast zur beweglichen σκηνή die Rede, sondern von εὑρεῖν σκήνωμα τῷ οἴκῳ Ἰακώβ. Diese Wendung verweist auf Ps 131,5 LXX[110] und bildet dort den Abschluss einer Bitte an Gott (Ps 131,1-5 LXX), sich an Davids Bemühungen für das Tempelbauprojekt zu erinnern. Interessant ist bei dieser Referenz vor allem der Unterschied bezüglich des Dativs τῷ οἴκῳ Ἰακώβ in Apg 7,46 und τῷ θεῷ Ἰακώβ in Ps 131,5 LXX.[111] Während David in Ps 131,5 LXX das Vorhaben formuliert, Jerusalem als festen Wohnort Gottes inmitten seines Volkes zu sichern, steht in Apg 7,46 erneut die Verbindung dieses Ortes (σκήνωμα) mit dem Volk Israel (τῷ οἴκῳ Ἰακώβ) im Vordergrund. Demnach bezeichnet σκήνωμα in Apg 7,46 weniger einen Wohnsitz für Gott, als vielmehr einen Ort für das Haus Jakob, an dem Gott ihm begegnet – analog und in Kontinuität zur σκηνὴ τοῦ μαρτυρίου.[112]

Inwiefern diese Kombination verschiedener Intertexte die Sinnpotentiale in diesem Redeabschnitt prägt, wird auch in der an sich neutralen Notiz von Salomos ‚Haus-Bau' in Apg 7,47 deutlich: Σολομῶν δὲ

---

109 Vgl. VAN DE SANDT, Presence, 46. PENNER, Praise, 314, Anm. 110 betrachtet sogar die gesamte Erzählung 2 Sam 7,1-17 als Intertext von Apg 7,46-47.
110 Auf Ps 131,5 LXX verweisen u.a. BARRETT, Acts, 372. SCHNEIDER, Apg, 466. PESCH, Apg, 256. ROLOFF, Apg, 125.
111 Daneben fällt auf, dass Ps 131,5 LXX das Anliegen Davids als Schwur bezeichnet, während Apg 7,46 es neutraler mit »bitten« formuliert. So rückt hier David mit seiner starken Motivation von Ps 131 LXX in den Hintergrund.
112 Vgl. VAN DE SANDT, Presence, 51-52. Damit erfüllt sich indirekt die Verheißung des Gottesdienstes »an diesem Ort« (Apg 7,7), da σκήνωμα innerhalb des verheißenen Landes die Fortsetzung der σκηνή der Wüstenzeit darstellt. Vgl. PENNER, Praise, 310.

ᾠκοδόμησεν αὐτῷ οἶκον.[113] Angesichts von Referenzen auf den Bericht über Salomos Tempelbau in 1 Kön 6,2a und das Tempelweihgebet in 1 Kön 8,19 enthält Apg 7,47 allerdings negative Implikationen, da Salomo hier ausschließlich in der Rolle des Erbauers dieses »Hauses«[114] betrachtet wird, nicht als »König« oder »Sohn Davids«. Besonders deutlich wird die kritische Bewertung von Salomos ‚Haus-Bau' vor dem Hintergrund des unmittelbaren Kontextes dieser Notiz und der dortigen Verwendung von Intertexten. Im Gegensatz zu Moses σκηνή und Davids σκήνωμα, die als bewegliche, dem Willen Gottes entsprechende Orte der Anwesenheit Gottes dargestellt werden, wird das »Haus« Salomos als festes Haus (οἶκος) charakterisiert, das noch dazu von Salomo selbst gebaut ist. Zu diesem negativen Bild von Salomo und seinem ‚Haus-Bau' trägt insbesondere die Vermeidung von οἶκος in Davids Bitte (im Unterschied zu 2 Sam 7,1-17) und die Übernahme von σκήνωμα aus Ps 131,5 LXX bei. Dadurch entspricht nämlich David in Apg 7,46 Gottes Zurückweisung eines οἶκος (2 Sam 7,5b-7), während Salomo laut Apg 7,47 genau das macht (ᾠκοδόμησεν αὐτῷ οἶκον), was Gott in 2 Sam 7,5b als Ort seiner Anwesenheit in der Geschichte Israels ablehnt (οὐ σὺ οἰκοδομήσεις μοι οἶκον τοῦ κατοικῆσαί με).

Explizit wird dieser ‚(Gottes)-Haus-Bau' durch Salomo im Kommentar der Erzählstimme (Stephanus) Apg 7,48 kritisiert: ἀλλ' οὐχ ὁ ὕψιστος ἐν χειροποιήτοις κατοικεῖ.

Insofern mit dem Adjektiv χειροποίητος an anderen Stellen Götzenbilder im Gegenüber zum wahren Gott Israels bezeichnet werden (vgl. Lev 26,1.30; Jes 2,18; Weish 14,8 u.a.),[115] wird der οἶκος Salomos auf eine Ebene mit diesen Götzenbildern gestellt. Dies wird auch daran deutlich, dass diese Stellungnahme des Stephanus zum οἶκος Salomos am selben Punkt ansetzt wie Jesu Tempelkritik (Mk 14,58). Dort wird nämlich der Tempel ebenfalls mit dem Attribut χειροποίητος bewertet, was

---

113 Zur Diskussion um das Verständnis von δέ und αὐτῷ in Apg 7,47 vgl. PENNER, Praise, 313. SPENCER, Acts, 78. WASSERBERG, Israels Mitte, 248-249. SCHIFFNER, Lukas liest Exodus, 380. WITHERINGTON, Acts, 263. FITZMYER, Acts, 383. JERVELL, Apg, 245.

114 Diese eher distanzierte Vorstellung Salomos entspricht der auch sonst im lk Doppelwerk zu beobachtenden Distanz zu Salomo. So wird Jesus in der Genealogie Lk 3,23-38 nicht auf die nachdavidische Linie Salomos und die ihm folgenden Könige des Südreichs zurückgeführt (im Unterschied zu Mt 1,6-11), sondern auf eine Nebenlinie über den Davidsohn Natan. Auch im Geschichtsabriss Apg 13,16-31 wird Salomo in der Reihe der Mittlergestalten nicht erwähnt.

115 Im Kontext der Stephanusrede ist hinzuweisen auf die Anfertigung des goldenen Kalbes in 7,40 (ἐμοσχοποιέω), die Freude der Israeliten über die Werke ihrer Hände (εὐφραίνοντο ἐν τοῖς ἔργοις τῶν χειρῶν αὐτῶν 7,41) und die Herstellung der Götzen in 7,43 (τοὺς τύπους οὓς ἐποιήσατε). Auch pagane Tempel werden als χειροποίητος bezeichnet (Jes 16,12; Apg 17,24). Vgl. VAN DE SANDT, Presence, 54. SIEGERT, „Zerstört diesen Tempel ...!", 112. GANSER-KERPERIN, Tempel, 249. BARRETT, Acts, 373.

durch die kontrastierende Ankündigung eines »nicht von Menschenhand gemachten« (ἀχειροποίητος) Tempels, die auf eine adäquatere Vorstellung verweist, unterstrichen wird.[116]

Bestätigt wird diese harte Kritik an Salomos Tempel in den Prophetenworten Apg 7,49-50: ὁ οὐρανός μοι θρόνος, ἡ δὲ γῆ ὑποπόδιον τῶν ποδῶν μου· ποῖον οἶκον οἰκοδομήσετέ μοι, λέγει κύριος, ἢ τίς τόπος τῆς καταπαύσεώς μου; οὐχὶ ἡ χείρ μου ἐποίησεν ταῦτα πάντα;

Diese führen mit einer fast wörtlichen Wiedergabe von Jes 66,1-2a[117] schöpfungstheologische Aspekte an, mit deren Hilfe über eine angemessene Haltung gegenüber dem Tempel als Ort der Anwesenheit Gottes reflektiert wird.[118] Was bisher innerhalb der Rede mit dem polysemen Begriff ὁ τόπος illustriert wurde, formuliert nun dieses Prophetenwort – ebenfalls unter Verwendung von ὁ τόπος – schöpfungstheologisch: dass der transzendente Gott nicht nur an »diesem einen Ort« anwesend ist, sondern an ‚jedem Ort auf der Erde und besonders im Himmel'.

Durch die Einspielung der Prophetenworte Jes 66,1-2 und durch feine Veränderungen dieses Subtextes werden also an dieser Stelle der Stephanusrede fundamentale Aussagen über Gott mit ebenso fundamentaler Kritik an unangemessenem Gottesbezug in der Geschichte Israels und implizit mit Kritik an den Gegnern des Stephanus verbunden. Dazu tragen zum einen schon die von Jes 66,1-2 übernommenen rhetorischen Fragen bei, zum anderen aber besonders die Umformulierung der einfachen Erklärung (γάρ) in Jes 66,2a zu einer weiteren rhetorischen Frage in Apg 7,50 (οὐχὶ ἡ χείρ μου ἐποίησεν ταῦτα πάντα; »hat nicht meine Hand das alles gemacht?«). Insofern diese indirekt zu einer bejahenden Antwort auffordert, führt diese kleine Veränderung des

---

116 Apg 7,48 kann auch als Widerlegung der Anklagen gegen Stephanus verstanden werden. Aufgrund des Bezugs zwischen Apg 7,48 und Apg 6,11.13-14 und Mk 14,58 kann darüber nachgedacht werden, welche Funktion die Übertragung des Tempelmotivs innerhalb des lk Doppelwerks vom Prozess Jesu auf die Stephanusepisode hat. Vgl. dazu BRAUN, Geschichte des Gottesvolkes, 350-352, 360-361.

117 Für eine Gegenüberstellung von Apg 7,49-50 und Jes 66,1-2a vgl. BRAUN, Geschichte des Gottesvolkes, 353-359, sowie die dort angegebenen Literatur.

118 Hier sind folgende Aspekte enthalten: 1. Kritisiert wird nicht grundsätzlich alles von Menschenhand für Gott Gemachte, sondern der οἶκος als fester Wohnort Gottes. (vgl. JESKA, Geschichte Israels, 181, 208. GANSER-KERPERIN, Tempel, 250. HAACKER, Stephanus in der Geschichte, 1538). 2. Der Tempel wird nicht prinzipiell als Heiligtum abgelehnt, sondern nur die Vorstellung, dieser sei einzig wahrer Wohnort Gottes. 3. Diese Relativierung der exklusiven Bedeutung des Tempels ist darin begründet, dass die Anwesenheit des transzendenten Schöpfer-Gottes auf keinen bestimmten Ort fixiert werden kann (vgl. VAN DE SANDT, Presence, 56-57. LARKIN, Acts, 118).

Gedankengangs von Jes 66,1-2 zu einer Aktualisierung der Kritik und bereitet damit auch den Übergang zu Apg 7,51-53 vor.[119]

3.5 Aktualisierende Vorwürfe gegen die Zuhörer Apg 7,51-53

Wenn Apg 7,51a mit dem doppelten Vokativ σκληροτράχηλοι καὶ ἀπερίτμητοι zu scharfen Vorwürfen gegen die Adressaten der Rede (ὑμεῖς) ansetzt, entsteht eine große Leerstelle zwischen Apg 7,47-50 und Apg 7,51, da nun aus der Schilderung der Vergangenheit der Geschichte Israels in die ‚Erzähl-Gegenwart' der Stephanusrede gesprungen wird. Dadurch kommt dem Prophetenwort in Apg 7,49-50 als (gewissermaßen allgemeingültiger) Abschluss der Geschichtsdarstellung besonderes Gewicht zu. Dasselbe gilt für die distanzierende Erwähnung des ‚Gottes-Haus-Baus' Salomos, zu der die Zuhörer durch diese Gestaltung in unmittelbare Verbindung gebracht werden.

Die Schärfe der Kritik an den Zuhörern ist schon in der Anrede mit σκληροτράχηλοι und ἀπερίτμητοι, die zum einen die Gottesrede von Ex 33,3.5, zum anderen diverse prophetische Anklagen aufnehmen (vgl. etwa Jer 6,10b; 9,1-25),[120] impliziert und wird dann in Apg 7,51b zunächst mit dem Vorwurf des permanenten Widerstandes gegen den Heiligen Geist in Kontinuität mit den Vätern Israels (ὑμεῖς ἀεὶ τῷ πνεύματι τῷ ἁγίῳ ἀντιπίπτετε) ausdrücklich formuliert. Auch dabei unterstreichen Referenzen auf Subtexte die Tragweite dieses Vergehens (vgl. Num 27,14),[121] die nicht zuletzt in ähnlicher Weise in prophetischen Texten ausgedrückt wird (vgl. Jes 63,10).[122] Insofern dieser pauschale Vorwurf im Kontext der Stephanusrede zunächst auf »eure Väter« bezogen wird, interpretiert er das im Geschichtsrückblick geschilderte Verhalten Israels zusammenfassend. Darüber hinaus wird aber zugleich die immer wieder implizierte Kontinuität zwischen den Vätern Israels und den Hörern nun explizit und zwar speziell im Hinblick auf das Fehlverhalten formuliert, indem der Zusatz καὶ ὑμεῖς die Adressaten der Stephanusrede auf eine Ebene mit den Vätern stellt. Was den Vätern – innerhalb der Stephanusrede – angelastet wird, kann auch auf die Hörer übertragen werden: Abwendung von Gott durch Göt-

---

119 Zum einen wird in Apg 7,51-53 die Anklage fortgesetzt – analog zu Jes 66. Zum anderen werden durch die rhetorischen Fragen, auf die eine bejahende Antwort erwartet wird, die Anklagen in Apg 7,51-53 betont. Vgl. KOET, Dreams, 66.
120 Für eine exakte Analyse der intertextuellen Referenzen vgl. BRAUN, Geschichte des Gottesvolkes, 363-366, und die dort angegebene Literatur.
121 Vgl. BARRETT, Acts, 376. SCHIFFNER, Lukas liest Exodus, 384, Anm. 248.
122 Vgl. BARRETT, Acts, 376. SPENCER, Acts, 80.

zendienst und eine unangemessene, dem Götzendienst ähnliche Haltung zum Tempel (vgl. besonders Apg 7,39.42-43.48-50).

Deutlich distanziert sich der Redner Stephanus an dieser Stelle allerdings, indem er von »euren Vätern« (οἱ πατέρες ὑμῶν) spricht – im Gegensatz zur Geschichtsdarstellung[123] –, und die Hörer mit ὑμεῖς anspricht.[124] Dem korrespondiert, dass im Widerstand gegen den Heiligen Geist auch das Verhalten der Hörer gegen Stephanus enthalten ist, da dieser in Apg 6,3.5.10 deutlich als Geistträger vorgestellt wird. In der Ablehnung von diesem konkretisiert und aktualisiert sich also der hier vorgeworfene Widerstand gegen den Heiligen Geist.[125]

Der Vorwurf des halsstarrigen Widerstandes in Apg 7,51 nimmt auch ein Motiv auf, das das gesamte lukanische Doppelwerk wie ein roter Faden durchzieht (Lk 2,30-32.34-35; Apg 13,43-47; Apg 18,1-8; Apg 28,16-31 in Aufnahme von Jes 6,9-11 LXX) und zur Reflexion über das Verhältnis zwischen Judentum und entstehendem Christentum anregt. Bei der Verkündigung Jesu als ‚Gottes Heil' für Israel und die Völker, die im Zentrum des lukanischen Doppelwerks steht, stellt sich zugleich die Frage nach der Akzeptanz dieser Heilsankündigung (vgl. Lk 2,30-32.34-35). Da Jesus und seine Verkündigung immer wieder von einem Teil der Juden an verschiedenen Orten abgelehnt wird (Apg 13,45; 18,6; 28,24), geht mit der universalen Heilsverkündigung zugleich ein Trennungsvorgang innerhalb Israels einher. Diese Trennung wird sehr deutlich in der Schilderung der Geschichte Israels im Sinne einer Geschichte des Abfallens von Gott in der Stephanusrede und im Vorwurf Apg 7,51. Dass Israel trotz dieses Trennungsprozesses nicht aus dem Heilshandeln Gottes ausgeschlossen ist und die Verstockung Israels heilsgeschichtliche Bedeutung hat, wie der weitere Kontext des lukanischen Doppelwerks zeigt, wird in Apg 7,51 allerdings offen gehalten. Dadurch regt der Text verstärkt zur Reflexion über das Verhältnis zwischen Judentum und entstehendem Christentum an und erweist sich auch hier als ein Schwellentext mit Scharnierfunkion innerhalb der Erzählung des „Weges des Heils".[126]

---

123 Dort bezieht sich Stephanus in der Regel deutlich in die Gemeinschaft mit seinen Hörern und folglich in diese Kontinuität zu den Vätern ein (Apg 7,2.11.12.15.19. 38.44.45), sogar im Kontext ihres Fehlverhaltens Apg 7,39.

124 Mit ὑμεῖς wird sogar der Vorwurf des Widerstandes gegen den Heiligen Geist gerahmt. Vgl. JESKA, Geschichte Israels, 150-151. WASSERBERG, Israels Mitte, 251. SPENCER, Acts, 79. GAVENTA, Acts, 129.

125 Dies bestätigt sich auch in Apg 7,54-60, zumal Stephanus in Apg 7,55 noch einmal ausdrücklich als πλήρης πνεύματος ἁγίου beschrieben wird. Implizit ist in diesem Vorwurf auch der Widerstand gegen Jesus enthalten, der im lk Doppelwerk besonders als Geistträger gezeichnet wird. Vgl. Lk 3,22; 10,21; 4,1.14.18-21 u.a.

126 Zum Verstockungsmotiv im lk Doppelwerk vgl. EISEN, Poetik, 210, 214. LEHNERT, Provokation Israels, bes. 123-124, 213-224, 235. KARRER, »Und ich werde sie heilen«, 255-271. RUSAM, Das Alte Testament bei Lukas, 438-445; WASSERBERG, Israels Mitte, 361-366. MUßNER, Traktat, bes. 243-249, 361. MUßNER, Die Kraft der Wurzel, 35.

Die rhetorische Frage in Apg 7,52 (τίνα τῶν προφητῶν οὐκ ἐδίωξαν οἱ πατέρες ὑμῶν), die eine generelle Verfolgung aller Propheten durch die Väter impliziert, fasst interpretierend zusammen, was im Geschichtsabriss anhand der Ablehnung des Propheten Mose (vgl. Apg 7,37) exemplarisch geschildert wird.[127] Nicht nur das biblische Motiv der Prophetenverfolgung[128] (z.B. die Tempelrede Jer 7,1-34[129]), wird hier für die Kritik an den Hörern der Stephanusrede verwendet, sondern sogar das Motiv vom gewaltsamen (Tötungs-)Geschick der Propheten, das darauf abzielt, die permanente Halsstarrigkeit Israels gegenüber Gottes Willen in gesteigerter Form zu illustrieren (vgl. Neh 9,6-37).[130] Apg 7,52 beschuldigt die Väter nämlich der Tötung der Propheten[131] und überträgt dies sogleich auf die Hörer mit der gesteigerten Anschuldigung, sie hätten sogar den von den Propheten angekündigten »Gerechten« (ὁ δίκαιος) verraten und getötet (οὗ νῦν ὑμεῖς προδόται καὶ φονεῖς ἐγένεσθε). Insofern mit dem Stichwort ὁ δίκαιος Apg 3,13-26 eingespielt wird und dort für das lukanische Doppelwerk in typischer Weise »Gerechter« in Anlehnung an den Gottesknecht in Jes 53,11-12 sachlich mit der Bezeichnung Jesu als Gottesknecht gleich gesetzt und sein Tod interpretiert wird, ist in Apg 7,52 auch eine Deutung des Todes Jesu enthalten.[132] Weiterhin wird mit der Bezeichnung der Adressaten der Rede als προδόται καὶ φονεῖς auf das Motiv des leidenden gerechten Gottesknechts angespielt, der von den Menschen verachtet wird. Zugleich wird dieser »Gerechte« als Prophet ausgewiesen, insofern er dasselbe Schicksal erleidet wie die Propheten, die sein Kommen angekündigt haben.[133] Mit dieser Kombination der Motive des leidenden gerechten Gottesknechts und des Propheten wie Mose, der das typische Prophetenschicksal erfährt, ist in Apg 7,52 eine christologische Aussage impli-

---

127 Analog dazu kann auch die Gegnerschaft gegen Stephanus als Beispiel dieser Prophetenverfolgung betrachtet werden, denn dieser wird ebenfalls als geistbegabte, prophetische Gestalt gezeichnet (Apg 6,3.5.10; 7,55), was auch an einigen Stellen seiner Rede zu sehen ist (Apg 7,37.42b-43.49-50).

128 Im Rahmen des deuteronomistischen Geschichtsbildes dient sie ursprünglich zur theologischen Deutung der Geschichte Israels, insbesondere der Katastrophen von 722 und 587 v. Chr. Vgl. WEIHS, Schicksal der Propheten, 20.

129 Vgl. dazu LANGE, Gebotsobservanz, bes. 29-30. Auf Analogien zwischen der Stephanusrede und Jer 7 hinsichtlich des polysemen Begriffs ὁ τόπος macht PENNER, Praise, 309, Anm. 98, aufmerksam.

130 Vgl. WEIHS, Schicksal der Propheten, 18-19. STECK, Israel, 77-80.

131 Prophetenverachtung und -mord wirft auch Jesus seinen Gegnern vor (vgl. Lk 11,38-51; 13,33-35). Vgl. BRAUN, Geschichte des Gottesvolkes, 378-380.

132 Zu ὁ δίκαιος im lk Doppelwerk vgl. MITTMANN-RICHERT, Sühnetod, bes. 89-96.

133 Der »Gerechte« wird auch durch die Anspielung auf Apg 3,22 als Prophet ausgewiesen. Denn dort wird Jesus, der Gerechte, mit dem angekündigten Propheten »wie« Mose identifiziert. Vgl. BRAUN, Geschichte des Gottesvolkes, 380-381.

ziert. Vor diesem Hintergrund wird hiermit also die Schuld der Zuhörer zusätzlich unterstrichen.¹³⁴

Äußerst scharf wird auch der nächste Vorwurf, das Gesetz nicht zu bewahren, in Apg 7,53 ausgedrückt: οἵτινες ἐλάβετε τὸν νόμον εἰς διαταγὰς ἀγγέλων καὶ οὐκ ἐφυλάξατε. Da die Formulierung εἰς διαταγὰς ἀγγέλων¹³⁵ im Rückgriff auf die Gesetzesgabe an Mose (Apg 7,38) auf die Kontinuität zwischen Mose, den Vätern Israels und den Adressaten selbst aufmerksam macht, und das Gesetz innerhalb der Stephanusrede durchweg positiv bewertet wird (vgl. die Umschreibung mit λόγια ζῶντα in Apg 7,38), wirkt das Nicht-Bewahren des Gesetzes umso verwerflicher. Die Qualität des Gesetzes und dementsprechend die Anstößigkeit des Verstoßes dagegen wird auch durch das Verb φυλάσσω ausgedrückt. Es begegnet nämlich häufig im Imperativ in Verbindung mit νόμος und formuliert dabei oftmals den Zusammenhang zwischen Erfüllung des Gesetzes und Heil bzw. Unheil bei Nicht-Erfüllen des Gesetzes, wie etwa in Dtn 7,9-12; 32,46-47 oder auch Lk 11,28.¹³⁶ Auch angesichts des Kontextes der Stephanusepisode zeigt sich die Bedeutung und gewissermaßen sogar Provokation dieses Vorwurfs der Gesetzesbeachtung, da sie die Anklage gegen Stephanus, er rede blasphemisch gegen das Gesetz (Apg 6,11.13-14) gegen die Ankläger umwendet.

Insgesamt wird in den Vorwürfen von Apg 7,51-53 mit der expliziten Verwendung des Schemas „wie eure Väter, so auch ihr" deutlich, dass der Sinn des Geschichtsrückblicks nicht nur in einem einfachen Nacherzählen besteht, sondern der Aktualisierung dient. Die Geschichte der Gottesbegegnung Israels, die schon durch die Art und Weise der Vergangenheitsdarstellung in der Stephanusrede mit Interpretationen versehen wird, wird nun noch einmal zusammenfassend in prophetischer Manier gedeutet und erhält damit aktuelle Bedeutung für das Verständnis der Gegenwart der Adressaten. Damit bildet sich also hier ausdrücklich der anamnetische Charakter biblischer Erzählung der „Geschichte der Gottesbegegnung"¹³⁷ ab. Wenn diese der Identitätsstif-

---

134 Vgl. WITHERINGTON, Acts, 274. Eine weitere Betonung der Schuld der Zuhörer erfolgt vor dem Hintergrund von Apg 3,13-15, wo ein ähnliches Kontrastschema verwendet wird. Vgl. dazu BRAUN, Geschichte des Gottesvolkes, 382-383.
135 Zwar kann der Empfang des Gesetzes durch die Anordnung von Engeln als Abwertung des Gesetzes begriffen werden, insofern es nicht unmittelbar von Gott kommt. Aber ebenso kann diese Aussage nach jüdischer Tradition auf den besonderen Wert des Gesetzes und die Transzendenz Gottes verweisen (z.B. Dtn 33,2 LXX; Gal 3,19; Hebr 2,2; Jub 1,27-29). Vgl. ZMIJEWSKI, Apg, 328. TIWALD, Hebräer, 330-331 u.a.
136 Vgl. BRAUN, Geschichte des Gottesvolkes, 384-385.
137 STEINS, Kanon und Anamnese, 121.

tung und -vergewisserung¹³⁸ dient und hier primär die Geschichte der Ablehnung Gottes und seiner Heilsmittler und Propheten konstruiert wird (die Verheißungen an Abraham, mit denen der Geschichtsrückblick beginnt, werden in Apg 7,51-53 nicht erwähnt), wirkt die Kritik an den Adressaten umso schärfer. Dadurch entsteht nämlich der Eindruck, ihre Identität gründe vor allem in dieser Unheilsgeschichte. Dieser Effekt wird zusätzlich dadurch unterstrichen, dass Stephanus sich hier zum ersten Mal konsequent von seinen Hörern abgrenzt (ὑμεῖς), während er sich – abgesehen von Apg 7,4 – innerhalb des Geschichtsrückblicks immer mit ihnen identifiziert (auch hinsichtlich der Geschichte von der Abwendung von Gott Apg 7,39-43). Demnach unterscheidet sich die Identität des Stephanus genau an dieser Stelle von der seiner Gegner, an der ihnen Widerstand gegen den Heiligen Geist und Tötung des Gerechten vorgeworfen wird. Im Umkehrschluss heißt das: Stephanus wird durch – hier nicht näher präzisierte – Akzeptanz des Gerechten charakterisiert, die zu seiner Identität dazugehört.

4. Folgen der Stephanusrede Apg 7,54-8,3

In den beiden Erzählstücken über die Folgen der Stephanusrede (Apg 7,54-8,1a und 8,1b-3), ist die Verwendung alttestamentlicher Texte zwar nicht mehr so offensichtlich wie in Apg 7,2-53, aber dennoch sind manche Anspielungen zu finden, die vor allem dem Bild von Stephanus sowie seiner Gegner schärfere Konturen verleihen.

Die Reaktion der Zuhörer auf die Stephanusrede in Apg 7,54 (διεπρίοντο ταῖς καρδίαις αὐτῶν ἔβρυχον τοὺς ὀδόντας) bestätigt zum einen den Vorwurf der inneren Unbeschnittenheit von Apg 7,51 durch den Rückgriff auf das lexem καρδία,¹³⁹ zum anderen illustriert die Formulierung ἔβρυχον τοὺς ὀδόντας die tiefe, innere Ablehnung von Stephanus. Diese Wendung als „Ausdruck hasserfüllter Gesinnung" und „höchster Wut"¹⁴⁰ erinnert nämlich an verschiedene Texte, in denen eine Gegenüberstellung von Gerechten und Frevlern, die durch Zähneknirschen charakterisiert werden, erfolgt (vgl. z.B. Ps 34,11-16 LXX; Ps 36,12 LXX; Ps 111,10 LXX; Ijob 16,9).¹⁴¹ Vor diesem Hintergrund wird mit dem Motiv des Zähneknirschens in Apg 7,54 die Opposition zwischen Ste-

---

138 Vgl. SCHNELLE, Historische Anschlussfähigkeit, 58, der davon spricht, dass Geschichtserzählung einen inneren Zusammenhang von Vergangenheitsdeutung, Gegenwartsverständnis und Zukunftsperspektiven herstellt.
139 Zugleich erfolgt eine Parallelisierung mit den Vätern Israels, insofern sich diese Formulierung an die Abwendung der Väter von Mose (Apg 7,39) anlehnt.
140 ZMIJEWSKI, Apg, 335.
141 Vgl. FITZMYER, Acts, 393. ZMIJEWSKI, Apg, 335. JERVELL, Apg, 251.

phanus und seiner Zuhörerschaft unterstrichen. Die Ablehnung des Stephanus durch seine Gegner wird dann nach der Vision des Stephanus (Apg 7,55-56) in Apg 7,57-58a durch Analogien zum Prozess Jesu laut Lk 23,13-25 und Mk 14,53-65 par. als in höchstem Maß gesteigert vorgestellt.[142] Mit der Steinigung vollziehen sie laut Lev 24,10-16 die Strafe für Blasphemie und laut Dtn 17,2-7 die Strafe für denjenigen, der in den Augen Gottes Böses tut, gegen den Bund verstößt oder anderen Göttern dient. Die Gegner des Stephanus folgen dabei aber nicht den genauen Regelungen für eine Steinigung in Dtn 17,4-7 – die Steinigung des Stephanus erfolgt nämlich ohne Feststellung des Tatbestandes und ohne formalen Urteilsspruch, also ohne geregeltes Gerichtsverfahren –, so dass sich ihr Vorgehen als unrechtmäßiges Handeln in Form von spontaner Lynchjustiz erweist.[143]

Für das Bild des Stephanus als prophetische Gestalt (in Analogie zu Jesus) ist besonders seine Vision Apg 7,55-56 aufschlussreich: Darauf weisen nicht nur die erneute Erwähnung seiner Geistbegabung (Apg 7,55: πλήρης πνεύματος ἁγίου)[144] – als Kontrast zu seinen Gegnern – und das Visionsgeschehen an sich hin, sondern auch die Präsentationsweise und der Inhalt der Vision. Dieser wird in Vers 55 von der Erzählstimme und in Vers 56 parallel dazu mit etwas anderen Worten in einer direkten Rede des Stephanus formuliert:[145]

Apg 7,55	Apg 7,56
εἶδεν δόξαν θεοῦ	ἰδοὺ θεωρῶ τοὺς οὐρανοὺς διηνοιγμένους
καὶ Ἰησοῦν ἑστῶτα	καὶ τὸν υἱὸν τοῦ ἀνθρώπου
ἐκ δεξιῶν τοῦ θεοῦ	ἐκ δεξιῶν ἑστῶτα τοῦ θεοῦ.

Die Beschreibung des ersten Visionsinhalts als δόξα θεοῦ (Apg 7,55) weist Analogien zum Offenbarungsgeschehen, das Mose in Ex 33,18-23[146] erfährt, auf. Die δόξα Gottes deutet zwar eine klare Trennung zwischen der transzendenten Heiligkeit Gottes und dem Menschen Stephanus an, aber zugleich zeigt sich, dass Gott sich gerade diesem Menschen und durch diesen Menschen offenbart, um ihn zu einer besonde-

---

142 Vgl. BRAUN, Geschichte des Gottesvolkes, 412-413.
143 Vgl. FITZMYER, Acts, 393. LARKIN, Acts, 122.
144 Damit wird nicht nur auf die Einführung des Stephanus in Apg 6,3.5.10 zurückgegriffen, sondern auch auf den Vorwurf gegen seine Hörer in Apg 7,51-52. Vgl. BRAUN, Geschichte des Gottesvolkes, 395-396. ZMIJEWSKI, Apg, 336. GANSER-KERPERIN, Tempel, 254.
145 Zwar ist Apg 7,56 keine wörtliche Wiederholung von Apg 7,55, aber die weitgehend parallele Satzkonstruktion bildet einen inneren Zusammenhang ab. Vgl. BRAUN, Geschichte des Gottesvolkes, 397-398.
146 Vgl. dazu DOHMEN, Exodus, 348-350. Zu den intertextuellen Referenzen vgl. BRAUN, Geschichte des Gottesvolkes, 398-400. Da auch lexematische Verbindungen zu Apg 7,2.30.38.44 bestehen, kann die Vision des Stephanus in die Linie kontinuierlicher Erscheinungen Gottes (ὁ θεὸς τῆς δόξης) von Abraham und Mose eingereiht werden.

ren Aufgabe zu berufen. Wie Mose fungiert also Stephanus als Prophet und Offenbarungsmittler, was schon in Apg 6,15 angedeutet wurde. So wird mithilfe dieser intertextuellen Referenz auf Ex 33 erneut die Frage nach der Gegenwart Gottes thematisiert und illustriert, wie sich diese zeigt. Noch deutlicher wird dies in der Beschreibung des ersten Visionsinhalts mit οἱ οὐρανοὶ διηνοιγμένοι[147] (Apg 7,56). Durch die Aufnahme von Gottes Aussage ὁ οὐρανός μοι θρόνος in Apg 7,49a[148] wird bestätigt und veranschaulicht, dass Stephanus Einblick in diesen wahren Ort Gottes bekommt, in dem sich Gott selbst mit seiner δόξα offenbart.[149]

In welcher Gestalt Stephanus die Herrlichkeit Gottes sieht, besagt der zweite Visionsinhalt, der in Apg 7,55 mit Jesus ('Ἰησοῦν ἑστῶτα ἐκ δεξιῶν τοῦ θεοῦ) und in Apg 7,56 parallel dazu mit dem Menschensohn (ὁ υἱὸς τοῦ ἀνθρώπου ἐκ δεξιῶν ἑστῶτα τοῦ θεοῦ) benannt wird. Damit entsteht insgesamt das Bild von Jesus als des Menschensohns, der zur Rechten Gottes steht. Vor dem Hintergrund, dass der erste Teil der Vision die Frage nach dem Sehen Gottes und nach seiner Gegenwart implizit thematisiert, drückt dieser zweite Visionsinhalt aus, dass ein »Sehen der Herrlichkeit Gottes« im Sehen Jesu als Menschensohn, der zur Rechten Gottes erhöht steht, erfolgt. Hierin sind auch folgende christologische Sinnpotentiale enthalten:

(1) Der Menschensohn Jesus wird als der leidende Gerechte dargestellt, der dem typischen Schicksal der Propheten entsprechend getötet wurde. Dies zeigen besonders Worte vom leidenden Menschensohn, auf die hier angespielt wird (Lk 9,22.43; 18,31; vgl. Apg 7,52).[150]

---

147 Laut ZMIJEWSKI, Apg, 337, unterscheidet Lk sonst nicht zwischen dem Singular ὁ οὐρανός und dem Plural οἱ οὐρανοί. GANSER-KERPERIN, Tempel, 253, sieht hier einen Rückgriff auf die traditionelle Motivik eines geöffneten Himmels (AscJes 5,7) und die Vorstellung vom himmlischen Thronrat Gottes (Jes 6; 1 Kön 22). Stephanus beschreibe also in apokalyptischer Manier den „Ort" Jesu im himmlischen Gefüge.

148 Schon die Angabe der Blickrichtung ἀτενίσας εἰς τὸν οὐρανόν in Apg 7,55, die ebenfalls Apg 7,49 aufnimmt, deutet an, dass Stephanus zum ‚Wohnort' Gottes blickt.

149 Durch die Kombination der Motive vom Sehen der δόξα Gottes und vom »Ort Gottes« spielt Apg 7,55-56 auch auf Ez 43,1-12 an. Vgl. dazu BRAUN, Geschichte des Gottesvolkes, 401, und die dort angegebene Literatur.

150 Dies lässt sich in die prophetenchristologischen Horizonte des lk Doppelwerks einordnen. Vgl. CHIBICI-REVNEANU, Himmlischer Stehplatz, 478, 484-485. Auch an anderen Stellen im lk Doppelwerk wird Jesus als ‚Gerechter' bezeichnet, wenn es um seine Passion geht (Lk 23,41.47; Apg 3,14; 7,52). Für den Zusammenhang des Christus- und des Prophetentitels vor dem Hintergrund der Darstellung Jesu als Gottesknecht vgl. MITTMANN-RICHERT, Sühnetod, bes. 287-289, 293-295.

(2) Die Vision Jesu als Menschensohn sowie die Gerichtssituation, in der sich Stephanus befindet, spielen Lk 12,8-12 ein,[151] wo die entscheidende richterliche Funktion des Menschensohnes Jesus im Endgericht angekündigt wird. Wegen der Verknüpfung des Menschensohnes mit dem eschatologischen Gericht vor dem Hintergrund von Dan 7,13f. kann die Menschensohnvision des Stephanus sogar als „Vorwegnahme des Parusiegerichts"[152] gedeutet werden. Demnach zeichnet Apg 7,55-56 insgesamt das Bild einer ‚doppelten Gerichtsszene': Zum einen steht Stephanus als Angeklagter vor dem weltlichen Gericht des Synedriums, zum anderen deutet sich in der Vision an, dass der Menschensohn als eschatologischer Richter über den Synedristen steht.

(3) Die auffällige Position des Menschensohnes Jesus, der zur Rechten Gottes *steht* (ἵστημι) – im Unterschied zum traditionell überlieferten *Sitzen* zur Rechten Gottes –, weist auf eine märtyrerchristologische Dimension[153] hin. Denn mit dem Motiv des Stehens wird auf biblische Aussagen über die Stellung von Gerechten und Blutzeugen im Himmel angespielt (vgl. z.B. Offb 3,21; 7,9-17; 20,4; Lk 15,7; 1 Kor 6,2).

Insgesamt wird in 7,55-56 also ausgesagt, dass der Prophet und Märtyrer Jesus als Menschensohn zur Rechten Gottes und zwar im Himmel steht. Damit wird zugleich implizit die Frage nach dem *Ort und der Präsenz Gottes* (Apg 7,50) beantwortet. Insofern Stephanus die Herrlichkeit Gottes in Gestalt dieses Menschensohns Jesus im Himmel erscheint, bestätigt Gott, was er durch das Prophetenwort Apg 7,49-50 bereits gesagt hat: Nicht der Jerusalemer Tempel ist privilegierter Ort Gottes, sondern der Himmel.[154] Präsent und sichtbar ist der Gott der Herrlichkeit im leidenden Gerechten und Propheten Jesus, der jetzt als erhöhter Menschensohn von seinen Jüngern, hier Stephanus, bezeugt wird. Die Gestalt des Stephanus wird also im Rahmen der Vision deutlich als Zeuge Jesu, nämlich als Verkündiger von Jesu Auferstehung und Erhöhung, präsentiert. Dies wird in der Steinigung des Stephanus

---

151 In Apg 7,55-56 wird Jesus durch einen ähnlichen Subjektwechsel mit dem Menschensohn identifiziert wie in Lk 12,8-9. Die Gerichtssituation, von der Lk 12,11-12 spricht, findet sich in der Situation des Stephanus wieder. Zu Lk 12,8-12 vgl. WOLTER, Lukasevangelium, 439-444. KLEIN, Lukasevangelium, 249.
152 ZMIJEWSKI, Apg, 337. Ähnlich JERVELL, Apg, 252.
153 Dass das Stehen des Menschensohnes auch als Anspielung auf das Martyrium Jesu verstanden worden ist, zeigen der unauffällige textkritische Befund zu Apg 7,55-56 sowie die Wirkungsgeschichte der ‚statio ad dexteram' und der ‚Schau eines ins Martyrium Vorangegangenen' in den Märtyrerakten. Vgl. CHIBICI-REVNEANU, Himmlischer Stehplatz, 487-488. Zur martyriumschristologischen Dimension in der lk Darstellung Jesu vgl. EBD., 484. BÖTTRICH, Proexistenz, 432. MITTMANN-RICHERT, Sühnetod, 87-110, 176-181.
154 MUßNER, Wohnung Gottes, 287, sieht von Apg 7,55-56 her eine Erklärung für die Polemik des Stephanus gegen »diesen heiligen Ort«. Vgl. auch LARKIN, Acts, 121.

bestätigt, die primär durch Referenzen auf die lukanische Darstellung des Todes Jesu geschildert wird.[155] Dadurch wird angedeutet, dass sich in der Stephanus und seinem Schicksal die in der Stephanusrede thematisiert Ablehnung prophetischer Gestalten in der Geschichte Israels bis hin zu Jesus fortsetzt und aktualisiert.

Nicht nur in der Steinigung des Stephanus, sondern auch im gesamten Erzählabschnitt Apg 7,54-8,1a wird mithilfe von Rückbezügen auf die Stephanusepisode in Kombination mit Referenzen auf diverse Intertexte die Geschichte Jesu als Geschichte Israels und Ort der Gottesbegegnung erinnert und aktualisiert. Besonders deutlich wird dies dadurch illustriert, dass das Bild einer doppelten Gerichtsszene gezeichnet wird: Einerseits treten die Gegner des Stephanus in Fortsetzung zu Apg 6,9-7,1 als weltliche Ankläger und Vollstrecker des unausgesprochenen Urteils auf (Apg 7,54.57-58.59a). Andererseits werden sie genau durch dieses Verhalten zu Angeklagten, denen der Menschensohn Jesus als eschatologischer Richter und als Fürsprecher für den Angeklagten Stephanus (Apg 7,55-56) gegenübergestellt wird, und für die Stephanus ebenfalls als Fürsprecher bei dem κύριος Jesus eintritt (Apg 7,60). Durch das Ineinandergreifen dieser beiden Gerichtsszenen wird weiterhin angedeutet, dass sich die Geschichte Jesu als Geschichte der Gottesbegegnung nicht nur aktualisiert, sondern auch fortsetzt, insofern der angekündigte Einfluss des Menschensohnes Jesus beim eschatologischen Gericht bestätigt wird. Damit wird außerdem auf die heilswirksame Bedeutung der Haltung zu diesem Menschensohn Jesus hingewiesen und mit Stephanus ein Beispiel für eine ideale Haltung zu ihm gegeben. Durch diesen Ausblick auf Jesus als endzeitlichen Richter und Anwalt verbindet diese Episode also zwischen der Vergangenheit der Geschichte der Gottesbegegnung mit Israel, der Gegenwart und der Zukunft. Daher kann ihr eine Schwellenposition zugesprochen werden.

5. Fazit

Eine kanonisch-intertextuelle Analyse von Apg 6,1-8,3 zeigt, dass verschiedene Arten von Schriftgebrauch zur Gestaltung der Stephanusepisode beitragen und ihre Funktion innerhalb der Apostelgeschichte bzw. sogar des lukanischen Doppelwerks formen.

In Apg 6,1-7 wird mithilfe struktureller und motivischer Analogien zu Num 11,13-17 eine ideale Konfliktlösung innerhalb der Jerusalemer Gemeinde gezeichnet. Stephanus wird dabei durch Motivanalogien zu

---

155 Für einen Vergleich von Apg 7,57 mit Lk 23,13-25.34.46 siehe BRAUN, Geschichte des Gottesvolkes, 412-413, 417-426, und die dort angegebene Literatur.

diversen Intertexten in Anlehnung an Propheten Israels und an Jesus als prophetische Gestalt eingeführt. Die prophetischen Züge des Stephanus bestätigen sich im weiteren Erzählverlauf, indem er beispielsweise mit Mose parallelisiert wird (vgl. Apg 6,15 mit Ex 34,29b) und in seiner Rede in prophetischer Manier verschiedene Vorwürfe an seine Hörerschaft richtet. Letztlich erfährt Stephanus sogar mit der Steinigung ein ähnliches Schicksal wie die häufig verfolgten und getöteten Propheten einschließlich Jesus. Auch die Gegner des Stephanus werden in Muster eingezeichnet, die von frevlerischen Gestalten Israels oder vom Volk Israel insgesamt bekannt sind. In der Stephanusrede wird außerdem überaus deutlich mithilfe der Schrift ein Bild der Geschichte Israels vor Augen gestellt, das zum einen als Verheißungsgeschichte und deren sukzessiver Realisierung präsentiert wird, zum anderen als Unheilsgeschichte, insofern das Volk Israel kontinuierlich von Gott, seinen Mittlern und seinem Gesetz abfällt. Besonders bedeutend ist, dass die Stephanusrede die für die religiöse Identität zentralen Themen Gott, Tempel und Gesetz mithilfe der Schrift behandelt und dabei jeweils durch unterschiedliche Formen des Umgangs mit den entsprechenden Intertexten eigene Akzente herausarbeitet. Demnach wird Geschichte hier nicht nur nacherzählt, sondern erinnernd vergegenwärtigt und aktualisiert, so dass die bleibende Bedeutung der Geschichte für die Gegenwart aufgezeigt wird. Somit trägt die Stephanusepisode unter anderem durch ihren Schriftgebrauch zur *Selbstvergewisserung religiöser Identität* bei und zwar an der Schwelle vor dem Eintreten in eine neue Etappe des „Weges des Heils". Daher nimmt die Stephanusepisode eine *Schwellenfunktion* innerhalb der Apostelgeschichte und des lukanischen Doppelwerks ein. Insofern nämlich die Aussagen über Gott, Tempel und Gesetz im Rahmen einer Erzählung der Geschichte Israels mithilfe von *Anspielungen auf und Parallelen zu alttestamentlichen Subtexten* erfolgen, zeigt sich ihre Übereinstimmung mit den Vorstellungen, die zum Selbstverständnis des Volkes Israel gehören. Durch *besondere Akzentuierungen* wird zugleich deutlich, welche Aspekte davon weiterhin (in der Jerusalemer Gemeinde) oberste Priorität besitzen und den Übergang der Verkündigung außerhalb Jerusalems vorbereiten. Da nämlich *Gott* überall anwesend ist, sind auch Gottesbegegnung und -dienst überall möglich, nicht exklusiv an den Tempel in Jerusalem und das verheißene Land gebunden. Außerdem können dann die *Verheißungen* Gottes, die laut Apg 1,1-11 in der Geistausgießung und Königsherrschaft Gottes bestehen, überall erfüllt werden.

Zur *Selbstvergewisserung der religiösen Identität* trägt primär die *Vergegenwärtigung der Geschichte* bei, die durch verschiedene Textstrategien und Gestaltungselemente erfolgt:

Schon dem Idealbild der Jerusalemer Gemeinde, das zum Teil in *Analogie zum Volk Israel* (vgl. Apg 6,2-3.7; 7,17.38; 8,1b.3) gezeichnet wird, kommt eine gewisse Vorbildfunktion zu. Insbesondere werden aber innerhalb des *Abrisses über die Geschichte Israels* in der Stephanusrede entscheidende Aspekte der Herkunftsgeschichte erinnernd vergegenwärtigt. Ausdrücklich zeigt sich das bereits in der Bezeichnung Abrahams als »unser Vater« (Apg 7,2b), womit von Anfang an der Bezug der Geschichtsdarstellung zu den Adressaten der Rede hergestellt wird. Auch im weiteren Verlauf wird die Kontinuität zwischen dieser Geschichte und den Hörern der Rede betont, indem die Israeliten meistens »unsere Väter« genannt werden. Zur Vergegenwärtigung der Geschichte trägt außerdem der kurze *aktualisierende* Hinweis auf die Identität des Landes, in das Abraham von Gott umgesiedelt wurde, mit dem der Hörer bei (Apg 7,4). Explizit wird die Geschichte Israels weiterhin gegenwärtig gesetzt, indem den Zuhörern in Jerusalem dieselben Vorwürfe gemacht werden wie »ihren Vätern«, wobei sich der Redner Stephanus nun von dieser Gemeinschaft mit den Vätern bzw. den Jerusalemer Juden distanziert (Apg 7,51-53). Im Rahmen dieser Anklagen zeigt sich sogar eine steigernde Fortsetzung der erzählten Geschichte, da die Verfolgung und Tötung der Propheten durch Verrat und Mord am »Gerechten« übertroffen wird.

Auch indirekt wird die Aktualität der Geschichte Israels für die Hörer der Rede durch verschiedene Strategien angedeutet: Im Geschichtsrückblick finden sich neben *strukturellen Analogien* und vielfältigen *Stichwort-* und *Motivverknüpfungen* zu Erzählungen aus alttestamentlichen Subtexten an manchen Stellen sogar wörtliche Übernahmen einzelner Passagen daraus. Abgesehen von der Verwerfung Moses durch einen Israeliten (Apg 7,27-28) handelt es sich dabei immer um eine direkte Gottesrede (Apg 7,6-7.32-34) oder von einem Propheten vermittelte Gottesrede (Apg 7,37.42-43.49-50). Häufig werden in diesen *wörtlichen Reden* vorher berichtete Ereignisse hinterfragt bzw. kritisiert und zum Teil Konsequenzen für die Zukunft formuliert (Apg 7,6-7.32-34.42-43). Die aus der Schrift bekannte Geschichte Israels wird also zum einen neu lebendig, indem sie mit ähnlichen Formulierungen präsentiert wird, zum anderen besonders indem sie mit diesen wörtlichen Gottes- bzw. Prophetenreden durchzogen ist. Denn die Gottes- bzw. Prophetenworte erhalten dadurch unmittelbaren Charakter, als wären sie aktuell an die Hörer der Stephanusrede gerichtet. Transparent für die Gegenwart wird die Geschichte außerdem durch die *Tendenz von Generalisierungen einzelner Episoden*, die von der konkreten Situation der Subtexte enthoben werden (vgl. Apg 7,23-29.33-34). Weiterhin dienen *Anspielungen auf reflektierende Intertexte*, wie z.B. in Apg 7,38.39.42a, und

Rednerkommentare' der deutenden Vergegenwärtigung der Geschichte Israels, denn sie interpretieren auf einer Art Metaebene die Erzählung der Geschichte (vgl. Apg 7,25.35.48).

Vergegenwärtigung der Geschichte erfolgt über Inhalt, Form und Gestaltung der Rede hinaus in der *Figur des Stephanus*. Als prophetische Gestalt wird Stephanus nämlich nicht nur durch seine Charakterisierung als Geisterfüllter, der Zeichen und Wunder tut und dem Gott eine Vision gewährt, und durch seine Rede, in der er Gott und seine Propheten zu Wort kommen lässt, gezeichnet, sondern auch durch seine Steinigung, die parallel zum typischen Prophetengeschick und zum Tod Jesu präsentiert wird. Demnach wird in Stephanus und seinem Schicksal die Geschichte der Propheten Israels fortgesetzt und vergegenwärtigt.

Inwiefern trägt nun die Stephanusepisode mithilfe dieser Strategien zur *Selbstvergewisserung christlicher Identität* bei?

Grundlegend ist, dass Apg 6,1-8,3 christliche Identität im Rahmen der Szenerie einer Gerichtssituation in einem Gegenüber zum ,Jerusalemer Judentum', das von den Gegnern des Stephanus – Volk, Älteste, Schriftgelehrte und Synedristen (Apg 6,12.15) – repräsentiert wird, konstruiert. Dabei trifft der Text sowohl Aussagen über die Identität der Jerusalemer Juden als auch über Stephanus als eines Repräsentanten christlicher Identität, da die hier erzählte Geschichte Israels von Abraham bis zu Jesus (und Stephanus) als gemeinsame Herkunft der Gegner *und* des Stephanus selbst skizziert wird.

Zur *Identität des Jerusalemer Judentums* gehört aus der Sicht des Textes als Basis der Gott der Herrlichkeit, der seine Verheißungen auf dem Weg Israels mithilfe seiner prophetischen Mittler erfüllt, und an jedem Ort anwesend ist, sogar trotz der Abwendung durch Israel. Besonders dieser ,Unheilsweg' wird ebenfalls als prägend für die Herkunft Israels und damit des Jerusalemer Judentums dargestellt. Als Bestätigung dafür dient die Steinigung des Stephanus als Verlängerung der Tötung der Propheten und Jesu in die Gegenwart hinein. Die Provokation, die in der Darstellung dieser Gewalttat als Element der Identität des Jerusalemer Judentums enthalten ist,[156] wird zusätzlich durch das Bild einer doppelten Gerichtsszene verstärkt (Apg 7,55-60), durch das die für das

---

[156] Aufgrund dieser Provokation kann zu Recht gefragt werden, ob Stephanus als ein „Symbol der Trennung zwischen Judentum und Christentum" (HAACKER, Stephanus in der Geschichte, 1517) zu verstehen ist, wie es ausgehend von F. C. Baur in der Auslegungsgeschichte bis ins 20. Jh. hinein verschiedentlich der Fall ist. Für weitere Beispiele dafür vgl. BRAUN, Geschichte des Gottesvolkes, 4-5. Zur Diskussion, inwiefern diese Traditionslinie von Apg 6,1-8,3 getragen wird, und wie das Verhältnis von Judentum und Christentum angemessener bestimmt werden kann, vgl. EBD., 460-469.

eschatologische Gericht entscheidende Bedeutung der Haltung zu Jesus Christus deutlich wird.

Gleichzeitig wird aber durch die Schilderung der Prophetentötung die Geschichte Jesu Christi in der Geschichte Israels verankert (vgl. Apg 7,52). Indem Stephanus Jesus also als Mittler Gottes vorstellt, der auf der Grundlage der Geschichte Gottes mit Israel zu verstehen ist, geht Stephanus einen anderen Weg als seine Zuhörer: Zwar ist die gesamte erzählte Geschichte Israels auch identitätsstiftende Herkunftsgeschichte von Stephanus, aber der halsstarrige Ungehorsam gegenüber dem Heiligen Geist in Form von Tötung der Propheten und Jesu (Apg 7,51-53) ist davon ausgenommen. Vielmehr verkündet er dagegen Jesus Christus als Teil der Verheißungen der Propheten Israels und deren Erfüllung. Die Identität des Stephanus ist also zusätzlich dadurch charakterisiert, dass er vorbildlicher Zeuge Jesu Christi ist. Dies äußert sich nicht nur in der Verkündigung des Todes Jesu, des leidenden Gerechten (Apg 7,52), sowie seiner Auferweckung und Erhöhung zum Menschensohn, in dem sich der Gott der Herrlichkeit zeigt (Apg 7,55-56). Darüber hinaus bezeugt Stephanus Jesus Christus auch in seiner konsequenten Nachfolge, die sich besonders in seinem Sterben als Nachahmung des Kreuzestodes Jesu manifestiert.

Der Unterschied der Identität der Jerusalemer Gemeinde und des Stephanus entscheidet sich demnach am Verständnis der Anwesenheit Gottes. Schon die Geschichte Israels zeigt, dass sich der Bezug zu Gott in der Haltung Israels zu Gottes Mittlern, zum Gesetz und zum Tempel spiegelt. Dasselbe gilt für die Haltung zu Jesus Christus: Er wird entweder abgelehnt oder als ein Ort bzw. eine Form der Anwesenheit Gottes bezeugt. Mit Stephanus wird also die Identität eines Zeugen Jesu Christi dadurch gekennzeichnet, dass vom ursprünglichen Weg Israels ein ‚neuer Weg' (Apg 9,2; 18,25f.; 22,4 u.a.) abzweigt, dessen Verlauf die Fortsetzung der Apostelgeschichte erzählt und als Ziel das »Ende der Erde« nennt.

Bibliographie

BACKHAUS, Knut/HÄFNER, Gerd, Historiographie und fiktionales Erzählen. Zur Konstruktivität in Geschichtstheorie und Exegese, Neukirchen-Vluyn 2007.

BARRETT, Charles K., A Critical and Exegetical Commentary on the Acts of the Apostles. Vol. 1: Preliminary Introduction and Commentary on Acts I-XIV (ICC), Edinburgh 1994.

BAUER, Walter, Griechisch-deutsches Wörterbuch zu den Schriften des Neuen Testaments und der frühchristlichen Literatur, hg. von Kurt und Barbara Aland, Berlin/New York [6]1988.

BÖTTRICH, Christfried, Proexistenz im Leben und Sterben. Jesu Tod bei Lukas, in: Frey, Jörg/Schröter, Jens (Hg.), Deutungen des Todes Jesu im Neuen Testament (WUNT 181), Tübingen 2005, 413-436.

BREYTENBACH, Cilliers/SCHRÖTER, Jens/DU TOIT, David S. (Hg.), Die Apostelgeschichte und die hellenistische Geschichtsschreibung. Festschrift für Eckhard Plümacher zu seinem 65. Geburtstag (AJEC 57), Leiden/Boston 2004.

BRAUN, Heike, Geschichte des Gottesvolkes und christliche Identität. Eine kanonisch-intertextuelle Auslegung der Stephanusepisode Apg 6,1-8,3 (WUNT II 279), Tübingen 2010.

CHIBICI-REVNEANU, Nicole, Die Herrlichkeit des Verherrlichten. Das Verständnis der δόξα im Johannesevangelium (WUNT II 231), Tübingen 2007.

CHIBICI-REVNEANU, Nicole, Ein himmlischer Stehplatz: Die Haltung Jesu in der Stephanusvision (Apg 7.55-56) und ihre Bedeutung, in: NTS 53 (2007) 459-482.

DOHMEN, Christoph, Biblische Auslegung. Wie alte Texte neue Bedeutungen haben können, in: Hossfeld, Frank-Lothar/Schwienhorst-Schönberger, Ludgar (Hg.), Das Manna fällt auch heute noch. Beiträge zur Geschichte und Theologie des Alten, Ersten Testaments (FS Erich Zenger) (HBS 44), Freiburg u.a. 2004, 174-191.

DOHMEN, Christoph, Exodus 19-40 (HThK.AT), Freiburg/Basel/Wien 2004.

DOHMEN, Christoph, Das Zelt außerhalb des Lagers. Exodus 33,7-11 zwischen Synchronie und Diachronie, in: Kiesow, Klaus/Meurer, Thomas, Textarbeit. Studien zu Texten und ihrer Rezeption aus dem Alten Testament und der Umwelt Israels, Festschrift für Peter Weimar (AOAT 294), Münster 2003, 157-168.

EGO, Beate/LANGE, Armin/PILHOFER, Peter (Hg.), Gemeinde ohne Tempel. Zur Substituierung und Transformation des Jerusalemer Tempels und seines Kults im Alten Testament, antiken Judentum und frühen Christentum (WUNT 118), Tübingen 2002.

EISEN, Ute, Die Poetik der Apostelgeschichte. Eine narratologische Studie (NTOA 58), Göttingen 2006.

FITZMYER, Joseph A., The Acts of the Apostles: A new Translation with Introduction and Commentary (The Anchor Bible, 31), New York u.a. 1998.

FREY, Jörg/SCHNELLE, Udo, Kontexte des Johannesevangeliums (WUNT 175), Tübingen 2004.

GANSER-KERPERIN, Heiner, Das Zeugnis des Tempels. Studien zur Bedeutung des Tempelmotivs im lukanischen Doppelwerk (NTA, Neue Folge 36), Münster/Aschendorff 2000.

GAVENTA, Beverly R., The Acts of the Apostles (Abingdon New Testament Commentaries), Nashville 2003.

HAACKER, Klaus, Die Stellung des Stephanus in der Geschichte des Urchristentums, in: ANRW II, 26/2 (1995) 1515-1553.

HIEKE, Thomas, Die Genealogien der Genesis (HBS 39), Freiburg u.a. 2003.

JACOB, Benno, Das Buch Exodus, Stuttgart 1997.

JACOB, Benno, Das erste Buch der Tora. Genesis, Berlin 1934.

JERVELL, Jacob, Die Apostelgeschichte (KEK 3), Göttingen 1998.

JESKA, Joachim, Die Geschichte Israels in der Sicht des Lukas. Apg 7,2b-53 und 13,17-25 im Kontext antik-jüdischer Summarien der Geschichte Israels (FRLANT 195), Göttingen 2001.

KARRER, Martin, »Und ich werde sie heilen«. Das Verstockungsmotiv aus Jes 6,9f. in Apg 28,26f., in: ders. u.a., Kirche und Volk Gottes, FS Jürgen Roloff, Neukirchen-Vluyn 2000, 255-271.

KEE, Howard Clark, To Every Nation under Heaven: The Acts of the Apostles (New Testament in Context), Harrisburg 1997.

KLEIN, Hans, Das Lukasevangelium (KEK 1,3), Göttingen ¹⁰2006.

KLEIN, Hans, Lukasstudien (FRLANT 209), Göttingen 2005.

KOET, Bart, Dreams and Scripture in Luke-Acts. Collected Essays (Contributions to Biblical Exegesis and Theology 42), Leuven u.a. 2006.

KOET, Bart, Isaiah in Luke-Acts, in: DERS., Dreams and Scripture in Luke-Acts. Collected Essays (Contributions to Biblical Exegesis and Theology 42), Leuven u.a. 2006.

LANGE, Armin, Gebotsobservanz statt Opferkult. Zur Kultpolemik in Jer 7,1-8,3, in: Ego, Beate/Lange, Armin/Pilhofer, Peter (Hg.), Gemeinde ohne Tempel. Zur Substituierung und Transformation des Jerusalemer Tempels und seines Kults im Alten Testament, antiken Judentum und frühen Christentum (WUNT 118), Tübingen 2002, 17-35.

LANGER, Gerhard, Herrlichkeit als kābōd in der hebräischen Bibel – mit einem Schwerpunkt auf dem Pentateuch, in: Kampling, Rainer (Hg.), Herrlichkeit. Zur Deutung einer theologischen Kategorie, Paderborn u.a. 2008, 21-56.

LARKIN, Wiliam J., Acts (The IVP New Testament Commentary Series, 5), Downers Grove u.a. 1995.

LEHNERT, Volker A., Die Provokation Israels. Die paradoxe Funktion von Jes 6,9-10 bei Markus und Lukas. Ein textpragmatischer Versuch im Kontext gegenwärtiger Rezeptionsästhetik und Lesetheorie (NTDH 25), Neukirchen-Vluyn 1999.

MITTMANN-RICHERT, Ulrike, Der Sühnetod des Gottesknechts. Jesaja 53 im Lukasevangelium (WUNT 220), Tübingen 2008.

MUßNER, Franz, Die Kraft der Wurzel: Jesus – Judentum – Kirche, Freibug u.a. ²1989.

MUßNER, Franz, Traktat über die Juden, Göttingen 2009.

MUßNER, Franz, Wohnung Gottes und Menschensohn nach der Stephanusperikope (Apg 6,8-8,2), in: Pesch, Rudolf u.a. (Hg.), Jesus und der Menschensohn (FS A. Vögtle), Freiburg/Basel/Wien 1975.

PENNER, Todd, In Praise of Christian Origins. Stephen and the Hellenists in Lukan Apologetic Historiography, New York/London 2004.

ROLOFF, Jürgen, Die Apostelgeschichte (NTD 5), Göttingen ²1988.

RUSAM, Dietrich, Das Alte Testament bei Lukas (BZNW 112), Berlin u.a. 2003.

RUSAM, Dietrich, Deuteronomy in Luke-Acts, in: Menken, Maarten J. J./Moyise, Steve (Hg.), Deuteronomy in the New Testament: The New Testament and the Scriptures of Israel (LNTS), London u.a. 2008, 63-81.

SCHIFFNER, Kerstin, Lukas liest Exodus. Eine Untersuchung zur Aufnahme ersttestamentlicher Befreiungsgeschichte im lukanischen Werk als Schrift-Lektüre (BWANT 172), Stuttgart 2008.

SCHNEIDER, Gerhard, Die Apostelgeschichte. I. Teil (HThK V/1), Freiburg u.a. 1980.

SCHNELLE, Udo, Historische Anschlussfähigkeit. Zum hermeneutischen Horizont von Geschichts- und Traditionsbildung, in: Frey, Jörg/Schnelle, Udo, Kontexte des Johannesevangeliums (WUNT 175), Tübingen 2004, 47-78.

SEEBASS, Horst, Genesis II. Vätergeschichte I (11,27-22,24), Neukirchen-Vluyn 1997.

SPENCER, F. Scott, Acts (Readings: A New Biblical Commentary), Sheffield 1997.

STECK, Odil, Hannes, Israel und das gewaltsame Geschick der Propheten. Untersuchungen zur Überlieferung des deuteronomistischen Geschichtsbildes im Alten Testament, Spätjudentum und Urchristentum (WMANT 23), Neukirchen-Vluyn 1967.

STEINS, Georg, Die „Bindung Isaaks" im Kanon (Gen 22). Grundlagen und Programm einer kanonisch-intertextuellen Lektüre (HBS 20), Freiburg i.Br. u.a. 1999.

STEINS, Georg, Kanon und Anamnese. Auf dem Weg zu einer Neuen Biblischen Theologie, in: BALLHORN, EGBERT/STEINS, GEORG (Hg.), Der Bibelkanon in der Bibelauslegung. Methodenreflexionen und Beispielexegesen, Stuttgart 2007, 110-129.

TALBERT, Charles H., Reading Acts. A Literary and Theological Commentary on The Acts of the Apostles, New York 1997.

TANNEHILL, Robert C., The Narrative Unity of Luke-Acts. A Literary Interpretation. Volume 2: The Acts of the Apostles, Minneapolis 1990.

TIWALD, Markus, Hebräer von Hebräern. Paulus auf dem Hintergrund frühjüdischer Argumentation und biblischer Interpretation (HBS 52), Freiburg u.a. 2008.

VAN DE SANDT, Huub, Why is Amos 5,25-27 quoted in Acts 7,42f.?, in: ZNW 82 (1991) 67-87.

VAN DE SANDT, Huub, The Presence and Transcendence of God: An Investigation of Acts 7,44-50 in the Light of the LXX, in: ETL 80 (2004) 30-59.

WASSERBERG, Günter, Aus Israels Mitte – Heil für die Welt. Eine narrativ-exegetische Studie zur Theologie des Lukas (BZNW 92), Berlin u.a. 1998.

WEIHS, Alexander, Jesus und das Schicksal der Propheten. Das Winzergleichnis (Mk 12,1-12) im Horizont des Markusevangeliums (BThSt 61), Neukirchen-Vluyn 2003.

WESTERMANN, Claus, Genesis, 2. Teilband: Genesis 12-36 (BK Altes Testament I/2), Neukirchen-Vluyn 1981.

WITHERINGTON, Ben III, The Acts of the Apostles: A Socio-Rhetorical Commentary, Grand Rapids/Cambridge 1998.

WOLTER, Michael, Das Lukasevangelium (HNT 5), Tübingen 2008.

ZENGER, Erich, Psalmen. Auslegungen. Bd. 3: Dein Angesicht suche ich, Freiburg u.a. 2003.

ZMIJEWSKI, JOSEF, DIE APOSTELGESCHICHTE (RNT 5), REGENSBURG 1994.

Frühchristliche Ansprüche auf die Schriften Israels

TOBIAS NICKLAS

Der Gedanke, dass Judentum und Christentum auch dadurch verbunden sind, dass sie in einem Teil ihrer Heiligen Schriften übereinstimmen, ist natürlich vollkommen zutreffend. Bereits bei der Bezeichnung dieses Corpus an Schriften jedoch zeigt sich, dass Juden und Christen unterschiedliche Zugriffe auf die gleichen Texte haben: Christen sprechen normalerweise vom Alten Testament, dem ein Neues Testament folgt. Diskutiert wurde und wird darüber hinaus immer wieder die Bezeichnung „Erstes Testament",[1] die m.E. jedoch mindestens genauso viele Probleme mit sich bringt, wie sie zu lösen sucht.[2] Aus jüdischer Sicht könnte man vom TaNaK sprechen, was für Tora, Nebiim (Propheten) und Ketubim (Schriften) steht, einen anderen Aufbau als ein heutiges christliches Altes Testament bietet und damit auch schon in sich eine andere, besonders stark an der Tora orientierte Hermeneutik verlangt.[3] Andere beliebte Ausdrücke, die versuchen, so neutral wie möglich zu sein, sind „jüdische Bibel", „Bibel Israels", „Hebräische Bibel" (trotz der in ihr enthaltenen aramäischen Anteile) oder auch (Heilige) „Schriften Israels". Wenn ich im Folgenden bewusst immer wieder den Begriff Altes Testament verwende, so ist dieser Wortgebrauch keineswegs negativ konnotiert, sondern versteht sich aus meiner heutigen, bewusst christlichen Perspektive, die die damit gemeinten Schriften – aus katholischer Sicht dem (so genannten) Kanon der Septuaginta[4] verpflichtet – als heilige Schriften hochschätzt, sie aber in Teilen anders liest und versteht, als Juden dies tun; wo ich von den „Schriften Israels" spreche, versuche ich die antike Perspektive einzunehmen, in der selbst

---

1 So v.a. ZENGER, Testament, sowie DERS., Heilige Schrift.
2 Entscheidend scheint mir vor allem das Problem, dass mit der Rede vom „Ersten" (und dann „Zweitem") Testament das abgeschlossene Zueinander von Altem und Neuen Testament aufgebrochen wird und die Möglichkeit eines „Dritten Testaments" impliziert ist.
3 Einführend hierzu ZENGER, Heilige Schrift, 22-27; ausführlich zu einer Hermeneutik der Jüdischen Bibel bzw. der Schriften Israels vgl. STEMBERGER, Hermeneutik.
4 Zum Problem des Septuaginta-Kanons vgl. HENGEL (& DEINES), Septuaginta; sowie knapper DERS., Septuaginta.

Kanongrenzen nicht in allen jüdischen Gruppen schon gleich gezogen wurden.[5]

Die Tatsache, dass Juden und Christen die in großen Teilen gleichen Texte als Grundlage des eigenen Glaubens lesen, wurde jedoch in den allermeisten Fällen nicht zur Basis gegenseitiger Toleranz und Anerkennung, sondern führte häufig eher zum Gegenteil, nämlich heftigen Auseinandersetzungen um die angemessene Leseweise der Schrift.[6] Wenn wir heute versuchen, voneinander zu lernen und aufeinander zuzugehen,[7] so darf dabei die Geschichte dieser Auseinandersetzungen nicht einfach verdeckt oder vergessen werden – im folgenden Beitrag geht es mir darum, einigen der frühesten Spuren dieser Konflikte nachzugehen und sie aufzudecken.

1. Vorbemerkungen und Einordnung in den größeren Rahmen

Wenn wir heute vom frühesten „Christentum" sprechen, so stellt diese Redeweise einen Anachronismus dar. Dies liegt nicht nur daran, dass das Wort „Christen" als Selbstbezeichnung der Anhänger Jesu von Nazaret erst sehr spät – vor allem im Rahmen antiker Märtyrerakten[8] – belegt ist. Dem widerspricht auch das Zeugnis der Apostelgeschichte – Apg 11,26 – nicht, denn die Bezeichnung Χριστιάνοι („Christen") wird der jungen Bewegung hier *von außen* beigelegt. Vor allem aber verstanden sich die Mitglieder der neuen Bewegung zumindest im 1. Jahrhundert (und viele auch noch deutlich später) sicherlich noch nicht (oder zumindest nicht überall) als eine eigenständige, vom „Judentum" getrennte Religionsgemeinschaft – lange Zeit war und blieben die bzw. viele der verschiedenen „christlichen" Gruppen auch trotz der Hei-

---

5 Man denke etwa an die Rolle des Buches Henoch, das zumindest bei einigen Autoren des frühen Christentums noch lange Zeit als heilige Schrift anerkannt wurde, bei anderen jedoch nicht.

6 Isaac KALIMI wird sich in einem Großprojekt „Fighting over the Bible" ausführlich mit diesen Fragen auseinandersetzen. Mein Beitrag kann in diesem Zusammenhang nur einen kleinen Impuls bieten.

7 Wichtige Impulse für eine angemessene Hermeneutik des Alten Testaments jenseits von Antijudaismus und Antisemitismus bietet DOHMEN, Hermeneutik.

8 Das Wort begegnet dann meistens im Rahmen des Verhörs, in dem die Angeklagten dann bekennen, Christen zu sein. Zu erwähnen jedoch ist auch Ignatius von Antiochien, der in seinen Briefen mehrfach „christliche" (Χριστιανισμός) und „jüdische Lebensweise" (Ἰουδαϊσμός) voneinander differenziert (vgl. z.B. *Magn.* 10). – Zur Entwicklung einer spezifisch „christlichen" Identität (bzw. Identitäten) in Abgrenzung von Judentum und griechisch-hellenistischer Welt vgl. einschlägig LIEU, Christian Identity.

denmission des Paulus mehr oder minder ein Teil des vielfältigen Judentums ihrer Zeit.⁹ Christusanhänger zu sein bedeutete somit einerseits in Kontinuität, andererseits in Diskontinuität zur nicht an Christus glaubenden jüdischen Umgebung zu stehen. Je nachdem, wo man sich in der zunächst zwar kleinen, von Anfang an aber differenzierten neuen Bewegung einordnete, bedeutete dies auch ein neues Verhältnis zu den „Schriften Israels". Das Verhältnis von Kontinuität und Diskontinuität zur jüdischen Wurzel konnte dabei je unterschiedlich interpretiert werden.

Für ein Extrem vollständiger Diskontinuität steht sicherlich Marcion von Sinope (Ende des 1. Jh.s – etwa 160 n.Chr.), der zwischen dem Gotte des Alten Testaments und dem Gott Jesu von Nazaret radikal unterschied und deswegen die Schriften Israels vollständig ablehnte.¹⁰ Sehr weit ging die Diskontinuität zu jüdischen Schrifthermeneutiken sicherlich auch in manchen „gnostisch"-christlichen Kreisen,¹¹ in denen zwar Texte des Neuen Testaments weiterhin eine Rolle spielten, in denen jedoch ebenfalls zwischen zwei Gottheiten identifiziert wurde. Der Gott Israels wurde dabei in manchen Gruppen als dämonischer, in anderen als eher dummer „Demiurg" angesehen, auf den die materielle Welt zurückging, aus der der Mensch bzw. die aus oberen Sphären stammenden Teile in manchen Menschen zu erlösen seien. Vor diesem Hintergrund verwendeten manche „gnostische" Schriften zwar weiter Aspekte der „Schriften Israels", z.B. die Schöpfungserzählungen der Genesis, deuteten sie aber radikal gegen den Strich gebürstet um.¹²

Auch wenn die Ideen Marcions und seiner Anhänger von der werdenden Mehrheitskirche abgelehnt wurden, blieben sie aktuell – Aspekte des marcionitischen Denkens lassen sich bis heute feststellen: Oft zitiert wird das Diktum Adolph von Harnacks, der in seiner Monographie zu Marcion die berühmte These vertrat:¹³ „Das Alte Testament im 2. Jahrhundert zu verwerfen, war ein Fehler, den die große Kirche mit Recht abgelehnt hat; es im 16. Jahrhundert beizubehalten, war ein Schicksal, dem sich die Reformation noch nicht zu entziehen vermochte; es aber im 19. Jahrhundert als kanonische Urkunde im Protestantis-

---

9   Hier vgl. u.a. die z.T. überraschend weit gehenden Beiträge bei BECKER/ YOSHIKO REED (Hg.), Ways.
10 Einführend zu Marcion vgl. RÄISÄNEN, Marcion; hoch interessant auch die Studie von MOLL, Arch-Heretic.
11 Der Begriff „Gnosis" ist mit Recht umstritten. Trotzdem scheint er mir momentan noch unverzichtbar zu sein. Zu meinem Verständnis des Begriffs vgl. NICKLAS, Gnostic ‚Eschatologies', 601-603.
12 Hierzu vgl. v.a. LUTTIKHUIZEN, Revisions.
13 VON HARNACK, Marcion, 217.

mus noch zu konservieren, ist die Folge einer religiösen und kirchlichen Lähmung."

Bittere Realität dagegen wurde die nahezu vollständige Abschaffung bzw. weitgehende Abwertung des Alten Testaments etwa in der so genannten „Botschaft Gottes", einer Art von Volksbibel, die im Jahr 1940 von mehreren Mitgliedern des in Jena ansässigen „Instituts zur Erforschung und Beseitigung des jüdischen Einflusses auf das deutsche kirchliche Leben" immerhin in einer Auflage von wohl 200.000 Exemplaren publiziert wurde.[14] Dieses Volkstestament stellt aus ihrem Kontext gelöste Aussagen des Neuen Testaments zusammen, deren Bezug zum Alten Testament, wo immer möglich, unkenntlich gemacht ist. Erschreckend ist z.B. die Tatsache, dass der Abschnitt mit den synoptischen Streitgesprächen als „Sein Kampf" tituliert ist.

Wir sehen: Die Frage nach dem christlichen Verhältnis zum Alten Testament, nach christlicher Hermeneutik der Schriften Israels ist kein rein akademisches Problem und schon gar keine harmlose Angelegenheit; für das Verhältnis von Judentum und Christentum bleibt sie dauernd aktuell. Die Abgründe lassen sich jedoch nicht nur in den beschriebenen Extrembeispielen festmachen; auch in den entstehenden Mehrheitskirchen, die weiterhin das Alte Testament als Heilige Schrift des Christentums verstanden, kam es sehr früh zu heftigen Auseinandersetzungen um das rechte Verständnis der Schriften Israels. Die Wurzeln dieser Auseinandersetzungen lassen sich bereits im Neuen Testament erkennen.

2. Frühchristliche Hermeneutik von Christus her bzw. auf Christus hin

Bereits bei der Untersuchung des womöglich ältesten christlichen Glaubensbekenntnisses, das uns im Neuen Testament erhalten ist, lassen sich einige wichtige Beobachtungen machen.[15] An den Ausgangspunkt seiner Argumentation um die Frage nach der Auferstehung der Toten stellt Paulus ein uraltes, bereits ihm überkommenes, dabei schon recht komplexes Glaubensbekenntnis (1 Kor 15,3b-5), das im Kern aus vier kurzen Abschnitten besteht, in denen es um das Sterben, Begraben werden, Auferweckt werden und Erscheinen Christi geht. Eine Dimension des Bekenntnisses besteht also in der Erinnerung des Christuser-

---

14 GRUNDMANN, Botschaft. Weiterführend hierzu: JERKE, Neue Testament, sowie HESCHEL, Aryan Jesus, 106-113.

15 Der zweite Kandidat für ein uraltes, dann wohl heidenchristliches Bekenntnis lässt sich in 1 Thess 1,9-10 finden. Die Rekonstruktionen dieses Textes sind jedoch umstritten.

eignisses, das jedoch bereits in der Rede vom „Auferweckt werden" eine Dimension der Deutung erfährt: Gott hat an dem Gekreuzigten gehandelt – und nur so sind die Erscheinungen vor Kefas und den Zwölf zu erklären.¹⁶ Damit jedoch ist der Reflexionsprozess, welcher hinter 1 Kor 15,3b-5 erkennbar wird, noch nicht vollständig beschrieben: Die Elemente 1 und 3 – Tod und Auferweckung – werden weiter ausgeführt und diese Ausführung mit der (für Paulus eher untypischen) Wendung κατὰ τὰς γραφάς („gemäß der Schriften") näher begründet. So wird das historische Ereignis des Todes Jesu, der als Christus verstanden ist (1 Kor 15,3b), als ein Sterben *für unsere Sünden* (ὑπὲρ τῶν ἁμαρτιῶν ἡμῶν) gedeutet. Der Satz erlaubt uns einen kurzen Blick in Reflexionsprozesse des frühesten Christentums: Dem Tod Jesu, dem großen Rätsel, das alles in Frage stellt, muss aufgrund der Erfahrungen von Ostern Sinn beigemessen werden. Dieser Sinn wird in der Lektüre von Texten der Schriften Israels aufgedeckt, welche sich in Bezug zu den erinnerten Ereignissen setzen lassen. Auch wenn hier keine letzte Sicherheit gewonnen werden kann, so scheint der Schlüssel für das hier zum Ausdruck kommende Verständnis des Todes Jesu in Jes 52,13-53,12, dem vierten Lied vom leidenden Gottesknecht, näherhin Jes 53,5-6.10-12, zu liegen.¹⁷ Dies ist kaum am Text alleine sicher festzumachen, der konkret eher vage Bezug lässt sich aber wahrscheinlich machen, wenn man bedenkt, welche Rolle Jes 52,13-53,12 auch in anderen frühchristlichen Versuchen der Deutung des Todes Jesu – sei es in den Passionsgeschichten der Evangelien oder sei es etwa in einem Hoheitstitel wie dem „Lamm Gottes, das die Sünde der Welt trägt" (Joh 1,29.35)¹⁸ – spielt.

Ähnliches gilt auch für Element 3, wo die Auferweckung am dritten Tage als schriftgemäß bezeichnet ist. Hier ist weniger der Intertext – Hos 6,2 – als die Frage umstritten, ob der Gedanke der Auferweckung am dritten Tag aus Hos 6,2 entwickelt wurde oder ob entsprechende Erfahrungen, von denen her auf die Auferweckung *am dritten Tag* geschlossen wurde, den Ausschlag für die Verbindung mit dem Prophetentext ergaben. Wahrscheinlich erscheint mir, dass es nach dem Tode Jesu zu Erfahrungen kam, die von den Anhängern Jesu im Sinne einer

---

16 Die Frage, ob die „Zwölf" bereits im ursprünglichen Bekenntnis erwähnt waren oder nicht, ist in der Forschung umstritten, spielt aber für unsere Frage keine Rolle. Weiterführend u.a. ZELLER, 1 Kor, 461-469 [Lit.!].
17 Vorsichtig kritisch hierzu allerdings ZELLER, 1 Kor, 463-464.
18 Zu dieser Deutung vgl. v.a. HASITSCHKA, Befreiung, 92. Für eine Übersicht zu anderen Deutungen, v.a. im Sinne der Paschalamm-Tradition vgl. NICKLAS, Ablösung, 144-152.

Auferweckung Jesu am dritten Tage gedeutet wurden. Dies wiederum konnte im Licht von Hos 6,2 als schriftgemäß begriffen werden.

Wie auch immer: Die Erfahrung des Christusereignisses verlangt nach Deutung; die Matrix einer solchen Deutung wird durch Texte der Schriften Israels vorgegeben, die sich auf unterschiedliche Weise mit dem Christusereignis in Verbindung setzen lassen.

Bereits damit jedoch ist ein erster Schritt in eine „christliche" Hermeneutik der Schriften Israels gemacht. Die Schriften Israels werden nun aufgrund von Fragen, die sich *vom Christusereignis her* kommend stellen, *auf das Christusereignis hin* gelesen.

Wie sehr sich dieser bereits in 1 Kor 15,3-5 zu beobachtende Vorgang auch in anderen Texten zeigen und mehr und mehr auf das gesamte Wirken Jesu beziehen lässt, zeigt sich an einer Vielzahl von anderen Beispielen. Hervorgehoben seien zwei, die besonders deutlich zeigen, wie die Autorität der Schriften Israels nun mehr und mehr in Bezug zur Autorität des Wortes und des Tuns Jesu Christi gestellt werden.

2.1 Die Tempelreinigungsszene des Johannesevangeliums (Joh 2,13-22)

Die *Tempelreinigungsszene des Johannesevangeliums* (Joh 2,13-22) lässt sich in zwei Abschnitte gliedern:[19]

Joh 2,13-17 Tempelaktion und Schriftdeutung
    Joh 2,13   Weg nach Jerusalem
    Joh 2,14-16 Eigentliche, mehrteilig geschilderte Tempelaktion
    Joh 2,17   Schriftwort (Ps 68,10 LXX)
Joh 2,18-22 Dialog mit den „Juden"
    Joh 2,18-20 Dialog und Missverständnis der „Juden"
    Joh 2,21   Deutung durch Erzählerkommentar
    Joh 2,22   Hinweis auf nachösterliche Reflexion der Jünger

Die Szene ist aus mehrerlei Gründen aufschlussreich. Anders als die synoptischen Evangelien setzt das Johannesevangelium die Tempelreinigung an den Anfang des Wirkens Jesu. Die in den Synoptikern erkennbare logische Verzahnung zwischen Tempelreinigung und Passion Jesu wird bei Joh jedoch nicht aufgegeben, sondern durch das in Joh 2,17 eingefügte, die in 2,14-16 geschilderte Aktion deutende Schriftwort hergestellt. Gleich mehrere Aspekte machen Joh 2,17 interessant. Der Text unternimmt einen Perspektivenwechsel – von der Erzählung der Ereignisse im Tempel zu Jerusalem (Joh 2,14-16) zur sicherlich späteren

---

19 Eine ausführliche Auslegung des Abschnitts habe ich in NICKLAS, Tempelreinigung, vorgelegt. Dort auch weiterführende Literatur.

Erinnerung der Jünger, die weder in der Szene selbst als anwesend geschildert sind, deren Erinnern jedoch hier noch nicht konkreter zeitlich eingeordnet ist (Joh 2,17). Joh 2,17 wiederum konfrontiert das zitierte „Wort der Schrift" mit dem erinnerten Ereignis. Ps 68 LXX wiederum, aus dem das angeführte Zitat stammt, wurde in verschiedenen Kontexten mit dem Tode Jesu in Verbindung gebracht. Besonders bekannt und weit verbreitet ist das Motiv der Speisung des Gekreuzigten mit Galle und Essig (Mk 15,23.36; Mt 27,34.48; Lk 23,36; Joh 19,28-30; EvPetr 16; *Barn.* 7,3.5 u.a.). Damit ist bereits eine erste assoziative Verbindung zwischen Tempelreinigung und Passion hergestellt. Dies geschieht natürlich auch auf der Ebene des Textinhalts, der vom „Verzehren" des Beters spricht: Während dieser Beter jedoch im Psalm selbst mit David verbunden ist, erfolgt nun eine Verschiebung: Die Deutung von Joh 2,14-16 mit Hilfe von Ps 68,10 LXX macht nur Sinn, wenn der Beter des Psalms – ursprünglich David – nun mit Jesus identifiziert wird. Hinzu kommt eine kleine Abänderung der Textform – aus dem Aorist in der Septuaginta-Vorlage des Psalms macht der Evangelist eine Futurform καταφάγεται.[20] Der Bezug zur in der Erzähllinie des Johannesevangeliums erst folgenden Passionserzählung kann dadurch noch deutlicher hervorgehoben werden.

Doch damit nicht genug: auch der zweite Teil des Textes endet mit einem Hinweis auf die Schrift. Der Dialog der Juden mit Jesus führt zu einem der für Joh typischen Missverständnisse, das sich am Verständnis des Begriffs ναός, „Heiligtum" (Joh 2,19-21) entzündet und für den Leser aufgrund des Erzählerkommentars in Joh 2,21 auflöst.

Bemerkenswert jedoch ist vor allem Joh 2,22:

ὅτε οὖν ἠγέρθη ἐκ νεκρῶν, ἐμνήσθησαν οἱ μαθηταὶ αὐτοῦ ὅτι τοῦτο ἔλεγεν, καὶ ἐπίστευσαν τῇ γραφῇ καὶ τῷ λόγῳ ὃν εἶπεν ὁ Ἰησοῦς.

Als er also von den Toten auferweckt worden war, erinnerten sich seine Jünger, dass er dies gesagt hatte, und sie glaubten der Schrift und dem Wort, das Jesus gesagt hatte.

Der Text verlässt hier die Perspektive der Jesuserzählung, die noch auf Kreuz und Auferweckung zuläuft und reflektiert über die eigene nachösterliche Perspektive.[21] Das Erinnern der Jünger Jesu wird nun explizit in die nachösterliche Zeit verlagert, es erhält so eine neue zeitliche, vor allem aber auch eine qualitative Perspektive, aus der erst der vorherige Dialog angemessen verstanden werden kann. In diese Perspektive hinein verlegt wird nun auch die Aussage über den Glauben der Jünger,

---

20 Eine detaillierte Analyse bietet z.B. THYEN, Johannesevangelium, 176-177.
21 Zur konsequent nachösterlichen Perspektive des Johannesevangeliums vgl. weiterführend HOEGEN-ROHLS, Der nachösterliche Johannes.

der sich nun auf die Schrift *und* das Wort Jesu bezieht. Beides – Schriftwort und Jesuswort – rücken so als Autoritäten nebeneinander.

Nur von einem Nebeneinander zu sprechen, würde dem tatsächlichen Sachverhalt jedoch nicht gerecht: Für das Johannesevangelium ist das Wort Jesu nicht einfach nur Wort einer irdischen, vielleicht prophetischen oder messianischen, aber letztlich doch rein menschlichen Autorität. Seit dem Prolog weiß der Leser des Johannesevangeliums, dass Jesus als der Fleisch gewordene, im Ursprung bei Gott seiende, göttliche Logos Gottes, als das Wort Gottes, zu verstehen ist (vgl. Joh 1,1-2.14). Im Verlauf des Evangeliums ist zudem zu lernen, dass alles Tun Jesu im Einklang mit dem Willen des Vaters steht (vgl. z.B. Joh 5,19-21) – und wenn die „Ich-Bin-Worte" Jesu in Epiphanien eingebettet sind, wie etwa in Joh 6,16-21 oder 18,1-11, so hängt das sicher damit zusammen, dass Jesu, des Gotteswortes, Worte letztlich als Wort Gottes verstanden sind.[22] Dann aber ist nicht nur nachzuvollziehen, warum das Johannesevangelium den Worten, die Jesus spricht (Joh 2,22), solch großes Gewicht beimisst, dann wird auch plausibel, warum Jesu Tun und seine Worte für Joh zum hermeneutischen Schlüssel werden, aus dem heraus Schrift von nun an verstanden wird. Dass dieser Gedanke auch enormes Konfliktpotenzial in sich birgt, wird sich im nächsten Abschnitt zeigen.

2.2 Erfüllungs- oder Reflexionszitate des Matthäusevangeliums

Durchaus vergleichbar, wenn auch in ihrer konkreten Funktionsweise etwas anders gelagert sind sicherlich die bekannten *Erfüllungs- oder Reflexionzitate des Matthäusevangeliums*. Da die sich damit verbindenden hermeneutischen Fragen allgemein bekannt sind, genügt es auch hier knapp zu bleiben. Dabei geht es um ungleichmäßig über das Evangelium verteilte Zitate, die mit der Formel (ἵνα) πληρωθῇ τὸ ῥηθὲν διὰ ... τοῦ προφήτου λέγοντος eingeleitet sind (vgl. Mt 1,22-23; 2,15.17-18.23; 4,14-16; 8,17; 12,18-21; 13,35; 21,4-5; 27,9).[23] Die Perspektive auf Christus hin, die den zitierten alttestamentlichen Texten verliehen wird, kann dabei unterschiedliche Funktionen haben.

2.2.1 In manchen Fällen geht es dem Text um die Deutung von zum Teil für sein eigenes Anliegen problematischer historischer Erinnerung. So baut Mt 4,12-17 auf der Erinnerung auf, dass Jesus von Nazaret zumindest eine Zeitlang in dem eigentlich unbedeutenden Kafarnaum

---

[22] Zu erwähnen ist darüber hinaus auch das Motiv der Erfüllung von Worten Jesu, wie es sich in der joh Passionserzählung findet (Joh 18,9.32).

[23] Für eine ausführlichere grundlegende Auseinandersetzung vgl. z.B. LUZ, Mt 1-7, 134-140.

gewirkt hat, auf. Ganz offensichtlich bereitet dieser Teil des Wirkens Jesu für ihn ein theologisches Problem, er hält die Erinnerung daran aber für so wichtig, dass er ihm in seiner Jesus-Erzählung umfangreichen Raum einräumt (vgl. anders Joh 2,12!). Um sie in sein theologisches Gesamtkonzept einbauen zu können, greift er zu einem Kunstgriff; er bietet nicht nur den einfachen Ortsnamen, der ihm keine Anknüpfungspunkte theologischer Deutung erlaubt, sondern schreibt von Kafarnaum, „das am See liegt, im Gebiet von Sebulon und Naftali" (Mt 4,13). An der Verortung in „Sebulon und Naftali" kann er nun ansetzen. Die Antwort auf seine Frage, warum Jesus von Nazaret ausgerechnet in Kafarnaum wirkte, findet er in einer leicht gekürzten Fassung von Jes 8,23-9,1:[24]

Mt 4,14-16:
... damit sich erfüllte, was durch den Propheten Jesaja gesagt worden ist: Das Land Sebulon und das Land Naftali, der Weg am Meer, (das Gebiet) auf der andern Seite des Jordan, das Galiläa der Völker: Das Volk, das im Dunkel lebt, hat ein großes Licht gesehen; denen, die im Schattenreich des Todes wohnen, ihnen ist ein Licht erschienen.

Damit aber wird nicht nur Jesu Wirken in Kafarnaum als Erfüllung einer Prophezeiung gedeutet, damit wird es gleichzeitig auch interpretiert: Was Jesus in Galiläa wirkt, bringt diesen Menschen ein Licht, das sie aus dem „Schattenreich des Todes" befreit. Dies wiederum lässt sich ausgezeichnet als Teil des matthäischen Gesamtkonzepts verstehen, das Jesus zwar als Messias Israels versteht, dessen Wirken aber mehr und mehr die Grenzen zu den Völkern überschreitet, so dass er als Auferstandener als von Gott selbst eingesetzter „Pantokrator" gezeichnet werden kann (Mt 28,18).[25]

2.2.2 Noch komplexer ist ein zweites Beispiel: Mt 8,16-17 bietet einen Sammelbericht, in dem von der Heilung vieler Besessener und Kranker die Rede ist. Dieser wird, anders als die Parallelen in Mk 1,32-34 und Lk 4,40-41, ebenfalls mit Hilfe eines Erfüllungszitats gedeutet:[26]

Mt 8,17:
... damit sich erfüllte, was durch den Propheten Jesaja gesagt worden ist: Er hat unsere Schwächen auf sich genommen und unsere Krankheiten getragen.

Auch hier setzt der Text sicherlich an der historischen Erinnerung an erfolgte wunderbare Heilungen durch Jesus an, die gedeutet werden

---

24 Zur genauen Form des Zitats MENKEN, Matthew's Bible, 15-33.
25 Zur matthäischen Christologie vgl. auch NICKLAS, Davidssohn.
26 Zur konkreten Textform vgl. wieder MENKEN, Matthew's Bible, 35-49.

soll.²⁷ Bereits die konkrete Wahl des alttestamentlichen Intertexts jedoch verleiht hier dem Erzählten eine Dimension, die nicht einmal explizit ausgesprochen werden muss. Dass Jes 53,4 aus dem vierten Lied vom leidenden Gottesknecht im frühen Christentum zu einem Schlüsseltext für das Verständnis der Passion Jesu wurde, zeigte sich bereits oben, bei der Besprechung von 1 Kor 15,3-5. Der Evangelist verbindet hier also zwei Dimensionen von Erinnerung miteinander: Im Licht des Kreuzes Jesu erhalten für ihn auch die Heilungen von Kranken und die Exorzismen eine neue Bedeutung. Bereits sie sind als Verweise auf Jesu Rolle in der Passion aufzufassen; dies wiederum wird erst durch die Verknüpfung von irdischem Heilswirken an Leidenden und Jesu (als heilvoll verstandenen) Leiden in der Passion über Jes 53,4 möglich.

2.2.3 Anders als in den beiden genannten Fällen schließen die Reflexionszitate des Textes jedoch bei weitem nicht immer an Erinnerungen um historische Fakten an. Dies ist sicherlich in besonderem Maße in den Kindheitserzählungen Mt 1-2 der Fall, wo solche Zitate ja gehäuft auftreten. Zwar lässt sich nicht ausschließen, dass das eine oder andere in den Kindheitsgeschichten Erzählte tatsächlich auch so oder in vergleichbarer Weise geschehen ist, in diesem Zusammenhang aber sind kaum verlässliche historische Beweisführungen möglich. Das Interesse der Texte jedoch liegt auf einem anderen Level; es geht ihnen vielmehr darum, das im Ereignis von Kreuz und Auferstehung über die Bedeutung des Lebens Jesu Erkannte auf die Geburt und die Kindheit Jesu auszudehnen. Im Hintergrund steht wohl der Gedanke, dass das, was sich in Tod und Auferweckung Jesu erwiesen hat, nicht nur für das Ende seines Lebens gilt, sondern für sein ganzes Dasein – bis hin zu seiner Zeugung und Geburt. Während Mk also die Gottessohnschaft Jesu von Nazaret erst unter dem Kreuz als voll erkennbar begreift (vgl. Mk 15,39),²⁸ drückt Mt in seinen Kindheitsgeschichten erzählerisch aus, dass Jesus Sohn Gottes von Anfang ist. Diese christologische Aussage wird mit Hilfe legendarischer Erzählungen, denen jedoch hohes theologisches Gewicht zukommt, zum Ausdruck gebracht:

Das sicherlich bekannteste der so einzuordnenden Reflexionszitate des Matthäusevangeliums findet sich sicherlich in Mt 1,22-23:

„Dies alles aber ist geschehen, damit sich erfüllte, was vom Herrn durch den Propheten gesagt worden war: Siehe, die Jungfrau wird ein Kind emp-

---

27 Klein, Wunder, hält die Sammelberichte gar für den Kern historischer Erinnerung an Wunder Jesu.
28 Zur markinischen Christologie vgl. NICKLAS, Der gekreuzigte Christus.

fangen und einen Sohn gebären, und man wird ihn bei seinem Namen Immanuel nennen, das heißt übersetzt: Gott mit uns."

Die Funktion des Zitats liegt auf zwei Ebenen: Einerseits wird dadurch die in Mt bereits am Ende der Genealogie angedeutete (Mt 1,16) und in Mt 1,18 ausgeführte, christologisch wichtige Idee der Jungfrauengeburt in der Schrift verankert, andererseits ist mit der Nennung des Namens „Immanuel" ein für den Gesamtplot des Matthäusevangeliums wichtiges Signal gesetzt, das in der Aussage des Auferstandenen in Mt 28,20 – „Ich bin bei euch alle Tage bis zum Ende der Welt" – wieder eingeholt wird. Die Bedeutung des Zitats für den Gesamtentwurf des Matthäusevangeliums kann so kaum überschätzt werden. Die Diskussion entzündet sich allerdings an seiner Textform. Mt zitiert hier Jes 7,14 in der Fassung der Septuaginta; zumindest sein erstes theologisches Anliegen, die Jungfrauengeburt in der Schrift zu verankern, ist bekanntlich nur über diese Textform möglich, die das hebräische עלמה, welches für „junge Frau" steht und im Griechischen üblicherweise mit νεᾶνις wiedergegeben ist, mit παρθένος, „Jungfrau", übersetzt. Hier davon zu sprechen, dass Mt einem Übersetzungsfehler aufgesessen wäre, jedoch würde der tatsächlichen Situation nicht gerecht. Einerseits scheint der LXX-Text hier bewusst eine Verknüpfung zu Jes 37,22 herzustellen, wo von der „Jungfrau Tochter Zion" die Rede ist,[29] andererseits wurde die Septuaginta ja nicht einfach als eine mehr oder minder beliebige Übersetzung wahrgenommen, der ein Urtext gegenüberstand, vielmehr lässt sich von frühjüdischen Texten ausgehend, verstärkt aber im antiken Christentum eine Entwicklung beobachten, die sie selbst als bis in den Wortlaut hinein inspiriert verstand.[30]

Mt versteht also den für ihn „inspirierten" Text der Septuaginta von Jesaja als Prophetie auf das Christusereignis hin, setzt ihn an einer entscheidenden Passage am Anfang seines Evangeliums ein, erklärt von daher einerseits den Ursprung Jesu und spannt andererseits einen Bogen bis ans Ende seines Evangeliums.

3. Konflikte um das rechte Schriftverständnis und die angemessene Textform

Dass die eben skizzierten Entwicklungen hin zu einer Hermeneutik der Schriften Israels mit Fragerichtungen, die sich von Christus her bestimmen, und Deutungen auf Christus hin nicht nur für die Entwick-

---

29 Vgl. hierzu WILK, Esaias, 2521-2522.
30 Eine einführende Übersicht zu entsprechenden Belegen bieten etwa SIEGERT, Hebräische Bibel, 26-30; TILLY, Einführung in die Septuaginta, 108-112.

lung „christlicher" Identität(en) von Bedeutung waren, sondern gleichzeitig ein hohes Konfliktpotenzial in sich bergen, wurde oben bereits angedeutet. Erste Entfaltungen dieses Konflikts zeigen sich bereits im Neuen Testament:

3.1 Wenn ihr Mose glauben würdet ... (Joh 5,46). Anzeichen für einen „christlichen" Alleinanspruch auf die Schriften Israels

3.1.1 Zumindest in Teilen dürfte das *Johannesevangelium* sich als Antwort auf einen dramatischen Konflikt der johanneischen Gemeinden mit der Synagoge verstehen.[31] Auch wenn die konkreten zeitgeschichtlichen Hintergründe, auf die der Text reagiert, wohl im Dunkel bleiben, so scheinen die johanneischen Gemeinden bereits die schmerzhafte Erfahrung eines Synagogenausschlusses mitgemacht zu haben (Joh 9,22; 12,42; vgl. auch Joh 9,34). Dass eine der Dimensionen des Konflikts sicherlich mit der hohen Christologie der johanneischen „Christen", die von der Seite der Synagoge als Gefährdung des Monotheismus und damit Blasphemie angesehen wurde, zu tun gehabt haben dürfte, ist unbestritten. Texte wie etwa Joh 10,30-39 sprechen eine zu deutliche Sprache. Damit einher jedoch dürfte auch eine Auseinandersetzung um das angemessene Verständnis der Schriften Israels gegangen sein. Der besondere Ansatz der nachösterlichen johanneischen Hermeneutik wurde bereits oben skizziert; dass man die Schriften auf Christus hin deutete, zeigt sich schon sehr früh im Text – etwa im Bekenntnis des Philippus, der Christus als den bezeichnet, „über den Mose im Gesetz und auch die Propheten geschrieben haben" (Joh 1,45). Eine Auseinandersetzung darüber, was es heißt, „Jünger dieses Menschen" zu sein und deswegen – aus der Sicht „der Juden" nicht „Jünger Mose" sein zu können (vgl. die Alternative in Joh 9,28) spiegelt sich besonders deutlich in den Dialogen, die sich an die Sabbatheilung des Blindgeborenen anschließen (Joh 9; vgl. besonders 9,24-34). Wie sehr in den Konflikten die Frage der Schrifthermeneutik eine Rolle spielt, wird jedoch besonders in der Jesusrede nach der Sabbatheilung des Gelähmten Joh 5,19-47 deutlich. Ausgangspunkt der Auseinandersetzung ist natürlich die (in der Erzählung erst nachgeschobene) Heilung des Gelähmten an einem Sabbat (Joh 5,9.16). Den Torabruch verteidigt Jesus mit Hilfe einer Aussage über seine Wirkeinheit mit dem Vater (Joh

---

31 Klassisch hierzu die Studien von MARTYN, History, und – im deutschsprachigen Raum –WENGST, Bedrängte Gemeinde. Beide Studien wurden inzwischen zu Recht in vielen ihrer Ergebnisse relativiert, der grundlegende Gedanke, dass das Johannesevangeliums in vielen Teilen als (sicherlich gebrochener) Spiegel eines Konflikts zwischen Synagoge und johanneischen Gemeinden zu lesen ist, bleibt aber relevant.

5,17), was von den „Juden" als Blasphemie ausgelegt wird und zu einem Tötungsbeschluss führt (Joh 5,18). Dies wiederum mündet in die erwähnte Rede des johanneischen Jesus über seine Vollmacht (Joh 5,19-47): Thematisiert dabei sind die Wirkeinheit Jesu mit dem Vater (Joh 5,19-30). Dies mündet in die Frage, aufgrund welchen Zeugnisses Jesus dies behaupten könne. Der Text spricht vom Zeugnis Johannes des Täufers (Joh 5,33-35), dem jedoch das Zeugnis des Vaters, das sich in den Werken, die Jesus vollbringt, erweist (Joh 5,36). Dem wird schließlich das Zeugnis der Schriften an die Seite gestellt (Joh 5,39):

Ihr erforscht die Schriften, weil ihr meint, in ihnen das ewige Leben zu haben; gerade sie legen Zeugnis über mich ab.

Die „Juden" – wohl die Mitglieder der örtlichen Synagogengemeinde(n) – sind für die johanneische Gemeinde offensichtlich bereits zu einem Gegenüber geworden. Dieses Gegenüber entzündet sich am Verständnis Jesu von Nazaret. Damit zutiefst verbunden jedoch ist nun auch ein unterschiedliches Verständnis der „Schriften". Diese werden aus Sicht der johanneischen Christusanhänger als Zeugnis für Christus gelesen. Neu jedoch zeigt sich, dass zumindest implizit die Schriftforschung der Gegenüber als sinnlos angesehen wird – sie „meinen" nur, in ihnen das ewige Leben zu haben, das – aus johanneischer Sicht – jedoch nur im Namen Jesu möglich ist (Joh 20,31; vgl. auch 11,25). Damit werden den jüdischen Gegenübern zwar noch nicht ihre Schriften entzogen, ihnen aber unterstellt, dass sie diese nicht angemessen verstehen – und diese ihnen deswegen nicht mehr zum Heil relevant sind.

Joh 5,45-47 geht noch weiter. Der Unglaube der Gegenüber des johanneischen Jesus – und darin gespiegelt die Haltung der jüdischen Gegner der johanneischen Gemeinden – führt zur Anklage durch Mose selbst, auf den die Schriften zurückgeführt werden (Joh 5,45).

Wenn ihr Mose glauben würdet, müsstet ihr auch mir glauben; denn über mich hat er geschrieben. Wenn ihr aber seinen Schriften nicht glaubt, wie könnt ihr dann meinen Worten glauben? (Joh 5,46-47).

Die in 5,39 genannten Schriften werden nun also auf die Tora des Mose konzentriert: Diese jedoch ist zumindest hier nur noch als Schrift „über mich", d.h. Christus im johanneischen Denken, verstanden. Dass es eine andere Leseweise der Schriften des Mose gibt, wird den Gegnern zumindest hier nicht mehr zugestanden – und schon gar nicht, dass diese legitim sein könnte. Die Schriften des Mose nicht auf Christus hin zu lesen, bedeutet in dieser Sicht, seinen Schriften „nicht zu glauben". Dies heißt nicht nicht, dass für Joh die Schrift nur noch auf eine

„Sammlung von Weissagungen auf Jesus Christus"[32] reduziert ist, der Umfang der Schrift bleibt gleich. Sie wird wohl auch weiterhin als Geschichte Gottes mit seinem Volk gelesen; dieser Gott jedoch kann für Joh nicht mehr ohne Christus gedacht werden.[33]

3.1.2. Vielleicht noch aufschlussreichere Parallelen zu diesem Denken jedoch finden sich in Texten der Apostolischen Väter.[34] Die Datierung der „mittleren Sammlung" der Briefe des *Ignatius von Antiochien* ist heute wieder umstritten.[35] Die Frage, ob sie als echt in die erste Hälfte des 2. Jahrhunderts oder pseudepigraphisch in die zweite Hälfte zu datieren sind, ist jedoch für die vorliegende Problematik wohl zweitrangig. Entscheidend ist, dass auch in den Schriften des Ignatius – sicherlich vor dem Hintergrund konkreter Auseinandersetzungen (auch) mit „judaisierenden" Christen[36] – immer wieder das Problem „christlicher" Hermeneutik der Schriften zum Tragen kommt. Was in den im Johannesevangelium erkennbaren Konflikten nur impliziert ist, wird bei Ignatius nun explizit ausgeführt. Im Zusammenhang mit einer immer wieder erkennbaren scharfen Abgrenzung von Judentum und judaisierenden Praktiken (vgl. v.a. *Magn.* 8-10) werden etwa „die Propheten" ganz dem Judentum entzogen. Diese hätten nicht der jüdischen Lebensweise (κατὰ Ἰουδαϊσμόν; *Magn.* 8,1) entsprechend, sondern Christus Jesus gemäß gelebt (κατὰ Χριστὸν Ἰησοῦν), sie seien dem Geist nach Jünger Christi gewesen (μαθηταὶ ὄντες τῷ πνεύματι), hätten auf Christus hin verkündigt (*Philad.* 5,2; 9,2) und ihn als Lehrer erwartet (beides *Magn.* 9,2; vgl. auch *Philad.* 5,2). Die Propheten können so selbst als an Christus Glaubende und in diesem Glauben Gerettete bezeichnet

---

32 So BAUER, Joh, 91. Sehr pointiert auch SÄNGER, „Von mir". Beide kritisiert bei THYEN, Johannesevangelium, 329.
33 Das Johannesevangelium steht mit dieser nochmaligen Zuspitzung frühchristlicher Schrifthermeneutik nicht alleine. Das apokryphe „unbekannte Evangelium" auf P.Egerton 2, eine Schrift wohl der ersten Hälfte des 2. Jahrhunderts, kombiniert in einer Streitszene Joh 5,39; 5,45 und 9,29 und dramatisiert damit den Konflikt noch einmal. Weiterführend zu diesem Text NICKLAS, ‚Unknown Gospel'; zum konkreten Problem NICKLAS, Evangelium.
34 Das dramatische Beispiel des *Barnabasbriefes* hat in ausgezeichneter Weise Prostmeier diskutiert, so dass hier alleine ein Querverweis genügen mag: PROSTMEIER, Antijudaismus.
35 Zur Kritik an der klassischen Auffassung, dass die Texte der mittleren Sammlung als echt aufzufassen seien, vgl. v.a. HÜBNER, Thesen, sowie LECHNER, Ignatius. Trotz der guten Argumente Hübners und Lechners, die hier nicht im Detail diskutiert werden können, neige ich weiterhin dazu, die Texte als echt aufzufassen.
36 Auch die Frage nach den konkreten, in den Ignatianen angegriffenen Gegnern ist umstritten. Sehr weit in seiner Identifikation der v.a. in *Magn.* 8-10 attackierten judaisierenden und/oder judenchristlichen Gegner geht etwa MYLLYKOSKI, Wild Beasts, der hier eine judenchristliche Gruppe vermutet, die Jesus als wahren und letzten Hohenpriester und Propheten Israels verstand (ebd., 358).

werden (*Philad.* 5,2), zusammen mit Abraham, Isaak und Jakob werden sie den Aposteln und der Kirche in eine Reihe gestellt (*Philad.* 9,1).

Vor diesem Hintergrund ist für Ignatius jede Hermeneutik der Schrift, die zum Judentum führt, abzulehnen. Besonders scharf formuliert *Philad.* 6,1: „Wenn euch aber jemand, auf Auslegung gestützt, Judentum verkündigt, den hört nicht an; denn es ist besser, von einem Beschnittenen Christentum zu hören, als von einem Unbeschnittenen Judentum. Wenn aber beide nicht von Jesus Christus reden, so sind sie für mich Grabsäulen und Totenhügel, auf denen nur Menschennamen geschrieben stehen."[37]

Geht Ignatius damit so weit, letztlich nur noch eine Auswahl der Schriften, die er auf Christus hin lesen kann, zu akzeptieren? Immerhin spricht er in *Magn.* 8,1 von Irrlehren und alten, wertlosen Fabeln (μυθεύματα), die zu einer jüdischen Lebensweise führten. Ist hier die Tora gemeint? *Philad.* 8,2 wiederum greift Gegner an, die sich auf die „Urkunden" (ἀρχεῖα) stützten, um ihren Glauben an das Evangelium zu begründen. Diese Argumentation kippt Ignatius um: „Meine Urkunden ... sind Jesus Christus, die heiligen Urkunden sein Kreuz und sein Tod, seine Auferstehung und der durch ihn geweckte Glaube."[38] Eine positive Aussage über das „Gesetz des Mose" (νόμος Μωϋσέως) – hier unterschieden von den „Worten der Propheten" – bietet immerhin *Smyrn.* 5,1; auch dies jedoch hat seinen Eigenwert nur im Blick auf Christus. Ignatius erstellt also sicherlich keine „alttestamentliche Auswahlbibel" auf Christus hin, die Tora bleibt für ihn Bestandteil der Schrift. Sie jedoch verliert allerdings ganz offensichtlich ihren Eigenwert und ist nur noch so weit von Bedeutung, als sie auf Christus hin kündet.

Dies zeigt sich durchaus auch konkret in seinen Schriften, die an keiner einzigen Stelle Zitate oder klare Anspielungen auf die Tora bieten, ja kein einziges markiertes Zitat auf eine Stelle des Alten Testaments. Die wenigen möglichen Anspielungen auf alttestamentliche Intertexte stammen aus Psalter, Sprichwörtern, Jesaja und Sacharja; in keinem Fall jedoch scheint eine Kenntnis dieser Texte nötig, um Ignatius' Argument nachvollziehen zu können.[39]

3.2 Textform und Schrifthermeneutik

Die Auseinandersetzungen jedoch konzentrierten sich nicht nur auf die Frage der angemessenen Schrifthermeneutik, zumindest in einigen

---

37 Übersetzung: LINDEMANN/PAULSEN, Väter, 221.
38 Übersetzung: LINDEMANN/PAULSEN, Väter, 223.
39 Die Stellen wurden überprüft anhand des (ausführlichen) Registers bei LINDEMANN/PAULSEN, Väter, 566-567.

Fällen paart sich damit tatsächlich auch der Konflikt um die rechte Textform. Dass es auf jüdischer Seite zu Überarbeitungen der griechischen Übersetzungen der Schriften Israels kam und sich das rabbinische Judentum letztlich von der Septuaginta abwandte,[40] hat sicherlich auch damit zu tun, dass diese Textform explizit von Christen in Anspruch genommen wurde.

Einen besonders detaillierten Einblick in Auseinandersetzungen nicht nur um die konkrete Auslegung von Texten, sondern auch zu gegenseitigen Vorwürfen über die bewusste Fälschung von Textformen bietet Justins *Dialog mit Trypho* (wohl 160 n.Chr.)[41]. Auch wenn sich der „Dialog" wohl nie in der aufgezeichneten Form abgespielt haben dürfte, in der Trypho nur als eine Art „Sparringspartner" der Argumente Justins gezeichnet ist, so spiegelt er doch Auseinandersetzungen, die wirklich stattgefunden haben. Die für die vorliegende Frage entscheidenden Abschnitte setzen in *dial.* 66 ein. In einem langen Argumentationsgang, der bereits auf *dial.* 43 zurückgeht, sucht Justin zu zeigen, dass sich Jes 7,10-17 nur auf Christus alleine beziehen könne; wichtig für die Argumentation wird zudem eine Einschaltung von Jes 8,4 werden. In *dial.* 66 zitiert er ausführlich diese Passage und legt anschließend großen Wert auf die Einzigartigkeit der jungfräulichen Geburt Christi.

Dem wiederum hält Trypho entgegen (*dial.* 67,1), dass Justin in Jes 7,14 eine falsche Textform zugrunde gelegt habe:[42] der zutreffende Text spreche nicht von einer „Jungfrau", sondern von einer „jungen Frau". Die Prophezeiung beziehe sich deswegen auf Ezekias (= Hiskia), in dessen Leben sie auch erfüllt worden sei. Die Auseinandersetzung weicht immer wieder auf „Nebenschauplätze" ab, die Kontrahenten eröffnen neue Fragen, kommen jedoch immer wieder auf Jes 7,14 zurück. Ich konzentriere mich deswegen auf die Argumente zum Thema: Eine Basis der Argumentation Justins besteht in der Vorstellung, dass die Übersetzung der Septuaginta – und zwar nicht nur der Tora – als glaubwürdige Basis der Argumentation mit der Schrift zu gelten habe, während einige jüdische Lehrer diese (offenbar in der Zeit Justins) bewusst abzuändern suchten (vgl. *dial.* 68,7; 71,1; vgl. auch Eusebius, *h.e.* 4,18,8); nur diese Änderungen wiederum machten die jüdische Deutung des Textes möglich. Dies wiederum gelte nicht nur für Jes 7,14,

---

40 Ausführlicher hierzu TILLY, Einführung, 113-121, der daneben eine Reihe weiterer Gründe anzuführen vermag.
41 Auch die Frage nach Justins Schrifthermeneutik wurde in der Forschung immer wieder diskutiert. Hierzu vgl. zuletzt CHILTON, Justin.
42 Dass er nicht auf die Einschaltung von Jes 8,4 eingeht, zeigt natürlich, wie sehr der erhaltene Text rein die christliche Perspektive Justins wiedergibt.

sondern auch für andere Stellen. Justin erwähnt eine (ansonsten nur bei Laktanz, *inst.* 4,18,22 belegte) Passage aus Esra (*dial.* 72,1), Jer 11,19, eine Passage, die allerdings noch in einigen jüdischen Bibelausgaben zu finden sei (*dial.* 72,2-3), ein wichtiger Parallelbeleg zu Jes 53,7, sowie einen anderen in den überlieferten Handschriften nicht belegten Abschnitt aus Jeremia (*dial.* 72,4), der gleichwohl bei Irenäus, *haer.* 3,20,4; 4,22,1 belegt ist und als Grundlage der Idee des *descensus ad inferos* dienen kann (vgl. 1 Petr 3,19; 4,6). Aus Ps 95,10 LXX wiederum seien die Worte ἀπὸ τοῦ ξύλου („vom Holz her") gestrichen worden, wodurch verdeckt worden sei, dass der Psalm vom gekreuzigten Christus spreche, der König unter den Heiden geworden sei (*dial.* 73,1-4).[43]

Es ist im Hinblick auf die vorliegende Frage sicher nicht nötig, hier die weitere Argumentation, die sich nun auch an der Auslegung von Ps 95 entzündet, nachzuzeichnen. In Justins Dialog treffen sich nicht nur verschiedene Schrifthermeneutiken, es wird auch die Auseinandersetzung um die rechte Textform der Schrift geführt.

Im Folgenden führt Justin Details aus Jes 7,10-17 und 8,4 an, die zeigen sollen, dass sich diese Prophezeiungen keineswegs auf Ezekias beziehen können: Besonders interessant ist etwa der Bezug, den er zwischen Jes 8,4 und der im Neuen Testament nur in Mt 2,1-12 überlieferten Szene von den Magiern aus dem Osten herstellt (*dial.* 77,3-4; 78). Um seinen Gegner (oder besser: seine Leser) von der Folgerichtigkeit seiner Argumentation zu überzeugen, muss er im Grunde selbst in den Jesaja-Text eingreifen. Die Einfügung von Jes 8,4 in den Fluss von 7,10-17 bleibt jedoch von Trypho unkommentiert; an ihr jedoch setzt Justin an: von niemandem außer Christus könne gesagt werden, dass er schon als „Kind, das weder Vater noch Mutter rufen kann, das Vermögen von Damaskus und die Beute von Samaria vor dem König der Assyrer in Besitz genommen habe" (*dial.* 77,3 in Auslegung von Jes 8,4). Erfüllt habe sich diese Prophezeiung jedoch bereits kurz nach der Geburt Jesu im Kommen und in der Anbetung Jesu durch die Magier. Mit dem in Jes 8,4 angesprochenen „König der Assyrer" sei Herodes gemeint (*dial.* 77,4). Es folgt eine mit Aspekten aus Lk 2,1-5 harmonisierte Erzählung von Mt 2,1-14.16, die durch zusätzliche Elemente wie die Herkunft der Magier aus der Arabia (*dial.* 77,4; 78,1.2.7) und die Geburt Jesu in einer Höhle (*dial.* 78,6; vgl. *ProtEvJac* 18,1) ergänzt und mit Schriftzitaten unterfüttert ist (Jes 33,13-19 [eingespielt aus *dial.* 70,2]; Jer 31,15). Die im Mt-Text nicht belegte Herkunft der Magier aus der Arabia ermöglicht Justin schließlich, den Bezug auf Jes 8,4 festzunageln – schließlich liege das in Jes 8,4 erwähnte Damaskus in der Arabia (*dial.* 78,9). Wir können

---

43   Hierzu weiterführend BRUCKER, Psalm 95[96], 1774-1775.

nicht ganz sicher sein, ob Justin ein Matthäusevangelium in der Form vorlag, in der wir es kennen, oder ob er aus einer Evangelienharmonie zitierte.[44] Es entsteht jedoch der Eindruck, dass auch er, um seine Argumente zu erhärten, keineswegs davor zurückschreckte, das zu tun, was er seinen Gegnern vorwarf: die Jesajazitate, auf den er seine Argumentation aufbaute, neu zu kombinieren und so in den Text einzugreifen und auch die (sicherlich noch nicht im späteren Sinne „kanonische") Schriften über Jesus mit Motiven, die wir heute „apokryph" nennen würden, zu ergänzen.

Insgesamt entsteht der Eindruck, dass sich im (nur sehr einseitig wiedergegebenen) Gegenüber von Justin und Trypho bereits zwei Welten gegenüberstehen, die sich weit voneinander entfernt haben:[45] Zwei Hermeneutiken des Verständnisses der Schrift(en), die sich gegenseitig bis in die Beeinflussung von Textpassagen hinein abstoßen, die offenbar bereits auf Auslegungstraditionen – wie etwa im Fall von Jes 7,14 – zurückblicken bzw. diese entwickeln, welche sich bestenfalls noch negativ im Versuch, sich voneinander abzusetzen, beeinflussen.

Justins Auseinandersetzung mit Trypho ist nur ein kleiner Ausschnitt einer Auseinandersetzung nicht nur um Hermeneutik, sondern auch um Textformen, die ihren Gipfelpunkt sicherlich in der Erstellung der Hexapla des Origenes fand.[46] Der Weg zurück zu einer gemeinsamen Leseweise der gleichen Schriften aber war bereits durch die bereits eingangs beschriebene Hermeneutik, die von Christus her liest und auf Christus hin versteht, verstellt.

4. Fazit: Gleiche Texte – unterschiedliches Verständnis – ein Gott

Die eben skizzierten Gedanken bieten natürlich nur wenige Linien eines Gesamtbildes, das unendlich komplexer ist als das hier Gezeichnete.[47] Für den jüdisch-christlichen Dialog jedoch ergibt sich bereits aus diesen wenigen Beispielen, dass die zunächst gut gemeinte Aussage,

---

44 Zur Diskussion um die Justin vorliegenden christlichen Schriften vgl. z.B. ALLERT, Revelation, 188-220, sowie SKARSAUNE, Justin.

45 Zur Bedeutung von Justins *Dialog* als Quelle der Aufspaltung dessen, was er „Judäo-Christentum" nenne, vgl. BOYARIN, Abgrenzungen, 46-107.

46 Hierzu weiterführend FERNANDEZ MARCOS, Septuagint, 204-222 [Lit.].

47 Wichtig ist v.a. der Gedanke, dass Judentum wie Christentum natürlich nicht einfach mit je *einer* Hermeneutik an TaNaK/Altes Testament herangehen, sondern sich im Verlauf der Geschichte verschiedene Zugänge – auch in gegenseitiger Beeinflussung und Abgrenzung voneinander – entstanden. Vgl. v.a. die differenzierten Darstellungen in DOHMEN/STEMBERGER, Hermeneutik.

Juden und Christen seien durch die gemeinsame Sammlung Heiliger Schriften – hier TaNaK oder hebräische Bibel, dort Erstes oder Altes Testament genannt – verbunden, zwar voll und ganz zutrifft, dass gerade diese Verbindung aber in der Suche nach der eigenen Identität in Abgrenzung und Gegenüber bereits im frühesten Christentum zu Auseinandersetzungen und Konflikten führte, die bis heute nicht gänzlich gelöst sind. Die historische Suche nach den Wurzeln dieser Konflikte kann dazu beitragen, die im heutigen Dialog manchmal zu beobachtende Naivität zu überwinden. Im Kern des Konflikts liegen die Probleme unterschiedlicher Hermeneutiken und – zumindest in manchen Fällen auch – unterschiedlicher Textformen (wie im Gegenüber von LXX und TaNaK sicherlich auch Textsammlungen). Während das Problem der unterschiedlichen Textformen nur – wenn auch wichtige – Einzeltexte trifft, wo eine erhöhte Sensibilität für die Vielfalt der überlieferten Texte, die bis in die frühesten Handschriften aus Qumran zurückgeht, schon weiterhelfen könnte.[48] Entscheidender jedoch scheint mir die Entdeckung, dass das vielleicht entscheidende Problem hinter den skizzierten Auseinandersetzungen darin liegt, dass implizit hinter ihnen die Idee steckt, dass die diskutierten Texte nur *eine* angemessene Leseweise zulassen, die zu dem *einen* Gott führt, der sich in ihnen offenbart. In dem Gedanken, dass (vor allem komplexe) Texte polysem sind, bahnt sich bereits eine auf der Ebene der Text- und Literaturwissenschaft liegende Lösung des Problems an: Die gleichen Texte können – innerhalb von „Grenzen der Interpretation" – auf unterschiedliche Weisen und dabei auf unterschiedliche Weisen angemessen gelesen und verstanden werden. Damit ist jedoch nur *ein* Teil des Problems gelöst – und m.E. der bei weitem geringere. Der entscheidende Schritt kann nur darin bestehen zu erarbeiten, dass beide Leseweisen nicht nur den Texten angemessen sind, sondern sich – auf unterschiedlichen Wegen und in unterschiedlichen Perspektiven – der lebendigen Wahrheit des *einen* Gottes Israels, der auch der Gott Jesu Christi und der Christen ist, annähern.[49] Dazu jedoch ist das grundsätzliche Bekenntnis dazu unabdingbar, dass der Bund Gottes mit Israel „niemals gekündigt" ist,[50] ja dass das Christentum unauflöslich mit Israel verbunden ist, ohne dabei „Israel" als Heilsvolk abgelöst zu haben.

---

48 Hierzu bereits die Einführung von TOV, Textual Criticism.
49 Es kann hier nicht darum gehen, diese Hermeneutik zu entwickeln. Entscheidende Gedanken bei DOHMEN, Konzept.
50 Vgl. LOHFINK, Bund.

Bibliographie

ALLERT, Craig D., Revelation, Truth, Canon and Interpretation. Studies in Justin Martyr's *Dialogue with Trypho* (VigChr.S 64), Leiden/Boston 2002.

BAUER, Walter, Das Johannesevangelium (HNT 6), Tübingen 1933.

BECKER, Adam H. /YOSHIKO REED, Annette (Hg.), The Ways That Never Parted: Jews and Christians in Late Antiquity and the Early Middle Ages (TSAJ 95), Tübingen 2007.

BOYARIN, Daniel, Abgrenzungen. Die Aufspaltung des Judäo-Christentums (ANTZ 10), Berlin/Dortmund 2009.

BRUCKER, Ralph, Psalm 95[96], in: Karrer, Martin/Kraus, Wolfgang u.a. (Hg.), Septuaginta Deutsch. Erläuterungen und Kommentare zum griechischen Alten Testament II: Psalmen bis Daniel, Stuttgart 2011, 1771-1775.

CHILTON, Bruce D., Justin and Israelite Prophecy, in: Parvis, Sara/Foster, Paul (Hg.), Justin Martyr and His Worlds, Minneapolis 2007, 77-87.

DOHMEN, Christoph, Das Konzept der doppelten Hermeneutik, in: ders./Stemberger, Günter, Hermeneutik der Jüdischen Bibel und des Alten Testaments (Studienbücher Theologie 1,2), Stuttgart et al. 1996, 211-213.

DOHMEN, Christoph, Hermeneutik des Alten Testaments, in: ders./Stemberger, Günter, Hermeneutik der Jüdischen Bibel und des Alten Testaments (Studienbücher Theologie, 1,2), Stuttgart u.a. 1996, 133-209.

DOHMEN, Christoph/STEMBERGER, Günter, Hermeneutik der Jüdischen Bibel und des Alten Testaments (Studienbücher Theologie, 1,2), Stuttgart u.a. 1996.

FERNANDEZ MARCOS, Natalio, The Septuagint in Contex. Introduction to the Greek Versions of the Bible, Leiden/Boston 2000.

GRUNDMANN, Walter (Hg.), Die Botschaft Gottes, Weimar 1940.

HARNACK, Adolf von, Marcion: Das Evangelium vom fremden Gott, Leipzig ²1924.

HASITSCHKA, Martin, Befreiung von Sünde nach dem Johannesevangelium (ITHS 27), Innsbruck/Wien 1989.

HENGEL, Martin, Die Septuaginta als von den Christen beanspruchte Schriftensammlung bei Justin und den Vätern vor Origenes, in: ders., Judaica, Hellenistica et Christiana. Kleine Schriften II (WUNT 109), Tübingen 1999, 335-380.

HENGEL, Martin (unter Mitarbeit von Roland DEINES), Die Septuaginta als ‚christliche Schriftensammlung', ihre Vorgeschichte und das Problem ihres Kanons, in: ders./Anna M. Schwemer (Hg.), Die Septuaginta zwischen Judentum und Christentum (WUNT 72), Tübingen 1994, 182-284.

HESCHEL, Susannah, The Aryan Jesus. Christian Theologians and the Bible in Nazi Germany, Princeton, NJ, 2008.

HOEGEN-ROHLS, Christina, Der nachösterliche Johannes. Die Abschiedsreden als hermeneutischer Schlüssel zum vierten Evangelium (WUNT II 84), Tübingen 1996.

HÜBNER, Reinhard M., Thesen zur Echtheit und Datierung der sieben Briefe des Ignatius von Antiochien, in: ZAC 1 (1997), 44-72.

JERKE, B., Wie wurde das Neue Testament zu einem sogenannten Volkstestament ‚entjudet'? Aus der Arbeit des Eisenacher ‚Instituts zur Erforschung und Beseitigung des jüdischen Einflusses auf das deutsche kirchliche Leben", in: Siegele-Wenschkewitz, Leonore (Hg.), Christlicher Antijudaismus und Antisemitismus: Theologische und kirchliche Programme deutscher Christen (ArTe 85), Frankfurt/Main 1994, 201-234.

KLEIN, Hans, Wunder bei den Synoptikern, in: Nicklas, Tobias/Spittler, Janet E. (Hg.), Glaubwürdig oder unglaubwürdig? Erzählung und Rezeption wunderbarer Ereignisse in der antiken Welt (WUNT), Tübingen 2013 [im Druck].

LECHNER, Thomas, Ignatius adversus Valentinianos? Chronologische und theologiegeschichtliche Studien zu den Briefen des Ignatius (VigChr.S 47), Leiden et al. 1999

LIEU, Judith M., Christian Identity in the Jewish and Graeco-Roman World, Oxford et al. 2004.

LINDEMANN, Andreas/PAULSEN, Henning (Hg.), Die Apostolischen Väter. Griechisch-deutsche Parallelausgabe, Tübingen 1992.

LOHFINK, Norbert, Der niemals gekündigte Bund. Exegetische Gedanken zum christlich-jüdischen Dialog, Freiburg et al. 1989.

LUTTIKHUIZEN, Gerard P., Gnostic Revisions of Genesis Stories and Early Jesus Traditions (NHMS 58), Leiden/Boston 2005.

LUZ, Ulrich, Das Evangelium nach Matthäus (Mt 1-7) (EKK I/1), Zürich/Neukirchen-Vluyn 1985.

MARTYN, James Louis, History and Theology in the Fourth Gospel, Nashville ²1979

MENKEN, Maarten J.J., Matthew's Bible: The Old Testament Text of the Evangelist (BEThL 173); Leuven 2004.

MOLL, Sebastian, The Arch-Heretic Marcion (WUNT 250) Tübingen 2010.

MYLLYKOSKI, Matti, Wild Beasts and Rapid Dogs. The Riddle of the Heretics in the Letters of Ignatius, in: Ådna, Jostein (Hg.), The Formation of the Early Church (WUNT 183), Tübingen 2005, 341-377.

NICKLAS, Tobias, Ablösung und Verstrickung: ‚Juden' und Jüngergestalten als Charaktere der erzählten Welt des Johannesevangeliums und ihre Wirkung auf den impliziten Leser (RStTh 60), Frankfurt am Main et al. 2000.

NICKLAS, Tobias, Das ‚unbekannte Evangelium' auf P.Egerton 2 und die ‚Schrift', in: SNTU 33 (2008), 41-65.

NICKLAS, Tobias, Der gekreuzigte Christus und der schweigende Gott: Gedanken zur Christologie des Markusevangeliums, in: Niebuhr, Karl-Wilhelm/Rogalsky, S./ Karakolis, Chrestos (Hg.), Gospel Images of Jesus Christ in Church Tradition and Biblical Scholarship (WUNT), Tübingen 2012 [im Druck].

NICKLAS, Tobias, Der matthäische Davidssohn und das Römische Reich, in: Van Belle, Gilbert/Verheyden, Josef (Hg.), Christ and the Emperor: the Evidence of the Gospels (Biblical Tools and Studies), Leuven 2013 [im Druck].

NICKLAS, Tobias, Die johanneische Tempelreinigung (Joh 2,12-22) für Leser der Synoptiker, in: ThPh 80 (2005), 1-16.

NICKLAS, Tobias, Gnostic ‚Eschatologies', in: Van der Watt, Jan (Hg.), Eschatology of the New Testament and Some Related Documents (WUNT II.315), Tübingen 2011, 601-628.

NICKLAS, Tobias, The ‚Unknown Gospel' on Papyrus Egerton 2 (+ Papyrus Cologne 255), in: Kraus, Thomas J./Kruger, Michael J./Nicklas, Tobias, Gospel Fragments (Oxford Early Christian Gospel Texts), Oxford et al. 2009, 11-120.

PROSTMEIER, Ferdinand R., Antijudaismus im Rahmen christlicher Hermeneutik. Zum Streit über christliche Identität in der Alten Kirche. Notizen zum Barnabasbrief, in: ZAC 6 (2002), 38-58.

RÄISÄNEN, Heikki, Marcion, in: Marjanen, Antti/Luomanen, Petri (Hg.), A Companion to Second-Century Christian ‚Heretics' (VigChr.S 76), Leiden/Boston 2005, 100-124.

SÄNGER, Dieter, „Von mir hat er geschrieben" (Joh 5,46), in: KD 41 (1995) 112-135.

SIEGERT, Folker, Zwischen Hebräischer Bibel und Altem Testament. Eine Einführung in die Septuaginta (Münsteraner Judastische Studien 9), Münster u.a. 2001.

SKARSAUNE, Oskar, Justin and his Bible, in: Parvis, Sara/Foster, Paul (Hg.), Justin Martyr and His Worlds, Minneapolis 2007, 53-76.

STEMBERGER, Günter, Hermeneutik der Jüdischen Bibel, in: ders./Dohmen, Christoph, Hermeneutik der Jüdischen Bibel und des Alten Testaments (Studienbücher Theologie 1,2), Stuttgart u.a. 1996, 23-132.

THYEN, Hartwig, Das Johannesevangelium (HNT 6), Tübingen 2005.

TILLY, Markus, Einführung in die Septuaginta, Darmstadt 2005.

TOV, Emanuel, Textual Criticism of the Hebrew Bible, Minneapolis 2001.

WENGST, Klaus, Bedrängte Gemeinde und verherrlichter Christus. Ein Versuch über das Johannesevangelium, München ⁴1992.

WILK, F., Esaias/Isaias/Das Buch Jesaja, in: Karrer, Martin/Kraus, Wolfgang u.a. (Hg.), Septuaginta Deutsch. Erläuterungen und Kommentare II: Psalmen bis Daniel, Stuttgart 2011, 2484-2690.

ZELLER, Dieter, Der erste Brief an die Korinther (KeK 5), Göttingen 2010.

ZENGER, Erich, Das Erste Testament. Die jüdische Bibel und die Christen, Düsseldorf ⁵1995.

ZENGER, Erich, Heilige Schrift der Juden und Christen, in: Einleitung in das Alte Testament, Stuttgart ³1998, 12-36.

Index of References

Old Testament (incl. Deuterocanonical Literature)

Genesis
   Gen 1,1-2,4a 211
   Gen 1-11 185
   Gen 1:26 27
   Gen 2:18 90
   Gen 4:20-21 256
   Gen 11:26-33 313
   Gen 11:31 313
   Gen 11:32 314
   Gen 12:1-8 319
   Gen 12:4 313
   Gen 12:5 315
   Gen 15:6 267
   Gen 15:13-14 316
   Gen 15:14 317
   Gen 18 22
   Gen 18:1 246
   Gen 18:2 27
   Gen 22 22
   Gen 23 1
   Gen 25:19 318
   Gen 28:10-11 179
   Gen 34 187
   Gen 43:9 111

Exodus
   Ex 1-24 192
   Ex 1:7-22 321
   Ex 2:3 321
   Ex 2:11-14 323
   Ex 3:1-10 323
   Ex 3:2 217
   Ex 3:12 317
   Ex 12 171
   Ex 15:26 27
   Ex 16 308
   Ex 19:1-24:11 194
   Ex 21 1
   Ex 22:29b 17
   Ex 23:20 286
   Ex 24 190
   Ex 24:12-18 186, 194
   Ex 31 190
   Ex 33,3-5 330
   Ex 33:7-11 325
   Ex 33:12-17 326
   Ex 33:18-23 336
   Ex 34,1 186

Leviticus
   Lev 4:21 255
   Lev 11 98
   Lev 17:3 4
   Lev 19:3 253, 254
   Lev 19:13 254, 255
   Lev 26 76

Numeri
   Num 10 1
   Num 11:13-17 309
   Num 17:6-15 171
   Num 27:1-14 92
   Num 36 92

Deuteronomy
   Deut 4:2 137
   Deut 4:44 5
   Deut 8:3 281, 283

Deut 9	190	1 Chronicles	
Deut 11:21-12:18	8	1 Chr 16:40	3
Deut 12	97		
Deut 12:5	7, 9	2 Chronicles	
Deut 13:1	137	2 Chr 23:18	3
Deut 14:3-20	98	2 Chr 25:4	3, 144
Deut 14:28-29	121	2 Chr 34:8-28	130, 131
Deut 15:1-18	120	2 Chr 34:31	136
Deut 15:7-11	99	2 Chr 35:12	91
Deut 16:16	92		
Deut 18:21-22	89	Ezra	
Deut 24:16	145	Ezra 7:10	139
Deut 25:4	91	Ezra 9:11-12	72
Deut 25:5-10	92		
Deut 27	76	Tobit	
Deut 27:2	5	Tob 1:3-2:24	97
Deut 27:4	9	Tob 1:17	98
Deut 27:2-7	8	Tob 1:19	101
Deut 27:13	9	Tob 1:20	101
Deut 28:25-26	100	Tob 2	98
Deut 28:26	99	Tob 2:1-4	87
Deut 28:49-50	195	Tob 2:6	86, 89
Deut 28:53	68	Tob 4:3-4	104
Deut 28:59	133	Tob 4:4-5	94
Deut 30	76	Tob 6:12	92
Deut 30:1-10	75	Tob 6:13	91
Deut 30:12	269	Tob 6:15	94
Deut 31:24	133	Tob 7	93
Deut 31:26	132	Tob 7:12	91
Deut 32	262	Tob 7:13	91
Deut 34	239	Tob 14:4	86, 87, 88, 89, 137
Deut 35	1		
		Tob 14:8-9	88
1 Samuel			
1 Sam 10:25	131	1 Maccabees	
		1 Macc 1:54-57	5
2 Samuel			
2 Sam 7,1-7	326, 327	2 Maccabees	
		2 Macc 2:1-12	234
2 Kings			
2 King 22:3-20	130, 131		
2 King 23:3	136		

Index of References

Job
- Job 4:12-17 — 31
- Job 6-8 — 252
- Job 9-15 — 252
- Job 21:11-12 — 256
- Job 27 — 252
- Job 28-38 — 252
- Job 30:31 — 255
- Job 38:1-40:2 — 32
- Job 39-40 — 252
- Job 40:6-41:26 — 32
- Job 41-45 — 252
- Job 46-53 — 252

Psalms
- Ps 6:8 — 290
- Ps 6:9 — 289, 290
- Ps 18:5 — 269
- Ps 28:3 — 312
- Ps 28:4 — 312
- Ps 31 — 273
- Ps 31:1-2 — 267, 274
- Ps 31:11 — 268
- Ps 42:23 — 268, 269, 274
- Ps 50 — 271, 274
- Ps 50:3 — 266
- Ps 50:6 — 265, 266
- Ps 68 — 353
- Ps 68:19 — 13
- Ps 68:23-24 — 270
- Ps 78:5-6 — 153
- Ps 79:2 — 195
- Ps 90 — 195
- Ps 90:11 — 282, 283
- Ps 95:10 — 363
- Ps 103:12 — 288
- Ps 117:26 — 290
- Ps 118 — 290, 291
- Ps 131:1-5 — 327, 328

Proverbs
- Prov 5:18-19 — 34
- Prov 6:1-15 — 111
- Prov 7:6-27 — 33
- Prov 8:22-31 — 31
- Prov 24:30-34 — 33
- Prov 30:3 — 179

Ecclesiastes/Kohelet
- Koh 7:23-29 — 36

Wisdom
- Wis 2:10-5:23 — 181
- Wis 2:12-15 — 169, 171
- Wis 3:10 — 172
- Wis 6:3 — 169
- Wis 6:9-11 — 169, 172
- Wis 8:7 — 150
- Wis 9:3 — 169
- Wis 10:1-11:1 — 174
- Wis 10:10 — 179
- Wis 10:18-21 — 180
- Wis 11:2-19:22 — 174
- Wis 12:15 — 169
- Wis 18 — 169
- Wis 18:9 — 171

Sirach
- Sir 1:11 — 162
- Sir 3:1-16 — 103
- Sir 7:27-28 — 103
- Sir 7:29-31 — 116, 119
- Sir 8:13 — 111, 112
- Sir 11:15 — 111
- Sir 13:2-23 — 119
- Sir 16:6-10 — 109
- Sir 17:1-12 — 109
- Sir 17:18 — 111
- Sir 19:13-17 — 109
- Sir 24 — 116
- Sir 24:33 — 124
- Sir 29 — 112

Sir 33:16-18	124	Jer 27[34]:11-12	71
Sir 36:1-22	156	Jer 33:10-11	71
Sir 36:22	157	Jer 36:10	130
Sir 38:34-39:1	143		
Sir 38:34	144	Baruch	
Sir 39	125	Bar 1:1-3:8	64
Sir 39:1	144	Bar 1:1-14	69
Sir 39:2-3	123	Bar 1:15-2:19	76
Sir 39:7-8	123	Bar 1:15-3:8	63, 67, 81
Sir 39:8	144		
Sir 48:7	110	Bar 1:19-21	76
Sir 49:8	118	Bar 2:2	67, 68, 69, 79
Sir 50:13	117		
		Bar 2:3	68, 70
Isaiah		Bar 2:20-23	70, 73, 75
Isa 5:24	132		
Isa 7:10-17	363	Bar 2:20	70, 71, 72
Isa 7:14	364		
Isa 8:4	363, 364	Bar 2:24	72, 73
Isa 8:23-9:1	355	Bar 2:28-35	75
Isa 11:10	273	Bar 2:34	72
Isa 26:19	285	Bar 3:9-5:9	64
Isa 29:18	285		
Isa 37:20	157	Ezekiel	
Isa 37:22	357	Ezek 11:25	133
Isa 42:18	285	Ezek 17:23	289
Isa 49:16	230	Ezek 40-48	117, 118
Isa 51:1-2	292		
Isa 52:13-53:12	351	Daniel	
Isa 53:4	356	Dan 7:15	154
Isa 53,7	269	Dan 9	69
Isa 53:-11-12	332		
Isa 55:8	20	Hosea	
Isa 61:1	285	Hos 6:2	352
Isa 66:1-2	329, 330		
		Amos	
Jeremiah		Am 5:25-27	324
Jer 1:18	230	Am 8:10	86, 87, 137
Jer 7:34	71		
Jer 8:1	73		
Jer 16:0	71	Jonah	
Jer 19:9	68	Jona 3:4	87

Micah			Nahum	
Mi 3:12	137		Nah 2-3	87
Mi 6:8	294			
Mi 7:6	286, 287		Maleachi	
			Mal 3:1	286

Early Judaism and Early Christianity

Dead Sea Scrolls			4 Esra	
4Q394 3-7ii: 14-15	4		4 Esra 3,4	211
4Q394 f8 iv: 9-11	10		4 Esra 3:25-27	211
4Q458	243		4 Esra 6:38	211
4Q552-553	242		4 Esra 7:6	237
11Q19 52:16	10		4 Esra 7:127	214
4QDb 4 8-11	114		4 Esra 8:1-8	237
			4 Esra 9:37	213
Book of Jubilees			4 Esra 12:27	213
Jub 1:27	195		4 Esra 12:37	216, 217
Jub 1:27-29	194		4 Esra 14	217
Jub 1:29	192, 193		4 Esra 14:5	217
Jub 2-50	185, 187		4 Esra 14:20	213
Jub 2:1	194		4 Esra 14:27-36	211
Jub 2:24	187			
Jub 2:33	191		2 Baruch	
Jub 6	186		2 Bar 1-77	229
Jub 6:10-22	200		2 Bar 2:1-2	230
Jub 6:22	187		2 Bar 3-86	226
Jub 6:23	195		2 Bar 4:2	230
Jub 6:35	201		2 Bar 4:3-6	230
Jub 12	11		2 Bar 6:3-8:2	241
Jub 15:25	201		2 Bar 10:5	235
Jub 15:28-29	201		2 Bar 46:1-6	237
Jub 23:9-31	194		2 Bar 76	239
Jub 23:32	195		2 Bar 77:11-26	246
Jub 30	192		2 Bar 78:2	245
Jub 30:10	197		2 Bar 84:1-7	239
Jub 30:11-13	196		2 Bar 84:2	240
Jub 49:16-21	197			
Jub 49:22	198			
Jub 50:1-13	199			

Testament of Job
  TestJob 12:4   253, 254
  TestJob 11-12   253, 254
  TestJob 14:1-5   255, 256

New Testament

Matthew
  Matt 1-2   356
  Matt 1:18   357
  Matt 2:23   72
  Matt 4:4   282
  Matt 4:10   283
  Matt 4:12-17   354
  Matt 4:14-16   355
  Matt 7:23   289
  Matt 8:16-17   355
  Matt 10:34   287
  Matt 10:36   286
  Matt 11:5   284
  Matt 13:32   288
  Matt 28:20   357

Mark
  Mark 4:32   288

Luke
  Luke 4:4   282
  Luke 4:8   283
  Luke 4:18-19   285
  Luke 7:22   284
  Luke 12:8-12   337
  Luke 12:52   287
  Luke 13:19   288
  Luke 13:27   289

John
  John 2:13-22   352, 353
  John 2:17   353
  John 5:19-47   358
  John 5:39   359
  John 5:45-47   359
  John 6:16-21   354
  John 10:30-39   358
  John 18:1-11   354

Acts
  Acts 1:1-11   339
  Acts 1:1-2   307
  Acts 1:4-8:3   307
  Acts 1:8   307
  Acts 6:1-8:3   305, 306, 307, 338, 341
  Acts 6:1-7   308, 310, 311
  Acts 6:1   308, 309
  Acts 6:2-6   309
  Acts 6:3-10   331
  Acts 6:5   310
  Acts 6:8-7:1   308, 310, 311
  Acts 6:9-12   310
  Acts 7:2-53   305, 311
  Acts 7:2-8   312, 313, 318, 319
  Acts 7:2   315
  Acts 7:3   314
  Acts 7:4   315, 334
  Acts 7:5   317
  Acts 7:6-7   316, 317
  Acts 7:8   318
  Acts 7:9-16   319
  Acts 7:17-19   319
  Acts 7:20-43   322
  Acts 7:35   323
  Acts 7:39   324

Acts 7:43	324, 325	Rom 4:3	267
Acts 7:45	326	Rom 4:7-8	267
Acts 7:46	327	Rom 8:36	268, 269
Acts 7:49-50	329, 330	Rom 9-11	262, 263
Acts 7:51-53	333, 334	Rom 10:8	269
Acts 7:52	332	Rom 11:5-6	263
Acts 7:54-8:1	338	Rom 11:9-10	270
Acts 7:54-8:3	334, 335	Rom 11:9	274
Acts 7:55-56	337	Rom 15:3	270
Acts 8:4-11:8	307	Rom 15:9-12	271
Acts 11:19-18:31	307	Rom 15:12	273
Acts 11:26	348		

Romans

1 Corinthians

Rom 1:3-4	272, 275	1 Cor 2:9	14
Rom 2-4	264	1 Cor 15:3-5	350, 351, 352, 356
Rom 2:20	266		
Rom 3:4	265, 266, 274		

Ephesians

		Eph 4:7-8	13

Index of Subjects

Abraham	11, 12, 17, 19-22, 27, 72, 90, 93, 97, 100, 103, 171, 174, 185, 191, 194, 200, 201, 217, 230, 238, 243, 244, 246, 264, 267, 268, 273; 291, 292, 313-322, 334, 335, 340-341, 361
Adam	90, 174, 181, 200 211, 230, 238, 243
Alexandria	12-13, 24, 45-49, 52-60, 148, 167-169, 173, 175-179, 181-182
Allusions	58, 65, 68, 72, 76, 77-79, 81, 85, 97, 98, 100, 103-105, 246, 261-262, 265, 266, 268, 279, 287-288, 290, 292, 294
Ancestor	76, 85, 94, 96, 97, 102, 105, 110, 117, 118, 168, 170, 171, 181, 202, 203, 256, 294
Angelus interpres	210, 241, 242
Apocalypse	194, 195, 225, 226, 228, 229, 230, 232, 233, 238, 239, 240, 241, 245, 246, 247, 248, 299
Apokryph	220, 360, 364
Aristeas/Ps-Aristeas	12, 13, 43-49, 51-59
Artaxerxes	140, 236
Assyria	23
Auferweckung	342, 351, 352, 353, 356
Autobiographical	86, 97, 101, 102, 104
Autorität/Authority	1, 4, 6, 10, 11, 12, 13, 14; 17, 18, 20, 30, 31, 34, 37-38, 46, 47, 49, 50, 53, 54, 56, 57, 58, 72, 86, 89, 90, 91, 92, 94, 95, 96, 102, 104, 105, 106, 122, 123, 129, 131-133, 135, 143, 145, 147, 154, 160, 161, 167, 168-173, 177-183, 186-195, 197, 198, 200, 202, 203, 207-213, 215-223, 225, 227-230, 234, 236-242, 244-248, 251, 257, 279, 282, 284-286, 288, 292, 295-297, 302, 303, 308, 352, 354
Authorship	46, 63, 178, 190
Batsheba	266
Beelzebul	295-296, 302

Buddhist	18
Canaan	23, 26, 100, 192, 200
Canon/canonical	24, 25, 31, 32, 38, 63, 85-87, 89, 93, 96, 97, 105, 109, 145, 167, 182, 183, 209, 210, 215, 216, 218, 220-222, 255, 257, 298, 347-349, 364
Citation	65-70, 72, 73, 76, 77, 78, 79, 81, 174, 175, 176, 267, 279-285, 287, 289-291, 300, 302
Covenant	5, 75, 91, 92, 132, 134, 136, 142, 144 171, 186, 189, 191, 194, 195, 196, 199, 200, 201, 204, 231, 239, 240, 244-246, 262, 318, 320, 335, 366
Creation	7, 10, 11, 13, 20, 21, 27, 58, 90, 190-195, 199-200, 202, 236, 265, 266, 269
Cult	9, 32, 95, 97, 101, 102, 120-122, 257
David	3, 8, 32, 96, 110, 130, 193, 211, 212, 243, 261-267, 269, 270, 272-277, 282, 326-328, 353, 355
Devil	279, 283, 302
Egypt	8, 27, 37, 47, 50, 51,75, 76, 99, 133, 148, 151, 168-170, 174, 177, 181, 182, 190 233, 253, 317, 320, 321
Elijah	99, 263, 285
Epicurus	20
Evangelium	266, 267, 273, 307
Exile/Exil	230, 237, 72, 74, 76, 82, 88, 98, 100, 101
Geschichtsschreibung	306, 307
Gnosis	349
Gottesfurcht	158, 163, 323
hebel	36, 37, 38
Herodotus	55
Hillel	6
Holy Spirit	26, 27
Homer	23, 160, 151, 161
Horeb	110, 317
Identity	7, 11, 44, 47, 55, 57-60, 70, 89, 98, 105, 149, 151, 154, 155, 161, 168, 170, 177, 178, 193, 202, 222, 223, 252, 257, 263, 261, 276, 284, 285, 292, 298, 306, 311, 318, 333, 334, 339, 340, 341, 342, 358, 365
Ignatius	348, 360, 361
Isaac	21, 72, 74, 90, 93, 98, 100, 200, 292

Islam	17
Jacob	72, 74, 90, 93, 98, 100, 102, 176, 179, 180, 181, 185, 196, 197, 200, 252, 292
Job	22, 24, 28, 31, 58, 74, 78, 105, 236, 251-257, 334
Josef	100, 181, 320, 321
Jonah	86, 88, 296, 297
Joshua	25, 100, 195
Judaism/Judentum	1, 2, 6, 8, 11, 12, 14, 17, 27, 44, 47, 50, 51, 59, 105, 123, 167, 207, 235, 236, 257, 296, 331, 341, 347-350, 360-362
Judgement	5, 72
Justice	19, 21, 22, 26, 28, 29, 51, 57, 78, 119-121, 270, 294
Justin	362-364
Kyrios	156
Lade	132
Law	3, 5, 44-59, 68-70, 74, 76, 79, 90-95, 103, 104, 105, 125, 130, 136, 138, 139, 140, 141, 144, 146, 157, 152, 157, 164, 169, 170, 172, 181, 182, 186-188, 190-194, 196, 197, 199, 200-203, 209, 212-214, 218, 219, 222, 234-240, 244, 247, 248, 253, 254, 268-269, 294-295, 310, 311, 333, 339, 342, 358, 361
Marcion	31, 349
Masada	2
Menschensohn	336-338, 342
Midrash	21, 26, 235
Mishnah	17
Mose	5, 133, 134, 137, 138, 139, 140, 148, 212, 213, 217, 219, 309, 311, 322, 323, 324, 326, 332, 332, 333, 336, 339, 358, 359, 361
Nahum	86-88, 137
Nebuchadnezzar	242
Nineveh	86-89
Noah	90, 186, 200, 299-301
Offenbarung	132-134, 137, 138, 139, 141, 142, 143, 154, 155, 160, 161, 164, 207, 209, 211, 213, 215, 216, 217, 219, 220, 221, 222, 223, 312-314
Palestine	13, 167

Patriarch	23, 32, 90, 93, 98, 100, 101, 104, 105, 171, 179, 180, 228, 236, 251, 291-292, 318-320,
Paul	25, 14, 261-269, 271-277, 307, 349-351
Pentateuch	9, 43-45, 47, 68, 76, 77, 79, 81
Pharisees	294
Polybius	55
Priesthood/Priest	3, 17, 18, 43, 47, 48, 50, 55,130, 131, 140, 141, 153, 230, 237, 276,
Pseudonym	43-47, 53-55, 57, 59, 213, 216, 220
Qumran	1-7, 12, 13, 78, 147, 167-168, 182, 188, 234, 236, 242, 243, 265, 365,
Quotation	2-4, 6, 13-14, 63-76, 78-80, 86-87, 90, 150, 174, 176, 230, 240, 245, 261-266, 268-277, 281, 283, 284, 290,
Quran	17
Rabbinic	5-7, 21, 231, 235, 236, 244, 248, 291
Righteous (Sufferer)/ Righteousness	50, 77, 262, 266-268, 270, 271, 274, 277, 293 298, 299, 300
Roman	1, 3, 5, 6, 7, 11, 227, 242, 252, 253, 257, 261, 262, 263, 264, 265, 266, 268-272, 274-277
Sabbath	191, 194, 199, 200, 202, 358
Sanctuary	9, 11, 120, 227, 229, 231, 232, 233, 235, 237, 238, 242, 246
Schriftgebrauch	305, 306, 318, 320, 338, 339
Schriftgelehrter	110, 111, 123, 125, 213
Schrift	129, 152, 207-210, 212, 215-223, 305, 306, 308, 311, 312, 319, 323, 339, 340, 348, 350, 353, 354, 357, 359, 360, 361, 363, 364
Shavuot	86, 101, 191, 199
Sinai	45, 52, 59, 110, 168, 170, 186-200, 202-204, 217, 311, 323, 327
Solomon/Ps-Solomon	28, 31, 78, 167-183, 193, 243, 297
Sondergut	280, 286, 300
Son of Man	296, 300, 301
Synagoge	358
Talmud	17, 37, 235
TaNaK	136-137, 142, 147-149, 157, 158, 162, 164, 182, 347, 365
Teacher	102

Index of Subjects 381

Temple	6, 7, 9, 10, 46, 54, 57, 69, 77, 88, 97, 116, 119, 121, 122, 192-194, 227, 231, 235, 241, 252, 253, 256, 282, 301
Tempelreinigung	352, 353
Tertullian	24
Theodizeefrage	214
Torah	1-11, 13, 14, 17, 46, 52, 75, 87, 90, 91-93, 95-96, 97, 99, 100, 104, 105, 109, 111, 114-116, 118-125, 132, 134, 135, 138, 142, 145, 161, 170, 172, 186-187, 189, 190-194, 196, 200, 202, 203, 209, 212, 213, 214, 215, 216, 217, 218, 219, 221, 222, 234, 236, 237, 238, 241, 244, 246, 248, 253, 282, 291, 347, 359, 361, 362
Translation	10, 12, 43-48, 50, 52, 53, 79, 226, 253, 257, 283
Tribes	8, 10, 97, 239, 246
Trypho	362-364
Witwen	308
Zechariah	298
Zion	30, 192, 193, 204, 235, 238, 265, 357

www.ingramcontent.com/pod-product-compliance
Lightning Source LLC
Chambersburg PA
CBHW050850160426
43194CB00011B/2094